This research has been supported by the Netherlands Organisation for Scientific Research (NWO), and the Dutch ministries of the interior (*Ministerie van Binnenlandse Zaken*) and justice (*Ministerie van Justitie*).

SCHENGEN INVESTIGATED

Schengen Investigated

A Comparative Interpretation of the Schengen Provisions
on International Police Cooperation in the Light of the
European Convention on Human Rights

by

Chantal Joubert

and

Hans Bevers

KLUWER LAW INTERNATIONAL
THE HAGUE / LONDON / BOSTON

A C.I.P. Catalogue record for this book is available from the Library of Congress

ISBN 90-411-0266-3

Published by Kluwer Law International,
P.O. Box 85889, 2508 CN The Hague, The Netherlands.

Sold and distributed in the U.S.A. and Canada
by Kluwer Law International,
675 Massachusetts Avenue, Cambridge, MA 02139, U.S.A.

In all other countries, sold and distributed
by Kluwer Law International,
P.O. Box 85889, 2508 CN The Hague, The Netherlands.

Printed on acid-free paper

Printed in the Netherlands

Preface

Émilie, notre puce chérie, merci pour le sursis.
Jouw lachen en huilen beschermen tegen alle stress.

In the midst of last minute checks and corrections, a sudden thought crosses our minds: the preface! We must still write the preface! It is far from easy to sit here, 48 hours before a deadline we were crazy enough to fix ourselves, and reflect on the last five years of our lives. Five intense years spent researching and writing, travelling and writing, reading and writing, listening and writing, learning and writing.

The process of gathering the information we hope you will find in this thesis would have been impossible without the help of numerous persons we came across in the course of this study. In the first place our supervising *promotores*, Tom Schalken and Jan Naeyé, who guided us through this project with their numerous comments and applause, mostly well-tempered and with humour, always encouraging. Furthermore, we would like to thank Cyrille Fijnaut, whom we at first feared for his knowledge, experience, fame and especially his competition in the fields of international police cooperation and comparative criminal law. It did not take long however, after having met him all over Europe, before he turned into a highly approachable and appreciated colleague. We were very glad and honoured that he, whom we almost considered our guru, was willing to become the external referee of our research. For the same reasons we would like to thank the other members of our manuscript committee, Brice De Ruyver, Jan-Watse Fokkens, Peter Tak and Bert Swart.

But it is impossible to accomplish such a project without help from outside the university. Policemen and women, judges or public prosecutors, all have furnished us with essential indications and have made it possible for us to gain insight on sometimes less accessible information. Their help was tremendous. In an attempt to be more specific and in great fear of forgetting someone, we would like to thank in first instance all the representatives of police forces here or abroad. We would like to begin by thanking Marijke Stevens for her help in the library of the Amsterdam police, Fred Mangelaars, Dick Bos and Marie-Thérèse Ford-Claessen of the CRI in The Hague for their cooperation and assistance in general.

Further, we would like to thank our contact persons in The Netherlands who helped us understand some of the practical aspects of police cooperation in border areas, Leander Witjes, Ton Rutting, Ted Peer, Tim Bremmers and Peter

Prince, as well as our contact persons abroad, *Kriminalrat* Clauer, Johan Scheers, Andrée Colas, Jacques Klein, Nicholas Schüller, *capitaine* Duflos, Jean-François Berthier, and *Polizeidirektoren* Dautert, Kröll and Helmers. Patrick Zanders, Gert Vermeulen, Ton van der Beken, Hartmut Aden, Marita Birgelen, Andrée Colas, Jacques Klein and Yves Reungoat were all willing to sacrifice their time for a control and revision of parts of our manuscript that deal with their respective law systems. We must however emphasize that we are the only ones who hold full responsibility for any mistake or fault in the text. We must also mention the numerous services abroad who were willing to receive us in their department in the course of this study and who helped us understand that police cooperation is more than a set of rules.

A preface would not be complete without the expression of our appreciation for the support, the ears and the advice given to us throughout the years by our direct colleagues in the department of criminal law at the Vrije Universiteit, in particular Klaas, Fleur, Michaël, Olaf, Jaap and Yvonne. Besides, we would like to make special acknowledgements and express our gratitude to our dearest American friend in Germany, Maryann Braciczewski, for correcting our English. Another special acknowledgement goes to our friends and families, particularly our parents who enabled and stimulated us to develop ourselves in directions and ways that brought us together personally and academically. We deeply regret that Liliane and Irene left too soon to be with us at this important moment of our lives.

In a more practical tone, we will conclude this preface adding that our choice for the use of masculine words in the text is a question of convention and not because men would be more inclined for police work. The text may be read as well by replacing these words with their feminine equivalent and still have the same scope. Finally, the text was generally updated until December 1, 1995, after which we were only capable of adding some basic references to mainly Dutch case-law, regulations and an incidental publication. The final manuscript was closed on March 20, 1996.

Amsterdam, April 1, 1996

Chantal Joubert & Hans Bevers

Short Contents[*]

[*] Chantal Joubert is first responsible for the contents of chapters 3, 5, 8, 9 and 10 and Hans Bevers for the chapters 2, 4, 6, 7 and 11. Both authors are responsible for chapters 1 and 12.

Table of Contents

List of Abbreviations

AAe	*Ars Aequi* (NL)
A.C.	*Arrêts de la cour de cassation* (B)
AID	*Algemene inspectiedienst* (NL)
al.	alinea
ANCPI	*Afdeling nationale coördinatie politiële infiltratie* (NL)
Anl.	*Anlage* (D)
APB	*Algemeen politieblad* (NL)
Appl.	application/applicant
APSD	*Algemene politie steundienst* (B)
art., artt.	article, articles
AWBi	*Algemene wet op het binnentreden* (NL)
B & P	*Bürgerrechte & Polizei* (D)
BayPAG	*Bayerisches Polizeiaufgabengesetz* (D)
BCN	*Bureau central national* (L, F)
Bd.	*Band* (D)
BDSG	*Bundesdatenschutzgesetz* (D)
BET	Benelux Extradition Treaty
BGBl.	*Bundesgesetzblatt* (D)
BGH	*Bundesgerichtshof* (D)
BGS	*Bundesgrenzschutz* (D)
BGSNeuRegG	*Bundesgrenzschutz-Neuregelungsgesetz* (D)
BKA	*Bundeskriminalamt* (D)
BKAG	*Bundeskriminalamtsgesetz* (D)
B.O.B.	*Bewakings- en opsporingsbrigade* (B)
BPolR	*Besluit politieregisters* (NL)
B.S.	*Belgisch Staatsblad* (B)
BT	*Bundestag* (D)
BtMG	*Betäubungsmittelgesetz* (D)
Bull. Ass.	*Bulletin des Assurances* (B)
Bull. Crim.	*Bulletin des arrêts de la chambre criminelle de la Cour de cassation* (F)
BVerfG	*Bundesverfassungsgericht* (D)
BVerfGE	*Bundesverfassungsgericht - Entscheidungen* (D)
BWPG	*Baden-württembergisches Polizeigesetz* (D)

Cass.	*Cour de cassation* (B, L, F)
(Cass.) Crim.	*Chambre criminelle de la Cour de cassation* (F)
CBO	*Centraal bureau opsporingen* (B)
CD	*Code des douanes* (F)
CDU/CSU	*Christlich-Demokratische Union/Christlich-Soziale Union* (D)
CELAD	*Comité européen de lutte anti-drogue*
Cfr.	Confer
CIC	*Code d'instruction criminelle* (L)
CID	*Criminele inlichtingendienst* (NL)
Civ.	*Chambre civile de la Cour de cassation* (F)
CMLR	Common Market Law Review
Corr.	*Tribunal correctionnel* (B, L, F)
CP	*Code pénal* (L, F)
CPP	*Code de procédure pénale* (F)
CR	*Computerrecht* (B, NL)
CRI	*Centrale recherche-informatiedienst* (NL)
CRS	*Compagnies républicaines de sécurité* (F)
CSP	*Code de la santé publique* (F)
D.	*Décret* (F)
DAR	*Deutsches Autorecht* (D)
D.C.P.J.	*Direction centrale de police judiciaire* (F)
DD	*Delikt & Delinkwent* (NL)
déb. Ass. Nat.	*débats de l'Assemblée Nationale* (F)
D.G.P.N.	*Direction générale de police nationale* (F)
diss.	*dissertatie* (NL)
D.P.	*Droit pénal* (F)
EC	European Community
ECD	*Economische controledienst* (NL)
ECHR	European Convention on Human Rights
ed./eds.	edition/editor, editors
EJCPR	European Journal on Criminal Policy and Research
ELR	European Law Review
EOrgKG	*Entwurf eines Gesetzes zur Bekämpfung der organisierten Kriminalität* (D)
et seq.	*et sequentia*, and following
et al.	*et alii*, and others
EU	European Union
Eur.J. Crime Cr.L. Cr.J.	European Journal on Crime, Criminal Law and Criminal Justice

FDP	*Freiheitlich-Demokratische Partei* (D)
FIOD	*Fiscale inlichtingen- en opsporingsdienst* (NL)
GA	*Goltdammer's Archiv für Strafrecht* (D)
Gaz. Pal.	*Gazette du Palais* (F)
GemW	*Gemeentewet* (B, NL)
GG	*Grundgesetz* (D)
GP	*Gemeentepolitie* (B)
GPP	*Gerechtelijke politie bij de parketten* (B)
GSO	*Groep speciale opdrachten* (B)
GVG	*Gerichtsverfassungsgesetz* (D)
GVNW	*Gesetz- und Verwaltungsblatt Nordrhein-Westfalen* (D)
GW	*Grondwet* (B, NL)
HR	*Hoge Raad* (NL)
HSOG	*Hessisches Gesetz über Sicherheit und Ordnung* (D)
HvB	*Hof van Beroep* (B)
IACP	International Association of Chiefs of Police
ICAct	Interception of communication act
ICPO-Interpol	International Criminal Police Organisation-Interpol
i.d.	*idem dito*
IG	*Instructions générales* (F)
IPA	International Police Association
IRG	*Internationales Rechtshilfegesetz* (D)
IRT	*Interregionaal rechercheteam* (NL)
ITCPR	International Treaty on Civil and Political Rights
J.C.P.	*Juris-Classeur Pénal* (F)
J.L.B.	*Jurisprudence de Liège et Bruxelles* (B)
J.O.	*Journal Officiel* (F)
J.T.	*Journal des Tribunaux* (B)
JV	*Justitiële Verkenningen* (NL)
KB	*Koninklijk Besluit* (B, NL)
KG	*Kammergericht* (D)
KJ	*Kritische Justiz* (D)
KLPD	*Korps landelijke politiediensten* (NL)
L.	*Loi* (F)
LCO/LIPO	*Landelijke contactgroep observatie/Landelijk informatiepunt politiële observatie* (NL)
LEP	*Loi sur l'étatisation de la police* (L)
LIFL	*Loi sur l'informatique, les fichiers et la liberté* (F)

LKA	*Landeskriminalamt* (D)
LOM	*Loi sur l'organisation militaire* (L)
MEK	*Mobiles Einsatzkommando* (D)
Mém.	*Mémoire* (L)
MEPolG	*Musterentwurf eines einheitlichen Polizeigesetzes* (D)
MOT	*Meldpunt ongebruikelijke transacties* (NL)
NCB	National central bureau
NCID	*Nationale criminale inlichtingendienst* (NL)
NCP	*Nouveau code pénal* (F)
Nds.GVBl.	*Niedersächsisches Gesetz- und Verwaltungsblatt* (D)
NGefAG	*Niedersächsisches Gefahrenabwehrgesetz* (D)
NJ	*Nederlandse Jurisprudentie* (NL)
NJB	*Nederlands Juristenblad* (NL)
NJCM	*Nederlands juristencomité voor de mensenrechten* (NL)
NJW	*Neue Juristische Wochenschrift* (D)
no./nr., nrs.	number, numbers
NRW	*Nordrhein-Westfalen* (D)
NSIS	National Schengen Information System
NStZ	*Neue Zeitschrift für Strafrecht* (D)
NWO	*Nederlandse organisatie voor wetenschappelijk onderzoek* (NL)
NWPolG	*Nordrhein-westfälisches Polizeigesetz* (D)
NZV	*Neue Zeitschrift für Verkehrsrecht* (D)
OIPG	*Operationeel contactpunt politiële gegevensuitwisseling* (B)
OLG	*Oberlandesgericht* (D)
OM	*Openbaar ministerie* (B, NL)
OrgKG	*Gesetz zur Bekämpfung der organisierten Kriminalität* (D)
OW	*Opiumwet* (NL)
OWiG	*Ordnungswidrigkeitengesetz* (D)
p., pp.	page, pages
P./Pas.	*Pasicrisie* (B, L)
Pan.	*Panopticon* (B)
par.	paragraph
PAuswG	*Personalausweisgesetz* (D)
PCO	*Point de contact opérationel* (B)
PolDÜVNW	*Polizeiliche Datenübermittlungsverordnung Nordrhein-Westfalen* (D)
PolW	*Politiewet* (NL)
POSA	*Peloton voor observatie, steun en arrestatie* (B)
pres.	president

R & K	*Recht & Kritiek* (B, NL)
RAID	*Unité de recherche, d'assistance, d'intervention et de dissuasion* (F)
rapp.	*rapporteur(s)* (B)
Rb.	*Arrondissementsrechtbank* (NL)
RCIC	*Regionaal communicatie- en informatiecentrum* (NL)
RDP	*Revue de droit pénal et de criminologie* (B)
Rev. Liège	*Jurisprudence de la Cour d'appel de Liège* (B)
Rev. sc. crim.	*Revue de science criminelle et de droit pénal comparé* (F)
RG	*Renseignements généraux* (F)
RhPfPAG	*Rheinland-pfälzisches Polizeiaufgabengesetz* (D)
RiStBV	*Richtlinien für das Strafverfahren und das Bußgeldverfahren* (D)
RiVASt	*Richtlinien für den Verkehr mit dem Ausland in strafrechtlichen Angelegenheiten* (D)
Rn.	*Randnummer* (D)
RO	*Wet op de rechterlijke organisatie* (NL)
RvdW	*Rechtspraak van de Week* (NL)
RVV	*Reglement verkeersregels en verkeerstekens* (NL)
R.W.	*Rechtskundig Weekblad* (B)
SC	Schengen Convention
SEK	*Spezialeinsatzkommando* (D)
SIE	*Speciaal interventie eskader* (B)
SIReNE	Supplementary information request at the national entry
SIS	Schengen Information System
SPD	*Sozialdemokratische Partei Deutschlands* (D)
SPolG	*Saarländisches Polizeigesetz* (D)
Sr	*Wetboek van strafrecht* (NL)
Stb.	*Staatsblad* (NL)
Stcrt.	*Staatscourant* (NL)
StGB	*Strafgesetzbuch* (D)
StPO	*Strafprozeßordnung* (D)
StV	*Strafverteidiger* (D)
StVO	*Straßenverkehrsordnung* (D)
StVollzG	*Strafvollzugsgesetz* (D)
StVZO	*Straßenverkehrs-Zulassungsordnung* (D)
Sv	*Wetboek van strafvordering* (B, NL)
Sw	*Strafwetboek* (B)
ThürPAG	*Thüringer Polizeiaufgabengesetz* (D)
TK	*Tweede Kamer* (NL)
Tr. Arr.	*Tribunal d'arrondissement* (L, F)
Trb.	*Tractatenblad* (NL)

TvP	*Tijdschrift voor de Politie* (NL)
UCLAF	*Unité communautaire de lutte anti-fraude*
U.K.	United Kingdom
UN	United Nations
UvA	*Universiteit van Amsterdam* (NL)
UZwG	*Unmittelbare-Zwangsgesetz* (D)
v.	versus
VE	*verdeckte Ermittler* (D)
VHW	*Voorlopige Hechteniswet* (B)
Vol.	Volume
VP	*Vertrauensperson* (D)
VR	*Verkeersrecht* (B, NL)
VRS	*Verkehrsrecht-Sammlung* (D)
VTSv	*Voorafgaande titel Wetboek van strafvordering* (B)
VU	*Vrije Universiteit* (NL)
VVPolGNW	*Verwaltungsvorschrift zum Polizeigesetz Nordrhein-Westfalen* (D)
WGP	*Wet op de gerechtelijke politie* (B)
WOB	*Wet openbaarheid van bestuur* (NL)
WPA	*Wet op het politieambt* (B)
WPolR	*Wet politieregisters* (NL)
WPR	*Wet persoonsregistraties* (NL)
WRW	*Wet op de rijkswacht* (B)
WVP	*Wet verwerking persoonsgegevens* (B)
WVR	*Wegverkeersreglement* (B)
WVW	*Wegenverkeerswet* (NL)
WWM	*Wet wapens en munitie* (NL)
ZRP	*Zeitschrift für Rechtspolitik* (D)

Part I

Context of International Police Cooperation

1 Introduction

Understanding a foreign law system has very much in common with learning a new language. Even after years of study, one cannot allege to have obtained the same insight as nationals. Moreover, a good knowledge of a foreign language, as of a foreign law system, demands much experience in practice. The fact that foreign law systems are not all available in the same language rather complicates the matter. Nevertheless, in this time of internationalization, one cannot go without the study of either foreign languages or law systems.

The countries of Western Europe have been growing closer since the end of World War II and have developed and intensified cooperation in an increasing number of domains. In the course of the eighties, Europeanization has been caught in a hurried pace of development. Even the last bastions of national sovereignty have not escaped this trend. Hastened by the growing fear of organized crime, institutional cooperation has reached criminal law. Consultation organs such as TREVI, Pompidou and all sorts of *ad hoc* committees make their appearance, while international organizations like the United Nations, the Council of Europe, the European Community and Union as well as the Benelux Union are increasingly involved in international cooperation in criminal matters.

One of the instruments created in this climate is the 1990 Schengen Implementation Convention (SC): This Convention, originally signed by Belgium, The Netherlands, Luxembourg, France and Germany, aims to implement the Schengen Agreement signed in 1985 by the same countries. The Convention, which at the origin essentially aimed at creating an internal market free of border controls for the European Community before the fateful year of 1992, has set up an elaborate set of rules designed to limit the consequences of the abolition of border controls. Among the innovations of the Schengen Convention is the setting up of a meticulous - and yet still general - framework for the operational cross-border police cooperation, including features such as cross-border observation and hot-pursuit, the incorporation of rules on the use of coercive measures in a foreign country and the creation of a computerized data bank, the Schengen Information System (SIS), which will be directly accessible to police services in the Contracting Parties.

1.1 Framework of the Study

The whole of the following study is based on the emergence, at least in its formal regulation, of a new form of police cooperation within Western-Europe: cross-border cooperation.[1] This topic has, in recent years, been privileged with a large amount of publicity. However, the discussion has been monopolized by the issue of drug trafficking. Although this is not completely undefendable considering the social problems associated with drug use, one cannot underestimate the problems related to other forms of criminality less blessed with media coverage.[2]

When discussing cross-border cooperation and crime repression, one can distinguish between crimes that can be investigated with the help of traditional methods, such as robberies, theft, homicide, murder and rape from crimes that cannot. The former are characterized by the fact that they involve direct victims and may be investigated on the basis of declarations of witnesses and victims, as well as of the traces left at the scene of the crime, while the latter escape investigation in the conventional manner. One can speak in this case of victimless or consensual crimes.

These crimes escaping conventional investigation are for instance consensual crimes (such as drug trafficking), relative consensual crimes (such as fraud and environmental crimes) and crimes that are related to the dependant character of the relationship between the criminal and the victim (for instance in trafficking in human beings, some types of prostitution, some types of sexual abuse, child pornography). Because of this, their investigation must rely on special policing techniques such as infiltration, the use of informers, technically advanced forms of observation, controlled delivery, the matching of data bank information, and anonymous witnesses. All these special policing techniques have in common their difficult if not impossible controllability.

The fact that drug trafficking monopolizes the media discussion is a questionable development for many reasons. Firstly, many of these methods are not regulated by any treaty and secondly, and most importantly, one underestimates in that way the impact of other forms of crime for which the cross-border police cooperation is meant and regulated. Moreover, it is a question well worth asking whether drug trafficking should indeed be repressed with the intensity

---

1   This does not mean, however, that cross-border police cooperation did not exist before its incorporation as an extension of police jurisdiction in the Schengen Convention, rather it was given a formal treaty basis.

2   It seems that it is difficult to find police data on issues such as arms trafficking. Drug trafficking even seems to monopolize national police registers in The Netherlands. This was pointed out by Fijnaut during his hearing before the Dutch parliamentary enquiry committee Van Traa in September 1995. He stated that he could not find any data on arms trafficking in the registers of the police.

this is being done. This only contributes to maintaining the market for the crime organizations without substantially solving the problem of drug abuse and suppliance criminality.

Nevertheless, it is important to study the international police cooperation more closely for the following reasons: First, international police cooperation already exists in practice. Second, this police cooperation has an impact on civil rights and liberties of the citizens, as well as on national sovereignty - and democratic legitimacy - of the Contracting Parties. Finally, it is clear that improving international cooperation in any domain, especially in a domain such as police cooperation, will benefit society in general. However, there are several reasons not to pretend that we have been able to cover and discuss the entire practice and regulatory system of international police cooperation. Although every single one of these reasons will certainly return in the course of this study, some of the most important ones may be mentioned at this early stage. Firstly, the phenomenon of cooperation in criminal matters has meanwhile taken on too many aspects and forms to inventorize all of them. Secondly, the subject is still strongly developing, not just its formal and institutionalized structure (as will be sketched in Chapter 2), but also informally. Thirdly, a constant impediment for a more or less complete overview and study of international police coope- ration is its basically secret and hidden character. This leads to a relative inaccessibility of material, especially regarding practical aspects but also with respect to internal regulations, guidelines, etcetera. As a result of this hidden character, lawyers in cases involving international cooperation are also forced to work with limited information and case-law does not reveal much of the practice either.

1.1.1 Aim and Problem Definition

In recent years, the signature of the Schengen Implementation Convention in 1990 has been the subject of numerous publications on international police cooperation.[3] Most of these publications essentially concern aspects of institu- tional, administrative or political cooperation: Few have considered a substan- tive, comparative study of the law applying to police powers.[4] The importance of mutual knowledge of rules and regulations in policing powers is indeed essential for an efficient and well grinded cross-border police cooperation in fighting cross-border crime. This is why we, on request of the *Nederlandse organisatie voor Wetenschappelijk Onderzoek* (NWO) and with the financial

---

3   One can, for instance, refer to Meijers *et al.*, 1991; Fijnaut *et al.*, 1992; Morié *et al.*, 1992; Benyon *et al.*, 1992; Anderson & Den Boer, 1992; D'Haenens & De Ruyver, 1992, as well as many articles in specialized periodicals.
4   Hofstede *et al.*, 1993 forms one of the rare exceptions to this.

support of the Dutch ministries of the interior and of justice, have been enabled to study these police powers since early 1991.

The original question as formulated in the many reports made to NWO in the course of the project was the following:

1. What is the law applicable to international police cooperation between Belgium, The Netherlands, Luxembourg, France and Germany (the original Schengen-countries)?
2. How does the cooperation function in the practice of crime repression?
3. Is a further regulation of this cooperation necessary, and to what extent?

After the first two years, additional questions rose:

4. Are the different national law systems in accordance with international treaties on police cooperation, and to what extent?
5. How do they offer sufficient guarantees in the light of the European Convention on Human Rights?

The central frame of the problem is the question as to which law is applicable for the police cooperation between the five original Schengen parties and whether this legal basis is sufficient to support the actual practice of the police cooperation.

These questions may be divided in three main studies: An inventory of the law in each country, an inventory of the actual practice and the analysis of the results of the first two studies to answer the question as to whether the legal framework is sufficient to support the practice. At the time this project started, it was thought that the Convention would come into force in early 1991 and that the practice of police cooperation on the basis of Schengen between the countries would form the bulk of the study. However, in the course of the first year of this project, it became apparent that the Convention would not be in force as soon as planned; finally, it was not in force until March 26, 1995. Moreover, the limited time of the study rendered illusionary the pretention to answer all of these questions in the given delay, therefore we felt the need to restrict the scope of this study considerably. Soon, the project was known in the corridors of the faculty of law, the ministries and NWO as "the Schengen-project." This designation was well chosen since we decided to concentrate on the 1990 Schengen Convention and the 1962 Benelux Extradition Treaty - it plays an important role in police cooperation between three of the original Schengen Parties - as the basis of what was seen as international police cooperation between the studied countries. Treaties and institutions as Interpol, TREVI and Europol, were only mentioned when relevant to certain issues.

One of the aims of the research, as was mentioned above, was to examine the legal framework of international cooperation in the light of the everyday police practice. It was thought that the lack of time could be partly compensated by directly interviewing police practitioners and scanning data found in police registers (for which we obtained authorization from the Dutch minister of justice) in border regions. However, this method did not prove to be as effective as we first thought, probably for the following reasons. There is still little experience with the Schengen Convention in practice, as it has not been in force very long. In this respect, we were still interested in information on cross-border problems before Schengen since such information can serve as a basis for the question whether Schengen has created a valid legal framework for existing problems. One of the further problems we encountered with the study was the limited information provided by the police of border regions, even after repeated requests. A possible reason for this might be perhaps the lack of cross-border problems, or at least the low frequency with which such problems occur: The information we did examine originating from the police registers only shows cross-border reactions of the police in answer to petty cross-border criminality and burglaries in cars and in houses. Another reason might be that the police either ignore the existence of the problems or are reluctant to supply such information to third parties. Nevertheless, the actual reason could not be established, and meanwhile, the ministry of justice has engaged another research of the first experiences with Schengen. A result of this for our project was, that several police forces in border areas could not provide us with information any more, since they were too busy cooperating with other projects.

Further, we have looked especially at what appeared to us as the innovation of the Schengen Convention (and the Benelux Extradition Treaty): The introduction of cross-border powers for police officers. We have concentrated on the operational cross-border police cooperation, active as well as passive cooperation: all forms of concerted police actions and the tolerance by national authorities of foreign police officers on their national territory. We have not considered issues of public order or illegal immigration: The police cooperation, which we have made the main issue of this study, is the cooperation in criminal matters and therefore we have excluded all forms of judicial cooperation (such extradition and judiciary assistance), administrative and policy cooperation, these being extensively described and analyzed in numerous works.[5]

The reason we have chosen not to consider the issue of immigration, despite the fact that this is sure to have an impact on the everyday police practice in the border regions, is primarily one of time limit. The issue of immigration and Schengen has been discussed in other works. Moreover, the magnitude of the

---

5   See for instance on criminal law enforcement cooperation such as extradition Stanbrook & Stanbrook, 1980; on mutual legal assistance by judicial authorities see Thomas, 1980 and Sjöcrona, 1990; on administrative and policy aspects of police cooperation in border areas see Claus, 1995.

remaining topic - international cooperation in crime repression - was such as to keep us busy for the entire time of the subvention period and beyond.[6]

Yet another restriction concerns the political, institutional and organizational side of police cooperation. The most important reason for this is the fact that it has been the subject of numerous books and studies.[7] Further, the institutional evolution of police cooperation is for the most part still in progress: When will the Europol Treaty be ratified? Which European or national institutions will exercise the judiciary control? What will be the scope of the jurisdiction? Will there be European rules of criminal procedure? Considering these institutional developments, the only option remaining for researchers of that field is to follow the evolution closely on the hand of the numerous articles published in legal periodicals and formulate criteria for this institutional cooperation.

Finally, we have decided to exclusively consider police powers, since in the light of the Schengen Convention this area of the police work will have the most repercussions on the everyday practice of cross-border cooperation. We have restricted the choice of the police powers to the following criterium: The police powers that will play a role in operational cross-border cooperation. These are observation, controlled delivery, hot-pursuit, apprehension, the use of physical force, bodily search, police interrogation and mutual legal aid by police officers. In occurrence, these are all independent police powers when the police enjoy the full initiative of the enquiry.

As we have stated above, it was thought in the first year of the study that it would be possible to make an evaluation of the first years of the Schengen practice as the Schengen Convention was thought to come into force in early 1991. However, since this proved not to be the case, there was still little known about the Schengen practice at the time this study was completed. Moreover, there was a total absence of case-law on the interpretation of the different provisions of the Convention. This is why, in the end, the study is not a comparison of national laws in the framework of the first experiences of the Schengen practice, but rather a theoretic interpretation of the Convention in the light of a comparison of the respective legal systems in the countries involved.

For this reason, the results of our study cannot be considered as a first evaluation of the Schengen Convention, but rather as previsions on the hand of a comparative analysis of the different official versions of the text of the Convention, leading necessarily to speculative elements. Indeed, this does influence the conclusions, suggestions and recommendations made at the end

6   For thorough discussions of Schengen and its implications for immigration, aliens and refugee law, see for instance Boeles, 1991; Bolten, 1991; Van Es, 1991; Hoogenboom, 1991; Steenbergen, 1991; Jessurun d'Oliveira, 1994, pp. 261-278; King, 1994.

7   See, among others, Anderson, 1989; Anderson & Den Boer, 1992; Fijnaut *et al.*, 1992; Benyon *et al.*, 1993; Anderson & Den Boer, 1994.

of this study. Nevertheless, we hope that this study as a whole, despite the absence of the evaluation of the practice that was originally intended, may have an impact on the practice of police cooperation.

Successful operational cross-border cooperation as aimed by Title III of the Schengen Convention can only be accomplished - and this brings us to a central hypothesis - when the problems of reciprocal knowledge and ignorance of the law of the different Contracting Parties have been solved.[8] Because this book may serve as a reference book and an interpretation tool, we hope it may be of some assistance in reaching that aim. Moreover, comparative police studies are a condition for proper international police cooperation.[9] Harmonization may not be an aim in itself, it must be, as it occurs, a consequence of intensive cooperation. Wanting hasty harmonization will paradoxically lead to tension and friction between countries and hinder harmonious cooperation.

1.1.2 Methods

Researching a topic that enjoys so much publicity and is in such evolution is a very trying experience. It involves constant revising, reviewing and rewriting and is always on the verge of falling in abeyance. Moreover, the growing interest for the so-called special policing techniques, which reached a peak (in The Netherlands) during the parliamentary enquiry of Fall 1995, has resulted in an avalanche of case-law and publications not only in specialized periodicals but also in newspapers and popular periodicals, especially concerning observation techniques, infiltration and exchange of police data. Because of this, we ended up with enough material to write a thesis on each of these topics alone. This was, however, but one of the problems we were confronted with since the beginning of the project in 1991.

Another problem we were confronted with involved the great cultural differences existing between the countries, leading to differences in their approach to crime, criminal law and criminal justice. This often lead to a great imbalance in information. Many items which are the object of formal statutes in one country are completely ignored in the statutes of another. To give just one classic example, the concept of suspicion is one that has been developed in great detail in countries as The Netherlands and Germany. However, in countries as Belgium, Luxembourg and France, this concept has not been

---

8   Nijboer, 1994, p. 22, stresses the importance of comparative law as means of increasing mutual knowledge and improving international cooperation.

9   See Fijnaut, 1994c, pp. 95 *et seq.*; the importance of comparative law in this field was also recognized by the Dutch parliament's enquiry committee on police investigations (the Van Traa committee) and the Dutch ministry of justice. Both ordered an extensive comparative research of undercover police methods; see Van Traa, 1996, App. V, pp. 455-524 and Tak *et al.*, 1996.

developed at all, neither in the literature nor in the case-law. The same differences in approach also lead to a difference in the regulation levels in the various countries. Because of this, we were often confronted with comparing (what seemed to us) apples and peaches.

A further problem concerned the difference in culture as to the accessibility of certain information. In some countries (particularly The Netherlands and Germany), the police seems to be seen in the first place as a public body which should be controlled. Because of this, most of the rules concerning its jurisdiction and powers are published in formal law. In other countries (France and, to some extent, Luxembourg), the police rather seems to represent one of the last bastions of the State sovereignty and security. In those countries, rules on the police, if existing, are found for an important part in (secret) circulars or directives. As the situation in Belgium seems to show, a combination of those two elements is possible as well.[10]

The relative secrecy in which the international police cooperation is discussed between the Contracting Parties caused yet additional problems. Many documents related to the practical implementation of Schengen are confidential. This may result in distortion as to the interpretation we give to the Convention and the actual interpretation given by the Contracting Parties. We have learned by accident, for instance, that one of the Schengen working groups has been set up to discuss issues as the concept and use of service weapons, the concept of self-defence and the concept of border region. Reports of this working group are confidential; this means that they cannot, in principle, be taken into account in our study despite their evident relevance.

We have encountered more fundamental problems as well, such as four different levels of language problems.[11] On the first level, we find three official languages in the five studied countries. Dutch in The Netherlands and Belgium, French in Belgium, Luxembourg and France and German in Germany and Luxembourg. This means that all of the special terminology used in the police law of these countries had to be given a valid English translation. We have been largely inspired in our choice of terminology by the English translation of the Schengen Convention published by the Benelux/Schengen secretariat in Brussels.[12] We have chosen to only use the English equivalent at the beginning of each chapter, with the original expression in the original language in parentheses. The second level of language problems is found between the different countries or country regionss which share the same language but do not use the same terminology. Dutch expressions used in The Netherlands do not necessarily

---

10   We discussed this more thoroughly in Bevers & Joubert, 1994, pp. 318-319.
11   This type of problem in comparative law has been sketched as well by Pradel (1995, pp. 37-39).
12   Published in Meijers *et al.*, 1991.

correspond to Dutch expressions in Belgium. The same goes for French express-ions in France, in Belgium and in Luxembourg.[13] We have managed to resolve this level of language problems by considering only the content of the express-ion, the *signified* - what the expression means - as opposed to the *significant* - the way it is being expressed - in order to find a valid and representative equivalent. The third level of problems is encountered when the expression used in the French, Dutch or German version of the Convention does not correspond to expressions used in the law of the country where the language concerned is an official language. The last level of language problems concerns the internal cohesion of the text of the Convention. It seems that the different versions of the Convention do not correspond with one another and that in some places the French version, for instance, may be interpreted differently than the Dutch version. The combination of this problems has caused some difficulty in the interpretation of the Convention and we have attempted to find a solution in each separate case.[14]

Table 1.1 Encountered Language Problems

Law language **Law source**	**National-national**	**National-international**	**International-international**
Same language	Countries sharing the same language	Texts of the same language	Int. texts of the same language
Different language	Countries of different languages	Texts of different languages	Int. texts of differ-ent languages

In trying to overcome the inherent problems of comparative law (culture, language, level of regulation, absence of equivalence and balance, apples and peaches syndrome etcetera), one can opt for different solutions. One solution is to have a number of researchers, scholars or learned practitioners from different countries give an overview of their own system in a common language according to a common schedule of analysis.[15] One of the risks inherent to this method, although a very worthy one, is the egocentric and ego-ethnic approach it may encourage. Despite the common schedule of analysis, many researchers may be tempted to add or discard issues according to their national situation. Inconsequent choices in translation is also a risk.

---

13   An example which will further be worked out in chapters 6 and 7: The expressions *aanhou-den/staandehouden* in the Convention as opposed to these same expressions in Dutch law have a legal meaning that the French and German expressions do not.

14   We have discussed this problem and its resolution further here below.

15   This method was used in a number of comparative studies, for instance Prakke & Kortmann, 1993; Osner *et al.*, 1993; Van den Wyngaert, 1993a; EC Commission 1994.

Another solution is to limit the amount of researchers working on a number of law systems which are not necessarily their own. One researcher studying two systems - none of which being his own - is in theory capable of analyzing both systems according to the same schedule and free of national pet hobby-horses. This approach does imply a substantial investment in full study time. However, what such a study might lack in thoroughness and detail knowledge, it gains in distance and it even may, in the best of cases, offer a refreshing look at old issues. This was the option for this project: limit the number of researchers to two, both having an active knowledge of each of the three relevant languages.

However, team work in legal research demands very close cooperation and solid arrangements. In some occasions, you may even ask yourself whether a third person should not be hired as an umpire. It is essential for the study that the two agree on a very strict schedule of analysis. We have lost track of the number of discussions and disagreements we have had over the years on divisions in the text, terminology, spelling (British or American?), lay-out, differences in opinion and visions and many other topics. What appeared to be coincidental agreements in the beginning eventually developed into structural cooperation.

The first agreement we were obliged to make concerned the areas of research and the division of the work load. In the first two years, we let our respective competence in different languages lead our choice: Countries with French as a legal language on one hand and Dutch and German languages on the other. Because there were five countries and two researchers we both shared The Netherlands. The first two years were essentially spent taking an inventory of the legal framework of the criminal procedure during the police enquiry in each country. In the last years, a division was made according to topics, more or less in a coincidental manner, according to preference and who was the first to chose a subject and begin a new chapter.

As for the actual research method used, we have made a rather classical choice: "study, discuss, travel, read and write."[16] We have more or less chosen a formal approach to legal systems, preferring formal legal sources to informal and incidental information. The order of preference in the sources was mainly the following: Written formal statutes and case-law in the first place, followed by lower levels of legislation inside the original system and framework. Literature follows, firstly in the original system or country, subsidiarily in a comparative framework. Other, less formal sources were, in the course of study trips, discussion with authorities, scholars and other local practitioners, and systematic as well as incidental practical visits in border regions. We completed

---

16   Nijboer, 1994, p. 23.

the information gathered on location with phone calls with contact persons in the studied countries and national practitioners of the international cooperation.

One of the most elaborate agreements that had to be made concerned the common denominators to be used in the comparative analysis of the different systems. We agreed on a common scheme for each topic, a common English vocabulary, a common point of reference or standard (the European Convention on Human Rights as the guardian of the rule of law), a common interpretation of treaties and finally a common analysis of questions. The common scheme is roughly embodied in each of the chapters concerning police powers. After the two introductory chapters on international police cooperation and the structure of criminal procedure in each of the countries, we have analyzed the police powers in a homogenous manner: an overview of the international law relative to that particular police power, followed by the applicable standards of the European Convention on Human Rights, an overview of the legal rules on that particular police power in each country, a comparative analysis and a conclusion of the particular aspect of the police cooperation in the light of the European Convention on Human Rights. In this way we hope to have achieved more than a description of the applicable law, rather than an analysis of the legal situation as a whole as well as a workable tool for the practice of police cooperation.

Indeed, in retrospective, the choice of the countries to be studied has come about in a rather uncommon manner. It was not based on a former hypothesis on the supposition that the countries would have particularly interesting legislation for the subject at hand[17] or that they belong to the same legal family,[18] but because the concerned countries have made a political choice to intensify their cooperation.[19] One alternative might have been to compare the Schengen system of cooperation with that of Scandinavian countries. Because of the fact that such research is being done at the rival University of Amsterdam (UvA), we have made a lucky choice in not considering this an option.[20] The ideal model of cooperation would perhaps be a combination of both systems.

The relative large number of countries[21] and of matters[22] we compared made it impossible to conduct a detailed study of the respective criminal procedure law systems. Because of that, we were faced with the obligation of

---

17 See Florijn, 1994, p. 46
18 Nijboer, 1994, pp. 43-46.
19 This was for instance the case for the countries chosen by Van den Wyngaert, 1993a; for a similar report edited by the EC, see EC Commission, 1994.
20 Mulder & Rüter, 1995.
21 In contrary to the studies done in Fennell *et al.*, 1995; Machielse, 1986; Lensing, 1988; De Doelder & Mul, 1994.
22 In contrary to for instance Lensing, 1988; Tak, 1990; Tak & Lensing, 1990; Fijnaut, 1991; Fijnaut, 1994a; Tak, 1994a.

making necessary concessions. However, despite these concessions as to the profundity of the study, we have seen the chance to look into a number of matters not yet or scarcely described.[23]

As we have said above, understanding a foreign law system is similar to learning a language: Reading statutes is not understanding their scope and function. "Notwithstanding his extensive coverage of foreign countries, Montesquieu remained conscious of the risk incurred by utilizing this (comparative; CJ/HB) method: Could one ever know so much about a foreign country that one could draw the correct conclusions? As he noted: 'Many things rule the behaviour of men - the climate, the religion, the laws, the maxims of government, the examples of things past, the morals, the manners; and therefrom results a general spirit which is thus formed' (....) Montesquieu's statement embodies the problem which remains unsolved more than two centuries later: How can one understand a political system without having fully grasped the general spirit of that system? Additionally, how can one assess the general spirit without a complete knowledge of the many different elements which compose that system?"[24]

To achieve a deeper understanding of the different law systems and their capacity to cooperate in the field of policing would necessitate a thorough comparative study of the historical, sociological and cultural-anthropological background of the five countries. The ideal research method in that view would be to spend at least one year in each of the countries, at best directly at the police. This comparative study would probably give insight into the reasons of the revealed differences and similarities. However, we have chosen to leave such a sociological study to others for the following reasons. Firstly, despite the fact that such a comparative cultural study of the police would contribute largely to an improvement in the actual cooperation, such a study is not essential for answering operational questions on the legal validity and applicability of treaties on international cooperation. Secondly, the allotted time for this project was not sufficient to permit this kind of study. Finally and foremostly in our opinion, we do not, as legal researchers, dispose of the proper scientific qualifications in social science to conduct such an important study. Because of the two former reasons, this last reason did not prove to be an impeachment.

We did however manage to obtain an impression of police and criminal law enforcement in all five countries, particularly by paying numerous visits to bodies and practitioners of law enforcement and international cooperation in each of the countries. Furthermore, we were so lucky to find criminal lawyers,

---

23 Matters such as cross-border hot-pursuit, observation, infiltration, exchange of police information, as well as a country which is far from being known: Luxembourg.
24 Koopmans, 1986; on comparative criminal law see Remmelink, 1993; Nijboer, 1994; Pradel, 1995.

police officers and scholars in each country who were willing to read and check our findings regarding their own legal system. This had become possible thanks to the fact that all our texts were in English, a language far more widespread than Dutch.

1.1.2.1 Schengen Convention and Benelux Extradition Treaty, a Combined Interpretation

When interpreting various versions of a treaty that do not seem to be compatible, one may chose to give all versions the meaning that will have the least incompatibilities with the others. This interpretation technique, which aims to interpret a text in such a way that there is no conflict between the different versions, is what German law calls a *Verfassungskonforme Auslegung*[25] and seems to conform to art. 33 par. 4 of the Vienna Convention on the Interpretation of Treaties.[26] Confronted with a number of interpretation problems in the course of this study, we have chosen to interpret the three official texts of the Schengen Convention and the two texts of the Benelux Extradition Treaty in a sense that gives all texts the same content. We feel, to take the different versions of art. 41 SC, that it is most logical to assume that foreign police officers, given the possibility to apprehend a suspect in order to hand the person over to the locally competent authorities, are also given the power to immobilize and retain the suspect until the local police arrive and, for their own safety, to handcuff him and proceed to his security search.[27]

This interpretation of the different versions of art. 41 par. 2 under b and par. 5 sub f SC is, as was stated above, is supported by other arguments as well. Art. 33 of the Vienna Convention on the Interpretation of Treaties addresses the issue of treaties that have been drawn up in two or more official languages. The first paragraph states that one should look firstly whether the Treaty provides for the solving of language-related interpretation problems. In the case at hand, it is to be regretted that the Schengen Convention does not. Secondly, it is possible that a version in another (unofficial) language may be consulted to shine light on the intention of the parties. This is, however, only possible when the parties have agreed on this method of interpretation, which does not seem to be the case here. Par. 3 states that all terms of a Treaty are presumed

---

25 The German constitutional court uses this technique, called literally "interpretation in conformity with the constitution," to interpret provisions that do not seem to be in complete accordance with the German constitution. In that way, they chose the interpretation that is most compatible with the constitution, excluding all incompatible interpretations but without annulling the provision entirely. Dworkin, 1986, p. 53, refers to this benevolent type of interpretation as "the principle of charity."

26 Vienna, May 23, 1969, Trb. 1977, 169.

27 This interpretation will be discussed in further details in chapters 6 through 10.

to have the same meaning in all authentic texts. Par. 4 states further that when the parties have not agreed on a solution and when the Treaty does not contain any clause resolving eventual language differences, one may seek advice in artt. 31 and 32. Only when this last method does not resolve the problem, one may give the problematic term the meaning that reconciles the different texts the best, taking the subject and aim of the Treaty into account. Reading artt. 31 and 32 of the Vienna Convention on the interpretation of treaties gives us a first indication of the context, the subject and the aim of the Treaty. By referring to the context, subject and aim of the Treaty, one may rely on additional sources such as the explanatory statements. These may be a good indication of the intention of the parties.

Reading the Dutch explanatory statement to the Schengen Ratification Act[28] does not shine any light on the matter and leaves the question open as to whether apprehension (in Dutch *staande houden*) must be understood in its strict Dutch definition or in a larger sense. Probably because of the fact that the French declaration with respect to the conditions of hot pursuit on their territory does not give any foreign officer the power to apprehend someone on French territory, the French explanatory statement does not contain any element that might help in solving the problem. However, one may read in this statement that foreign officers will not be allowed to arrest suspects on French territory, demonstrating in that way how the expressions are used loosely.[29] The Luxembourg explanatory statement does not bring any new element that would permit us to conclude one or another option.[30] The Belgian explanatory statement does not help us any further,[31] nor does the German.[32]

When trying to interpret a treaty in three languages, all of which are official, the Vienna Convention states in its art. 33 par. 4 that in the case that the differences cannot be worked out in the light of explanatory statements and other official sources, one must seek an interpretation that reconciles these texts in the best possible manner in the light of the aim and subject of the treaty.

The Schengen Convention aims to establish a zone where free circulation of goods and persons can be achieved. In doing so, the Contracting Parties have adopted a series of compensatory measures designed to palliate a possible threat to the internal security of the different states caused by the lifting of border controls. Title III aims to regulate police cooperation in the newly created

---

28 *Memorie van Toelichting Goedkeuringswet Overeenkomst van Schengen*, TK 22 140, nr. 3.
29 See *Assemblée Nationale*, no. 2055 (1990-1991), p. 36: "*En France, les agents de la police étrangère poursuivant ne pourront pas procéder eux-même à l'arrestation du malfaiteur, la police française seule disposant de ce pouvoir.*"
30 See *Chambre des députés*, nr. 3567 (1991-1992), p. 6.
31 See *Sénat de Belgique, Session extraordinaire*, 1991-1992, nr. 464/1.
32 Explanatory statement (*Begründung zum Vertragsgesetz*), BT-Drucksache 12/2453.

Schengen territory. The purpose of art. 41 is to regulate cross-border hot pursuit and sub-paragraph 5 f intends to provide rules for the case where the locally competent authorities are unable to intervene in time. If foreign officers in that case have the power to stop the fleeing suspect, is it not logical that they also have the power to maintain him in place, and if necessary to handcuff him, at least until the arrival of the locally competent authorities? In our opinion this would be the interpretation that reconciles the three versions in the most logical way. Assuming our interpretation of this disposition is a true reflection of the intention of the contracting parties and with the necessary reserves as to this interpretation, we will examine the different national law systems and the Schengen Convention in the light of this interpretation.

1.1.2.2 The Rule of Law and the European Convention on Human Rights as a Common Standard

In the course of this book, we often refer to the rule of law as a universal standard. Indeed, one of the things the studied countries have in common is that they all abide by the rule of law. Moreover, they have obliged themselves by treaty to respect the principles of the rule of law.[33] Historically, the rule of law simply signifies the subjection of the royal power to ordinary law.[34] This idea, along with the idea of democracy, was debated fiercely during the seventeenth century throughout Europe.

We have chosen the European Convention on Human Rights as an inspiration for our vision of what the rule of law should represent. It is possible to distinguish between two main conceptions of the rule of law in modern times. The first, representing a more positivist way of looking at law, tends to limit the rule of law to its purely formal and logical component: The rule of law is the formal subjection of the State to ordinary law.. This is embodied in the second paragraphs of the articles guaranteeing the right to privacy, right to freedom of thought, freedom of expression and freedom of pacific reunion (artt. 8-11 ECHR), in which the Convention sets as a condition for the restriction to a right or freedom the existence of a formal law. Other rights such as the right to life (art. 2), and the right to liberty and security (and art. 5) are subject to

---

33 Every member State of the European Convention on Human Rights is a member of the Council of Europe. The obligation to respect the rule of law is both expressed in art. 3 of the statute of the Council of Europe (Statute of London, May 5, 1949, published as an appendix in Manual of the Council of Europe, 1970, pp. 299-312; Dutch text in: Stb. J. 341 (1949, p. 569)) as well as in the preamble of the European Convention on Human Rights; see also Van Dijk & Van Hoof, 1990, p. 191.

34 Brun & Tremblay, 1985, p. 476.

yet stricter norms.[35] The prerequisites of this formal law have been developed especially in the cases Kruslin and Huvig, where a number of conditions were stated. Par. 2 of art. 8 ECHR, "requires firstly that the impugned measure should have more basis in domestic law (than general case-law); it also refers to the quality of the law in question, requiring that it should be accessible to the person concerned, who must moreover be able to foresee its consequences for him, and compatible with the rule of law." The positivist view of the rule of law rests on the premise that each act of the State must be justifiable by some kind of superior norm. This view gives the rule of law an essentially formal content. The hierarchy of the different State functions may be summarized as follows: predominance of the legislative over the judiciary and the executive. The rule of law is then restricted to its expression in the principle of legality.

The second, inspired from the theories of natural law, gives the rule of law a more elaborated material content, which is that of the minimal standards of justice.[36] In principle, the formal content of the principle of legality is sufficient to guarantee the rule of law in a State. However, one can imagine that formal legality is not necessarily the only factor guaranteeing the predominance of law. A government that would constantly invoke special laws or govern by decrees in order to restrict the rights of its citizens would indeed respect the principle of legality. Such a government would dispose of unlimited arbitrary power which it would abuse. This is why many have advocated the recognition of minimal guarantees as being part of the rule of law, law being in that sense a higher universal norm. International law of the protection of human rights generally insists on this aspect of the rule of law. The European Convention on Human Rights, for instance, enumerates fundamental rights, some of which may not suffer any restriction.[37] Those which can be restricted are submitted to a number of formal and material conditions to legitimize the violations.[38] One can view the rights and freedoms as guaranteed by the European Convention on Human Rights as a blanket protecting each individual in the Member States. These fundamental rights and freedoms may be seen as the expression of higher norms binding the States. Secondly, the member States are bound to

35 This has been acknowledged by the Court in McCann and Others v. U.K., September 27, 1995, Series A, 324, p. 41 of the judgement.
36 Brun & Tremblay, 1985, p. 480.
37 This is the case for instance of the protection against torture, inhuman or degrading treatment or punishment (art. 3) and the protection against slavery (art. 4).
38 As we have stated above, this is the case, for instance, for the right to privacy, freedom of thought, freedom of expression and freedom of peaceful reunion (artt. 8-11) which can only be restricted according to law (formal condition) and when it is necessary in a democratic society (material condition). The right to life (art. 2) and the right to liberty and security (art. 5) are submitted to yet more formalities, whereas the protection against torture, degrading or inhuman treatment or punishment cannot suffer any restrictions.

a more formal rule of law: Restrictions to these rights and freedoms may only occur as the formal prescriptions of the Convention are followed. Finally, all Member States of the Council of Europe have obliged themselves to recognize and respect the rule of law. Formal legality is necessary for the democratic control, as well as for the foreseeability and accessibility, while the rule of natural law is necessary for limiting the power of the legislative.[39]

Although the principles of the rule of law discussed above apply to all the domains of State action, its repercussions for areas such as substantial criminal law, criminal procedure and police law are evident. Actions of the State in that area are liable to infringe upon the rights and liberties of citizens. In our opinion, the rule of law signifies at least the fact that the State is bound by law to the same extent as ordinary civilians and therefore it cannot operate beyond or above the law. We believe that the State should not, in principle, engage in activities which, carried out by ordinary citizens, would lead to criminal prosecution. If the State chooses to infringe upon this principle, it should do so only on the basis of formal law, therefore after having this choice and the extent of the infringement publicly controlled by parliament. But this formality alone should not suffice to legitimize the systematic resort to the violation of fundamental rights. The necessity of such violations should be demonstrated in a democratic society.

1.2 Historical Evolution of the Project

In retrospect, one of the factors that has positively influenced our writing stamina was the obligation towards our sponsors, one of them being the Dutch ministry of the interior, to produce a full report at the end of the first two years. In order to meet this obligation, we were obliged to immediately begin writing. We promptly started to collect material and visit seminars and congresses to orientate ourselves. In that first year, we managed to arrange a number of visits to police services in border regions in four of the countries to be studied.[40]

---

39 Dworkin (1986, p. 93) defines the rule of law as follows: "Law insists that force not be used or withheld, no matter how useful that would be to ends in view, no matter how beneficial or noble these ends, except when licensed or required by individual rights and responsibilities flowing from past political decisions about when collective force is justified." Dworkin seems in that way to reunite two apparently opposed positions. On the one hand, he insists on the necessity of the respect of individual rights and on the other hand, the need for political decisions as a more "formal" prerequisite.

40 In that first year, we visited the Luxembourg *gendarmerie* in Dudelange, the German police in Saarburg and the French *gendarmerie* in Metz, Thionville and Sierck-les-Bains, all in the Moselle region. Later, we managed to arrange visits in Kortrijk to the Belgian *gendarmerie*, municipal police and judicial police and to the French police in Lille. In addition, we paid several visits to documentary centres and libraries, such as the documentation centre of the *Gendarmerie Nationale* and the *Institut de Hautes Etudes en Sécurité Intérieure* in Paris, the

The visits were aimed at becoming acquainted with the everyday police practice in border regions in these four countries. As a result of this writing craze at the end of the second year, we confronted our directors with a manuscript of 900 pages.

The fact that the ministry of the interior expected a report so soon is a circumstance we saw mostly as an advantage: It contributed largely to our motivation in putting our findings on paper. Furthermore, it offered a definite deadline, much more tangible than the vague knowledge that a doctorate thesis must be completed within four years. However, it may prove to have had some unpleasant consequences. Time for a thorough legal and factual orientation in the study material was lacking because writing had to be started immediately. Ironically, the material and financial means placed at our disposal for the purpose of the research could not be used optimally because of this time limit. The possibility to spend more time with the police forces in border regions was reduced to a minimum, despite elaborate financial means available.

A preliminary version of the interim report was presented to representatives of the ministries of justice and the interior on June 1, 1993. For the occasion, an expert meeting was organized and a number of authorities from different areas of criminal law and police practice were invited to assist us in formulating further aims of the research.[41]

One of the most important conclusions of this meeting was that the report in its original form was far too voluminous whereas, at the same moment, many of the various participants thought that the inventory made was still incomplete. In the light of this, it was further concluded that the research should not be directed at any professional group in particular, but that it rather should develop its scholastic character. In that way, the study could reach all the professional groups involved with the practice of criminal procedure at the same time. Furthermore, the research should concentrate on typical problem areas of the police cooperation related to the collection of evidence. It was also suggested that a field research of the practice of police cooperation would be an interesting complement to the inventory of legal regulations. The results of the first part of the research as well as preliminary conclusions were published in Dutch in the beginning of 1994.[42]

---

documentation centre of the Amsterdam Police, the Police Study Centre in Warnsveld, the Detective School in Zutphen, the Police Direction Academy in Münster, the Peace Palace and the Central Criminal Intelligence Centre (CRI) in The Hague, and the library of the *gendarmerie* in Brussels.

41 At this conference, the following persons were present: M. Bakker, M. van den Berg, J.K. Boissevain-Marinus, P.A. Bosch, S. Eschen, W. Franssen, S. van de Geer, M.I.C. Hoefman, L.F. Keyser-Ringnalda, H.V. Koppe, G.A.H. Mangelaars, J. Naeyé, A.A.M. Orie, L.C.W.J. Romeijnders, T.M. Schalken, J.M. Sjöcrona, F.W.M. van Straelen and A.H.J. Swart.

42 Bevers & Joubert, 1994.

Finally, at the suggestion of the *Directie Politie* of the Dutch ministry of justice, police corps of the border regions have been approached to cooperate with the research. With their assistance, a number of examples of the police practice have been collected and were used to illustrate common problems and general police cooperation. Indeed, the CRI, central police authority where the NCB Interpol is located, has been involved since the beginning and has offered us much assistance.

With the results of the expert meeting in mind, we proceeded further with the analysis of the data we had collected in our first book. Because of the international character of the research and to facilitate the control of the data in the countries, we decided to continue in English, this language being, moreover, the second language of both of us.[43] After re-setting a common scheme for the analysis of the data described above, we continued writing. A number of incidental visits were made in the studied countries for collecting complementary information, but the last year was mostly dedicated to writing. Regrettably, due to the end of the project it was not possible to thoroughly process and discuss some highly interesting research results published during the first months of 1996. As a consequence, a comparative research of special policing techniques in Germany, France, Italy, Norway and Denmark could only be scarcely referred to,[44] and the asme is the case with the impressive report (4900 pages!) the Dutch parliamentary inquiry committee Van Traa published on these methods.[45]

1.3 Overview of this Book

For this book, we have chosen a more or less chronological approach of the policing practice in the five studied countries. However, we begin with two introductory chapters: an introduction to the international police cooperation, followed by an introduction to the structure of the criminal procedure in the pre-trial phase. The introduction to the international police cooperation gives an overview of the current situation in this field. Organizations and treaties such as Interpol, Schengen, Maastricht and Europol are sketched and put in their international context in relation to police cooperation (Chapter 2). The introduction of the structure of the criminal procedure in the pre-trial phase is mainly composed of two parts: aspects of the actors and their role followed by an overview of the place of the police enquiry in the criminal procedure (Chapter 3).

---

43   Moreover, as we mentioned above, it allowed us to have our texts read, checked and commented by foreign specialists, who do not all manage to read Dutch.

44   Tak *et al.*, 1996.

45   Van Traa, 1996 with 11 appendices.

In each of the following Chapters (4-11), the police power concerned is sketched and analyzed with regards to both international police cooperation and the European Convention on Human Rights. The consequences of the differences in law in the different countries for the international police cooperation play a central role in the analysis. The chapters are roughly constructed as follows: an introduction of the applicable international law of international police cooperation, followed by a short analysis of the applicable provision of the European Convention on Human Rights and its case-law. We next proceed to a description of the legal situation in the studied countries and conclude by both comparing the legal situation and analyzing it in the light of the international police cooperation and the European Convention on Human Rights. As we have mentioned above, we have tried to follow a chronological criterium in the order we have chosen to analyze the police powers.

We started with two police investigative powers, which mostly play an important role in the grey area between suspicious behaviour and the actual commission of a criminal offence. Moreover, these policing techniques are most often used in the repression and investigation of the so-called consensual criminal offences. We have first examined observation, also called surveillance, a secret investigative police power where the police play a passive role which is limited to the mere observation, with or without the use of technical means. Observation was analyzed in the light of cross-border police cooperation and of art. 8 ECHR (Chapter 4). The second police power evolving in this grey area and the cause of much controversy are special techniques where the police play a more active role as actors, co-actors or guides in the commission of criminal offences: Techniques as controlled delivery, infiltration and the use of informers are analyzed in Chapter 5 in the light of existing international rules and art. 8 ECHR.

The study continues with an analysis of the power of cross-border hot-pursuit (Chapter 6) in the light of artt. 41 SC and 27 BET. We offer an interpretation of these two provisions in the light of the different official versions of the treaty texts and the national laws. A logical consequence of hot-pursuit is the power to apprehend, arrest and perform a control of identity (Chapter 7). In this chapter, we first look at the different provisions of the Schengen Convention and the Benelux Extradition Treaty and sketch the legal situation as to cross-border apprehension, arrest and control of identity. On the basis of the possible interpretations of these treaties, we offer a workable interpretation for the pursuing police officers. We proceed with an analysis of artt. 5 and 8 ECHR and their consequences for the legal situation.

The following three police powers may be seen as related to one another. The use of physical force and arms, bodily search and interrogation are described in Chapters 8 to 10. These powers are all a possible follow up to the power of cross-border hot-pursuit and the relevant provisions of the Schengen

Convention and the Benelux Extradition Treaty will be analyzed as such. The use of physical forces will be considered in the light of the relevant provisions of the European Convention on Human Rights (artt. 2, 3, 5, 6 and 8).

Finally, we have devoted one chapter to the direct mutual legal aid by police officers (Chapter 11). The implications of artt. 39 and 46 SC, as well as artt. 18 and 26 BET will be analyzed. Further art. 8 ECHR, the Data Protection Convention and the Recommendation on Police Data will give the relevant standards as to the respect of human rights. The chapter will give an overview of the national norms on the collecting, storing and (especially international) exchange of police data and the consequences for cross-border cooperation.

We will conclude with an analysis of the different questions raised in the preceding chapters and answer these questions in the light of the international police cooperation, the European Convention on Human Rights and the rule of law. Finally, we make suggestions on possible national and international frameworks to redress and improve the situation.

2 Developments in International Police Cooperation

During the last decades, the intensification of the fight against cross-border crime has caused a tremendous international activity. Practically every international organization has to some extent tried to exercise its influence and power in order to contribute to combatting international crime. The United Nations, the Council of Europe, UNESCO, the Commonwealth, the European Community, the Benelux and numerous other organizations have made their contribution. The first result of these activities is an impressive amount of bilateral and multilateral agreements, treaties and commitments. Part of these addresses forms of cooperation in general, such as extradition, recognition of foreign penal sentences, mutual legal assistance in criminal matters and informational cooperation between law enforcement bodies, while others focus on specific crime categories: terrorism, drugs, money laundering, trafficking human beings, fraud, etcetera.

In this context, it is impossible to even mention all these international instruments, let alone to discuss them.[1] The single aim of this chapter will be to give a brief sketch of the international legal and political framework within which the international police cooperation between Belgium, The Netherlands, Luxembourg, France and Germany takes place and will continue to develop. We do not intend to offer a thorough and critical analysis of these developments. Particularly where it concerns Interpol, Schengen and the Maastricht Treaty on European Union, this has been done already, and in much more detail than would be possible in this study.[2] Regarding the most recent twig on the trunk of international policing, Europol, it is hard to describe or discuss anything definite. Since there is no Europol Convention in force yet (and we will explain why it is still doubtful that this will change in the near future), there is not yet enough objective information available to conduct a thorough analysis of Europol today. It is surely possible to develop an idea of the form and contents

---

1   Fortunately, this has been done in a great number of publications already; where this is relevant, we will refer to them more specifically.
2   For Interpol, we refer to Anderson, 1989; Bresler, 1992; for Schengen, to Meijers et al., 1991; Fijnaut et al., 1992; Pauly, 1993; for Maastricht, to O'Keeffe & Twomey, 1994. In a more general sense, it is worth mentioning Benyon et al., 1993; Anderson & Den Boer, 1994 and Busch, 1995.

the future Europol should have, but that subject has already been the central issue of many a publication.[3]

The international developments in the field of crime, law enforcement cooperation and even cooperation in general have led to a partial harmonization of criminal law. In economic criminal law this was mainly instigated or even forced by the European Community;[4] in the field of crime related to psychotropic substances (including money laundering) it was forcedly based upon treaties from bodies such as the United Nations and the Council of Europe.[5] A general harmonization of substantive criminal law seems to be much further away. In a 1970 report on request of the Council of Europe, even the idea of drafting a model penal code was rejected.[6] The topic has not been put on the agenda of an international organization ever since. To a certain extent, a gradual harmonization of criminal procedure is also taking place, mostly due to the European Convention on Human Rights and the case-law regarding the application of this Convention by the Member States.[7]

Obviously, international cooperation in criminal law enforcement matters may take place at a number of levels, in countless forms and between numerous bodies and authorities. What we intend to focus on in this study is cross-border cooperation between police forces and between individual police officers, even more specifically operational cooperation. Therefore, unless it is of direct interest to the main subject, in this chapter we will not deal with international bodies and treaties concerning other forms of international criminal law enforcement cooperation, such as extradition,[8] mutual legal assistance by judicial authorities,[9] or administrative and policy aspects of police cooperation in border areas.[10]

In the following paragraphs, we will sketch some developments in international policing, using two models of international (police) cooperation. Firstly, there is what we call the interpolice model, referring to cooperation that has emerged and is organized on the level of and between police forces. The second model is the intergovernmental model, consisting of initiatives of police cooperation taken at the level of national governments among each other. Since they will usually all have a right to veto, each of these governments is answer-

---

3   We may refer to, for instance, Van Outrive & Enhus, 1994; Swart, 1995; Verbruggen, 1995; Den Boer, 1995; Busch, 1995, pp. 332-350.
4   Lensing, 1993, pp. 220-225; Sieber, 1994, pp. 86-104.
5   See for instance Keyser-Ringnalda, 1992, pp. 499-515 and Keyser-Ringnalda 1994, pp. 165-180.
6   Enschedé, 1990; see also Keyser-Ringnalda, 1992, pp. 502-505.
7   Lensing, 1993, pp. 217-220; Verbruggen, 1995, p. 198.
8   See for instance Stanbrook & Stanbrook, 1980.
9   See for instance Thomas, 1980 and Sjöcrona, 1990.
10 See Claus, 1995.

able to their national parliaments for the decisions they have taken unanimously with their foreign counterparts. A third model that could be mentioned here is the model of communitary police cooperation, dealt with by one or several bodies of the European Community, in particular the Commission, the Court of Justice and the European Parliament. It is true that these bodies are increasingly involved in affairs concerning the police, and EC structures such as UCLAF (fraud), CELAD (drugs) and the EC Drugs Task Force seem to have considerable influence on the European police forces.[11] Strictly spoken, they only imply coordination, do not address operational policing and will therefore be left out of consideration. The same applies to all Council of Europe initiatives concerning international police cooperation, such as the Pompidou group on narcotic drugs.[12] A fourth intergovernmental model of police cooperation, of which numerous examples may be found, is bilateral cooperation. In some cases, bilateral cooperation has served as a starting point for multilateral cooperation (an example of this is the German-French Agreement of Saarbrücken, which became the basis for the Schengen framework). Sometimes bilateral agreements are rather the elaboration of other forms of cooperation (such as the arrangements containing details about the Schengen cooperation in border areas).

2.1 Interpolice Cooperation

During our research, we often had the impression that the police, as an organization, can be characterized by its strong team spirit, an attitude that even carries across national boundaries. This international "colleague-concept" may be illustrated by the fact that a police officer always seems to refer to another police officer, close or far, known or unknown, as "a colleague." As a consequence, it is only logical that police services in different countries but facing the same or similar problems have developed ways to cooperate. As long as this cooperation is based upon arrangements between police forces, services or officers, it may be called interpolice cooperation. Depending on the degree of formalization and the decision level where the arrangements were concluded, they may be distinguished in informal and formal agreements. We will mention and sketch some forms of informal interpolice cooperation as well as the best-known and best developed formalized interpolice cooperation body, Interpol.

2.1.1 Informal Police Cooperation

Especially in border areas, the police have probably always been tempted to work with their cross-border colleagues, and this for several reasons: Firstly,

---

11   Van der Wel & Bruggeman, 1993, pp. 65-70.
12   Van der Wel & Bruggeman, 1993, pp. 72-83.

a cross-border social and cultural life existed long before the beginning of Europeanization of political life; as a result, police officers on both sides of the border were as familiar with each other as "ordinary" citizens. Secondly, the presence of a border attracts and creates crime, and criminals have always tried (and succeeded) to take advantage of differences in (especially) economic and fiscal legislation (alcohol, tobacco, butter smuggle). Consequently, some sort of contact and cooperation has always been necessary and evident.

These contacts may take any imaginable form and contents, social and cultural as well as educational and operational. They may vary from joint courses concerning legal, technical or language issues, social events, mutual informing about recent developments, exchanges of personnel (liaisons and others) and regular meetings of police chiefs to joint alarm procedures, joint traffic campaigns, regional bulletins on several subjects of policing, exchanges of radio equipment. Furthermore, because of the often almost accidental course of the borderline, there are some examples of police authorities on one side of the border granting their foreign neighbours the right of way: For practical reasons they could cross the territory of their neighbour State in order to go from one part of their national territory to another, instead of staying in their own country and making a detour.[13] Despite their evident importance for the every-day police practice, the legal status of these interpolice arrangements often raises questions. This is especially the case if parts of the contents of the arrangements have been regulated later in more formal documents, such as statutory law or international treaties, or if one or more of the partners to the arrangement formally does not exist any longer, such as the Dutch municipal and state police, which were replaced by the new regional police. Does the coming into force of statutory or treaty legislation replace all informal agreements in the same field, and do regional police forces inherit the arrangements of the municipal and state police forces which they have replaced?

A central role in the development of international police contacts is played by numerous police organizations, the best-known probably being the International Police Association (IPA) and the International Association of Chiefs of Police (IACP). As to the cooperation in the Dutch-German-Belgian Rhine-Meuse area, an organization that may not remain unmentioned is NEBEDEAG-POL. Within the structural cooperation platform between police officers realized by this *Nederlands-Belgisch-Deutsche Arbeitsgruppe Polizei*, many possibilities

---

13 An example of this may be found in a letter of June 27, 1986, concerning an agreement between the Dutch state police and the Belgian *gendarmerie*, allowing the Dutch police to cross Belgian territory in order to go from one part of their jurisdiction (Zundert) to another (Nieuw-Ginniken). Similar arrangements have been made on December 15, 1966 for the territory of the Belgian enclaves in the Dutch Baarle-Hertog, including the arrest and transport of the arrestee through foreign territory.

of international cooperation have been developed, some of which have had a considerable influence on the development of cross-border policing in bodies such as Schengen.[14]

2.1.2 Interpol

Since the first time it was established (in 1914), the International Police Congress has evolved from a conference with participants from 17 countries into the International Criminal Police Commission with 20 members in 1923, and via an organization controlled by the Nazis into a newborn, post-war International Criminal Police Organization (ICPO-Interpol). After the Second World War, the number of members increased impressively, from 78 in 1963 to 150 in 1990 and more than 170 in 1993.[15] Note that, although strictly spoken Interpol's members are not States but police forces, the organisation can be considered to have an intergovernmental status anyway.[16] This is expressed in for instance art. 4 par. 2 of its Constitution, stating that a request for the Interpol membership must be submitted by or on behalf of the government.[17] Furthermore, Interpol is related to several other international organizations, governmental, such as the International Civil Aviation Organization, as well as non-governmental, such as the International Society of Criminology.[18]

The aims of Interpol may be found in art. 2 of its Constitution:

> 1. To ensure and promote the widest possible mutual assistance between all criminal police authorities within the limits of the laws existing in different countries and in the spirit of the Universal Declaration of Human Rights.
> 2. To establish and develop all institutions likely to contribute effectively to the prevention and suppression of ordinary law crimes.

Art. 3 adds some important restrictions to this task, explicitly forbidding Interpol from assisting in cases with "a political, military, religious or racial character," thus trying to assure the neutral ideological character of the organization.[19]

As to the structure of the organization, Interpol has its central headquarters in Lyon (France), with a general secretariat and four divisions (general administration, liaison & criminal intelligence,[20] research & studies and technical support). The liaison & criminal intelligence division consists of five depart-

---

14 Bönninghaus, 1992; Van der Wel & Bruggeman, 1993, pp. 123-131.
15 Benyon *et al.*, 1993, pp. 121-122; for an elaborate discussion of Interpol's fascinating history, we refer to Anderson, 1989 and Bresler, 1992.
16 Anderson, 1989, pp. 57-58.
17 See further Gallas, 1981, pp. 187-188.
18 Gallas, 1981, p. 187; Benyon *et al.*, 1993, p. 125.
19 Benyon *et al.*, 1993, pp. 122-123.
20 This division is also called the police division; Van der Wel & Bruggeman, 1993, pp. 23-24.

ments, respectively general crime, economic & financial crime, drug trafficking, criminal intelligence and the European secretariat, which also has a direct link to the general secretariat. From a global point of view, Interpol is divided into nine regions, each of which organizes its own regional conferences. The only region with its own secretariat is Europe. The European Secretariat was set up in 1986 and deals with all criminal matters with a European dimension, except drugs. It also has a special focus on developing law enforcement in recent Member States from eastern Europe.[21] In addition, perhaps the most important part of Interpol is its National Central Bureaux, the contact offices in each of the members that can be considered the roots of the organization. It may be noted that this network does not only benefit police cooperation but also plays a role in judicial cooperation.[22] As an example, art. 16 par. 3 European Convention on Extradition and art. 15 par. 5 European Convention on Mutual Legal Assistance in Criminal Matters both mention Interpol as a possible way of sending requests between States.[23]

Different from the impression the general public still seems to have, Interpol activities do not include any form of executive policing or investigating.[24] Apart from its various supporting tasks, especially in the field of technical assistance and several types of research, the main function of the organization is to serve as a communication platform between member police forces. This may include passing requests for criminal information as well as requests for a specific kind of assistance. Furthermore, the general secretariat's liaison & criminal intelligence division analyses computerized and other criminal information.

The organization as well as its functioning have often been subjected to a wide range of criticism. On the one hand, claims have been made that Interpol works inefficiently and with too many delays due to its size; on the other hand, too many members could become dictatorships or countries related to international terrorism, which might constitute an insecurity for confidential information.[25] Furthermore, within Interpol there would be too much emphasis on European cases. The organization has become a great deal less European than it used to be in the beginning of its history, police forces from European countries now accounting for around 20% of its members. However, still 80% of the messages sent through Interpol concern European cases, causing "a lack of symmetry between Interpol's members and its users."[26] In the near future

---

21 Benyon *et al.*, 1993, pp. 127-128.
22 Cameron-Waller, 1993, p. 101.
23 Gallas, 1981, p. 187.
24 Benyon *et al.*, 1993, p. 122.
25 Benyon *et al.*, pp. 130 and 223.
26 Benyon *et al.*, 1993, p. 130.

this might be changed by closer cooperation within other European structures, such as Schengen and the EC, resulting in an Interpol with a highly improved availability for its non-European members. This would certainly also have a positive influence on the size and the flexibility of the organization. Efficiency has further been improved by technical measures such as new computer and telecommunication systems,[27] although one may wonder whether all Member States will be able or willing to make the effort to use these new technologies.[28]

2.2 Intergovernmental Police Cooperation

International police cooperation may be given a formal structure in arrangements between the governments of participating countries. Several models of this intergovernmental policing are possible, four of which will be mentioned here: the Scandinavian, the Benelux, the Schengen and the Europol model.

2.2.1 Nordic Council

In the Nordic Passport Control Agreement (1957), Denmark, Finland, Norway, Sweden, and (later) Iceland have abolished passport controls at their common borders. In 1962, this Agreement was followed by the Nordic Cooperation Agreement, which deals with subjects such as police and judicial cooperation.[29] As a consequence of linguistic, cultural and historical affinities between the countries concerned rather than as a result of an explicit choice, the Nordic cooperation model is based on mutual trust and recognition of criminal law enforcement systems.[30]

All participating States recognize a relatively wide territorial jurisdiction and together they have adopted some uniform legislation (especially on extradition, transfer of sentenced persons and proceedings as well as mutual legal assistance), but in general every country has maintained its own legislation, structure and powers.[31] In order to solve conflicts between two States, the uniform legislation contains a conflict settlement regulation.

Within this model, there is an intense police cooperation that only has a limited basis in formal agreements or statutory law.[32] This cooperation includes not only procedures (which request must be addressed to which authority?), but

---

27   Benyon *et al.*, 1993, pp. 224-226.
28   In this sense also Bresler, 1992, pp. 361-362 and Van der Wel & Bruggeman, 1993, p. 34.
29   Fode, 1993, p. 63-64.
30   Fode, 1993, p. 65; Mulder & Rüter, 1995, p. 23.
31   Mulder & Rüter, 1995, pp. 24-26.
32   Fode, 1993, p. 65.

also possibilities to conduct interrogations in other Nordic States, to have a citizen of another State identified, judicial records sent or fines collected. In the context of a foreign request from another Nordic State, the police may in principle apply the same coercive measures as their national law allows for a domestic investigation. Furthermore, the information that the police are allowed to exchange with their national colleagues, may be exchanged with their Scandinavian counterparts as well.[33] Although they may also use a detailed network of liaison officers, direct contacts at any level are possible between police forces of two Nordic Council States, and may even permit extradition without the involvement or notification of respective ministries of justice.[34]

2.2.2 Benelux

From the beginning of their unification in 1944, the Benelux States (Belgium, The Netherlands and Luxembourg) have thought of their organization as a model or experiment for European cooperation between independent, sovereign countries.[35] Seeking the abolition of their internal borders after having become a customs union in 1948, they have drafted a number of treaties regulating the practical consequences that the disappearance of border checks might have for criminal law enforcement. On June 27, 1962 they signed the Benelux Treaty on Extradition and Mutual Legal Assistance in Criminal Matters (hereafter Benelux (Extradition) Treaty or BET), with the intention of "extending the possibilities of extradition of criminals to a greater number of offences, simplifying formalities related to this and enabling mutual legal assistance in criminal matters to an extent beyond what is allowed by existing treaties."[36] The treaty also introduces the possibility that, in urgent cases, a suspect of an extraditable offence who has been discovered in one Benelux country, may be pursued onto the territory of another Benelux country where, under certain conditions, the pursuing police officer may proceed to the suspect's apprehension.[37]

In 1968, this treaty was followed by the Benelux Treaty on the Execution of Judicial Decisions in Criminal Matters,[38] and in 1969 by the Benelux Convention on Administrative and Criminal Cooperation in Matters Related to the Aims of the Benelux Economic Union.[39] A final instrument of criminal law enforcement cooperation between the Benelux countries is the 1974 Treaty

---

33 Mulder & Rüter, 1995, pp. 29-30.
34 Fode, 1993, p. 66.
35 Kruijtbosch, 1993, pp. 32-33.
36 Trb. 1962, 97.
37 The whole of the treaty has been commented in detail by De Schutter, 1967/1968, pp. 1937-1946.
38 September 26, 1968, Trb. 1969, 9.
39 April 29, 1969, Trb. 1969, 124.

Regarding the Transfer of Proceedings in Criminal Matters, which is not in force yet.[40]

2.2.3   Schengen

Historical Background

In 1984, Germany and France reached an agreement in Saarbrücken, in which they expressed their intention to slowly proceed to the abolition of checks at their common border.[41] The Benelux Member States, the common territory of which had been free of border checks since 1960, were allowed to join their surrounding neighbours, and on June 14, 1985, the five signed the so-called Schengen Agreement.[42] This agreement, which was named after the Luxembourg village on the Mosel where it was signed, contains a declaration of intention to abolish internal border controls, thus creating an experimental garden for the cooperation between the ten members the European Community counted at that moment. In the following years, the expressed intentions were elaborated in what was to become the Schengen Implementation Convention.

Meanwhile, in 1986, the ten EC members agreed on the Single European Act, launching the idea of "Europe 1992," the common market that would no longer be interrupted by border control. This intention would be elaborated in the 1992 Maastricht Treaty, which will be discussed below. In order to maintain its intention to become an experimental garden for a united European Community, the Schengen group was to try to make sure that its Schengen area would be free of border checks in 1990.

When in the fall of 1989, the signature of the Schengen Implementation Convention (hereafter: Schengen Convention or SC) was pending, the world was suddenly surprised by the fall of the Berlin Wall. For the Schengen group, this meant that the German territory (and thus the Schengen area) would eventually be extended to the former German Democratic Republic and a new external border would be added (with Poland). As a compensation for the diminution of the travelling area of the Polish because of the disappearance of the East-German State, a Polish-German non-visa agreement was signed. After the text of the Schengen Convention was adapted, it was finally signed in Schengen on June 19, 1990.[43]

---

40   May 11, 1974, Trb. 1974, 184.
41   July 13, 1984, BGBl. II 1984, 786 and J.O. 1984, 2565.
42   Trb. 1985, 102.
43   Trb. 1990, 145.

Aim and Content

The main aim of the Schengen Convention is, to realize the abolition of checks at the internal borders and consequently free movement of persons (art. 2). This abolition of border control is accompanied by a set of compensatory measures, such as an intensification of checks at the external borders (artt. 3-8), partial harmonization of legislation on visas, residence permits and organized travel (artt. 9-27) as well as of asylum procedures (artt. 28-38). Furthermore, a great deal of measures in the field of police and security (artt. 39-91), more specifically police cooperation (artt. 39-47), modernization of some central aspects of international cooperation in criminal matters (artt. 48-69), narcotic drugs (artt. 70-76) and firearms and ammunition (artt. 77-91). In addition, the Convention provides for the introduction of a joint information system, the Schengen Information System, in order to maintain public order and security (artt. 92-119), including its own privacy protection regime (artt. 102-118). Economic affairs have been dealt with in Title V on transport and movement of goods (artt. 120-125), whereas Title VI contains a general harmonization of the law on protection of personal data (artt. 126-130). An Executive Committee of representatives of the governments of all Member States has been entrusted with the implementation and interpretation of the Convention (artt. 131-133).

Police Cooperation

Among this multitude of themes, we will almost exclusively focus on the first Chapter of Title III, the artt. 39-47, dealing with police cooperation, and with art. 73, dealing with monitored or controlled delivery in the field of narcotic drugs. In the following, we will give a short sketch of the contents of artt. 39-47 and 73 SC; in particular the artt. 39, 40, 41, 46 and 73 will be discussed meticulously in Chapters 4-11 of this study so that it will be sufficient to only introduce them here. Art. 39 SC contains a general provision that the police authorities of the Schengen Member States will, within the limits of their respective national legal systems, provide their foreign counterparts with all kinds of assistance requested for the purpose of preventing and detecting criminal offences. The provision mainly serves as a basis for informational police cooperation.

In art. 40 SC, cross-border observation has been regulated. This will primarily take place with, but in urgent situations also without prior permission of the country where the observation will lead to. A number of general conditions may be found in par. 3, the most important ones being the obligation to comply with the law of the Contracting Party where the operation takes place and to report to the authorities of this country afterwards. Observation with prior permission is possible for all extraditable offences, whereas without permission the observation is restricted to thirteen severe offences explicitly mentioned in par. 7. Par. 4 contains a specification of police officers who are entitled to conduct a cross-border observation, and par. 5 mentions the authorities to whom a request for prior permission must be sent and notified of non-requested observations.

In accordance with art. 41, police officers of one Schengen country may continue a hot pursuit of a suspect who was caught in the act or has escaped from provisional custody or a custodial sentence into another Schengen country. In a kind of *à la carte* construction, several aspects were left to the choice of every single Contracting Party: whether or not the pursuing officer will have the right to proceed to the pursued person's apprehension (par. 2), whether and to what extent the pursuit by a foreign police officer will be bound to a restriction in distance or time (par. 3) and whether the pursuit may take place in case of the commission of any extraditable offence or only of offences mentioned in a catalogue (par. 4). General conditions comparable to those for cross-border observation may be found in par. 5, and the competent police officers are mentioned in par. 7. Between the Benelux Member States, basically the pursuit regulation of the 1962 Benelux Extradition Treaty will remain in force.

The legal position of the officers concerned in a cross-border operation has been addressed in artt. 42 and 43 SC. Regarding criminal offences committed against or by them, art. 42 states that the legal position of a cross-border operating police officer will be the same as the position of the police officers of the country where the operation takes place. Art. 43 adds that the country of origin bears full civil liability for damages caused by their police officers during the course of a mission on foreign territory.

Technical details of international cooperation have been dealt with by art. 44, aiming at a standardization, harmonization, and exchange of communication equipment, in particular in border areas, in order to improve the transmission of information for the purposes of cross-border observation and pursuit. Art. 45 obliges the Contracting Parties to introduce a registration of aliens (including Schengen and EC citizens) in hotels and other lodging and letting establishments. The declaration forms used for this registration will be collected by the competent authorities for the prevention of threats, for criminal proceedings and to ascertain what has happened to missing persons or accident victims. Art. 46 addresses the spontaneous sending of information to the police of another Schengen country for purposes of prevention, and art. 47 mentions the possibility of the secondment of liaison officers on the basis of bilateral agreements.

A provision in the Convention's chapter on illicit drug, that also immediately touches the topic of operational police cooperation is art. 73. It states that the Contracting Parties must, within their national legal systems, allow monitored deliveries of illicit drugs to take place. In individual cases, each of the States concerned will be asked for prior authorization, and every single State retains responsibility and control over the operation and will remain entitled to intervene.

In general, the regulation of most operational aspects of cross-border policing has a dominantly subsidiary character, explicitly recognizing national sovereignty during the operations: Cross-border policing is only possible if and to the extent which it is allowed by national law; police officers are bound to local legal provisions, and an extension of the cooperation on a bilateral basis will always remain possible.

Criticism

The emergence of the Schengen Convention was greeted with strongly mixed feelings. On the one hand, the provisions on international police cooperation could be considered an important achievement. For the first time, it was decided that the international police cooperation should not be left the possibility to develop freely from any international legal intervention or framework but instead it should be an explicitly legalized and (thus) regulated. In the Explanatory Memorandum of the European Treaty on Mutual Legal Assistance in Criminal Matters, it was still stressed that it was "best not to force the existing practice of the police into a rigid mould."[44] On the other hand, the Schengen Convention has also been the subject of fierce criticism from the moment it was published (and even before).[45]

The changes in the field of aliens and asylum policy were criticized for being too harsh and inhuman. Especially in an era of increasing numbers of refugees, it is hardly acceptable if a group of the world's richest countries would start building a "fortress Europe."[46] Furthermore, it is bitter for all citizens of Eastern European countries that, once the Iron Curtain has fallen and their freedom of movement finally returned, they would be restricted in that movement because the Western societies would not let them enter their territories. And this despite the fact that these same Western countries had always criticized the fact that Eastern European countries did not let their people leave their territories.[47]

Three closely related aspects of Schengen that have encountered a great deal of criticism are the secret atmosphere in which Schengen has emerged and the lack of openness it still is surrounded by, as well as the built-in impossibility of a sufficient democratic control and the role of the Executive Committee. This Committee has been entrusted with the fundamental task of ensuring the

---

44 Heimans, 1994, p. 138, who indirectly refers to Fijnaut, 1992a, p. 98.
45 Such as Mols, 1990, which forms the report of a conference held on November 10, 1989.
46 See for instance Boeles, 1991; Bolten, 1991; Hoogenboom, 1991; Steenbergen, 1991; Jessurun d'Oliveira, 1993, pp. 166-182; Jessurun d'Oliveira, 1994, pp. 261-278; King, 1994.
47 Van Es, 1991.

application and explanation of the complex Schengen matter, a task which certainly implies binding rule-making and interpretation of the whole field covered by the Convention.[48] In short, the Committee's tasks will be a mixture of legislation and jurisdiction, without however being public and without any form of direct and specified control by a democratically elected body.[49] This objection may be partly neutralized by the possibility, offered by art. 132 par. 3 SC, that at the request of the representative of one Member State, the final decision on a draft decision by the Executive Committee may be postponed two months. Meanwhile, the national parliament may be consulted as to the final decision to be taken. During the discussions on the Schengen Ratification Act, the Dutch government has been forced by an amendment to inform the Dutch parliament about every concept-decision of the Committee.[50]

Another important objection concerns the absence of a common, independent judicial control.[51] This could be remedied by entrusting the final judicial control on the application and interpretation of the Convention in individual matters to the EC Court of Justice. This possibility is being researched at the request of the Dutch government, but it seems that Belgium and Italy are the only other Member States who would consider this an acceptable solution.[52] A criminal law aspect of the Schengen regulation that has been regretted in several places is the total absence of a role for the defence, especially in combination with the lack of any form of international, harmonizing judicial control on the international cooperation in criminal matters.[53] Finally, the restrictive impact Schengen might have on the individual's private life was also an aspect of Schengen that had to endure a great deal of criticism.[54] Especially the Schengen Information System was said to constitute such an infringement concerning privacy that associations with Orwell's Big Brother were made.[55]

In spite of all criticism, the Schengen Convention did finally come into force, although much later than the originally intended year of 1990. The delay was partly due to developments in Central and Eastern Europe: The disappearance of the Iron Curtain meant a change for the entire Western world and all aspects of its security concept. Another reason for several delays was formed by political and legal problems in most Member States. In The Netherlands and

---

48 Meijers, 1991, pp. 5-6.
49 Groenendijk, 1993, pp. 391-402; Curtin & Meijers, 1995, pp. 391-442.
50 In this sense art. 2 Schengen Ratification Act, Stb. 1983, 138. Meanwhile, a procedure for this has been proposed in TK 19 326, nr. 125.
51 Meijers, 1991, pp. 5-6; Mols, 1995.
52 In this sense the Dutch parliament was informed by the government; see for instance TK 19 326, nrs. 54, 69 and 83.
53 Swart, 1991b, pp. 108-109; Orie, 1991, p. 761; Verbruggen, 1995, p. 189.
54 Verhey, 1991; Schattenberg, 1993; Boeles, 1993.
55 Baldwin-Edwards & Habenton, 1994.

Germany, fundamental changes in the law on aliens and refugees were judged necessary but met considerable political resistance. Belgium had not yet introduced a privacy protection legislation and in France, the Convention was to face repeated political reticences and legal impediments.[56] Moreover, technical obstacles occurred in the form of the Central SIS computer in Strasbourg refusing to function properly. By the time all these problems were solved, it was decided that as of March 26, 1995, the Schengen Convention would be applied for an initial period of three months between all Member States fulfilling the required conditions. At this moment, the countries where Schengen is in force are Belgium, The Netherlands, Luxembourg, Germany, France, Spain and Portugal. Especially France, being terrorized by severe bomb attacks by supposedly Algerian muslim fundamentalists and irritated by the international consequences of the Dutch liberal drug policy, has shown little enthusiasm about Schengen being in force. It has therefore expressed its wish to prolong the initial period with another six months - a proposal which has been rejected by all other Member States - and has decided that for reasons of public policy and national security that checks at the internal borders will be carried out again.[57]

As to the extension of the Schengen cooperation, it must be mentioned that Italy and Greece have signed and ratified the Convention as well, but still need to adapt and extend some essential parts of their legislation. Austria, since January 1995 fulfilling the EC membership condition of art. 140 SC, is likely to be the next country where the Convention will be applied.[58] Meanwhile, talks are going on about the question whether, under which conditions and in which form Denmark, Finland, Sweden (who already has the observer status) and maybe even Norway and Iceland could join the Schengen group.[59]

2.2.4   From TREVI to Europol

TREVI
Since 1975, the ministers of the interior and of justice of the Member States of the European Community have met regularly in order to discuss problems concerning public order and internal security. In 1976, they decided to set up a number of working groups of functionaries with the task of encouraging international cooperation in combatting international violence. The initiative was

---

56   Sketched in detail by Keraudren, 1994, pp. 123-144.
57   This possibility is offered "for a limited period" by art. 2 par. 2 SC; explanation was given to the Dutch parliament in TK 19 326, nr. 119.
58   The Protocol admitting Austria as the next member was signed on April 18, 1995; Trb. 1995, 176 and 177.
59   In this sense a letter by the Dutch state secretaries of foreign affairs and justice, TK 19 326, nr. 134.

given the name TREVI, supposedly named after the fountain in Rome where it started, combined with the fact that one of the initiators was a Dutch director-general of police named Fonteijn. TREVI may also be considered an acronym for the French *Terrorisme, Radicalisme, Extremisme et Violence Internationale*.[60]

TREVI developed as an intergovernmental board in the field of police policy, its main goals being the improvement of possibilities for the international exchange of information and the realization of a better cooperation between the police forces in its Member States. Although originally it especially focused on terrorism,[61] soon its focus was extended to include policing drug crime and other forms of severe organized crime, eventually completed by law enforcement problems that would result from opening the borders in the European single market and the establishment of a European Drugs Intelligence Unit.[62] This unit was entrusted with tasks such as collecting information on international drug trafficking and money laundering, as well as improving the international exchange of information on this subject.[63]

Europol
In 1992 the Treaty on European Union (the so-called Maastricht Treaty) was signed in order to elaborate and realize the intentions expressed in the 1986 Single European Act.[64] Besides regulating details of the Common Market, the Maastricht Treaty introduced a second and a third pillar in the EC structure, respectively containing the Common Foreign and Security Policy and the Common Justice and Home Affairs. The third pillar will also incorporate TREVI's activities, turning post-Maastricht TREVI into a "third pillar working group."[65] Furthermore, in the Maastricht Treaty it was decided that the former TREVI European Drugs Intelligence Unit was to be transformed into the European Drugs Unit/Europol.[66] With this European police unit, an old ideal of especially the German police seemed to slowly approach its realization.[67] Nevertheless, it has not yet been established whether Europol should eventually

---

60   Fijnaut, 1987a, p. 310; Benyon *et al.*, 1993, p. 152.
61   For a study of TREVI's activities in this field, we refer to Le Jeune, 1992, pp. 105-176.
62   Benyon *et al.*, 1993, p. 152.
63   Benyon *et al.*, 1993, pp. 155-156.
64   February 7, 1992, Trb. 1992, 74. The Maastricht Treaty is dealt with very thoroughly in O'Keeffe & Twomey, 1995.
65   Verbruggen, 1995, p. 197.
66   For a general discussion of recent developments concerning the third pillar and police co-operation in the European Union, we refer to Fijnaut, 1994b, Den Boer, 1995 and O'Keeffe, 1995.
67   Benyon *et al.*, 1993, pp. 158-159.

be developed in the direction of the Interpol model or of the FBI model.[68] The second model, a European Bureau of Investigations with (its own or derived) operational powers on the entire territory of the Community, has been strongly advocated from the German side, but still meets considerable resistance in most other EC Member States.[69]

Aim and Content

The initial tasks of the European Drugs Unit/Europol were established in a ministerial agreement signed in Copenhagen at June 2, 1993 and confirmed in a Common Action of January 24, 1995.[70] They were limited to the exchange of information for the investigation of drug related crime and the so-called strategic analysis of criminal intelligence (not related to individual persons). Since March 10, 1995, as a result of the summit in Essen (Germany), the Europol mandate was extended to include international car theft, the traffic of nuclear material and the traffic of human beings. On the basis of the ministerial agreement, Europol now provisorily functions through liaison officers of the Member States who have been seconded in The Hague (The Netherlands) where they may directly exchange police information with their counterparts of the other EC States.[71] The secondment of the foreign liaisons and their legal status is the subject of bilateral agreements between host country The Netherlands and the respective officers' home countries.[72]

Recent Developments

In order to formalize the establishment of Europol and further extend its tasks, the EC Member States have been negotiating the status of Europol and its place in the EC structure for several years. Central moot points were from the beginning, whether and to what extent democratic and judicial control of Europol should be entrusted to the European Parliament and Court of Justice. The call for a control task for the Parliament was sacrificed relatively easily by most Member States,[73] but a role for the Court was strongly emphasized, particularly because of the interest of the harmonizing effect a common judicial interpretation would have.

---

68 For this model, see for instance De Feo, 1994 and Verbruggen, 1995, pp. 152-180.
69 Benyon et al., 1993, pp. 158-159.
70 Council document 12321/1/94 REV 1 CK 4; see Klip, 1996, p. 5.
71 According to information we received from Europol and CRI officers, all EU countries except Luxembourg would have sent at least one liaison officer. The Dutch parliamentary enquiry committee has however reported that Europol would host 32 liaison officers from all member states except Austria; see Van Traa, 1996, App. V, pp. 429-430.
72 Klip, 1996, p. 5.
73 This minimalization of democratic control over Europol was strongly criticized by for instance Van Outrive & Enhus, 1994; Swart, 1995, p. 80, Curtin & Meijers, 1995.

Especially the British government insisted that any involvement of the Court of Justice in Europol affairs would be unacceptable since it would imply that Europol would no longer be an intergovernmental but a Community matter. This would not be different if individual States would decide to mention this role of the Court in a separate protocol. Due to the British opposition, it was impossible to reach a general agreement during the June 1995 summit in Cannes, France. When the Europol Convention was finally signed on July 26, 1995 in Brussels, fourteen out of fifteen Member States expressed in a common declaration their intention to have questions of interpretation settled by a preliminary ruling of the Court of Justice. The Benelux States have stressed once more that, in order to enable the Convention to come into force, a solution to this problem must be reached before June 1996. Without a satisfying solution for the role of the Court in the settlement of conflicts with respect to the police coordination, The Netherlands will not ratify the treaty.[74] At a press conference at the end of the Cannes summit however, the British prime minister Major already indicated that in a year the British opinion would remain unchanged.

The Convention describes the main objective of Europol as "to improve (....) the effectiveness and cooperation of the competent authorities in the Member States in preventing and combating terrorism, unlawful drug trafficking and other serious forms of international crime where there are factual indications that an organized criminal structure is involved and two or more Member States are affected by the forms of crime in question in such a way as (....) to require a common approach by the Member States." Initially it will continue focusing on the prevention and repression of illicit drug trafficking, crime connected with nuclear and radioactive substances, illegal immigrant smuggling, international car theft and money laundering related to these forms of crime. The Convention entrusts the European Council with the decision (to be taken unanimously) to extend Europol's powers to several terrorist activities and to other forms of crime which are listed in an annex to the Convention. This annex contains a catalogue of crimes against life, physical integrity and personal freedom, as well as against property, public goods and fraud and against the environment.

The Convention does not provide for operational or executive police powers, but only regulates informational powers and several forms of support, such as technical advice, special expertise and efficiency consults. This means that Europol will makes its official start as an organization of the Interpol rather than the FBI model, and the treaty would need to be amended in order to change that situation. However, one may wonder what is the exact course of the thin line between non-operational and operational support, a question that seems to be a practical matter for those working at Europol as well: "Meanwhile, with

---

74   In this sense the Dutch government in a parliamentary discussion of June 22, 1995, TK 21 501-02/21 501-20, p. 6.

its extended mandate (since March 10, 1995 including the traffic of nuclear material and cars as well as of human beings), the Europol Drugs Unit deals with around 600 cases per semester, some of which are increasingly approaching the operational cooperation."[75]

---

75 This was revealed by Europol Assistant Coordinator Bruggeman (1995b, p. 451). This was confirmed by the Dutch Van Traa committee, who revealed that, during the first six months of 1995, Europol's liaisons have received 660 requests for information and provided 4103 replies; see Van Traa, 1996, App. V, pp. 429-430.

3 Structures of Criminal Law Enforcement

In this chapter, we will give a compact overview of the structure of the criminal law enforcement in Belgium, The Netherlands, Luxembourg, France and Germany.[1] For this purpose, we have made a number of arbitrary choices. Firstly, we have chosen to divide the chapter into three paragraphs: paragraph 1 on the actors of the criminal procedure, in which we describe in turn the police, the public prosecutor, the investigating judge and the suspect in the five chosen countries. This manner has the advantage of being simple to refer to when studying the police powers being analyzed in the remainder of the book. Paragraph 2 sketches the course of the pre-trial enquiry, which, in our opinion, has the advantage of placing the police powers in their respective legal framework. Paragraph 3 will draw conclusions and roughly make an inventory of the differences that may have consequences for the police cooperation.[2]

Secondly, we have made choices as to the vocabulary we used to designate all the different parties and concepts. In principle, we have chosen an English translation of the concept, the most literal possible, with the principle expression in its original language in brackets. As for the different actors of the criminal procedure, we have chosen to translate the function (with its equivalent in the original language), sometimes alternating with a literal translation.

3.1 Compact Overview of the Judicial Organization

Before we proceed to the first paragraph of this chapter describing the actors of the criminal procedure, it is useful, if not essential, to sketch the judicial organization of each country. As a whole, criminal proceedings may be divided into two main parts: the pre-trial and the trial proceedings. In the pre-trial phase, we mostly see the police, the public prosecutor, the investigating judge and the suspect, whereas during the trial we see the apparition of the trial judge or judges, the suspect becoming the accused and being, at this stage, most often represented by an attorney. We will concentrate here on the organization of the judiciary in the stage of trial proceedings.

---

1   For a more detailed overview of this subject, see for instance Van den Wyngaert, 1993a; EC Commission, 1994 and Bevers & Joubert, 1994, pp. 39-315.
2   More substantial conclusions will be drawn in the following chapters where police powers will be analyzed, especially in the last concluding chapter of this work.

3.1.1 Belgium

In Belgium, the judicial organization follows this described dichotomy very closely. Courts with a pre-trial jurisdiction are the investigating judge and the courts of investigation, the latter being composed of the court in chambers (*chambre du conseil/raadkamer*) in first instance and the court of indictment (*chambre des mises en accusation/kamer van inbeschuldigingstelling*) in appeal.[3] Courts with a trial jurisdiction are divided according to the distinction of criminal offences in substantive criminal law. Offences being divided in *crimes*, *délits* and *contraventions* in accordance with the French Napoleonic model.[4] *Crimes* were, according to the Napoleonic system, to be judged before the assize court (with a jury), *délits* before the *tribunal correctionnel* (college of professional judges) and *contraventions* before the police court (single judge). In recent years, however, only serious *crimes* punishable with a life sentence are judged before the assize court, the remaining being judges before the *tribunal correctionnel*. Through a process called *correctionalisation* other *crimes* are converted into *délits* and therefore judged before the *tribunal correctionel*. Finally, *contraventions* are judged before the police court. However, in recent years, many statutes have given jurisdiction to the police court to judge certain *délits*.[5] The court of appeal (*cour d'appel*) is composed of three judges and the cassation court (*cour de cassation*) is composed of three chambers, each of which has two departments (French and Dutch) each consisting of five judges.

3.1.2 The Netherlands

The Dutch criminal law distinguishes between two categories of criminal offences: *misdrijven*, the most severe offences, and *overtredingen*, the minor offences. In the pre-trial phase of the proceedings, we find the investigating judge (*rechter-commissaris*) and the court in chambers (*raadkamer*). As in Belgium, the jurisdiction *ratione materiae* of the different Dutch courts is related to the distinction of the offences. *Overtredingen* are judged in first instance by a sub-district court (*kantongerecht*). *Misdrijven* are judged by a district court (*rechtbank*), composed of three judges. Simple cases may be tried before one member of this district court, the so-called police judge. Appeals of the sub-district court decisions are made before the district court, whereas appeals of the district court decisions are brought before the court of appeal (*Gerechtshof*).

---

3   Van den Wyngaert, 1993b, pp. 9-10.
4   See sub-section 3.2.1.1 for a definition of these offenses; see also Van den Wyngaert, 1993b, p. 10.
5   See Van den Wyngaert, 1993b, pp. 10-11.

The organization is dominated by the cassation court (*Hoge Raad*), which is the highest court in The Netherlands.[6]

3.1.3   Luxembourg

Courts which have jurisdiction during the pre-trial stage in Luxembourg are the investigating judge (*juge d'instruction*), the judicial council of the court of first instance (*chambre du conseil*) and the judicial council at the court of appeal. As for the trial phase, the jurisdiction *ratione materiae* of the courts corresponds to the tripartite division of criminal offences:[7] The police court (*tribunal du juge de paix* sitting as a *juge de police*) hears cases involving *contraventions*, the correctional chamber of the *tribunal d'arrondissement* (*chambre correctionelle*) hears those involving *délits* and the criminal chamber of the *tribunal d'arrondissement* (*chambre criminelle*) tries cases involving *crimes*. The correctional chamber hears appeals of the police judge, the criminal chamber hears appeals of the correctional chamber and appeals of the criminal chamber of the *tribunal d'arrondissement* are heard by the criminal chamber of the court of appeal.[8] The court of cassation (*cour de cassation*) has been at the top of the judicial hierarchy since 1980. The court is composed of one chamber where five judges sit for hearings.[9]

3.1.4   France

Pre-trial jurisdiction is shared by the investigating judge (*juge d'instruction*) and the court of indictment (*chambre d'accusation*) at the court of appeal.[10] The trial phase in first instance follows the division between criminal offences.[11] *Contraventions* are tried by the police judge (*juge de police*). *Délits* are judged by the correctional court (*tribunal correctionel*), which is a part of the *tribunal de grande instance*. *Crimes* are presented before the assize court (*cour d'assises*), the court at the territorial level of the *département*. This court is composed of three professional judges and nine jurors. The decisions of both the police judge and the correctional court are heard in appeal before the *chambre des appels correctionnels* which is part of the court of appeal. There is no appeal possible of the decisions of the assize court, although a case may be referred

---

6   See Swart, 1993b, pp. 287-288.
7   See sub-section 3.2.1.3.
8   See Spielmann & Spielmann, 1993, p. 264.
9   Thiry, 1984, pp. 213 *et seq.*
10 Note that this court might in the future be replaced by a so-called *tribunal criminel départemental*, composed of one president, two judges and two civilian evaluators, see La semaine juridique, 1995-40.
11 See sub-section 3.2.1.4.

to the criminal chamber (*chambre criminelle*) of the court of cassation (*cour de cassation*).[12] The court of cassation is composed of six chambers, of which only one has jurisdiction for criminal cases. The criminal chamber is presided over by one judge and is composed of advisers with or without deliberating vote and of general advocates. The criminal chamber may only render a judgement when five members with deliberating votes are present.[13]

3.1.5   Germany

The first instance court in trial proceedings in Germany is the local or sub-district court (*Amtsgericht*) for offences sanctioned with a penalty not exceeding a maximum of 3 years. The district court (*Landgericht*) has first instance jurisdiction in cases where neither the sub-district court or high court (*Oberlandesgericht*) have jurisdiction. The high court only has first instance jurisdiction in severe crimes such as high treason and assault against the highest representatives of the state.[14] Appeals of the sub-district court are heard by the district court and appeals of the district court are heard before the high court. Cassation (*Revision*) is possible, with permission of the court, before the federal court (*Bundesgerichtshof*). Constitutional complaints (*Verfassungsbeschwerde*) may be brought before the federal constitutional court (*Bundesverfassungsgericht*) with the permission of the court.

3.2 Actors of the Criminal Procedure

In this paragraph, we will proceed to sketch an overview of the different actors of the criminal procedure at the pre-trial phase of the enquiry. We begin with the police for several reasons. Firstly for chronological reasons, as one most often thinks of warning the police when a criminal offence has been committed and secondly, because the police are the object of this study. We will continue with the public prosecutor, as his work is closely linked to that of the criminal police. We will continue by describing the tasks of the investigating judge and conclude with an overview of the concept of suspect in the countries of this study.

3.2.1   Police

The police may be seen as the executive arm of law enforcement. For the public, the expression police designates in the first instance the corps of civil servants

---

12 See Pradel, 1993c, pp. 113-114.
13 Stefani *et al.*, 1993, pp. 373 *et seq.*
14 See Kühne, 1993, pp. 141-142.

charged with the fundamental task of enforcing general prescriptions, with the aim of achieving the higher goal of tranquillity, security and public salubrity.[15] As a part of the criminal investigation organization, the police may be seen as the fundamental pillar of evidence gathering in the first instance. Although the public prosecutor plays an active role in leading the enquiry and, in most countries, disposes of extensive investigation powers, it is often the police who will be sent on location to make the first acknowledgements.

In this sub-paragraph, we will present an overview of the organization of the police in each of the studied countries. The organization of the police is indeed of particular interest when looking at international police cooperation. It enables insight into the structures of a particular corps and, in the context of international cooperation, it will be a factor increasing understanding for each other's situations on both sides of the border.

3.2.1.1 Belgium

There are three distinct police forces in Belgium carrying out investigative tasks: on the one hand, the approximately 16,000 municipal police officers (*police communale/gemeentepolitie*) and the 15,000 *gendarmes* (*gendarmerie/rijkswacht*) on the one hand, are competent for both maintaining the peace as well as for investigating crimes and, on the other hand, the approximately 1,400 judicial police officers of the *parquet* (*police judiciaire près les parquets/gerechtelijke politie bij de parketten*) who only have competence for investigating crimes.[16] The organization of these three forces are regulated foremostly in the Municipal Act (GemW), the Act on the *Gendarmerie* (WRW) and the Act on the Judicial Police (WGP), though many provisions are contained in a number of special statutes.[17] These three acts contain provisions concerning organization. Further, the Police Function Act (*Loi sur la fonction de police/Wet op het politieambt -* WPA) contains provisions regulating the police tasks, the cooperation between the different forces and the application of means of constraint.[18] Finally, a number of provisions concerning the judicial competences of the police may be found in the Code of Criminal Procedure (*Code d'instruction criminelle/Wetboek van strafvordering - Sv*).

---

15 See Stefani *et al.*, 1993, p. 273.
16 Bevers & Joubert, 1994, p. 47; see also Van den Wyngaert, 1993b, p. 5; for an entertaining historical overview of the Belgian police forces, see Van Outrive *et al.*, 1992, for the most recent developments in the Belgian police organization, see Fijnaut, 1995, pp. 67-101.
17 Van Outrive *et al.*, 1992.
18 Act of 5 August 1992, B.S. 22 December 1992.

Besides these three police forces, there are between 60 and 70 specialized services competent in Belgium to exercise secret police tasks.[19] Although these specialized services only have restricted police powers, most, such as the railway police, the financial inspection and the special fiscal inspection, have their own regulations concerning organization and control.[20]

The Gendarmerie

The *gendarmerie* or *rijkswacht* finds its origin in its French counterpart and was, until January 1, 1992, one of Belgium's armed forces.[21] Because of this, its organization, management and finances fell under the responsibility of the ministry of defence. Since 1992 this has been the responsibility of the ministry of the interior. Although this brought about great internal changes, not much of this change is apparent for the public: Its internal organization, uniform and equipment have remained unchanged.[22] However and despite the demilitarization, the *gendarmerie* will continue performing certain military tasks such as those contained in artt. 58-62 WRW.

The most important tasks of the *gendarmerie* are maintaining the public order and enforcing the law (art. 1 WRW). The statute distinguishes, on the one hand, between preventive and repressive police tasks and, on the other hand, between ordinary and extra-ordinary tasks. The ordinary police tasks may be carried out *ex officio*, while the extra-ordinary tasks may only be performed upon a request of the State.

The ordinary and extra-ordinary police tasks may be of an administrative (maintaining the public order) as well as of a judicial nature. When performing its judicial duties, each district of the gendarmerie is assisted by a "Monitoring and investigating brigade" (*Bewakings- en opsporingsbrigade* - BOB) that concentrates on carrying out more specialized investigative tasks (art. 5 WRW). The *gendarmerie* is also assisted by "Surveillance, support and arrest squads" (*Peloton voor observatie, steun en arrestatie* - POSA), one for each of the five regions[23] and, on a national level, a special intervention squad (SIE, also called "the group Dyane," after the vehicle they have been using mostly).[24]

---

19   See Ponsaers & De Cuyper, 1980, pp. 88-100.
20   See Tobback, 1989, p. 5.
21   See on the demilitarization of the *gendarmerie* Bruggeman, 1992, pp. 45-52 and Van Outrive, 1993, pp. 125-128.
22   Van Outrive, 1993, p. 127; on the further plans to modify the *gendarmerie* we refer to Bruggeman, 1995a, pp. 239-240.
23   The territorial and mobile units of the *gendarmerie* of one or more provinces form together five regions: one for the metropolitan Brussels region and four for each two provinces (art. 7 WRW).
24   See Van Parys & Laurent, 1990, pp. 226-231 and Bruggeman, 1992.

The duties and powers of the *gendarmes* as of the other Belgian police officers are, since January 1, 1993, detailed in the Police Function Act (WPA). The statute also contains specific provisions on the way the different police powers must be exercised. It distinguishes between ordinary and extra-ordinary police tasks, the former being carried out on account of the officers' own initiative and the latter only upon request of the State. The ordinary police tasks mostly consist in the investigation of criminal offences[25] and the search for persons that must be arrested or objects that must be seized. The extra-ordinary police task mostly involve assisting the State with "the strong arm," accompanying persons at public ceremonies and serving notice of and executing judicial decisions.

Art. 15 WPA gives the *gendarmerie* the duty to investigate criminal offences. This duty is executed primarily by the officers and other higher ranking under-officers that have obtained, on the basis of art. 16 WRW, the competence of officer of judicial police, auxiliary to the public prosecutor. Artt. 8 and 9 Sv give the auxiliaries to the public prosecutor jurisdiction over criminal investigations, whereby their tasks are directly controlled by the public prosecutor's department and indirectly by the minister of justice.

The *gendarmes* have jurisdiction *ratione loci* on the whole of the Belgian territory (artt. 15 WRW and 45 WPA). To this jurisdiction must be added that, according to international treaties, the *gendarmes* have in some cases a certain jurisdiction on Dutch, Luxembourg, French and German territory (artt. 27 BET and 40, 41 SC).[26]

The Municipal Police
The Belgian Municipal Act states that each of the Belgian municipalities, indifferent of its size, must have its own police that, like the *gendarmerie*, has jurisdiction *ratione materiae* to perform administrative as well as judicial police tasks. Depending on the size of the municipality, it will be called urban or rural police. When a municipality has more than 10,000 inhabitants, it will usually have an urban police force, that, placed under the control of the mayor, will be organized and commanded by a police chief (art. 172 GemW). The smaller municipalities have most often a rural force of municipal police, that is sometimes solely composed of one officer. Small rural police forces usually form a brigade with other neighbouring small forces.

Since the Police Function Act has come into force, the tasks of the municipal police coincide almost entirely with those of the *gendarmerie*, the most

---

25   The expression "criminal offense" has been chosen by the authors to designate in the most general manner all actions that may be considered illegal, indifferent of the classification of offenses made in each legal system.

26   This will be discussed further in paragraphs 6 and 7 especially.

important exception being that the *gendarmerie* perform military tasks as well, while the municipal police only performs administrative and judicial tasks.[27] The judicial task of the municipal police is performed by (or directed by) the police officers that have obtained the capacity of officer of judicial police, auxiliary to the public prosecutor (*officier van gerechtelijke politie/hulpofficier van de procureur des Konings*). Only these officers have jurisdiction *ratione materiae* to draw up police reports of their findings.[28] Other officers are only habilitated to draw up ordinary reports that must be submitted to the auxiliary to the public prosecutor. According to art. 202 GemW, the auxiliaries to the public prosecutor in the municipal police force are the adjunct-commissaries (*adjunct-commissarissen/commissaires adjoints*), commissaries (*commissarissen/commissaires*) and chief commissaries (*hoofdcommissarissen/commissaires en chef*).

The jurisdiction *ratione loci* of the officers of the municipal police is restricted, in principle, to the territory of their own municipality or, in rural forces, to the territory of their brigade. In certain cases, the provincial governor may extend their jurisdiction outside the territorial limits of their employment (art. 45 par. 2 sub 1 WPA). In the past few years, this intermunicipal policing has known some strong evolutions: Two 1994 circulars have been issued in order to explain and elaborate art. 45 WPA,[29] and as a result, for instance the provincial governors of West and East have already extended the territorial competence of municipal police officers in their provinces to all municipalities in these provinces. Furthermore, it is possible for the police to transgress the territorial limits when acting in hot pursuit of a suspect or escaped person while the urgency of the situation does not permit warning the locally competent authorities in time.

The cooperation between the different (urban and rural) municipal police forces tended to differ depending on the region and, indeed, on the municipality. Nevertheless, some municipalities have achieved well functioning cooperation by means of agreements. These agreements may concern organizational arrangements as well as the operational level: On the one hand, there may be agreements on the intensification of the cooperation by the use of the same radio frequencies and, on the other hand, officers of different municipal forces may be able to assist each other on an informal level during a criminal investigation. It may be possible, for instance, that a police officer of one municipality carries

27 See Hutsebaut, 1993, pp. 106-113.
28 These are admitted in court as evidence and attest to their content.
29 The circulars Pol 31bis, July 20, 1994, B.S. July 27, 1994, pp. 19390-19393, and Pol 47, September 16, 1994, B.S. September 24, 1994, pp. 24363-24373.

out a search on the territory of another municipality, provided the police report is drawn up by a locally competent colleague.[30]

Note that this territorial competence may, in certain circumstances, even be extended outside the national limits of Belgium. Police officers of the municipal police may, on the basis of the Benelux Extradition Treaty (art. 27 BET) and the Schengen Convention (artt. 40 and 41 SC), observe and pursue a suspect or an escaped person onto Dutch, Luxembourg, French and German territory. Indeed, this concerns municipalities situated no further than 10 kilometers from the border.[31]

Police Judiciaire Près les Parquets
Besides the two above mentioned police forces, Belgium also maintains yet another police force, the judicial police of the public prosecutor (*gerechtelijke politie bij de parketten/police judiciaire près les parquets*), whose status is regulated by the Judicial Police Act of 1919 (*Wet op de gerechtelijke politie/Loi sur la police judiciaire* - WGP). This police force, with no administrative police tasks, is organized in 23 brigades, one national and 22 which are linked to the public prosecutor's department in the court's districts (art. 7 WGP).

The most important duty of this national brigade (also known as the 23rd brigade) is the investigation of terrorism-related crime and of internationally organized crime. It is assisted in this task by a specialized unit for undercover operations (*Groep voor schaduwing en observatie*). This special national brigade is part of the general office (*Commissariaat-Generaal/ Commissariat Général*) of the judicial police in Brussels. Two public prosecutors stand at the top of the brigade as national magistrates and as such, their most important task consists of coordinating the investigations of terrorism and organized crime.

The police officers of the judicial police are either officers or agents of judicial police (*gerechtelijke officieren* and *gerechtelijke agenten/officiers judiciaires* and *agents judiciaires*) with the investigation of criminal offences as their single task (artt. 1 WGP and 14 WPA). They must, however, report any information they might encounter that may be of importance to the administrative police and the administrative authorities (art. 14 par. 4 WPA). The judicial police may investigate on request of the public prosecutor's department or *ex officio* all criminal offences that come to its knowledge. It is, moreover, the only police force disposing of local and regional, technical and scientific forensic laboratories.

The officers and higher ranking agents of judicial police have jurisdiction *ratione materiae* as auxiliaries to the public prosecutor and dispose of all the

---

30   This was reported to the researchers by the chief commissary of the municipal police of Kortrijk; see also Fijnaut, 1992a, pp. 227-231.
31   This will be discussed further in Chapters 4 and 6 especially.

powers reserved as such in the Code of Criminal Procedure (art. 8 WGP). *Ratione loci*, the judicial police has jurisdiction on the whole of the Belgian national territory (art. 45 WPA). On the basis of international treaties, this jurisdiction may, in certain urgent cases, extend to the outside of the Belgian territory (art. 27 BET, artt. 40 and 41 SC).[32]

Cooperation

In principle, the three Belgian police forces are balanced horizontally as well as vertically. The fact that the municipal police are decentralized and the *gendarmerie* and judicial police are centralized forms the horizontal balance, while the fact that the judicial and administrative tasks are supervised by the (local and national) judicial and administrative authorities forms the vertical balance.

In practice, this balance always was somewhat difficult to find. Since the 1960s, the *gendarmerie* has seen its influence as a police force increase on the one hand because of the improvement of the legal framework in which its officers operate as well as, on the other hand, due to an increase in the number of its members and systematic investment. Because, in the same period of time, the different forces of municipal police depended (and still do) on (politically) unstable municipal administrations, the horizontal as well as the vertical balance disappeared out of sight.[33] The demilitarization of the *gendarmerie* as well as the harmonization of the police powers as regulated in the Police function act, however seems to have been an improvement of this situation. In any case, the legal situation of both forces now has more in common than was the case in the past.

There are, however, other characteristics of the Belgian police organization that may be the source of problems in the cooperation between the different police forces. Specifically the fact that both the *gendarmerie* and the municipal police share the same jurisdiction *ratione materiae* without the law defining a distinct jurisdiction *ratione loci* for any of the three forces is the cause of many ambiguous and problematic situations. In essence, there are always two police forces sharing jurisdiction on administrative matters and in judicial matters even three. The choice of the police force that will investigate a given matter will depend on the choice of the person calling "the" police. In the event that a criminal investigation has been started, the public prosecutor might be tempted to have it carried out by his own police force, the judicial police, even if it was originally in the hands on the *gendarmerie*. In that case, it is probable that the *gendarmerie* will cooperate, albeit reluctantly, with the investigation of the judicial police.

32 This will be discussed further in Chapters 4 and 6 especially.
33 See Tobback, 1989, p. 11; Daniels, 1989, p. 448 and Denis, 1989, pp. 3-22.

In attempting to solve the problems, the ministry of the interior published a circular (OOP 13), which tried to distinguish between the (principle) tasks of the municipal police and those of the *gendarmerie* in administrative policing.-[34] This circular has chosen a system of primary police tasks for both police forces, meaning that certain tasks, depending on local circumstances, will be reserved, though not exclusively, to either the municipal police or the *gendarmerie*.[35]

Though the circular also has certain implications for the cooperation in criminal investigations, that was never its aim. The Police function act, however, that was introduced two years later, does indeed contain certain provisions designed to improve the cooperation between police forces in both maintaining the peace and investigating criminal cases. Firstly, art. 9 WPA states that the ministers of the interior and of justice must coordinate the general policy concerning the *gendarmerie*, the municipal police and the judicial police. In this context, by the end of 1995, the minister of the interior issued a circular, introducing the concept of interpolice zones (*Interpolitiezones*).[36] According to this circular, the provincial governors are entrusted with the task of creating zones of cooperation in which all three regular police forces must cover the entire police task together.[37] As a result, it is likely that the task division envisaged by circular OOP 13 will be abolished and, depending on local circumstances, municipal police and *gendarmerie* will both fulfill specialized as well as more general tasks.[38]

Secondly, art. 10 par. 1 WPA stipulates that pentangular meetings must take place in each court district, where the mayors and public prosecutors must confer with the police chiefs of *gendarmerie*, municipal and judicial police. This body has been elaborated in more detail in a Royal decree and a circular,[39] which address two levels of pentangular meetings. At a local level (the level of the interpolice zones), the concertations must stimulate an integrated administrative, judicial and police policy on matters of public order and security, whereas pentangular meetings on a provincial level mainly fulfil policy and advisory tasks for the local meetings.

---

34 Circular of April 26, 1990, B.S. April 27, 1990, "*houdende de algemene richtlijnen betreffende de coördinatie van het optreden van de gemeentepolitie en de rijkswacht in het kader van de bestuurlijke politie.*"
35 The list contained in the circular is a list of priorities and not enumerative.
36 Circular IPZ 1, *Richtlijnen inzake de indeling van het grondgebied per provincie in Interpolitiezones (IPZ)*, December 5, 1995, not published.
37 According to Fijnaut, 1995, p. 82, this would also imply the end of the distinction between rural and urban municipal police forces.
38 In this sense also Fijnaut, 1995, pp. 98-101.
39 Respectively of April 10, 1995, B.S. June 6, 1995, pp. 17620-17622, and of May 22, 1995, B.S. June 6, 1995, pp. 17646-17664.

Finally, since 1994, a general police support service (*Algemene Politie-steundienst/service général d'appui policier* - APSD) was created by Royal decree.[40] According to art. 2 KB APSD, it has been charged with improving the cooperation between and coordination of the three regular police forces, as well as the coordination of the police policies of the three ministries involved (justice, the interior and defence). The APSD consists of four divisions: one responsible for operational support, one for international police cooperation, one for telematics and one for police policy support.[41] Part of this last division is a service, charged with the coordination of the pentangular meetings. The division international police cooperation plays a central role in particularly the international exchange of police information, which will be discuseed in Chapter 11.

In an agreement of July 4, 1994, the ministers of justice and the interior have introduced operational contact points in the border areas (*operationele invalspunten in de grensregio's* - OIPG). These contact offices have been entrusted with the task of providing Belgian as well as foreign police services with operational and informational assistance regarding international cooperation in the border areas. The OIPG's could perhaps be considered as the border area representatives of the APSD-division for international police cooperation, on which they can rely for assistance and support themselves.

3.2.1.2 The Netherlands

Since April 1994, the Dutch police have undergone great changes in their organization.[42] Before this time, the Dutch police were, as were the police of other European countries (Luxembourg, Belgium, Spain, etc.) strongly influenced by the Napoleonic Era. An important characteristic of this was the presence of two regular police forces.[43] Before April 1994, the larger municipalities in the Netherlands had their own decentralized municipal police force (*Gemeentepolitie*), placed under the management of the local mayor and financially dependent on the ministry of the interior, while smaller towns were served by the national police force (*Rijkspolitie*), which was the responsibility of the ministry of justice.[44] The latter national police force did not operate outside its own territory and in that way, did not interfere with the municipal

---

40 KB July 11, 1994, B.S. July 30, 1994, pp. 19658-19664; the decree will be referred to in the following as KB APSD.
41 We refer also to Fijnaut, 1995, p. 97.
42 See Bevers, 1994.
43 See the Police Act (*Politiewet* - PolW) of 1957; for a detailed overview of the Dutch police forces and their development, see Boek, 1995 and Elzinga, Van Rest & De Valk, 1995.
44 See for the situation before April 1994, Perrick, 1989; Swart, 1993, pp. 286-287 and Bevers & Joubert, 1994, pp. 39-41.

police. A third police force, the royal military police (*Koninklijke marechaussee*), under the responsibility of the ministry of defence still exists. Although a direct descendant of the French *maréchaussée*, its role as a regular police force may not be compared to that of the French *gendarmerie* of today.

Assisting the two general police forces, a number of centralized police services were financed and managed by the ministry of justice, providing the regular police forces with specialized techniques, knowledge, experience and material: These were for instance the Central criminal intelligence service (*Centrale recherche-informatiedienst* - CRI), the General Road Traffic Service (*Algemene verkeersdienst*), the Waterway Police (*Rijkspolitie te water*) and the Royal House Security (*Veiligheidsdienst koninklijk huis*).

Regional Police Forces
The new Police Act has been in force since April 1994. In essence, it has replaced both the municipal and national police with 25 regional police forces (*Regiopolitiekorpsen*), all of which share the same jurisdiction *ratione materiae* as well as *loci*. These regional police forces are managed by a regional police director as well as a national police management council and are financed by the ministry of the interior. Besides these 25 regional polices forces, another force was created to assist the regional forces: the 26th or national police force (*Korps landelijke politiediensten* - KLPD), managed and financed by the ministry of justice.

One of the most important reasons for the re-organization was the need to act effectively against increasing over-local, national and international crime. The cooperation between the numerous municipal police forces was often difficult and an organization with a reduced number of bigger forces was seen as a solution. Indeed, financial reasons also played an important role in the decision making process since 25 police forces require much less overhead expenses than 150. The reorganization was also seen as a good opportunity to increase the influence of the public prosecutor on the internal organization and management of the police, since he depends highly on the reliability, organization and equipment of the police for his own functioning. What may also have played a role is the "tribal battle" going on at the time between the ministries of justice and the interior to gain as much influence as possible on the police.[45]

In addition to the regional police forces and their supporting services, the general police task within the Dutch armed forces is entrusted to the centralized military police, the *Koninklijke marechaussee*. This military police force is financed and managed by the ministry of defence. Moreover, several ministries have their own specialized enforcement agencies, such as the Agricultural

45   See Van de Vijver *et al.*, 1992, p. 78.

Inspection (*Algemene inspectiedienst* - AID), the Economic Control Service (*Economische controledienst* - ECD), the Fiscal Intelligence and Investigation Service (FIOD) and customs and excise. Note that the police powers and jurisdiction of these services are limited to their own domain.[46]

The regional police forces are each managed by a regional police manager (*korpsbeheerder*), who is the mayor of the provincial capital or, in the event that this city is outside the region, the mayor of the most populated city in the region. Assisted by the chief of the regional police, they discuss the management of the police regularly with the public prosecutor in what is known as the "tripartite meetings" (*driehoeksoverleg*). Unlike the Police Act 1958, the regional public prosecutor (*hoofdofficier van justitie*), as head of the prosecutor's department (*parket*) of the court district (*arrondissement*) in the region, has been given an important role in the management of affairs as well.

The task of the police officer is defined in art. 2 of the Police Act 1993. The police, following orders of the competent authorities as well as the law, must ensure maintenance of the public order and grant help to those in need.[47] Besides maintaining the legal order, including the prevention of criminal offences according to the explanatory statement,[48] art. 1 PolW distinguishes a number of judicial police tasks: carrying out the legal provisions under the responsibility of the minister of justice, the administrative settlement of legal infractions of regulations (as long as the enforcement of these provisions has been entrusted to the responsibility of the public prosecutor), the service of criminal procedures, the transport of persons legally deprived of their liberty and to serve the courts.

Although the regional police forces do have a certain degree of autonomy as for their internal organization, there are some units all forces have in common. Three of those policing units will be mentioned briefly in this context. The criminal intelligence departments (*Criminele inlichtingendiensten* - CID's) have as a main task the gathering and processing of information on suspects and possible future suspects of severe and organized crime, in order to enable intervention by operational police units.[49] The organisation and functioning of these intelligence branches played a central role in the parliamentary inquiry on special policing techniques.[50] Tactical or operational units in each region

---

46   With regard to these services, see also Van Traa, 1996, pp. 342-351.
47   "*De politie heeft tot taak in ondergeschiktheid aan het bevoegde gezag en in overeenstemming met de rechtsregels te zorgen voor daadwerkelijke handhaving van de rechtsorde en het verlenen van hulp aan hen die deze behoeven.*"
48   TK 1991-1992, 22 562, nr. 3, p. 8.
49   They should therefore not be confused with the British CID's, which are regular detective units.
50   They are being discussed in Van Traa, 1996, pp. 303-318.

56

have the task of overtly investigating criminal offences.[51] Closely related to these two units are the observation units, which carry out specialized observation and surveillance measures for both CID's and tactical units.[52] Five of these units have been entrusted especially with cross-border observations in the context of the Schengen Convention.[53]

In carrying out his duty, the Dutch police officer has jurisdiction *ratione loci* in the whole of the Dutch territory, but in principle he will restrict his actions to the territory where he is employed (art. 7 PolW). In the event that he is legally acting on duty, he is authorized to use force and other means of constraint (art. 8 PolW). In order to carry out judicial police tasks, all police commissaries, chief inspectors and police chiefs fulfil the function of auxiliary to the public prosecutor (*hulpofficier van justitie*). Lower ranking police officers may also have this function by decree of the minister of justice. As auxiliaries to the public prosecutor, these police officers act as a bridge between the public prosecutor's department and the police, while they may also carry out a number of tasks in the name of the public prosecutor.

Korps Landelijke Politiediensten
As stated previously, a national and specialized 26th police force was created to assist the 25 regional forces. This force is placed under management of the ministry of justice, assisted (on decisions with regard to for instance the internal organization, budget, personnel and policy) by a council for the KLPD.

The KLPD is organized in five divisions: The Dutch royal house and diplomats division (assures the security of these notables), the Mobility division (includes the Road Traffic and Waterway Police), the Logistics division (entrusted with connections and transport within and between the regional police forces), the General support division (which deals with several types of special-ized support for the regional police forces ranging from air-police, communica-tions, technology and materials for the training of dogs and horses).[54] Finally, the fifth division is the Central criminal intelligence service (CRI).

The CRI is accountable for international police cooperation as well as the international exchange of police information, maintaining the contact with Dutch liaison officers abroad and with foreign liaison officers in the Netherlands. Further, the CRI is responsible for maintaining the contact with the centralized special investigation forces of the other ministries such as the AID, the ECD,

---

51 Van Traa, 1996, pp. 318-323.
52 See Van Traa, 1996, pp. 327-328.
53 See Van Traa, 1996, p. 323; on cross-border observation, see further chapter 4 of this study.
54 The functioning of this *Dienst technische operationele ondersteuning* (DTOO), that played an important role in the parliamentary enquiry on policing techniques, was discussed thoroughly in Van Traa, 1996, pp. 329-330.

the FIOD and customs. In order to carry out its international task, the CRI also accommodates the Dutch National central bureau of Interpol, the National criminal intelligence department (NCID), the National Schengen information system (NSIS) and SIReNE,[55] and many specialized departments (dealing with such subjects as international police cooperation, financial crime and coordination of infiltration). To improve their accessibility as a support service for the regional police forces, the CRI also has five deconcentrated offices, called *Afdeling recherche-informatiedienst* (ARI).[56]

Cooperation
The regionalization of the Dutch police forces was designed to improve the cooperation between the different forces: Indeed, it is to be expected that the cooperation between 25 police chiefs is much easier than between 150. However, the 25 regional police chiefs find themselves with much more power than ever before. Cooperation problems have also occurred in the five interregional detective teams on organized crime, which were supposed to begin investigating in 1993.[57] In these interregional detective teams or "nucleus teams", several police regions co-operate in investigating specific forms of international or organized crime.[58] Some problems of these teams seem to have been related to the fact that some police chiefs of most rural areas did not want to lose any personnel to these teams, especially after having already given a substantial part of their force to urbanized regions.[59] In addition to these interregional teams, a national detective team (*Landelijk rechercheteam*) is now being set up, that will be charged with mainly auxiliary and coordinatory tasks for regional and interregional detective teams. It is however not excluded that its officers might also obtain operational tasks, especially in investigations on a national or international scale.

Problems of this kind will certainly play a role in the evaluation of the police reorganization, that has been announced by the Dutch government already. Another aspect that will (again) cause a great deal of discussion during

---

55 This Supplementary information request at the national entries enables the police forces of the Schengen countries to directly and bilaterally ask for additional information in the event that they find a person or object reported in the SIS.

56 See about these ARI's further Van Traa, 1996, App. VI pp. 96-97.

57 See the report of the Wierenga Committee (*Rapport van de bijzondere commissie IRT*), Ministry of the interior, The Hague, 1994. The whole affair has led to the resignation of the ministers of justice as well as of the interior. We will discuss the problems of this interregional detective team in more detail in Chapter 5.

58 Their functioning, as well as that of a national detective team that is still to be installed, has been evaluated in LRT in Van Traa, 1996, pp. 334-342; see also Van Traa, 1996, App. VI, pp. 138 *et seq.*.

59 *Vorming "superpolitie" in alle regio's moeizaam*, de Volkskrant, January 27, 1994.

that evaluation, will be the democratic vacuum in which the regional police functions, hanging between the provincial and the municipal levels of adminis- tration.[60] For this reason, the minister of the interior has frequently expressed his hope that a new reorganization will lead to provincial police forces.[61]

3.2.1.3 Luxembourg

An important characteristic of the Luxembourg legal and police system is the language. Although the Luxembourg language (*Letzebuergisch*) is the spoken language of the country, it only obtained the status of official language in 1989. Because of many historical reasons, French and German are still official languages and the only ones in which official documents are published. All legal statutes are exclusively published in French, while police reports are drawn up in German. Since the language of the courts is French, police reports and other procedure coming from the police must be translated when used in court.[62]

Luxembourg has, as many European countries since Napoleon, two police forces, one with a civil (*police*) and one with a military origin (*gendarmerie*). The *police*, although originally a civil organization, were militarized in 1930.[63] Both police forces are now under the organizational responsibility of the ministry of defence (*ministère de la force publique*). Two other ministries are also responsible for the public force, the ministries of the interior (*ministère de l'intérieur*) and of justice (*ministère de la justice*).

The inter-weaving of the two forces is not only apparent in the fact that the ministry of defence is responsible for both organizations, but also in the promotion rules applicable for officers of both police forces. According to art. 70 par. 2 of the Military Organization Act (*Loi concernant l'organisation militaire* - LOM), an officer of the *police* will be promoted to the same rank in the *gendarmerie*: For instance, a captain of the *police* due for promotion will become captain in the *gendarmerie*. In the course of their careers, officers will go from one force to another and in this escalation, the rank of the *gendarmerie* will be higher than the corresponding rank in the *police*. The head of both organizations is the colonel of the *gendarmerie*.

---

60 See on this democratic deficit for instance Bevers, 1995.
61 For instance *Dijkstal: Misschien al in 1997 provinciale politie*, Ng-magazine January 19, 1996, p. 15. In the northern province of Friesland, the decision to provincialize the police has been taken by the municipalities; see *Friesland: provinciale politie en nieuwe taken voor gemeenten*, Ng-magazine January 19, 1996, pp. 16-17. Objections against such a provicialization have come from for instance mayors, police chiefs and parliamentarians; *'Provinciale politie zet de wereld op zijn kop'*, Ng-magazine January 26, 1996, pp. 20-21.
62 See Bevers & Joubert, 1994, p. 58.
63 Police Centralization Act (*Loi sur l'étatisation de la police* - LEP), Mém. 1930, nr. 933.

The maximum strength of both forces is fixed by law and is now 449 for members of the *police* (of which about 20 women) and 590 for the *gendarmerie* (of which about 20 women). In the past years, the actual number of police officers has stabilized to approximately 470 for the *police* and 580 for the *gendarmerie*.[64]

The agents and officers of both forces are habilitated to carry out tasks of judicial policing and, in this capacity, most of them are competent to act as auxiliaries of the public prosecutor (*agent* or *officier de police judiciaire*) according to artt. 9, 10 and 13 CIC. The difference between agents and officers of judicial police depends on the rank one has in the police force.

The officers of judicial police are those with the rank of officer in the *gendarmerie* and in the *police* (art. 10 CIC). They have the power and the duty to acknowledge the commission of an offence, to investigate it and search for the culprits (art. 11 par. 1 CIC). They carry out enquiries according to the provisions set out in artt. 46-48 and 30-40 CIC. As soon as the officer of judicial police knows that a crime has been committed, he must notify the public prosecutor (*procureur d'État*). Agents of judicial police are police officers with a limited power of investigation. They are the remaining police officers that do not have the habilitation of officer of judicial police (art. 13 par. 1 CIC). They will assist the officers of judicial police in carrying out investigations (art. 13 par. 2 CIC).

According to art. 9 CIC, the tasks of judicial policing are carried out under the supervision of the public prosecutor, himself being controlled by the council chamber of the court of appeal (*chambre du conseil de la cour d'appel*). The tasks of judicial policing consist in acknowledging an offence has been committed, collecting evidence *ex officio* and searching for the culprits as long as the investigating judge (*juge d'instruction*) has not officially opened the judicial enquiry, called *instruction* (art. 9-2 par. 1 CIC). As soon as such an enquiry has been officially opened, the judicial police lose their power to initiate investigations and must await orders of the investigating judge.

The Gendarmerie

The *gendarmerie* has jurisdiction *ratione loci* on the whole of the Luxembourg territory. Its organization has been established in the Military Organization Act of July 23, 1952, which has been often amended since then.[65] It is habilitated to exercise tasks of both administrative and judicial policing, as well as military

---

64 See also artt. 59, 60 and 70 LOM, Mém. 1989, nr. 22, April 18, 1989.
65 The last amendment is of 1989.

police tasks.[66] Moreover, the *gendarmerie* assists the army in maintaining the interior security of the country, intelligence and emergencies (art. 58 LOM).

The ministry of defence is responsible for its organization, management, professional training and discipline, whereas the ministry of justice is responsible for tasks concerning the maintaining of the public order and the judicial police (art. 58 LOM). Note that the performing of judicial police tasks is controlled by the public prosecutor (art. 9 CIC). At the top of the hierarchical pyramid of the organization is a colonel, commander of the *gendarmerie* and the public safety forces (*commandant de la gendarmerie et de la sûreté publique*)[67] who is also the highest ranking officer of the *police*.

The *gendarmerie* is territorially divided into three districts which correspond with the police districts. Each district is served by a number of brigades covering a number of municipalities. The strength of the different brigades depends on the size of the population. The *gendarmerie* is composed of a total of 37 brigades: The district Diekirch (north) has 13 brigades and is responsible for the safety of the grand-ducal family, the district Luxembourg (centre) is composed of 12 brigades that is responsible for the safety of the airport, immigration and the transfer of prisoners to the national prisons and, finally, the district Esch-sur-Alzette, which is composed of 10 brigades.

The Police Grand-Ducale

The largest municipalities in Luxembourg (there are nineteen) have, besides a unit of the *gendarmerie*, also headquarters of the *police grand-ducale*. The ministry of defence is responsible for its organization, management and professional training, while the ministry of the interior has jurisdiction over the *police* carrying out tasks of administrative policing. When performing tasks of judicial policing, the *police* answers to the ministry of justice (art. 68 LOM). In the past, the *police* was a civilian organization under the responsibility and control of the mayor. In 1930, it became a national force but remained under the responsibility of the mayor for their policing tasks on a local level.[68] In 1953, it became a military force and, since 1968, the state carries all costs and expenses regarding equipment as well as 60 % of the salaries (the remaining 40 % is paid by the municipalities).[69]

The police officers have national jurisdiction *ratione loci*, but note that when carrying out judicial police tasks they are subject to the control of the public prosecutor (art. 9 CIC). The execution of tasks of judicial policing is

---

66 See artt. 11 *et seq.* of the Royal Decree on the *gendarmerie* of January 30, 1815 (*Arrêté souverain sur le service de la maréchaussée*); see also Semerak & Kratz, 1989, p. 105.
67 In German: *Kommandant der Gendarmerie und der öffentlichen Sicherheit.*
68 See art. 3 LEP.
69 Semerak & Kratz, 1989, p. 102.

regulated by the ministry of defence, assisted by the director of the *police*. At the hierarchical top of the police force is the police director (*directeur de la police*), seated in Luxembourg city.[70] The police force is divided in three districts (Centre, North and South), corresponding to the districts of the *gendarmerie*. The headquarters are placed under the hierarchical control of the mayor of each of the nineteen municipalities. The districts North and South each have their own criminal investigating units.

Cooperation

There are a number of services that are directed by the commander of the *gendarmerie* and assist both police forces in their tasks, carrying out specialized requests for the district units. These are the service of the judicial police (*service de la police judiciaire*), the different technical services and the special units.

The members of the service of the judicial police (not to be confused with the tasks of judicial police that may be carried out by all police officers) are composed of plain clothes police officers who are competent to perform judicial tasks on the whole of the Luxembourg territory. This service, hosting the criminal police (*police criminelle/Kriminalpolizei*) and the national central bureau of Interpol, is divided into eight sections, all specialized in a specific area of criminality.[71] The service of judicial police is mostly solicited by the public prosecutor's department (*parquet*) for carrying out big scale or international investigations. Formerly only accessible for members of the *gendarmerie*, it has been open for members of the *police* as well since 1992.

Further, art. 78 LOM stipulates that measures should be taken to improve and intensify the cooperation, coordination and concentration of both police forces in their activities. As a result, both police forces share a number of services designed to help them carry out their tasks more efficiently. As a result, a number of services have been placed under the common management of both the police and the *gendarmerie*.[72] Moreover, both police forces share the same

---

70 Semerak & Kratz, 1989, p. 103.
71 For instance crimes against persons or goods, crimes against the public safety, drugs, and financial crime.
72 These are the *Service des transmissions et de traitement des informations*, directed by both the *commandant de la gendarmerie* and the *directeur de la police*, and composed of the following services: *Service de transmission de l'information*, the radio terminal, the computerized data service (*Datenfunk*), the telex, the emergency alarm system, the switchboard, the information network for Interpol and TREVI, and press contacts (*Gendapol*); the service of information processing and exploitation, the national central bureau of Interpol (BCN-Interpol/TREVI), which is part of the *gendarmerie* and is responsible for the daily contacts on an international level and the service for the processing and registration of information (*Service de traitement et d'enregistrement*).

training school, the *École de la gendarmerie et de la police* (art. 63 LOM) and both forces may be requested to set up big scale common operations.[73]

The public prosecutor is responsible for the way an investigation is carried out by the different police forces: He will determine which police services will be carrying out a particular investigation and whether a preliminary judicial enquiry (*information*) will be opened. In the event that this happens, the investigating judge will be further responsible for the investigation and for the choice of the police service carrying out the enquiry. Although this situation may create friction between the two police forces because, for instance, of the fact that an investigation started by one police force will be transferred to another force, it does not pose great problems in coordination.[74]

The fact that both police forces have a military status and that they are hierarchically dependant of the same ministries tends to guarantee a certain unity in the way police tasks are being carried out by both forces. However, discussions with officers of both forces show differences in mentality and a certain degree of competition between the two, leading to a certain extent to cooperation problems. A proposed merger of the two forces into one national police force has been dismissed for these reasons.

3.2.1.4 France

The French police force is composed of two separate police corps: the *gendarmerie nationale*, a police force with a military status known before the revolution of 1789 under the name *maréchaussée*[75] and the *police nationale*, a non-military police force.[76] As a military organization, the *gendarmerie* is under the responsibility of the minister of defence as to its organization and carries out police tasks in both the army and the civilian society. On the contrary, the *police nationale*, under the responsibility of the minister of the interior, is only competent for police tasks within the civilian society.[77]

Despite its relative significance and its limited police powers, the municipal police (*police municipale*) should be mentioned at this point. Although the *gendarmerie* has jurisdiction *ratione loci* as a regular police force in municipalities counting less than 10,000 inhabitants, the municipal council may, when public security renders this necessary, decide to set up a municipal police force

---

73   Decree of 1985; see Semerak & Kratz, 1989, p. 102.
74   This has been confirmed by sources in both the *gendarmerie* and the *police*.
75   The *maréchaussée* finds its origins as military police in the 12th century. It obtained its non-military police tasks in 1536 from François I.
76   The *police* appeared after the revolution in 1789 as counterweight to the military force of the *gendarmerie*. See Jammes, 1982, p. 115.
77   See also Pradel, 1993c, pp. 105-136 and Meyzonnier, 1994, pp. 119-178

(art. L.131-2 *Code Communal*). The police officers of this force have the restricted police powers of adjunct agents of judicial police (*agent de police judiciaire adjoint*) and only have jurisdiction *ratione materiae* for acknowledging the commission of criminal offences and the apprehension of suspects caught in the act. The mayor is not habilitated to extend this jurisdiction to other police powers.[78] The police chief of municipalities counting more than 5.000 inhabitants must be part of the *police nationale*. As a result, the chief of police of these municipalities has jurisdiction as an officer of judicial police and is empowered to carry out certain tasks beyond the jurisdiction of adjunct agents of judicial police. Because of its limited importance on an international level, we will further disregard the municipal police in our study.

In general, it is said that the *gendarmerie* is especially active in rural areas, whereas the *police nationale* is active predominantly in urbanized centres. However, no act gives to one or another police force exclusive jurisdiction *ratione loci* or *ratione materiae*.[79] Both police forces carry out the same police tasks concurrently. Although the *gendarmerie* is said to have national jurisdiction,[80] one cannot speak of an exclusive competence since many services of the *police nationale* also have national jurisdiction.[81] When carrying out tasks of judicial policing, both forces are subject to the control of the public prosecutor's department (*ministère public*) and are obliged to assist one another (art. D-1 *et seq.* CPP).

Police officers of both police forces have jurisdiction *ratione materiae* to act as an auxiliary to the public prosecutor (*agents* or *officiers de police judiciaire*). In this capacity they dispose of powers of judicial policing. All [police officers acting in this capacity, according to art. 15 CPP, are subject to the authority of the public prosecutor (*procureur de la République*). All officers of judicial police have the same legal responsibilities and privileges, notwithstanding their allegiance to one or another police force. Both the investigating judge (*juge d'instruction*) and the public prosecutor may decide which of the two police forces will be carrying out the investigation. This means that a case may be transferred from one force to another. The officers of both police forces are obliged to assist each other (art. D.2 CPP). In some circumstances, the law suggests to the investigating judge to rely on the specialized services of the central direction of the judicial police, a specialized service of the *police*

---

78 Decocq, Montreuil & Buisson, 1991, p. 112.
79 See Stefani *et al.*, 1993, pp. 278 *et seq.*
80 Art. 28 of the Law of the 28 Germinal Year VI (April 18, 1798) states that the *gendarmerie* is especially suitable for maintaining the peace in rural areas and on country roads. Moreover, the decree of May 20, 1903 stipulates that the *gendarmerie* carries out its tasks on the whole of the French territory.
81 See Decocq, Montreuil & Buisson, 1991, p. 115.

nationale.[82] In the event that services of the *gendarmerie* and the *police nationale* are working on a case together, the investigating judge responsible for the investigation will decide on matters regarding coordination and progress of the investigation (art. D.5 CPP).

Art. 16 CPP states which state officers are empowered to act as officers of judicial police (*officier de police judiciaire*). The main tasks of the judicial police is the registration of criminal offences, collecting evidence and searching for the culprits. Agents of judicial police (*agents de police judiciaire*) are the *gendarmes* and inspectors (*inspecteurs*) who do not have the power to act as officers of judicial police.

The Police Nationale
The organization of the *police nationale* is both centralized and specialized. It is centralized because the whole organization is placed under the direction of the minister of the interior. It is specialized since it is composed of a large number of services each focusing on specific offences and activities. Its organization is also fairly complicated, because of the different levels of coordination.[83]

The designation "*police nationale*" is used to identify the whole of the police services subject to the hierarchical direction of the ministry of the interior (art. 1 Act of July 9, 1966).[84] The *préfecture de Paris*, although enjoying a particular status because of historical reasons, is part of the *police nationale* and an important number of its services are subject to the authority of the *Direction générale de police nationale* (D.G.P.N.).[85]

Starting in 1990, a large-scale re-organization of the *police nationale* was initiated, later to be abandoned in 1993.[86] In short, the *police nationale* is organized as follows: At the top we find the minister of the interior and of

---

82 The special circumstances referred to by the law deal mainly with cases regarding human and arms trafficking, counterfeiting and cases where special techniques must be used. In other circumstances, however, the judge may chose the specialized services of the *gendarmerie*, as they are specialized in other domains. One of these is, for instance, the study of insects, an important technical knowledge in pathological forensic science.

83 For a historical summary of the development of the *police nationale*, see Meyzonnier, 1994, pp. 126-132.

84 This includes the officers of the former *Sûreté nationale*, as well as those of the *Préfecture de Paris*. With the law of 1966 and the creation of the *Direction générale de police nationale*, in contrary to the one of 1941 organizing the *Sûreté nationale*, the overlapping between the *Sûreté nationale* and the *Préfecture de Paris* ceased to exist. See Stefani *et al.*, 1993, pp. 278 *et seq.*

85 Decocq, Montreuil & Buisson, 1991, p. 116.

86 Meyzonnier, 1994, p. 133.

development of the territory,[87] followed in the hierarchy by the general director of the *police nationale*. There are intervention units directly attached to the general director, such as the coordination unit for repression of terrorism (*unité de coordination de la lutte anti-terroriste*), the unit of investigation, assistance, intervention and dissuasion (*unité de recherche, d'assistance, d'intervention et de dissuasion* - RAID), and the security service (*service de sécurité*). On the second level of organization, we find on the one hand two administrative directions[88] and, on the other hand, nine directions and active services, the most relevant of which for this study are: the central direction of judicial police (*Direction centrale de police judiciaire* - D.C.P.J.),[89] the central direction of city police forces (*Direction centrale des polices urbaines*) and the central service of the air and border police (*Service central de la police de l'air et des frontières* - P.A.F.).[90]

Since June 1993, the *préfet* is the only authority responsible for public order. He is assisted in his tasks by the departmental director of public security (*directeur départemental de la sécurité publique*), who is a high ranking police officer and also departmental director of city police forces (*directeur départe-*

---

87 *Ministère de l'intérieur et de l'aménagement du territoire* is the new name of the ministry of the interior since April 1993.

88 They are the direction responsible for personnel and training in the *Police nationale* (*Direction du personnel et de la formation de la police*) and the logistics direction (*Direction de la logistique de la police*). We will not insist on these directions since they are not relevant to the study at hand.

89 This central direction is composed of a multitude of specialized services grouped in four sub-directions: the sub-direction of technical and scientific police (*sous-direction de la police technique et scientifique*), the sub-direction of criminal affairs (*sous-direction des affaires criminelles*), the sub-direction of economical and financial crimes (*sous-direction des affaires économiques et financières*) and the sub-direction of financial resources and liaisons (*sous-direction des resources et liaisons*); see Decocq, Montreuil & Buisson, 1991, p. 124.

90 Long-term plans have been made to integrate this service into a new police direction: the central direction of the fight against illegal immigration and employment (*direction centrale de lutte contre l'immigration et le travail clandestins*). Other services are: two intelligence services, the central direction of general intelligence (*direction centrale des renseignements généraux*) and the direction of territory surveillance (*direction centrale de la surveillance du territoire*), which may both be brought under a common direction since June 1993, followed by the general inspection (*inspection générale de la police nationale*), the central service of the republican state security police force (*service central des compagnies républicaines de sécurité*), the service of international technical police cooperation (*service de coopération technique internationale de police*) and the service for official visits and the safety of important personalities (*service des voyages officiels et d la sécurité des hautes personnalités*). For more details on these services and on the complete organisation of the *police nationale*, we refer to Decocq, Montreuil & Buisson, 1991, pp. 116-136.

mental des polices urbaines).[91] On the same level, the departmental director of the general intelligence service (*renseignements généraux*) and the departmental director of the air and borders police will report both to the *préfet* and their respective central directions in Paris, at the ministry of the interior. On the contrary, the judicial police as well as the direction of territory surveillance will not report to the *préfet*, since they are directly managed in Paris.[92]

The main tasks of the *police nationale* include those of the judicial and administrative police and of maintaining order. Judicial policing, assisting the public prosecutor, essentially repressive, consists in establishing the commission of criminal offences, collecting evidence, searching for suspects and executing requests of the public prosecutor (*procureur de la République*) and of the investigating judge (*juge d'instruction*). These tasks are mostly carried out by police officers subject to the central direction of judicial police and of the central direction of city police forces. Police chiefs and inspectors are empowered to act as officers of judicial police (*officiers de police judiciaire*). Agents of judicial police (*agents de police judiciaire*), a qualification that has been recently given to officers of the peace (*gardiens de la paix*), are auxiliaries of the officers of judicial police and assist them in this capacity in their judicial tasks.[93]

The Gendarmerie

The French *gendarmerie*, a centralized military institution subject to the authority of the ministry of defence, is organized according to the Act of May 20, 1903. The *gendarmerie* has jurisdiction to act as military police but is also competent for regular police tasks such as maintaining the public order and investigating criminal offences. It is composed of two main branches, the departmental *gendarmerie* (*gendarmerie départementale*) and the mobile *gendarmerie* (*gendarmerie mobile*). It is further composed of a number of specialized units, such as the air and air transport *gendarmerie* (*gendarmerie de l'air et des transports aériens*), the marine *gendarmerie* (*gendarmerie maritime*) and the republican guard (*gardes républicaines*).[94] The general direction of the *gendarmerie* (*direction générale de la gendarmerie*) is at the head of the organization and is composed of a number of administrative divisions such as the general inspection, the training school commandment and the technical centre.

---

91   This has been reiterated in the Security Orientation and Programming Act of January 21, 1995 (*Loi no. 95-73 du 21 janvier 1995 d'orientation et de programmation relative à la sécurité*), J.O. January 24, 1995, p. 1249 (*Loi sécurité*).
92   Meyzonnier, 1994, p. 133.
93   See Meyzonnier, 1994, p. 134; note also the *Loi sécurité*.
94   Decocq, Montreuil & Buisson, 1991, p. 137.

The national French territory is divided into six military regions,[95] in each of which both branches of the *gendarmerie*, the departmental and the mobile *gendarmerie*, are placed under the responsibility of one high ranking officer.[96] There is a *groupement de gendarmerie départementale* in each department, composed of a number of *compagnies*, one in each court district. The *compagnies* are each responsible for the coordination and hierarchical leadership of the different territorial *brigades*, present in all the *cantons*. Each *brigade* is composed of six to forty under-officers and *gendarmes* and is commanded by a chief warrant officer, a warrant officer or a marshal.[97]

Cooperation
The territorial organization of the police officers habilitated to carry out tasks of judicial policing seems to be the source of problems and friction: The multitude of specialized services with overlapping jurisdictions in both the *gendarmerie* and the *police nationale* often leads to a climate of competition between the different competent services, which often hinders the coordination of the investigation. Additionally, problems of competition between public prosecutors may arise in cases where more than one public prosecutor has jurisdiction, for instance, because a number of offences have been committed in different areas by the same suspect(s).[98] For these reasons, it is often advocated in the doctrine for the recognition of a national jurisdiction for all officers of judicial police.[99]

In recent years, perhaps under the influence of the growing internationalization in the police field, the cooperation between the different police services has improved. In both the *gendarmerie* and the *police nationale*, services have developed with overlapping and competing jurisdictions, specialized in different areas. This is the case, for instance, of the technical and scientific police service of the *gendarmerie* (*police technique et scientifique*), which specializes in the pathological forensic science. In the event that a public prosecutor or an investigating judge needs an expert opinion concerning a found corpse, he may call on this service to establish facts such as the time and place of death. In cases involving organized crime, it is often the specialized services of the regional *police nationale* (*service régional de police nationale*) that are called upon.

---

95 See Stefani *et al.*, 1993, pp. 284 *et seq.*
96 The centres of these regions are: Paris, Lille, Rennes, Bordeaux, Metz and Lyon. The regions are each commanded by a colonel and are subdivided into 21 departments, which are each composed of a number of court districts (*arrondissements*); see Stefani *et al.*, 1993, pp. 284 *et seq.*
97 Decocq, Montreuil & Buisson, 1991, pp. 136 *et seq.*
98 Examples of this are found in Moréas, 1985, written by a former police commissionary.
99 See for instance Denis, 1974, pp. 191-209; Decocq, Montreuil & Buisson, 1991, p. 79.

The public prosecutor or the investigating judge decides, depending on the circumstances of the case, which service will carry out the investigation (art. D.1 CPP). In the event that one of these authorities is of the opinion that the service which has started the investigation is not appropriate for the case, they may decide to transfer it to another service (artt. D.3 *et seq.* CPP). In that case, all police reports and files must be transferred to the service continuing the investigation.[100]

3.2.1.5 Germany

The Federal Republic of Germany is a federal State composed of sixteen provinces since the unification of the Federal republic with the Democratic republic in October 1990.[101] The Constitution (*Grundgesetz* - GG) divides the different tasks of the State, such as jurisdiction over the police, between the federal government and the provinces. It does not, however, provide for an answer to the question concerning which body has the general legislative jurisdiction on the police tasks.[102] According to art. 70 GG, this competence is left to the provinces since the provinces are competent to legislate in areas not explicitly reserved by the constitution for the federal legislator. Most of the legislation on the subject is indeed provincial. Each province has its own acts on the police regulating the organization and (in part) the jurisdiction of the police in each of the provinces.[103] Note that the police have been wearing the same uniform in the whole of Germany since the end of the seventies.

The fact that the provinces have jurisdiction to legislate on police organization has indeed resulted in the situation where each of the sixteen provinces has its own statute regarding the organization of the police. Also, concerning the regulation of police powers, each province has taken a somewhat different stance; although since 1972 the provincial ministers of the interior have agreed on a Model Police Act (*Musterentwurf eines einheitlichen Polizeigesetzes* - MEPolG) there is increasingly more interest for harmonization.[104]

Although, in principle, the police task belongs to the domain of legislation of the provinces, it would be untrue to conclude that the federal government only plays a secondary role in this domain. Art. 73 GG also contains a number of dispositions reserving some areas of policing to the legislative power of the federal state, such as the cooperation between federal and provincial levels in

---

100 See also Bevers & Joubert, 1994, pp. 147-148.
101 We have chosen the word province instead of the German word *Land/Länder*, in order to facilitate the use of adjectives such as provincial.
102 See Götz, 1991, p. 28.
103 The competence of the police during its investigative tasks is exclusively regulated by federal law, such as the Code of Criminal Procedure (*Strafprozeßordnung* - StPO).
104 See Götz, 1991, p. 33; see also Drews/Wacke/Vogel/Martens, 1985, p. 89.

criminal investigation and the international fight against crime. Art. 74 GG, moreover, stipulates that both the federal and the provincial legislators are competent to regulate certain police tasks, such as traffic regulation on land and water.

The management of the police in Germany is completely in the hands of the federal and provincial ministers of internal affairs. When it comes, however, to their task in the criminal procedure, it is the public prosecutor (*Staatsanwalt*) who exercises the hierarchical control and is responsible for the investigation. He may give direct orders to the auxiliaries of the public prosecutor (*Hilfsbeamten der Staatsanwaltschaft*), who must be designated by provincial law (art. 152 GVG).[105]

Despite their legal obligation to the public prosecutor, the German police enjoy a certain degree of autonomy in the exercising of their tasks. The jurisdiction of the public prosecutor over the police is limited to the criminal procedure.[106] The decision concerning the moment to send a police report to the public prosecutor, which decision formally puts an end to the autonomy of the police, is entirely up to the police. This also means that the public prosecutor is entirely dependent on the information transmitted by the police.[107]

Those police officers who are auxiliaries to the public prosecutor have special investigating powers otherwise reserved for the public prosecutor himself or the investigating judge (*Ermittlungsrichter*). The jurisdiction to act as such is given in urgent cases (*Gefahr im Verzug*) when the circumstances of a particular case are urgent enough to justify resorting to more extensive police powers.[108] Because the assessment of the situation is done by the police officer himself, it remains possible for him to escape or delay the supervision of the *Staatsanwalt*.

As a rule, the police officers have jurisdiction *ratione loci* in the area where they are assigned (*Kreis, Station* or *Stadt*). However, in provinces such as Baden-Württemberg, Bavaria and Hessen, the territorial jurisdiction of the police officers stretches to the limits of the provincial borders. In the remaining provinces, this rule is subject to a number of exceptions. In all cases, police officers are authorized to enter the territory of another when this is necessary for urgent reasons. This is authorized as well when assistance is needed.[109]

Because of the mere fact that the police are the recipients of the powers given to them by the law of their province of assignment, they are, as a rule, not allowed to act in another province. This rule has exceptions as well, in part

---

105 Kleinknecht/Meyer-Goßner, 1995, pp. 1449-1451.
106 Kleinknecht/Meyer-Goßner, 1995, p. 1449.
107 See for instance Körner, 1992, pp. 130-133.
108 The special position of *Gefahr im Verzug* shall be discussed further in this chapter.
109 Götz, 1991, p. 205.

regulated by federal law, such as the obligation of provinces to give each other assistance in case of necessity (artt. 35 par. 2 and 3 and 91 GG). Further, art. 167 GVG provides for the possibility to pursue a fleeing person across a provincial border in order to arrest him. This possibility is also often embedded and extended in the laws of the province. Furthermore, there are treaties between provinces providing for cross-border police powers. The powers of the waterways police especially are often extended in that way. The police statutes of each province often contain rules on the crossing of provincial borders by police officers.[110]

The Federal Police Services

a. The Federal Criminal Police Office (BKA)

Art. 73 par. 10 GG gives the federal legislator the exclusive jurisdiction over the cooperation between the federal and provincial authorities in criminal investigations. Further, this provision enables the federal government to create a federal criminal police. The federal government has used this possibility in 1951 and regulated its organization and competencies in the Act on the Federal Criminal Police Office (*Gesetz über die Einrichtung eines Bundeskriminalamtes* - BKAG).[111] This institution, seated in Wiesbaden, is directly subject to the authority of the federal minister of the interior (*Innenminister*) regarding its organization and management as well as for the execution of its tasks.

The task of the federal criminal police may be summed up as follows: combatting criminals (potentially) active internationally or in more than one province (art. 1 BKAG). With this goal, the BKA, also the German central national bureau of Interpol, collects, analyses, processes and distributes information and develops methods and techniques (art. 2 BKAG).[112] The federal criminal police also acts in the field of crime prevention (art. 5 par. 1 BKAG), although this field belongs, in principle, to the competence of the provinces. It also assists the provincial criminal police forces (LKA), which have as one of their tasks the improvement of cooperation (art. 3 BKAG).

The agents of the federal criminal police also have the power, and in some cases the obligation, to carry out investigations personally. This happens particularly in cases of inter-provincial criminality, political violence and internationally organized arms and drugs trafficking and counterfeiting (art. 5 par. 3 BKAG). In other cases, the agents of the federal criminal police may be

---

110 See Götz, 1991, pp. 406 *et seq.*; this question shall be discussed later in Chapter 6.
111 BGBl. I, 1951, p. 3393; note that a new law is pending; see for more information, Steinke, 1995, pp. 212 *et seq.*
112 See Götz, 1991, p. 184.

requested by the authorities of one province, the federal minister of home affairs or the federal public prosecutor (*Generalbundesanwalt*) to continue an investigation initiated by the police of one province. In that case, the police of the province in which the investigation is taking place must follow the instructions and carry out orders of the federal criminal police (art. 5 par. 3 BKAG). Furthermore, the BKA may decide to transfer an interprovincial investigation to one of the concerned provincial criminal police offices.[113]

b. The Federal Border Police (BGS)

A second important federally organized police agency is the federal border police (*Bundesgrenzschutz* - BGS). Its organization and tasks are to be found primarily in the 1994 Federal Border Police Act (*Gesetz zur Neuregelung der Vorschriften über den Bundesgrenzschutz* - BGSNeuRegG).[114] This statute finds its justification in art. 73 par. 5 GG that gives exclusive jurisdiction to the federal parliament to legislate on matters of toll and border protection.

The first and foremost important task of the federal border police is the protection of the borders of the Federal Republic of Germany and the control of cross-border traffic. This task is carried out by the border security service (*Grenzschutzeinzeldienst*) that is directed by the *Grenzschutzdirektion* in Koblenz and is subdivided into 18 agencies. In many border regions, the security of the border is guaranteed by the federal border police as well as by customs officers (*Zöllner*) or in Bavaria by the Bavarian border police.[115]

The agents of the federal border police are police officers and as such, carry out tasks of the criminal police with the same powers. The majority of them are subject to the provincial law as auxiliaries of the public prosecutor to which extended powers and jurisdiction are recognized.[116]

c. Other Federal Police Agencies

Besides the federal criminal police and the federal border police, the federal government has a number of possible police resources at its disposal to help maintain the federal influence in police matters. In urgent cases, for instance, the *Inspekteur der Bereitschaftspolizeien* (under the direct supervision of the federal minister of the interior) is entitled to the immediate assistance of a special police force.[117] There is also the special police force of the *Bundestag*

---

113 Drews/Wacke/Vogel/Martens, 1985, p. 64.
114 BGBl. I, 1994, 2978.
115 Götz, 1991, p. 182; Drews/Wacke/Vogel/Martens, 1985, p. 68.
116 Götz, 1991, p. 184.
117 Drews/Wacke/Vogel/Martens, 1985, p. 69.

which is directly controlled by the parliament and embodied under the supervision of the president of the parliamentary assembly.[118] Finally, note the existence of several federal services, such as the federal rail police (*Bundesbahnpolizei*), river and shipping police (*Strom- und Schifffahrtspolizei*), air police (*Luftpolizei*) and customs investigating service (*Zollfahndungsdienst*), while the civil servants employed by the bureau for the protection of the constitution (*Bundesamt für Verfassungsschutz*) and those employed by a number of other federal institutions dispose of some police powers.[119]

The Provincial Police Forces

As mentioned earlier, the German constitution reserves jurisdiction for police matters to the provinces. The different provinces have all provided for their own police organization and passed acts with this aim.[120] The distinctions between the different provinces on that matter are not limited to details but are rather often present at the basis. The concept of what in one province is understood by "the police" may greatly vary from one province to another. In some provinces the word police is used also when speaking of a number of administrative bodies with controlling powers, while in other provinces the term is used exclusively concerning agencies with executive police powers that may take direct measures against citizens.[121]

All of the provinces have one provincial police force with general police powers, although many had known municipal police forces. These were all abolished after the Second World War, the last one in 1975 in Munich.[122] The executive police of each province may be subdivided into a number of services: patrolling and maintaining the peace are done by the uniformed *Schutzpolizei*, criminal investigations by the *Kriminalpolizei*, maintaining the public order, the prevention of insecurity and riots as well as managing important events are eventually performed by the special units of the *Bereitschaftspolizei*. In addition, each province has its own police for its waterways (*Wasserpolizei*).

The territorial jurisdiction of the police may be extended to the territory of another border country on the basis of art. 41 SC. This provision of the Schengen Convention authorizes police officers of both the provincial and federal police forces as well as, in certain cases, the specialized *Zollfahndungs-*

---

118 Drews/Wacke/Vogel/Martens, 1985, p. 71.
119 Drews/Wacke/Vogel/Martens, 1985, pp. 73-86.
120 Some provinces have regulated the organization as well as police powers in the same law while others have passed different texts. For example, Baden-Württemberg and Saarland each have passed a single law providing rules for the organization as well as powers of the police, while both Rheinland-Pfalz and Nordrhein-Westfalen have done this in two different laws.
121 See Drews/Wacke/Vogel/Martens, 1985, pp. 48 et seq. and Götz, 1991, pp. 24 et seq.
122 See Götz, 1991, pp. 176 et seq.

dienst to cross the national border as long as they are *Hilfsbeamten der Staats-anwaltschaft*.[123]

a. *Schutzpolizei*

In most of the provinces, the uniformed police force charged with general executive police tasks such as patrolling is called the Schutzpolizei. It has jurisdiction in all cases where specialized services, such as the *Kriminalpolizei* or the *Bereitschaftspolizei*, have no exclusive jurisdiction. In general, the *Schutzpolizei* is responsible for maintaining the peace and law enforcement in traffic offences and other minor transgressions. The *Schutzpolizei* is subdivided into smaller units which, depending on the province, often correspond to the administrative subdivisions of the districts.[124] In each of the provincial *Schutzpolizeien*, we find a *Spezialeinsatzkommando* - SEK, composed of heavily armed police officers under the responsibility of the provincial ministers of the interior. These special units have tasks in the intervention against such serious events as the taking of hostages and terrorism.

b. *Kriminalpolizei*

With the specialization of police techniques and the developments of forensic sciences since the end of the 19th century the investigative task of the police, the so-called "criminal police" (in German *Kriminalpolizei* or in short the "*Kripo*" as opposed to the *Schutzpolizei*, the "*Schupo*"), have distinguished themselves from the general police task. Both the *Kripo* and the *Schupo* are organized in the same way and present in each precinct on a local level.[125] However, there remains a sharp division between the two: for instance, their respective size in personnel are independent from one another, officers of the *Kripo* seldom transfer to the *Schupo* and vice versa and they both endorse a different ranking system with no correspondence to one another.[126]

The only task of the *Kripo* is to investigate important crimes. It does so by using the technical means made available by the provincial criminal police offices, which are present in each province and placed under the responsibility of the provincial ministries of the interior. The provincial criminal police keep

---

123 This shall be extensively discussed in Chapter 6.
124 See for an overview of the provincial *Schutzpolizeien* relevant for the Schengen partners Bevers & Joubert, 1994, pp. 89-90.
125 It is a subject of discussion whether the *Kripo* is a specialization of the general police force (see Drews/Wacke/Vogel/Martens, 1985, p. 92) or a specialization alongside the general force (see Götz, 1991, p. 178).
126 Kuijvenhoven, 1990, p. 337.

74

in contact with each other and with the federal criminal police. Exercising disciplinary control over the local detective teams as well, they have the jurisdiction to give them orders.[127] Furthermore, the provincial criminal police house diverse specialized services and laboratories and their officers carry out investigations personally when it comes to offences related to radioactivity, explosives, counterfeit currencies, state security, narcotics, severe economic crime and environmental criminality.[128] Finally, the *Mobile Einsatz Kommandos* (MEK), set up by the provincial ministers of the interior, are also part of the diverse *Kriminalpolizeien* and are available for observation actions against severe criminality.

c. *Bereitschaftspolizei*

Each of the provinces has its own special unit of public order police (*Bereitschaftspolizei*), organized and managed according to the classical centralistic model and quartered in barracks. This police force is directly under the control and administration of the provincial ministers of the interior who also have jurisdiction to give direct orders for its mobilization. In some provinces the minister of the interior is even the only person habilitated to give orders related to its mobilization. With the interaction of the *Inspekteur der Bereitschaftspolizei*, the federal minister of the interior may also make use of this police force. Service for the *Bereitschaftspolizei* is also a part of the training for young police officers.[129]

d. *Wasserpolizei*

In the same way that the criminal police have distinguished themselves from the general police tasks, the police for the waterways (*Wasserpolizei*) have also developed independently. Their most important responsibility is the supervision of professional and civil traffic on the waterways, but in the last few years the *Wasserpolizei* heve become increasingly involved in the investigation of environmental crimes. The division of jurisdiction between the provincial *Wasserpolizei* and the federal *Strom- und Schifffahrtpolizei* is contained in a number of intergovernmental conventions between the federal and provincial governments.[130]

---

127 Drews/Wacke/Vogel/Martens, 1985, p. 92.
128 Semerak & Kratz, 1989, p. 93.
129 See also Drews/Wacke/Vogel/Martens, 1985, p. 93.
130 Drews/Wacke/Vogel/Martens, 1985, pp. 79 and 93.

3.2.2   Public Prosecutor

The public prosecutor is responsible for the prosecution of criminal offences and, in most countries, for leading the pre-trial investigation before an official preliminary judicial enquiry has been opened. In all but one of the studied countries (Germany), the public prosecutor's department is designated by the terms public ministry (*ministère public, openbaar ministerie*) as well as by *parquet* (or *parket*). This last appellation originates from the time known as the "old regime" (*ancien régime*), when the procurers and advocates of the King in France did not operate on the same level as the judge, but rather on the same level as the audience, the suspect and his representative: on the floor, covered with wood, the parquet. This name stayed although the magistrates of the public prosecutor's department now often operate on the same level as the judge: on top of a kind of podium.[131] The following sub-paragraph contains a short description of the organization and tasks of the prosecutor and his department.

3.2.2.1 Belgium

The public prosecutor is a member of the public prosecutor's department, which is the agency responsible for the prosecution of criminal offences and application of the criminal statutes. This includes the following tasks: First, carrying out the criminal procedure by starting the procedure before the judge. The public prosecutor's department has a monopoly on the criminal prosecution of criminal offences (see artt. 1 and 2 VTSv). Second, presenting evidence before the courts. Since the suspect is presumed innocent, he does not have to present any proof. The public prosecutor's department is assisted in this task by the police. Third, the public prosecutor's department is the instigator of the execution of the imposed sanction.[132]

The members of the public prosecutor's department are part of a hierarchical body, on the outside operating as one block. This body is organized as a pyramid in each court of appeal district with the prosecutor general (*procureur général/procureur-generaal*) as the head of the organization. He is assisted in his tasks by the advocates general (*avocats généraux/advocaten-generaal*) and his substitutes as well as, at the level of the judicial district (*arrondissement*), by the public prosecutors (*procureurs du Roi/procureurs des Konings*) and their substitutes. The prosecutors general and their substitutes constitute the general prosecutor's department (*parquet général/parket-generaal*) while the public prosecutors and their substitutes (*magistrats du parquet/parketmagistraten*) are

---

131 Stefani *et al.*, 1993, p. 101.
132 See Van den Wyngaert, 1994, p. 440; regarding the public prosecutor, see also Declerq, 1994, pp. 9-28 and Verstraeten, 1994, pp. 38-50.

considered the prosecutor's department (*parquets/parketten*). These magistrates are designated by the King (art. 153 GW). Although they are part of the judiciary, they may under no circumstances be confused with the sitting magistrates, the judges.

The prosecution policy is determined by the general prosecutor's department and the lower departments, not by the ministry of justice, although this has been questioned in recent years. The minister of justice may order a prosecution, but he cannot stop or prevent prosecution in individual cases. It is said that "he has authority but no power," although there is much discussion about what this would imply.[133] In the original interpretation, the prosecutors-general inform the minister on his request about the prosecution policy in their ressort; in spite of his political responsibility, he does not determine the prosecution policy.[134] There is however a strong tendency to consider the prosecution policy a public task of the minister of justice, who must develop a criminal policy with priorities that should be imposed on the prosecutors-general.[135] The main channels through which the minister of justice may influence the prosecution's policy are the assembly of prosecutors-general (*college van procureurs-generaal*) and the so-called national magistrates (*nationale magistraten*). The assembly of prosecutors-general, for which the 1995 Coalition agreement (*Regeerakkoord*) has announced a legal basis, is assisted in its tasks by the recently introduced Criminal policy service (*Dienst voor het strafrechtelijk beleid*) of the ministry of justice.[136]

The national magistrates both have a special position in the prosecution of terrorists, authority over the 23rd (national) brigade of the prosecution office's judicial police (specialized in severe crime with a possible national or international impact), and the coordination of combat of severe crime and of application of special policing techniques. They are the central coordinating authority in the Schengen circular of March 16, 1995, but oddly enough, they have not been mentioned in the Schengen Convention itself, although they did already function at that time.[137] As for their functioning, they depend on and operationally represent the assembly of proscutors-general.[138] Note that, on March 22, 1996, the cabinet accepted a bill on the *nationale magistraten*, which will regulate their function, task, position and powers, and rebaptize them *federale magistra-*

---

133 Verstraeten, 1994, p. 49.
134 Verstraeten, 1994, p. 49; Van den Wyngaert, 1994, p. 441.
135 For more discussion and references, we refer to Verstraeten, 1994, p. 49.
136 KB January 14, 1994, B.S. March 3, 1994, pp. 5236-5238. Regarding the Coalition agreement and its content on police and judicial matters, we refer to De Ruyver, 1995, pp. 14-16.
137 De Hert & Vanderborght, 1996, p. 5.
138 De Hert & Vanderborght, 1996, p. 9.

ten. The bill also intends to create a formal legal basis for the assembly of prosecutors-general, and to give a decisive position to the minister of justice.

The magistrates of the public prosecution department play a crucial role in the criminal procedure. They are habilitated to act as officers of judicial police (*officiers de police judiciaire/officieren van gerechtelijke politie*) on the basis of art. 9 Sv and have a general competence to investigate crimes. In theory, they have the same powers as police officers but as a rule they are the ones leading the investigation and deciding on actual prosecution in the case.[139]

3.2.2.2 The Netherlands

The public prosecutor's department is responsible for leading the criminal investigation, prosecuting suspects and executing court decisions. The public prosecutor's department is a hierarchic agency with, according to the law, the minister of justice at the top who is politically responsible. The department is directed by the assembly of prosecutors-general (the so-called *P-G-vergadering*), presided by the prosecutor-general of The Hague. In general, the prosecutor's department likes to stress its independence from the minister and the whole issue as to the position of the minister is a controversial one.[140]

There is a chief officer of justice (*hoofdofficier van justitie*) at the head of each judicial district. At the lower level of sub-districts and districts, the department is represented by the public prosecutors, the so-called officers of justice (*officier van justitie*) while at the appellate and supreme courts it is represented by prosecutors general and advocates general.[141] Furthermore, it is worth mentioning that at this moment, a national prosecution department is being established that will be entrusted with the authority over the national detective team and house the three national public prosecutors (*landelijke officieren van justitie*). These prosecutors have a mainly coordinatory task regarding respectively the fight against terrorism, the fight against money laundering and the international police cooperation.

All the members of the standing magistrature (*staande magistratuur*) have the same powers. There are, however, differences in the extent to which each officer of justice will use them. For instance, a chief officer of justice will

---

139 See Van den Wyngaert, 1994, pp. 440-441; on the role of the public prosecutor during the police enquiry, see Verstraeten, 1994, pp. 115-117.

140 See Swart, 1993b, p. 287; the position of the prosecution and its relation with the minister of justice has been discussed more detailedly in Schalken, 1991; 't Hart, 1994 and De Doelder *et al.*, 1994.

141 See Frielink, 1992, pp. 93 *et seq.*; Swart, 1993b, p. 287; Van der Grinten, 1995, pp. 21 *et seq.*

seldom be directly involved in the prosecution of an average case but might be closely following a widely publicized one.[142]

The first and best known task of the public prosecutor's department is initiating the criminal prosecution. In addition, it also plays an important role in the police investigation, art. 148 Sv even stating that the public prosecutor leads the investigation.[143] The officer of justice representing the public prosecutor's department is empowered to give orders to the police concerning the investigation. In most cases, however, the officer of justice will rarely intervene with the police investigation as the police officers are already bound by general lines of investigative conduct established in the law and in guidelines by the public prosecutor's department.[144]

Because of the fact that the expediency principle, or *opportuniteitsbeginsel*, is embedded in the Dutch Code of Criminal Procedure, the Dutch legal order has seen the development of a particular form of rule-making: policy, or *beleid*. According to the expediency principle, the public prosecutor enjoys a large amount of discretion on deciding whether a crime should be prosecuted. In order to make sure that this discretion is applied in a more or less homogenous manner across the country, the public prosecutor's department and the ministry of justice draw up guidelines on its application. In the beginning, it was thought that the public prosecutor had to prosecute, except when this did not serve the general interest. Since the seventies, this principle has been inverted: The public prosecutor only prosecutes cases when their prosecution serves the interest of the society. This is the practical translation of the idea that the criminal justice system is not the only way to solve problems of criminality.[145]

3.2.2.3 Luxembourg

The public prosecutor's department is hierarchically organized, indivisible, independent and non-dismissable.[146] According to art. 16 CIC, the public prosecutor's department is responsible for the prosecution of criminal offences and law enforcement. It must be represented at each level of jurisdiction of the criminal courts and must be present at the debates before each trial jurisdiction (art. 16-1 CIC). According to art. 19 CIC, the minister of justice may order the department to prosecute a particular offence. In that way, there is a hierarchical

---

142 Frielink, 1992, pp. 93-94.
143 The relationship between the public prosecutor and the police is the subject of many discussions. We have chosen not to go into the discussion here in order to present a general view.
144 Frielink, 1992, p. 96.
145 See Frielink, 1992, p. 99; Swart, 1993b, p. 284.
146 See Spielmann & Spielmann, 1993, p. 267.

link between the minister and the department. However, the minister may not order the department to drop charges or to stop an investigation.[147]

The department is represented in the lowest court (the police court) by the substitute of the department (*substitut du parquet*) or by a judicial officer (*attaché de la justice*). At the first instance court in each judicial district (*arrondissements*), it is the State prosecutor (*procureur d'État*) or one of his substitutes that will represent the public prosecution before the trial court as well as before the investigating judge. The State prosecutor general (*procureur général d'État*) or one of his advocates general will prosecute before the appellate courts.[148] He may also directly require the assistance of the police when in function (art. 18 par. 3 CIC) and has authority over all officers and agents of judicial police (artt. 20 and 21 CIC).

The prosecutor of the State is the one who represents, personally or through his substitutes, the public prosecutor's department. He studies all complaints and denunciations and decides on their follow-up. He accomplishes all the necessary investigation and prosecution acts or orders them to be accomplished. In doing so, he leads the activities of the judicial police of his jurisdiction. He has all the powers with which an officer of judicial police is invested. When in function, he may directly require the assistance of the judicial police. In that sense, he is the one leading the criminal enquiry (artt. 22 *et seq.* CIC).

3.2.2.4 France

The prosecution of criminal offences is done in France by magistrates, members of what is sometimes called the standing magistrature, as opposed to the sitting magistrature, the real judges. The members of the public prosecutor's department are appointed by decree by the president of the French Republic on proposal of the *Garde des sceaux*, the minister of justice.[149]

The public prosecutors are removable and revocable, which is to say that their conduct is controlled by a committee of discipline.[150] Before the police courts, there is no *parquet* as such, the department being represented either by the prosecutor of the Republic (*procureur de la République*) or by a police commissionary (artt. 45 and 46 CPP). Before the *tribunaux correctionnels*, the department is represented by the prosecutor of the Republic assisted by his adjuncts. Before the court of appeal (*chambre d'accusation, chambre des appels correctionnels*) the *parquet* is composed of the prosecutor general by the court of appeal (*procureur général près la cour d'appel*) and, depending on the

---

147 *Chambre des mises* January 24, 1972, P. 22, 110.
148 See Spielmann & Spielmann, 1993, pp. 266-267.
149 See Stefani *et al.*, 1993, pp. 100 *et seq.*
150 *Ordonnance* 58-1270, December 22, 1958, *relative au statut de la magistrature*.

importance of the case, of a number of general advocates and substitutes of the prosecutor general (artt. 34 and 510 par. 2 CPP). Before the court of cassation, the public prosecutor's department is composed of a first advocate general and of other advocates general, of which six are attached to the criminal chamber (see artt. 620 and 621 CPP).[151]

As a hierarchical institution, the public prosecutor's department is placed under the responsibility of the government.[152] As opposed to the sitting magistrature that does not receive orders from anybody, the magistrates of the department are subject to the orders of their immediate superiors: The magistrates of the *parquet* are placed under the direction and control of their hierarchical superiors and under the authority of the *Garde des sceaux*,[153] the minister of justice. Although not an actual member of the department, he is the uncontested chief of the institution.[154]

Further, the department is indivisible, independent, unchallengeable and not liable. The members of the department of the same *parquet* are considered by law to be and act as one and the same person. They act independently of the judging and instructing jurisdiction as well as of the victim. They are unchallengeable because they are indispensable and necessary parties to the criminal process (art. 669 par. 2 CPP).[155] Finally, the department cannot be liable for the damage caused to and costs incurred by the accused in the case of an acquittal.[156]

The public prosecutor's department plays a central role in the investigation of criminal offences. The public prosecutor may even request from the investigating judge that all investigations, which he deems necessary for the determination of the truth, be carried out (art. 82 par. 2 CPP). Refusal of the judge must then be motivated in writing. He also has the power to control the investigation. He always has, for instance, the power to request that all acts of procedure be communicated to him for the prosecution. He may be present during the interrogations and confrontations of suspects (art. 119 CPP)[157] and during searches (art. 92 CPP).

---

151 See Stefani *et al.*, 1993, p. 101.
152 Stefani *et al.*, 1993, p. 103.
153 Translation of art. 5 of the *Ordonnance relative au statut de la magistrature*.
154 Stefani *et al.*, 1993, pp. 103-104.
155 See *Crim.* April 7, 1976, D. 1976 and Stefani *et al.*, 1993, p. 107.
156 See Stefani *et al.*, 1993, p. 107.
157 He may not be present when witnesses are being heard.

3.2.2.5 Germany

The prosecution of criminal offences in Germany is done by a hierarchical agency of the judiciary, the public prosecutor's department (*Staatsanwalt-schaft*).[158] Therefore, its officers do not have the privilege of personal and material independence as recognized to judges. The officers of the public prosecutor must obey the service directives given by their superiors (art. 146 GVG). The individual official of the public prosecutor does not act with his own full mandate but acts rather as a representative for the higher ranking superior officer of the *Staatsanwaltschaft* (art. 144 GVG), which always has the power to take over a particular case himself or to delegate it to another officer (art. 145 GVG).[159]

The general federal prosecutor (*Generalbundesanwalt* at the federal court, the *Bundesgerichtshof*) has the initial competence to prosecute matters relating to state security and terrorism. In particular cases he may transfer these cases to the provincial prosecutors.[160] Because of the fact that, for the rest, the organization of the public ministry is a provincial legislative prerogative, the general federal prosecutor is not hierarchically superior to the provincial prosecutors. The administrative control over the general provincial prosecutors belongs to the respective provincial ministers of justice. The general provincial prosecutor is the hierarchical superior of the highest ranked officer of the public prosecutor (*Leitender Oberstaatsanwalt*) of the provincial court of his district (*Bezirk*). In turn, this highest ranking public prosecutor is the superior of the different officers of the provincial courts (artt. 142 par. 1 and 147 GVG).[161]

The tasks of the public prosecutor in criminal matters may be summarized as follows. The public prosecutor must receive denunciations and complaints (art. 158 StPO), conduct or direct the criminal investigation (artt. 160 *et seq.* StPO), control or carry out temporary arrests, seizures, searches, control of identity, etc. His primary task, however, is the investigation of crimes and in that context searching for incriminating as well as discharging elements (art. 160 par. 2 StPO). He has limited discretionary prosecuting power : If sufficient evidence is present, the case must be brought to court (the so-called principle of legality, art. 152 par. 2 StPO).[162] Nevertheless, the court is not competent to proceed with the case without the formal bringing of the charge by the public

---

158 The position of the public prosecutor in German procedure has been discussed by Tak, 1992b.
159 See Roxin, 1993, pp. 45 *et seq.*, and for a general summary in English Kühne, 1993, p. 141.
160 Roxin, 1993, p. 46.
161 Note that the federal German Code of Criminal Procedure does not use the expressions *Generalstaatsanwalt* and *Oberstaatsanwalt* as they originate provincial law. See Roxin, 1993, p. 46.
162 See Roxin, 1993, pp. 48-50.

prosecutor. The discretionary power of the prosecutor is limited to petty crimes which may be dropped (artt. 153 *et seq.* StPO).[163] The prosecutor must, moreover, be present at court proceedings as the representative of the state.

3.2.3 Investigating Judge

In many countries in continental Europe, the investigating judge plays a central role. Following a reform of the criminal procedure in the aftermaths of the *Révolution*, this function was introduced in France to replace the accusation jury (*jury d'accusation*), which had been introduced by the revolutionary authorities. With the Act of 7 *Pluviôse an* IX, the *juge d'instruction* was introduced, and charged with hearing witnesses separately and in the absence of the suspect.[164] This institution was "introduced" in a number of European countries by *Napoléon*. We will limit ourselves to describing this actor as he plays an important role in the pre-trial enquiry. However, except in incidental cases, he will further be ignored throughout the whole of this study and is described here for the sole purpose of orientation.[165]

3.2.3.1 Belgium

In principle, the basic criminal procedure in Belgium prescribes the *instruction* by the investigating judge. In practice, however, the enquiry is most often led by the public prosecutor and the police (the enquiry is then called *information*), the *instruction* being reserved for complicated cases or cases where special means of constraint are needed.[166]

The investigating judge is considered an auxiliary of the public prosecutor (*officier de police judiciaire*) with the important exception that he is not empowered to start an investigation *ex officio*. He must wait for the official request, the *saisine*, the order originating from the public prosecutor or the victim, unless he is acting *in flagrante delicto*. Not only is the investigating judge not free to begin an investigation as he wishes, he is also restricted to the

---

163 See for an illustration of this discretionary power the judgement on the constitutionality of the criminalization of cannabis products, BVerfG March 9, 1994, StV 1994, pp. 295 *et seq.*, also published in NJW 1994, pp. 1577 *et seq.* In this decision, the court judged that the prosecution of a person for possession of a small quantity of cannabis products for his personal consumption can be disproportional.

164 See Stefani *et al.*, 1993, pp. 67 *et seq.*

165 The question of whether or not the enquiring role of the investigating judge should be abolished has been dealt with in for instance Fijnaut & Kolthoff, 1991.

166 Note that in its report the committee for the criminal procedure recommends to give the examining judge more independence by taking away his power to act as assistant of the public prosecutor; see Franchimont, 1994, p. 8.

scope of the investigation request: He is only competent for the investigation of the offence referred to him (art. 61 Sv). He may, however, freely chose the powers he uses in his investigation: The Code of Criminal Procedure does not regulate this aspect in great detail but only generally states that the investigating judge has a general power to carry out all investigations he deems necessary. The court of cassation has recognized this power, stating only that the judge may carry out all investigation acts not forbidden by law and not incompatible with the dignity of his profession.[167]

As an auxiliary of the public prosecutor, the investigating judge is submitted to the control of the prosecutor-general at the court of appeal (art. 279 Sv). This control is only exercised on his acts as an auxiliary of the public prosecutor and not on his judicial acts such as the issuing of warrants.[168]

3.2.3.2 The Netherlands

One finds at least one investigating judge (*rechter-commissaris*) in each district court in the Netherlands (*rechtbank*). They are appointed by the court on suggestion of its president after the chief public prosecutor (*hoofdofficier van justitie*) has been heard (art. 59 RO). In the past, this was done by the court of appeal (*Gerechtshof*), but this rather elaborate procedure was abolished in 1992.[169] The investigating judge is chosen among the sitting judges of the court.[170]

The investigating judge is assisted by the court clerk (*griffier*). In urgent cases, the investigating judge may appoint someone else as clerk, for instance when a number of searches must be carried out simultaneously. In that case, the investigating judge most often appoints police officers who he subsequently swears in as clerks (art. 171 RO). The clerk will draw up the report (art. 172 par. 1 RO), which will be countersigned by the investigating judge (art. 176 RO).

The celerity of the procedure is controlled by the district court (art. 180 par. 1 RO). The investigating judge carries out the judicial preliminary enquiry personally, according to the letter of the law. This premise is the expression of the relative superiority of the judicial preliminary enquiry over the police enquiry. As the latter is carried out by subordinate police officers under the supervision of or by the public prosecutor personally, it is thought to lack the guarantees of independence that a judge might offer. The investigating judge hears witnesses and experts, orders the use of means of constraint and conducts

---

167 *Cass.* May 2, 1960, Pas. I, 1020.
168 See Van den Wyngaert, 1993b, pp. 6-7; for an overview of the *instruction*, see Van den Wyngaert, 1994, pp. 628 *et seq.*; Verstraeten, 1994, pp. 154-162 and Declercq, 1994, p. 108.
169 Act of June 3, 1992, Stb. 1992, 278.
170 See Corstens, 1995, pp. 287-289.

other acts of investigation. The legislator has, however, given him the possibility to delegate his actions to police detectives and other auxiliaries of the public prosecutor (art. 177 par. 1 Sv). This power of the judge may also be used outside the framework of the judicial preliminary enquiry. One may think for instance of the case where the judge might want to see some questions answered before deciding on the remand in custody of a suspect.[171]

3.2.3.3 Luxembourg

In each judicial district (Luxembourg and Diekirch) there is one or more investigating judge. The president of the investigating judges in each district assigns a particular judge to a case (art. 54 CIC). In principle, the judicial preliminary enquiry is mandatory in the cases of *crimes* (crimes are punishable with sentences of a minimum of eight days artt. 7 and 25 CP) and not for *contraventions* (art. 49 CIC).[172] The ju maydge only begin his enquiry after a formal requisition (*réquisitoire*) has been submitted by the public prosecutor (artt. 27 and 49 CIC) or after the victim has presented a complaint before the judge (art. 56 CIC).

The investigating judge has the power to have all investigations carried out which he deems necessary for the finding of the truth (art. 51 CIC). In this role, he must be on the lookout for incriminating as well as discharging evidence (art. 1 CIC). In the event that the investigating judge is present during the investigation of a case in *flagrante delicto*, he will take over the control and direction of the operations. When the investigating judge is unable to proceed to the acts of investigation, he may order the judicial police, the auxiliaries of the public prosecutor, with a *commission rogatoire*, to carry out these acts (art. 52 CIC). Note the hierarchy contained in artt. 41 and 42 CIC in an enquiry done *in flagrante delicto*: When the public prosecutor is present, he takes over the direction of the enquiry started by officers of the judicial police. The moment the investigating judge makes his entry on the scene of the crime, the public prosecutor as well as all other officers present are relieved of their leading role.

The public prosecutor is the one who initiates the judicial preliminary enquiry. The order, the *réquisitoire*, may concern a particular suspect or remain anonymous (art. 50 par. 2 CIC). The public prosecutor may at any time demand that additional investigations be made with the help of a *réquisitoire supplétif*.

The investigating judge instructs the enquiry and carries out the investigations he deems necessary for the finding of the truth (art. 51-1 CIC). He may delegate certain acts of investigation to the judicial police, in their capacity of

---

171 Corstens, 1995, p. 289.
172 One exception is art. 132 CIC: in the case of less severe *crimes* upon requisition of the public prosecutor.

auxiliaries of the public prosecutor, through a *commission rogatoire*. The police are not authorized to interrogate a suspect after he has appeared before the investigating judge (art. 52-2 CIC).[173]

3.2.3.4 France

The aim of the *instruction* is in the first instance to find the probable culprit and second to decide whether enough evidence is present for bringing the case to trial. Not all cases are brought before the investigating judge. The Code of Criminal Procedure prescribes mandatory *instruction* for *crimes* and optional for *délits*. *Contraventions* are not brought before the investigating judge except upon request of the public prosecutor.[174]

The investigating judge is in present times a member of the *tribunal de grande instance*. Following a decree of the *Président de la République*, upon the advice of the *Conseil supérieur de la magistrature*, the investigating judge is appointed for a renewable period of three years.[175] He may be revoked as an investigating judge, but as a sitting magistrate he is non-revocable and irremovable. In general, the preliminary judicial enquiry is carried out by the specially appointed investigating judge, but another judge may be temporarily appointed if necessary.[176]

The investigating judge is independent. In the past, in the 1808 Code of Criminal Procedure (*Code d'instruction criminelle* as it was called), the investigating judge was, as an officer of judicial police (*officier de police judiciaire* or auxiliary of the public prosecutor), subordinated to the public prosecutor (*procureur de la République*). Today, this is seen as incompatible with his responsibilities in carrying out acts of investigations and making decisions on a judiciary level: finding evidence and assessing it in relation to the question as to whether the case should be brought to court. For this reason, the investigating judge is no longer an auxiliary of the public prosecutor and as such is not submitted to the power of control and supervision of the latter. Furthermore, it is no longer the public prosecutor who is responsible for assigning cases to one or other investigating judges, but the president of the court. Moreover, the president of the court is also empowered to reassign the case to another judge. Finally, he is free to carry out all acts of investigation he deems necessary and may even chose to ignore requisitions of the public prosecutor.[177]

---

173   See also Thiry, 1971, pp. 172 *et seq.*
174   Stefani *et al.*, 1993, p. 342.
175   See Stefani *et al.*, 1993, p. 343.
176   See Stefani *et al.*, 1993, p. 344.
177   Stefani *et al.*, 1993, p. 348.

The judge is referred to a case by the public prosecutor or by the victim (art. 1 par. 1 CPP). He carries out acts of investigation such as questioning the suspect, hearing witnesses, search and seizure, identification line-ups, telephone taps, etc.

3.2.3.5 Germany

The German investigating judge (*Ermittlungsrichter*) does not lead an enquiry, rather he controls the legality and authorizes investigation acts to be used by the public prosecutor. Although the public prosecutor is said to be master of the preliminary enquiry and he possesses a number of investigative powers to carry out his task, there are specific investigation acts he may not so easily resort to: The law imposes that they be submitted to the authorization of a judge. The institution of the investigating judge has been created to authorize the use of sensitive investigation methods during the enquiry of the public prosecutor, while keeping the public prosecutor master over it.[178]

The public prosecutor or the police request the use of certain necessary investigations before the judge at the district court (*Amtsgericht*) of the district where the investigation act should be carried out (artt. 162 par. 1 sub 1 and 163 par. 2 *in fine* StPO). The judge only has jurisdiction over the legality of the investigation (*Zulässigkeit*), which means for instance the proportionality of the act. He may not control the pure opportuneness of the act, judging for instance that it be obsolete or useless.[179] The investigating judge will act, in principle, on requisition of the public prosecutor but may act of his own initiative in the special procedure of "danger in delay" (*Gefahr im Verzug*), in which case he will act as the public prosecutor in his replacement (*Notstaatsanwalt*).[180]

3.2.4 The Suspect

The suspect is not a condition *sine qua non* of the police enquiry. When his identity is not known, the investigation will focus on his discovery. In that case, a crime will have been committed and the police will be investigating reactively. In another situation, the police may have a suspect in view who has not (yet) committed a crime. In that case, the police will be investigating pro-actively. However, the application of certain means of constraint is usually subordinated

---

178 The position of the German prosecutor and judge since the abolition of the enquiry investigating judge (in 1974) has been addressed in detail by Tak & Lensing, 1990, pp. 15-62 and Tak, 1992b.
179 See Roxin, 1993, p. 61.
180 See for instance Tak, 1992b, pp. 680-681.

to the question as to whether one is a suspect and whether an offence has already been committed, both being necessary to justify resorting to these means.

The state of suspicion is a question of police experience, but some countries have introduced more or less objective criteria for the determination of whether a person may legally be considered a suspect and whether particular means of constraint may be applied. These rules or their absence will be the subject of this sub-paragraph.

3.2.4.1 Belgium

The legal question as to when it is possible to speak of a suspect is a matter that is left unaddressed in legislation or case-law and has not been the subject of many discussions in the literature.[181] Art. 41 par. 2 Sv mentions a person "pursued by public clamour", assimilating this situation to an *in flagrante delicto* situation[182] (for example to a situation where the suspect has been caught red-handed); this means that witnesses around this person state that he is the culprit.[183] In addition, the same provision states that the suspect may be some-one found, shortly after the commission of the offence, in possession of objects, instruments, tools, papers or weapons indicating that he presumably is the culprit or has participated in the offence. Finally, art. 2 VHW states that outside the *in flagrante delicto* situation there must be "severe indications of guilt" for the remand in custody of a person.

Besides the expression "suspect," the law mentions terms such as "defend-ant" (*beklaagde*) and "accused" (*beschuldigde*). However, the difference in the legal meaning between the two is not clear and neither is the relation between these terms and the expression "suspect".[184]

3.2.4.2 The Netherlands

The concept of suspicion is a central one for the Dutch criminal procedure. For the application of the means of constraint put at the disposal of the public authorities by the Code of Criminal Procedure, the law demands that there be a reasonable assumption that an offence has been committed. Suspicion in criminal law is present from the moment a reasonable assumption of guilt (*redelijk vermoeden van schuld*) towards a particular person has arisen (art. 27 Sv). Suspicion is a central material condition for the application of investigation powers. It is also the moment a person is guaranteed a very important right.

---

181 Fijnaut, 1991a, p. 56.
182 The investigation procedure *in flagrante delicto* will be studied in 3.2.2.
183 See D'Haenens, 1985 and Vandeplas, 1979, p. 10.
184 See Bevers & Joubert, 1994, p. 116.

Once a person is considered a suspect, he may not be interrogated before having been informed of his right to remain silent, the so-called *cautie* (art. 29 par. 2 Sv).

The existence of a reasonable assumption of guilt in the sense of the law is determined by a trilogy of cumulative factors:[185] Firstly, the assumption must be a consequence of facts and circumstances; this means that vague indications or rumours are not sufficient. A certain degree of probability in the facts and circumstances must also be present in this. Secondly, the reasonable assumption must be objective; consequently, the simple impression of a police officer in not enough to justify the assumption. Finally, suspicion must be directed towards a specific criminal offence. This means that a preliminary police enquiry may not be started for the investigation of an offence that has not (yet) been committed.[186]

Besides this reasonable assumption of guilt, the criminal procedure also contains other gradations of suspicion, such as aggravated suspicion (*ernstige bezwaren*, artt. 56 par. 1 and 67 par. 3 Sv) and sufficient indications for guilt (*voldoende aanwijzingen van schuld*, art. 250 par. 5 Sv). The aggravated suspicion is of significant importance for the police enquiry: It may lead to the application of more infringing means of constraint, such as a search of the clothes or body of the suspect and his remand in judicial custody. Because of the infringing nature of these means of constraint on the fundamental rights of the suspect, more serious conditions have been imposed for the suspicion in relation to the severity of the reproached offence. In addition, suspicion must be severe enough to justify the application of these means of constraint and the nature of this aggravated suspicion must, moreover, be relevant to the nature of the offence.[187]

3.2.4.3 Luxembourg

The concept of "suspect" is foreign to Luxembourg law as a formal prerequisite for the start of an investigation. Only during the *in flagrante delicto* procedure, which is initiated when a person has been caught red-handed, does the law speak of "serious and corroborating indications" (*indices graves et concordants*) of a nature justifying charges (art. 39 CIC). From this moment on, the "suspect" enjoys certain rights mentioned in paragraphs 3 to 7 and he may be remanded twenty-four hours in police custody.

Upon his remand in police custody, the suspect may have a person of his choice contacted, have a doctor examine him and consult an attorney before

---

185 Schalken, 1981, p. 6.
186 Bevers & Joubert, 1994, p. 101.
187 Schalken, 1981, pp. 7 *et seq.*

interrogation (art. 39 CIC). In general, one is considered a suspect the moment one legally has the benefits of the rights enacted for the *instruction contradictoire*.[188] During the preliminary judicial enquiry by the investigating judge, the law speaks of a charged or accused person (*inculpé*): This gives the judge the power to charge "any person who has taken part as an author of or an accomplice to the facts being investigated" (art. 50 CIC).

3.2.4.4 France

Although the concept of "suspect" has not enjoyed much discussion in the literature,[189] the French Code of Criminal Procedure does contain a certain number of provisions from which it is possible to attempt a definition.

In certain circumstances, the officer auxiliary to the public prosecutor may detain a person, in principle no longer than twenty-four hours. According to artt. 63 and 77 CPP, this is authorized only for persons against whom "indications exist that they have or have attempted to commit an offence" (the so-called *garde à vue*); the retention of others is not allowed for longer than "the necessary time." From that moment on, the Code of Criminal Procedure guarantees him a number of rights: He must be informed of these rights and of the maximum duration of his retention. He may telephone home, be examined by a physician and speak to an attorney after the first twenty-four hours of *garde à vue* (artt. 63 - 63-4 CPP).[190]

During the preliminary judicial enquiry, the suspect is considered the person against whom a complaint (with *constitution de partie civile*) is lodged, the accused (*réquisitoire introductif d'instance*) or the person against whom indications are present on which the assumption can be based that he has been involved as the author or as an accomplice in the commission of an offence (artt. 80-1 - 80-3 and 86 CPP). In the latter case, the suspect is known as the person under examination (*mis en examen*).

---

188 This was confirmed to us by officers of the Luxembourg ministry of the interior.

189 Note that in the first 1993 law reforming the criminal procedure law (nr. 93-2, January 4, 1993, *portant réforme de la procédure pénale*), later amended and partly replaced by the law of August 24, 1993, a discussion was initiated on the expression to use in designating the person against whom certain procedures are taken. The legislator had wanted to replace expressions such as *inculpé* or *inculpation* by *"personne mise en examen"* (person placed under examination). See Joubert, 1994, p. 261, Pradel, 1993b, 299-306.

190 See for more details and a short history on the reform leading to these articles Joubert, 1994, pp. 248-271.

3.2.4.5 Germany

The concept of suspicion plays a central role in German criminal procedure. It is a condition for the receivability of a complaint, a denunciation or a request for prosecution: There must be an assumption that a criminal offence has been committed.

The German expression to designate the suspect changes throughout the criminal procedure. He is called the *Verdächtiger* when there is certain degree of probability (*Verdacht* or *Tatverdacht*) present based on facts and circumstances. The *Verdächtiger*'s position in the criminal procedure is not regulated, he has no special rights or guarantees and does not have to be informed of his state.[191] However, when a police enquiry is launched against the suspect, he becomes the person charged (*Beschuldigter*) and is then guaranteed a number of rights.[192] From the moment the public prosecution has been initiated against this person, he is called the *Angeschuldigter* and at the beginning of the main court hearings at the trial, he becomes the accused or *Angeklagter* (art. 157 StPO). Last, the convicted suspect is called the *Verurteilter*.[193]

The Code of Criminal Procedure distinguishes between different terms designating various degrees of suspicion: the simple suspicion (*einfacher* or *Anfangsverdacht*), the suspicion based on certain facts (*verfahrensträchtiger Verdacht*), the sufficient suspicion (*hinreichender Verdacht*) and the aggravated suspicion (*dringender Verdacht*). For the simple suspicion that may lead to prosecution, the law demands that there be "enough factual references" (art. 152 par. 2 StPO). The mere existence of suppositions is not sufficient, but, surprisingly enough, the German literature and case-law have not specified this concept any further.[194]

A police enquiry may be started as soon as there is a suspicion based on facts justifying the enquiry. If the indications and evidence present are so important as to create a sufficient suspicion, the public prosecution may be initiated and the case brought to trial. The aggravated suspicion justifies the use of severe means of constraint, such as pre-trial custody.[195]

---

191   Kleinknecht/Meyer-Goßner, 1995, pp. 14-15.
192   Kleinknecht/Meyer-Goßner, 1995, p. 15; on the problems these rights cause for the police, see Roxin, 1993, pp. 169-170.
193   Kleinknecht/Meyer-Goßner, 1995, p. 563.
194   Kühne, 1989, p. 971.
195   Roxin, 1993, pp. 266-267.

3.3 The Preliminary Enquiry

The expression preliminary enquiry is used to designate the pre-trial phase of the investigation. As we have seen above, the police play a central role in this phase. In principle, the legal framework of the preliminary enquiry is based upon the principle that a criminal offence has been committed. However, in recent years, a practice has evolved towards pro-active policing. What exactly is meant by this expression may vary, but in general the expression pro-active policing designates the gathering of information in relation to a crime that has not yet been committed with the purpose of either prosecuting the authors or collecting as much information as possible on particular groups in order to prosecute at a later date. Pro-actively collected data may not only serve to gain insight into the criminal scene but also to prevent the commission of severe crimes and to justify, before the investigating judge, resorting to special techniques such as telephone tapping.

In this paragraph, we will sketch the legal framework of the basic preliminary enquiry. The whole of the pro-active activity of the police will be ignored as it evolves in the secret sphere of police tactical information and thus is not very accessible in most countries. However, when rules exist and when relevant, they will be mentioned in the respective paragraphs.[196]

3.3.1   General Principles

This sub-paragraph will concentrate on the general principles of the preliminary enquiry. We will begin with a definition of the different criminal offences in substantive criminal law and continue with an overview of the structure of the whole of the criminal procedure, beginning with the start of the police enquiry and the importance of the police report. Finally, the relevance of the concept of opportuneness of criminal proceedings versus the concept of legality in the various countries will be discussed.

3.3.1.1 Belgium

Belgian criminal law distinguishes between three sorts of criminal offences of which the enumeration is found in art. 1 of the Criminal Code (*Strafwetboek -* Sw): crimes (*misdaden/crimes*), delicts (*wanbedrijven/ délits*) and petty offences

---

196   The subject of pro-active policing has been discussed recently by for instance Weßlau, 1989; Fijnaut, 1994a; Naeyé, 1995a and Brants & Field, 1995.

(*overtredingen/contraventions*). They are sanctioned respectively with criminal, correctional and police sentences.[197]

One may distinguish between two stages in the Belgian criminal procedure: the enquiry taking place before the actual trial, also called preliminary enquiry and the substantial enquiry, which takes place during the trial. The aim of the preliminary enquiry is the gathering of as much evidence as necessary for bringing the case to trial.[198]

There are two procedures for gathering evidence. The first one is through the police enquiry led by the public prosecutor and the second is the enquiry of the investigating judge. However, in both cases, the public prosecutor plays a central role since he is the one to decide whether a preliminary enquiry will take place and whether the enquiry will be carried out by the police under his direction or by the investigating judge as a judicial preliminary enquiry.[199] As we have noted above, the investigating judge is not empowered to act of his own initiative but is dependant on the *saisine* of the public prosecutor. In order to decide whether and in which way an offence will be investigated, the public prosecutor must be informed of each criminal offence established by the police (art. 29 Sv).

Police officers draw up reports of all the complaints and denunciations they receive, as well as of their personal acknowledgements; these reports are sent to the public prosecutor's department (artt. 53 Sv and 40 WPA). A police report is a document in which a police officer registers all useful information in relation to a criminal offence: what he has seen, heard or acknowledged personally.[200]

In principle the report is only an authentic document in form, not in content. This means that it does not have, in principle, a more probative force as evidence than other evidence brought before the judge. The public prosecutor will have to prove its content. Some police reports, however, may be given special weight as evidence. Because of the fact that police reports in many cases are given a special place in the evidence, not every police officer is empowered

---

197   Criminal sentences longer than five years and fines higher than 25 Belgian francs, correctional sentences are no longer than five years and police sentences last five to seven days and fines of to 25 francs; see Van den Wyngaert, 1994, pp. 136-141. On plans to modify the categories of criminal offenses and to abolish the death penalty, see De Ruyver & Hutsebaut, 1995.

198   Van den Wyngaert, 1994, pp. 576-577; note that the committee for the reform of the criminal procedure law has set as one of its goals to give a legal framework to the pre-trial police enquiry - the *information* - as it is the usual course of criminal proceedings to begin with the police enquiry; furthermore, the committee has formulated proposals as to the secrecy during the pre-trial enquiry; see Franchimont, 1994, pp. 7 *et seq.*

199   Van den Wyngaert, 1994, p. 578.

200   Van den Wyngaert, 1994, p. 580; Verstraeten, 1994, pp. 120 *et seq.*; and Declercq, 1994, pp. 123 *et seq.*

to produce one. In principle, only the police officers with the powers of auxiliaries of the public prosecutor are entitled to draw up official police reports. In recent years, however, this rule has admitted some exceptions: The power to draw up reports has been granted more and more often to officers not empowered to act as auxiliaries of the public prosecutor.[201]

Once the police report has been sent to the public prosecutor, he may decide to refrain from prosecuting, the so-called *sépot*. He may always go back on his decision although the offence might be prescribed after a certain time.[202] The *sépot* does not rest on a legal basis but has developed in practice from the idea that the public prosecutor has the right and the privilege to prosecute but is not obliged to do so. This rests on the principle of expediency, the so-called "principle of opportuneness" (*opportuniteitsbeginsel*): The public prosecutor's department decides on the opportuneness of the prosecution in a particular case.

There are no legal conditions for the decision not to prosecute a certain suspect. All criminal offences, whether they are *crimes* or *délits*, are liable to be the object of such a decision. It is possible to distinguish between the technical *sépot* and the policy *sépot*. When the prosecution of a particular case is either impossible because of technical reasons or would probably not lead to a conviction, one speaks of a technical or procedural *sépot*. This is the case, for instance, when the investigation indicates that the reproached facts do not constitute a criminal offence, the facts are prescribed or prove to have a special immunity, the suspect is deceased or cannot be identified.[203]

Further, a case may evade prosecution because of policy reasons. That is the so-called policy *sépot* (*beleidssepot*). The criterion is usually that of the public interest, not that of the victim or the suspect, although they are often taken into account. A policy *sépot* may rest on motivations such as: the facts are not serious, the consequences of prosecuting would not important enough in comparison to those of not prosecuting or the report on the suspect's situation (for example *reclassering*) gives favourable prospects.[204]

3.3.1.2 The Netherlands

The Dutch Criminal Code (*Wetboek van strafrecht* - Sr) divides criminal offences into two categories: the more serious offences contained in book two (called *misdrijven*) and the petty offences mentioned in book three (called

---

201 Van den Wyngaert, 1994, p. 581; Verstraeten, 1994, pp. 120 and 412 *et seq.* and Declercq, 1994, pp. 458 *et seq.*

202 Van den Wyngaert, 1994, p. 469; on the police *sépot*, see De Nauw, 1990, p. 71 and Verstraeten, 1994, p. 43.

203 Van den Wyngaert, 1994, p. 470; on the police sepot, see Verstraeten, 1994, p. 43.

204 See Van den Wyngaert, 1994, pp. 469 *et seq.* and Verstraeten, 1994, pp. 43-44.

overtredingen). A definition of these two concepts does not exist in the law. Note, however, that prison sentences do not exist as a sanction for *overtredingen*. This designation is, furthermore, of no great relevancy for the starting of a preliminary police enquiry (*opsporingsonderzoek*). Each criminal offence may generate the start of an enquiry. Of more relevancy is the question as to whether a criminal offence may justify pre-trial custody. In case the law makes provisions for the possibility of pre-trial custody, more infringing means of constraint may be used against the suspect.[205]

The preliminary police enquiry is one crucial part of the first stage of the Dutch criminal procedure. The first stage is divided into the preparative enquiry (*voorbereidend onderzoek*) on the one hand and the final enquiry on the other hand (*eindonderzoek*). The preliminary police enquiry as well as the preliminary judicial enquiry of the investigating judge belong to this preparative enquiry.[206]

The preliminary police enquiry begins as soon as the police are alarmed of the commission of a criminal offence, either by denunciation or by the discovery of a red-handed suspect. The aim of this enquiry is to gather indications, elements and evidence relating to the offence and relevant for what is called the "fact-finding" (*waarheidsvinding*). During the enquiry, the police may gather information on the committed crime by hearing witnesses, looking for traces as well as material clues and consulting experts. The results of this enquiry will be committed to paper in the police report (*proces-verbaal*). There is no requirement as to the literal transcription of the declarations of witnesses and experts: In principle these reports contain summaries of the legally relevant excerpts.

As this police report may be presented as evidence in court, it is subject to strict rules as to its content. This is why, for instance, the police report must be written, signed and dated by the reporting officer under his professional oath. It is important that the report be drawn up as soon as possible and sent to the public prosecutor. Unless the public prosecutor finds that further investigation is necessary, the work of the police officer in relation to a particular criminal offence is finished after the report has been sent to the prosecutor.[207]

The public prosecutor with jurisdiction in a particular case will decide on the action to be taken and has in this a certain margin of discretion. He will decide whether the case should be prosecuted. There might be technical reasons to refrain from prosecuting, for instance when there is not enough evidence or

---

205   For an English summary of the Dutch criminal procedure see Swart, 1993b, pp. 279 *et seq.*; for a French overview of the preliminary enquiry in The Netherlands, see Corstens & Roording, 1995, pp. 247-255; see also Corstens, 1995.

206   Tak, 1992a, p. 52.

207   See artt. 148, 152, 153, 344 Sv; Minkenhof/Reijntjes, 1990, p. 146; Tak, 1992a, p. 53.

other factors rendering conviction improbable. This is called a technical *sepot*.[208] Technical *sepots* are to be distinguished from the so-called policy-*sepot*, which is a consequence of the principle of expediency (art. 167 par. 2 Sv). "It may be refrained from prosecution for reasons of general interest." This discretion has given rise to the development of a true prosecution policy in the last years.[209]

In the beginning, the rule was that prosecution would take place unless there were reasons to refrain from prosecuting. This policy has slowly been reversed and prosecution now only takes place when there are reasons for it. The negative application of this principle of expediency has evolved into a positive application and in that way, the exception became a rule.[210]

It is a topic of discussion whether a legal basis exists or should be created for the application of this discretion by the police. It has, however, been acknowledged that the police apply a certain degree of discretion in practice.[211] This "police-*sepot*" is the consequence of, on the one hand, the limited manpower and means of the police and, on the other hand, the fact that the public prosecutor does not prosecute every criminal offence because of policy reasons; thus, one cannot expect the police to start an investigation on all the reported criminal offences. Therefore, the public prosecutor makes a choice out of the selection of reports drawn up by the police.[212]

3.3.1.3 Luxembourg

As many States on which the Napoleonic codification has been imposed, Luxembourg law distinguishes between three categories of criminal offences (art. 1 CP): the *crimes*,[213] the *délit*,[214] and the minor infraction (*contravention*).[215] This distinction is relevant for the start of a police enquiry as only *crimes* and those *délits* for which the law prescribes an imprisonment sentence may justify the start of an enquiry and the use of the investigation methods provided for in the Code of Criminal Procedure (see artt. 30, 31 and 40 CIC).

---

208 Minkenhof/Reijntjes, 1990, p. 38.
209 Minkenhof/Reijntjes, 1990, p. 37.
210 Schalken, 1985, p. 155.
211 Minkenhof/Reijntjes, 1990, p. 38; HR January 31, 1950, NJ 1950, 668; Schalken, 1984, pp. 5 *et seq.*.
212 Minkenhof/Reijntjes, 1990, p. 38.
213 Sanctioned by a criminal sentence (*peine criminelle*), ranging from a minimum of five years reclusion or imprisonment to forced labour.
214 The *délit* is sanctioned by a correcting sentence (*peine correctionnelle*), a minimum of eight days to five years emprisonment.
215 Minor offenses are sanctioned by police sanctions (*peine de police*), fines and between one and seven days of custody.

The Luxembourg criminal procedure is composed of two phases: a pre-trial phase and a trial phase. The pre-trial phase is either conducted by the public prosecutor (*information*) or by the investigating judge (*instruction*). The pre-trial phase is said to be inquisitorial whereas the trial phase is said to be accusatorial.[216]

The judicial police, those police officers who are auxiliaries of the public prosecutor, have jurisdiction to conduct investigations as long as no official enquiry has been opened. They act under the direction of the public prosecutor (art. 9 CIC) and are supervised by the State prosecutor general. They are, moreover, controlled by the judicial council and the court of appeal (art. 9-1 CIC). The police must acknowledge criminal offences and gather evidence as long as an enquiry has not been opened, in which case the investigating judge and the judicial council will lead the enquiry (art. 9-2 CIC). The investigating judge will only act if the case has been referred to him by the public prosecutor or by the victim unless the case has been submitted to him via an *in flagrante delicto* procedure.[217]

The task of the police changes during the course of the criminal procedure. In the first pre-trial stage of the procedure, before the *information* and before the police report has been sent to the public prosecutor, the police have extensive investigation powers. The police conduct investigations, *in flagrante delicto* or in other cases (artt. 30 *et seq.* and 46 *et seq.* CIC), of their own initiative.

The police report plays an important role in the criminal procedure as it can be used as evidence. Police officers draw up reports of all complaints and denunciations they receive and of their personal acknowledgements. These reports are then sent to the public prosecutor who decides on the further course of action. In this report, the officers register all relevant information, what they have heard, seen, witnesses' declarations or acknowledged personally.[218] Because these reports can be given a special weight in court, not every police officer is empowered to draw one up: In principle, only the police officers that have the special competence of auxiliaries of the public prosecutor may draw up *procès verbaux*. In some circumstances, the law even prescribes the mandatory content of a police report: For instance, in case of a remand in police custody, the time and the length of the questioning and of rest periods must appear in the report (art. 39 CIC), as well as the date and exact time of day of

---

216 Spielmann & Spielmann, 1993, pp. 269-270 and 18-23.
217 Spielmann & Spielmann, 1993, p. 263.
218 Spielmann & Spielmann, 1993, pp. 269 *et seq.*

the beginning of the retention and the date and time of day that the suspect has been brought before the judge (art. 39-8 CIC).[219]

The public prosecutor will decide of the further course of action as soon as he has received the police report. He may decide to stop the enquiry and refrain from prosecuting. This power is not based on any legal provision but rather on the fact that the public prosecutor has jurisdiction to prosecute but is not obliged to do so. This is called the principle of expediency or the principle of opportuneness.

3.3.1.4 France

The new French Criminal Code (*Code pénal*), in force since March 1994, classifies criminal offences into three categories: *crimes, délits* and *contraventions* (art. 111-1 CP).[220] The law determines the *crimes* and the *délits* and provides for a sanction whereas the regulation (*règlement*) determines the *contravention* (art. 111-2 CP). This distinction is relevant for the investigation powers as only *crimes* and *délits* may constitute the cause for a police enquiry *in flagrante delicto* (artt. 53 CPP *et seq.*). For the beginning of a police enquiry outside of the particular case of the *flagrante delicto*, the distinction does not play a very important role (artt. 75 CPP *et seq.*).

The French criminal procedure is divided mainly into a pre-trial phase and a trial phase.[221] In the pre-trial phase, one may distinguish between the police phase and the preliminary judicial enquiry (*instruction préparatoire*) led by the investigating judge. The judicial police, as auxiliaries of the public prosecutor, play in these various phases a different role, losing their autonomy as the enquiry formalizes. The police are required to acknowledge the commission of criminal offences, gather evidence and find their authors as long as no official judicial enquiry (*information*) has been started (art. 14 CPP). Once an *information* has been opened, the police will follow the instructions given to them by the judge.

The main characteristic of the pre-trial police phase is, as a principle, that no coercive measures may be used. Searches may only be carried out after the

---

219 In art. 154 CIC, for instance, the law distinguishes between reports against which no testimonial evidence may be brought, save by *inscription de faux* and reports against which contrary evidence may be presented, but with a reverse onus. The former are reports drawn up by officers empowered to act as auxiliaries to the public prosecutor, whereas the latter are drawn up by other officers, mentioned in art. 154 CIC.

220 Although the "old" Criminal Code has not ceased to be in force and will remain so in the following years, the judge being free to apply the one or the other according to his interpretation of transitory law, the authors will only discuss the new provisions.

221 See Rassat, 1990, p. 171; in English, see Pradel, 1993c, pp. 124 *et seq.*

police have obtained the authorization of the concerned party. The police may, however, use coercive measures during the enquiry done *in flagrante delicto*.

The police draw up police reports of their findings which are sent to the public prosecutor. He will decide of the course of action to take and may decide to either prosecute or to drop the case. If he choses to prosecute, he may opt for one of the following three choices: He may apply for an *ordonnance pénale*, whereby the case will be brought before the police judge (*juge de police*) for judgement and sentencing will take place with neither a hearing being held, a motivation being given nor an attorney being present. This is possible for *contraventions* only.[222] If the offence is either a *délit* or a *contravention*, he may convoke the suspect directly via a *citation directe*, whereby the case will be brought directly to trial. Finally, in the case of a *contravention* or a *délit*, he may refer the case to the investigating judge for the holding of preliminary judicial enquiry.[223]

All the information given to the police by the public will be registered in the official police report (*procès-verbal*). The *procès-verbal* may be defined as the document drawn up by the public prosecutor or an officer of judicial police (in the sense of a police officer acting as auxiliary of the public prosecutor) having jurisdiction *ratione materiae* and *ratione loci*, in which the officer records his findings and other actions in judicial matters (such as questioning, searches and seizures) as they are being accomplished.[224]

According to art. 19 CPP, the officers auxiliary of the public prosecutor must send their reports to the public prosecutor as soon as their operations have ended. Along with the reports, they must send all relevant documents and acts drawn up at the same time, as well as all seized objects. Every police report must state the official capacity of the officer drawing it up. Further, he will make a different report for each investigative act carried out (art. D.10 CPP).

The report has a relative value when it is produced in court as evidence. When reports are used to acknowledge the fact that a *crime* has been committed, they have the value of a simple piece of information. When it comes to the acknowledgements of the commission of *délits*, police reports have the value of a simple piece of information, save where the law provides otherwise. In that case the law often states that the report is evidence unless contrary proof is presented or it is contested in the special procedure *inscription de faux*. As for the reports acknowledging the commission of *contraventions*, they are evidence unless contrary proof is presented (artt. 430, 431, 433 and 537 CPP).[225]

---

222 Pradel, 1993c, pp. 131-132.
223 According to Pradel, 1993c, p. 125, the direct convocation is most often used (80%) whereas the preliminary judicial enquiry is only held in about 8% of the cases.
224 See Decocq, Montreuil & Buisson, 1991, p. 503.
225 Decocq, Montreuil & Buisson, 1991, pp. 517-518, see also Stefani *et al.*, 1993, pp. 297-298.

The principle of the expediency of criminal proceedings (*principe de l'opportunité des poursuites*) is expressed by art. 40 par. 1 CPP: "The public prosecutor receives complaints and denunciations and assesses the steps to be taken." The public prosecutor evaluates further the consequences to be given to the police reports and documents he receives (art. 40 par. 2 CPP). This principle is only valid at the very beginning of the proceedings, when the public prosecutor is evaluating the course to take as to a particular offence. Once the investigation by the investigating judge has begun or the prosecution has been initiated, this possibility disappears.

Once a criminal offence has come to his attention, the public prosecutor is faced with three possibilities: He may firstly drop the case and classify the file (*classement sans suites*). He does this for instance for reasons such as the following: the prescription of the offence, elements of the offence are missing or the burden of the proof placed on the State is not feasible. He may also decide to drop the case when he is of opinion that prosecution is not opportune. One important thing to remember is that this decision can be temporary: As long as the offence is not prescribed, prosecution may still occur.[226] Secondly, he may decide for mediation, but this decision does not necessarily have an effect on the prosecution.[227] Finally, he may decide to prosecute. Contrary to the decision to classify the case, he may not go back on this decision.[228] A more sensitive issue concerns whether police officers have discretion as to the opportuneness of their investigative actions (*opportunité des actes de police*).[229]

3.3.1.5 Germany

German law distinguishes between two categories of criminal offences (art. 12 StGB):[230] *Verbrechen*, sanctioned with a minimum prison sentence of one

---

226 Stéfani *et al.*, 1993, p. 451.
227 Stéfani *et al.*, 1993, p. 452.
228 See Stéfani *et al.*, 1993, p. 452.
229 The expression is borrowed from Decocq, Montreuil & Buisson, 1991, p. 269. A decision of the *Conseil d'État* seems to have attempted to put an end to the discussion by stating that: "Administrative authorities have the duty to appreciate the conditions of the execution of a judicial decision as long as in their opinion a danger exists for order and security." Further, it considers that the necessities of public order evaluated in each particular case may justify the public forces refraining tfrom acting. Finally, it seems that the discretionary power of the police for the acknowledgement of criminal offences is not incompatible with the discretion belonging to the public prosecutor; see *Conseil d'État*, June 3, 1938, in: D. 1938, 3, 65; for more on this discussion, see also Decocq, Montreuil & Buisson, 1991, pp. 269-270.
230 German law recognizes yet one more category of offence: the administrative offence (*Ordnungswidrigkeit*). We are not taking these into account since these offences are processed administratively and they are, therefore, not relevant in the context of this research.

year, and *Vergehen*, sanctioned with lesser sentences. This distinction is not relevant for the start of an investigation.[231]

German criminal procedure is divided into three main phases: the investigation (*Ermittlung*), the intermediate proceedings[232] (*Zwischenverfahren*) and the trial (*Hauptverfahren*).[233] In principle, the prosecutor will start an enquiry when he suspects that a criminal offence has been committed. In practice, however, the police will play the central role in the investigation, transmitting their reports to the prosecutor once they have gathered sufficient data. According to art. 163 StPO, the police must investigate criminal offences and must carry out all the necessary investigations and measures that cannot be delayed. They must send their findings to the public prosecutor's department as soon as possible.

A police report (*Protokoll*) does not have any special value as evidence in German law although this has been the subject of many discussions. According to art. 261 StPO the evidence must be evaluated by the personal impression of the judge. The lecture of a police report relating the impressions of a witness is not admissible in court (art. 250 StPO).[234]

Once the public prosecutor has received the reports from the police, he has a number of choices: He may return the report to the police for further investigations, he may drop the case for technical reasons or he may decide to bring the case directly to court. If he choses to prosecute, the case will be brought before the competent court. Before the main hearings start, there is an intermediate procedure: In these proceedings, the court will answer the question as to whether the case should be brought to trial and whether further investigations are necessary (artt. 199-212b StPO). Although the suspect has no right to appeal this decision, the prosecutor may do so.[235]

As mentioned above, the public prosecutor may decide to drop the case for technical reasons such as lack of evidence or if the facts do not constitute an offence in criminal law. This is the only legal justification for dropping the case, as German criminal law applies the principle of legality (*Legalitätsprinzip*). On the one hand, this principle implies that the prosecutor must start an enquiry as soon as legal suspicion (that a criminal offence has been committed, the so-called *Tatverdacht*) is present, on the other hand, he has the legal obligation to prosecute once he has acknowledged, after further enquiry, that the suspicion has been confirmed.[236] The principle of opportunity only applies to offences

231 Bevers & Joubert, 1994, p. 164.
232 The translation is from Kühne, 1993, p. 153.
233 See on German procedure, particularly the pre-trial stage, Tak & Lensing, 1990, pp. 15-62.
234 See Roxin, 1993, pp. 319-329; for an overview of the situation in the German literature, see Garé, 1994, pp. 54-64.
235 Kühne, in 1993, pp. 153-154.
236 Roxin, 1993, p. 75.

of lesser severity, the "trifle cases" (*Bagatelldelikte*), and under strict conditions (artt. 153 *et seq.* StPO).

3.3.2   Beginning and Course of the Investigation

The following sub-paragraph will concentrate on the way information on criminal offences is given to the police by citizens in the form of the complaint and the denunciation. We will then sketch the general course of events and conclude with the special procedure initiated when criminal offences are discovered while being committed: *in flagrante delicto* or in the act.

3.3.2.1 Belgium

As we have stated above, it is the public prosecutor who has jurisdiction to decide whether a criminal investigation should be carried out. In order to decide, he must be kept informed of the commission of criminal offences. This is why art. 29 Sv specifies that every civil servant who comes across the commission of a *crime* or *délit* in the course of duty has the legal obligation to inform the public prosecutor as soon as possible.[237]

The ways the public prosecutor and the police obtain information on committed criminal offences are numerous; one might think for instance of complaints, denunciations, police investigations, suspects being caught red-handed, informers and even the media.[238] The Code of Criminal Procedure distinguishes between three categories: the complaint (*klacht*), the denunciation by citizens (*aangifte*) and the denunciation by civil servants (*ambtelijke aangifte*).[239]

A complaint is made by the victim of a criminal offence or another inconvenienced person, after which a report is drawn up by the police (artt. 53 and 54 Sv). On the basis of this report, the public prosecutor will assess the necessity of a criminal investigation. A complaint is not enough in itself to initiate a criminal investigation, as the prosecutor may always decide to drop the case. However, the victim may chose to use the possibility given by the law (art. 63 Sv) to present a complaint before the investigating judge as a civil party (*klacht met burgerlijke partijstelling*). In this case, the investigation will start with the complaint and the prosecutor no longer has jurisdiction to drop the case. On the other hand, there are criminal offences where an investigation may only be initiated after a complaint has been lodged (art. 2 VTSv).

---

237 It is not clear whether this obligation exists when the civil servant is not on duty.
238 Bevers & Joubert, 1994, p. 114.
239 Van den Wyngaert, 1994, pp. 578-582.

One speaks of denunciation when a citizen (viz. not a police officer) informs the State of the commission of a criminal offence, of which he has acquired knowledge because for instance he has witnessed it or heard about it. The police must draw a report of this as well (art. 39 WPA). Moreover, art. 30 Sv obliges everyone who witnesses either an assault on the life or property of a private individual or an attack against public security, to inform an auxiliary of the public prosecutor.

In addition to the denunciation by citizens, Belgian law also recognizes the denunciation of *crimes* and *délits* by civil servants.[240] This denunciation follows the obligation set in art. 29 par.1 Sv. This obligation holds not only for offences which the civil servant has acknowledged personally, but also for offences he has come across via citizens.[241]

The only preliminary enquiry regulated in the law is the one by the investigating judge. The enquiry carried out by the police under the direction of the public prosecutor is left in a legal vacuum.[242] Although a number of acts such as the Code of Criminal Procedure as well as the act on pre-trial custody contain certain provisions on the powers of the public prosecutor and his auxiliaries, these are of a rather general nature and apply almost exclusively to the situation where an offender has been caught in the act (*in flagrante delicto*). Although the law does not provide a list of investigation powers that may be used by the police, there are many such powers at the disposal of the police.[243] These powers may be divided into two categories: Investigations related to persons and acts related to objects. Since January 1, 1993, many of these powers have obtained a legal basis in the Police function act.[244]

Investigations Related to Objects

One of the first investigations that may be carried out after the police have been informed of a crime is the investigation at location: the *locus delicti*.[245] This investigation is legally regulated in the case of *in flagrante delicto* discoveries of committed crimes, but it is generally accepted that this may also be done during the general police enquiry.

During this operation, the *locus delicti* will be isolated in order to protect and control eventual evidence that may remain and to prevent risking the loss

---

240 *Contraventions* are excluded from the scope of this obligation.
241 See also De Nauw, 1990, pp. 65-74 on the moment the prosecutor ought to be informed.
242 Arnou, 1990/1991, p. 975; see also Van den Wyngaert, 1994, pp. 601-602.
243 See Fransen, 1986, p. pp. 15-16 and De Nauw, 1990, p. 66.
244 See also for an overview of the Belgian criminal procedure in English Van den Wyngaert, 1993b, pp. 1-49.
245 Van den Wyngaert, 1994, p. 608; in the absence of legislative texts and case-law on the general police enquiry in Belgium, we have mainly used (unpublished) study material of the Koninklijke Rijkswachtschool in Brussels for this section on investigation acts.

of important indications due to people coming and going on the site. It is also at this point that a first selection of witnesses and suspect(s) may occur. These will be taken from the scene of the crime as soon as possible and put under the responsibility of a police officer in order to prevent them from influencing each other. Other persons present will be asked to leave the site.[246]

After the situation at the *locus delicti* has been established and recorded with the help of drawings, descriptions and photographs, the police may proceed to the search of the premises. As long as the search takes place in a public place, every auxiliary of the public prosecutor is authorized to proceed on the basis of art. 26 WPA. This is also the case for vehicles when there is serious suspicion that the vehicle has been used for the commission of the offence. In the event that the place to be searched is a private location, it may only be searched in the framework of an enquiry *in flagrante delicto* upon the requisition of an investigating judge or with the explicit authorization of the resident.

Indeed, as the location is being searched, the police may come across objects related to the commission of the offence. These will be seized, preferably in the presence of the suspect(s) as he may then be asked immediately to identify and comment on the objects. The police report will make accounts of the objects found and seized as well as of the reactions of the suspect(s) during the operation and when confronted with the objects.

Further, once the location has been isolated, it may be necessary to carry out technical investigations: take samples, fingerprints, footprints, handprints, traces of gun use, blood and hair samples, etc. All these samples may be submitted to analysis and comparisons by experts. For the taking of samples that require special training, special teams of experts may be called in, such as the *gendarmerie*'s BOB: the surveillance and investigation brigades. Other experts may be called in, such as the specialized scientific services of the judicial police of the public prosecutor and external experts of all kinds: doctors, sworn translators, locksmiths, etc.[247]

Investigations Related to Persons
Every Belgian citizen must be able to establish his identity on the request of the police.[248] When police officers arrive on the scene, they have the power to control the identity of possible witness(es), suspect(s) and other present persons (art. 34 par. 1 WPA).[249] There are many forms of limitations of liberty possible in Belgium. Besides the administrative arrest or the arrest of persons sentenced for detention, there is also the police arrest, *in flagrante delicto* or

246 Bevers & Joubert, 1994, pp. 118-119.
247 See Bevers & Joubert, 1994, p. 120.
248 See art. 1 of the Royal Decree of July 29, 1985.
249 The Belgian control of identity will be analyzed in more detail in Chapter 7.

as a special measure and the arrest following an order of the judge. Once a person has been arrested, he may be submitted to a security search.[250]

In Flagrante Delicto

The discovery of a criminal offence *in flagrante delicto* initiates a procedure which takes a central place in the Belgian criminal procedure. This procedure is, along with the preliminary judicial enquiry, the only legally regulated type of pre-trial enquiry. The Belgian legislator has linked the red-handed discovery of a criminal offence to a series of police investigation powers.[251]

An offence is considered *in flagrante delicto* when it is discovered as it is being committed or immediately after (art. 41 Sv).[252] The expression immediately (*terstond*) must be understood as restricting the time between the commission and the discovery to a short period of time.[253] The law categorizes two other situations as discovered *in flagrante delicto* (art. 41 par. 2 Sv): as the suspect is being pursued by the clamour of the crowd or when he is discovered with objects, weapons, tools or papers indicating that he may be the culprit or an accomplice, providing this happens shortly after the offence has been committed.

The discovery *in flagrante delicto* of a criminal offence gives the public prosecutor and implicitly his auxiliaries the power to carry out certain investigations without a warrant and without the prior authorization of the concerned person. This is the case for instance for the arrest of the suspect,[254] search and seizures of a house and bodily searches. A search of a place not accessible to the public (such as a house) may in that case be carried out without a search warrant from an investigating judge and without the authorization of the occupant (artt. 36 and 39 Sv).[255] Restrictions as to the time of day do not stand in that case either, which means that such a search may also be carried out between 21:00 and 05:00. The same type of exception applies to the bodily search which, in the absence of a *flagrante delicto* situation, must be authorized by the judicial council.[256]

---

250 See further Chapter 9 on the different forms of physical searches.
251 On the enquiry *in flagrante delicto*, we refer to for instance Verstraeten, 1994, pp. 143 *et seq.* and Declercq, 1994, pp. 118 *et seq.*
252 The concept of *flagrante delicto* and its consequences for international police cooperation is developed further in Chapter 6.
253 See Spriet, 1991, p. 22.
254 Although in this case not only the public prosecutor and his auxiliaries are empowered to arrest the suspect, but every private person as well.
255 See Van den Wyngaert, 1994, pp. 609-610.
256 Van den Wyngaert, 1993b, pp. 27-28.

3.3.2.2 The Netherlands

The first task of the police according to the law is to draw up reports on the criminal offences they have investigated (art. 152 Sv). Although the police discover many offences themselves, they also rely on the complaints and denunciations they receive from the public. Any person that acquires knowledge of the commission of an offence may lodge a complaint or make a denunciation (art. 161 Sv). In principle, this is even considered an obligation according to art. 160 Sv. In general every person has the faculty to give information to the police, orally or otherwise, even anonymously, and this information may always initiate a police enquiry.[257] Further, the police are obliged to formally receive and record the complaint or denunciation (art. 163 par. 4 Sv).

Dutch law makes a difference between complaints and denunciations, giving complaints a higher level of formalism. A denunciation is receivable no matter which form it takes, whereas a complaint is subject to a number of rules as to its receivability.[258] Not observing the rules may lead to the nullity of the complaint (art. 164 par. 3 Sv). It is not necessary that the complaint be directed against a particular person, but it is essential for the receivability that the victim (or a person of her choice with a written mandate) lodge the complaint personally and that it be recorded by a competent police officer.

Once the police have been informed of the commission of a criminal offence by a complaint, a denunciation or otherwise, they may begin an enquiry, since the beginning of a police enquiry finds its justification in the suspicion that a criminal offence has been committed. This does not mean that every criminal offence will in fact lead to a police enquiry. The public prosecutor, as we have stated above, has the jurisdiction to drop the case either for technical reasons or for reasons of policy. Further, the police may have technical reasons not to investigate a particular case.[259]

Once the police or the public prosecutor has decided to investigate a particular case, the law puts many powers at their disposal. They are known by the Dutch Code of Criminal Procedure as the "means of constraint" (*dwangmiddelen*) as their use most often constitutes a violation of some fundamental right or freedom. Investigation powers may also be found in other statutes, such as the Opium Act (*Opiumwet* - OW) and Act on Weapons and Ammunition (*Wet wapens en munitie* - WWM). In principle, these means of constraint may only

---

257 The question as to whether a complaint or denunciation has been made is only relevant for the determination of the commission of a false complaint or denunciation (artt. 188 and 268 Sr). See Minkenhof/Reijntjes, 1990, p. 149.

258 Minkenhof/Reijntjes, 1990, p. 150.

259 See Bevers & Joubert, 1994, p. 101.

be applied on the suspect, but in exceptional cases they may be used against third parties.

Investigations Related to Objects

One of the first things the police may chose to do when they are informed of the commission of a criminal offence is to go to the *locus delicti*. Once on location, there are many investigations of a material nature to be carried out in order to answer important questions of fact, one of them being indeed the question as to whether an offence has actually been committed.

The public prosecutor has jurisdiction to visit any place at any time in order to inspect the state of a location or an object (art. 150 Sv). This is called the survey (*schouw*). However, he has no jurisdiction to enter a private home when its access is refused by the occupant unless he is acting *in flagrante delicto* or the criminal offence in question is a crime for which pre-trial custody is authorized.

During a survey, the public prosecutor will scan the location, inspect and scrutinize and eventually have photographs taken. As he comes across objects that may be relevant for his investigations, he may proceed to their seizure (art. 97 Sv). He has no jurisdiction to enter private homes to which access is refused. He may have himself assisted by such persons as police officers, experts or witnesses whom he will appoint personally. In the event that the situation calls for immediate action and it is not advisable to wait for the arrival of the public prosecutor, auxiliaries of the public prosecutor may act in his place (art. 158 Sv).[260]

During a search, in opposition to during the survey, a location will be meticulously combed through: During a search, the walls and floors may even be torn apart.[261] In principle this search is a prelude to a judicial preliminary enquiry, the opening of which must be requested by the public prosecutor (art. 181 Sv). The search is done in expectation of the enquiry of the investigating judge.[262] The search is possible only in a *flagrante delicto* situation or when the facts concern an offence for which pre-trial custody is possible and when it is of a pressing necessity (*dringende noodzakelijkheid*). When the location is a private home, a special procedure must be respected, described in the General Act on Trespassing (*Algemene Wet op het Binnentreden* - AWBi).[263] From these provisions follows, for instance, that the officers carrying out the search identify themselves and request authorization to enter. Upon refusal, the officers must have a warrant and, when possible, they must show it.

---

260   See also Melai, note on art. 150 Sv and Minkenhof/Reijntjes, 1990, pp. 143 *et seq.*
261   Melai, note 2 on art. 150 Sv.
262   Minkenhof/Reijntjes, 1990, p. 118; Melai, notes on art. 97 Sv.
263   This law came into force in June 1994 and has abrogated artt. 120-123 Sv (Stb. 572).

Investigations Related to Persons

One of the most significant characteristics of the Dutch criminal procedure is the difference that is made between the concept of apprehension (*staande houden*) and arrest (*aanhouden*).[264] The apprehension is a very temporary measure, lasting only the time necessary for the officer to ask a suspect his name, whereas the arrest may last up to fifteen hours.

As mentioned above and as will be discussed in greater detail in Chapter 7, the concepts of suspect and suspicion play a central role in the exercise of the power to apprehend. Art. 52 Sv gives police officers jurisdiction to apprehend a suspect in order to ask him for his name and address. If the officers are of opinion that the suspect should be interrogated, he may be arrested for hearing purposes (art. 54 Sv). Note that it is the public prosecutor himself who has jurisdiction to arrest the suspect, whereas the law authorizes auxiliaries of the public prosecutor or even simple police officers to carry out arrests when it is not advisable to await the arrival of the public prosecutor himself.

Dutch law also provides for regulations concerning bodily searches on and in the body of a person. Other special acts provide for yet other types of bodily searches: the security search of the Police Act (art. 8 PolW), the identification search for foreign suspects (this search is further not considered), the drugs search (art. 9 par. 5 OW), the weapon search (art. 52 par. 2 WWM), the arrest search and the incarceration search, prior to cell custody.

The most important condition for the investigative bodily search mentioned in the Code of Criminal Procedure (art. 56 Sv) is the presence of an aggravated suspicion. The public prosecutor may request that the suspect be searched on his body and clothes, whereas police officers may only have a suspect's clothes searched. The security search is regulated in art. 8 PolW and may be done by every police officer when facts and circumstances indicate an imminent danger for the officer himself or of third parties.[265]

As we have said above, the suspect may be held at the police station for interrogation purposes for a period of six hours (maximum of fifteen hours, the nightly hours included). After this period, he must either be set free or be presented to the (auxiliary of the) public prosecutor. This authority will decide whether the suspect should be kept in police custody. This measure is only authorized for offences for which pre-trial custody is possible. The suspect may not be held more than three days, and must be presented before the investigating judge before the end of the third day or be released.[266] If the judge decides that the suspect must be kept longer at the disposition of the justice, he may

---

264 These two terms, the differences between them and their consequences will be discussed in detail in Chapter 7.

265 See further Chapter 9 on security search and investigative search.

266 See further Chapters 7 and 10.

decide to place him in pre-trial custody (art. 60 Sv). This may also be decided directly after the arrest. In that case, the suspicion must be of an aggravated nature (*ernstige bezwaren*) and indeed, only when the reproached offence is one for which pre-trial custody is authorized.

In Flagrante Delicto

When a suspect has been caught in the act, police officers has an array of more extensive powers at his disposal. One finds a definition of the concept of *in flagrante delicto* (*heterdaad*, literally: in hot action) in art. 128 Sv, which speaks of an offence being discovered "during or immediately after its commission" or "shortly after" its commission. The jurisdiction of the police officers during a situation of *flagrante delicto* being an exceptional one, the concept is usually interpreted restrictively. Whereas most of the police powers described above are only allowed for offences for which pre-trial custody is possible, this is not the case for *in flagrante delicto* situations.

The extended jurisdiction of police officers applies to the arrest (art. 53 Sv, which jurisdiction is, moreover, recognized to anyone witnessing an offence being committed), trespassing on private locations for the purpose of a seizure (art. 96 Sv), to the survey or the search and seizure (art. 97 Sv), trespassing on special locations, investigation of traces on the body (art. 195 Sv). Furthermore, police officers may enter any place for the purpose of arresting the suspect (art. 55 Sv).

3.3.2.3 Luxembourg

One of the first tasks of the police is defined by artt. 9-2 and 46 CIC: The agents and officers of judicial police have the task of acknowledging the commission of offences, gathering evidence and seeking the criminally responsible. As auxiliaries of the public prosecutor, these police officers carry out preliminary enquiries either under the direction of the public prosecutor or of their own initiative as long as an official enquiry has not been initiated. The public prosecutor is the authority with jurisdiction to receive all complaints and denunciations (art. 22 CIC). From this follows that every public authority or agency coming across a criminal offence is obliged to inform the public prosecutor (art. 22 par. 2 CIC) who decides upon the further course of the enquiry. As we have noted above, he has discretion as to prosecute the case or not on the basis of the principle of opportuneness of court proceedings. However, a denunciation as a civil party will oblige the prosecutor to initiate a preliminary judicial enquiry and he will transfer the case to an investigating judge.

If the case is prosecuted further, the law leaves a number of investigation means, or means of constraint at the disposal of the police, depending on whether they are acting of their own initiative or under the direction of either the public prosecutor or the investigating judge.

Investigations Related to Objects

Save in case of a enquiry *in flagrante delicto*, it is the investigating judge who has jurisdiction to proceed to a survey of the *locus delicti* first hand. The public prosecutor may accompany him as well as the suspect and his legal counsel (art. 63 CIC) who must be informed one day in advance. Indeed, the judge may be of opinion that it might be unwise to have the suspect present because the survey must take place immediately or because there are reasons to believe that elements may disappear. In that case he may proceed without informing the suspect.

Note that in principle there is a hierarchy in the authorities habilitated to carry out investigations during the criminal procedure. When the police are first on location, they carry out investigations within the limit of their jurisdiction. They are, however, relieved of their responsibilities as soon as the public prosecutor arrives (art. 41 CIC). If the investigating judge arrives, the public prosecutor loses his authority and it is the judge who will take over the enquiry (art. 42 CIC).

Once on location, the judge may proceed to a search and seizure, in which case all the legal formalities must be respected, unless he is acting in an enquiry *in flagrante delicto* (art. 65 CIC). In principle, the search must be done with the authorization of the occupant and during the so-called legal hours (between 06:60 and 20:00), according to the formalities stated by artt. 33 to 38 CIC. However, the authorization of the occupant is not mandatory when the judge is doing (or ordering) the search himself or when the suspect has been caught red-handed. When the police are acting of their own initiative, they must obtain, prior to the search and seizure, the written and express authorization of the occupant which will be recorded in the police report (art. 47 CIC).

Investigations Related to Persons

One of the first investigations that may be done by the police is the identity control of the suspect. This procedure, regulated by art. 45 CIC, gives the police extensive means of constraint. The person who is the object of the control may be brought to the police station and held there as long as necessary for his identification. Fingerprints and photographs may even be taken. The entire procedure must be accounted for in a detailed police report.[267]

The suspect may be searched, either for investigation purposes or for security reasons. These forms of bodily searches are not extensively regulated

---

267 See further Chapter 7.

in the law: On the one hand, the investigative search is considered a *perquisition*, from which follows that the special provisions on searches must be respected except in the event that of a procedure *in flagrante delicto* (artt. 33 to 38 CIC). On the other hand, the security search is considered inherent to police practice and is not regulated at all.[268]

In Flagrante Delicto

As in other systems of criminal procedure, the fact that an offence has been discovered in the act gives rise to the start of a particular procedure called *in flagrante delicto*. This procedure is characterized by the fact that the investigating authorities enjoy more extensive enquiring powers.

An offence is considered in the act when it is discovered as it is being or has just been committed (art. 30 CIC). The law also understands as having been discovered *in flagrante delicto*, the person who, at a time close to the commission of the offence and pursued by the clamour of the crowd, is discovered in possession of particular objects or tools or is marked by particular traces or clues which may lead to the assumption that he has participated in the commission of the offence. The law makes the same assumption of the person who has been denounced by the head of a household when the offence has been committed inside a home.

In case an offence is discovered in the act, it is the auxiliary of the public prosecutor (*officier de police judiciaire*) who has immediate jurisdiction to proceed to the first investigation acts. He will be present at the *locus delicti* and will take all the necessary measures (artt. 31 *et seq.* CIC). He has jurisdiction to search and to seize objects he finds. He may even proceed to the search of a home, as prescribed by art. 33 CIC, regardless of the legal hours and of whether the occupant has given his authorization.

Moreover, the auxiliary of the public prosecutor has extensive powers as to means of constraint against individuals. He may forbid that anyone leave the scene of the crime (art. 37 CIC) and may retain and interrogate all persons whom he suspects will be able to give relevant information. In this, he even has the power to force a person to appear before him as he may request the assistance of the public forces with the permission of the public prosecutor (art. 38 CIC). With the authorization of the public prosecutor, he may further place the suspect in police custody for a period not exceeding twenty-four hours (art. 39 CIC), where he may be subjected to a bodily investigative search. The suspect possesses at that moment of a number of rights: He may have a person of his choice informed that he is being held, be examined by a physician and be assisted by a legal counsel.[269]

---

268 See Chapter 9.
269 See further Spielmann & Spielmann, 1993, pp. 270 *et seq..* See also Chapters 7 and 10.

3.3.2.4 France

According to art. 14 CPP, the judicial police, in their function as auxiliaries of the public prosecutor, have jurisdiction to discover criminal offences,gather evidence and to track down their authors as long as no preliminary judicial enquiry has been opened. As auxiliaries of the public prosecutor, the (higher ranked) officers of judicial police that have jurisdiction to lead the police enquiry in the first instance, according to the conditions laid down in the law (artt. 17, 53-67 and 75-78 CPP). They receive the complaints and denunciations and they may be directly assisted by the public forces.

The officers of judicial police may start a police enquiry of their own initiative or upon the request of the public prosecutor. The information relative to a criminal offence comes to them by coincidence, as a result of particular investigations or in the form of a complaint or a denunciation by a citizen. The police receive the complaint or denunciation and inform the public prosecutor as soon as possible, along with all the police reports and documents relative to the offence (art. 40 CPP).[270] The police have jurisdiction to initiate an enquiry in order to ascertain that a criminal offence has been committed with the important restriction that no means of constraint may be used. In practice, the police usually wait until they have gathered enough evidence before they inform the public prosecutor.[271]

What may happen as well, is that the public prosecutor's department, after having been informed of the commission of an offence by a complaint or a denunciation, orders the police to start an enquiry by means of a *réquisition*. In that case, the department will seize all the results of the enquiry that have been gathered until that day and transfer them to a particular public prosecutor who will coordinate the enquiry in a more direct fashion (art. C.134 IG).

The length of a police enquiry is variable: It may be wrapped up very quickly or go on for weeks or months. The police officers must report regularly to the public prosecutor or directly to the department and stop their investigations as soon as a preliminary judicial enquiry has been started.[272]

Investigations Related to Objects
The officers of judicial police as auxiliaries of the public prosecutor may travel to the *locus delicti* for a survey of the location. However, every search and seizure they judge necessary may only be carried out with the express and written authorization of the occupant (art. 76 CPP). Save the case where the

---

270 As a public authority, the police have the legal obligation to inform the public prosecutor of all criminal offences that come to their knowledge.
271 See Rassat, 1990, p. 172.
272 Decocq, Montreuil & Buisson, 1991, p. 329.

police are acting *in flagrante delicto*, they may not rightfully proceed to a search and seizure against the will of the occupant unless they have obtained a warrant from the investigating judge.[273] Moreover, the investigating judge, once he has legally obtained jurisdiction to investigate a particular case, is always competent to proceed to a survey of the *locus delicti* or to a search and seizure (artt. 92 *et seq.* CPP).

Since 1985, the judicial police may be assisted by experts during a general police enquiry (artt. 60 par. 2, 77-1 and 157 CPP).[274] These experts may be consulted to carry out special investigations for which a certain ability or craftsmanship is necessary. Their reports are not considered *expertise* in the legal sense, but are rather used to acknowledge certain fact findings that cannot allow any delay. The *Cour de cassation* and the *Cour d'appel* have the task to draw up a list of judicial experts to serve in this function. The police may assign experts other than those appearing on the list, but in that case they must take an oath (artt. 77-1 and 60 par. 2 CPP).[275]

As we have stated above, no means of constraint may be used during the police enquiry, except when the police is acting *in flagrante delicto*, with the concerned citizen's permission or with a warrant of the investigating judge. Before the police may proceed to a search of a location that is to be legally considered a home, they must obtain the express and written authorization of the head of the household (art. 76 CPP). However, with the help of a warrant from the investigating judge (*commission rogatoire*), the police may be habilitated to carry out a search even upon the refusal of the occupant (art. 94 to 98 CPP). Indeed, relevant documents and objects may be seized during the search. In principle, the search and seizure must be done in the presence of the person whose house is being searched (art. 57 CPP).

The search must be done during the legal hours, meaning that no search should be done between 21:00 and 06:00 (art. 59 and 95 CPP). However, this rule permits a number of exceptions: Save the exception formed by the *flagrante delicto procedure*, a search may also take place during nightly hours when the reproached offences are related to narcotics (art. L.627 CPP) or to prostitution (artt. 59 CPP and 334 CP).

---

273 Crim. May 30, 1980, in: D. 1981. 533, note from Jeandidier; crim. June 1987, in: Bull. crim. nr. 267.
274 Act nr. 85-1407 of December 30 1985, published in J.O. December 31, 1985.
275 See also Lasalle, 1990, p. 18.

Investigations Related to Persons

There is no legal provision regulating the bodily search itself,[276] as it is considered a search of a home (*perquisition*). One may distinguish between two kinds of bodily searches: *perquisition* and security search (*fouille de sécurité*). The investigative body search, as a *perquisition*, may only be carried out with the authorization of the suspect unless the police is acting *in flagrante delicto* or the investigating judge has issued a warrant.[277] Further, the security search, as a simple act of police, may be carried out for instance when the suspect is being placed in police custody (art. C.117 IG) or when he has been caught in the act.[278]

The judicial police have further the power to retain in police custody anyone who may have information on a particular case or are suspect because of certain indications (artt. 77 and 78 CPP). The suspect may not be held longer than twenty-four hours; this period may be extended for another period of twenty-four hours with the authorization of the public prosecutor (art. 77 CPP). Since 1993, the law also obliges the police to inform the suspect of a certain number of rights (artt. 63-1 to 65 CPP): to have a third party informed of the retention, to have oneself examined by a physician and to confer with an attorney at law after the first twenty-four hours have elapsed.[279] A person who is not a suspect may only be retained the time necessary for his statement.[280]

In Flagrante Delicto

As we have already mentioned, the fact that an offence has been discovered in the act gives the police extended powers to investigate the case. In that case, not only the police, but anyone discovering the offence may apprehend the suspect (art. 73 CPP), in which case the application of means of constraint to compel the suspect to appear before the competent public authority is authorized (art. 327 CP).

One speaks of such an offence *in flagrante delicto* if it has been discovered or as it is being - or just has been - committed. An offence is also discovered in the act when a person is pursued by clamour of the crowd or is discovered, shortly after the commission, to be in possession of objects or bearing marks or clues justifying the assumption that he has participated in the commission of the offence. An offence is furthermore treated as such when it has been

---

276 Called most often *fouille corporelle*, *fouille sur la personne* or *fouille à corps*.
277 Cass. crim. January 22 1953, in: D. 1953, 1, 533 with note Lapp; J.C.P. 53, II, 7456 with note Bronchot; see also Decocq, Montreuil & Buisson, 1991, p. 301.
278 See also Chapter 10 of this study.
279 For an overview of the reform and counter-reform accomplished in 1993, see Joubert, 1994, pp. 248 *et seq.*
280 See Chapters 7 and 10.

committed inside a home and the head of the household requests the assistance of the police to acknowledge its commission (art. 53 CPP).

The special *in flagrante delicto* procedure may only be initiated when the offence committed is one sanctioned with a detention sentence (artt. 67 CPP). The officer of judicial police must immediately inform the public prosecutor and travel to the *locus delicti* for a survey in order to make all the necessary fact findings. He will ascertain that all clues and pieces of evidence that are susceptible to get lost be kept in security. Further, he will seize all tools and weapons, as well as anything that seems to be the product of the offence and he presents them to the suspects for recognition. He may also proceed to a search (artt. 54 and 56 CPP).

Moreover, the officer of judicial police may remand a person in police custody when this person is a suspect or is expected to have information that may interest the enquiry. The *garde à vue* of the suspect may last twenty-four hours whereas the simple witness may only be held the necessary time for his deposition (art. 63). Persons remanded in custody have been accorded a number of rights listed in the artt. 63-1, 63-2, 63-3, and 63-4 CPP, of which the suspect must be informed the moment his retention begins.[281]

3.3.2.5 Germany

As the public prosecutor is considered the "head with no hands" (since he does not possess executive powers), the police, and in particular the officers with the power to act as auxiliaries of the public prosecutor, have the task of assisting the prosecutor in his enquiries. As we have seen above, however, the police are not subordinates of the public prosecutor but of the minister of the interior of each province. The police act on two accounts: They may begin enquiries of their own initiative as soon as they are informed of the commission of a criminal offence, or may be requested by the public prosecutor to carry out enquiries.[282] According to German law, the police enquiry may be started in three ways: through an offence being discovered by an officer on duty (*amtliche Wahrnehmung*), by denunciation (*Strafanzeige*) and by request for prosecution (*Antrag auf Strafverfolgung*).[283]

German law obliges police officers to open an enquiry when they are informed of the alleged commission of a criminal offence (artt. 160 and 163 StPO). The way they have obtained the information is not relevant for this obligation: It may be information from a witness or facts they have witnessed

---

281 For an overview of the reform and counter-reform accomplished in 1993, see Pradel, 1993b; Joubert, 1994, pp. 248 *et seq.* See further Chapters 7 and 10 of this study.
282 See Roxin, 1993, pp. 51-60.
283 See Roxin, 1993, pp. 262 *et seq.*

themselves, records that have been transferred, news clippings originating from newspapers or other sources. A police officer who has acquired knowledge of the commission of an offence while he was on duty and who fails to start an enquiry, may be found guilty of a criminal offence (*Strafvereitelung*, art. 258a StGB).[284]

Most of the criminal offences reach the police by means of denunciations.[285] A denunciation can be made either directly to the public prosecutor, to the police or to the district court. The denunciation may be made in writing or orally, in which case the police officer receiving the denunciation must draw up a report and have it signed by the declaring party (art. 158 par. 1 StPO). Although factual information that, in the opinion of the declaring party, justifies the start of a police enquiry is considered a denunciation, it is the task of the police to determine whether the facts actually justify the start of an enquiry.[286] A denunciation may also come with a request for prosecution, in which the requesting party will express his explicit wish to see the case prosecuted (art. 158 par. 2 StPO). The request is pincipally made in writing, but may be made orally at the public prosecutor's department or at the district court. In that case, a report of the request must be drawn up and it must be signed by the requesting party.[287]

Once the police enquiry is opened, it is possible that more investigative powers are necessary. The law gives the police the possibility to use a number of means of constraint directly: control of identity (art. 163b StPO), arrest (art. 127 and 164 StPO) and gathering of fingerprints, photographs and other measures for the recognition of the suspect (*erkennungsdienstliche Maßnahmen*, art. 81b StPO).

Investigations Related to Objects

According to art. 161 StPO, the public prosecutor may carry out all investigations he deems necessary. Concerning the investigation to be carried out on the *locus delicti* (*Tatort*), there is little to be found in the Code of Criminal Procedure. However, the guidelines (*Richtlinien*) do contain general provisions on the way this investigation must be carried out.[288]

The investigation at the *locus delicti* may be carried out by the public prosecutor personally, although he may request the police to proceed. He will thereby retain the general direction of the enquiry, leaving the police with a large amount of discretion as they are generally better equipped technically and

---

284   See Roxin, 1993, pp. 262 *et seq.* and Metzner, 1992, pp. 64-65.
285   Roxin, 1993, p. 263.
286   Kleinknecht/Meyer-Goßner, 1995, p. 564.
287   See Roxin, 1993, p. 263.
288   Kleinknecht/Meyer-Goßner, 1995, pp. 575-576.

tactically.[289] He may also request the assistance of the investigating judge or special services such as the financial officers and the federal criminal police.[290]

Once on location, the situation will be recorded in detailed reports and sketches; drawings as well as photographs will also be made (art. 69 StPO).[291] The police will then search for clues, traces and evidence. These may be material clues, such as objects that can be seized (artt. 94, 102 and 103 StPO), as well as non-material clues, such as statements of victims, witnesses and neighbours.[292]

Save the situation where there is danger in delay (*Gefahr im Verzug*), the search and seizure of a home is only possible with a warrant from the judge. During the search, artt. 102-110 StPO should be respected. In the event that a search must be carried out in a house which is not that of the suspect, it may only be done with the intention of arresting the suspect or when there are indications that particular objects, traces or piece of evidence are to be found there (artt. 102 and 103 par. 1 StPO). Furthermore, a search may only be carried out during the day, which means in the summer between 04:00 and 21:00 and in the winter between 06:00 and 21:00.

As a principle, one tries to inform the guardian of the location of the aim of the search and will have him present during the operation (art. 106 StPO). The police officers will give a written account of the search upon his request (art. 107 StPO). These regulations are, however, to be considered as indications and not as obligations, and their neglectance will therefore not have any legal consequences.[293] According to art. 108 StPO, not only objects found in relation to the criminal offence being investigated, but also those found by coincidence and possibly related to other criminal offences may be seized. In that case, however, the public prosecutor's department must be informed immediately.[294]

Special or technical investigations may be necessary during the course of the enquiry. In that event, the public authority leading the enquiry will call upon specialized services. Indeed, the larger police corps will rely on their own services, but the smaller units will be able to rely on the services of either the provincial criminal police or the federal criminal police.[295] The public prosecutor may also call on external expert services when specific expertise is necessary (artt. 161a and 163a StPO). However, RiStBV 69 specifies that the decision to resort to an external expert (*Sachverständiger*) may only be taken when this is

289 Kleinknecht/Meyer-Goßner, 1995, pp. 575-576.
290 Kleinknecht/Meyer-Goßner, 1995, p. 576.
291 Kleinknecht/Meyer-Goßner, 1995, pp. 207-208.
292 Kleinknecht/Meyer-Goßner, 1995, pp. 8-11, pp. 261-265 and pp. 307-312.
293 Kleinknecht/Meyer-Goßner, 1995, pp. 316-317.
294 See Roxin, 1993, pp. 241-246.
295 Bevers & Joubert, 1993, p. 171.

inevitable. The expert will record his findings in a report which will be presented orally during the trial (art. 250 StPO).[296]

Investigations Related to Persons

Many investigative means are at the disposal of the police if the name or whereabouts of a suspect is not known.[297] In order to identify a suspect, the law authorizes the police to take all necessary measures. This means that the suspect must state his name and show his identification papers when requested by the police. If the identification of the suspect is not possible or when problems arise as to his identification papers, he may be searched. In the event that his identification is not possible otherwise, the police may take measures for the identification (*erkennungsdienstliche Maßnahmen*), in which case photographs and fingerprints may be taken even against his will (art. 81b StPO). The identification control of persons other than a suspect is also possible, but in that case they must be informed of the reason they are being controlled (art. 163b StPO). However, because of the principle of proportionality, other measures for the identification of non-suspects will not be authorized. A person being retained for identification purposes must be brought before a judge as soon as possible (art. 163c StPO). He may be authorized to contact a person of trust (except when there is a danger of collusion) and may not be held more than twelve hours.[298]

Furthermore, persons may be interrogated. There are according to German law two types of interrogation: the interrogation of witnesses or persons who otherwise are liable to have relevant information for the police (*informatorische Befragung*) and the deposition of the suspect (*Vernehmung*).[299] Before the end of the police enquiry, the suspect must have the opportunity to express himself on the course of the events (art. 163a par. 1 StPO).[300] In principle, only the judge has jurisdiction to decide whether a suspect may be held in remand or in pre-trial custody (art. 104 GG). This rule allows a small number of exceptions, in which case the suspect must, however, be brought before a judge as soon as possible (artt. 112, 112a, 113 and 128 StPO).

In addition to the above mentioned investigative possibilities, a suspect may also be searched. German law makes a strict difference between the bodily search of a person (*Durchsuchung einer Person*), regulated by art. 102 StPO and the bodily investigation (*körperliche Untersuchung*), regulated in artt. 81a to 81b StPO. The principle, nevertheless, is that both the bodily search and the bodily investigation must be ordered by a judge.

---

296 Kleinknecht/Meyer-Goßner, 1995, pp. 792-793.
297 Bevers & Joubert, 1994, pp. 171-172.
298 Kleinknecht/Meyer-Goßner, 1995, pp. 598-600.
299 Kleinknecht/Meyer-Goßner, 1995, p. 15.
300 See further Chapters 7 and 10.

In Flagrante Delicto
There are two situations giving special jurisdiction to the public prosecutor and the police as to means of constraint that may be used against a person: One of them is the situation where there is danger in delay (*Gefahr im Verzug*), the other is the *in flagrante delicto* situation (*Flagranz*). Danger in delay is the situation where there is a certain risk that particular investigative operations (such as arrest, search and seizure) can not be carried out with success should the operations be delayed.[301] Danger in delay is a justification for extending jurisdiction that would otherwise be reserved for the judge to the public prosecutor or his auxiliaries in the police forces. One may think for instance of the decision on the opportunity of a search and seizure (artt. 105 and 98, 11e par. 1 StPO), temporary arrest (art. 127 par. 2 StPO) and the bodily searches and investigations (artt. 102 and 105 StPO).

Reference to extended jurisdiction when a criminal offence is discovered *in flagrante delicto* (*frischer Tat* or *Flagranz*) is made in artt. 104 and 127 StPO. When a person is caught in the act of committing a criminal offence, anyone may apprehend him temporarily. This is the case when a person is discovered while committing a criminal offence or immediately after at the *locus delicti* or in the immediate proximity. There is also *Flagranz* when, the suspect not being at the scene of the crime, direct indications and clues lead the police to the suspect.[302]

3.4 Conclusion

An important pillar of efficient international police cooperation is the mutual understanding of each other's systems of criminal law.[303] In this chapter we have sketched the structure of the criminal procedure in five neighbouring countries, stressing the pre-trial phase and its most important actors: the police, the public prosecutor, the investigating judge and the suspect. In this paragraph we will make a number of very general comparative remarks.

3.4.1 Police

What is striking at first view when comparing the different police forces is their diversity. Not only are they different from one country to another, but also most of the countries each have a plurality of police forces working at law enforcement. Indeed, for the most part this is a heirloom of the French occupation. The

---

301 See Tak & Lensing, 1990, p. 35 and Fijnaut, 1991a, p. 70.
302 Kleinknecht/Meyer-Goßner, 1995, pp. 430-431.
303 This need for mutual understanding is also stressed in the foreword of Van den Wyngaert, 1993, p. ii.

dichotomy between police (a civilian police force under the authority of the ministry of the interior) and *gendarmerie* (a military force under the authority of the ministry of defence) has its origin in the concern for the preservation of a balance of power. One police force is often seen as an undue risk for the security of democracy.

Table 3.1 Police Forces and Authorities

	Police forces	Management authority	Investigation authority
B	* Gendarmerie/ Rijkswacht	* Ministry of the interior	* Public prosecutor
	* Police communale/ gemeentepolitie	* Mayor/provincial governor	* Public prosecutor
	* Gerechtelijke politie	* Public prosecutor	* Public prosecutor
NL	* Regiopolitie	* Mayor of central municipality	* Public prosecutor
	* Korps landelijke politiediensten	* Ministry of justice with ministry of the interior	* Public prosecutor
	* Koninklijke marechaussee	* Ministry of defense	* Public prosecutor
L	* Gendarmerie	* Ministries of defense and justice	* Public prosecutor
	* Police	* Ministries of defense, the interior and justice	* Public prosecutor
F	* Gendarmerie	* Ministry of defense	* Public prosecutor
	* Police nationale	* Ministry of the interior	* Public prosecutor
	* Police municipale	* Mayor	* Mayor/public prosecutor
D	* Federal police (BKA & BGS)	* Federal ministry of the interior	* Public prosecutor
	* Provincial police forces	* Provincial ministries of the interior	* Public prosecutor

This disparity inside each country can also be seen in the jurisdiction of the services. It seems, however, that with the influence of international police cooperation most countries are tending to diminish this disparity. Indeed there is still a long way to go to eliminate all competition conflicts. The countries with the most apparent[304] cohesion are The Netherlands and Luxembourg: The executive police forces are all directed, managed and controlled by the same

---

304 The expression "apparent" is used because it seems that competition between services is very difficult to eliminate.

ministries. Belgium and France seem to represent the other extreme, although the last reorganization in Belgium can be seen as an step towards more cohesion. The dichotomy in the French police system seems to be the source of an overlapping of jurisdiction. Here again, the last years have seen an improvement in the cooperation between the two forces. The situation in Germany is of a different order. One is confronted with a plurality of independent police forces. The separation of jurisdiction between provincial and federal police services seems clear although there is a certain degree of overlapping.

3.4.2 Public Prosecutor

In all of the studied countries, the public prosecutor's department is organized as a hierarchical agency. Their executive members are magistrates who have, in principle, the direction of the pre-trial enquiry of the police. Although in most of the countries except Germany, the public prosecutor possesses investigative powers personally; the practice is such that the police are usually entrusted with the care of (at least) the first phase of the pre-trial enquiry.

The biggest and most important difference between the countries is the fact that all but Germany share the same principle in their prosecution policy: the principle of opportuneness or expediency of criminal proceedings. The public prosecutor is not obliged to prosecute, he has jurisdiction to do so. He enjoys in most countries a great deal of discretionary power as to whether a case should be prosecuted. On the contrary, the German public prosecutor is obliged to prosecute, unless there are technical reasons not to.

This situation is liable to cause friction between cooperating police forces: As most countries most certainly have developed a certain more or less prosecution policy or priorities, it is not said that it is the same everywhere. A quick look at newspaper clippings of the last few years show clear disagreements between countries as to which criminal offences should have priority.

3.4.3 Investigating Judge

As was stated above, the institution of the investigating judge is one with a common origin. However, this institution has not remained unchanged in all countries over the years. In Belgium, the investigating judge is considered an auxiliary of the public prosecutor, an officer of judicial police, and he has no power to initiate an investigation. In his investigating powers, he is limited to the *saisine*, the submission of the case to him by the public prosecutor. In Luxembourg and in The Netherlands, although not an auxiliary of the public prosecutor, the judge is dependant of the *réquisitoire* (or *vordering* in Dutch) of the public prosecutor. Although this is also the case in France, it is the president of the court who can dismiss him or transfer the case to another judge.

The relation with the public prosecutor is therefore less direct. In Germany, finally, the judge does not lead an enquiry at all, but is there only to authorize the use of certain means of constraint. There is not one judge in charge of a particular case, rather it is one judge among other judges who is on duty at the moment a judge is needed.

3.4.4 Suspect

In countries such as Belgium, Luxembourg and France, the concept of suspicion is not discussed very much, neither in the literature nor in the case-law. The suspicion does not have to be personalized for the start of an enquiry. However, as soon as certain means of constraint must be applied, the law provides certain indications as to who the suspect is. Most of these indications are found in the beginning of the enquiry *in flagrante delicto* and are linked to the rights a person has once he is considered a suspect. In France, the situation is somewhat different since the police may compel a non-suspect to appear before the auxiliary of the public prosecutor. But as soon as this person becomes a suspect in the course of his hearing, he must be informed of a number of rights. In The Netherlands and in Germany, the concept of suspect or suspicion plays a central role. In both these countries, there is a gradation of suspicion justifying more infringing means of constraint.

3.4.5 Police Powers and Autonomy

Concerning the categorization of criminal offences, the studied countries are divided into two groups: one with a tripartite and the other with a bipartite distinction of criminal offences. The first group, composed of Belgium, Luxembourg and France, still distinguish, according to the Napoleonic model, between *crimes*, *délits* and *contraventions*. The Netherlands and Germany compose the second group and make a distinction resembling that between severe criminal offences and misdemeanours. In general, the fact that a criminal offence is a *crime*, a *délit* or a *misdrijf* is not a good criterion for international police cooperation as it varies from one country to another. The choice made by the Schengen Convention, either the extraditable offence criterium or an offence catalogue may be considered intricate, but is, nevertheless, a more practical choice.

In the pre-trial phase, it is possible to make a distinction between proactive and reactive police action. When comparing police enquiries it is possible to make the following general statements. As explained above, the difference between proactive and reactive policing lies in the question as to whether a criminal offence has (already) been committed. Indeed, in countries where the police enquiry follows few formal rules, the liberty to act even in the absence of a criminal offence is great. On the contrary, where rules do exist, they are often there to restrict the scope of action of the police. In most countries with few rules, the use of means of constraint is usually forbidden during the first phase of the police enquiry (save in *flagrante delicto* situations) and the results of enquiries inadmissible in court. The information gathered is rather used to justify and obtain the authorization from the judge to resort to the use of more coercive means. In countries with more rules on the police enquiry, such as The Netherlands, the law imposes a certain degree of suspicion as a prerequisite for the use of more coercive means.

In principle, in all of the studied countries, the police have great liberty in their investigations, as long as no means of constraint are used and the privacy of citizens is respected. However, the autonomy of the police in the first pre-trial phase varies from one country to another. One may notice a gradation going from police officers in Luxembourg and Belgium to those of Germany, passing by France and The Netherlands. In a normal situation, thus not *in flagrante delicto* cases, the Luxembourg police may not use any means of constraint during their enquiries save a security search and an identity control unless they have the authorization of the concerned party or act upon requisition of the public prosecutor or the investigating judge. Belgian police officers may carry out a survey, a bodily search, a search of a vehicle on their own and of their own initiative. French police officers also have the power to convoke non-suspects for questioning. Dutch police officers may keep a suspect in police custody for six hours, carry out a search and seizure in a place accessible to the public and in urgent cases even private premises, apprehend and arrest a suspect and carry out a security search and an investigative search of the clothes of a suspect. Finally, German officers have the most autonomy in their investigations: They may carry out almost all investigations of their own initiative, especially in urgent cases. These include indeed the survey of the *locus delicti* and the search and seizure, but also the search in computerized data banks, technical investigations, arrest, the taking of photographs and of fingerprints.

In cases where a suspect has been caught red-handed, the differences are not as great. Police powers of all five countries include search and seizure of all places, even those not accessible for the public, bodily searches, photographs and fingerprints and keeping a suspect in police custody.

Whether these differences will have an impact on the international police cooperation is a complicated matter, but they may indeed be expected to have an impact on the mentality of the police services. It is probable that police officers who are used to working with a large amount of autonomy may be inclined to act without asking themselves whether they have jurisdiction. This may be the source, at least in the beginning of cross-border practice, of international friction. This, however, must be verified in the years following implementation of the practice of cross-border police operations.

Part II

Police Powers and International Cooperation

4 Observation

The Schengen Convention is the first international treaty to introduce cross-border observation as a police cooperation technique.[1] In international police cooperation this technique could become an important novelty, even though it is likely that it has already been used internationally before the adoption of a legal basis. In paragraph 4.1, we will discuss the conditions, possibilities and limits of the regulation provided by the Schengen Convention, and sketch the limits of observation as provided by the European Convention on Human Rights. Paragraph 4.2 will give an overview of the legislation and regulation concerning observation in Belgium, The Netherlands, Luxembourg, France and Germany. A systematic comparison of these regulations will be given in paragraph 4.3, and with the results of this comparison we will offer a new look at some aspects of the Schengen provisions in the last paragraph. Some attention will also be paid to the question, whether a policing technique as observation ought to be based on statutory or other legal provisions.

As for the terminology that will be used: In some languages and countries, the subject of this section would be called "surveillance,"[2] whereas other languages and countries prefer "observation" for especially directed "watching and listening" and use "surveillance" for general police patrol. In this text, we will use the word "observation," mainly because this terminology is used by the English texts of the Schengen Agreement and Convention as provided by the Schengen Secretariat in Brussels.

Observation in the largest sense might be described as "watching without being watched," which is a policing technique that - in the form of general street surveillance - has been among the first activities applied by state forces fulfilling police tasks: The members of the city guards used to walk around, watching the events happening with or without them being watched, with or without them being recognized as guardians, in order to intervene if necessary.

During the twentieth century, and for Northwest Europe especially during the last three decades, the character of crime has changed, the most important

---

1   Competences such as cross-border hot pursuit and controlled delivery, which have been elaborated in the Schengen Convention as well, are not completely new: They were introduced before by the 1962 Benelux Extradition Treaty, respectively the 1988 UN Psychotropic Substances Convention.

2   Marx, 1988, p. 12, describes "passive surveillance" as a covert, non-deceptive police action. "Surveillance" is also used by Helsdingen, 1987, pp. 22-25 and Tabarelli, 1987, pp. 97-84.

change being the increase of severe and organized (cross-border) crime.[3] Traditional police powers and investigative techniques have shown to be insufficient for the investigation of organized crime: This is mainly due to the fact that the commission of organized crime offences is not often reported to the police, either because there are no victims (for instance consensual crime like most drug offences, smuggling of arms and other contraband) or the victims are so numerous and anonymous that they are unaware of the crimes (such as in fraud or environmental crime cases).[4] This leaves the police with very few traces and evidence, particularly against the leading people in the background. They run their criminal organisation like a commercial enterprise, prepare their activities a long time in advance and have the real criminal offences committed by others, much lower in the hierarchy.

In order to gather evidence on the involvement of certain persons in these types of crime, police forces have developed more intensive and more efficient ways of gathering information, ways that are strongly inspired by the working methods of secret and state intelligence services: observation techniques.[5] These techniques may be generally qualified as "non-deceptive covert policing techniques," which terminology distinguishes them from "non-deceptive, overt techniques" (like uniformed patrol), "deceptive, overt techniques" (such as trickery by persons whose police identity is known) and "deceptive, covert police actions" (like infiltration).[6]

One may distinguish numerous types of observation: public or private, static or dynamic, short-term or long-term, with or without the use of technical aides, construction of motion patterns of a specific person or vehicle. It is evident that these different forms can also be combined, conducted in teams and in cooperation with foreign police forces. It is likely that, thanks to technological developments, the influence of technical devices has increased enormously and will continue increasing. More refined, sophisticated techniques and devices will be available, which will also be applied and used in order to improve not only the possibilities but also the results of observation. Technical means one may think range from simple binoculars or hearing-aids to telescopic devices, hidden body transmitters (on a so-called wired infiltrator), long distance and parabolic microphones, and even satellites to enable seeing or hearing events that could not be seen or heard otherwise or follow persons, vehicles or objects unnoticed. In addition to this monitoring, audio and video recorders enable the storage of gathered information in a practical way, as well as the relatively easy and reliable reproduction of this information. As far as the information is gathered

---

3   See Kaiser & Albrecht, 1990; Van Duyne *et al.*, 1990 and Fijnaut & Jacobs, 1991.
4   In the same sense Marx, 1988, p. 13.
5   See also Helsdingen, 1987, pp. 22-25; Fijnaut & Marx, 1995a, pp. 1-16.
6   This distinction is made by Marx, 1988, p. 11-12.

or stored in the form of digital data, there is a considerable risk of it being manipulated, which would challenge the reliability of the results.[7] A feature of the use of automatic equipment that might be interesting in times of budget cuttings, is that these devices allow the continuous observation of a place without a police officer even being present. In brief, the use of technical devices and technological developments can enormously widen the possibilities and results of police observation.

The information gathered by observation can be used for several purposes: In the first place to construct evidence against a suspect of a crime that has been committed (repressive) or still is to be committed (proactive). The information can also be used to analyze the structure of a criminal organisation or to support other police actions against the organisation (for instance to keep an eye on an infiltrator). Thirdly, it can serve to prevent the actual commission of an offence (like in case of armed robbery) or to enable that criminals be caught in the act. Finally, observation techniques may also have an important function in the protection of active undercover operations such as infiltration.

4.1 International Norms

Several sources of international law contain provisions that are to some extent relevant for police observation and its cross border appliance. A central position with respect to this should be given to the Schengen Convention, which will be discussed in section 4.1.1. Since in the context of this research the cross border appliance of observation stays restricted to the Schengen countries, fundamental criteria of the admissibility of observation in all these countries may be found in the European Convention on Human Rights and the case-law of the European Court and Commission regarding the interpretation of this Convention. This second spectrum of international norms will be dealt with in section 4.1.2.

4.1.1   International Norms on Police Cooperation

One of the first international instruments on police cooperation in criminal matters is the 1962 Benelux Extradition Treaty. However, this treaty will be left without further consideration in this context, since it does not explicitly address the subject of cross-border observation. Some have indeed argued that

---

7   A major risk of the recent developments in the field of computerization and virtual reality techniques seems to be, that images could also be manipulated or even manufactured; an impressive example of the latter is shown in Steven Spielberg's motion picture *Jurassic Park*.

observation could be based on the Benelux Treaty implicitly,[8] but it may doubted if, according to today's standards, an implicit legal basis would be sufficient for such a strong infringement with both national sovereignty and the individual's right to privacy. Furthermore, it seems that in the eyes of those who drafted the Schengen Convention, the Benelux Treaty did not address the method of observation. Unlike the situation for cross-border pursuit, Schengen does not refer to relevant Benelux provisions which will or will not be changed or influenced by the Schengen regulation.

Article 40 of the Schengen Convention, as far as relevant here, reads as follows:

> 1. Police officers of one of the Contracting Parties who, within the framework of a criminal investigation, are keeping under observation in their country, a person who is presumed to have taken part in a criminal offence to which extradition may apply, shall be authorized to continue their observation in the territory of another Contracting Party where the latter has authorized cross-border observations in response to a request for assistance previously been submitted. Conditions may be attached to the authorization. On request the observation will be entrusted to officers of the Contracting Party in whose territory it is carried out. (....)
>
> 2. Where, for particularly urgent reasons, prior authorization of the other Contracting Party can not be requested, the officers conducting the observation shall be authorized to continue beyond the border of the observation of a person presumed to have committed offences listed in paragraph 7, provided that the following conditions are met: (....)

This article provides a basis for border-crossing by police-officers during observation of a presumed criminal, when a certain number of conditions are fulfilled.

The first condition is that the observed person be "presumed to have taken part in a criminal offence to which extradition may apply." The "extradition-element" of this condition is relatively clear,[9] the "participation-element" is not. The explanatory statement of the Dutch government states that the provision not only allows the observation of a person who is under suspicion of having committed such a criminal act, but also the proactive observation of a person who is presumed to prepare the commission of criminal offences in the (near)

---

8   See for instance Fijnaut, 1991b, p. 770 and Vermeulen et al., 1994; they however seem to refer to hand-over observation, which is no real cross-border observation since the entire construction indeed excludes that the border will actually be crossed.

9   Note that, in art. 61 SC, France has considerably diminished the number of offences for which extradition will be possible, by raising the minimum limit to two years, thus breaking the uniformity of the observation regulations; see Vermeulen et al., 1994, p. 54, footnote 106.

future,[10] including everyone with whom this person stands in contact.[11] This interpretation however does not seem to find sufficient support in the respective authentic texts of the Convention. Literally, the French, German and Dutch wordings all demand that the offence be already committed and the observation take place "within the framework of a criminal investigation,"[12] of which one can only speak after a suspicion of a committed crime has risen. Furthermore, the wordings in which the three authentic languages of the Convention state that the observed person should be "presumed to have taken part" or "to have committed" do not seem to be exact equivalents of each other.[13] The Dutch *betrokkenheid bij* and the German *beteiligt sein an* (both literally meaning: involvement in) might perhaps leave an opening to criminal activities that are being prepared to be committed in the (near) future, but the French *avoir participé* or *avoir commis* (literally meaning: having participated or having committed) does not leave any flexibility towards proactive observation. This terminology clearly and doubtlessly implies that the criminal offence involved has taken place already and cross-border observation is allowed for repressive goals only. Furthermore, it is supported by the fact that in art. 46 SC, a provision that does indeed concern proactive policing, an entirely different terminology is applied than in art. 40 SC.

The second condition is the authorization of the cross-border observation by the state on whose territory the observation will take place. This authorization, that may be subject to conditions,[14] must be given in response to a request for assistance which has previously been submitted.[15] Officers observing a person presumed to have committed one of the offences listed in the seventh paragraph of the article,[16] may also continue their observation without

---

10   In its decision in the Lüdi case, the European Court on Human Rights called this "the preliminary stage of an investigation, where there is good reason to believe that criminal offences are about to be committed;" ECHR June 15, 1992, Series A 238.

11   Explanatory statement of the Dutch government, TK 1990-1991, 22 140, nr. 3; see also Fijnaut, 1991b, p. 776; Den Boer, 1991, p. 15.

12   The English phrase has been taken from the non-authentic translation from the Schengen secretariat. In Dutch, German and French respectively called *opsporingsonderzoek*, *Ermittlungsverfahren*, and *enquête judiciaire*.

13   These English phrases have been taken from the Schengen secretariat translation in English as well.

14   For instance regarding the possibility to carry weapons or the moment the observation must be joint or taken over by locally competent police officers.

15   The fact that a central role has been created for this procedure, that has been introduced for international cooperation after the commission of an offence, also seems to support the interpretation that no proactive observation was intended.

16   These are: assassination, murder, rape, arson, counterfeiting, armed robbery and fencing, extortion, kidnapping and hostage taking, traffic in human beings, illicit traffic in narcotic drugs and psychotropic substances, breach of the law on arms and explosives, use of explosives and illicit carriage of toxic and dangerous waste.

prior permission of the other state when, due to the urgency of the case, this permission cannot be requested beforehand. In that case, the authorities of the territory on which the observation takes place must be notified immediately of the crossing of the border and a request for their assistance must be submitted to them without delay. The observation shall be interrupted either upon request of the competent authorities or, in case no reaction to the notification or the request is obtained, five hours after the border has been crossed. For police and judicial authorities, it will however be difficult to control at what time exactly the border was crossed and if indeed the observation was stopped five hours later.

Furthermore, the cross-border observation is only allowed under a number of general conditions: The officers conducting the observation must be able to establish their official function and have to carry a document certifying that authorization has been granted (unless they crossed the border without permission in case of an urgency). During the observation the officers must comply with the provisions of art. 40 of the Convention, as well as with the law of the state on whose territory they operate. They may carry their service weapons unless the requested state specifically decided otherwise. The Netherlands and France have declared that foreign police officers carrying out a cross-border observation on their territory may not carry other service weapons than those which are common for the local police forces.[17] The weapon may only be used in case of legitimate self-defence. The observing officers are neither allowed to enter private homes and places not accessible to the public nor to challenge or arrest the person under observation. Control on cross-border observations is exercised by the local authorities, to whom the observing officers must report after the observation is finished. Local authorities may also require that the observing officers appear in person and authorities in the officers' country of origin are obliged to provide assistance to further investigations, judicial proceedings included.

Most of these general conditions are quite clear and indeed seem to be very practical, but some of them need to be commented more closely: One can wonder what an officer is supposed to do with his service weapon when, during an observation in his own country, he suddenly has to cross the border and is not allowed to cross the border with it? He can not reasonably be obliged to throw it away or bring it to a police station before continuing the observation. Police services in border areas will have to ascertain that their officers who might get involved in cross-border observations are not equipped with other weapons than those which may be carried across the border. And what if an officer is an eye witness to a criminal act by the person he is observing during

---

17 *Note du groupe de travail I "Police et sécurité"*, Brussels, June 2, 1995, SCH/I (94) 17, 8ème rév.

a cross-border observation? Is he entitled to arrest this red-handed suspect, just as any civilian (national or foreigner), or is this forbidden in accordance to art. 40 par. 3 f? It must be considered a deficiency of the Convention that it does not contain any answers to the question of the consequences in case one or more of the general conditions are not fulfilled. Will all the information gathered be considered as illegally obtained and, if so, will this information be excluded from the evidence? Or will it be used anyway, and in that case why have these conditions been formulated in the first place?[18] A third remark to be made is that the observing officers are supposed to comply with the legal provisions of the state where they operate, whereas they have only been schooled in working with their own national laws. Therefore, they will have to be trained in working with the law of neighbouring countries as well.[19]

A more serious problem is that the Convention does not explain what is to be understood by observation and therefore it is unclear which police activities may be covered by this term. The word is not mentioned among the definitions given in art. 1 of the Convention, nor does any other provision give an indication of the sense in which the term should be interpreted. The Schengen circular of the French minister of justice does mention some measures and activities that will be allowed, but altogether they may not be considered more that an indication. The Belgian and German governments have not tried to explain the concept of observation at all. In their explanatory statement to the Schengen Ratification Act, the Dutch government described observation as "watching without being watched." This definition suggests that "observation" would only cover the visual experience of another person's activities and therefore excludes the experience of acoustically transmitted information. However, in practice it will be very difficult, if not impossible, to separate visual observation from acoustical eavesdropping. A police officer who tries to watch without being watched will necessarily also hear without being heard. Moreover, both kinds of spying on an individual's activities can lead to similar infringements with his right to privacy. On the other hand, even the purely visual "watching without being watched" is so vague that even policing techniques

---

18 The Dutch government, being interrogated on this subject by members of parliament, explained that the reaction would depend on the national law of the judge confronted with this problem. They also added that Convention did not contain any regulation of this matter because the members states had willingly not striven for a harmonisation of criminal law and procedure. TK 1991-1992, 22 140, nr. 12, pp. 64-65 and nr. 14, p. 17.

19 In the same sense Fijnaut, 1991a, p. 774. However there are indications that in some countries the schooling has ben modified as to include some basic knowledge of the national law of the neighbour countries. The Police School in the Dutch Heerlen has for instance developed a common education program for the Belgian, German and Dutch police schools in the Meuse-Rhine-region; see *Grensoverschrijdende politiesamenwerking is een must*, in: APB 1994-9, p. 11.

like controlled delivery and infiltration could be considered as special forms of observation. The fact that the contracting parties have judged it necessary to draft a special regulation for controlled delivery (art. 73 SC), shows however that they most likely did not intend to use the word observation for other policing techniques. For that reason it can be concluded that art. 40 of the Schengen Convention cannot serve as a basis for cross-border infiltration.

Another question regarding the interpretation of the term observation in the Convention is whether the use of technical apparatus such as cameras, binoculars, telescopes, infra-red cameras, "bugs" or long-distance microphones, hidden position transmitters or radio beacons ("beepers") and audio and video recorders during a cross-border observation is allowed or not. The text of the Convention itself does not contain or suggest an answer to this question and, different from art. 41 SC with regard to cross-border pursuits, it does not explicitly restrict the cross-border observation to land borders, which might imply that observation with the help of satellites or other kinds or air observation is allowed.[20] Considering the fact that the observing officers must comply with the law of the state on whose territory the operation takes place, this will therefore mostly depend on the local legal provisions. Local legal provisions also rule the individual legal position of police officers carrying out observations or pursuits on a foreign territory. According to art. 42 SC, they are considered as local police officers with respect to offences committed by or against them. This implies that resistance against their interventions shall be regarded as a criminal offence, but also that under certain conditions, they may ignore regulations without committing an offence. The most important category of such exceptions, traffic dispensations, will be discussed in detail in Chapter 6.

A special form of observation, to which we referred already above, is mentioned in art. 73 SC: As far as possible under their constitution and national legislation, the Schengen countries are obliged to allow the exercise of controlled deliveries on their territory. This method, that was previously introduced by the UN anti-drugs treaty of 1988, implies that intervention against illegal (drug) transports is postponed, for instance in order to get to know more about the organisation behind the transports or to be able to arrest the persons behind the couriers as well. The final decision to allow controlled delivery is left to the local authorities who will also stay competent to intervene at any moment. Here again one could wonder whether or not this term has the same meaning in all of the contracting countries. Finally, it has to be mentioned that this policing technique seems to encourage the phenomena of forum shopping: By letting a transport pass through more liberal countries, police and judicial authorities can ascertain that drug traffickers are arrested in the country with

---

20   This suggestion was supported by a well-informed Belgian police officer.

the most severe penalties.[21] The subject of controlled delivery will be discussed more elaborately in Chapter 5.

An important novelty is introduced by art. 92 SC: the Schengen Information System (SIS). This computerized international database, fed by all participating countries, will contain information on persons and objects wanted by the participants or against whom the participants want to warn the authorities of their neighbouring countries. Especially the possibility to inform police officers abroad about persons or vehicles involved in the commission or preparation of severe offences (art. 99) is likely to become a great help in cross-border policing in general and observation in particular.

4.1.2   The European Convention on Human Rights

The main aim of observation by the police is the collection of information regarding the activities and contacts of the persons under observation, whether these have a public character or not. This means that observation can easily infringe the individual's right to privacy. Like most police activities it especially concerns the informational aspect of the right to privacy, the right to decide what can be done with information about the individual. Besides this, depending on the methods that are used observation can also affect the spatial aspect of the privacy, the right to decide who is admitted into the private atmosphere.

The right to respect for the private life is guaranteed by art. 8 of the European Convention on Human Rights, to which treaty all five countries studied are parties.[22] Article 8 ECHR reads as follows:

> 1. Everyone has the right to respect for his private and family life, his home and his correspondence.
> 2. There shall be no interference by a public authority with the exercise of this right except such as is in accordance with the law and is necessary in a democratic society in the interests of national security, public safety or the economic well-being of the country for the prevention of disorder or crime, for the protection of health or morals, or for the protection of the rights and freedoms of others.

The fact that several forms of observation can restrict the individual's privacy also seems to have been acknowledged by the legislators of the countries studied here. As we will see, Dutch, German, French and Luxembourg law contain criminalizations of overhearing private meetings with technical means, and the legislation in Belgium at least recognizes the privacy of the residence. But does this also implicate that art. 8 of the Convention requires that restriction of this

---

21   Mols & Spronken, 1990, p. 48.
22   The subject has also been discussed by Fijnaut, 1994a, pp. 28-54, in particular pp. 52-54, and in a more general sense in Naeyé, 1995 and Brants & Field, 1995.

right by observation be in accordance with the law? In order to answer this question, the case-law of the Court and the Commission on this article will have to be studied more closely.

The article has been explained and interpreted by the European Court as well as the European Commission on Human Rights, especially in the cases of Patricia Hope-Hewitt & Harriett Harman v. United Kingdom[23] and Kruslin and Huvig v. France.[24] In the first case, the European Commission decided that "secret surveillance activities for the purpose of gathering and storing on file information concerning an person's private life (...) constitutes an interference with this right." The observation therefore had to be in accordance with the law, and the guidelines on which the operation in this case was based could not be considered as "law," being too brief and not providing legally enforceable rules.[25] Evidently, this same argument can be used against the guidelines on which the Dutch practice is based,[26] whereas it applies even stronger to the situation in Belgium, where the texts of the guidelines are officially confidential. After the Commission judged the complaint well-founded, a decision of the European Court has to be waited for.[27]

In the other cases relevant here, the (joint) cases of Kruslin v. France and Huvig v. France, the final Court decisions have been taken already: According to the decision in the Kruslin and Huvig cases, "there must be a measure of legal protection in domestic law against arbitrary interferences by public authorities with the rights safeguarded by paragraph I" (of art. 8 ECHR). The Court adds that "especially where a power of the executive is exercised in secret, the risks of arbitrariness are evident" and states that "a severe interference with private life (...) must accordingly be based on a "law" that is particularly precise. It is essential to have clear, detailed rules on the subject, especially as the technology available for use is continually becoming more sophisticated." Although both the Kruslin and the Huvig case were about telephone tapping, it is evident that the interpretation that the Court uses, also applies to observation; the last argument recited even seems to refer explicitly to observation with the use of "continually becoming more sophisticated technology." In view of this case-law of the Commission and the Court, the conclusion is inevitable that art. 8 of the Convention requires a legal basis for most forms of police observation.[28]

23   European Commission on Human Rights, Appl. no. 12175/86.
24   European Court on Human Rights, April 24, 1990, Series A, 176-A and 176-B.
25   Cited in Fijnaut, 1991c, pp. 69-85.
26   In the same sense Fijnaut, 1994a, pp. 53-54.
27   Harteveld, Keulen & Krabbe, 1992, p. 132.
28   This was also concluded by the Dutch parliamentary enquiry committee on policing methods; see Van Traa, 1996, pp. 433-434.

4.2 National Norms

In order to research whether and to what extent the police in the Schengen countries have the power to observe, it is necessary to examine several fields of law that may contain competences or restrictions. In the first place, police power limits can be found in law on police powers and tasks, like Police Acts and Codes of Criminal Procedure. In the second place, because the rule of law implies that the police are not allowed to commit criminal offences either, limits of their powers can be derived from rules that prohibit certain kinds of behaviour. Thirdly, police activities can be limited by provisions in ministerial decrees, directives and circulars, that can have a public as well as a secret character. Finally, it is obvious that their powers are restricted by general rules and principles (such as those found in constitutions), which also function as a source of inspiration for the other categories of regulation. In this paragraph, the existence and purport of regulation on observation in the five countries will be examined.

4.2.1   General

4.2.1.1 Belgium

Until recently, Belgium did not know any statutory regulation of covert policing techniques such as observation. The first official and public acknowledgement of the existence and the use of observation was the signing of the Schengen Convention in 1990, followed and explained in 1995 by the Schengen circular. However, this does not mean that the Belgian police forces had never used any such method before. In the seventies and eighties some remarkable cases were promulgated in which, besides infiltration, also observation played a central role.[29] Moreover, the Belgian police forces know a number of special units that are mainly or entirely specialized in observation. The 23rd brigade of the judicial police (*Gerechtelijke politie*) has its "Group for shadowing and observation" (*Groep voor schaduwing en observatie* - GSO) and the *gendarmerie* knows comparable units at three different levels. Small-scale and static observations are carried out by the "Monitoring and investigating brigade" (*Bewakings- en opsporingsbrigade* - BOB) in each of the districts, the "Platoon for observation, support and arrest" (*Peloton voor observatie, steun en arrestatie* - POSA) is

---

29   A parliamentary committee (the so-called *Bendecommissie* or Gang Committee) examined the (mal)functioning of the Belgian justice system during the investigation of some severe gang crimes and political terrorism in the seventies and eighties. See Van Parys & Laurent, 1990, p. 39-148. See also Fijnaut, 1983; Ponsaers & Dupont, 1986; Coveliers, 1992; Fijnaut, 1995, pp. 67-73. The subject of infiltration will be dealt with in detail in Chapter 5.

entrusted with larger-scale, mobile and static observations in each of Belgium's regions, and observations in large and important cases are done by the national "Special Intervention Squad" (*Speciaal interventie eskader* - SIE). The POSA and SIE are specialized in bigger-scale (for example international) observations and only operate on demand of other units of the *gendarmerie*.[30] Apart from these, most of the bigger municipal police forces have some kind of specialized observation service.[31]

Although observation has been applied by the Belgian police forces for a while now, there is little information on the subject. In legislation and case-law it has always been absent and in the legal and criminological doctrine it has hardly ever been discussed or even mentioned. Exceptions to this are the already mentioned book on the François case, the report of the Parliamentary Gang Committee and the report of the Dutch Van Traa committee, which all pay substantial attention to the phenomenon.[32]

As to the regulation framework in which police observation takes place, it was stated already that Belgium does not know any statutory regulation of this policing technique. In 1990, guidelines for the use of the covert policing techniques have been partly regulated in a number of confidential circulars, drafted by the ministry of justice.[33] In order to break the confidential character of these guidelines, the most important rules they contained were published in 1992, when an amendment was proposed to add these rules to the Police Function Act that was pending in parliament.[34] A complete statutory or otherwise publicly accessible regulation of these techniques has not yet been realized but the first step in that direction has been made. Since the summer of 1994,

---

30   Although this has not yet been confirmed, it is likely that this will *a fortiori* be the case for the SIE. On the relationship between the different Belgian observation units, see Brammertz *et al.*, 1993, pp. 21-22.
31   See for instance Boon *et al.*, 1991, pp. 111-119.
32   See Fijnaut, 1983; Van Parys & Laurent, 1990; and Van Traa, 1996, App. V, pp. 463-467.
33   Directives concerning special techniques of investigation to fight severe or organised crime (*Richtlijnen betreffende bijzondere opsporingstechnieken om de zware of georganiseerde criminaliteit te bestrijden*), April 24, 1990, Nr. 7/SDP/690/MN NIX/RB6/6. It seems that these directives have been amended and extended on March 5, 1992; see Hofstede *et al.*, p. 30 and Demanet, 1994, p. 157.
34   *Gedrukte stukken* 1991-1992, nr. 409/8; the proposal was rejected but thanks to Coveliers, most of the contents of the circulars was published anyway. Without referring to Coveliers' rejected proposal, some have shown their regrets that the Police Function Act does not contain any regulation regarding the covert policing techniques; see Hubin, 1994, p. 132 and Demanet, 1994, pp. 142 and 157. On certain issues, the amendment slightly differs from the circulars but in general it completely represents the ideas and principles of the circulars. Therefore the amendment itself will be left out of consideration.

Belgium knows a legal basis for telephone tapping and other forms of eaves-dropping and monitoring by the police and investigating authorities.[35]

In the circular, observation is defined as "an investigative technique during which the police uses persons and means in order to discretely gather information or evidence concerning certain persons or affairs" (nr. 10.1). The circular distinguishes between short-term and long-term observation and binds long-term observations as well as observations with the use of technical aides to more severe conditions: Besides proportionality and subsidiarity, these are mostly procedural conditions. Furthermore, the circular contains a general prohibition of the use of legally forbidden technical means. It is nevertheless unclear which means are illegal, since the new Interception of Communication Act seems to be the first one to prohibit overhearing, filming and other ways of spying without permission. The only exception to this lack of regulation is the secret of telephone conversations, which has been protected by a criminalization since 1930.

The use of observation and other special policing methods have to be restricted to the (repressive as well as proactive)[36] investigation of organized and severe gang crime.[37] This condition may also be found in nr. 10.2.2 of the circular and is, in a more detailed form, repeated in the second paragraph of art. 90ter par. 2 Sv as introduced by the Interception of Communication Act, which contains a catalogue of offences. Other than the directives however, the text of the Interception of Communication Act seems to exclude the use of observation for proactive purposes.[38] Long-term observation and observation with the use of technical means is only allowed when executed under supervision of the public prosecutor or investigating judge, who have the power to put the operation to an end when an irresponsible infringement of the privacy of individuals occurs (nrs. 10.3.1 and 10.3.2 of the circular). The Interception of Communication Act has introduced an even more severe restriction, stating that these methods can only be applied with a previous permission of the investigating judge (art. 90quater Sv).

According to nr. 10.3.3, other local police forces must be warned by special messages that an observation is going on in order to prevent problems of them intervening. In nr. 10.3.4, the circular underlines that the aim of observation should be that the gathered information may be used in court. This provision

---

35   Interception of Communication Act (ICAct), B.S. January 24, 1995, in force since February 3, 1995.

36   At least, no rule seems to stand in the way of proactive observation against these categories of offences; in the same sense Hofstede *et al.*, 1993, p. 31.

37   In the same sense already the minister of justice under whose supervision the circulars were drafted, M. Wathelet in the Report of the Gang Committee; see Van Parys & Laurent, 1990, p. 231.

38   In the same sense (to his own regrets) Berkmoes, 1994.

could be seen as a safeguard that the law and the directives will be respected by the police officers involved in the operations. However, because of the confidential character of the circulars, courts will not be able to put the evidence and the way it has been gathered to the test of the circulars.

Belgian police officers who are competent to proceed to a cross-border observation are those of the public prosecutor's judicial police, the *gendarmerie* and the municipal police. On the basis of bilateral agreements, for cases of crime concerning illicit drugs, arms and explosives, and illicit carriage of toxic or dangerous waste, customs officers may be entitled to cross-border observations as well.[39] In the following however, customs officers will be left out of consideration.

4.2.1.2 The Netherlands

Even though observation is a basic policing technique that - in the form of patrol - every police officer is familiar with, some forms of this technique, such as long-term observation (more than 24 hours without interruption, more than a week with interruptions) and observation with technical instruments have also become a specialisation.[40] Therefore, the Netherlands have founded specially selected, trained and equipped observation units. The activities of these units have been coordinated by the National contact group on observation (*Landelijke contactgroep observatie* - LCO) since 1972.[41]

Dutch legislation has never created any explicit statutory basis for observation. Like in Belgium, this policing method is the subject of ministerial guidelines, but other than the Belgian situation, the Dutch guidelines have been published officially in the form of a ministerial decree.[42] Another difference is that the Dutch guidelines deal with observation in an implicit way only. Their main subject is the gathering of criminal intelligence in general and the functioning of the criminal intelligence department (*Criminele inlichtingendienst*

---

39 A bilateral agreement of this kind was concluded with France in Schengen, June 19, 1990, J.O. 1995, p. 16443.

40 Figures about the frequency with which various observation methods and techniques have been applied in The Netherlands may be found in Van Traa, 1996, pp. 170-172.

41 Helsdingen, 1987, p. 23. Nowadays, this LCO is called LIPO, which stands for *Landelijk informatiepunt observatie* (National information point on observation). A similar contact service exists for cross-border observation; both are to be found at the CRI in Zoetermeer.

42 Furthermore, on December 21, 1995, the assembly of prosecutors-general introduced a number of terminological definitions for "special investigation methods" such as observation and infiltration, including criteria about examination, registration and control of the use of these methods. The list of terminology was published in for instance NJB 1996, pp. 107-108.

- CID),[43] which especially focuses on severe or frequently committed offences and organized crime. Information on suspects and eventual future criminals (proactive registration) may be registered and elaborated, whereas information on so-called grey field-subjects (persons regarding whom it is yet unsure whether they might become a CID-subject soon, for instance because they seem to stand in close contact with people already registered as CID-subjects), may be registered and elaborated provisorily.

The Dutch Supreme Court has decided that police officers are entitled to carry out observations on the basis of their general task description in art. 28 PolW 1957 (at present art. 2 PolW 1993), even before a criminal offence has actually been committed (proactive observation).[44] More generally, the right to privacy in the Netherlands is guaranteed by art. 10 of the Constitution (*Grondwet* - GW), as well as by some prohibitions in the Criminal Code. Exceptions to these prohibitions have been made for telephone tapping during a criminal inquiry, as well as for the overhearing of telephone and other private conversations by the secret service. Statutory law on similar exceptions for overhearing private conversations by the police is pending.[45] However, since the beginning of 1994, all forms of covert policing in The Netherlands are being discussed and criticized strongly. No new legislation on covert policing will be introduced before the closing debates about the parliamentary enquiry on policing methods in Spring 1996, and until then, the eavesdropping bill pending in the Senate will not be voted.

The Dutch police officers who are entitled to carry out cross-border observations are, according to art. 40 par. 4 SC, the officers of the state police (*rijkspolitie*) and the municipal police (*gemeentepolitie*). However, both these police forces were abolished and replaced by regional police forces in April, 1994. According to a declaration of the Dutch government, the relevant powers of state and municipal police will from that moment be exercised by "the officers, employed for the police task."[46] This refers to all officers of the regular, regional police forces and those of the National police services agency KLPD.[47] As did the original wording, the new text excludes cross-border observation by the *marechaussee*, who are indeed "charged with" several police tasks (art. 6 PolW 1993) but not "employed for the" police task. In addition, art. 40 par. 4 SC refers to the officers of the Fiscal information and research

---

43   1994 CID Regulation (*CID-regeling*), March 31, 1995, Stcrt. 1995, 74. These departments, which do not have any operational task, should not be confused with the British CID's (Criminal Investigation Departments).

44   HR October 14, 1986, NJ 1987, 564 and HR October 14, 1986, NJ 1988, 511.

45   *Wijziging van het Wetboek van Strafvordering in verband met de regeling van het opnemen van gesprekken met een technisch hulpmiddel*, TK 23 047, nrs. 1-2.

46   Declaration of November 25, 1994, Trb. 1995, 5, p. 2.

47   See art. 3 par. 1 PolW 1993.

service (FIOD) responsible for entry and excise. On the basis of bilateral agreements, they may be entitled for cross-border observation in cases of crime regarding drug, arms and explosives and toxic or dangerous waste.[48] A formal legal basis for cross-border observation by other special enforcement services does not exist, although in practice, such observations do seem to occur.[49]

4.2.1.3 Luxembourg

In Luxembourg, general provisions of statutory law or of another nature with regard to observation during criminal inquiries do not exist. In practice the use of this method is considered allowed on the basis of the general regulation of police powers as found in art. 9-2 CIC: "The criminal police is (...) charged with the constatation of offences against the Criminal Code, the collection of evidence and the investigation of the authors (...)." However, the use of technical means for the interception of communication for investigative purposes does have a legal basis in art. 88-1 CIC.

According to Luxembourg police officers, the Grand Duchy knows a practice of observation that is mainly based on the same rules as the ones that are written down in the Belgian guidelines, in which practice specialized general observation units (such as the *gendarmerie*'s *Groupe d'observation*) play a role as well.[50] Luxembourg does not know any general constitutional provisions on privacy, but the Protection of Private Life Act criminalizes breaches of privacy by overhearing or observing conversations or meetings in private places.[51] The same provisions also protect the privacy of letters and states that telephone tapping and opening of letters can be allowed under certain circumstances.

Luxembourg police officers who are competent to carry out cross-border observations are those of the *gendarmerie* and the police. Furthermore, on the basis of bilateral agreements, customs officers may be entrusted with the same tasks as far as it concerns illicit traffic and carriage of drugs, arms and explosives, and toxic and dangerous waste.[52] In the following, customs officers will however be left out of consideration.

---

48 Until the end of December 1995, such bilateral agreements were unknown.
49 In this sense Van Traa, 1996, App. V, pp. 442-444.
50 Rambach, 1993, pp. 462-463.
51 Artt. 2-3 of the *Loi concernant la protection de la vie privée*, August 11, 1982, Mém. 1982, 1840.
52 The only bilateral agreements of this kind known was concluded with France in Schengen, June 19, 1990, J.O. 1995, p. 16444.

4.2.1.4 France

General statutory or other provisions on police observation in general do not exist in French law. Indeed, there are statutes on the use of static video cameras on the streets and the use of wire tapping, but these regulations, which will be discussed later, do not have a general character. Under certain conditions, the use of observation in general as a policing technique has been allowed by the courts, as long as no compulsory methods are used and the dignity of justice is respected. This may also contain a certain respect for the privacy, a right which is not explicitly mentioned by the Constitution, but has been recognized by the Constitutional Council as being one aspect of the individual liberty as guaranteed by the 1789 declaration of rights.[53] Furthermore, some privacy protection is offered by provisions in the new Criminal Code (*Nouveau Code Pénal* - NCP) that, just like its predecessor, criminalizes the breach of domicile and the privacy of letters, as well as the overhearing or observing of conversations or meetings in private and public places with technical means, if this infringes the privacy of the participants.[54] The French Schengen circular does surprisingly mention the use of observation on French territory by foreign police officers,[55] and somewhat elaborates the concept of observation.[56] It specifies that observing officers may for instance make various acknowledgements and photographs, may record spontaneous statements of witnesses and seizes objects offered voluntarily; they may however not proceed to the interception of telecommunication.

France does not know any specialized observation units, although some services evidently have more experience in this field than others.[57] According to a spokesman, the main reason for not having specialized units is the fact that most of the general police forces do not have the technical and financial means to systematically execute long-term observations. A general allowance to carry out such measures is considered to be contained in the police's general task description in art. 75 CPP: "(They) carry out preliminary enquiries, be it according to the public prosecutor's directions or ex officio."[58]

---

53 *Conseil constitutionnel*, January 12, 1977, published in Favoreu & Philip, 1991, pp. 258-260.
54 Respectively in artt. 226-4, 226-15 and 432-9, and 226-1 CP. The new Criminal Code of France has been in force since March 1, 1994. Art. 368 of the former *Code Pénal* did not forbid the overhearing or observing of private meetings in public places.
55 As well as the observation by French officers on foreign territory.
56 *Circulaire du 23 juin 1995 commentant des dispositions des articles 39, 40 et 41 de la convention signée à Schengen le 19 juni 1990*, NOR: *JUSA9500149C*.
57 A police unit with special experience in this field is for instance the Anti-gang Brigade, as described in Moréas, 1985.
58 Lasalle, 1990, nrs. 42 and 55; Lorenz, 1993, p. 336.

In art. 40 par. 4 SC, the competent French police officers for cross-border observation have been mentioned. The first among them are the officers and agents of judicial police (*agents et officiers de police judiciaire*) of both the *gendarmerie* and the police and. In addition, France has recently published bilateral agreements with Belgium, Luxembourg and Germany stating that, with respect to their powers regarding illicit traffic in drugs, arms and explosives, and toxic or dangerous waste, observations in the sense of art. 40 SC may be carried out by customs officers as well.[59] Customs officers will however be left out of consideration in the rest of this study.

4.2.1.5 Germany

In Germany, the federal Constitutional Court (*Bundesverfassungsgericht*) has decided that the constitutional protection of individual freedom (as guaranteed by the articles 1 and 2 of the Constitution (*Grundgesetz*) also implies an individual right to informational self-determination (*informationelle Selbstbestimmung*), the right to decide and to know for which purposes personal data are to be used.[60] An important consequence of this decision is that a basis in statutory law is required for every police measure infringing the private life of individuals. The German legislation on this matter therefore contains, both on a federal level and in the statutory law of the provinces (*Länder*), a great number of more or less detailed rules as to the gathering of personal data by police operations, including observation.

The matter is dealt with in the (federal) Code of Criminal Procedure (*Strafprozeßordnung* - StPO), that was altered in this sense by the Organized Crime Act,[61] as well as in the Police Acts (*Polizeigesetze*) of almost each of the sixteen provinces.[62] The federal rules are restricted to situations of repressive policing (that is after a suspicion has risen that a crime has been committed), whereas the provincial acts are not meant to regulate criminal proceedings but to create rules and powers for preventive and proactive policing. As we will see later on, German law also distinguishes different types of observation. Apart from these provisions on procedure and powers, the German

---

59   Agreements concluded in Schengen, June 19, 1990, J.O. 1995. pp. 16443-16445.
60   BVerfG December 15, 1983, BVerfGE 65, 1; also published in NJW 1984, pp. 418 *et seq*.
61   Act for Combatting the Illicit Traffic of Narcotic Drugs and Other Manifestations of Organized Crime (*Gesetz zur Bekämpfung des illegalen Rauschgifthandels und anderer Erscheinungsformen der Organisierten Kriminalität*), BGBl. I, 1992, 1302. It has been in force since September 22, 1992.
62   Note that the situation in Germany, where this matter is regulated in more than twenty different statutes (Constitution, Criminal code, Code of criminal procedure and the legislation on the federal police forces (BKA and BGS), and Police Acts of 16 federal provinces), is too complicated to present more than a rather generalised summary.

Criminal Code (*Strafgesetzbuch* - StGB) also protects the privacy of citizens by prohibiting the breach of domicile, the infringement of the privacy of letters and the overhearing of telephone and other private conversations without permission.[63]

It should be remarked that the fact that proactive policing is regulated in provincial law has caused and still causes a great deal of discussion. Dogmatically, it cannot be regulated in the (federal) Code of Criminal Procedure, since this can only be used after the "threshold of suspicion" (*Verdachtsschwelle*) of art. 152 StPO has been crossed by the constatation of an offence that has been committed.[64] Objections against this are that proactive policing finally does have a criminal investigative intention (the prosecution of future criminal offences) and, as long as it is not a part of criminal procedure but of police law, the judicial authorities have very few means of control and the police has a great deal of autonomy.[65]

Germany knows different types of observation units: Based on a decision of all the ministers of the interior together, every German province has a so-called Effective mobile unit (*Mobiles Einsatz Kommando* - MEK). These units do not operate in the general field of severe crime, but were founded and trained especially for cases of kidnapping and terrorism. In addition to these MEK's, the provincial criminal police offices (LKA's) of most provinces also know observation teams that work on drug-cases and other sorts of crime,[66] and offer technical and tactical support to the MEK's. At a federal level, observation teams entrusted with severe, organized, interprovincial and international crime may be found within the federal criminal police office BKA.[67]

Regarding cross-border observation, art. 40 par. 4 SC states that this is entrusted to all officers of both the federal and the provincial police forces. Furthermore, in cases of illicit drug traffic and traffic in arms and explosives, those officers of the customs investigation service (*Zollfahndungsdienst*) who are auxiliary officers of the public prosecutor may carry out cross-border observations as well.

---

63 These may be found in artt. 201-205 StGB.
64 Roxin, 1993, p. 265.
65 For this discussion, we refer to for instance Weßlau, 1989; Wolter, 1991, pp. 30-33; Hund, 1991; Kniesel, 1992; Denninger, 1992, pp. 169-173; Busch, 1995, pp. 169-179.
66 Tabarelli, 1987, p. 81.
67 According to a high-ranked German police officer near the Belgian and Dutch borders, there have been numerous cases of cross-border observation in the past. However, since there was no official regulation and German ministers of the interior opposed against cross-border observations by German police officers, they were not documented or registered as such. In individual cases, they were usually approved by the judicial authorities afterwards.

4.2.2   The Use of Technical Means

As we have noted above, art. 40 of the Schengen Convention states that a cross border observing police officer is both bound to the provisions of the Convention and to the national law of the country where he is operating. Furthermore, he will indeed be bound to the law of his own country as well. Therefore, in order to know which observation methods a cross-border observing officer is authorized to use, we have to study the Convention as well as the law of all five of the countries. Art. 40 of the Schengen Convention does not contain any conditions as to the methods that are used during observation. The Convention therefore neither allows nor excludes the use of technical devices during cross-border observation, whereas recent developments show that at least some operational tendencies in this direction do exist, especially in the field of enabling cross-border telephone tapping.[68]

In this section, we will discuss the regulation regarding observation methods with technical means in the five countries. This will include legal provisions criminalizing the use of some techniques, but also - as far as existing - statutory legislation containing concrete police powers and relevant provisions in other than statutory regulations such as guidelines.[69] In order to enable comparison of the regulations, we decided to divide the regulations with the help of two criteria: the place where the measure is used (because of the different extents of the intrusion) and the type of technical means: optical or acoustical (mainly because this division can be found in the legislation of most countries as well).

4.2.2.1 Optical Devices in Public Areas

The first type of sophisticated observation to be discussed is the use of optical devices in public areas, which may range from binoculars and photo cameras to automatic video equipment with telescopic lenses and infra-red light.

---

68   An inquiry of this possibility was proposed by the former Dutch minister of justice, E.M.H. Hirsch Ballin and is actually being discussed within the so-called K.4 Committee.

69   This distinction between "weak" allowances, that are based on the lack of a prohibition, and "strong allowances," based on an explicitly created power, can be found in for instance Soeteman, 1994 p. 71. See also Cleiren, 1992, p. 17-18 who, for the distinction between "primary rules of obligation" and "secondary rules," refers to Hart, 1961.

146

Belgium
The use of optical devices during police investigations has not been regulated in Belgian statutory law.[70] This does not mean that such techniques are not applied: the report of the Gang Committee shows that at least they are used by the *gendarmerie*'s SIE, be it under control of an officer of judicial police and with permission of the judicial authorities.[71]

The only regulation on this subject in force at this moment are the above mentioned confidential guidelines, nr. 1 of which restricts the application of so-called "special investigative techniques" to cases of organized crime.[72] Nr. 10.1 of these guidelines states that observation with technical means potentially infringing the privacy of the observed or others is allowed and may be applied against a suspect of a criminal act and in order to gather evidence of this. In comparison to short-term observation and observation without technical means, this method is bound to special conditions. The special conditions aimed at are mentioned in 10.3: besides proportionality and subsidiarity, they include an important role for the public prosecutor and the investigating judge. These magistrates have to be notified of every long-term or technical observation at the moment the operation starts or as soon as possible afterward. They may decide that the operation must be interrupted or stopped in case the infringement is too invasive.

Nr. 10.2 of the guidelines states that the use of legally forbidden technical devices is not allowed, but the guidelines do not explain for which devices such is the case or even where such criminalizations could be found. As to the use of cameras, the Belgian Criminal Code does not contain any prohibitions, and numerous types of technically advanced photo and video equipment are freely available.[73] Moreover, guideline nr. 2.4 also allows that in some situations criminal offences be committed by the police, as long as this is in accordance with the public prosecutor's department.[74] In practice, this accordance seems to be hard to reach.[75]

---

70   Note that the Schengen circular, when referring to the obligation that "technical documents, such as photo's and audio or video tapes be added to the reports," recognizes the possibility that such techniques are used during observation.

71   Van Parys & Laurent, 1990, pp. 322-324. More recent examples of the use of cameras in public, for reasons of prevention as well as for criminal investigation and public order, are mentioned by Gutwirth, 1995, p. 3.

72   In the same sense the minister of justice under whose supervision the circulars were drafted, M. Wathelet in the report of the Gang Committee (Van Parys & Laurent, 1990, p. 231).

73   De Hert, 1994, p. 15.

74   Rambach, 1993, p. 39, also seems to come to the conclusion that exceptions to the prohibition to use legally forbidden equipment can be imagined.

75   At least, a complaint in this sense was uttered by the commander of the *gendarmerie*'s central investigation office *Centraal Bureau Opsporingen* (CBO); see Berkmoes, 1994.

According to the guidelines, the aim of the use of observation and other special investigative methods is to gather information that can be admitted in court (for instance in nr. 10.3). The admissibility of evidence gathered with the use of technical observation devices will always be judged by the court. Has a rule been broken that intends to protect the rights of the suspect as a party in the procedure, then the evidence gathered should be excluded (exclusionary rule).[76] The exclusionary rule however only protects the rights of the suspect as a party to the trial and does not offer any protection of privacy against activities such as gathering information with video equipment.[77] Central criteria will be, if the principles of proportionality and subsidiarity were respected: Therefore the measure must not be too severe in comparison to the investigated crime and the same result can not be realized with other methods.

Since February 1995, however, when the new Interception of Communication Act came into force, art. 314bis Sw offers a criminalization of recording, eavesdropping or spying on "any form of private communication or telecommunication," as long as the interception takes place with a technical device whatsoever, and except for the situation that all participants to the communication agree. Higher penalties have been introduced for police and other public officers who commit one of these offences within the framework of their task (art. 259bis Sw) and in both cases, preparing the commission of the offence is criminalized as well. In addition, art. 90ter Sv has created an explicit statutory basis for a police power to record, eavesdrop or spy on "any form of private communication or tele-communication" with the help of a device of any kind. Main condition for the use of this power is that the application of such measures be necessary for combatting one of the criminal offences mentioned in art. 90ter par. 2 Sv, which provision contains what the government summarized as "severe crime, especially terrorism, gang crime and organized crime."[78] According to the Belgian government, the word private should be interpreted extensively; the only decisive yard-stick on this point will be the character of the communication.[79] Therefore, the interception of a conversation in a person's living-room

---

76 Van den Wyngaert, 1994, pp. 760-761; Cass. August 17, 1979, Pas. 1979, I, 1309.
77 De Wilde, 1988, p. 70 and footnote 53; Holsters, 1990, pp. 5-6.
78 Explanatory statement, *Gedrukte stukken* 1992-1993, nr. 843/1, p. 12; the article itself contains a detailed catalogue of criminal offences that may be investigated with this technique: Assault and conspiracy against the royal family and the government, the taking of hostages, some severe threatenings, threatening with nuclear substances or theft of such substances in order to do so, indecent assault on or prostitution of minors, manslaughter, murder, armed robbery, aggravated theft or extortion, money laundering, severe arson, several organised drug offences, illegal traffic of firearms, as well as attempt to one of these offences (par. 3).
79 Explanatory statement, *Gedrukte stukken* 1992-1993, nr. 843/1, p. 3.

can be just as much a criminal offence as the interception of the same conversation on a lively square in the center of a city.[80]

Both the criminalizing and regulating provision apply to all kinds of communication in every type of language (the government has used the word utterance (*taaluiting* or *énoncé*) to express this).[81] On the one hand, this large interpretation of the word communication means that all sorts of modern communication techniques, such as radio waves, telefax and computer mail or e-mail, are included as well. On the other hand however, this language-bound interpretation excludes the application of both provisions to general actions and activities. Does this mean that the police (and, actually, any ordinary citizen) are allowed to spy on private actions that can not be qualified as communication, such as buying and selling, negotiating, preparing transports? And how about registering the frequency with which a certain place is visited by people with raincoats and violin cases, or spying on people's behaviour inside their own residences, as long as the "spy" does not infringe with the domestic peace? These actions do not seem to be covered by the criminalization, nor by the regulated power, whereas they certainly do invade the individual's private sphere.

A restriction in the proposed bill is that it only applies to the interception with the help of a technical device. As a consequence, the observation of private communications without the use of technical means will not be criminalized, notwithstanding the infringement with the privacy that such an action implies.

The Netherlands
Dutch law does not offer much information on the use of optical devices in public. A regulation in statutory law or even in guidelines of this observation technique does not exist, and the criminalization in art. 441b Sr only applies to filming or video-taping with cameras in shops, cafes and restaurants by the owner or manager without this use being mentioned to the public.[82] The bill on eavesdropping that is pending in parliament since spring 1993 does not intend to introduce a regulation of this method either.

Since the method in general is not explicitly prohibited, it could be considered as being in principle allowed. The Dutch Supreme Court has even decided explicitly that photographs, taken from an alleged suspect who was

---

80   In that case however, it will be more difficult to establish the private character of the communication.
81   Explanatory statement, *Gedrukte stukken* 1992-1993, nr. 843/1, p. 7.
82   In this sense Wesselius, 1994, p. 18.

observed in public, could be admitted as evidence.[83] This might imply that the police are even entitled to apply "fishing expeditions," investigating persons and waiting for them to commit a criminal offence.[84] In any case, there is no doubt that the central criteria will be, if the principles of proportionality and subsidiarity were respected. The measure must not be too severe in comparison to the crime and there must be no other, less intrusive ways that could lead to the same result.

In a civil case, the Dutch Supreme Court once had to judge the activities of a man who had gathered information on the social and private life of a female neighbour on welfare, which information he had given to the local welfare department. The court decided that this operation was illegal, because of the infringement with the woman's right to privacy according to art. 8 ECHR.[85] Because of this, one can wonder whether the police may use non-stop and long-term video observation of the entrance to a private house that is frequently visited by persons who are under suspicion of criminal activities. Since this is a rather obvious infringement with the right to privacy as protected by art. 10 of the Dutch Constitution and art. 8 ECHR, a statutory basis seems to be necessary.[86] This applies even stronger to the method of filming what happens inside a private place with a technical device installed outside of this place, that is to say, if this can still be considered as using optical instruments "in public."[87]

Luxembourg

A regulation of observation with the use of technical devices has existed in Luxembourg since 1982. It introduced the power to apply technical means during the observation of "all kinds of communication," if such is necessary for the investigation of a crime that can be punished with imprisonment of at least two years (art. 88-1 CIC). This regulation apparently does not cover the use of optical techniques for spying on a suspect or alleged suspect, unless the activity that is being watched could be considered a form of communication.

The Luxembourg Penal Code does not contain a criminalization of spying on an individual's non-communicative activities and therefore does not seem to stand in the way of this investigative method. According to experts, the power

---

83 HR June 25, 1985, NJ 1986, 109, with annotation by Th.W. Van Veen; HR October 13, 1992, NJ 1993, 223, and HR May 9, 1995, NJ 1995, 672, both with annotation by T.M. Schalken. According to Wesselius (1994, p. 18), this would also be the case with films or video registrations originating the illegal use of a camera in a shop or restaurant.

84 See T.M. Schalken in his annotation to HR October 13, 1992, NJ 1993, 223, particularly p. 832.

85 HR January 9, 1987, NJ 1987, 928, with an annotation by E.A. Alkema.

86 See Corstens, 1995, pp. 279-280.

87 Van Traa, 1994, p. 24; see also Naeyé, 1995b, pp. 269-284.

introduced by art. 88-1 CIC is used only for the interception of verbal or written communication, such as telephone calls, letters, and telex and telefax messages.[88] However, there are some indications that the Luxembourg police do indeed also apply cameras for observation.[89]

France
Since January 21, 1995, France knows an explicit statutory basis for the use of optical observation techniques in public.[90] On the basis of this *Loi sécurité*, the public authorities may install video cameras at the public road wherever they judge this necessary for the protection of public interests and security. Most important restriction regarding the position of the cameras is, that they may not be specifically aimed at entrances to private domiciles or show the interior of such premises. Note that the *Loi sécurité* only regulates static observation and does not address the subject of mobile observation of an individual followed or otherwise focused upon by the police.

Article 226-1 of France's new Criminal Code prohibits several forms of observation with a technical device, unless the device is used overtly. It distinguishes between optical and acoustical observation: The first is criminalized when it includes photographing or filming of a person in a private area without this person's consent. For the latter, not the place of the observation but its private character is decisive. Therefore one can conclude *a contrario* that the French legislator did not want to introduce a criminalization for optical observation in public areas and therefore filming or photographing a suspect by police officers is an essentially allowed investigative method.[91] In fact, this technique is even widely used against traffic offenders, an aim that is now also mentioned explicitly in the *Loi sécurité*.

As a consequence, evidence gathered with the help of modern optical registration devices in principle can be admitted in court.[92] This is confirmed by the Schengen circular of the French minister of justice, which does indeed (although in a strongly limited sense) address the observation with optical means, stating that foreign police officers in France may for instance use photo cameras. Other optical devices such as video equipment are left unmentioned, but the circular recalls the condition that French law must be respected.[93] Like all types of evidence this kind of information will be put to the test of the

---

88   These experts were interviewed by Rambach (1993, p. 463).
89   This was related to us by a police officer and confirmed by a other sources.
90   *Loi no. 95-73 du 21 janvier d'orientation et de programmation relative à la sécurité*, J.O. January 24, 1995; see De Hert & Gutwirth, 1995, pp. 221-224.
91   This means a correction of the view expressed in Bevers, 1993, p. 92.
92   For instance Crim. July 23, 1992, Bull. Crim. nr. 274.
93   *Circulaire du 23 juin 1995 commentant des dispositions des articles 39, 40 et 41 de la convention signée à Schengen le 19 juni 1990*, NOR: *JUSA9500149C*.

general principles of French criminal law (loyalty, dignity of justice, secrecy and non-coercive character of the investigation). In case these principles were not respected, the information will have to be excluded.

Germany

An explicit statutory basis for photographing and filming an individual's activities as a police investigation method exists on a federal level (for the investigation of already committed crimes) as well in most of the provinces (where the measure must serve a preventive or proactive purpose).[94] It will always depend on the case in question if the gathered information is accepted as evidence. Central criteria will be the principles of proportionality and subsidiarity, thus the measure must not be too severe in comparison with the investigated crime and no less intrusive methods might lead to the same result.

According to German law, gathering information of what happens inside a private domicile,[95] even when this observation is done with a technical apparatus placed on the outside, is considered as observation in a private area.[96] By some provincial legislators, this form of observation has been submitted to other provisions and conditions.[97] According to the Federal Court of Justice (*Bundesgerichtshof*), a specific statutory basis is necessary for long-term video observation of the entrance to a private residence as well since such an operation would constitute an infringement with the privacy of the individual.[98] However, since the introduction of art. 100c StPO by the Organized Crime Act, such a statutory basis does exist.

4.2.2.2 Optical Devices in Private Areas

When it comes to observation with optical devices in private areas, the situation is quite different since the inviolability of the home is involved. This right is explicitly guaranteed by art. 8 of the European Convention and in fact all five countries know criminalizations of the infringement with the domestic privacy,

---

94 See for instance artt. 100c par. 1 StPO, 15 and 17 NWPolG, 25b RhPfPVG, and 27-28 SPolG.

95 In the interpretation given to art. 13 GG, this concept is not restricted to the house only, but also includes such places as basement, garage, inner court or garden, caravan, tent, boat. It even extends to working areas, as long as they are not accessible for the general public; Pieroth & Schlink, 1989, p. 225.

96 Roxin, 1993, p. 55.

97 See for instance art. 17 par. 2 NWPolG, that restricts the use of this method to cases of danger for a person's life, physical integrity or freedom.

98 BGH May 14, 1991, published in NJW 1991, pp. 2651-2652 and Kruse, 1993, p. 183. Different from the opinion of the *Bundesgerichtshof*, Kramer (1992, pp. 2732-2738) concludes that the application of this technique would be allowed on the basis of the general investigation power regulated in art. 163 StPO.

combined with exceptions for investigative measures like search of premises by police or judicial authorities.[99]

Belgium

The Belgian guidelines on observation allow the use of technical means for the repressive and proactive combatting of organized and severe gang crime, as long as this happens under direct supervision of the public prosecutor or the investigating judge and unless legally forbidden technical devices are used. Whether the results can be admitted as evidence will depend on the proportionality and subsidiarity in the concrete case. The new Interception of Communication Act will only be applicable to optical observation methods in the almost hypothetical situation that an image reveals some form of communication, like two people using sign language or writing down information for each other. In that case, the new statute imposes some strict norms regarding the cases in which communication may be intercepted: Art. 90ter par. 2 Sv restricts this to severe offences in the sphere of organized crime and terrorism and submits the application of this interception to previous permission by the investigating judge (art. 90quater Sv).

According to Belgian statutory law, secret photographing or filming of an individual's activities is not explicitly forbidden or penalized, irrespective as to this photographing or the activities take place in private or public areas. When the observation takes place in or from a private area without the consent of the occupant, the operation should be considered as breach of domicile, which is criminalized by art. 439 and 440 Sw and therefore not allowed as an investigative method. Observation from a public into a private place could perhaps be considered allowed on the basis of the permissive rule, since no offences are being committed.[100] On the other hand, one could wonder whether this infringement with the privacy of domestic and family life without an explicit and clear legal basis is in accordance with art. 22 of the Belgian Constitution and the European Court's case-law on the right to privacy guaranteed by art. 8 ECHR.

The Netherlands

Under Dutch law, the use of secretly taken photographs of a person in a private place is criminalized under art. 139f Sr, when this can possibly damage the legal interests of the person being photographed. The provision also restricts the

---

99 The question has been asked, whether or not art. 8 ECHR forces the member states to legally protect the inviolability of the home, for instance by criminal legislation on infringements with the domestic privacy. This question will not be addressed in this context but is discussed by Cohen-Jonathan, 1993, p. 427.

100 In this sense Dierkens *et al.*, 1991, p. 494.

possibilities for the police to take photographs during a criminal inquiry: When a criminal is caught in the act, pictures of the scene may be used as evidence, but filming an alleged criminal in his home in order to gather information about his contacts or his way of life has to be considered an illegal breach of his privacy and is therefore not allowed.[101] Moreover, such an operation would form an illegal infringement with the observed's privacy,[102] and as a result the information gathered would not be admissible as evidence in court.[103]

Evidently, this is also the case when optical technical means are used in a private area without permission of the occupant, since such an operation would in general mean a breach of domicile as criminalized by art. 138 Sr. In that case, pictures of a caught in the act-situation would not be admissible as evidence either, since they would be obtained by criminal offence. In case the video equipment had been installed by a shop-owner or a manager of a restaurant without an explicit warning to the clients, this person would commit a criminal act according to art. 441b Sr. Nevertheless, this would not necessarily mean that the information gathered this way would not be admissible as evidence, unless the police were aware that the camera had been installed or used.[104]

A specific form of optical observation in places which are not accessible to the public has recently been the cause of fierce discussions. It was revealed that the police exercised so-called peeking operations (*(in)kijkoperaties*) in such places, for instance in order to verifying if it is worth asking an official search warrant for the premises.[105] According to the Supreme Court, such a peeking operation could be based on art. 9 par. 1 sub b of the Dutch Opium Act (OW), which allows police officers to enter places where a drug offence is being committed or suspected to be committed.[106] According to the minister of justice, operations are illegal if they involve entering private houses or other forms of breach of domicile.[107] Note that after the initial commotion around this method, the assembly of prosecutors-general issued a confidential manual for peeking operations.[108]

---

101 In the same sense Remmelink, commenting this provision in Noyon/Langemeijer/Remmelink.
102 In this sense HR January 9, 1987, NJ 1987, 928, annotated by E.A. Alkema.
103 In this sense for instance Knoester, 1994, p. 565.
104 In this sense Wesselius, 1994, p. 18.
105 These operations were criticized by for instance Corstens, 1994a, pp. 497-498 and Blom & Mevis, 1995, pp. 5-27, while they were supported by for instance Pieters & Revis, 1995, pp. 401-407. See also Van Traa, 1994, pp. 21-23 and 68, as well as Naeyé, 1995a, pp. 25-27.
106 HR May 31, 1994, NJ 1995, 29 with annotation by G. Knigge; in the same sense the Court of Appeals, Amsterdam, December 1, 1994, NJ 1995, 159.
107 In this sense, a question of members of parliament Kalsbeek and Stoffelen was answered on April 5, 1994, TK *Aanhangsel van de Handelingen* 1993-1994, nr. 417. This restriction seems to be respected, as was concluded in Van Traa, 1996, p. 183.
108 December 7, 1994; it has meanwhile been published in Van Traa, 1996, App. I.

Besides the verification whether it is worth asking a search warrant and return for a catch in the act, peeking also seems to be carried out for other, more tactical goals such as placing cameras, or more trivial ones such as changing the batteries of a position transmitter.[109] Whether this will be allowed on the basis of the same legal provision is however more disputable.[110] The same is the case with peeking operations during other than drug investigations. Some state that this would be possible in the context of the power of prosecutor and police to carry out a survey (*schouw*) as referred to in artt. 150 and 158 Sv,[111] but meanwhile the Supreme Court has decided that this is not a sufficient basis for such operations.[112]

Luxembourg
On the basis of art. 88-1 CIC Luxembourg investigating police officers may control and intercept any type of communication, in public as well as in private, provided that such is necessary for investigating a crime punishable with imprisonment of two years or more and only with permission of the investigating judge. However, as we saw above this provision only applies when the optically observed scene can be considered a form of communication, like gestures and written utterances. A legal provision of statutory law or of another nature, creating a general investigative power to apply optical technical devices during an observation operation at private or public places, is unknown.

On the other hand, Luxembourg law does contain a criminalization that could be applied in such situations. Art. 2 sub 2 of the Private Life Act prohibits "the observation (...) with any technical instrument, of a person in a place that is not accessible to the public and without the person's consent, by setting or transmitting his picture (...)."[113] According to this provision, the decisive element whether or not photographing a person in a private place is a criminal act, is the permission of the photographed.

It is obvious that permission cannot be said to have been given in case the observation was only possible thanks to breach of domicile (which is criminalized by art. 148 CP). Moreover, the offence would also be committed by someone who, standing outside the house, would make a photograph of the occupant's activities inside without the observed person's permission. Evidence gathered this way would not be admissible in court.

---

109   *Bij inkijkoperaties worden vooral batterijen gewisseld*; in: de Volkskrant, February 9, 1995.
110   See also Blom & Mevis, 1995, p. 5 footnote 2.
111   Pieters & Revis, 1995, p. 404.
112   HR December 19, 1995 (Zwolsman-case), publication forthcoming in NJ 1996 with annotation by T.M. Schalken.
113   Private Life Act (*Loi concernant la protection de la vie privée*), August 11, 1982; Mém. 1982, 1840.

France

In his Schengen circular, the French minister of justice addresses the observation with optical means, stating that foreign police officers in France may for instance use photo cameras. Other optical devices such as video equipment are left unmentioned, and the circular does not explicitly mention the use of cameras in private places, but it does recall the condition that French law must be respected.[114]

Art. 226-1 CP contains a clear prohibition of photographing or filming a person in a private area without his consent.[115] Statutory law or other legal provisions creating an exception to this criminalization for purposes of criminal investigation do not exist. The *Loi sécurité* mentioned above explicitly excludes that video cameras be aimed directly at private premises, particularly the interiors of private domiciles,[116] and the Schengen circular is not sufficiently specified to create such an exception. Therefore, it is irrelevant to consider the fact that breach of domicile in order to make such pictures, would also be a criminal offence itself (artt. 226-4 and 432-8 CP).

Germany

Secretly taking photographs of an individual, even in private places, is not explicitly forbidden or penalized under German criminal law unless, of course, this action is combined with breach of domicile, this being a criminal offence under art. 123 and 124 StGB. In the German system of criminal investigation powers, this does not imply however that the application of this type of operation by the police is allowed. As we have shown above, the use of a video camera for observation of the outside of the entrance to a private residence is considered an infringement to the privacy that ought to find its basis in statutory law.[117] Thus it is obvious that this is *a fortiori* the case for optical observation inside a private area. Art. 100c StPO does offer a legal basis for the use of optical instruments during observation. In his explanatory statement on the Organized Crime Act the Federal council (*Bundesrat*, that represents the provinces of the federation and took the initiative for this bill) explains that the possibility to apply this technique is restricted to areas that are not protected

---

114 *Circulaire du 23 juin 1995 commentant des dispositions des articles 39, 40 et 41 de la convention signée à Schengen le 19 juni 1990*, NOR: *JUSA9500149C.*

115 See art. 226-1 CP. Some authors used to think that this criminalization did not stand in the way of interferences with the private life when these interferences were carried out by or based on an order given by the investigating judge. However, since the judgement of the European Court on Human Rights in the Kruslin & Huvig cases, it is clear that this interpretation cannot be considered in accordance with art. 8 of the Convention; see Blontrock & De Hert, 1991, pp. 865-871.

116 De Hert & Gutwirth, 1995, p. 223.

117 BGH May 14, 1991, NJW 1991, pp. 2651-2652.

by art. 13 GG, this provision aiming at the protection of the privacy of the home. Therefore, art. 100c StPO may not be considered a sufficient legal basis for this technique as a criminal investigation method. For the same reason, it is not allowed to use photo or video apparatus outside a private home with the intention of recording the activities taking place inside.[118] This will indeed be different if there is no indication that the observed person intends to protect the private character of his activities, for instance if he may be seen easily from the street through an open window.[119]

Most of the German provinces have allowed the use of photo and video observation techniques in private areas for the prevention of immediate danger.[120] Moreover, in some of them this technique may also be used for collecting information on persons who are under suspicion of preparing an offence out of a catalogue of severe crimes (proactive observation in the context of preventive crime-fighting).[121]

4.2.2.3 Acoustical Devices in Public Areas

When observation operations are executed in public areas, the use of acoustical devices causes a more severe intrusion of privacy than the use of optical devices. Whereas the latter usually only magnify or record scenes that in principle can be seen anyway, the former makes it possible to amplify and record sounds that normally would be impossible to hear. Moreover, usually the words expressed by a person give more information with regard to his (future) intentions than his gestures do. Maybe partly due to this difference, the legislators generally have paid more attention to the regulation of the use of acoustical devices in public than to the use of optical devices.

A very specific type of acoustical observation device, that is used in public but does not help transmitting or recording conversations, is the beeper or position transmitter. It transmits a signal that is received by the observing police officers and frequently indicates the position of the followed person or object. With the help of a beeper it is much easier to trace an observed person's address or shelter, contact persons or hide-out for contraband or ransom. According to the Dutch government, the Schengen partners intend to use the same frequencies for position transmitters in the future.[122]

---

118   Roxin, 1993, p. 55.
119   In a similar sense, Kleinknecht/Meyer-Goßner (1995, p. 303) state that it will be allowed to
        register a conversation in public that can be overheard without any special efforts.
120   For instance artt. 17 par. 2 NWPolG and 28 par. 4 SPolG.
121   For instance artt. 33 par. 2 BayPAG and 25b RhPfPVG.
122   TK 22 140, nr. 12 p. 35.

Belgium

Since early 1995, a prohibition of the technical interception of communications with a private character may be found in art. 314bis Sw. This prohibition was introduced by the Interception of Communication Act, which also covers the use of acoustical devices during an observation operation in public (art. 90ter Sv). This provision creates a police power to use technical devices in order to intercept and record or otherwise register all forms of private communication, when such an operation is necessary for the investigation of one of the severe criminal offences mentioned in the second paragraph of art. 90ter Sv. The use of this eavesdropping technique will be bound to prior permission by the investigating judge (art. 90quater Sv). Since art. 314bis Sw criminalizes the interception of private communication without all participants knowing, the procedure of art. 90ter Sv must be respected for the use of an infiltrator carrying a body transmitter (wired infiltrator) as well.[123]

The Interception of Communication Act does not create a power for proactive eavesdropping, since the legislator only intended to regulate eavesdropping in repressive investigations. The criminalization of art. 314bis Sw does however not distinguish between repressive, proactive or other goals intended. The proactive overhearing and recording of private conversations, which seemed to be possible on the basis of the guidelines before 1995, are criminalized now and therefore not allowed anymore.[124]

Not being explicitly forbidden, the use of position transmitters may be considered allowed as a technical means on the basis of the guidelines, be it under the special conditions of supervision by the investigating judge or public prosecutor and only for combatting severe organized and gang crime.[125] Because a position transmitter may not be considered a means of communication, the Interception of Communication Act did not change the basis of this method in the guidelines. Indeed, if a position transmitter is applied that may serve the interception of communication as well, the new statute does apply.

Netherlands

In Dutch legislation, overhearing of private conversations in public areas with the help of a technical device is clearly prohibited, unless the overhearing takes

---

123 Therefore, with respect to this method, the conclusions of Bosly & Vandermeersch (1995, p. 305) and Van Traa (1996, App. V, p. 466) must be rejected.

124 This was regretted by *gendarmerie* lieutenant-colonel Berkmoes, 1994. See also Van den Wyngaert, 1994, p. 658; Huybrechts, 1995, p. 49; Verstraeten, 1995, p. 617.

125 According to a leading officer of the *gendarmerie*, some police vehicles are permanently equipped with such instruments, and do the Belgian police forces sometimes also use a satellite of the German BKA. Furthermore, it was reported that the *gendarmerie*'s SIE frequently invoke the assistance of the Dutch KLPD in order to install position transmitters; see Van Traa, 1996, App. V, p. 467.

place with the consent of at least one of the participants to the conversation (art. 139b Sr). This exception is based on the fact that the cooperation of one of the participants who simply reveals the contents of the conversation afterwards would already be sufficient to break the private character of the meeting. Therefore, in the opinion of the government overhearing the meeting by using technical devices with this person's permission would not increase the damage done to the confidential character of the conversation.[126] However, one may wonder if this is a valid argument: The fact that a participant to a conversation must be aware of the possibility that one of the other participants leaks information to a third person does not imply yet that he has to be prepared for a confrontation with a complete and undeniable recording of his own words.[127]

In extension to this, art. 125a Sv as proposed by the above mentioned eavesdropping bill, intends to create a clear and sufficient legal basis for the use of technical means to record all kinds of private conversations without the presence of a wired police undercover. Condition for the application of this technique will be the previous authorization of an investigating judge, which may be given if the measure is necessary for the investigation of a criminal offence punishable with imprisonment of more than four years (proposed art. 125a par. 2 Sv). The use of these eavesdropping techniques will not only be allowed for the repressive investigation of such crimes, but also when this is necessary for their proactive investigation, meaning that conversations may be registered in order to gather intelligence and evidence with regard to the probable commission of such crimes in the (near) future (proposed art. 126g Sv).[128] Regarding the efficiency and possible success attributed to direct eavesdropping, it is interesting to see that, in the restricted number of known cases in which the technique was used in spite of the prohibition, the method did not provide any useful information.[129]

There is no doubt that in the Netherlands beepers are used, even though there is no regulation by law or guidelines and the police used to be highly reticent in admitting in public or even in court that they have been used.[130]

---

126 Answering statement, TK 9419, nr. 4, p. 6.
127 In the same sense Remmelink in Noyon/Langemeijer/Remmelink, annotation 4 on art. 139a Sr; Knoester, 1994, p. 563.
128 The parliamentary discussion of the bill, that has been accepted by the Second Chamber already, has however been suspended until the end of the parliamentary enquiry; see also Van Traa, 1994, pp. 18-20.
129 Van Traa, 1996, p. 176.
130 See for instance Borsboom & Spronken, 1993, p. 163-164; Van Traa, 1994, p. 25. Recently, a person under observation warned the police after discovering a hidden device under his car he thought was a bomb. The officers warned were initially unaware about the observation and had already engaged explosion detection experts before they were warned about the real nature of the device and the person involved. Due to these circumstances, the latter had to be arrested in an earlier stage of the investigation than originally planned. See *'Bom' onder*

Meanwhile the Amsterdam Court of Appeals has judged that the use of position transmitters as an investigative technique is not illegal but must be documented in the police reports.[131] Furthermore, the Van Traa parliamentary enquiry committee has shown that the use of these devices is even rather frequent: in 1995, 212 requests for installing position transmitters were rewarded.[132]

Luxembourg

In art. 88-1 CIC, the Luxembourg legislation contains an explicit police competence for the technical surveillance of all sorts of communication with a private character, in public as well as in private areas.[133] Provided the previous authorization of an investigating judge, this power may be used for overhearing conversations if this is necessary for the investigation of a criminal offence that may be punished with imprisonment of two years or more. This technique may be used only with regard to conversations in which the suspect of the crime himself or persons who are supposed to receive or send information on his behalf participate, and is restricted to situations in which, because of the nature of the crime, other investigation methods have proven to be ineffective.

According to some Luxembourg experts, this power is only used for telephone tapping, not for direct eavesdropping on conversations in public or private.[134] Others suggested differently, explaining that "officially, the Luxembourg police forces do not use microphones when investigating, but at least they did buy some."[135] Whether the Luxembourg police forces apply position transmitters for tracing criminals, contraband or ransom is not clear.

France

A statutory or other kind of provision creating a basis for overhearing or recording conversations with a private character is unknown to French law. Moreover, according to art. 226-1 CP eavesdropping on conversations of a confidential or private nature without the consent of all participants to the conversation is a criminal offence, regardless of the area where the conversation takes place. Since no statutory exception for investigation or other goals has been made, it has to be concluded that French law does not allow the use of acoustical technical eavesdropping instruments during observation operations.

---

auto blijkt peilzender van politie; in: de Volkskrant, January 17, 1996.

131   December 1, 1994, NJ 1995, 159 (Zwolsman-case); the Supreme Court has accepted this judgement in its decision of December 19, 1995, publication forthcoming in NJ 1996 with annotation by T.M. Schalken.

132   One of these beepers was even built into a bicycle! See Van Traa, 1996, pp. 178-179.

133   This is a slight correction of the situation sketched in Bevers, 1993, p. 94.

134   Rambach, 1993, p. 463.

135   This was related to us by a police officer we spoke several times, and confirmed by another source.

Notwithstanding this clear legal prohibition, several indications exist that the French police do indeed overhear private communications with the help of technical devices. In that case, information gathered is not used as evidence, but presented to the investigating judge with the aim of getting a search warrant or an authorization for telephone tapping. As a source of the information, the police refer to confidential informants.[136] Information on the eventual application of beepers by the French police could not be obtained, but one may assume that these are used as well, the results of their use being hidden in a similar way.

Germany
The unauthorized overhearing or recording of private conversations is criminalized according to German law by art. 201 StGB, whether these conversations take place in private or in public. Nevertheless, since the character of the conversation is determining, it is not criminalized to register a conversation in a public place that may be overheard without any special effort.[137] However, special competences for overhearing such conversations as a criminal investigation method have been created by the Organized crime act, that has introduced the new art. 100c StPO. On the basis of the second paragraph of this provision, the police may use acoustical technical means in order to overhear and register "non-overt utterances" for the investigation of one of the offences mentioned in art. 100a StPO, at least when this investigation is useless or substantially impeached without the use of these techniques.[138]

According to art. 100d StPO, a decision to apply direct eavesdropping techniques must be taken by a judge. In case of urgency, the public prosecutor and his auxiliaries are competent to take this decision as well, but then a judge should confirm the decision within three days. Par. 1 sub b of art. 100c StPO creates a clear legal basis for the application of beepers or position transmitters to investigate crimes of considerable importance or to trace suspects of such crimes. Decisions to use beepers may be taken by the police themselves.

Moreover, most of the provincial Police Acts contain such competences for the prevention of danger, including the possibility to use overhearing techniques for the proactive gathering of information on alleged criminals.[139] This is usually limited to persons who stand under suspicion of wanting to

---

136 This practice was revealed in interviews with officers and former officers of the French police forces, including some of the *renseignements généraux*, the intelligence branch of the *police nationale*. It was also referred to by Nadelmann, 1993, pp. 240-241.
137 Dreher/Tröndle, 1993, p. 1138; Hofman, 1995, p. 448.
138 See also Hofman, 1995, pp. 409-412.
139 See for example artt. 18 par. 1 NWPolG, 25b par. 1 RhPfPVG and 28 par. 1 and 2 SPolG.

commit crimes of considerable importance (*Straftaten von erheblicher Bedeutung*[140]) and the persons they are in contact with, and only allowed if the use of the method is necessary for proactive policing, the so-called preventive crime fighting (*vorbeugende Kriminalitätsbekämpfung*) or intelligence investigation (*Vorfeldermittlungen*). Most of the provincial Police acts reserve the decisive power regarding the application of proactive observation with acoustical instruments to the head of the detectives' department.

4.2.2.4 Acoustical Devices in Private Areas

When acoustical techniques are applied in order to eavesdrop on or register private conversations that take place in an area that is not accessible to the public, this constitutes not only an infringement with the character and confidentiality of the conversation (the informational privacy), but also an infringement with the spatial privacy of the home. The intensity and severeness of such activities have inspired the legislators of all studied countries to legislate on this subject. This is especially the case with the most common and well-known method of overhearing private conversations, telephone tapping.

A special way of using acoustical devices in private as well as public areas, which has been mentioned several times already, is the attachment of a micro transmitter or body recorder to an infiltrator or other undercover agent in order to ensure his protection.[141] The legal status of this technique, that may also be used for overhearing private conversations as long as they take place in the presence of a wired undercover agent, is diverging.

Belgium

The Interception of Communication Act was the first Belgian statute to introduce a regulation concerning the overhearing or recording of private meetings in criminal law. Besides a criminalization of overhearing and registering private communication, the Interception of Communication Act has also introduced in art. 90ter Sv a regulation for the use of such techniques by the police forces as a criminal investigation method. The use of technical devices to register private communication is restricted to the repressive investigation of one of the severe criminal offences mentioned in art. 90ter par. 2 Sv, and prior permission of the investigating judge is required. The legislator has not wanted to enable

---

140   Some police acts contain a more detailed definition of what is meant by this phrase, like art. 8 par. 3 NWPolG. See with regard to defining "crimes of considerable importance" and "organized crime" Rachor, 1992, pp. 233-240.

141   Among experienced undercover agents, the use of being "wired" is highly discussed: Some insist on being wired because of the alleged protection, others refuse to do so because of the alleged danger. This was confirmed by the national coordination for infiltration, R. Karstens.

the proactive use of communication interception techniques in order to investigate the preparation of severe offences.[142]

The regulation proposed by the government does not mention any possibility or restriction as to where and how eavesdropping equipment may be installed. However, in their explanatory statement to their proposal, the government explained that the new police power will not include an allowance to enter a computer system against the user's will.[143] The government also explicitly excluded the use of burglary or other breaches of domicile and entries against the occupant's will or without him knowing to enable the installation of bugs.[144] An important way left to have a conversation in a private place intercepted will then be the use of a wired infiltrator, who enters the premises with permission of the tenant and thus does not have to commit breach of domicile. Since this implies that communication will be overheard without the permission of all participants, this kind of eavesdropping in private can no longer be based upon the guidelines, but must be permitted by an investigating judge.[145]

Until the introduction of the Interception of communication act, Belgium was the only member of the Council of Europe that did not know legislation on overhearing and recording telephone conversations during a criminal inquiry. The only Belgian exception to the secret character of telecommunication was the investigative power to trace phone calls to or from a certain telephone over a period of time (art. 88bis Sv). This call registration with a so-called *Zoller-* or *Malicieux*-apparatus (pen register) creates the possibility of controlling whether telephone contacts between certain connections have taken place and how long they have lasted.[146] Now that the Interception of Communication Act has come into force, a remarkable gap between Belgium and its neighbours has been filled: The Belgian police and judicial authorities will finally be able to proceed to telephone tapping, probably the most common form of interception of communication.[147]

---

142 See also Van den Wyngaert, 1994, p. 658; Huybrechts, 1995, p. 49; Verstraeten, 1995, p. 617. The need of this possibility had been stressed during a congress at the *Vrije Universiteit* Brussels by *gendarmerie* lieutenant-colonel Berkmoes; see Berkmoes, 1994.

143 *Gedrukte stukken* 1992-1993, nr. 843/1, p. 11.

144 *Gedrukte stukken* 1992-1993, nr. 843/1, p. 15.

145 In this sense, we do not share the opinion of Bosly & Vandermeersch, 1995, p. 305 and Van Traa, 1996, App. V, p. 466.

146 For a more detailed discussion of this investigation method, see Deruyck, 1991/1992, pp. 10-15; Rambach, 1993, p. 41 and Van den Wyngaert, 1993b, pp. 28-29.

147 To our surprise, all commentators on the new act only stress the long awaited possibility of wire tapping (see for instance Van den Wyngaert, 1994, pp. 656-661; Huybrechts, 1995, pp. 41-57; Bosly & Vandermeersch, 1995, pp. 301-343; Verstraeten, 1995, pp. 610-621), and apparently ignore the fact that, with the possibilities for other types of communication interception, Belgium is ahead of most of its European partners.

Netherlands
Under Dutch law, the use of acoustical aides when observing a meeting in a private area is criminalized, unless the permission of the overheard has been given (art. 139a Sr). As was shown above, this permission means that the consent of only one of the participants to the meeting is sufficient, as to allow the use of acoustical aides in combination with a police infiltrator or informant.[148]

Apart from this overhearing construction, the Dutch eavesdropping bill mentioned above intends to create a power to overhear and record conversations in private places without any of the participants knowing, as well as the power to overhear conversations in private places like houses, cars, boats, airplanes and hotel rooms (proposed art. 125a Sv). Recording conversations in a private place is allowed for the investigation of a criminal offence punishable with imprisonment of four years or more, committed by an organisation or in such a connection with other crimes that the legal order is endangered. An additional condition is that the use of eavesdropping techniques is reasonably necessary in order to solve the crime or arrest the suspect. Besides this context of repressive investigation, conversations in private areas may also be recorded if one of the participants is a person who, according to facts and circumstances, is believed to be involved in the organized plotting of such criminal offences; this proactive investigation is to be introduced by the proposed art. 126g Sv. In both cases, prior permission should be given by an investigating judge.

For the purpose of recording private conversations, the police will also be allowed to enter private places without the occupant's knowledge and commit any kind of breach of domicile, including burglary, in order to hide microphones and other equipment.[149] The use of this auxiliary method will be bound to some more restrictions: The crime in case must be punishable with imprisonment of eight years or more, must be committed or plotted by an organisation and the permission to enter the place should be given separately and explicitly by the investigating judge (proposed art. 125a par. 4 Sv). It is however possible that the legislator has too much confidence in this new method: In those cases where direct eavesdropping was applied despite the prohibition, it did not provide the success hoped for.[150]

Since 1971, the Dutch Code of Criminal Procedure provides regulations on investigative techniques as the use of pen registers (125f Sv) and telephone tapping (125g Sv). The former creates the possibility of tracing telephone

---

148 More information on infiltration can be found in Chapter 5.
149 There have been indications that, in the recent past, this has also been done during the so-called peeking operations mentioned above.
150 Van Traa, 1996, p. 176.

contacts between certain connections and their length,[151] while the latter regulates the overhearing and recording of conversations through the telephonic system. Since 1993 the provision also covers the interception of computerized communication and telefax messages, but tapping of mobile telephone communication (which functions through normal radio signals) was excluded until recently.[152] Thanks to recent technical developments, enabling the separation of the signals of a specific mobile telephone from the signals of other mobile telephones, this is technically possible since January 1, 1996.[153] Besides this, a bill is pending that proposes to enable the proactive use of telephone taps as well.[154]

Luxembourg

Article 2 sub 1 of the Luxembourg Private Life Act criminalizes the overhearing of meetings in a private area with the use of acoustical techniques unless there is consent of the participants. The statute requires that the permission be given by the person whose words are being overheard, which means in practice that the consent of every participant to the meeting will be necessary and overhearing the conversation with the help of an infiltrator that attends to the meeting will not be allowed.

In the Luxembourg Code of Criminal Instruction, art. 88-1 offers an investigation power to overhear and register all kinds of communication, if such is necessary (that is, other methods have proven insufficient) for the investigation of crimes punishable with imprisonment of two years or more. The method may be used only against persons who, on the basis of specific facts, are under suspicion of having committed or participated to the offence or of receiving or transmitting information for such a suspect or accused. Eavesdropping and recording private communication according to this provision is allowed only on the basis of prior permission of an investigating judge.

In spite of the large wordings of this provision, the possibility of directly eavesdropping or recording private conversations does not seem to be applied by Luxembourg investigating authorities.[155] As we mentioned above, there are however some indications that at least they do have purchased the equipment for direct eavesdropping. With regard to the interception of spoken communication, the main use of this provision is telephone and telefax tapping,[156] whereas pen registers may be applied in practice as well. Because the Luxembourg police

---

151 See Borsboom & Spronken, 1994, pp. 162-163.
152 See Van de Reyt, 1993, pp. 523-533; Swart, 1993a, p. 304 and Corstens, 1995, p. 415.
153 Van Traa, 1996, p. 172.
154 TK 23 251, nrs. 1-2.
155 In this sense Rambach, 1993, p. 463.
156 See also Spielmann & Weitzel, 1991, p. 163-173 and Spielmann & Spielmann, 1993, pp. 273-274.

(at least officially) do not use infiltration,[157] the technique of observation through wired infiltrators is not applied and therefore seems to need no regulation.

France

Unless permission of the participants has been obtained, article 226-1 of the French *Nouveau Code Pénal* considers the direct overhearing of a conversation in a private area with the use of technical aides as a criminal offence. Since the text requires that the permission be given by the person whose words are being overheard, in practice the consent of every participant to the meeting will be necessary and overhearing a conversation with the help of a wired infiltrator would thus not be allowed either.[158] The only French publication paying attention to this technique that could be found, states that such operations would not be allowed unless in highly exceptional cases, on the basis of a statutory regulation and with a judge's warrant.[159] Some tend to expect that a statutory regulation of this investigation technique will soon follow, because of the general developments in France, that sensitive subjects should be given an explicit regulation.[160] In our opinion, one can wonder to what extent this would apply in the case of direct eavesdropping since, according to specialists in and around the French police forces, these techniques are not used, at least not for the gathering of information that is meant to be used as evidence in court.[161]

Until the Kruslin and Huvig decisions of the European Court on Human Rights, telephone tapping by the French police was done on the basis of general principles and with an order by the investigation judge.[162] After Kruslin and Huvig, it was clear that the protection of privacy according to art. 8 ECHR demanded that telephone tapping have a legal basis that is accessible, sufficiently clear and particularly precise. As a result to this, the French legislator has created a statutory regulation for repressive telephone (and telefax) tapping in art. 100 through 100-7 CPP,[163] as well as for preventive (also called administrative or security) telephone tapping, the latter being embodied in a separate

---

157   In Chapter 5, the method of infiltration is discussed more elaborately.
158   An elaborate discussion of infiltration by the police may be found in Chapter 5.
159   Delmas-Marty, 1991, p. 196.
160   In this sense Lorenz, 1993, p. 338.
161   As Nadelmann (1993, pp. 240-241) points out, "even as the courts have debated the legality of wiretaps, the French police routinely have used wiretaps for purposes of gathering intelligence on criminal matters," which intelligence was used "for instance, to obtain a legal search warrant from the *juge d'instruction*."
162   April 24, 1990, Series A 176. With regard to this jurisprudence, see Swart, 1991a, pp. 160-168 and Blontrock & De Hert, 1991/1992, pp. 865-871.
163   See Lorenz, 1993, pp. 338-349 and Pradel, 1993c, pp. 123-124.

166

law.[164] Repressive telephone tapping is allowed on the basis of warrant issued by an investigating judge, which may be given only if the interception is required in the context of an investigation of a crime punishable with imprisonment of two years or more (art. 100 CPP). Note that the French circular on the interpretation and application of the Schengen Convention explicitly excludes that foreign police officers proceed to wire tapping during an observation on French territory.[165]

According to art. 3 of the Telephone tapping act, what is called the preventive interception of telecommunication can be ordered if this is necessary for national security and interests of science and economy, as well as for the prevention of terrorism and organized crime.[166] Orders of this kind should be given by the prime minister or one of his two especially appointed delegates, on motivated request by the minister of defence, interior or customs, or one of their special delegates (art. 4).

Germany

Overhearing and recording conversations in private areas as a criminal investigation technique is often referred to in German doctrine as *großer Lauschangriff* (big eavesdropping attack). This technique has been a central discussion theme in Germany since the end of the eighties, during which not only the constitutionality but also the usefullness and practical need of the measure were put up for debate.[167] Crime fighters stress the necessity of these methods, whereas human rights defenders state that such would be an inadmissible infringement with the constitutional protection of the home.[168] According to the general German opinion however, at least an amendment of art. 13 GG would be required before such investigation power could be created in accordance with the Constitution: Besides search and seizure, the only restriction of the privacy of the home allowed by art. 13 GG is a restriction that is necessary to eliminate an immediate danger for a person's life.[169]

---

164 *Loi no. 91-646 du 10 juilliet 1991 relative au secret des correspondances émises par la voie des télécommunications*, J.O. July 13, 1991, pp. 9167-9169.

165 *Circulaire du 23 juin 1995 commentant des dispositions des articles 39, 40 et 41 de la convention signée à Schengen le 19 juni 1990*, NOR: *JUSA9500149C*.

166 According to Corstens, 1994b, this preventive wiretapping also includes the proactive interception of telecommunication.

167 See for instance Seifert, 1992, pp. 355-363, Lisken/Caesar, 1993, p. 67, Böttger & Pfeiffer, 1994, pp. 7-17 and Schelter, 1994, pp. 52-57.

168 Note that both crime fighters and human rights defenders can be found among all parties, organizations and authorities which play a role in the criminal procedure.

169 In this sense politicians from the social democrats (SPD) as well as the christian democrats (CDU/CSU) during the debate on the Organized Crime Act on June 4, 1992, *BT-Sitzung* 12/95, p. 7827. See also Wolter, 1988, p. 77, Lisken/Caesar, 1993, p. 67, Kruse, 1993, p. 187 and Schelter, 1994, p. 55.

Until today, no statutory provisions on bugging private places in criminal inquiries have been accepted. The original proposal of the Organized Crime Act did intend to introduce a possibility to use a wired infiltrator carrying a hidden microphone to enable private conversations to be overheard as an investigation power.[170] However, this so-called *kleiner Lauschangriff* (small eavesdropping attack; main difference with a big eavesdropping attack is, that in case of the former the conversation concerned is overheard anyway because of the presence of the infiltrator) was seriously criticized already and, in order to avoid jeopardizing the entire bill, the federal government preferred taking this provision out of the proposal, which means essentially that eavesdropping in private residences is forbidden according to art. 201 StGB.[171]

The German discussion on direct eavesdropping in private domiciles is still going on and in the heat of the electoral battle of 1994 ("the 16 elections year"), the main political parties all showed their (political) interest in legislating on this subject. The coalition parties (CDU/CSU and FDP) proposed a joint crime fighting bill,[172] which was supported and taken over by the government and came into force on December 1, 1994.[173] The main change this bill involves for investigative policing and eavesdropping possibilities, concerns the criminal offences mentioned in art. 100a StPO, to which catalogue they would eventually add a number of other offences, such as money laundering and several forms of fraud. The main opposition party (SPD) proposed another bill, that did indeed contain an amendment of art. 13 GG and intended to introduce new and more invasive eavesdropping powers for criminal investigations, including the big eavesdropping attack,[174] but it was rejected by the coalition.[175] A third proposal, done by the provinces of Bavaria and Baden-Württemberg, also intended to enable the use of technical means for eavesdropping conversations in private places including the private home, was rejected as well.[176] The discussion about the subject still continues, and now seems to focus on the question whether a more general amendment of art. 13 GG should be preferred to a more

---

170 The method of infiltration is discussed in detail in Chapter 5.

171 The opinion of the federal government is expressed in their explanatory statement to the Organized Crime Act (*Begründung der Bundesregierung zum EOrgKG, BT-Drucksache* 12/989, pp. 39-40 and 58; see also Hilger, p. 462; Gropp, 1993b, p. 29 and Lisken, 1993, pp. 121-124; Hofman, 1995, p. 410.

172 The proposal of CDU/CSU and FDP was done at January 1, 1994 and followed by the definitive version at February 3, 1994. The proposal is discussed in Bandisch, 1994, pp. 153-159 and Wächtler, 1994, pp. 159-161.

173 *Verbrechensbekämpfungsgesetz*, October 28, 1994, BGBl. I, 1994, 3186.

174 The social democrat proposal was presented at January 27, 1994 and is discussed by Welp, 1994, pp. 161-168.

175 Particularly within the liberal FDP, there is a great deal of resistance against an amendendment of art. 13 GG and the infringement with the privacy of home.

176 May 24, 1994; see Hofman, 1995, p. 415.

restricted one.[177] The FDP has recently changed its opinion and dropped its resistance against the bugging of private homes, but this has led to the resignation of their own minister of justice, who did not want to take responsibility for the eventual introduction of the measure.

Exceptions to the criminalization of overhearing private conversations have already been created by most of the provincial Police acts, in which a police competence for the bugging of private places is regulated. Main condition for overhearing conversations in private areas according to most of the provincial police acts is that this be necessary for the prevention of immediate danger to society or the life of a person.[178] However, in some of the German provinces this technique may also be applied for collecting information on persons under severe suspicion of preparing an offence mentioned in a catalogue of severe crimes (proactive observation).[179] Except in case of urgency, a judge's permission is required. In combination with a search warrant, issued by the same judge, the police may also be entitled to enter private places without the occupant's knowledge in order to install technical eavesdropping equipment.[180] For the prevention of the lives of infiltrators, most police acts also allow that under covers be wired in order to enable the overhearing of what happens inside the area where they operate.[181] Because this measure is considered purely preventive, no judiciary permission is needed.

With regard to the use of the telecommunication network for purposes of criminal investigation, the German legislator has created two possibilities: telephone call registration by pen registers and telecommunication interception or tapping. The former is the possibility of controlling whether telephone contacts between certain connections have taken place and how long they have lasted without overhearing or recording the contents of the communication itself,[182] while the latter, regulated in artt. 100a and 100b StPO, was on the contrary introduced in order to enable this interception of the contents of

---

177 The former has recently been advocated by Hund (1995, pp. 334-338), who proposes that a new art. 13 GG should differentiate between the general protection of the domicile (which may be limited) and a specific protection of the intimate sphere within the domicile (to which no restrictions would be allowed). The latter has been proposed by Hofe, 1995, pp. 169-171.
178 Bäumler, 1992, pp. 587-588; see for instance artt. 17 and 18 NWPolG, 15 par. 4 HSOG, 28 par. 4 SPolG, 35 par. 2 NGefAG; in the same sense Rüter, 1995, pp. 601 and 603.
179 This is the case according to artt. 34 par. 1 BayPAG, 25b par. 2 RhPfPVG and 35 par. 1 ThürPAG; Bäumler, 1992, p. 588. In German terminology, this is called *vorbeugende Kriminalitätsbekämpfung* (preventive crime fighting).
180 Note that none of the German police acts explicitly mentions the possibility of this combination, which according to law enforcement practitioners is nevertheless used.
181 With regard to this for instance artt. 15 par. 6 HSOG, 17 par. 4 and 18 par. 4 NWPolG, 18 par. 4 SPolG and 34 par. 3 BayPAG.
182 Art. 12 Telephone Hardware Act (*Gesetz über Fernmeldeanlagen*). See Klesczewski, 1993, pp. 382-389.

telecommunication. It regards the interception of not only telephone communication, but also of all other forms of telecommunication, like telex, telefax and telegraph.[183] Besides, the Federal court has decided that the criminalisation of telephone tapping was not be infringed with by a police officer who could overhear a conversation between an criminal and an informer thanks to the informer's permission.[184] Observation through the telecommunication network is allowed only with repressive, not with preventive or proactive intentions.[185]

4.3 Comparing National Norms

4.3.1 Observation in General

Because of the sensibility of observation from a privacy point of view, one of the important aspects in the light of art. 8 par. 2 ECHR is the legal framework in which observation as a policing method can be placed. With regard to this, one can distinguish two different systems of regulation of police powers. The system of legality, which may be found in the European Convention on Human Rights, in Germany and, at least to some extent, in the Netherlands, implies that every action by the police, and especially those actions which restrict the fundamental freedoms of the individual citizen, should have an explicit basis in the domestic law. On the other hand, in the system of permissiveness, used in Belgium as well as, to some extent, in the Netherlands, France and Luxembourg, the police are entitled to proceed to every action that is not explicitly prohibited without a specific regulation existing. In the second system, the legal framework of the police powers is not only created by regulations of criminal procedure, but also by the mere fact that a type of behaviour or activity has (or has not) been criminalized. This is indeed a clear and easy system for the investigating police, who will usually be well aware of what is criminalized and what is not. From a point of view of the protection of the individual's rights, however, there are several disadvantages to the system of permissiveness, the most important one being the built-in lack of control on activities that do not lead to evidence on trial. Furthermore there is no guarantee either that, during the operation, the acceptability of the methods will be examined and judged by authorities who may be trusted to be more impartial than the police. Moreover, this system does not protect the citizen from privacy infringements by techniques that are too

---

183   Kleinknecht/Meyer-Goßner, 1995, p. 294.
184   The so-called *Mithörjurisprudenz*, BGH November 8, 1993, StV 1994-2, pp. 58-62; see Tak *et al.*, 1996, p. 119.
185   Hofman, 1995, p. 406; Rüter, 1995, p. 603; this restriction is however being discussed as well; see for instance Mann & Müller, 1995, pp. 180-185.

new to have been criminalized already, even if a criminalization would be desirable.

Evidently, in both systems a central position should also be given to constitutionally protected rights of the individual. With regard to the protection of the privacy, a general provision on the protection of privacy can be found in the constitutions of four countries. The constitutions of Belgium and The Netherlands mention it explicitly, whereas it has been read into the french and German constitutions. As was stated above, the individual privacy also finds protection in art. 8 of the ECHR, which treaty is in force in all five countries.

It seems to be mainly due to the influence of the judgements of the European Court on Human Rights and of other courts that legislators have created more and more statutory law on techniques and activities that the police may apply during observation operations. All five countries studied here have legislation on telephone tapping, whereas the use of other, even more sophisticated observation techniques is regulated explicitly in Germany, Luxembourg and Belgium. Note that in Belgium, part of this matter is also regulated in secret directives of the ministry of justice, while relevant directives in the Netherlands have been published. If and to what extent the other countries know or have known secret regulations with regard to observation techniques is unknown, but it can certainly not be excluded.

Table 4.1 Observation in General

	B	NL	L	F	D
Type of norm					
Statute	+	-	-	-	+
Statute pending	-	+	-	-	-
Directives	+	+	-	-	+
Secret directives	+	-	-	-	-
General task description	+	+	+	+	-

Legislation on observation without special technical devices only knows a statutory regulation in Germany; in the other countries, this is accepted on the basis of the general task description of the police. In the Netherlands, this task description has been interpreted in that sense by the Supreme Court, whereas a general basis may also be deduced from a public directive of the ministries of justice and the interior. In Belgium, secret directives contain a provision on this method, that is also allowed on the basis of the permissive rule.

4.3.2 Observation with Technical Devices

The only country of the five where observation with optical devices in public has been regulated by statutory law is Germany: Both federal and provincial law in Germany address these policing operations. In France, a statutory basis exists for the use of static video cameras in public, and a Schengen circular mentions the possibility of using cameras during cross-border observation. In the Netherlands, case-law has decided that photo and video observation may be allowed on the basis of the general task description, whereas in Belgium a basis can be found in the ministry of justice's secret directives. As far as known, Luxembourg has no regulation of the use of optical devices in public, and this kind of spying has not been criminalized in any of the five countries.

Table 4.2 Optical Devices in Public

	B	NL	L	F	D
Type of norm					
Statute	-	-	-	+	+
Guidelines/directives	+	-	-	+	-
Case-law	-	+	-	-	-
Published	-	+	-	+	+
Conditions					
Proportionality/subsidiarity	-	+	-	-	-
Proactive	+	+	-	-	+
Repressive	+	+	-	+	+
Control before	+	-	-	+	+
Control during	+	-	-	-	+
Control afterward	+	+	+	+	+
Organized/severe crime	+	-	-	-	+
Gathering evidence for trial	+	+	-	-	+
Gathering intelligence	-	+	-	-	+
Suspects and contact persons	+	+	-	-	+

172

Observation with optical devices in private has been the subject of legislation in the German provinces only. This police power must also be considered allowed on the basis of the Belgian directives, unless its application is accompanied by breach of domicile, which is criminalized in all five countries. In France, observing a person in private with the help of an optical device is a criminal offence itself, like also in The Netherlands, at least if the person's legal interests are damaged. This implies that the use of optical devices in private for criminal investigation purposes will usually not be allowed, unless for instance in a caught in the act-situation, in which case the damaged interests would not be legal.

Table 4.3 Optical Devices in Private

	B	NL	L	F	D
Type of norm					
Statute	-	+	-	-	+
Guidelines/directives	+	-	-	-	-
Published	-	+	-	-	+
Conditions					
In flagrante delicto situations	-	+	-	-	-
Proactive	+	-	-	-	+
Repressive	+	+	-	-	-
Control before	+	+	+	-	+
Control during	+	-	+	-	+
Control afterward	+	+	+	-	+
Specific crimes	+	-	+	-	-
Organized/severe crime	-	-	-	-	+
Gathering evidence for trial	+	+	-	-	+
Gathering intelligence	-	+	-	-	+
Suspects and contact persons	+	-	-	-	+

Three of the five countries have created a statutory basis for observation with acoustical devices in public as an investigation method for the police: Luxembourg, where in practice the technique does not seem to be used, Belgium, and

Germany, where legislation can be found on a federal as well as on a provincial level. In The Netherlands, a bill intending to introduce legislation on this policing technique is still pending in parliament. To some extent, all countries know a criminalization of technical overhearing of private conversations. France is the only country where no exception to the criminalization of acoustical eavesdropping in public has been created, and where this method is therefore not allowed at all.

Table 4.4 Acoustical Devices in Public

	B	NL	L	F	D
Type of norm					
Statute	-	-	+	-	+
Guidelines/directives	+	-	-	-	-
Published	-	-	+	-	+
Conditions					
Proactive	+	-	-	-	+
Repressive	+	-	+	-	+
Control before	+	-	+	-	+
Control during	+	-	+	-	+
Control afterward	+	-	+	-	+
Specific crimes	+	-	+	-	+
Organized/severe crime	-	-	-	-	+
Gathering evidence for trial	+	-	+	-	+
Gathering intelligence	+	-	-	-	+
Suspects and contact persons	+	-	+	-	+

The Dutch criminalization of eavesdropping contains a special exception stating that overhearing or recording private conversations is not criminalized when done with permission of at least one of the participants to the conversation. Therefore, this criminalization, different from the others, leaves an opening for eavesdropping private meetings through a wired infiltrator who participates at the meeting. In Belgium and Germany, this is only allowed thanks to respectively the Interception of Communication Act and provisions in the provincial police acts. In France it is not allowed and in Luxembourg it is illegal as well, but since Luxembourg allegedly does not apply infiltration, this prohibition can be considered irrelevant. Another special measure of observation with acoustical technical devices, the use of beepers or position transmitters, has only been given a statutory basis in German law. In Belgium the directives seem to provide a regulation for the use of beepers, whereas in the Netherlands, a basis may be found in case-law. About the use of beepers in Luxembourg and France, nothing is known, the field of what is known as "police tactics" being fully confidential.

Table 4.5 Acoustical Devices in Private (Wire Tap Excluded)

	B	NL	L	F	D
Type of norm					
Statute	-	+	+	-	+
Guidelines/directives	+	-	-	-	-
Published	-	+	+	-	+
Conditions					
Proactive	-	+	-	-	+
Repressive	+	+	+	-	+
Control before	+	-	+	-	+
Control during	+	-	+	-	+
Control afterward	+	-	+	-	+
Specific crimes	+	-	+	-	-
Organized/severe crime	+	-	-	-	+
Gathering evidence for trial	+	-	+	-	+
Gathering intelligence	+	-	-	-	+
Suspects and contact persons	+	-	-	-	+

The most invasive observation method, observation with acoustical devices in private areas, has been partly regulated in all five countries (see *Table 4.5*). In its most common form (telephone or wire tapping) this kind of observation is allowed as an investigative measure in all five countries, and all have criminalized telephone tapping and direct overhearing and recording of private conversations without consent outside of the legal procedures. In The Netherlands, consent of only one of the participants is sufficient to remove the criminal character; in the other four, this may only be reached in case all participants

175

agree. As a consequence, the Dutch police do not need a specific power for overhearing private meetings where a wired infiltrator is present. German police law knows some specific legal rules with regard to this method for preventive (and proactive) reasons, and under Belgian law this is allowed for investigative purposes only. French law does not allow this method at all and Luxembourg allegedly does not apply infiltration, which would also exclude the use of wired infiltrators.

Under German, Luxembourg and Belgian law, powers have been created to enable the police to eavesdrop meetings in private places, a regulation that the Luxembourg authorities only seem to apply for telephone tapping. The Dutch legislator has been working on the introduction of such powers for their police as well; for the time being, the Dutch regulation will be the only one to explicitly allow their police the commission of burglary in order to install bugs. The Belgian legislator has explicitly excluded this possibility during parliamentary debates, whereas the German police legislators have left the possibility open that an eavesdropping warrant be combined with a search warrant.

4.3.3 Limits of the Application

Two general restrictions for the application of such special policing techniques as observation can be found in all countries, even though they are sometimes phrased in a different form or hidden in another rule. These two are the principles of proportionality and subsidiarity, implying that intrusive techniques may only be applied in case of severe crime and only when their application is necessary for the success of the investigation. This usually implies that the investigation of the crime involved would be more difficult or less likely to be successful without using these methods.

Apart from these two general limits, one may also distinguish two more specific groups of limits to the application of observation techniques, both of which might be considered as specifications of the proportionality principle. On the one hand, the investigation with the help of these techniques is sometimes restricted to certain crimes or crime types, on the other hand the phase of the investigation in which application of observation is allowed may be limited. This second limit also seems to have consequences for the aims that observation might have.

4.3.3.1 Crime Types

Because of the intrusiveness to private life that can be made by police observation, especially when using techniques spying and listening devices, but also because of the costs and intensive work involved in these methods, the application of systematic observation is often restricted to certain cases. For this reason, some of the countries studied here have included more or less detailed criteria for the application of observation techniques in their legislation or guidelines. On the one hand, these criteria may contain detailed catalogues of offences for which certain forms of observation are allowed, on the other hand they may also be general conditions or limits, such as the restriction that a method ought to be used only in case of offences for which pre-trial detention is allowed.

Art. 40 par. 1 SC restricts the possibility of cross-border observation with prior permission of the neighbour state to criminal offences which may lead to extradition. Cross-border observation without prior permission of the country on which territory it will be carried out, is only allowed in case of one of the offences listed in par. 7 of the same article, which is a severe restriction of the first crime category and contains:

> Assassination, murder, rape, arson, counterfeiting, armed robbery and receiving of stolen goods, extortion, kidnapping and hostage taking, traffic in human beings, illicit traffic in narcotic drugs and psychotropic substances, breach of the laws on arms and explosives, use of explosives and illicit carriage of toxic and dangerous waste.

The studied countries themselves have also restricted the possibilities of application of special techniques to certain criminal offences, for which they have mainly used three methods: general description of types of crime, specified and detailed catalogues of offences.

The first method has been applied in the Belgian directives ("organized and severe gang crime"), the German Code of Criminal Procedure's regulation on optical devices, and most of the German police acts (the sometimes more or less specified "crimes of considerable importance"). This method has the advantage of being flexible (it can be interpreted in accordance with the necessities of society), but also the disadvantage of being unclear and not offering a sufficient legal security.

The second restriction method connects the crimes that may be investigated with certain observation techniques to the maximum punishment that the crime may be liable to. In this sense, the Luxembourg and French Codes of Criminal Procedure only allow the interception of communication respectively telephone tapping for crimes punishable with a maximum of 2 years imprisonment or more. The Dutch code demands that the investigated crime be punishable with a maximum of at least 4 years imprisonment for telephone tapping and (in the future) eavesdropping, whereas it proposes a limit of 8 years or more for eavesdropping in the private home. It is evident that, in this system, there can be no doubt as to whether or not the use of an observation method is allowed for the investigation of a certain crime. However, among the crimes that may be investigated by observation, there may be several offences that can not reasonably be investigated with such methods, especially offences committed by one author only. In these cases this restriction method would allow the use of intrusive observation methods, even though this could not reasonably lead to the crime being solved. Moreover, in case an offence for which the maximum penalty is raised above the 2, 4 or 8 years limit, this would automatically open the possibility of using more intrusive methods of investigation, even if this was not the intention of the legislator. Note however that in the Netherlands, the application of the eavesdropping bill is generally restricted to crimes that are committed in an organized crime context, whereas the Luxembourg and French law demand that the interception of the conversations be "necessary for the inquiry." In this way, all three countries seem to have excluded most of the possibly problematic cases.

The most specific method of restriction to certain crimes is the use of a detailed catalogue, in which all the offences for the investigation of which a certain technique may be used are mentioned explicitly. This method is used in the Belgian Interception of communication act, as well as in the German regulations on wire tapping and overhearing private conversations. Not only this method is at least as clear as the second one, but it also avoids the risk of an unintended introduction of special investigation techniques for crimes that can not reasonably solved that way.

According to art. 40 SC, cross-border observation with prior permission of the authorities of the other state is allowed for the investigation of offences for which the author may be extradited. This category is much wider than the categories of crimes for which each of the five countries allow observation with optical or acoustical devices. In case of prior permission of the country the border of which is about to be crossed, the authorities who have given permission will also have been able to check whether and to what extent the application of technical instruments is allowed for the crime to be investigated.

If prior permission for cross-border observation can not be obtained because of the urgency of the case, the observation may continue if the investigation concerns one of the offences mentioned in the seventh paragraph of art. 40. However, not all five legislations allow that these criminal offences be investigated with the help of advanced technical observation devices. Belgian law for instance, does not allow this for the investigation of counterfeiting, whereas the German Code of Criminal Procedure does not permit the use of optical observation devices for investigating rape or the illicit transport of toxic and dangerous waste. Furthermore, the Belgian Interception of Communication Act and the Dutch eavesdropping bill both demand that the crimes to be investigated by such eavesdropping techniques be committed by a group of persons, not just by one individual. These differences, that may eventually lead to the illegal gathering of information that might be excluded from the evidence in court, are so detailed that it will be indispensable that the observing officers be aware of the national regulations.

4.3.3.2 Repressive, Preventive or Proactive

In the beginning of this chapter on observation, reference was made to a discussion as to whether or not art. 40 SC allows cross-border observation during "the preliminary stage of in investigation, where there is good reason to believe that criminal offences are about to be committed," the so-called proactive and preventive types of observation. Other than most other opinions, we concluded that art. 40 only offers a basis for cross-border observation in a repressive context, that is to say, after a suspicion has risen that a crime has been committed. It is, however, interesting to examine to what extent the legislation of the five countries at the basis of the Schengen Convention contains provisions allowing the use of observation techniques in the proactive stage of an investigation.

In their regulations regarding observation techniques, three out of the five studied countries pay attention to the concept of investigating criminal offences before they have actually been committed. Luxembourg and Belgian law exclude this field of application, although the secret directives in Belgium at least seem to leave an opening for other than repressive investigations. Further, no rule of Belgian law seems to stand in the way of proactive observation in general. The Dutch CID-guidelines, eavesdropping bill and other proposals explicitly intend to regulate the gathering of intelligence for proactive purposes. The provincial police acts in Germany contain regulations on eavesdropping for the prevention of a directly imminent danger, which is usually described in a detailed manner, and most of these police acts also create a police power to gather intelligence for proactive reasons. The French Telephone Tapping Act addresses prevention for purposes of national security and interests of science and economy, as well as prevention of terrorism and organized crime.

It is uncertain what is meant exactly by the preventive purposes referred to by the French act. Possibly, this only refers to a strictly preventive approach of persons who are under suspicion of preparing the commission of criminal offences, in the sense that the crime finally does not take place. This would be an interpretation close to the German provisions on preventive observation, for which no legal basis is or will be provided in Belgium or the Netherlands. On the other hand, it might also refer to a more proactive approach of the commission of the crime by gathering evidence on the preparation of the crime before it has been committed, aiming at an increased amount of evidence against the future suspects after the actual commission of the crime. This interpretation would be closer to the German provisions on proactive crime fighting and to the provisions to be introduced by the Dutch eavesdropping bill. Both of these countries seem to understand by proactive investigations, the investigations during which information is gathered, eventually being used to prove a criminal offence still to be committed.

One may wonder whether these proactive investigations aiming at the gathering of evidence are allowed on the basis of the second paragraph of art. 8 ECHR. This paragraph only mentions the prevention of (disorder or) crime as a goal justifying privacy restrictions, which implies that the aim of the operation ought to be that the final commission of the offence does not take place. In the Lüdi case, the European Court on Human Rights accepted the use of an infiltrator in the preliminary stage of an investigation as being "aimed at the prevention of crime." Strictly spoken, however, it would be more correct to distinguish between preventive policing as "trying to avoid the actual commission of a crime" and proactive policing as "anticipated repression, planning and evidence gathering for an efficient prosecution after the commission of a crime."[186]

4.4 Conclusion

As to the powers for observing police officers that have been or will probably soon be created, the Dutch police seems to be the most gifted. The only observation type they may not be entitled to during an observation operation, is the use of optical devices in private areas, unless the observed situation is the actual and red-handed commission of a criminal offence. With regard to the overhearing of private conversations, the Dutch police will in the near future even be given the power to the secret installation of bugs in private houses in certain cases. Both this eavesdropping technique and the more conventional telephone tapping will be allowed for repressive as well as for proactive purposes. The German and Belgian police must work with more limited powers already. In Germany, optical and acoustical technical devices may only be used in private places for preventive and (in some provinces) proactive purposes, whereas telephone tapping is restricted to repressive investigations. Tendencies to enlarge the police's powers on these points do indeed exist, but concrete proposals have not been done recently.

In Belgium, on the basis of the ministry of justice's confidential guidelines, the police may in principle use every kind of technical device for observation, whereas a legal basis has been created for all types of interception of communication in public as well as in private, including telephone taps. Differently than the guidelines, the proposal restricts the use of technical overhearing devices to repressive goals. The Belgian legislator has not shown any intention to allow burglary by the police in order to install bugs or otherwise facilitating the investigations. The Luxembourg and French regulation are far more restricted than the three others: They only allow the interception of communication. The

---

186 In this sense also Weßlau, 1989, pp. 56-76 and 335, as well as Denninger, 1992, pp. 169-170.

Luxembourg law has a wider scope with regard to the overhearing techniques that may formally be used, since it includes the direct overhearing of conversations with a private character; in practice however, the police only seem to apply telephone tapping. The French law is broader in the sense that it does not only allow overhearing for repressive purposes, but also for preventive and proactive ones.

In order to be acceptable in the light of art. 8 ECHR, the powers with which the police may intrude an individual's private life must be "necessary in a democratic society," and "a restriction is in conformity with the Convention only when it is necessary in the light of the interests advanced as weighed against the requirements of a democratic society."[187] For the interpretation of this condition, the Court allows the national authorities a very broad margin of appreciation, affected mainly by the nature of the activities involved as well as by the aim of the restriction.[188] On this ground, most intrusions with the privacy as allowed by the five countries will be admitted by the Court in Strasbourg as well, if their application remains within the limits of proportionality and subsidiarity. There is however one aspect to the Dutch eavesdropping proposal that might be doubtful in the light of art. 8 ECHR: the possibility to allow the police the commission of burglary for the installation of bugs. One can imagine that this power, an activity that has never been allowed in a criminal investigation context in any of the other countries, is applied by secret services dealing with the essential interests of national security, in which case the margin left to the country's appreciation is extremely wide.[189] However, neither the Court nor the Commission has ever been asked to judge the acceptability of burglary for the interests of national security.[190] One may wonder if such a power, maybe the most intrusive infringement with the domestic privacy one can imagine, would be allowed for reasons of criminal investigation at all, let alone the use of such techniques before a crime has even been committed.

In the light of the second paragraph of art. 8 ECHR along with the judgements of the Court on the conditions justifying an infringement with the right to privacy, it is relevant to examine the quality of the regulations as they exist in the studied countries, by putting them to the test of the criteria formulated by the Court in its Kruslin and Huvig decisions.[191] According to these

---

187 Van Dijk & Van Hoof, 1990, p. 583.
188 According to the Court in the Dudgeon case, October 22, 1981, Series A, 45, p. 21. For more information on the margin of appreciation, we may refer to Macdonald, 1993, pp. 83-124.
189 Van Dijk & Van Hoof, 1990, pp. 579-580.
190 Cohen-Jonathan (1993, pp. 427-429) indicates that "there is hardly any jurisprudence by the Court on the protection of the home" at all.
191 April 24, 1990, Series A, 176A and 176B (Kruslin and Huvig v. France), commented by Swart, 1991a.

decisions, infringements with the right to privacy ought to be in accordance with the law, which means firstly that the measure "should have some basis in domestic law," secondly that this law "should be accessible" and thirdly the law should have a minimum foreseeability and quality, "requiring it to be compatible with the rule of law."

The German legislators (on both federal and provincial levels) have created a great deal of legislation on observation, mostly obliged by the federal constitutional court. In combination with some general prohibitions existing already in the Criminal Code, the exceptions created as police powers form a clear and admirably detailed legal framework. With regard to use of observation techniques, the legislation contains detailed regulations of which techniques are allowed, under which circumstances and for the investigation of which crimes. For the repressive use of such techniques, the crime types are mentioned in detailed catalogues, whereas for preventive and proactive use, crime type restrictions are given in general definitions, some of which have been explained in detail. The regulations existing and being introduced in The Netherlands are just as clear, except where it concerns the use of optical devices and the use of position transmitters. Both have only been referred to in case-law, whereas neither of them is included in the eavesdropping bill. The use of acoustical devices knows a detailed regulation as to which techniques may be used; the crimes that may be investigated with these techniques are referred to in a concrete and enumerative offence catalogue.

Regarding optical observation by the police, the legislations of Luxembourg and France do not contain any regulation other than a prohibition to do so in private places. The legislation of these countries with respect to acoustical observation, especially telephone tapping, contains sufficiently clear regulations of what is allowed, in which cases and under which circumstances. Since the Interception of Communication Act coming into force, the situation will be similar for acoustical observation in Belgium. The Belgian situation for other types of observation still is less clear, especially since the regulations are confidential and not restricted to detailed categories or even a catalogue of crimes. Moreover, the only restriction they do contain with regard to the use of technical devices, is a prohibition to apply technical means that are legally forbidden. It must be regretted that the situation with regard to optical observation methods will remain unclear, since they are neither explicitly prohibited nor explicitly accepted. Altogether, this does not seem to be a sufficiently clear basis in the light of art. 8 ECHR.

The last important item to be compared is the control that may or may not be exercised on police observation. This control may be divided in three aspects:[192] control before the operation (which includes the power to order the start of such an operation), control during the operation itself and control afterward. With regard to the overhearing and recording of conversations, control before or during the operation is exercised by an investigating judge in Belgium, The Netherlands, Luxembourg and France. The Belgian directives also allow that previous control be exercised by the public prosecutor. In Germany, most legal provisions also allow previous control by the prosecutor but, in his absence, the prosecutor's control task may be fulfilled by his auxiliaries. In both cases, this low-level control is compensated by German law demanding that such provisory order or permission be confirmed by a judge. Note however that, as long as the Dutch eavesdropping bill is not in force yet, eavesdropping with other techniques than telephone tapping is controlled by the police only.

Less detailed provisions exist on the previous control of observation with optical instruments, especially since this technique has only been regulated by German legislation. The German regulation for control on this type of observation is very similar to the one for acoustical observation. As to the other countries, control might be exercised to a certain extent by he public prosecutor, who is supposed to supervise criminal inquiries in general; in Belgium, this rule is also found in the secret directives. The other type of control on observation by the police, the control after the operation has been finished, is in all five countries exercised by the court, at least when it comes to a criminal prosecution and the observation method is being discussed. If this is not the case, for instance because the observation was aimed at gathering intelligence rather than evidence, usually no control afterward takes place. The main reason for this lack of control is that, in most of these cases, the person who has been observed is not aware of this, and even if he has been informed about the observation of his activities or the tapping of his telephone, it will be difficult for him to obtain complete information on the results, the methods and the extent of the observation. Especially where the police seem to apply non-authorized methods to gather intelligence which they use to obtain legal warrants,[193] there should be a possibility to control this intelligence and the way it was gathered. In order to answer to the demands of the European Convention at this point, all five countries know at least some regulation on the protection of privacy against the

---

192   On the basis of the Klass case, Cohen-Jonathan (1993, p. 421) concludes that a "review of surveillance must intervene at three stages: when the surveillance is first ordered, while it is being carried out or after is has been terminated."

193   Like the Dutch police inspecting whether it is worthwhile requesting for a search warrant and the French police wiretapping in order to get information of a "confidential informer." The fact that the courts accept these uncontrollable "confidential informers" to be used, almost seems to provoke constructions.

registration of computerized data. A detailed examination of the national legislations and the international regulations on this point (like the Council of Europe Data Protection Convention), which would be necessary to assess to what extent these regulations are sufficient in the light of art. 8 ECHR, would however go beyond this research.

All of the five countries at the origin of the Schengen Convention allow and use observation as a method of criminal inquiry, at least to a certain extent. The only country in which practically every type of observation is based on statutory provisions is Germany. The interpretation that the Constitutional Court has given to the privacy and the individual freedom led to the situation that Germany now has an extremely detailed and vast system of legislation on breaches of the privacy by the state in general and on observation in particular, which could be an example to all democracies abiding by the rule of law. One must regret that the other countries have not yet arrived at this point of privacy protection, especially since not only the German Constitution but also the European Convention on Human Rights asks for more detailed regulation of this matter. Practically speaking, the creation of an explicit legislation on observation powers by the police would also bring more clarity into the unclear terminology used in the Schengen Convention and clear up the legal position and situation in which observing police officers might find themselves (in their own country as well as abroad). Furthermore, it would enlarge the possibilities of controlling the activities of the police in the highly sensible field between the common interest of criminal investigation and the individual interest of privacy. One may wonder seriously whether the use of intensive observation techniques by the police without a statutory basis is in accordance with the right to privacy as guaranteed by art. 8 ECHR.[194]

It is obvious that the German legislation is in accordance with this already. The legislators of the other countries will soon have to create legal bases too, since the guidelines in the Netherlands and Belgium, for different reasons cannot be considered "law" in the sense of art. 8 ECHR, whereas Luxembourg and France do not know any domestic regulation for observation at all. It is however worth noticing that France is the only of the five countries to have paid some attention in its Schengen circular to the concept of cross-border observation. Whether or not the provisions of art. 40 SC may be considered a legal basis for observation within the national borders is doubtful as well, let alone the question whether this article is sufficiently detailed with regard to the observation methods and techniques that may be used. Apart from the necessity of a

---

194 See the cases of Patricia Hope-Hewitt & Harriett Harman v. United Kingdom (European Commission on Human Rights, Appl. no. 12175/86) and Kruslin and Huvig v. France (European Court on Human Rights, both April 24, 1990, Series A, 176A and 176B, as well as Fijnaut, 1994a, pp. 52-53.

legal basis to the background of the European Convention there are other reasons for creating an explicit legislation on observation powers by the police: It would bring more clarity into the unclear terminology used in the Schengen Convention and clear up the legal position and situation in which observing police officers might find themselves (in their own country as well as abroad). Finally, it would enlarge the possibilities of controlling the activities of the police in the highly sensitive field between the common interest of criminal investigation and the individual interest of privacy. Thus, it would benefit the rule of law as contained in the European Convention.

5 Controlled Delivery, Infiltration and Informers

As we have seen in the preceding chapter, the police use a wide range of techniques in order to gather information on activity in the criminal world. Rather then passively observe suspects, the police may want to play a more active role in the investigation to get a better view inside a particular criminal organization. One may construct an almost continuous line depending on the degree of involvement of the police: from a simple omission to intervene, via the guiding or sending of civilian informers, to deep cover infiltration techniques.

Once the police has obtained information on a specific transaction concerning allegedly illegal activities, they may decide to see it carried out without intervening and in that way try to catch drug or arms dealers red handed. This is known as controlled delivery. The passive nature of the observation operation may change in a more active operation, as police officials themselves take part in the activity as undercover agents. In that case one speaks of flash rolls, (reverse) sting operations or infiltration. The difference between the three is not as clear cut as one may want to believe. Flash rolls and sting operations may be limited to short periods of time but it is obvious that they involve infiltration as well.

Infiltrators may not only be undercover police officials but may be informers as well: criminals already active in an organization or civilians with no criminal background. In that context, the use of listening devices may be an important issue.[1] To help us understand the role of police officials in these policing methods, one may distinguish on the one hand overt and covert police actions where the methods used **are not** deceptive in their art (one thinks then of uniformed patrols or passive surveillance) and on the other hand overt and covert police actions where the methods used **are** deceptive in their nature (for instance in the case of trickery where the identity of the police officer is known or undercover policing in general).[2] In this context one may consider controlled delivery as a non deceptive covert method and infiltration, flash rolls and (reverse) sting operations as deceptive covert methods.

---

1   We refer the reader to the preceding chapter where this question has been discussed.
2   This distinction is made by Marx, 1988, p. 12.

In recent years in Europe, it seems that the use of covert investigation methods has not only increased, but that the use of these special policing techniques has shifted from a form of infiltration aimed exclusively at investigating and prosecuting crimes to one aimed principally at the gathering of information on a criminal organization.[3] The most significant difference between the two approaches is the size of the operation, which tends to be larger scale and multi-disciplinary.[4] Simultaneously, these techniques have also been shifting from police infiltration to civilian infiltration.[5] Countries have been experimenting with this "new" way of policing and have experienced successes as well as failures.

There are various ways of sorting out the different possible forms of infiltration techniques. One may distinguish on the one hand between different kinds of infiltrators: the police infiltrator and the civilian infiltrator, whether criminal or not and on the second hand, one may distinguish according to the nature of the infiltration missions. It may be a one-time short term action, like in sting and reverse stings, this type of mission being mostly aimed at the gathering of evidence for criminal prosecution. It may also be project-wise operations which constitutes a series of short term infiltration actions linked to one another. Further, it may even be longer term infiltration operations in which cover-up companies are set up, the so-called front-stores, or yet what is known as deep cover infiltration operations.[6]

Indeed, all these policing methods may be seen in a reactive context as well as in a proactive context. The trend, however, is to see them in a proactive context as we have noted above that the principal aim of these methods is shifting from the investigation and prosecution of specific crimes already committed to the gathering of information on criminal activities in general. Consequently, one could make a distinction between the reactive and proactive investigations in the following way: The one is looking for the authors of a committed and acknowledged crime, while the other is seeking insight on the (alleged) crimes committed by known persons. Be that as it may, it seems that in the practice of law enforcement one seldom sees purely proactive or reactive undercover operations, the two being intimately intertwined.[7]

---

3   As far as The Netherlands are concerned, this is for instance acknowledged by the reports of the working group infiltration (De Wit, 1994) and the parliamentary working group investigating methods (Van Traa, 1994). Both reports will be discussed further below.

4   See Naeyé, 1995a, p. 12.

5   This was acknowledged in The Netherlands by the parliamentary working group Van Traa, 1994.

6   We use in this the distinctions used by the working group De Wit, 1994.

7   As this was related to us in Düsseldorf by *Kriminalrat* Clauer at the LKA in Nordrhein-Westfalen.

In short, it is perhaps wise to note that in the end, there will be as many forms of investigating techniques as there are inventive police and justice officials.[8] In this chapter, we will limit ourselves to first sketching the international norms on the subject and the minimum standard offered by the European Convention on Human Rights. We have chosen to discuss the matter of covert deceptive policing techniques in three phases: We will take an inventory of national norms on the subject of controlled delivery, infiltration (including all variations of this technique) and the use of informers, before we conclude by a comparison of these different norms in the light of police cooperation. Finally their concordance with the European Convention on Human Rights will be tested.

5.1 International Norms

5.1.1 International Norms on Police Cooperation

Looking for international norms on the matter is a trying enterprise. Controlled delivery was introduced internationally for the first time by art. 11 of the United Nations Convention Against Illicit Traffic in Narcotic Drugs and Psychotrope Substances.[9] The Schengen Convention (SC), which in some aspects provides for detailed norms on police cooperation, contains only one provision that might serve as a basis for international cooperation on that matter.

An analysis of art. 73 of the Convention shows us that only one form of passive observation of drug deliveries is addressed in very general terms: The Contracting Parties engage themselves to adopt measures to permit controlled deliveries on their territories in matters of illicit drug trafficking. The decision to resort to controlled delivery, according to the treaty, should be taken in each particular case on the basis of a previously obtained authorization of all concerned Contracting Parties. Still according to art. 73 SC each Contracting Party has control and direction of the operation taking place on his territory.

Although the term "controlled delivery" could be used to designate an operation involving infiltrating police officials as well as a strictly passive form of delayed intervention one should note that in the light of the French version of art. 73 of the Schengen Convention - where the terminology used differs from that of the German and Dutch versions - more active forms involving undercover

---

8 Moreover, not only police officers may resort to these secretive techniques, but also other organizations, as illustrated by a newspaper clipping (de Volkskrant, September 9, 1995): A "sting-team" of the international organization BSA, an organization which combats soft-ware piracy across the world, is said to have dismantled a network involved in the traffic of illegal soft-ware.

9 Vienna, December 20, 1988, published in The Netherlands in Trb. 1989, 97.

agents are excluded from the scope of the Convention.[10] The French version refers to the term "*livraison surveillée*," an expression also used in French legislation, designating a technique not involving police infiltrators, in opposition to "*livraison contrôlée*," a technique involving infiltrating officers. This interpretation is confirmed by the French version of art. 11 of the UN Convention, which also uses the term "*livraison surveillée*." France is moreover one of the only studied country having already adopted legislation on surveilled (or observed) as well as controlled delivery. This means to say that the expression controlled delivery is probably used in international context in this restricted sense. There are no treaties to this date that address the issue of infiltration.

The fact that this difference in terminology may be source of great difficulties is well illustrated by the following example: One may imagine a controlled delivery started in Spain with the help of one (or more) infiltrators. Arriving at the French border, the infiltrator(s) must leave the convoy, as France does not allow this type of operation on its territory and, according to the above mentioned treaties, is not obliged to do so. Upon the arrival of the convoy in Belgium, the infiltrators may, if they are still alive and are still trusted by their "fellow" criminals, reintegrate the group.[11] This interpretation of the Convention raises yet another question: What is the legal position of a controlled delivery infiltrated by a civilian infiltrator? By an informer? These questions cannot be answered by the existing treaties and may be the source of many future diplomatic problems.

In addition, it seems that par. 3 of art. 11 of the UN Convention does provide a basis in international law for a more active type of State action. On the basis of this provision,

> Illicit consignments whose controlled delivery is agreed to may, with the consent of the parties concerned, be intercepted and allowed to continue with the (drugs) intact or removed or replaced in whole or in part.

States seem to be authorized to let drug shippings enter the black market with the aim of identifying persons involved in drug trafficking.

In that it does not necessarily oblige the agents of the Contracting Parties to seize the transport, this provision seems to have been at the origin of the controlled transports responsible for the introduction of thousands of kilograms of narcotic drugs on the Dutch market during the IRT-case we will discuss later.

---

10 This has already been acknowledged as a real problem by W. Bruggeman, one of the coordinators of the Europol Drugs Unit.

11 Example given by W. Bruggeman at the congress "*Collaboration internationale en matière pénale et protection juridique*," Brussels, May 5, 1995; this is implicitly confirmed by the explanation given to observation in the French Schengen circular of June 23, 1995 (NOR: *JUSA9500149C*).

Par. 1 of art. 11 states that controlled deliveries are authorized when "permitted by the basic principles" of the respective domestic legal systems of the Contracting Parties. However, both art. 11 of the UN Convention and art. 73 SC do not contain prescriptions but guidelines to the Contracting Parties. The difference between prescriptions and guidelines can be stressed by stating that a prescription suggests a transfer of sovereignty from a State to an international norm whereas guidelines do not. They do not directly create a competence for the respective public prosecutors or the police, rather they bind States as to take measures enabling controlled deliveries and transports to take place. Because of that, these two provisions may not be considered a legal basis in themselves.

Finally, whether art. 40 SC may serve as a basis for cross-border infiltration operation is a question well worth asking. One could interpret the word observation as to include some forms of infiltration: observation from inside a criminal organization. Most of the conditions posed by the many provisions of this article could serve as a framework for cross-border infiltration.[12] Considering that some of these conditions are somewhat impractical in the context of infiltration, such as the fact that officers must be in the position to prove at any moment their official quality, this article was probably not meant to serve as an international legal basis for cross-border infiltration.[13] Moreover, in the eventuality that this article could serve as an international norm for cross-border infiltration, it offers very few guarantees in the view of the European Convention on Human Rights.

5.1.2   European Convention on Human Rights

Concerning international norms, it is surely relevant to look upon the case-law of the European Court of Human Rights. One question may arise when glancing through the case-law of the Court: Does the Convention impose on the member States that the use of techniques such as controlled delivery and infiltration be based on statutory law? One may wonder in this context whether the use of such techniques consists in a violation of art. 8 of the Convention concerning the right to privacy.

---

12   Art. 40 states some of the following conditions for a cross-border observation: It must be in the framework of a judiciary enquiry and after a request for mutual legal assistance, the visited country must have the guarantee that only police officials may be used as observers, the police officers must at any moment be in a position to prove their official quality and finally, the officers may not trespass on private premises; Schürmann (1995, p. 349, footnote 4) notes that the use of German infiltrators on foreign territory must be done in accordance to the provisions of judiciary assistance.

13   Nevertheless, some high-ranking practitioners seem to believe that it could, as was related to us by sources inside the French *gendarmerie*.

The standard case on infiltration is the Lüdi case.[14] Lüdi was a Swiss national against whom the Swiss authorities, tipped by the German authorities, launched an undercover operation with the help of a Swiss infiltrator and telephone tapping. Both methods had a basis in national Swiss law. The defence pleaded that the use of an infiltrator against Lüdi had infringed his right to privacy as guaranteed by art. 8 of the European Convention on Human Rights. The Court held that there was no violation of Lüdi's private life as one cannot invoke this protection while engaging in cocaine deal. An infiltrator in the context of a cocaine deal is not a violation of art. 8 of the Convention and consequently it was not found relevant, despite the terms of par. 2 of art. 8, to address the issue of the quality of the norm on which the policing technique was based. The argument used was that the applicant "must have been aware that he ran the risk of encountering an undercover police officer whose task would be to expose him."[15] The Court did not address the question of sufficient law,[16] rather it seemed to distinguish between two moments: the moment one is not involved in criminal activities and the moment where one does engage in criminal activities. In this way, the protection of art. 8 of the Convention would be granted solely to the former. It seems that this restrictive view of the concept of privacy could be considered inconsistent with judgements of the Court regarding telephone tapping where the court stated that the use of such method must be based on sufficient law.[17] If someone engaged in criminal activity should reasonably be expected to knowingly run the risk of running into an undercover agent, then this person could also be expected to knowingly run the risk of being eavesdropped or spied on by means of a telephone tap, which according to the Court must be based on sufficient national law. According to the actual (incomplete) reasoning of the Court in Lüdi, this would not be the case for infiltration which, one may argue, could be considered at least as infringing in one's right to private life as telephone tapping, moreover because of the direct involvement of the authorities in the person's actions. The fact that someone presumably engages in a criminal activity should in fact be irrelevant to the question of whether someone may (or may not) be observed in his private life without his knowledge by any means.

The right to privacy does not disappear during a cocaine deal, rather its violation may be justified by the circumstances when done in accordance with the rule of law: In order to acknowledge the alleged criminal activities, one has

---

14   June 15, 1992, Series A 238.
15   See nr. 40 of the Lüdi case.
16   See also Swart, 1993a, p. 182.
17   See the Kruslin and Huvig cases discussed below. Marx (1988, p. 147) notes as well that undercover operations share with wiretapping the invasion of privacy, without the restraint or inherent limitations imposed by judicial warrants in the United States.

to violate the privacy of the suspect. The right to privacy is not a right that appears and disappears to facilitate the work of the investigating authorities. It exists as such, as a continuing protection englobing all our private activities, but is not absolute. This is why the drafters of the Convention stipulated in par. 2:

> There shall be no interference by a public authority with the exercise of this right except such as is in accordance with the law and is necessary in a democratic society in the interests of national security, public safety (...) for the prevention of disorder or crime (...)

This paragraph authorizes national authorities to violate the right to privacy, as long as it is in accordance with the law and necessary in a democratic society. These issues are ones to be debated in each parliament as the legislator ponders on the opportuneness of such law.

Furthermore, considering this rule of law as expressed by par. 2 of art. 8 ECHR and present in the spirit of the whole of the Convention one may wonder about the consequences of such a decision which denies the existence of privacy during (alleged) criminal activities. This would mean for instance that, considering that according to Lüdi criminals have a lesser expectation of privacy than law abiding citizens, the rule of law would only apply to actions of the authorities in relation to the rights of law abiding citizens. Violations of the right to privacy of law abiding citizens would need to be based on sufficient law whereas violations of the right to privacy of criminals would not. This interpretation is not acceptable as it would leave a great deal of areas that would not be covered by the rule of law and would let the guarantee of the rule of law depend on factors (for instance that someone is either a law abiding citizen or a criminal) that have not yet been legally established. Considering that it could not have been the intention of the authors of the Convention to restrict the protection of the guaranteed rights as to dispense their violation from the requirements of the rule of law one may chose to interpret extensively the rights guaranteed by the Convention. Since one can suppose that policing techniques such as telephone taps and infiltration were not foreseen at the time the Convention was signed it is not impossible that such techniques are covered by the protection of art. 8 ECHR, this at least to prevent arbitrary violations of art. 8.[18]

Let us consider the consequences of the affirmation that criminals would not have a reasonable expectancy of privacy. As noted above, this would lead us to conclude that the right to privacy would only be recognized to law-abiding

---

18   With special thanks to K. Rozemond, who helped us develop this point of view with his adverse opinions.

citizens. As a violation of this right would, according to par. 2, have to be based on a law bearing the characteristics discussed in the cases Kruslin and Huvig, a violation of this right on alleged criminals would not need a basis in formal law. Considering the preceding, when would the State need to make violations of this nature? Indeed, it is to be hoped that the State will not go about breaching the right to privacy of law-abiding citizens, but will concentrate scarce resources on alleged criminals. Would this not render the legislation obsolete? Moreover, especially in these secret policing techniques, the police is expected to blend in the criminal world, committing the same crimes they are sent to investigate. For all these reasons it is preferable to adopt a more extensive interpretation of the right to privacy, giving the benefit of art. 8 par. 2 ECHR to a wider range of interventions of the State.

Once we have acknowledged the fact that suspects have a right to privacy, it goes without saying that persons who are no suspect in the meaning of the criminal procedure have this right as well. The application of techniques such as infiltration, proactive or reactive, are a violation of this right, notwithstanding the issue as to whether one is a suspect or not. Moreover, the application of these techniques potentially violate the presumption of innocence. The presumption of innocence will be discussed in greater detail in Chapter 10, but we can comment at this stage that contacts between the infiltrating police officer and the suspect can be seen as the questioning by the police of an unaware suspect. The question of from which moment the suspect should be recognized this right has been answered by the Neumeister case. The Commission stated that the relevant stage of the procedure "is that at which the situation of the person concerned has been substantially affected as a result of a suspicion against him."[19] In our opinion, encounters between infiltrating police officers and unaware suspects may have such consequences for the suspect, for instance because of the ability of the undercover officer to manipulate the intention and actions of the suspect, that the protection of the presumption of innocence must be given to the suspect even at that early stage. Even more so in proactive undercover operations. Although some may argue that this right is not absolute and that it can be restricted, the restriction of such a fundamental right must be at the very least based on sufficient domestic law.

The Court had stated in the cases of Kruslin and Huvig, cases which may be considered as standard cases on the rule of law, that telephone tapping was a violation of art. 8 ECHR and was as such "an interference by a public auth-

---

19 Report of May 27, 1966, Neumeister, B.6 (1966-1969) p. 81; this view was eventually confirmed by the Court; see judgments in the Foti case of December 10, 1982 (A 56, p. 18) and in the Oztürk case of February 21, 1984 (A 75, p. 21); see also Van Dijk & Van Hoof, 1990, p. 329.

194

ority" with the exercise of the applicants' right to respect for their..."private life."[20] Such an interference contravenes art. 8 unless it is "in accordance with the law, pursues one or more of the legitimate aims referred to in paragraph 2 and furthermore is necessary in a democratic society in order to achieve them." According to the Court, the expression "in accordance with the law" within the meaning of art. 8 par. 2 "requires firstly that the impugned measure should have more basis in domestic law; it also refers to the quality of the law in question, requiring that it should be accessible to the person concerned, who must moreover be able to foresee its consequences for him, and compatible with the rule of law." Regarding the quality of the law, the Court states further that "Especially where a power of the executive is exercised in secret, the risks of arbitrariness are evident." The Court continues: "Tapping and other forms of interception of telephone conversations represent a serious interference with private life and correspondence and must accordingly be based on a law that is particularly precise. It is essential to have clear, detailed rules on the subject, especially as the technology available for use is continually becoming more sophisticated." If this is the case for telephone tapping that requires no direct intervention of police authorities, then one could hardly argue that policing techniques that aim at the manipulation of the actions of the suspect without his knowledge would not correspond to this definition.

5.2 National Norms

In giving an overview on the legal framework of these special policing techniques in the five countries at the origin of the Schengen Convention, we have chosen to begin with sketching the general legal situation (section 5.2.1). We then proceed to discuss three different variations of covert police work: controlled delivery (section 5.2.2), infiltration (section 5.2.3) and the use of informers (section 5.2.4). We realize that this distinction between these policing methods is an artificial one, as controlled delivery can be done with undercover police officers as well as with the help of informers sent by the police or public prosecutor. However, this distinction has been made to enable the sketching of the legal framework.

5.2.1 General

When it comes to comparing norms on covert policing techniques one is first struck by the difference in conceptions of policing in the different countries. Some States consider these as public domain while others consider them as

---

20   April 24, 1990 (Series A 176), also published in The Netherlands in NJCM-Bulletin, 1990, pp. 6-7.

matters of State security, the aims of which are liable to be frustrated by publicly accessible statutes, or even as simple matters of police technique not needing any regulations at all. The types of norms considering these policing techniques are very diversified as well as their quality. This may have consequences for the controllability of the norm and of the police actions, as well as for the international police cooperation. In contrast, what seems to be a general trend in the studied countries is that political scandals caused by irregularities in or disagreements on investigating techniques often act as catalyst for some type of legislative activity.

5.2.1.1 Belgium

There are no statutes regulating these policing techniques in Belgium, which does not mean that Belgian police officials refrain from using them. The François case,[21] in which during the second half of the 1970's an infiltrating *gendarmerie* officer found himself buying and selling drugs in order to recover a sum of money that had been lost in the beginning of the operation, and the creation of a special commission set up to study the case initiated the debate on that subject.[22] The minister of justice at the time, stated on that occasion that the use of policing techniques such as sting operations and infiltration engender such potential risks and costs that they should only be allowed in the specific context of the fight against organized crime.[23] The use of these special undercover policing techniques was finally regulated by (confidential) circular.[24]

Besides the circular, the principles of the Belgian police investigations must be taken into account as the Belgian judge will control the legality of the investigating techniques used on the only basis of these principles.[25] This means for example that the exclusionary rule has to be observed, of which follows that everything is allowed if it is not forbidden.[26] One must also regard such principles as the prohibition of provocation, the principles of

---

21   See Fijnaut, 1983.
22   Van Parys & Laurent, 1990.
23   Van Parys & Laurent, 1990, p. 231.
24   *Omzendbrief betreffende bijzondere opsporingstechnieken om de zware of georganiseerde criminaliteit te bestrijden* (Circular concerning special techniques of investigation to fight severe or organized crime), ministry of justice, April 24, 1990, Nr. 7/SDP/690/MN NIX/RB6/6. Part of the circular was rendered public through its publication as proposed bill of law (*Gedrukte stukken* 1990-1991, 1637/1).
25   See Chapter 3 on the structure of criminal law enforcement.
26   Consult on evidence in general Van den Wyngaert, 1994, pp.759-768; Holsters, 1990, pp. 2-5.

proportionality and subsidiarity,[27] as well as the contact with and the written rapport to the judicial authorities. Finally, there is a certain degree of tolerance granted to criminal acts committed by police officials.[28]

These special techniques seem to be very used in Belgium. According to official sources inside the *gendarmerie*, special investigation teams are even present in each public prosecutor's department, not unlike the ones present in the United States and The Netherlands.

5.2.1.2 The Netherlands

Although there are no statutes concerning these particular policing techniques in the Netherlands, the case-law and the competent ministries have adopted a number of guidelines. In the particular issue of undercover policing the case-law requirements regarding the principles of proportionality and subsidiarity will be higher than for other policing techniques because these imply a larger measure of intervention on the part of the State.[29] This is the case for instance where the investigation of severe crimes cannot be achieved with the help of less drastic means. The admissibility of undercover policing will be tested in each individual case on the basis of the principles of proportionality and subsidiarity on the one hand and, on the other hand, on other principles such as conscientiousness and fair play. This particular issue is regulated as well by means of directives, some of which are confidential. We will address these below.

The discussion on the admissibility of these investigating methods has recently reached its peak in the aftermath of what is known as the "IRT-scandal." As an answer to an increase in organized crime, the IRT, short for "inter regional police detective team" (*interregionaal rechercheteam*) was set up in 1987. Because of alleged disagreements on policing techniques, the team was dismantled in 1993. It seems that not everybody was satisfied with the final turn of events as a series of press releases rose doubt on the official reasons behind

---

27　The concepts of proportionality and subsidiarity are very important in the law systems of a number of continental European Countries. By proportionality, one refers to the action of the officer which must be in proportion to the reproached actions; see Van den Wyngaert, 1994, p. 14. By subsidiarity, one refers to the action of the officer which must moreover be the least infringing, the least violating of the basic rights of the suspect while still achieving the aimed result: the necessary action. See Van den Wyngaert, 1994, p. 9.

28　Dierkens *et al.*, 1991, p.454.

29　Corstens (1995, p. 282) writes that these principles must be respected in the use of these special undercover practices as they must be respected in all the State's actions of criminal procedure. The use of such a serious means as infiltration is only justified when the aim, investigating severe crimes, justifies it; other, less violating means, have proven not effective to reach the aim.

the dismantlement of the team: Accusations of corruption and insinuations about illegal policing methods were made.[30] Finally, this led to the setting up of an enquiry to shine more light on the circumstances leading to the end of the investigation team.

The conclusions of this enquiry (published in the so-called report-Wierenga) led to the fall of the two police ministers (justice and the interior) because they had failed to exercise the right control on the team.[31] A parliamentary working group (the working group-Van Traa, named after its chairman) was set up to decide on the opportuneness of starting a parliamentary enquiry committee on policing methods. The working group answered positively to this question and has extensively addressed the issue of the acceptability of certain policing methods in a democracy, as well as the need for statutory regulation.[32] In addition, to what the working group had already done, the committee has taken an inventory of the investigating methods used in The Netherlands and has noted a shift from police infiltration to civilian infiltration, as well as the fact that a combination of different methods is used.[33]

Since these events, revelations have been made about the methods used by the team, which do not fail to have international implications. It has been suggested that narcotics have been imported to Great Britain under the hospice of the Dutch public prosecutor's department.[34] It is during the hearings of the

---

30 See for instance: *Minister kende plan IRT voor import coke* (de Volkskrant, March 31, 1994) *IRT-drugs zijn niet op straat beland* (de Volkskrant, April 2, 1994) *IRT-team Haarlem van corruptie beschuldigd* (de Volkskrant, April 1, 1994). It seems that the CID of Haarlem ran an informer since 1994 in order to gain insight on organized crime. In this operation, 20.000 kilos of soft drugs have been introduced on the market (NRC-Handelsblad, April 18, 1995). As we have seen above, this approximation seems to have been conservative as subsequent newspaper clippings show that in fact up to 400 thousand of not only soft drugs but also hard drugs have been hitting the streets as a result of this investigation method (de Volkskrant, June 16, 1995). See also De Telegraaf and Algemeen Dagblad, April 20, 1995. This was apparently no reason to stop using these techniques since even after the dismantlement of the IRT, the prosecutor general of Amsterdam decided to continue using the "dubious" investigation method (later known as the Delta method), leading to the introduction of yet more thousands of kilos of soft drugs on the market (Het Parool, April 20, 1995); indeed, a detailed overview of the events leading to the dismantlement of the detective team can be found in Van Traa, 1996.

31 See Wierenga, 1994.

32 See Van Traa, 1996, with 11 Appendices of altogether nearly 5000 pages.

33 Van Traa, 1996, pp. 72-292.

34 The Dutch public prosecutor's department had apparently let a criminal informer climb the hierarchy of a criminal organization which had imported ten thousands of kilos of marijuana, as well as synthetic drugs like XTC and amphetamines, into Great Britan. This in order to infiltrate the top of the organization. See question by members of parliament Kalsbeek-Jasperse, Scheltema-de Nie, Korthals and Soutendijk-Van Appeldoorn, *Kamervraag-IRT*, in: TK 1994-1995 - *Aanhangsel van de Handelingen* nr. 404, also published in NJB 1995, 9,

parliamentary committee that, officially, more light was shed on the method used by the police at that time. The method, called controlled transport (*doorleve-ring*), aims the analysis of the activities of criminal organization. Although the minister of justice has explicitly forbidden resorting to this method, but there are indications that this method is still being used in The Netherlands.[35]

5.2.1.3 Luxembourg

Although there is neither a statute in Luxembourg regarding undercover policing techniques such as controlled delivery or infiltration, nor any (known) circular or directive on the subject, Luxembourg does permit that controlled deliveries originating foreign countries take place on its territory.[36] Furthermore, it is not excluded that certain confidential circulars do exist, especially since Luxembourg seems to have adopted some of the same forms of special policing techniques that are used in Belgium. Their existence is however purely speculative and has not been confirmed.

Although policing techniques such as controlled delivery do not seem to find obstacles in Luxembourg law, the situation is not clear as to whether infiltration may occur on Luxembourg ground. According to sources in Luxembourg, it is not excluded that foreign infiltrating officers operate on Luxembourg territory in the framework of cross-border controlled deliveries and according to agreements in international legal assistance. This is true especially when one notes the ambivalent position of Luxembourg internationally: Luxembourg has on the one hand obliged itself according to art. 73 SC to let controlled deliveries take place on its territory and, on the other hand, is a member of an international forum on infiltration.[37] The practical consequences of this are not known.

---

p. 332; see also Middelburg & Van Es, 1994 and Naeyé, 1995, p. 54.

35 It seems that this method was thought to be legal because of the interpretation of the 1990 circular on infiltration which did not mention the aim of the operation as being the apprehension of the suspects and the seizure of the illegal goods. Because this was not explicitly mentioned, it was thought that the gathering of information was a justification for the bringing on the market of large amounts of illegal psychotropic substances. On December 21, 1995, the assembly of prosecutors-general introduced a number of terminological definitions for "special investigation methods" such as observation and infiltration, including criteria about examination, registration and control of the use of these methods. The list of terminology was published in for instance NJB 1996-3, pp. 107-108.

36 This was confirmed by officials of the Luxembourg police.

37 See Kastel, 1989, p. 215.

5.2.1.4 France

Before the adoption of the statute of December 10, 1991 (Anti Drugs Act) concerning controlled deliveries (in the text called **surveilled** deliveries) and infiltration (called **controlled** deliveries),[38] the situation was not clear as to the admissibility of evidence gathered with the help of policing techniques involving a form of provocation. The courts were willing in some cases to consider police provocation as a legal exception for prosecution, but in other cases refrained to do so.[39] What caused the French legislator to pass the Anti Drugs Act was in fact the prosecution of customs officers by examining judges in Lyon and Dijon for drug trafficking in March and April 1991. The ministry of justice immediately reacted by passing a directive (June 19, 1991) allowing police infiltration. According to this directive, the examining judge had to be kept informed on all activities of the infiltrating officers.

In general the French courts hold as a principle that only the results of lawful policing methods or methods ratified by an examining judge may be considered as evidence in court.[40] The remaining less formal factual elements may only be considered as general information that may be of use for the public prosecutor upon deciding on the relevancy of assigning an examining judge to conduct a preliminary judicial enquiry. This type of information may also eventually lead to the delivering of orders for telephone taps or search warrants by the examining judge.

5.2.1.5 Germany

The German federal constitutional court stated in 1983 in an important judgment that individuals must be protected by the State against unlimited collecting, storing, using and transmitting of personal data.[41] Although this right is not absolute, it does follow that its violation must rest on a rule of law that offers the necessary guarantees limiting the violation.

The judgment of the court has led to large scale legislative operations, especially with respect to the protection of privacy: Every German province has its own statute on data protection, above which also exists a federal statute on that matter. Because of the fact that the police usually collect data that by nature

---

38   *Loi relative aux renforcements de la lutte contre le trafic des stupéfiants*, J.O. December 20, 1991, nr. 296, p.16593 (Anti Drugs Act), partly incorporated in special statutes such as the *Code de la santé publique* and the *Code des douanes*, before being incorporated in art. 706-32 CPP.

39   See Pradel, 1992, p. 229.

40   For an overview of the limits of the liberty of evidence in France see Leclerc, 1992, pp.15-29.

41   *Volkszählungsurteil* (census judgement), December 15, 1983, BVerfGE 65, 1, also published in NJW 1984-8, pp.419-428.

regards especially sensitive areas of the personal lives of individuals, this led to great legislative changes, on federal as well as provincial levels of legislation concerning police and criminal procedure, in all the rules regarding police powers that may potentially violate the personal life sphere. The resulting codification activity has given to date, although partly still in progress, a statutory basis to a great number of police powers.

The necessity to adapt existing statutory provisions regarding the police and adopt new ones was emphasized by the practice of the police when it began to be confronted in the early eighties with an increase in organized crime. In the fight against crime, the accent came to rest more and more on extending police powers in the sphere of proactive crime repression (*vorbeugende Kriminalitätsbekämpfung*).[42] Because of the secret manner of collecting information in these proactive policing activities, and considering the case-law of the federal constitutional court, it was necessary to provide these new techniques with a formal statuary basis. The resulting discussion attempting to determine the moment in which proactive policing evolves in repressive policing and the subsequent question regarding which level of statutes (provincial or federal) should embody the provisions on that matter is still vivid.[43] For all these reasons, the German doctrine and case law, as well as statutory provisions, have to this day worked out proactive policing in the minutest detail.

Ten of the eleven "old" provinces had in early 1993 statutory provisions regarding proactive policing techniques. The eleventh one, Niedersachsen, has adopted new legislation on that matter which did not legalize this practice.[44] The majority of the "new" eastern provinces have also adopted new legislation concerning special policing methods. There is also a federal law, which recently came into force, regarding observation, treatment of computer data and other policing techniques.[45]

German statutes have introduced a special terminology to designate and differentiate actors in the above mentioned policing techniques, although this terminology may vary from province to province, or from province to federal legislation. When an undercover police officer is involved the term hidden

---

42 See among others Weßlau, 1989, Götz, 1990, pp. 46 and 73-74; Ring, 1990, p.373; Hund, 1991, p.463.

43 See among others Wolter, 1988, pp. 49-90 and pp. 129-142; Weßlau, 1989; Ring, 1990, pp. 372-379; Hund, 1991, pp. 463-468; Wolter, 1991, pp. 30-33; Strate, 1992, pp. 29-37; Fischer, 1992, pp. 7-13 and Kniesel, 1992, pp. 164-167.

44 See Law on the repression of danger (*Niedersächsisches Gefahrenabwehrgesetz*-NGefAG), April 14, 1994, Nds. GVBl. Nr. 0/1994; see also Gössner, 1992, p. 19.

45 Law on the repression of illegal drug trafficking and other expressions of organized crime (*Gesetz zur Bekämpfung des illegalen Rauschgifthandels und anderer Erscheinungsformen der Organisierten Kriminalität* - OrgKG): July 15, 1992, BGBl. I, 1992, 1302; the statute came into force on September 15, 1992; see also Hilger, 1992, pp. 457-463 and 523-526.

investigator or infiltrator (*Verdeckte Ermittler*) is used. It is striking, however, that expressions such as sting operations (*Scheinankaufen*) and agents provocateurs (*Lockspitzel*) are not found even though they too involve the assignment of police officials or others under false identities.[46]

5.2.2 Controlled Delivery

Controlled delivery can be defined as the monitoring by the police of an illegal transport with delayed intervention. It may involve the use of an infiltrator but we will not discuss this possibility here. It is thus a covert, non deceptive policing method where police officials refrain from intervening in order to gather information on certain criminal activities in general and in particular on the responsible persons for these activities.

5.2.2.1 Belgium

The above mentioned confidential circular defines controlled delivery as a "guided transport" (*begeleide zending*) or a "postponed seizure" (*uitgestelde inbeslagneming*) set up by a police corps within the context of an judicial enquiry controlled by a magistrate (nr. 8.1). The police let a transport of illegal goods take place without intervening in order to intercept the transport at its destination or a point of control. This definition seems to exclude carrying out controlled transports (the transport of goods without police intervention aimed at the gathering of information) since the aim of the operation remains the intervention of the police.

Controlled deliveries may only take place when they satisfy the principles of proportionality and subsidiarity and are subject to written authorization of the competent magistrate of the place where the operation begins as well as of the place of destination (nr. 8.3). The national magistrate is competent to decide on disagreements between the different magistrates (nr. 8.4). Where a controlled delivery is to occur on the territory of another country, the decision of postponing the seizure must rest on the previously obtained authorization of the competent foreign authority as well as on the guarantee that the illegal goods will be intercepted before they hit the street and the culprits can be prosecuted (nr. 8.4.2). Where a controlled delivery originating another country must take place on Belgian ground, the foreign authorities are expected to give all the necessary information to the competent magistrate in Belgium in order to enable him to take the decision of postponing the seizure.

---

46   See Löwe/Rosenberg, 1989, art. 163, nr. 55.

The public prosecutor of the place of intervention acts as the competent magistrate in charge of the enquiry and takes all decisions related to the execution of the operation (nr. 8.5.1). The public prosecutor's department competent in the places along the route of the illegal transport must be kept informed of the operation (nr. 8.5.2). If control on the illegal goods or concerned persons is in danger of being lost, the auxiliary public prosecutor in charge of the operation may resort to intercepting the transport in order to seize the goods (nr. 8.5.3). The final intervention must be executed with great care with respect to the seizure of the illegal goods, the gathering of evidence and the prosecution (nr. 8.5.4).[47]

5.2.2.2 The Netherlands

One cannot speak of judicial police action in the Netherlands without stressing the importance of the principles of proportionality and subsidiarity.[48] Applied to the question of controlled delivery it may be said that the nature of the catch as well as its size will be significant in the evaluation of the appropriateness of the operation, especially if there is no other way of efficiently prosecuting the suspects. It must be said as well that Dutch criminal law does not stand in the way of postponed seizure of illegal goods because of the principle of the appropriateness of prosecution.[49] In any case this technique is not only used and accepted but is also addressed in the above mentioned 1991 directive.[50] Note that nothing stands in the way of using this technique to monitor deliveries of all kinds of illegal goods, from illegal drugs to child pornography or illegal arms.

The 1991 directive on infiltration intends to regulate controlled delivery as well.[51] It makes a distinction between controlled delivery where the police only plays a role as an observer and controlled delivery where the police and the ministry of justice play an active role by providing for a delivery service run by an infiltrator. The directive finds it not necessary to set conditions for the former type of controlled delivery but it sets a number of conditions for the latter.

The use of controlled delivery is subjected to the demands of the principles of proportionality, subsidiarity and diligence. In general terms, controlled

---

47 On controlled delivery in Belgium, see further Van Traa, 1996, App. V, pp. 469-470.
48 Since we have spoken about these principles in Chapter 3 we will not discuss this matter further. See further Corstens, 1995, 281.
49 The power of the public prosecutor to decide whether or not prosecution is appropriate. This principle has been discussed in Chapter 3, to which we refer the reader.
50 Tabarelli, 1987, p. 80.
51 Infiltration directive (*Richtlijnen Infiltratie, vastgesteld in de vergadering van procureurs generaal*), February 20, 1991.

delivery is authorized when specific elements indicate the (future) commission of crimes that can be accounted to the organized or career criminality or when these crimes cannot reasonably be investigated otherwise for other reasons.

One method has been the object of much publicity in The Netherlands since the beginning of the hearings of the parliamentary committee Van Traa: The controlled transport or *gecontroleerde doorlevering* of narcotic drugs (soft and hard), aimed at the gaining of insight in the criminal world and its organization as opposed to the interception and seizure of the illegal transport. Controlled transports, in combination with the use of informers who are guided and paid by the police, and even encouraged to climb the hierarchy of the criminal organization led to the IRT-scandal. The use of this method, the so-called Delta-method, has resulted in the importation on the Dutch market of hundreds of thousands of kilograms of soft and hard drugs without interception.[52] As mentioned above, it was thought that because of the fact that apprehension of the suspects and seizure of the illegal goods was not mentioned explicitly in the 1991 circular on infiltration as aim for the use of special investigating methods, the gathering of information could be a justification. The minister of justice has pronounced a moratorium on this method on the eve of the committee hearings, but hearings of high ranking police officials have not excluded the possibility that this method is still being used.[53]

5.2.2.3 Luxembourg

Luxembourg permits cross-border surveilled deliveries on its territory.[54] Indeed, its legislation does not seem to pose great difficulties on that matter. According to the principle of opportuneness of criminal proceedings it is quite possible for the competent authorities to refrain from intervening in the commission of a crime if they find this opportune. The absence of legislation on the subject may have as a consequence that there is no restriction as to the nature of illegal goods the transport of which may be monitored, nor as to whether the illegal goods must be seized. Whether these possibilities are used by the authorities is unknown and non documented. Controlled deliveries originating neighbouring countries are allowed to cross Luxembourg borders as Luxembourg has obliged itself with art. 73 of the Schengen Convention as well as with the Vienna U.N. Convention of 1988 to let controlled deliveries take place on its territory.

---

52 This Delta method was judged absolutely irresponsible and unacceptable by the parliamentary enquiry committee; see Van Traa, 1996, pp. 161-168.
53 See hearing of J. Wilzing in Van Traa, 1996, App. II, p. 66.
54 This has been confirmed to us by sources inside the Luxembourg police.

5.2.2.4 France

The Anti Drugs Act distinguishes, as stated above, between *livraison surveillée* (par. 1 of art. 706-32 CPP, concerning the monitoring of a drug delivery) and *livraison contrôlée* (par. 2, where undercover police officers are also involved) and gives these two policing methods a legal basis.[55] The first paragraph limits itself to giving the auxiliary public prosecutors and, under their supervision, their adjuncts the power to observe and monitor the drug delivery after obtaining the authorization of the competent public prosecutor.[56]

As France knows the principle of opportuneness of criminal proceedings, it is not sure whether controlled delivery needed a basis in French law. In any case, the law does not seem to stand in the way of such operations but it is uncertain what effect this provision will have on the legality of (non regulated) controlled deliveries of other illegal goods.[57] Whether controlled transports may be authorized by the law is another question. We have explained above how the redaction of the circular on infiltration in The Netherlands was understood by certain as to leave an legal opening for the controlled transport of narcotic drugs. In France, however, the law explicitly states that these operations may only be set up for the purpose of acknowledging the commission of an offence, identifying the suspects and preceding to the seizure of the drugs.

---

55 See also Pradel, 1992, p.231; originally, these provisions was incorporated in art. L.627-7 CSP and 67*bis* CD, but was later incorporated in the (new) *Code pénal* by the law 92-1336 of December 16, 1992.

56 "(...) *les officiers de police judiciaire* (...) *peuvent* (...) *procéder à la surveillance de l'achemi-nement des substances ou plantes classées comme stupéfiants(...).*"

57 Since surveilled deliveries of illegal psychotropic substances are explicitly allowed, it may implicitly exclude surveilled deliveries of other illegal transports, such as child pornography or arms; note that, considering the present crusade against drug trafficking in France, it is to be expected that the investigation and prosecution of other crimes than drug related offences will not be a priority in near future. This crusade against drug trafficking seems to have reached a new peak with the intention of the French government to modify the criminal law in adding new provisions criminalizing acquaintances of drug dealers with a standard of living which they are unable to justify by legal means. In this way the onus of proof will be reversed: These persons will be guilty of this new offence unless they can answer for their financial situation in a legal manner (see de Volkskrant, September 16, 1995).

5.2.2.5 Germany

A published guideline provides a legal basis for the practice of controlled delivery.[58] Indeed, German formal law does not explicitly stand in the way of such a technique as controlled delivery, which is even used and accepted.[59] although, this does seem incompatible with the principle of legality,[60] it need not be so considering that police intervention is only postponed and that the transport will eventually be intercepted.[61]

The guideline distinguishes between three categories of controlled deliveries: controlled transport (*kontrollierte Durchfuhr*), a guided illegal transport originating a foreign country passing through the German territory and exiting to a third country;[62] controlled export (*kontrollierte Ausfuhr*), a guided illegal transport originating Germany entering another country and controlled import (*kontrollierte Einfuhr*), a guided transport into Germany. Such operations are possible for transports of such illegal goods as psychotropic substances, arms, stolen and fencing goods. As Germany follows the principle of legality very strictly in that every violation of the law must be prosecuted, controlled delivery needed a legal basis since it is seen as an omission to prosecute (immediately). Consequently, the law prescribes great care.

This type of operation is only authorized when it is not possible to investigate or achieve prosecution in another way. The supervision is done in such a way that arrest of and interception is assured.[63] Moreover, in the case of controlled import and export, the foreign States must make the following declarations: that they have agreed to the controlled import or export, that they will control the transport, that all the criminally responsible will be prosecuted and the illegal goods will be seized, excluding the method of the so-called controlled transport used in The Netherlands. Finally, The foreign authorities must be able

---

58 Guidelines for the criminal procedure and fines (*Richtlinien für das Strafverfahren und das Bußgeldverfahren* (RiStBV)), nrs. 29a-29d; ratified by: Baden-Wüttemberg, Bayern, Berlin, Hamburg, Hessen, Mecklenburg-Vorpommern, Niedersachsen, Nordrhein-Westfalen, Rheinland-Pfalz, Saarland, Sachsen, Schleswig-Holstein, Sachsen-Anhalt, Thüringen and the federal government.

59 See Tabarelli, 1987, p. 80.

60 See Chapter 3 on police enquiries.

61 In this sense also Tak *et al.*, 1996, pp. 207-208; on controlled delivery in Germany, see further Van Traa, 1996, App. V, pp. 485-486.

62 It is therefore not the controlled transport as understood in The Netherlands and which implies the possible introduction of illegal goods on the illegal market and which aims the gathering of information on criminal organizations and not the seizure of the goods.

63 Although the text of the guideline does not contain an obligation to intervene, this is strongly suggested in nr. 29a: "*Die Überwachung ist so zu gestalten, daß die Möglichkeit des Zugriffs auf Täter und Tatgegenstände jederzeit sichergestellt ist.*"

to assure the German authorities that they will be kept informed of the criminal procedure.

5.2.3   Infiltration

As we have seen above, when considering infiltration as a policing method, one may distinguish between for instance short term and long term, sting operations, flash roll, front stores, deep cover etc. Usually one considers methods such as sting operations and flash roll as short term infiltration, whereas long(er) term infiltration is usually known as infiltration. In any case the term infiltration is used to designate many kinds of covert deceptive policing methods where police officers play an active role.

5.2.3.1 Belgium

The afore mentioned circular provides very specific regulation: Infiltration is referred to by the Belgian minister of justice as the police action, incognito and for a restricted period of time, inside a criminal network or organization aiming the acquisition of information about and evidence regarding the commission of (or the attempt to commit) criminal offences.[64] Only police officials are permitted to take part in undercover policing activities (nr. 9.1). This limitation is explicitly repeated in nr. 9.4.3 of the circular which also provides for the eventual assigning of foreign officials on Belgian ground for infiltration purposes. As for the duration of an infiltration mission should require, it should only be a short period of time (nr. 9.2.4). There is no indication as to how short this period should be nor as to which limit should not to be transgressed.

Belgian courts have been called upon on a number of occasions to decide on the admissibility of these special policing techniques. Infiltration is permitted according to this case-law because there is no provision in the law which prohibits it explicitly. However, the court stressed that its accordance with the following criteria must be examined:

Firstly, the use of undercover missions should only be tolerated in cases of severe criminal situations where objective facts have given reason to presume that particular individuals have been engaging (or are planning to engage) in criminal activities. Secondly, the undercover activities must be consistent with the general principle of due administration on the part of the concerned State officials. In particular, one should be aware of the following necessities: The assignment of the undercover agent must serve only to protect the menaced interest and the agent should act in an impartial manner. The undercover agent

---

64   Van Parys & Laurent, 1990, p. 233; for more information on infiltration in Belgium, we refer to Van Traa, 1996, App. V, pp. 470-471.

should not commit criminal offences except when strictly necessary and the superior officer must closely control the actions of the undercover agent.[65] Thirdly, the undercover agent may not provoke the potential criminal into committing the criminal offence, for example by using deceitful means to trick an individual into committing a crime.[66]

The ministry of justice's circular is partly inspired by the case-law and partly a complement to it. The circular contains not only provisions to regulate police infiltration but also to ensure that the risks will be limited to an acceptable level. A police official may operate under a false identity in order to infiltrate a group of persons, concerning which there is objective indications of their involvement in committing severe crimes or as members of a group involved in criminal activity (nr. 9.1). Undercover agents are forbidden to use provocation (nr. 9.2.1) and the circular stresses again the importance of the principles of proportionality and subsidiarity (nr. 9.2.2).[67] Note, however, that the circular specifically prohibits the commission of serious crimes. Finally the circular limits undercover actions to short term operations (nr. 9.2.4).

Further, the circular offers provisions regarding the manner in which an undercover action should be performed (nr. 9.3.7). It is forbidden to take action in an undercover mission without the written permission of the public prosecutor. He must be informed thoroughly and precisely in a written and confidential report of an auxiliary public prosecutor about the facts on which the request is based as well as about the pursuit and conclusion of the operations. This report is submitted by the auxiliary public prosecutor in command of the operation. The public prosecutor's department may decide at any point to terminate the operation. Undercover operations may only be executed by specially trained and experienced police officers, among which foreign police officers may be included.

The circular also distinguishes between two forms of short term infiltration operations: sting and flash roll operations. An undercover police officer may simulate interest to buy goods on the basis of an offer concerning for example drugs, weapons or stolen goods (sting operation). Often it may also be necessary to be in possession of large sums of money in order to convince the other party

---

65   On the commission of criminal offences by undercover agents, see HvB Brussels, November 30, 1984, R.D.P. 1985, p. 688, J.T. 1985, p. 729; Cass. February 27, 1985, R.D.P. 1985, p. 694; De Nauw, 1988b, pp. 447-454.

66   HvB Brussels, November 19, 184, RW 1984-1985, p. 2463-2572 and the annotation by J. Scheers; Cass., February 5, 1985, nr. 9277 (not published; see Van Parys & Laurent, 1990, p.234); Fransen, 1986, p. 25.

67   These two principles act then as a test the eventual criminal actions committed by police officials: If the commission of these crimes proves to be proportional and subsidiary, they shall remain unpunished.

of one's seriousness, a technique that is called flash roll. It is necessary to obtain written permission from a magistrate prior to these operations.

The utmost limit of police undercover action is provocation of criminal offences. The Belgian case-law sees the prohibition of provocation as a test for the admissibility of elements of evidence deriving from undercover policing actions. The *Hof van Beroep* (Court of appeal) of Brussels has developed some criteria for determining the extent to which the police may stimulate the commission of an offence without being taxed with provocation. Police provocation is defined as the use of "deceitful means" designed to make someone commit a crime. The use of "deceitful means" may be defined as the use of material or moral pressure, gifts, promises, menaces and other cunning devices influencing the free will in order to provoke the commission of a criminal action. To avoid this, the person against whom pressure is exercised may not be driven to such a situation where the only choice remaining is unlawful conduct.[68]

Police provocation is defined as the generation or encouragement of the criminal intention in the potential offender (nr. 2.2.2). In accordance with the case-law, the public prosecutor's department must be able to refute any allegation of provocation emanating from the accused (nr. 2.2.4).[69] The Brussels court recognizes the necessity and the legality of such undercover techniques with the prior authorization and under the control of the public prosecutor's department, as long as this technique is used once a crime has already been committed or is in the process or on the point of being committed (*sur le point de*), excluding undercover infiltration as a police technique for the gathering of insight on crimes that have not yet been committed (proactively).[70]

Note that, although the circular does not authorize the use of civilian infiltrators, this does not seem to be excluded in practice as sources inside the *gendarmerie* confirm the use of civilian infiltrators. Nevertheless, most of the undercover operations in Belgium are stings and incidently, bigger scale use of front-stores.[71]

5.2.3.2 The Netherlands

As we have seen above, the issue of investigating methods such as infiltration has reached the political agenda in a rather noisy way. The IRT-scandal has been responsible for a detailed assessment of the factual use of this investigation

---

68   HvB November 19, 1984, R.W. 1984-1985, p. 2563.
69   HvB Brussels, March 3, 1987, RW 1987-1988, pp. 640-643.
70   Brussels, September 7 1994, J.L.B., 1994, 135, nr. 268, 25 and with note by C. De Valkeneer and G. Haarscheer; see also Corr. Namur, January 5, 1994.
71   This has been confirmed by Belgian legal and police practionners.

method, as well as for an inventory of the actual methods used.[72] The legal basis of this method is contained in a directive.[73]

Following a study set up by the Dutch public prosecutor's department in 1985, a directive was issued concerning infiltration as a method of police enquiry. This directive was replaced in 1991 by a new directive, distinguishing between infiltration and sting operations, infiltrator and informer.[74] Infiltration is defined as a form of entry into particular groups in the criminal world, with or without the use of a false identity, by outsiders (which means by people originating from outside the allegedly criminal group), in order to investigate and prosecute.[75] Sting operations represent an often used form of infiltration that consists in the purchase of a particular good in order to facilitate the prosecution of the offenders or of others that have committed crimes in relation with that good. It is also possible to sell goods with the intention of gaining the trust of offenders.[76] To this date the existence of at least one more directive, on the money paid to informers, to show at deals or to secure an illegal transaction,[77] has been confirmed by official sources and the literature although it remains confidential.[78]

For the purpose of creating an undercover identity it is possible to use false papers such as driving licenses, passports and permits.[79] It is, however, not clear whether the State employees working at the different governmental agencies such as the population registers can be expected (or obliged) to cooperate with the police or public prosecutor. In the same way it is not known whether an undercover agent is permitted to take part in such transactions as to found a company or enter a contractual relationship under his adopted identity.

As was stated earlier, infiltration and sting operations must be in accordance with the principle of proportionality: The nature of the criminal act that is to

---

72 See Wierenga, 1994 and Van Traa, 1994. A realistic assessment of the situation is also found in De Wit, 1994.

73 According to the conclusions of the working group Van Traa, infiltration should regulated in statutory law; see Van Traa, 1996, pp. 435-436.

74 Stcrt. 1985, 236. This directive has been replaced in 1991 by a new directive that remained confidential until 1993. Meanwhile, they have been published in *Richtlijnen openbaar ministerie, Strafrecht*, Sdu, Den Haag.

75 For more information on infiltration in general in The Netherlands see Frielink, 1990, Corstens, 1995, pp. 280-283, Van Traa, 1996, pp. 232-274.

76 Information originating from the CRI, in particular from the *Afdeling Nationale Coördinatie Politiële Infiltratie*, which will be called ANCPI in this study.

77 *Regeling Tip-, toon- en voorkoopgelden* (*brief van 16 december 1985, kenmerk directie politie* R85/85/4), published in Van Traa, 1996, App. I.

78 Existence of secret directives on special policing techniques and in particular of one directive concerning infiltration was confirmed by official sources.

79 Information originating from the ANCPI.

be investigated must justify the means employed.[80] Although there is no catalogue in the directive detailing which criminal acts justify the resort to infiltration as investigating technique, the 1991 directive specifies that there must be specific factual elements which indicate the commission or preparation of a criminal act in the context of organized or career oriented crime. It is explicitly forbidden to infiltrate the criminal milieu without specific cause to do so and the demand for specific factual elements can be seen, according to the directive, as a way to make sure it does not happen.

As for the principle of subsidiarity, the directive States that infiltrating undercover officials may solely be assigned on a case when the specific criminal offence cannot be investigated in another responsible manner.[81]

Another important condition to the use of infiltrating undercover officers is the controllability of the actions during the operation. According to the directive it is mandatory that the public prosecutor give its permission and that the action be controlled on the afore-mentioned criteria by the commanding officer before the operation is set up. The commanding officer then evaluates this control together with what is called a "guiding team" (*begeleidingsteam*) in the directive. In this evaluation, the investigative methods are discussed *in concreto* both substantially and technically. If this evaluation gives positive results, the commanding officer will discuss it once more with the public prosecutor. The public prosecutor will carry the final responsibility for the investigative method used. The terms of the agreement between the public prosecutor's department and the police will be put in writing.

The guiding team, composed of one or more guides, will assist the infiltrator during the undercover operation. The team will begin by preparing the operation (gathering information, describing the aim, developing a strategy) and will act as an intermediary between the commanding officer and the infiltrator. The team will also guide and direct the infiltrator during and after the operation and finally, it will take the necessary measures to ensure the safety of the infiltrator.

A guiding committee is set up in each jurisdiction and composed of representatives of the public prosecutor's department of that jurisdiction, the different commanding officers of the infiltration teams and the national division on the coordination of infiltration of the CRI. This committee sets the framework for the strategies to be followed, is responsible for the exchange of information between the different competent prosecutor's department and sets directives in criminal procedure, for instance regarding the procedure to be followed to hear the infiltrator as a witness. Finally, the committee will evaluate the operation.

---

80   See also Frielink, 1990, pp.120-130.
81   See also Frielink, 1990, pp. 130-131.

The assignment of undercover agents not belonging to the police force must be limited to those few cases where the use of police officers is not possible. They may be allowed to act in the Netherlands under the supervision of the public prosecutor's department and are bound by the provisions of the directive and by Dutch law. This may happen for instance as undercover agents are, while assigned in another country, unsuspectedly obliged to travel to the Netherlands in the course of their mission.[82] Because of the rising international cooperation in crime fighting an international forum on infiltration was created in 1987 which meets two to three times a year and in which the Netherlands participate.[83]

According to the directive it is unavoidable that undercover agents, while trying to take on the same colour as his environment, commit criminal offences. This is acknowledged provided they remain within specified limits. It is therefore necessary that there be a direct link between the offence to be committed and the undercover mission. The principles of proportionality and subsidiarity must be taken into account as well and the commission of the offence must take place under the supervision of the commanding officer with the previously obtained permission of the competent public prosecutor.

Because sting operations and infiltration are mostly used to gather evidence it is imperative that the undercover agents bear in mind that the operation will be granted openness.[84] This means that the information gathered with the help of the infiltrating officer, as well as working methods will be subject to control and available to be tested during the hearing before the judge.

Another way of preventing the danger of "sliding" for infiltrating officers is to restrict the time they may be assigned on an infiltrating mission. The 1985 directive provided that infiltrators only be assigned for a short period of time. This restriction has not been repeated in the 1991 directive.[85]

The parliamentary working group-Van Traa acknowledged the following assignment duration for undercover agents: two years for the Amsterdam municipal police and four years for the national police force, whereas the working group "infiltration" suggests an assignment time of three years (pre-

---

82 See Frielink, 1990, pp.143-144; HR September 14, 1981, NJ 1981, 643; HR January 17, 1984, NJ 1984, 405 and AAE 1984, p.631.

83 Kastel, 1989, p. 215. Other participating countries are Norway, Denmark, Sweden, Belgium, Luxembourg, France, Germany, Great-Britain and Canada.

84 Kastel, 1989, p. 215.

85 Before the reorganization of the police forces in the Netherlands, full-time officers from the *gemeentepolitie* (municipal police forces) could only be assigned to infiltrating missions for a maximal of two years. The *rijkspolitie* (state police) assigned only part-time infiltrating officers who could stay active for a period of four years. The situation today has been changed considerably. Special police infiltration teams (PIT's) have been created in consultation with the CRI (ANCPI); see Van Traa, 1996, pp. 236-237.

ceded by a one year training period and followed by a one year reinsertion program).[86]

The limits of police intervention in the commission of a criminal offence were set in the *Tallon* case by the *Hoge Raad*, the Netherlands' highest court. The police officers may not entice the suspect to committing other criminal actions than the ones for which he had the general intention to commit.[87] The directive repeats and specifies the *Tallon* principle: The infiltrating officer may set the stage for some specific actions of the suspect, but it must appear that these actions would have been committed even without the intervention of the infiltrating officer. The intention of the suspect must appear from factual intelligence emanating a source that has in the past proved reliable, for instance an informer. The only role of the infiltrating officer is to render the criminal intention of the suspect visible. Provoking is thus not necessarily unlawful, as long as it is limited to guiding the general intention of the suspect towards the commission of a particular criminal offence.[88]

It is preferable that only specially trained police officers be assigned to controlled delivery missions. The use of civilians is, according to the directive, less desirable and shall be restricted to these special cases where the use of a police officer is not possible. The parliamentary working group Van Traa has, however, acknowledged that the use of (criminal) civilians for such operations is increasing in the Netherlands.[89]

Note that the Dutch courts seem to have changed their attitudes toward transparency and controllability of the investigation method since the IRT scandal. Where courts before the IRT seemed to find that in some occasions the aim justified the means, they are at present increasingly questioning them. Public prosecutors refusing to reveal the methods used during the investigation have been faced with the court declaring them not competent to prosecute.[90]

---

86 Van Traa, 1994, p. 28.
87 HR December 4, 1979, NJ 1980, 356 (with note Th.W. van Veen).
88 See also Frielink, 1990, p. 29 and pp. 138-143.
89 Van Traa, 1994, p. 71.
90 An example of the attitude of courts before the IRT-scandal is illustrated in the following case where the Court of appeal of Amsterdam did not demand transparency of the investigation and that consequently it was declared that there was no obligation to have investigation methods were appear in the police report. This omission did not lead to the declaration of incompetence of the public prosecutor (Hof Amsterdam, February 4, 1993) The court seems to be more critical in the following case: The lack of openness in the gathering of the evidence led to prosecutor being declared incompetent to prosecute. The case involved a sting-operation where a false fax-message was used in deal negotiations with the suspects. The message was neither mentioned by the informer nor authorized by the police. In that way it was not possible to establish the way agreement was reached for the sum of ƒ200.000 (Rb Utrecht, September 23, 1993). Another example is given by the court in Rotterdam: The court had refused to condemn the suspects because the public prosecutor refused to reveal information on the

Moreover, a central control committee for special investigation techniques (*Centrale toetsingscommissie voor bijzondere opsporingsmethoden*) has been set up since December 1994 (to start on January 1, 1995) for the control before-hand of policing techniques such as infiltration and deals with criminals. This committee, set up by the assembly of prosecutors general, controls the legality of all national and international project-wise infiltration operations except for those one time or short term operations. Further, the committee will control the legality of all actions such as stings, controlled deliveries and front stores. Besides regulating and guiding long-term infiltration operations, its main tasks are concentrated on gaining insight on the use of special policing techniques on a national level. The committee must report to the assembly of prosecutors general and the minister of justice.[91] Note that this commite is composed of members of the public prosecutor's department, the chairman (the head of the public prosecutor's department in Den Bosch), two advocates general and three public prosecutor's, which is reason to doubt of its independent character.[92]

The 1991 circular seems to limit itself to short term infiltration techniques such as sting operations, although other types of infiltration techniques are not excluded. In the practice of crime investigation, one notes a shift from this shorter term limited concept of infiltration towards a longer term more extensive concept. This is probably caused by the necessity of gathering as much information as possible on organized and carrier crime and has led to more project-wise infiltration operations. The aim of this type of infiltration, mostly done proactively, is not primarily the prosecution as it has been in the past, but essentially the gathering of information in itself.[93] Although the 1991 directive

investigation techniques (De Volkskrant, May 18, 1995).

91   See news release of the public prosecutor's department of December 6, 1994 (*Persverklaring van de vergadering van Procureurs-Generaal, Centrale toetsingscommissie voor bijzondere opsporingsmethoden van start*).

92   The opinion of this committee is not always followed by the minister. It seems that the minister of justice has ordered the stop of one infiltration operation despite positive advise given by the committee. The operation was launched after 2 years of unsuccessful investigations against a particular group. According to official sources, the import of many tons of soft drugs into The Netherlands would make the minister's political position precarious, would a scandal occur (De Gelderlander, July 1, 1995).

93   De Wit, 1994, p. 3; the working group describes further the open and closed criminal intelligence methods. The former is said of gathering information with the help of observers, infiltrators and informers which may be used directly in the criminal investigation and are noted in the police report. The latter designates the method, previous to the open method, where informants, observers and infiltrators are used to improve one's information position with the aim to have the criminal activity terminated. In principle, this method is excluded from the control of the public prosecutor and does not appear in the police report (p. 5).

marks a definite preference for the use of police officers as infiltrators, the practice seems to show a different trend.[94]

Finally, according to the confidential report-De Wit, most infiltration operations are not successful; Of the 78 undercover operations launched by the police in the Netherlands in 1994, only 16 have had a positive result. 56 were stopped because the they did not amount to anything and six are still in progress. The bad results seem, according to the working group, to find their source in the short term decision making, leading to the end of an investigation or a change of priorities at a moment where the police infiltrators had put a lot of time and energy and had managed to infiltrate the sub-top of criminal organizations. The working group concludes that, based on the experience to date, police infiltrators should not be sent in deep-cover infiltration operations in which they must take on a false identity and mingle for long periods of time with the criminal world. One of the problems pointed out by the working group is the fact that in such deep cover operations, new recruits in a criminal organization are often forced to start off in the section of the organization responsible for violent crimes and contract killings. Another problem seems to be too many ways of thinking and methods among the police infiltrators. The working group seems to be more for the sending of criminal infiltrators in deep cover operations. The criminal infiltrator has the advantage of having a criminal past and the capacity to move around easier in the criminal world. Sending criminals must be done with great care, according to De Wit and especially the practice of letting the criminal profit from his illegal activities, ie: that he may keep what he gained while working for the police, must be brought to an end. There has been too many stories in the past about criminals working for the public prosecutor's department that have been able to grow inside an organization thanks to the State. The working group seems to be enthusiastic about the setting up of front-stores in a number of operations launched in 1993. The first front-store was set up on request of Canadian authorities. The operation with the code name Contrat was successful. Ever since, a unknown number of front stores have been set up in The Netherlands, active in sectors such as transport and financial services. They are so successful that the working group proposes to set up a fund. The Netherlands officially infiltrates since 1985. In those days, the police used mostly short term actions such as stings. It seems that these methods have lost their efficiency especially in the 1990's, as criminal organizations caught on. Of the 75 training vacancies are only 25 filled. The working group advises to expand the number of infiltrators as soon as possible to 60. With that number, it would be possible, according to the working group, to at least honour requests from foreign countries. It seems that the U.S have

---

94   See Van Traa, 1996, pp. 273-274; note that the committee found that infiltration by civilians
      should be avoided altogether (Van Traa, 1996, p. 274).

protested three times last year because the Netherlands had no available infiltrators.[95]

5.2.3.3 Luxembourg

Where police officials are called upon to play a more active role as infiltrators, Luxembourg is very secretive. According to official sources, Luxembourg does not permit the setting up of sting operations on its territory. This form of policing technique is considered an unlawful provocation in the sense of art. 66 CPL.[96] It is said that other forms of infiltration are not being exercised because of the small size of the country and the limited number of available police officers.[97]

Although Luxembourg does not seem to organize infiltration operation itself, it is likely that infiltration does take place to a certain extent, at least with regards to foreign police officers. This possibility has been suggested to us by sources in the Luxembourg police. Moreover, it would be compatible with the fact that Luxembourg participates in an international forum on infiltration that was created in 1987 and which meets two to three times a year.[98]

An overview of Luxembourg's criminal law may offer more light. The definition of "provocation" might open a legal door to infiltration or at least seems to offer some legal flexibility: "Will be prosecuted as offender the one who, with the help of gifts, promises, menaces, use of authority and power or intentional use of tricks or stratagems **directly** provokes the commission of a crime or delict."[99] Officers that have not **directly** provoked the commission of an offence, for instance because the actions of the police were limited to setting the scene, would not necessarily be guilty of provocation and would most likely avoid effective prosecution. Indeed, whether the police and the public prosecutor in practice use such possibilities is purely speculative.

5.2.3.4 France

Police officers with the power to act as auxiliary to the public prosecutors may infiltrate the drug scene according to the 1991 Anti Drugs Act and in doing so may even resort to committing criminal offences themselves while still avoiding

---

95 This information was leaked to the Dutch national newspaper De Volkskrant (June 15, 1995).
96 See the definition of provocation below.
97 This information originates officials of the *police* as well as of the *gendarmerie grand-ducale*.
98 Kastel, 1989, p. 215.
99 Art. 66 CP: "*Seront punis comme auteurs d'un crime ou d'un délit: (...) Ceux qui, par dons, promesses, menaces, abus d'autorité ou de pouvoir, machinations ou artifices coupables, auront directement provoqué à ce crime ou à ce délit.*"

prosecution. The statute, embodied in the code of criminal procedure, states that auxiliary public prosecutors and their adjuncts under their supervision will not be held criminally responsible when they deal in drugs, which includes buying, possessing, transporting or delivering narcotics or products which are normally used for the fabrication thereof (art. 706-32 CPP).[100] They may assist the suspect(s) in providing them with means of transport, deposit, storage, conservation or communication. They may even provide these persons with "judicial means" (*moyens de caractère juridique*). What exactly is meant with this expression is not clear, but it does suggest for instance that the granting to informers of temporary new identities as well as setting up of cover-up companies or institutions (the so-called front stores) is possible. As for infiltrating officers the statute is silent but it does not seem impossible that they be provided with temporary new identities. It seems, however, excluded that their names be kept secret once they appear in judicial procedures. What may in practice possibly happen is that one or more names are not inscribed on the written procedure in order to avoid "burning" an infiltrating officer.[101] The letter of these provisions does not seem to exclude the proactive use of infiltration as an investigative method. The statute imposes, however, that they beforehand solicit and obtain the authorization of the public prosecutor or the assigned examining judge (who must advise the public prosecutor's department, the *parquet*).[102] This authorization may not concern activities which may be determinant for the commission of the criminal offence. These investigating powers are also given to customs officers (art. 67*bis* CD). Note that there is no mention as to the duration of the operation. Although the text of the article suggests that infiltration is allowed at least for the duration of the drug delivery, one may consider as well the time needed to be trusted by the drug dealers. It is not excluded that even long term infiltration operations would be tolerated by the courts, especially if it is done under the supervision of the public prosecutor.[103]

---

100 "*Ils ne sont pas pénalement responsables lorsqu' (...) ils acquièrent, détiennent, transportent ou livrent ces substances (...).*"

101 Although neither confirmed nor denied by official sources, this was related o us by former police officers.

102 This seems to include both proactive and reactive use of infiltration: With the authorization of the public prosecutor it would seem possible to investigate before a particular criminal offence has been committed, especially when one interprets the latter provision with the term art. 75 CPP, which gives police officers the power to conduct enquiries they or the public prosecutor find appropriate. None of these provisions demand the existence of suspicion, as long as a fundamental right is not violated, for instance by a search or an arrest (artt. 76 and 77 CPP).

103 This is true although operations seem to be limited to short term stings, reverse stings and flash-rolls in practice. Deep cover investigations do not seem to take place in practice. The existence of a (confidential) circular on the application of the Anti Drugs Act has been confirmed to us (*Lettre circulaire du 14 avril 1992 ayant pour objet l'application de la loi*

Provocation used by the police in order to trap a suspect is a controversial topic. Although the Anti Drugs Act (art. 706-32 CPP) forbids provocation, it is not certain to which extent the undercover agent may stimulate the commission of a criminal offence. Art. 706-32 par. 2 CPP *in fine* states that the public prosecutor may not give authorization for actions that are determinant for the commission of the offence. This suggests that the undercover agents may guide the suspect in a particular direction as long as the general criminal intention of the suspect is present at that time. This interpretation is in accordance with former case-law prior to the Anti Drugs Act concerning provocation. This question is debated in each particular case and in general the case-law states that the police have not provoked the criminal offence when its commission is not **caused** by acts of the police. The judge must be convinced of the existence of the criminal intention prior to the intervention of the undercover agent. This criminal intention may be inferred from facts such as telephone taps, certain patterns of travel observed by shadowing officers or prior convictions for drug trafficking.[104]

In principle, the courts disapprove of provocation but they sometimes tend to deviate from this premise, providing the case in question concerns a severe criminal offence. This is the case for instance when that would serve the interest of society or when the suspects involved indulge in incessant or organized crime.[105] What seems important for the courts is the weight of the different interests: In some cases the goal seems to justify the means. It is not clear whether the Anti Drugs Act has changed the case-law on that point as far as drug enforcement is concerned.

As both the *Gendarmerie* and the *Police Nationale* may infiltrate on the basis of the Anti-drugs act, a strategy has been established to determine specialities in investigation. According to this strategy, the *Police Nationale* concentrates on the repression of drugs import from foreign countries (the international offer), while the *Gendarmerie Nationale* concentrates on the local repression (the local offer) on a departmental level.[106]

---

du 19 déc. 1991 relative au renforcement de la lutte contre le trafic des stupéfiants, NOR: *JUSD9230010C*). This circular specifies the will of the legislator: The circular contains details on implementing these new means of investigation in each investigation section on the level the Court of appeal. It stresses, further, the importance of the public prosecutor's role in avoiding overlapping jurisdiction. This was related to us by official sources.

104 Pradel, 1992, p.234.
105 Cass. crim. May 22, 1908, D.P. 1909, 1, 328; Cass. March 2, 1971, Bull. crim. nr. 71; March 16, 1972, Bull. crim. nr. 108; October 20, 1979, Bull. crim. nr. 266.
106 This has been related to us by official sources inside the *Gendarmerie Nationale*.

5.2.3.5 Germany

As we have seen earlier, Germany being a relatively decentralized federation, legislation is divided between federal and provincial levels, and between formal statutes and regulations.[107]

a.   Federal Laws:

Since 1991 a federal statute regarding repression of organized crime (Organized Crime Act - OrgKG) has been in force offering a statutory basis for infiltration by the police.[108] The Organized Crime Act applies strictly to matters concerning the repression of organized crime and not, as the provincial acts, to matters of prevention and proactive activity.[109]

Art. 110a par.1 StPO (in which most of the OrgKG has been embodied), restricts the scope of application of infiltration to criminal offences of particular severity without offering a precise description of these offences: drug related offence, trafficking in arms and money, offences against State security, professionally committed crimes or crimes committed by criminal organizations. An undercover investigator may also be assigned on cases where there exists a fear based on factual circumstances of repetition of certain crimes. Undercover investigators may only be assigned to a mission when the concerned crime could not or would with undue difficulty be elucidated in other ways. Paragraph 3 of art. 110a StPO describes the possibility of constructing and granting a legend (an alleged identity) to an undercover investigator.

The public prosecutor's office must give its written permission before an undercover investigator may be assigned to a particular case (art. 110b StPO). In urgent situations (danger in delay or *Gefahr im Verzug*), it is possible to act without this written permission, in which case the public prosecutor's department must be notified within three hours. In cases where an undercover action is directed against one particular person or involving trespassing of places that are

---

107   The topic of infiltration in Germany is being dealt with as well by Tak *et al.*, 1996, pp. 184-201 and Van Traa, 1996, App. V, pp. 486-488.

108   Act for Combatting the Illicit Traffic of Narcotic Drugs and Other Manifestations of Organized Crime (*Gesetz zur Bekämpfung des illegalen Rauschgifthandels und anderer Erscheinungsformen der Organisierten Kriminalität*), published in BGBl. I, 1992, pp. 1302-1312. The statute has been in force since September 22, 1992. Since the adoption of the OrgKG, the number of investigations involving undercover infiltrators and informants does not seem to have increased. This was related to us by *Kriminalrat* Clauer of the LKA Nordrhein-Westfalen in Düsseldorf, October 20, 1994.

109   It seems, however, that although a theoretical distinction can be made between proactive and reactive policing in Germany, purely proactive investigations are not very common in practice. Both proactive and reactive investigations are usually "intermeshed." This has been related to us by *Kriminalrat* Clauer, LKA NRW, Düsseldorf, October 20, 1994.

not generally accessible to the public, the judge's permission is mandatory. In cases of danger in delay, however, the public prosecutor's department has the competence to decide on that issue (art. 110b par. 2 StPO). The undercover investigators may enter homes and other places not generally accessible to the public under their false identity provided they have the permission of the occupant. If they do so they are subject to all statutes and regulations applying to trespassing (art. 110c StPO).

The persons against whom an undercover mission had been set up must be notified of this as soon as the mission has resumed unless this would endanger the purpose of the enquiry, the public security, life and limb of persons or the assigning of the infiltrating officer in another case. Until these conditions are fulfilled, the documents and reports relating the mission are kept and supervised by the public prosecutor's department (par. 2). Art. 110e StPO states finally that the collected data resulting from the undercover mission may be used by police and justice officials to help elucidate other criminal offences as described in art. 100a StPO.

It is also worth mentioning that the case-law as well as the literature give a large amount of liberty to persons acting as agents provocateurs (Lockspitzel). Considered as such is a person that "under the orders or authorization of the investigating or prosecuting officials, gives a person the opportunity to commit a criminal offence or influence such a person so that the offenders may be apprehended."[110] The limit of this liberty is provocation: A provoking agent may not motivate a person in a way that is not in accordance with the principles of the rule of law (Rechtsstaat),[111] which means that the acceptability of a provocation will depend on factors such as the character and the importance of the suspicion, the danger created by the crimes to be investigated and the expected possible difficulties, the scope and the goal of the provocation and the action already taken by the person to be provoked.[112] In practice this means that provocation of a person that has not to this date committed any criminal offence is not permitted,[113] even in cases involving a person with criminally oriented tendencies.[114] It seems, however, that even in the latter case, the use

---

110   This definition is borrowed from Löwe/Rosenberg, 1989, art. 163, nr. 63.
111   Roxin, 1993, pp. 56-58.
112   Löwe/Rosenberg, 1989, art. 163, nr. 69.
113   Roxin, 1993, pp. 56-57.
114   Fischer, 1992, p.11; some authors believe that the OrgKG failed in providing for sufficient norms regarding such definitions as undercover investigators and informants; see for instance: Hund, 1993, pp.379-381.

of provocation does not have any effect on the legality of the prosecution, but rather leads to an eventual reduced sentence.[115]

b.   Provincial Laws:

Only police officials may be assigned as undercover infiltrators according to the Police Act of Nordrhein-Westfalen (*Polizeigesetz Nordrhein-Westfalen*, art. 20 par. 1 PolGNW). An infiltrator may be granted a false identity (called cover-up - *Deckmantel* or legend - *Legende*), to which purpose official government agencies may even issue official documents establishing the alleged identity. This new identity enables the infiltrator to take part in such normal activities as buying cars, renting an apartment or founding a company.[116]

The use of an infiltrating agent is permitted when, in accordance with par. 1 of the same provision, this is necessary to combat a specific danger of bodily harm, life or liberty of a person or to prevent the commission of serious crimes. For this purpose there must exist elements of factual evidence that these crimes are likely to be committed.

The infiltrating agent is not allowed to commit criminal offences himself, which raises the question of his ability to temporarily take part in the commission of the offence in order to prevent its completion.[117] The infiltrating agent must take great care that he not provoke the commission of the crime: This could lead to the liberation of the suspect or a low sentence especially in cases where there are no prior convictions.[118]

Trespassing on premises not accessible to the public is permitted according to par. 3 of the same provision as long as the undercover investigating officer has the permission of the rightful occupant. In that case the trespassing does

115   See BGH, January 12, 1995, in StV, 1995-5, pp. 247-249), where informers took advantage of the accused's poor financial situation despite the fact that they knew the accused had never before been involved with psychotropic substances. They offered the accused a way to get rid of his debts by bringing him in contact with an undercover investigator. Newspapers are also a source of examples: The German police (Rheinland-Pfalz) seems to have provoked three Dutch inhabitants in trafficking in large quantities of drugs. The accused were first offenders and needed the money to pay certain debts, in: de Volkskrant, May 11,1995). Note also BGH, March 16, 1995, 4 StR 111/95, where the principle according to which an infiltrating investigator must be sent in the only cases where a suspicion (art. 160 par. 1 StPO) is present is repeated as well as the principle that provocation of the offence is a factor not to be ignored in the sentencing. Note that this situation is the subject of criticism: see Danwitz, 1995, pp. 431 *et seq.*

116   Heise/Tegtmeyer, 1990, p. 178.

117   Heise/Tegtmeyer, 1990, p. 181; Weßlau, 1991, p. 44; Caeser, 1991, p. 242; Meertens, 19926, p. 206, Lesch, 1993, pp. 94-97.

118   BGH, NJW 1080, 1761 and BVerfG, NStZ 1985, 131; BGH 32, 345 and Roxin, 1993, pp. 56-59.

not constitute an extra violation because the occupant agrees. If the officer were to gain access with the help of a trick or a stratagem or if, when let inside, he were to search the premises without permission, it would then constitute a violation and would not be allowed.[119] According to par. 4, the decision to assign an undercover investigator is left to the commanding officer (*Behörden-leiter*).

In Rheinland-Pfalz the statute places the assignment of undercover agents on the same level as the use of hidden technical devices. This means that the same conditions have to be fulfilled with regards to the person against whom one or more of these actions are to be taken. This also means that the same restrictions and possibilities apply concerning trespassing in homes and that the individual in question must be informed subsequently of the measures taken against him.

The Rheinland-Pfalz Police Act does not say which authority is competent to decide whether an undercover investigator should be assigned on a particular case. For this reason it is not probable that the decision need only be taken by a judge. Another significant difference between the statute of Nordrhein-Westfalen and that of Rheinland-Pfalz is that the statute of the latter seems to permit the assignment of infiltrating investigators who are not members of the police force. But it is not likely that this difference has relevance in practice as the *Gemeinsame Richtlinien*,[120] according to which infiltration is only allowed when done by police officers, are also in force in Rheinland-Pfalz.

The Police Act of Saarland is more explicit: Par. 2 al. 4 and par. 3 of art. 28 provide that only police officers may be assigned to undercover missions. The decision to initiate such an operation rests exclusively on judges of the county court (*Amtsgericht*) except in urgent cases (danger in delay - *Gefahr im Verzug*). Collecting information in or out of homes is solely permitted with the permission of the rightful occupant and only in order to prevent danger to limb and life or other menacing dangers (par. 4).

Art. 19c of the Police Act of Baden-Württemberg allows assignment of undercover investigators under the same conditions as the other special methods of collecting data (*Besondere Mittel der Datenerhebung*). The law provides for a certain number of prescriptions relating to the possibility of keeping an under-cover agent's identity secret and of issuing official documents bearing his fictive

---

119 Heise/Tegtmeyer, 1990, pp. 181-182.
120 Common directives of the provincial ministers and senators of justice and ministers and senators of the interior on the resort to informants, as well as on the assignment of undercover investigators in criminal prosecution *(Gemeinsame Richtlinien der Justizminister/-senatoren und der Innenminister/-senatoren der Länder über die Inanspruchnahme von Informanten sowie über den Einsatz von Vertrauenspersonen (V-Personen) und Verdeckte Ermittlern im Rahmen der Strafverfolgung)*.

identity (art. 19e). Furthermore, the law allows undercover investigators to enter homes with the permission of the rightful occupant.

c.   Regulations:

As we have seen above, one of the guidelines on criminal procedure also addresses the uses of informers and of infiltrators (*Gemeinsame Richtlinien*). [121] The changes in the expressions of organized crime in the society has encouraged the development of adapted means of repressing crime. One of these adapted methods is the operational assignment of infiltrators (*Verdeckte Ermittler*). Infiltrators are defined as specially chosen and equipped police officers infiltrating the criminal scene under the cover of a "legend" - a fabricated identity - and attempting to gather clues in order to enable criminal prosecution. Their identity shall be kept secret during the procedure.

The authorities will resort to this method of investigation for the repression of severe or organized criminality, drug and arm trafficking or criminality endangering the State security only in cases where other methods have failed, proven ineffective or non proportional. Each case must be evaluated with care, according to the guideline. One important limitation to the actions of the undercover investigator is that they are not allowed to commit crimes.Infiltrators may not commit criminal offences.

As for the procedural aspect, the public prosecutor's department must be solicited for his authorization. If this authorization cannot be solicited in time, the public prosecutor must be notified as soon as possible. The infiltrator is not exempted from his obligation of investigating the criminal offences he witnesses (art. 163 StPO). However, tactical reasons, such as the expectation of new clues or evidence of criminal offences, may justify the delay of certain investigative measures. This does not apply when, because of the severity of the newly discovered crime, immediate action is necessary.

Finally, although only police officers are allowed to act as infiltrator, it is not excluded that civilians are used as infiltrators. As far as provocation is concerned, the exploitation of a suspect's readiness to commit an offence is well accepted. [122] This is very well illustrated by the case where an *agent provocateur* - paid according to his successes - was sent against a first offender. Although clearly beyond legality, the court stated that this was not in itself

---

121   Ratified by the federal government, Baden-Würtemberg, Bayern, Berlin, Brandenburg, Hamburg, Niedersachsen, Nordrhein-Westfahlen, Rheinland-Pfalz, Saarland and Schleswig-Holstein. Note that the ratification of this guideline by Niedersachsen in combination with its refusal to include infiltration in its law on special investigation techniques, results implicitly in the prohibition in that province of proactive use of this technique.

122   This was confirmed in talks we had with the Aachen lawyer Martina Birgelen.

the dismissal of the criminal proceedings or even for not sentencing the suspect.[123] This view on provocation was also present in what is known in Germany as the Bomb-scandal (*Bombenschwindel*): The German secret services made the headlines of the world with a plutonium sting in Russia in the aftermath of the fall of the iron curtain. It seemed, however, that the German secret services had set the whole story into scene and provoked the suspects into furnishing them plutonium.[124]

5.2.4   Use of Informers

A very important source of - usually secret - information, informers play a crucial role in police enquiries and often in the grey zone preceding an official police enquiry. Whether they be incidental or regular informers, they can supply the police with important information regarding a particular case or even inside information originating the organized crime scene. They can be found for instance in hotels, pubs and restaurants, they may be taxi drivers, neighbours or sex shop goers, just people on the street or even criminals.[125] They find the police, or a particular agent or the police finds them: The contact methods are very diversified. The biggest problem is, however, the reliability of these informers: On the one hand the information consists often of hearsay or is inaccurate and, on the other hand, some informers may gain advantage of the tip they give,[126] placing the police official in an ethically difficult position.

Informers, criminal or not, may also play an active role in the investigation of criminal offences when sent by the police or the public prosecutor (or both) to infiltrate a criminal organization. They may be asked to act on the orders of the State inside the organization (when this informer is already part of the criminal organization) and may even avoid prosecution on the basis of special amnesty regulations for cooperative suspects. Although effective, very flexible and relatively cheaper than specially trained police officers, this particular investigative method may give rise to deep ethical conflict on the political level.[127]

---

123   BGH, October 13, 1994 - 5StR 529/94.
124   See Der Spiegel, April 10, 1995, and de Volkskrant, May 11, 1995 where the suspects confirm the story.
125   Van der Vegt, 1989, p. 49.
126   To stabilize a drug monopoly for instance, to get someone out of the way or just for revenge.
127   A good example of this is the IRT-scandal, where the hearings of the parliamentary committee Van Traa revealed that an informer, protected by the police and the public prosecutor, was sent to climb up the hierarchy of a particular criminal organization. Because this organization was only involved in trafficking of hennep products and because this did not fit in the Dutch policy of prosecution, the informer was told to try and get the organization to traffic in other, harder, psychotropic substances. See Van Traa, 1996, pp. 75-99 and pp. 161-168, where the

5.2.4.1 Belgium

As for the other previously mentioned special policing techniques, Belgium provides for a very detailed solution. The above mentioned confidential circular also provides guidelines for the use of informers. Chapter 3 of the circular enacts a code of conduct for the relationship of police officials with informers, Chapter 4 describes the role of the public prosecutor's office in these matters and Chapter 5 concerns the payment of "information money" (*tipgelden*). According to the circular, payment of information money may only apply to persons that presumably are part of an organized criminal organization or from whom can be expected that they came across the information in a manner that is more than coincidental (nr. 3.1.1.1).

Most of the provisions regarding informers concern organizational aspects like the setting up of an informers administration (*informantenbeheer*, nr. 3.2.2.1), background and motivation of the enquiry (nr. 3.2.2.2), contact keeping with informers (nrs. 3.2.2.3-3.2.2.6) and the internal responsibility regarding informers. After each contact with the informer the police official must report to the informer administration to enable supervision (nr. 3.2.2.4). A copy of the report must be sent to the regional informer administration (nr. 3.2.5.2). In addition to these rules, the circular contains provisions regarding the legal situation of the informer. It stipulates that the identity of the informer must be protected and that all documents and reports relating to him must strictly refer to him with means of a local identification number (nr. 3.1.3). However, even this local identification number often remains confidential.[128] The public prosecutor, in his quality of hierarchic superior, may require that the identity be revealed to him,[129] after which the obligation of confidentiality will rest on him as well. This protection will also be valid for the court but it is important to state that the informer may not be heard under oath in this case (nr. 323 Sv).

In order to prevent abuses on the part of the informer the circular provides for his evaluation as reliable informer (nr. 3.2.2.7) and sets up an computerized data bank to control the reliability of informers (nrs. 3.2.3.1-3.2.3.4). Every time an informer proves to be unreliable after evaluation, his identity is registered in the data bank in order to avoid any further contact with him (nr. 3.2.4).[130]

---

committee judges this so-called Delta method as absolutely unacceptable.

128 It is common practice based on nr. 3.2.5.2 that the copy of the report to be sent by the *informantenbeheer* to the regional information service (*informatiedienst*) not mention this identification number.

129 De Wilde, 1988, pp. 66-67.

130 On informers in Belgium, see also Van Traa, 1996, App. V, pp. 467-469.

5.2.4.2 The Netherlands

Although there are no statutes providing the use of informers by the police with rules, the police are not left without specific guidelines on the subject. The (confidential) directive on money for tips, flash-rolls and transactions (*tip-, toon-en voorkoopgelden*) sets guidelines for police officials regarding the payment of sums of money to informers of the criminal scene.[131]

This directive defines the informer as a person procuring police officials with solicited or unsolicited information about present or future crimes provided he remain anonymous.[132] One may distinguish between two sorts of informers, the incidental and the customary one. Customary informers may even in some cases make their living out of providing the police with interesting information.

In rewarding useful information, justice and police officials may use information money. These rewards may consist of sums of money for incidental informers that have witnessed more or less by coincidence the commission of an offence, but may even consist of public announcements of reward money depending on the budget of the official authority involved.[133] However, these sums may be part of a deal with informers of the criminal milieu. Note that the amount of the available budget for these rewards is unknown as well as the manner and criteria used to pay these sums. Police officials may also "protect" these special informers from other individuals of the milieu as a means of reward.[134]

The directive refers to tip, flash-roll and transaction money as the money, emanating from public authorities or not, offered to an informer for information that has led to the identification of suspects in a committed or attempted crime, or to the prevention of a crime, the principle being: No suspect, no pay. Promises of reward to the informer may only be made by police officials provided the information has led (in part) to the apprehension of the suspect(s) in a given case or has helped to identify him (them). In concert with the public

---

131 This directive came forth during the meeting of *Procureurs-Generaal* on August 28, 1985; the confidential and sensitive character of this subject is well illustrated by the fact that even the members of the parliamentary committee Van Traa, commissioned to get insight on the size of organized crime, were not given access to neither informers nor infiltrators. The public prosecutor's department refused to give the authorization because, according to the department, the confidentiality of the identities cannot be guaranteed in a satisfactory manner (De Volkskrant, January 21, 1995). Moreover, allegations have been made of the use of asylum seekers, refugees and "tolerated" refugees as informers by the ministry of Justice. The state secretary Schmitz did not give any answers, which is yet another example of the sensitive character of the use of informers (Rotterdams Dagblad, March 8, 1995); meanwhile, this directive is published in Van Traa, 1996, App. I.

132 According to Van der Vegt, 1989, p. 50.

133 See Roest, 1991, p. 325.

134 Verbraak, 1991, pp. 25-24.

prosecutor's office, it is possible that some exceptions be made to these rules. This may be the case for example when the information has led to the tracing of irreplaceable goods (such as art masterpieces or stolen jewelry) or to the prevention of the commission of severe crimes. In cases where the information proves to be accurate without leading to the tracing of the suspect (provided the informer is not responsible for this) the reward might be paid anyway. Money may also be paid in order to keep structural contacts warm (*inspan-ningsgelden*, literally: effort money) while at the same time paying the costs made by informers.[135]

All payments made must be reported in the CID book-keeping (the book-keeping of the criminal intelligence service) kept for internal purposes only. The directive contains also a code of conduct concerning among other things promises, margin of discretion regarding decisions, method of payment and also stipulates the periodical reviewal of the value keeping the contact with a particular informer warm. In relation with the latter, the CID keeps and updates a black list of informers that have proven unreliable.[136]

Another possibility consists of making deals with criminals: In exchange of information concerning an offence the public prosecutor may demand for a lower sentence during the sentencing hearing, engage himself to refrain from appealing, overlook some factual evidence or request the suspect's pre-trial liberation.[137] A letter from the assembly of prosecutors general to the chief public prosecutor (July 1, 1983) prescribes a particular procedure for making deals with criminals. According to this letter such deals are only acceptable in matters of life and death as well as matters of equivalent severity. One may think in this case of such matters as concerning the security of the State or the public health. Another condition is that it be impossible to achieve the proposed aim in another way and that the participation offered by the criminal be essential to that aim. The promised benefit contained in the deal may not be granted before the accuracy of the information has been proven. Such deals may only be made in concert with the public prosecutor's office, the prosecutors general of the court and eventually with the justice department.[138]

Note that the identity of the informer may be kept secret in spite of the law concerning openness of administration (*Wet openbaarheid van bestuur*- WOB).[139]-

---

135 Roest, 1991, pp. 277-278.
136 Van der Vegt, 1989, pp. 56-57; informers and their position in Dutch law have been discussed thoroughly in Van Traa, 1996, pp. 207-231, who conclude that a specific statutory basis for the use of informers is desirable (pp. 434-435).
137 Pijl, 1988, p. 414; Roest, 1991, p. 326.
138 The parliamentary enquiry committee concluded that these guidelines have been outdated by the practice and that in general a legal basis for such deals with criminals would be necessary; see Van Traa, 1996, pp. 435 and 465.
139 *Tipgevers van politie zijn gerustgesteld*, in: Algemeen Dagblad, October 24, 1990.

The identity may be kept confidential with regards to the administration of the evidence even during the trial hearing.[140] This confidentiality seems to be so sacred that even the members of the parliamentary committee have been denied the possibility to interview informers.[141]

5.2.4.3 Luxembourg

The use of informers seems possible in Luxembourg as well. Every particular *policier* or *gendarme* probably has its own informer, although no guidelines seem to be provided regarding procedural aspects. On the basis of art. 326 CP the court may grant an informer a reduced sentence which may eventually serve as a basis for deals with criminals. Whether informers may be rewarded (in money or otherwise) for their services is not likely, as they is no budget for these expenses. The payment of incomers is the subject neither of legislation nor of an official budget item.[142] Moreover, it is likely that the identity of informers may not be kept confidential once their name appear on police reports. In practice, it is not excluded that informers are not mentioned on police reports in order to protect their anonymity.

5.2.4.4 France

It had already been accepted by the case-law that since both *police* and *gendarmerie* officials pursue their investigations in civilian clothes, they may also rely on informers and disguises.[143] Use of these methods, however, is left to the appreciation of each commanding officer and depends greatly on the financial or technical means of each particular service. In general neither the police nor the *gendarmerie* have large sums of money at their disposal in order to enable them to financially compensate informers. In practice it may happen that a particular police service brings its informer in contact with customs officers, as many criminal offences have their corresponding customs' offences. This is done because customs have greater financial means at their disposal

---

140 HR March 17, 1981, NJ 1981, 382 with note by Th.W. van Veen.
141 *Enquêtecommissie mag tipgevers niet spreken*, in: NJB 1995, p. 332.
142 This has been confirmed to us by sources inside the police.
143 Cass. crim. July 6, 1894, D.P. 99, 1 171; April 4, 1924, D.P. 1925, 1, 10; Paris, April 3, 1987, Juris-Data nr. 023426; February 12, 1988, Juris-Data nr. 023105.

originating from what they call a "*droit de touche*"[144] and in this way the informer may be granted larger sums of money.[145]

Another method of paying off informers is to give them some advantage, such as a reduced sentence granted by the trial judge (for instance art. 268 CP or 450-2 CPN). It is not excluded that this article may serve as a basis for deals with criminals, although this is not documented. Indeed, nothing stands in the way of the police to be more tolerant towards a worthy informer. Traditionally, it seems that the police dispose of both positive as negative ways of gathering information from civilians. Positive ways are mostly expressed in the form of tolerance towards, for instance, owners of drinking establishements, foreigners and prostitutes. As these categories of persons depend on the police for the regularity of their situation, they may be rewarded by a tolerant application of the law. This dependency may also be exploited in a more negative way: The identity of clients of a drinking establishment owned by an uncooperative potential witness may be systematically controlled, that of a known foreigner in irregular situation or of the clients of a prostitute. The threat of this control may be enough to generate numerous tips.[146]

One thing seems certain, the identity of informers may not be kept confidential once they appear in police reports. It is likely that some police officials may be tempted to refrain reporting the presence of informers in order to protect their anonymity. In any case there are no official records on these types of practices and the tip is part of the grey zone preceding other "official" investigating methods. The police officer may write in his report to the public prosecutor that he has obtained information from "a reliable source."[147]

The direct use of informers as infiltrators in France - legally - is doubtful, as the 1991 Anti Drugs Act only refers to the use of police, *gendarmerie* or customs officers as such. However, the indirect use of informers, in the grey zone of pro-activity, might very well evade all control, since it will not appear in the police report. Moreover, this type of grey information might be used to convince an examining judge to authorize the use of other more legally recognized investigating methods as telephone taps and infiltration.

---

144 Literally: "right to receive." This concerns the possibility given to customs officers to deduct a certain percentage of the value of confiscated goods. Use of this method was confirmed to us by a former police commissionary; see art. 391 CD and *Décret* nr. 57-520, April 15, 1957, J.O. April 24, 1957, p. 4243.

145 This was related to us by a former police commissary.

146 Lévy, 1987, pp. 19-25.

147 The cliché expression: "...*de source sûre, j'ai appris que...*" will then appear in the police report.

5.2.4.5 Germany

In general, the statutes distinguish between informers (*Informanten*, literally: informers) and regular informers (*Vertrauensperson*, literally: persons of trust).[148] The former designates an informer that is ready to divulge confidential information to the police on an incidental basis, whereas the latter concerns an informer disclosing information on a more regular and organized basis. Although on the federal level the rules concerning informers are not set in formal law, most of the German provinces have incorporated provisions on regular informers in statutes.

In the Police Act of Nordrhein-Westfalen (NWPolG) the rules concerning informers are contained in artt. 19 and 20. Art. 19 NWPolG stipulates that information on criminal activity may be acquired through "persons whose cooperation with the police is not known to thirds." These informers or "persons of trust" (*V-Personen*) may be used to gather information on the same persons with respects to whom use of hidden picture and sound equipment is permitted. The persons of trust may only be used to gather information on specific persons and concerning a previously set objective. Furthermore, the situation must be such that specific danger for life, limb and freedom is present, or that the information is necessary to prevent the commission of severe criminal actions. This situation ought not to be confused with the (incidental or customary) declaration of witnesses or tipsters. These are not acting on behalf of the police seeking information on a specific (past, present or future) crime but are in principle acting on their own initiative and give information usually on crimes that have already been committed.[149]

In general these persons of trust will be ordinary civilians so as to enable them to dispose of their own free will when deciding to cooperate with the police. This also has as consequence that persons of trust do not dispose of police powers although they may in some occasions be sent in an operation with hidden listening devices (wires, in German: *Personenschutzsender*).[150] According to the second paragraph of art. 19 the decision to send a person of trust rests on the chief of service but this decision making power may be delegated.

---

148 The law makes a clear difference between undercover investigator (VE) and informant (VP) but in theory one cannot exclude the possibility of the police infiltrating through informers and in that case, the difference is negligible. Furthermore, the control of these methods by the trial judge, public prosecutor or examining judge will depend on whether the methods are known. In that sense, the difference between VP and VE in the trial is that the informer must appear as a witness while the infiltrator may be ignored. This was related to us by *Kriminalrat* Clauer, LKA NRW, Düsseldorf, October 20, 1994.

149 See Heise/Tegtmeyer, 1990, pp. 173-174.

150 Heise/Tegtmeyer, 1990, p. 74; see Chapter 4 for more information on wired infiltrators.

The person forming the object of the operation must be informed of this after the termination of the operation. This, however, may be omitted if the aim of information gathering, the use of the concerned informer at a later date or life and limb of thirds are endangered. This is also the case when the gathered information gives rise to a police enquiry (art. 19 par. 3).

The statutes of Rheinland-Pfalz and of Saarland do not have such detailed provisions as that of Nordrhein-Westfalen. Art. 25b of the statute of Rheinland-Pfalz only vaguely mentions the possibility of gathering non public information with the help of covert means or persons. In this province informers are considered in the same manner as hidden listening or filming devices, which means that they are subject to the same conditions contained in art. 25b RhPfPVG.[151] The statute of Saarland seems to distinguish persons of trust from informers: They are considered beside one another.

Baden-Württemberg does not provide for any rule concerning persons of trust or informers. Because it is hardly possible that informers are not used one may assume that informers are seen as ordinary witnesses or tipsters.

As we have said above, the federal Organized Crime Act (OrgKG) does not mention the possibility of relying on informers. However, there exists a directive since 1986 specifying the manner of enquiring. This directive (Gemeinsame Richtlinien) does distinguish between persons of trust and informers. The informer is seen as an incidental or structural tipster whose information upon request may be handled in confidentiality (art. I.2.1 Anl. D RiStBV). The person of trust is a civilian that is sent in a particular case in order to gather information. His identity along with his relation to the police will always in principle be kept confidential. However, the granting of confidentiality must be in accordance with the principles of subsidiarity and proportionality, which usually means that these criteria will be fulfilled in cases involving severe or organized crime. The decision concerning the granting of confidentiality rests solely on the responsible authority of the public prosecutor's department or in urgent cases of the police (art. I.5).

There is no information as to whether financial or otherwise rewarding of tips on a federal level is permitted, nor is there anything known on the making of deals with criminals. Some provisions are contained in the Drug Act (Betäubungsmittelgesetz - BtMG) and in the regulations regarding chief witnesses (Kronzeugenregelung).[152] They contain rules concerning deals with a specific

---

151 According to this article, trespassing on private premises is subject to a court order as well, which is rather peculiar when one considers that informers may be invited to trespass on private grounds by the owner or occupant.

152 Gezetz zur Änderung des Strafgesetzbuches, der Strafprozeßordnung und des Versammlungsgesetzes und zur Einführung einer Kronzeugenregelung bei terroristischen Straftaten,, June 9, 1989, BGBl. I, 1059.

category of criminals, offenders of the Drug Act and terrorists, who offer substantial help in the prevention or solution of criminal actions. The Drug Act authorizes the trial court either to diminish or to suspend the sentence when the accused has played an important role in the prosecution of other suspects (art. 31 BtMG). Since 1989, Germany has also known a general chief witness program, which was originally introduced as a temporary measure against terrorist crimes. Although its field of application was slowly extended to other types of crime, according to our latest information it was expected to expire on December 31, 1995.[153]

In addition, a number of provisions exist in the above mentioned federal guidelines on the use of informers and infiltrators (*Gemeinsame Richtlinien*). Mainly because of the fact that the rule-making competence of the federal State is limited to the sphere of the official criminal investigation, the guidelines mostly address the issue of guaranteeing confidentiality. This is guaranteed in case of severe and organized criminality, illegal trafficking in drugs and arms, counterfeiting of money or crimes against the State security. They may only be used when there is no other way to obtain certain information and to achieve prosecution by gathering evidence. The confidentiality is only guaranteed for cases when the fact that a particular informer has collaborated with the police would be dangerous for the informer. The guideline forbids also the use of minors as informers.

The public prosecutor as well as the police are bound by the assurance of confidentiality. The guarantee of confidentiality is lifted when the information proves to be knowingly false, when the informer ignores instructions and in other ways cannot be relied on, participates in the commission of a criminal offence or commits a criminal offence himself. The guideline states further that when an informer is assigned to a particular case in the framework of a criminal investigation, the guarantee of secrecy may only be given after authorization of the public prosecutor's department. If this authorization cannot be solicited timely, the public prosecutor's department must be notified without delay. The guideline provides for further procedural details.[154]

5.3 Comparing National Norms

This overview of the existing norms regarding special policing techniques in the five countries at the origin of the Schengen Convention leads to the following remarks. There is no consensus on the necessity of having detailed legislation on that matter. Techniques such as controlled delivery, infiltration, sting

---

153   Tak *et al.*, 1996, pp. 201-204.
154   For information on the use of informers in Germany, see Van Traa, 1996, App. V, pp. 483-485.

operations or the use of informers are subject to varying forms of regulations, if any. In a few countries, such as Germany and France, some or all of these techniques are subject to statuary legislation, generally accessible to the public and are assured a certain degree of controllability by the courts. In the other studied countries, these techniques are, when regulated at all, confined in circulars and directives that, not only may be amended in very informal manners escaping parliamentary control, but even evade court control aftermath because of their secret character (see *Table 5.1*). When they are not regulated, it is left to the courts to decide whether police officials have transgressed their limits. In doing so the courts very often resort to flexible criteria which vary according to the seriousness of the offence.

There seems to be two ways of looking at the use of special investigation techniques involving actual participation of police officers. They are seen either as a tactical question or an exception to the general rule that the police must abide the law. As a tactical question, the need for normative provisions is accessory, the courts being seen as the sole guardian of the limits not to be trespassed. In the contrary, as an exception to the rule of law, these methods are seen as highly sensitive issues needing legislation to legitimate the actions of the State. Belgium, The Netherlands and Luxembourg belong to the first group characterized by the lack of statutes, although not to the same degree. Luxembourg is a good example of that first group as it denies the existence of all legislation and its participation in any operation, despite its participation to an international forum and its international obligations. Belgium and The Netherlands have both adopted circulars for internal use, but the fact that in The Netherlands these are published demonstrates the turn that this country is making towards the second group.

The second group is characterized by its formal legislation. Despite this apparent similarity, one notes the difference in reasoning towards the necessity of adopting statutes. France adopted legislation to cover the members of its police force, while Germany did so under the pressure of its constitutional court. One could argue that both States see in the law a justification for violations of the law by the State: Committing criminal acts or violating the right to privacy are both acts that, when done by a citizen, are punishable. The State would lose all credibility in the public opinion. Note, however, that the passing from the first group to the second often has to do with events independent to the will of the State's authorities: Public dismay as to a particular scandal or situation often acts as a catalyst for formal legislation.

Table 5.1 Infiltration in General

	B	NL	L	F	D
Type of norm					
Statute	-	-	-	+	+
Guidelines/directive	+	+	-	-	+
Published	-	+	-	+	+
Conditions					
Proportionality/subsidiarity	+	+	-	-	+
Organized/severe crime	+	+	-	-	+
Drug offences only	-	-	-	+	-

There is no consensus on whether these techniques should be applicable to a wide range of criminal offences or to a very limited one, nor is there a consensus on the way to go about restricting the scope of application of these special techniques. In most of the studied countries the choice has been made to avoid limiting the crimes justifying these policing techniques, reserving this action to what is vaguely known as severe, organized or career criminality. In other countries, however, such action is limited to a number of crimes set up in a catalogue in the statute (Germany) or to only one category of crimes, such as (in France) drug related crimes (*Table 5.1*).[155]

5.3.1   Controlled Delivery

Most of the countries demand authorization of the public prosecutor's department for controlled deliveries (see *Table 5.2*), although the need for formal legislation is not seen as strongly. This is probably due to the relatively small amount of involvement of the State in the operation. When controlled delivery is limited to the observation of illegal transports, the action of police officers is limited to a very passive one as observers. Indeed, this relative passivity is misleading when one notes the responsibility of the State in letting illegal goods enter the free market. This is probably why the countries of group two have adopted some kind of normative framework on an internal level.

---

155   The question regarding whether or not one state should embody a catalogue of offences in the law in opposition to a general clause is briefly discussed in Gropp, 1993b, p.35.

234

Table 5.2 Controlled Delivery

	B	NL	L	F	D
Type of norm					
Statute	-	-	-	+	-
Guidelines/directives	+	+	-	-	+
Published	-	+	-	+	+
Conditions					
Permission of judge/public prosecutor	+	+	-	+	+
Proportionality/subsidiarity	+	+	-	-	+
Organized/severe crimes	+	-	-	-	+
Drug offences only	-	-	-	+	-

5.3.2   Infiltration

Here again, one notes the division in two groups, the one group seeking its normative framework in the form of guidelines, the other in formal legislation (*Table 5.3*). As we have said above, this underlines the difference of perception of the rule of law in the different States.

In all countries where the use of infiltration is officially acknowledged, however, the assignment of infiltrating investigators is subject of some kind of normative framework - be it formal or informal - and to the authorization of the public prosecutor, or more generally to the public prosecutor's office. Most of the countries provide for the (formal or informal) possibility to grant temporary identities to infiltrating officials, although not in the same degree (see *Table 5.4*). Only one of the studied countries, Germany, provides for the formal obligation of notifying a person afterwards of the fact that he or she has been put under the surveillance of an undercover agent. This obligation greatly increases the controllability of the measure but was not present in any of the other countries.

What is striking in this overview is the disparity (in quantity and in quality) of norms regarding the use of such special policing techniques (*Tables 5.5* and *5.6*). There are no standards and few common denominators. This is striking on the one hand because we find ourselves in an area that flirts with the limits of the law and on the second hand because the studied countries would all describe themselves as abiding by the rule of law. Controllability is left to the good will of the different actors in the criminal systems of national States. In the crime fighting climate of today, priority is given to the granting of more extensive policing powers and not to extensive legislation protecting the rights of the unaccused.

Table 5.3 Infiltration

	B	NL	L	F	D
Type of norm					
Statute	-	-	-	+	+
Guidelines/directives	+	+	-	-	+
Published	-	+	-	+	+
Conditions					
Depends on method	-	+	-	-	+
Permission of judge/public prosecutor	+	+	-	+	+
Proportionality/subsidiarity	+	+	-	-	+
Organized/severe crimes	+	-	-	-	+
Drug offences only	-	-	-	+	-

5.3.3   Informers

The practice of using informers is widespread throughout the studied States although not regulated in the same way. Some countries provide substantial financial means for this purpose, others may "look the other way" when it comes to deciding about prosecuting them. Yet others provide detailed codes of conducts or are silent as to the official treatment of the informer. Some countries even have formal provisions enabling judicial officials to reduce the sentence of a "cooperative" criminal (*Table 5.4*). The concept of informer is, furthermore, a concept subject to vary. Whether one speaks of incidental informer or of "running" an informer may be just the difference between simply observing and infiltrating. This makes the definition of the concept tedious and complicated.

236

Table 5.4 Use of Informers

	B	NL	L	F	D
Type of norm					
Statute	-	-	+	+	+
Guidelines/directives	+	+	-	-	+
Published	-	-	+	+	+
Conditions					
Proportionality/subsidiarity	+	+	-	-	+
Informer from criminal milieu	+	-	+	+	-
No suspect/no pay	-	+	-	-	-
Denunciation before prosecution	-	-	-	+	-
Denunciation before committing crime	-	-	+	-	-

5.4 Conclusion

As illustrated in *Tables 5.5* and *5.6*, all the countries, Luxembourg excepted, have regulated the use of short-term infiltration in one form or another. The question of long(er) term infiltration, deep cover as well as contact with informers seem to be of a more sensitive nature. All the countries show a strong preference towards police officers as infiltrators, although it seems that the practice is shifting towards civilian infiltration. Moreover, the factual differences between infiltration on the one hand and the "running" of informers on the other seem to be increasingly few. With this development, the State may avoid directly committing criminal offences through its executive agents. However, the State is still involved since these criminal offences are being committed under the control, direct or indirect, of the very same State through the public prosecutor's department. One may wonder whether the State is not guilty of encouraging crime. In any case, it operates in very dark alleys.

Table 5.5 Regulated Infiltration Items by State I

	Methods	Supervision	Actual infiltrator	Time limit
B	* contr. delivery * sting operations * infiltration * informers	* public prosecutor	* police officers (poss. foreign)	* exclusively short term (no specification)
NL	* contr. delivery * sting operations * infiltration * front stores * informers	* commanding officer, with public prosecutor, authorization by ministry	* police officers (poss. foreign) * civilians	* short term
L	-	-	-	-
F	* contr. delivery * infiltration * front stores	* directed by commanding officer with authorization of public prosecutor	* police officers (police, *gendarmerie*, customs)	* no specification
D	* contr. delivery * infiltration * informers	* public prosecutor	* police officers	* exclusively short term, legend may be used longer

Further, as pointed out in *Table 5.6*, the public prosecutor plays a very active role in the authorization and supervision of special investigating techniques in most of the studied countries. Because the public prosecutor must test in each case whether the use of these techniques is in accordance with principles of law and, because he is the one to determine whether a case will be prosecuted, he may at one time or another find himself judge and party in the same case. It is not far fetched to imagine a case where special investigating methods, which use was authorized by the public prosecutor (or the department), have got out of hand. Would it not be tempting for the competent public prosecutor not to prosecute the case? In our opinion, problems of this sort might easily be avoided by subjecting the authorization to the control of a judge.

Table 5.6 Regulated Infiltration Items by State II

	Offences by infil-trators	Limit of actions	Special training	Openness
B	* only when strictly necessary	* provocation	* special training must be given	-
NL	* within set limits	* provocation	* special training must be given	* must be controllable
L	-	* provocation	-	-
F	* buy, sell, possess, transport or deliver narcotics	* provocation	-	* will appear in police report
D	* no offences	* provocation	* special training	* openness

Before one addresses the question of whether and which legislation is needed in this field, one should address the issue of whether these enquiring methods are necessary in a democratic society[156] and whether they are effective. This discussion needs to be held in public, at best in each national parliament. Once the society has decided that the use of such policing techniques is necessary, the rule of law obliges the national parliament to adopt legislation on the subject. In a second phase, and because criminality knows no borders, it will be necessary to adopt an international framework in which cooperation will be facilitated. There is no need for harmonization in our opinion, simple conflict rules are sufficient.

To answer the first question, whether these enquiring methods are needed in a democratic society, we must first ask ourselves whether criminalyzing the actions these special techniques aim at prosecuting serves a purpose. If the answer is yes, we should pursue by asking in which ways exist to investigate these crimes and in which way it is necessary to investigate these crimes. Once we have taken an inventory of all the investigation methods available, we should ask whether a legal basis is needed for the chosen investigation methods. At that point, the discussion should be directed at which form this legal basis should take.

---

156 As observed by G.P.M.F. Mols during the annual assembly of the Dutch Association of Jurists (Nederlandse Juristenvereniging) on June 9 1995, in itself, the setting out of rules in the law concerning a special method of investigation is a good thing. However, a statute does not answer the question as to whether an investigative method is necessary. Especially where the violation of a fundamental right is important, the necessity to resort to this method must be as important in relation to the pursue aim.

In an attempt to answer the first question, one may take a glance at the results of the war on drugs in the United States. This glance might convince some that more extensive policing powers are not the sole answer to organized crime:[157] Measures designed to render institutions less fragile for corruption or preventive measures designed to make products less attractive for organized crime such as decriminalization of the use of psychotropic substances may at least help in getting rid of organized crime and make this problem at least manageable while limiting the impact on everyday life in general and public health in particular. Note as an illustration the following comment: In a meeting of the Dutch police chiefs on drugs policy, organized are a very timely moment - after the Haarlem police admitting having let in recent years a great amount of drugs enter the free market - the chairman of the assembly at the time, admitted that the war on drugs had failed in The Netherlands, since it only makes criminals richer.[158]

Furthermore, comparing the relative dangers of these delicate techniques with the factual results may also lead us to review the position that undercover policing methods are necessary in a democratic society.[159] Although practices such as controlled delivery (not involving direct intervention of undercover police officials) may not cause great execution difficulties, the fact that infiltrating police officers run great risks while jeopardizing the State's credibility needs little illustration: A public official makes use of stratagems, false identities based on false papers and so-doing commits crimes in the name of the State that employs him. The undercover agent endangers his life and may even resort to turning criminal himself.[160] Quoting an ex-police detective implicated in the François case in Belgium:[161] "There's just too much money involved in that (criminal) world and that's something you'll never be able to beat as an ordinary policeman." Let us suppose that these policing techniques were

---

157 In The Netherlands, it was publicly acknowledged by the police chief in The Hague, J. Brand, that the war on drugs had been lost; see NRC-Handelsblad, June 24, 1995 and *De Raad, de media en de War on drugs*, APB, 1995, pp. 4-5.

158 NRC-Handelsblad, June 10, 1995

159 See among others, the former Rotterdam police chief Blaauw, 1985 pp. 243-253. Moreover, there are no guarantees as to the efficiency of these methods. Criminal organizations are very aware of the arsenal at the disposal of the state to combat them. As an illustration, one story in the Dutch newspapers suggested that criminal organizations send youngsters in the police school to learn to be infiltrators (De Telegraaf, April 15, 1995). They even send threatening letters to the police and public prosecutors (NRC-Handelsblad, April 14, 1995; De Telegraaf, April 14, 1995; Trouw, April 15, 1995). It is rather a question of whether the State should play the same game as criminal organizations while at the same time repeating that the game is illegal. In the absence of substantial results, one must wonder whether a democratic society should get involved in that game.

160 See on that subject Van Parys & Laurent, 1990 and Fijnaut, 1983 and Pels, 1993, pp. 4-7.

161 This was reported by Blaauw, 1985, p.250.

indispensable for the fight against (organized or career) crime. National legislation would be imperative because of the rule of law: The use of techniques such as infiltration is not only a violation of the right to privacy as we have shown above, but an exception to the general rule that no one is above the law. The State, passing as a criminal, acts as an exception to that rule. In committing crimes, the State might be able to invoke self-defence or urgency incidentally, but this is not enough when such techniques are used structurally.

Furthermore, considering the European Convention on Human Rights, we must acknowledge, as we have stated above, that all these special policing techniques are liable to violate the right to privacy as guaranteed by art. 8 ECHR for the following reasons: Firstly, because these special policing techniques - especially when we look at the pro-active use of these techniques - aim the gathering - and storing - of information. The right to privacy, moreover, must be given an extensive interpretation that includes the protection against intrusions by an undercover agent: Infiltration is a violation of art. 8 because if it were not, art. 8 would have no practical application. In addition, such covert investigating methods may potentially violate the presumption of innocence and with this violation, the suspect's right to remain silent. The suspect's encounter with the undercover agent can have such consequences for him that it would go against the Convention to restrict this right in the absence of a legal basis.

Setting aside the vague provision on controlled delivery contained in art. 73 SC and the existence of an international forum on infiltration, police cooperation in the matters discussed above is left in the grey zone of agreements between public prosecutors, examining judges and governments. One may even wonder whether art. 73 SC may be used as a basis for international cooperation at all since it only encourages the Contracting Parties to engage themselves to adopt measures enabling controlled deliveries to take place on their territories in matters of illicit drug trafficking. When it comes to police operations that go beyond the mere observation of drug transports, the silence is total. Although there is no doubt about the fact that a certain degree of cooperation takes place between countries in these matters, there is no way to get official data on the subject. The international cooperation is left to the arbitrariness of the different mutual, secret agreements between police officials and judiciary authorities. The judiciary control of these procedures often escape the courts completely.[162]

The consequences of the different national approaches to covert deceptive policing methods are difficult to sketch. Because of their secretive character, official sources hesitate to divulge specific information. Nevertheless, note that the disparity in the sort of norms is not a factor to help cooperation. In addition,

---

162 Schürmann (1995) states a number of problems encountered by the German infiltrators and informers acting on foreign territories, one of them, and not the least, being the recognition or absence of recognition of false identity papers used for legends.

the fact that these methods may only be used in specific kinds of offences that may differ from State to State. Note that all countries (Luxembourg excepted) see drug trafficking as ground for police infiltration. Another difficulty arises when one notes that some countries do and others do not accept foreign undercover police officials on their territory.

The greatest difficulty seems, however, the confidential character of some of the provisions.[163] Although it is not certain to which extent the confidentiality is extended to competent police officials of the different countries among themselves, there is no doubt that it is not a situation that encourages cooperation. It pushes these issues to case by case evaluation behind the scenes of diplomacy, escaping in that way any form of impartial control. Another important question is whether the use of these types of policing techniques should be left solely to the discretion of police and prosecuting authorities. They constitute such a far reaching interference with one's private life[164] as well as an ethical risk for the State that its use should be allowed only on the basis of detailed statuary law.

Finally, there might also be other reasons for adopting clear and precise statutes on this subject: Clear legislation will, firstly, help concerned police officers by telling them how far they may go (important for their criminal as well as their civil liability) while helping courts to play their controlling role. Secondly, detailed statutes, rather than (confidential) circulars, will help international cooperation in making knowledge of each others normative framework independent of personal contacts between different authorities. Setting up an international framework for this cooperation with simple conflict rules belong to the possibilities which may very well help short term cooperation. National legislation would then be the first step in that direction.

---

163 Some may argue that this confidential character has the advantage of not binding the judge who is then free to evaluate the evidence on the basis of general principles of fairness. This is, however, true when the investigating methods have been revealed and made controllable for the judge. In cases where the prosecuting authorities remain secretive, this control is impossible. This point came forth during a discussion with Mr Zanders of the Belgian *Gendarmerie*.

164 This was also strongly stressed by public prosecutor Körner (1985, p. 423) in his comment to the Drug Act (*Betäubungsmittelgesetz*): "*Das Ansetzen eines V-Mannes an einen Tatverdächtiges ist der umfassendste und schwerwiegendste Eingriff in die Grundrechte eines Bürgers.*"

6 Hot Pursuit

The necessity to pursue criminals and alleged criminals often implies that the police officer following the suspect must leave his own area of competence, and is forced by the urgency of the situation to ignore laws that he would have obeyed usually, such as traffic regulations. The legislators of the five countries studied here all have provided statutory exceptions for these situations, whereas they have even created possibilities for a pursuing police officer to cross the national borders and continue their pursuit in a neighbouring country. In this paragraph, we will discuss these international and national regulations, the possibilities they create and the problems they might possibly cause.

6.1 International Norms

In international law, not much legislation, case-law or jurisprudence on cross-border hot pursuit can be found. The main reason for this is that only a few countries have allowed state officials of other countries to cross their borders and infringe with their national sovereignty by exercising foreign powers on their territory.[1] Regarding the international norms which do indeed exist, we will mainly focus on norms regarding police cooperation. Because of its general relevance in criminal and police matters, as well as its harmonizing influence in these fields in all of the studied countries, some attention will be paid to the European Convention on Human Rights as well.

6.1.1 International Norms on Police Cooperation

International norms with regard to cross-border hot pursuit by the police may be found in several treaties, especially in the 1990 Schengen Convention (SC)

---

1 For this reason, Poulantzas, who has defined the right of hot pursuit generally "as the right of a state to continue the pursuit of wrongdoers outside a) its territorial waters, b) the air space above its territory and territorial waters, and c) its land frontiers - or outside areas over which the state has jurisdiction - upon the high seas or into the air space over the high seas, or into a no man's land, or, if agreement exists thereon, into the territory of another state, provided in all these cases that the pursuit has started immediately after the violation in these areas and has continued without interruption beyond the said domains," has especially focused on hot pursuit into areas where no national sovereignty exists. See Poulantzas 1969, pp. 1-2.

and the 1962 Benelux Extradition and Mutual Legal Assistance Treaty (BET).[2] In the 1990 Schengen Convention, the Benelux countries, France and Germany have established the possibility of cross-border hot pursuit in art. 41, the first paragraph of which reads as follows:[3]

> Officers of one of the Contracting Parties following, in their country, an individual apprehended in the act of committing one of the offences referred to in paragraph 4 or participants in one of those offences, shall be authorized to continue pursuit in the territory of another Contracting Party without prior authorization where given the particular urgency of the situation it was not possible to notify the competent authorities of the other Contracting Party by one of the means provided for in article 44 prior to entry into that territory or where these authorities have been unable to reach the scene in time to take over the pursuit.
> The same shall apply where the person pursued has escaped from provisional custody or while serving a custodial sentence.
> The pursuing officers shall, not later than when they cross the border, contact the competent authorities of the Contracting Party in whose territory the pursuit is to take place. The pursuit will cease as soon as the Contracting Party on the territory of which the pursuit is taking place so requests. At the request of the pursuing officers, the competent local authorities shall challenge the pursued person so as to establish his identity or to arrest him.

It is therefore necessary that the pursued person be either an escaped prisoner or apprehended in the act, and that this act be one of the offences referred to in art. 41 par. 4 SC.[4] This paragraph obliges the Contracting Parties to define these offences, leaving a choice between:

> (a) the following offences: assassination; murder; rape; arson; counterfeiting; armed robbery[5] and receiving of stolen goods; extortion; kidnapping and hostage taking; traffic in human beings; illicit traffic in narcotic drugs and psychotropic substances; breach of the law on arms and explosives; use of explosives; illicit carriage of toxic and dangerous waste; taking to flight after an incident which has resulted in death or serious injury.

and

---

2   *Beneluxverdrag aangaande de uitlevering en de rechtshulp in strafzaken*, Brussels, June 27, 1962, Trb. 1962, 97. The 1958 High Sea Convention also regulates a very specific form of hot pursuit: the pursuit on high sea of a vessel that has committed a crime in the territorial waters of a party to this treaty. In the following, this treaty will however be left without consideration.

3   Non-authentic translation by the Benelux secretariat, published in Meijers *et al.*, 1991, pp. 167-169.

4   That is to say, in cross-border pursuits in which at least one non-Benelux member state is involved; for situations between Benelux member states, we refer to the sub-section 6.1.1.2.

5   On the basis of the Dutch, French and German versions of the Convention one must conclude that the right English translation would have been: aggravated theft and robbery.

(b) extraditable offences.

With the obvious exception of the last offence, the list under (a) contains the same offences as the ones for which cross-border observation without a previous authorization is allowed according to art. 40 par. 7 SC. It is worth noticing that not all of these offences are equally probable to be discovered in-the-act. Especially concerning crimes like assassination, murder and rape this is rather unlikely. The catalogue of extraditable offences referred to under (b) is much larger than the list under (a); it is the same as the group of offences for which cross-border observation with a previous authorization is allowed and essentially, it contains all offences punishable with imprisonment of a year or longer.[6] The choices made by the respective countries will be discussed in section 6.2.2, where the national norms of each of the countries in this field are explained. Here we would however like to remark that the offences that may lead to cross-border pursuit are not considered equally important in all five countries. Especially when the pursued person has been apprehended after a cross-border pursuit leading into a country where the offence involved is not given high priority by police and judicial authorities, the latter will not automatically be enthusiastic to cooperate and hear the account of the pursuing officers. In this sense, the fact that for instance the possession of small proportions of soft drugs is considered allowed in the Netherlands is likely to be a source of (even more) tensions in the border regions with Belgium and Germany.[7]

Confusion concerning the pursuit of escapees could still be caused by the interpretation to be given to the various authentic versions leading to the English translation "custodial sentence," as mentioned in art. 41 par. 1 SC. The question as to whether these versions have specific meanings in the respective legal systems of the Contracting Parties and whether or not such differences might have legal implications, will be discussed later. A similar question is, what is exactly meant by the words "provisional custody," or more specifically by its counterparts in the three authentic languages. Finally, we would like to draw attention to the fact that the text on pursuit from provisional custody has been

---

6   According to art. 2 of the European Convention on Extradition (Paris, December 13, 1957, Trb. 1965, 9). Until this day, this Convention has not been ratified by Belgium, but between Belgium and the other Schengen countries it will nevertheless be applied on the basis of art. 60 SC. Moreover, a bill of ratification of the Extradition Convention is actually pending in Belgian parliament.

7   In Germany, the legal situation regarding this offence tends to develop in the direction of the Dutch soft drug policy, since the Constitutional Court has decided that it may be disproportional (and therefore unconstitutional) to prosecute a person possessing a small quantity of cannabis products for his personal use; BVerfG March 9, 1994, published in for instance StV 1994, pp. 295-303. According to Rüter, 1996, pp. 85-86, most German provinces meanwhile have a drug policy that is comparable to the Dutch policy.

drafted regardless of any differences in modalities and conditions for provisional custody between the Contracting Parties.

Art. 41 adds that the pursuing officers shall, before crossing the border, try to notify the competent authorities of the other Contracting Party by one of the means of communication provided for in art. 44 (telephone, radio, and telex lines and other direct links). In case it is not possible to obtain prior authorization due to the urgency of the situation, the border may be crossed without authorization. In a declaration as referred to in art. 41 par. 9, the countries have specified whether or not the pursuing officers, once the border has been crossed, are empowered to apprehend the suspect according to par. 2. The apprehension and the declarations made with respect to this measure will be discussed in Chapter 7 of this study.

In a declaration according to par. 9, the Contracting Parties also have to define in which way the pursuit itself may be carried out or limited, for which the Convention provides them with the choice between:

(a) in an area or during a period as from the crossing of the border, to be established in the declaration

and

(b) without limit in space or time.

Again, the respective countries' choices with regard to this aspect will be part of the discussion of the legal situation in each of the countries.

Paragraph 5 of art. 41 SC contains the general conditions to which the cross-border pursuit are subjected; some of these conditions are similar to the general conditions for cross-border observation, whereas some others partly differ from these or even regard questions that are typical for pursuit rather than for observation. For both forms of cross-border policing, the officers must comply with the provisions of the treaty and with the law of the country where the pursuit takes place (for this reason, the law of every country with respect to pursuit will be discussed below), and entry into private homes and places not accessible to the public is prohibited.

Due to the different nature of both forms of policing, the hot pursuit regulation as designed in the Schengen Convention contains several conditions which (at least partly) differ from the conditions regarding observation. Such is the case with regard to the service weapons of the border crossing police officers: The Contracting Parties may not make any restrictions as to carrying a service weapon in case of a hot pursuit. As for observation, using the weapon is only allowed in case of self-defence. A condition made uniquely for hot pursuit is that the pursuit may only take place over what the Convention calls land borders. It is not difficult to understand why the drafters of the text have wanted to exclude hot pursuit through the air and over high sea, but one can wonder whether and why this restriction should also exclude a pursuit over the numerous border rivers, such as the Moselle, the Scheldt, the Maas, the Rhine, and the Ems. Besides, why would this restriction not have been made for observation?

Another specific hot pursuit condition may be found in art. 41 par. 5 sub d SC, stating that the

> pursuing officers shall be easily identifiable, either by uniform or by means of an armband or by accessories fitted to their vehicle.

Since the nature of observation is incompatible with such a condition, it is easy to understand that this condition was not mentioned in that context. During a pursuit however, the pursued person will (at least most of the time) be aware of the fact that he is followed, and it may be very helpful that the public (and the locally competent police) be aware of the police pursuing an alleged criminal. On the other hand, the explicit presence of foreign police uniforms and cars might also cause unrest under the local population.[8]

After the operation has been finished, the pursuing officers must present themselves before the local competent authorities and give an account of their mission; if so requested, they must remain at the local authorities' disposal. Unless the suspect's apprehension and arrest takes places in the country from which he is a national citizen, the country where the pursuit started may request his extradition (par. 7). If the suspect appears in court after such an extradition, the trial judge will have to be able to verify whether the pursuing officers have respected the law of the country of apprehension. Therefore, not just the pursuing officers but also members of the judiciary must be aware of central parts of the national legislation of their neighbour states. With regard to observation, the officers' appearance in person is not *a priori* demanded; a written report to the authorities will usually be sufficient. The officers who are competent to carry out a cross-border hot pursuit are mentioned in art. 41 par. 7 SC. They are the same officers as the ones declared competent for cross-border observation, and will be discussed in more detail per country in paragraph 6.2.

According to art. 42 SC, during a cross-border pursuit, the officers shall be regarded as officers of the country where they operate with respect to offences committed against or by them. This implies on the one hand that their quality of a police officer may be an aggravating circumstance with regard to

---

8   In this sense also Brammertz *et al.*, 1993, pp. 18-19 (also published in French). Many Dutch for instance seem to feel uneasy when they notice a German uniform in The Netherlands; see for example Huizing, 1994, p. 17.

offences committed by them, such as theft by an officer in function, whereas insulting or physically resisting a public officer may constitute a specific criminal offence. On the other hand, it implies that these specific provisions do not apply when the officer was not entitled to carry out the operation during which the offence took place.

It is stated in article 41 par. 8 SC that, as far as the internal relations of the Benelux countries are concerned, the regulation of art. 27 BET will remain unchanged. In their declarations with regard to art. 41 par. 9, all three of the Benelux countries have repeated their intention to have hot pursuit operations across their mutual borders carried out according to the above mentioned art. 27, "as far as this concerns the apprehension, its territorial scope and the offences involved."[9] One might wonder in what way the two treaties will interfere. On the one hand, some state that the Benelux Treaty drafters have not thought about or did not want a regulation in such detail as the drafters of the Schengen Convention wanted.[10] Thus, every restriction regulated in Schengen without having been mentioned in the Benelux Treaty would apply to cross-border pursuits between Benelux countries as well. On the other hand, one could say that some Schengen restrictions concern subjects that have not been addressed in the Benelux provision that will stay in force (art. 27), and as a consequence the Schengen regulation (which constitutes a restriction) does not apply here. To us, such an interpretation also seems to be a logical consequence of the spirit of the Schengen Convention expressed in for instance artt. 39 par. 4 and 5, 40 par. 6, and 41 par. 9 and 10, being that the existing practice and regulation of international police cooperation is supposed to be changed in an extensive, not in a restrictive sense.[11] The same intention seems to be expressed in art. 41 par. 8 SC and the declarations according to par. 9, which also seem to have resulted from the fact that the Benelux countries have not wanted to exchange their achievements in this field for a more restrictive regulation.

In art. 28, the Benelux Treaty contains a second provision concerning cross-border pursuit, which seems to be overruled by the fact that art. 41 SC will be **without prejudice** to art. 27, without art. 28 being mentioned. Therefore, *a contrario*, art. 41 SC will be **with prejudice** to art. 28. The latter mainly regarded the (legal) position of the cross-border operating officers, rather than the way this operation may or shall be carried out. It regulated that the officers

---

9   These declarations were published (in each country's respective language) in Trb. 1990, 145, pp. 235-240. According to art. 30 par. 2 of the Vienna Convention on the Law of Treaties (May 23, 1969, Trb. 1972, 51), in that case the treaty that is referred to must prevail.

10   In this sense Brammertz *et al.*, 1993, p. 11; see also Fijnaut, 1991b, p. 771.

11   According to several functionaries in the Dutch ministry of justice who participated in the Schengen negotiations, the intention of art. 41 par. 8 SC was indeed to avoid that Schengen would constitute a restriction for the Benelux cooperation.

shall be regarded as local officers with respect to offences committed by or against them (almost literally the same provision as in art. 42 SC) and demanded that the pursuing officers be able to prove that they were acting in official capacity (as in art. 41 par. 5 sub d, last sentence). Furthermore, art. 28 BET **allowed** that the officers wear their uniform (whereas art. 41 par. 5 sub d SC goes further, **obliging** them to be easily identifiable by uniform or accessories) and carry their service weapon (as in art. 41 par. 5 sub e), and in case of emergency, use means of force and defence to the same extent as the locally competent officers, which seems to be a much wider allowance than the self-defence mentioned in art. 41 par. 5 sub e SC.

It is clear, however, that the provision stating that for the Benelux countries art. 27 of their treaty will remain unchanged, will affect some important aspects of the Schengen (hot) pursuit regulation as discussed above. The first aspect to be affected is, that art. 27 BET does not demand that the pursued suspect be apprehended in the act. He may also be recognized as a suspect of a crime discovered after it was committed, which seems to (at least theoretically) enlarge the field of application of cross-border pursuit. Unlike art. 41 par. 4 SC, the Benelux Extradition Treaty does not leave a choice as to the categories of offences for which cross-border pursuits may take place,[12] this is possible for every offence to which extradition may apply. Again, this category is significantly larger than the extraditable offences according to the European Convention on Extradition, which applies to (most of) the Schengen partners: it contains essentially every offence punishable with imprisonment of six months or longer. Another difference is that the Schengen Convention only allows border crossing

> where given the particular urgency of the situation it was not possible to notify the competent authorities of the other Contracting Party (...) or where these authorities have been unable to reach the scene in time to take over the pursuit,

whereas art. 27 BET authorizes to cross the border (in any case) and only demands that the locally competent authorities be called upon for assistance immediately.[13]

As for the persons who are competent to carry out a cross-border pursuit, the Benelux Treaty (at least originally) is more reticent and restrictive than the provisions of the Schengen Convention: The only municipal police forces whose officers were competent to pursue across the border, were the forces of municipalities within ten kilometres of the common border. Since the latest police reorganization, this cannot be applied to the Dutch police anymore, the munici-

---

12   It therefore remarkable that, in their declarations regarding the mode of enforcement of the cross-border pursuit, they have expressed a choice for the 'extraditable offences' anyway; see Trb. 1990, 145, pp. 236-240.
13   In this sense also Fijnaut, 1991b, p. 771.

pal police forces having been abolished.[14] Moreover, the Schengen members have created a possibility to extend the scope of the pursuit on a bilateral basis, which (according to par. 7) applies to the categories of competent officers as well. Hitherto however, the only country that has made such bilateral extensions is France; the contents of these extensions will be discussed below.

Regarding those aspects of pursuit that were not regulated in the Benelux Treaty but have been in the Schengen Convention, the latter changes the situation as the Benelux countries have known until recently, because *lex posterior derogat legi anteriori*.[15] This change regards aspects of the way the pursuit should be carried out as well as aspects of control after the pursuit has been finished.

As for the former aspect, it must be noted firstly that the Benelux Treaty did not mention the possibility of pursuing escaped prisoners across the border, this extension being added by the Schengen Convention. Secondly, the Benelux Treaty did not explicitly bind the pursuing officers to the law of the country where they operate, which is thus newly introduced by art. 41 par. 5 sub b SC. The fact, however, that the Benelux Treaty did not contain such a provision did not mean that the officers were not bound to these rules. This condition seems to be so evident that it does not need to be mentioned explicitly in order to be applicable. Besides, the Benelux Treaty did not contain an explicit prohibition for the pursuing officers to enter into private homes and places not accessible to the public. This does, however, not necessarily imply a change within the Benelux, since such an action according to the law of all five countries is only allowed on the basis of the national law. Finally, neither art. 27 nor art. 28 BET contains a restriction that "the pursuit shall be solely over land borders," as mentioned in art. 41 par. 5 sub b SC. The introduction of such a restriction of the existing regulation within the Benelux would be against the Benelux intention that the cooperation between their countries be not limited by the Schengen Convention. Therefore this restricting provision does not apply within the Benelux, and between these countries not only a pursuit by boat across the Maas or Scheldt between the Netherlands and Belgium, but even one by helicopter or by boat along the North Sea coast would be allowed.

As for controlling the pursuit, the Benelux Treaty did not demand that the pursuing officers present themselves before the locally competent authorities or to remain at their disposal if so requested (as in 41 par. 5 sub g SC). An obligation that the country from which the pursuing officers have come shall, if so requested, assist the inquiry subsequent to the operation in which they took part, as stated in art. 41 par. 5 sub h, could not be found in the Benelux Treaty

---

14 See Bevers, 1995, pp. 45-46.
15 "The later law amends the earlier one;" this adage has also been expressed in art. 30 par. 3 Vienna Treaty Convention.

either. Both obligations however seem to be a logical consequence of the wish for cooperation between the treaty partners, this entirely in the spirit of both treaties.

In general, one can conclude that the cross-border pursuit regulation in the Benelux Treaty contains less provisions regarding restrictions, control and influence of superiors than the Schengen regulation.[16] Since the Schengen regulation is a newer one, this would have implied that for the Benelux countries, the new regulation would constitute a restriction of the existing situation. However, in the general spirit of both treaties and according to their intention expressed during the negotiations of the Schengen Convention, the Benelux countries have been able to avoid this by creating sufficient exceptions.

Regarding the frequency of cross-border hot-pursuits occurring in practice, only little information is available. According to a survey among police officers in the Belgian-German-Dutch border region, only 25 % of the Dutch and 20 % of the German police officers interviewed said they were ever involved in a cross-border pursuit,[17] even though a legal basis in international or national law for cross-border pursuit to or from Germany did not exist. The pursuits seem to take place especially when it concerns car theft, escape after causing a car accident and avoiding traffic or alcohol control.[18] As to the officers of the Belgian police, 47 out of the 57 interviewed thought that cross-border hot pursuits never occur. Complaints regarding cross-border pursuing police officers mainly seem to concern police officers, who "go to far into their neighbour country" or "convert privileges to their own use."[19]

6.1.2   European Convention on Human Rights

Essentially, the European Convention on Human Rights does not contain any provisions relevant to cross-border hot pursuit by police officers. The use of this power by the police does not seem to conflict with any objective interest of a citizen, let alone a human right or fundamental freedom safeguarded by this convention. However, this does not mean that the rules the member states of the Council of Europe have established and have bound themselves to are completely irrelevant with regard to this matter. As we mentioned before, due to the special character of a hot pursuit, police officers might be urged to break rules, especially those regarding traffic. This would be against the central

---

16   In this sense also Fijnaut, 1991b, p. 771.
17   Hofstede et al., 1993, pp. 33-34.
18   Note that in case of the two latter offences a cross-border pursuit would not be allowed, the Schengen Convention being in force or not.
19   Hofstede et al., 1993, pp. 55-56.

principle of the rule of law, binding not only the citizens but also the State and its representatives to the law, including its criminal prohibitions.

The European Convention itself does not contain any provision with regard to a general application of the rule of law in the Council of Europe's member States. The principle has only been recognized implicitly in the second paragraphs of almost every provision guaranteeing an individual's right or fundamental freedom, these second paragraphs regulating whether and to which extend exceptions may be made on the basis of the law. However, every Contracting Party to the European Convention is also a member of the Council of Europe, and according to art. 3 of the founding Statute of this body,[20] every member state "must accept the principles of the rule of law." Therefore, one must conclude that a member State of the Council of Europe that wants to allow its police officers to break the law in urgent situations should at least create a basis in the law for this.

6.2 National Norms

In order to illustrate the context of the comparison of national norms on hot pursuit and territorial restrictions of police powers, this paragraph will discuss the legal situation with regard to hot pursuit per country. In this context, it will also be necessary to describe the concept of caught-in-the-act or flagrancy in each of the countries, this concept being a central notion in the hot pursuit regulation of art. 41 SC. Because the actual situation of a hot pursuit might in some cases demand that the pursuing officer does not entirely comply with the law (especially when it comes to for instance obeying traffic rules during a car chase), it will be useful to study the possibly existing regulations of the police being allowed to break the law.

6.2.1 Territorial Restrictions

Since the pursuit of a person is a great deal less static than most other police powers, which are normally being carried out at a certain spot, the phenomenon of pursuit is closely related to the territorial restrictions to which a police officer is subjected. Therefore, these restrictions will be studied here for each country separately.

Furthermore, such territorial restrictions may also be found in international treaties regulating cross-border pursuits. On the basis of the Schengen Convention, the following five types of restrictions may be distinguished: The pursuit is allowed within a certain distance from the place where the border was

---

20   This so-called Statute of London (May 5, 1949) is published as an appendix in *Manual of the Council of Europe*, 1970; the Dutch text may be found in Stb. J. 341 (1949, p. 569).

crossed; the pursuit is allowed within a certain zone; the pursuit is allowed in the entire country, but the apprehension of the pursued only in a certain zone; the pursuit in allowed in the entire country, but the apprehension only within a certain time limit; the pursuit as well the apprehension are allowed in the entire country.

6.2.1.1 Belgium

The possibility of the police pursuing a person has been given an explicit statutory basis in the Belgian Police Function Act (*Wet op het Politieambt* - WPA),[21] that mentions this police power especially in the context of the territorial restrictions of the Belgian police forces. In this context, it is necessary to make a distinction between on the one hand the *gendarmerie* and the prosecutor's judicial police, and the municipal police forces on the other hand. The first and second may essentially exercise their powers on the entire country's territory, whereas the territorial competence of the third is in principle restricted to their own municipality or brigade. However, on the basis of art. 45 WPA and the circulars Pol 31bis and Pol 47 referred to in Chapter 3, the territorial competence of municipal police officers may be extended to all municipalities in their province, as has been done in for instance East and West Flanders.

With regard to this restriction, a structural and an incidental exception have been created. The first is the possibility according to art. 45 sub 1 WPA that, on request of the municipal councils concerned, the provincial governor may entitle a municipal police officer to assist the municipal police in another than his own municipality. In addition, on the basis of art. 45 sub 2 WPA, municipal police officers may also operate outside of their own territory when pursuing suspects of criminal offences or escaped prisoners, as long as the situation's urgency does not allow that locally competent police services be warned in time. In this case, they may also apprehend the pursued person. The law does not require that the pursued person be caught in the act, nor does it contain any restrictions as to categories of offences for which this inter-municipal pursuit may take place.[22] It is necessary, however, that the pursuit has started in an area where the pursuing officer is competent;[23] on the other hand, this does not imply that the offence of which the pursued is suspected, must have been committed in that area.[24]

---

21 August 5, 1992, B.S. December 22, 1992, in force since January 1, 1993.
22 Bourdoux & De Valkeneer, 1993, p. 294.
23 In this sense Huybrechts, 1988/1989, pp. 331-333; Bourdoux & De Valkeneer, 1993, p. 294.
24 Bevers & Joubert, 1994, p. 233.

On the basis of the Benelux Treaty and the Schengen Convention, foreign police officers of the neighbouring countries may also continue a pursuit onto the Belgian territory. The conditions for this cross-border pursuit may differ depending on the country where the officers come from. For Dutch and Luxembourg officers, the Benelux Treaty allows the pursuit of suspects of any offence for which extradition is possible, whether the commission of this offence was discovered in the act or not. On the basis of the Schengen regulation, cross-border pursuit between these countries may also take place in case of escaped prisoners. The pursuit itself between the Benelux countries is not restricted to land borders or bound to limits in space or time, but the apprehension of the pursued is only allowed within a zone of ten kilometres from the border.[25] The pursuing officers are entitled to enter private places to the same extent as local officers.

As for German and French police officers carrying out a pursuit in Belgium, their position and powers have been regulated by the Schengen Convention and the declarations the Belgian government has made with regard to the appliance of this provision. As a consequence, German officers may cross the Belgian border to pursue an escaped prisoner or a suspect of an offence that may lead to extradition, provided the offence was discovered in the act. French officers may also continue the pursuit of escaped prisoners across the Belgian border, but the hot pursuit of a suspect who was caught in the act is allowed only when the offence involved is mentioned in the catalogue ex art. 41 par. 4 sub a SC. Both German and French police officers may continue their pursuit without limits in time or space, but only the German officers are entitled to proceed to the apprehension of the pursued, as long as this happens within 30 minutes after crossing the border. Other than for the officers of Belgium's Benelux partners, hot pursuit into Belgium by French or German officers is allowed across land borders only, and is restricted to situations in which it is impossible to notify the local authorities or these are unable to reach the scene in time to take over the pursuit.

6.2.1.2 The Netherlands

The law of the Netherlands does not mention the pursuit as an independent police power.[26] Pursuit must rather be considered as being implicitly included in such measures of constraint as apprehending and arresting a suspect or escapee. A person disobeying an order to stop, may be forced to do so by for

---

25 For more details on apprehension after cross-border pursuit we may refer to Chapter 7 of this study.

26 Hofstede *et al.*, 1993, p. 27.

254

instance pursuing, forcing his car into the kerb, and by road blocks.[27] It is evident that such physical constraint may only take place in accordance with the principles of subsidiarity and proportionality.[28] Since the pursuit itself has not been regulated explicitly, no restrictions as to crime categories have been made, nor is it necessary that the pursued suspect be caught in the act.

As to their territorial competence, Dutch police officers with investigative tasks are entitled to carry out their task in the entire country (art. 7 par. 1 PolW 1993), but according to par. 2 they will refrain from operating outside of their own region. Exceptions to this general rule have been made for cases where the law or the competent authorities (depending on the task involved, this is the mayor or the public prosecutor[29]) have decided otherwise, and for cases of emergency. This emergency, that was mentioned explicitly in the former Police Act 1957 (in force until April 1994) and in the first draft of the new Act, has been left out in an amendment to the text, that did however not have the intention to change the legal position, but only to simplify the way this was formulated.[30] As a consequence, emergency may still be considered a valid reason for a police officer to cross the regional border and continue his operation in another region. Under the Police Act 1957, the concept "case of emergency" was not defined by law, but in a 1959 circular of the minister of justice, it was interpreted as "cases in which the officer may reasonably judge that the interest of the investigation does not tolerate further delay."[31] It is obvious that this clause includes the apprehension of suspects of severe criminal offences or escaped prisoners, thus the pursuit of such a person in order to enable his apprehension is a justification for a police officer operating outside his own region.

With respect to international cross-border pursuits on Dutch ground, two regulations must be taken into account: the 1962 Benelux Treaty for pursuits by Belgian officers,[32] and the 1990 Schengen Convention if the pursuit takes place by German officers. The Benelux Treaty allows that a suspect of any extraditable offence, whether discovered in the act or not, as well as (according

---

27   See Naeyé, 1990, p. 443.
28   More information on physical force may be found in Chapter 8.
29   See Bevers, 1994, pp. 326-334 and Bevers 1995.
30   Adapted amendment by members of parliament Van der Heijden and Stoffelen, TK 22 562, nr. 60.
31   *Aanschrijving van de minister van justitie aan de procureurs-generaal, fungerend directeuren van politie*, May 27, 1959, APB 1959-12.
32   And Luxembourg officers! The Benelux Treaty does not restrict the cross-border continuation of a pursuit to a country's neighbour States. Therefore, although it is rather hypothetic, art. 27 BET it allows that Luxembourg police officers pursue a suspect through Belgium into The Netherlands (in the same sense Klip, 1996, p. 2 and footnote 7). They will however not be allowed to proceed to the pursued person's apprehension, since they will have left the 10 kilometre zone along the Luxembourg border.

to the Schengen provisions) a person who has escaped from prison, may be pursued across the Belgian border. This pursuit is not bound by any limits in space or time, whereas the pursuing officers may proceed to the apprehension of the suspect within a ten kilometre zone along the border. During their pursuit, the Belgian officers are entitled to enter private places to the same extent as Dutch officers are.

On the basis of the Schengen Convention and the declarations the Dutch government has made with regard to the appliance of its provisions, German police officers may also carry out a pursuit in the Netherlands, under the condition that they are unable to notify the Dutch authorities or these are unable to reach the scene in time to take over the pursuit. They may cross the Dutch border to pursue an escaped prisoner or a suspect of an offence that may lead to extradition, provided this offence was discovered in the act, and it is not possible to notify the local authorities or these are unable to reach the scene in time to take over the pursuit. The pursuing officers may continue their pursuit within a zone of ten kilometres along the common border, where they may also apprehend the pursued person.[33]

6.2.1.3 Luxembourg

An explicit regulation of the pursuit of suspects or other persons is unknown to Luxembourg law; pursuit has to be considered as a power that is inherent to more specific powers, as for example apprehension. The territory of the Grand-Duchy is so small that territorial limits of the competence of the police and *gendarmerie* officers would hardly be possible, therefore they are allowed to carry out their tasks in the entire country.[34] Since the pursuit has not been regulated, it is not submitted to any formal restrictions as crime categories or the crime concerned being discovered in the act.

The 1962 Benelux Treaty and the 1990 Schengen Convention have created the possibility that foreign police officers carry out a pursuit on Luxembourg territory. On the basis of the former, Belgian police officers may continue the pursuit of a suspect of an offence for which he may be extradited, whether this

---

33 In addition to the general restriction to ten kilometres, the police authorities of the northern Dutch police regions and the northern German province of Lower Saxony have stated in an internal service order, that a pursuit may not be continued beyond the range of the radio contact with the home basis; see *Mobilofoon-procedure KTS-net/Funksprechverfahren KTS-Netz*, December 12, 1993 (bilingual agreement).

34 For the police, this is regulated in art. 8 LEP, July 20, 1930, Mém. 1930, 933, whereas for the *gendarmerie*, a regulation does not exist, but the national competence follows from the fact that this is a force with a national character.

offence was discovered in the act or not.[35] On the basis of the latter, the pursuit of an escaped criminal is allowed as well. Between the Benelux countries, the pursuit is not restricted to land borders or bound to limits in space or time. The apprehension of the pursued by the pursuing Belgian officer is however allowed only within a zone of ten kilometres along the border.

Police pursuit in Luxembourg by officers of the French and German police forces has been regulated in art. 41 SC. Cross-border pursuit according to this convention is limited to persons who have escaped from prison and suspects of one of the offences mentioned in the catalogue of art. 41 par. 4 sub a, provided this offence has been discovered in the act, and the Luxembourg authorities could not be warned in time or take over the pursuit themselves. For both the German and the French officers, the area where they may carry out the pursuit is more restricted than for their Belgian counterparts, since they may only continue their pursuit within a ray of 10 kilometres from the place where they entered Luxembourg territory. Within this circle-like zone, German police officers are entitled to proceed to the apprehension of the pursued, whereas French officers have to leave this to their Luxembourg colleagues.

6.2.1.4 France

French law does not know an explicit regulation for pursuit of a suspect by the police; therefore such a pursuit must be considered inherent to other police powers. The exercise of these powers by a police officer is generally restricted to a certain part of the French territory, which implies that these territorial restrictions also constitute an important limit for their pursuing competence.

The regulation of territorial competence for the French police is very complicated. According to art. 18 CPP, those police officers who are auxiliaries to the public prosecutor may operate "within the territorial limits where they fulfil their usual tasks." For some centralized services, this territory is the entire French Republic,[36] but for most police services this description refers to administrative districts (*circonscriptions*) that are created, divided and adapted by the government.[37] The *circonscriptions* of the *gendarmerie* coincide completely with the administrative divisions of *régions*, *départements* and *arrondissements*, whereas those of the *police nationale* are created by the

---

35 Although this is mainly hypothetic, the same is allowed to Dutch police officers, to the same extent and for the same reason as a Luxembourg officer may operate on Dutch territory.
36 Such as the *direction centrale de police judiciaire* and the *compagnies républicaines de sécurité* of the *police nationale*, as well as the *gendarmerie mobile*.
37 See Decocq, Montreuil & Buisson, 1991, pp. 225-230.

decentralized administrative authorities and only partly correspond with this division.[38]

In some cases, art. 18 CPP allows however that police officers without a general national competence operate outside of their own *circonscription*, especially when ordered by the civil or judicial authorities, and in cases of "emergency, urgency and flagrancy." An additional condition is, that the officer may only **continue** a task, which implies that they were carrying out the task within their *circonscription* already.[39] A specification of the extension of the territorial competence in case of flagrancy has been given in the decree that has led to art. D.12 CPP. This provision states that a pursuit may only be continued across the border of a *circonscription* when it concerns a more or less severe criminal offence (*crime* or *délit*);[40] a police officer may not leave his own *circonscription* to pursue the author of a *contravention*. The condition that the person to be pursued must be a suspect who has been caught in the act seems to exclude that an escapee be pursued outside of the officer's original *circonscription*. However, such a pursuit is allowed since escape from prison has been criminalized as a *délit* itself by artt. 434-27 and 434-28 CP. According to par. 2 and 3 of art. D.12 CPP, a police officer who leaves his own territory while pursuing a suspect must immediately contact the local judicial or police authorities of the *circonscription* where he is continuing his pursuit. Furthermore, continuation of a pursuit is allowed in case the prevention of a *crime* or *délit* urges an intervention outside the original circonscription.[41]

Police officers from Belgium, Luxembourg and Germany may continue a pursuit across the French border if the pursued person is an escaped prisoner or has been apprehended in the act of commission of one of the offences mentioned in the catalogue of art. 41 par. 4 sub a SC, provided the French police could not be warned in time or was unable to intervene. Cross-border pursuit may be carried out across the land borders only and the pursuing officers of all three neighbouring countries do not have the right to enter private places or areas not accessible to the public. Belgian and German police officers may continue their pursuit on French territory without limits in space or time, whereas officers from Luxembourg are bound to a pursuing circle with a 10 kilometre ray form the place where they crossed the common border. The French government has strictly reserved the right to apprehend the pursued for the locally competent officers.

---

38   See Decocq, Montreuil & Buisson, 1991, pp. 230-231.
39   Bevers & Joubert, 1994, p. 237.
40   Art. 111-1 CPP distinguishes three categories of criminal offences in French law; these are the two most severe ones; the third category is formed by the *contraventions* (misdemeanours in the British sense of the word).
41   See Decocq, Montreuil & Buisson, 1991, p. 245.

6.2.1.5 Germany

Police pursuit in Germany has not been regulated as a police power explicitly, but must be considered inherent to other police powers. Nevertheless, some important legal provisions with regard to pursuit by the police do exist, especially in the field of the territorial competence.

Apart from the officers of the federal police forces *Bundesgrenzschutz* and *Bundeskriminalamt*, who are entitled to operate in the entire country, the competence of German police officers is based on the law of the province where they are employed, since according to art. 70 GG, the accent of police legislation lies with the provinces.[42] Therefore, in principle the German police are not allowed to carry out their tasks outside of their own province,[43] and most provinces have even restricted this territorial competence to one district (*Bezirk*).[44]

However, both the federal constitution and provincial law have created several exceptions to this regulation, for instance for assistance in case of immediate danger and calamities, transport of prisoners, and operations on request of the authorities of another province. Interprovincial agreements also provide possibilities for the waterway police to carry out their tasks on rivers and canals that (partly) form the borders between the provinces. In the field of criminal procedure, a special exception has been created by art. 167 of the Judicature Act (*Gerichtsverfassungsgesetz*, GVG), which allows police officers of the provincial police forces to continue the pursuit of a fugitive across the border to another province, where the pursued may also be arrested by the pursuing officer.

A fugitive in this context may be a suspect of a punishable act (be he caught in the act or not), but also an escaped prisoner or a person who tries to avoid a control of his identity.[45] The pursuit itself is not restricted to following the fugitive in order to pass him, but may include making detours and using road blocks in order to stop him or wait for him.[46] It is not necessary that the pursuit be restricted to one province; it may also be extended over more than

---

42 Götz, 1991, p. 28.
43 Art. 63 par. 3 BWPG states that "*Im Gebiet eines anderen Bundeslands können die Polizeidienststellen Amtshandlungen nur vornehmen, wenn dies durch ein dort geltendes Gesetz oder von der zuständigen Behörde eines Bundeslandes zugelassen ist.*" (Police services may only carry out police tasks on the territory of another province, if such has been allowed by a valid law or the competent authorities in that province), thus expressing "a general principle of federal constitutional law." See Drews/Wacke/Vogel/Martens, 1985, p. 111.
44 Götz, 1991, pp. 205-206.
45 Löwe/Rosenberg, 1989, art. 167 GVG, nrs. 5-7; Kleinknecht/Meyer-Goßner, 1995, p. 1457.
46 Löwe/Rosenberg, 1989, art. 167 GVG, nr. 6.

one.[47] Police operations in another province than their own are being regulated by the law of the province where the operation takes place.[48] However, when it concerns the criminal investigation task of the police, provincial law only completes the federal provisions of criminal procedure. The legislation of some provinces therefore provides an extension or more detailed regulation in addition to art. 167 GVG,[49] whereas additional regulations with regard to other measures of criminal investigation have been created in an interprovincial convention on the extension of the police competence.[50]

International hot pursuit on the territory of Germany has been regulated in the Schengen Convention. On the basis of art. 41 SC, Dutch, Belgian, Luxembourg or French police officers may continue a pursuit across the German border if the pursued person has been caught in the act of the commission of an offence that may lead to extradition according to the European Treaty on Extradition, or is an escaped prisoner. An additional condition for this cross-border pursuit is, that it must be impossible to notify the local authorities or they must be unable to reach the scene in time to take over the pursuit. Cross-border pursuits in Germany may continue without limit in space or time over the entire German territory,[51] and the officers pursuing are entitled to apprehend the pursued person everywhere in the country.

6.2.2 Offence Categories

The Schengen Convention has provided the participating countries with a choice as to the offences for which a cross-border pursuit may take place. Essentially, they had to choose between the enumerative catalogue of offences mentioned in art. 41 par. 4 sub a on the one hand, and the more flexible and larger group of all offences which may lead to the pursued person's extradition. This second group, however, may vary depending on the mutual regulations of extradition between each two neighbouring countries. In order to sketch the extent of the various offence categories chosen, as well as the differences between them, a comparative description will be offered in the following.

---

47   Löwe/Rosenberg, 1989, art. 167 GVG, nr. 8.
48   Hofstede et al., 1993, p. 27; an example of this may be found in art. 103 HSOG.
49   For instance artt. 102 and 103 HSOG.
50   This *Abkommen über die erweiterte Zuständigkeit der Polizei in den Bundesländern* has been published in for instance GVNW 1970, 243, and is in force in for instance the provinces of Nordrhein-Westfalen, Niedersachsen, Hamburg and Bremen; see Götz, 1991, p. 208.
51   In an internal service order, the police authorities of the northern Dutch police regions of Groningen, Drenthe, IJsselland and Twente have stated that a pursuit into the northern German province of Niedersachsen may not be continued beyond the range of the radio contact with the home basis; see *Mobilofoon-procedure KTS-net/Funksprechverfahren KTS-Netz*, Nordhorn, December 12, 1993 (bilingual agreement).

Unlike the Benelux Treaty, the Schengen Convention also creates the possibility to pursue escaped persons across the national borders. With regard to this category, the Convention does not leave the Contracting Parties any discretion: The pursuit of a person who has escaped from provisional custody or serving a custodial sentence may be continued, indifferent to the severeness of the offence he is suspected of or condemned for, or the duration of the sentence he was serving. The three authentic languages of the Convention, however, do not seem to apply equivalent terms for "provisional custody" and "custodial sentence." Therefore, we will include a comparison of this aspect as well.

6.2.2.1 Belgium

According to Belgian law and legal doctrine, the words *voorlopige hechtenis* as used in the Dutch text of the Convention, are used specifically to designate the deprivation of liberty that an investigative judge may order in the interest of the investigation.[52] The expression used in the French text of art. 41 SC, *arrestation provisoire*, on the other hand seems to refer to the terminology used for the arrest in urgent cases, where a judge's order could not be obtained.[53] As for the concept of custodial sentence, mentioned in the English translation, we remark the following: Where the Dutch text of art. 41 uses the word *gevangenisstraf*, this seems to correspond to the sentence mentioned in art. 7 Sw, a liberty sentence which according to Belgium's Penal Code may vary from 1 day to 10 years (artt. 25 and 28 Sw).[54] The words used in the French version of the Convention (*peine privative de liberté*) have a far more general meaning, which seems to be covered entirely by the English version.

In their declaration regarding the offence categories for which a pursuit of a suspect may be continued across the Belgian border, the Belgian government has made a specification per neighbouring country. Police officers coming from Benelux partners Netherlands and Luxembourg may enter Belgium when pursuing a suspect of an extraditable offence according to the 1962 Benelux Extradition Treaty, which implies that this is allowed for suspects of almost any offence that may be punished with imprisonment of six months or more.

With regard to the German police, the Belgian declaration also allows the cross-border pursuit for all extraditable offences, but the actual situation is much

---

52 Van den Wyngaert, 1994, p. 680.
53 De Valkeneer & Winants, 1992, p. 62-69.
54 Other, more severe sanctions have been codified under terms like *hechtenis*, *dwangarbeid* and *opsluiting*. According to Van den Wyngaert (1994, p. 311), the original distinction between these sanctions used to be in the different penitentiary disciplines where they were executed; nowadays however, the only relation remaining is the one to the duration of the sanction.

more complicated. On the one hand, the Benelux Extradition Treaty does not apply since Germany does not belong to the Benelux, whereas on the other hand, Belgium has not (yet) ratified the European Convention on Extradition.[55] The only international regulation on extradition between the two countries would therefore be the German-Belgian Treaty on extradition and mutual assistance in criminal matters of January 17, 1958, which contains an enumeration of 38 extraditable offences. However, art. 60 SC states that "In relations between two Contracting Parties, one of which is not a party to the European Convention on Extradition (....), the provisions of the said Convention shall apply (....)." On the basis of the same art. 60, that seems to have been drafted originally for Belgium,[56] the European Treaty on Extradition will apply between Belgium and Germany as soon as the Schengen Convention will be in force. As a result, hot pursuit by German police officers across the Belgian border will be allowed for practically every offence punishable with imprisonment of one year or more.

With regard to the Belgian-French extradition relations, art. 60 will also introduce the European Convention. This will not, however, have any consequences for hot pursuit by French police officers across the Belgian border, since this has not been restricted to the category of extraditable offences, but to the much more limited catalogue of fourteen offences mentioned explicitly in art. 41 par. 4 sub a.

In Belgian case-law, the status of the offence may be relevant for the question as to whether the pursuing officers are competent to cross the border. According to the Antwerp Court of appeal, defending oneself against an arrest by a Dutch police officer, carrying out a cross-border pursuit for a non-extraditable offence does not constitute the specific offence of resistance, because the officer concerned is not in his legal function.[57] However, in a similar case the court in Liège seems to have decided in the opposite sense.[58] Another interesting, recent example of this is the case of the pursuit of a Dutch car across the Belgian border for ignoring the speed limit, an offence punishable with 2 months imprisonment whereas the minimum limit for extraditability is 6 months.[59] It should be noted that, in case of a hot pursuit by a foreign officer in Belgium, this will not be judged in Belgium and Belgian law will not be the main yardstick to be used.

---

55 Paris, December 13, 1957, Trb. 1965, 9. However, the bill to have this treaty ratified is pending in Belgian parliament.

56 It should be reminded that nowadays art. 60 also applies to Portugal, which joined the Schengen group later and is not a party to the European Convention on Extradition either.

57 March 8, 1984, R.W. 1983/1984, pp. 2965-2966.

58 Unpublished decision, referred to by Bourdoux & De Valkeneer, 1993, p. 295, as Liège (6th chamber), October 16, 1991.

59 Case reported to our colleague J. Timmer by the prosecutor-general's office in Den Bosch.

6.2.2.2 The Netherlands

As follows directly from the text and system of Dutch legislation (art. 67 Sv), the words *voorlopige hechtenis* are used exclusively for the pre-trial measure of deprivation in the interest of the investigation, as ordered by the investigative judge. It does therefore not include those forms of detention or arrest applied in earlier stages of the enquiry. Dutch law and doctrine would also lead to a very restrictive interpretation of the word *gevangenisstraf* as used in art. 41 SC: The Dutch legislator has distinguished this custodial sentence strictly from a second form, called *hechtenis*. Whereas the duration of the latter has been restricted to a maximum of 1 year (art. 18 Sr), the first may last 15 years and can even be a life sentence (art. 10 Sr). In addition, they should be executed in penitentiary centres with different disciplinary systems.

As to the offence categories which may lead to cross-border pursuit into the Netherlands, the situation for police officers originating from Belgium is different from that of the German police. Police officers from Belgium may continue a pursuit on Dutch territory, provided the pursued person is under suspicion of having committed an offence for which his extradition would be possible. According to the Benelux Treaty, this means that the offence must be punishable with imprisonment of six months or more.

German police officers may also continue a pursuit across the Dutch border of a suspect of an extraditable offence, but these are not necessarily the same in the German-Dutch extradition relationship as in the Belgian-Dutch extradition relationship. Between Germany and the Netherlands, the 1957 European Convention on Extradition applies, which has been simplified and implemented in the bilateral Convention of Wittem.[60] This second treaty does extend the category of persons who may be extradited from Germany to the Netherlands (and *verso*), but this extension only concerns persons who have been condemned already. Thus, with respect to a suspect, the extradition (and therefore a hot pursuit across the border to the Netherlands) is allowed if the person is suspected of an offence that may be punished with imprisonment of one year or more, as stated in the European Convention on Extradition.

In this context, it is also worthwhile to note the existence of a bilingual police agreement, created between the Dutch and the German police forces on both sides of the border in the northern regions of the Netherlands with the intention of elaborating and facilitating the cross-border police cooperation as meant by the Schengen Convention. It is remarkable that, in spite of the text

---

60 *Overeenkomst tussen het Koninkrijk der Nederlanden en de Bondsrepubliek Duitsland betreffende de aanvulling en het vergemakkelijken van de toepassing van het Europees Verdrag betreffende uitlevering van 13 december 1957*, August 30, 1979, Trb. 1979, 142; this convention has been in force since January 31, 1983.

of art. 41 SC, the Dutch version of this treaty intends to restrict the pursuit of escaped prisoners to those who are convicted of an extraditable offence, a restriction that seems to be unnecessary and a likely cause for confusion.[61]

6.2.2.3 Luxembourg

The term *arrestation provisoire* as used in the Schengen Convention does not literally correspond to a concept of Luxembourg criminal procedure. It does however suggest a link with arrest by police officers or other early-stage measures of deprivation of liberty. Where art. 41 SC applies the terminology *peine privative de liberté*, no direct reference to a legally restricted concept of Luxembourg law is made. The wording rather seems to imply the general concept of custodial sanctions.

On the basis of the Benelux Extradition Treaty, Belgian police officers are entitled to enter Luxembourg while pursuing a suspect of an extraditable offence. This implies that the offence must be punishable with a maximum imprisonment of six months or more. In their declaration regarding the offences for which German and French police officers may pursue a suspect across the Luxembourg border, the Luxembourg government has chosen for the fourteen offences mentioned in the catalogue of art. 41 par. 4 sub a SC.

6.2.2.4 France

Where the French version of the Schengen Convention mentions escapees from *arrestation provisoire*, the text does not contain a direct reference to a specific concept of French law. It is nevertheless strongly suggested that this concerns all stages of pre-trial custody, including police custody. The words *peine privative de liberté* on the other hand may only be interpreted as the most general description of custodial sanctions.

In its declaration, the French government has made no distinction between Belgian, Luxembourg and German police officers with respect to the definition of offences for which foreign officers may continue a hot pursuit in France. None of them is entitled to cross the French border in other cases than the fourteen offences referred to explicitly in the catalogue of art. 41 par. 4 sub a SC.

---

61   The German version of this agreement (*Mobilofoon-procedure KTS-net/Funksprechverfahren KTS-Netz*, Nordhorn, December 12, 1993) does not mention this restriction.

6.2.2.5 Germany

Art. 41 SC in the German version allows that a person may be pursued across the national borders of the Schengen states if he has escaped from *Untersuchungshaft* or *Strafhaft*. From the text and system of Germany's Code of Criminal Procedure, it follows clearly that the forementioned word *Untersuchungshaft* is a specific legal term which only applies to pre-trial detention ordered by a judge (artt. 112-114 StPO).[62] This would mean that the pursuit of an escapee from a police office would be excluded from being continued across the border. *Strafhaft* is not a word used in German legal documents, but as a general description it refers to all types of custodial sanctions imposed by a judge.

Regarding the category of suspects who may be pursued by Dutch, Belgian, Luxembourg and French police officers across the border to Germany, the declaration of the German government states that such is allowed for offences that may lead to the person's extradition. For all four countries, the European Convention on Extradition will apply, even though this has not been ratified by the Belgian parliament yet and notwithstanding the above mentioned Convention of Wittem between Germany and the Netherlands. Therefore, police officers from the Netherlands, Belgium, Luxembourg and France are entitled to continue a hot pursuit if the pursued person stands under the suspicion of having committed an offence for which he may be punished with imprisonment of one year or more.

Regarding the pursuit of escapees, the Schengen Convention does not make any restriction as to the severeness of the underlying offences. Unlike the Dutch version, the German text of a bilingual agreement between the Dutch and the German police authorities on both sides of the border in the northern regions of the Netherlands, does not intend to restrict the pursuit of an escaped prisoner to convicts of an extraditable offence.

6.2.3 Competent Officers

In the seventh paragraph of art. 41, the Schengen Convention mentions the officers who are competent to carry out a cross-border pursuit on the territory of their Schengen neighbours. Here, again, some slight differences exist between the Schengen Convention and the Benelux Treaty, this time because the categories of investigative officers referred to in the former are larger than those referred to in the latter. Firstly, the Benelux Treaty only regards police officers of municipalities within 10 kilometres of the common border, whereas the Schengen Convention also includes all other municipal police officers. Secondly,

---

62   In this sense also Creifelds, 1988, p. 1179.

on the basis of the Schengen Convention the group of competent officers may be extended by bilateral agreements, especially regarding officers with investigative tasks in the field of illicit drugs, arms and toxic and dangerous waste.[63]

6.2.3.1 Belgium

The officers competent for cross-border pursuit from Belgium are the members of the public prosecutor's criminal police and the *gendarmerie*, as well as those of the municipal police forces. By bilateral agreement, an extension with customs officers is possible, with respect to their powers regarding illicit traffic in narcotic drugs and psychotropic substances, traffic in arms and explosives, and the illicit carriage of toxic and dangerous waste. The only example of such an agreement with Belgium that is known, concerns the Belgian and French customs and excise officers. On the basis of a 1962 convention between Belgium and France, Belgian customs and excise officers also have the power to exercise control in international trains on French territory,[64] whereas a bilateral agreement on the basis of art. 41 SC allows Belgian customs officers to continue a hot pursuit on French territory in cases of crime involving drugs, arms and explosives and toxic or dangerous waste.[65]

6.2.3.2 The Netherlands

With regard to the Dutch officers who are competent for cross-border hot pursuit in the Benelux and Schengen contexts, both treaties mention the members of the municipal and the state police. However, these have meanwhile been abolished and replaced by regional police forces, which have inherited the tasks and powers of their predecessor.[66] As a result, all investigative officers of the regional police forces must be considered competent for cross-border pursuits now.[67] In addition, bilateral agreements may create the same power for officers of the fiscal information and research service (FIOD), with respect to the illicit

---

63   To date, the only agreements of this kind we know about, concern the French borders with Belgium, Luxembourg and Germany; the contents of these agreements will be dealt with per country.
64   Cass. April 16, 1980, R.D.P. 1981, pp. 595-597.
65   Schengen, June 19, 1990, J.O. 1995, 16443.
66   Meanwhile, this has been confirmed internationally by a declaration of the Dutch government to their Schengen partners; November 25, 1994, Trb. 1995, 5, p. 2.
67   It is likely that the members of the future National Detective Team will be entrusted with this cross-border pursuit power as well, especially since one of their explicit tasks will be to combat international crime.

traffic in narcotic drugs and psychotropic substances, traffic in arms and explosives and the illicit carriage of toxic and dangerous waste.[68]

It may be considered remarkable that those Dutch law enforcement services which traditionally were most charged with border control tasks, the Royal *marechaussee* and the *douane* (customs and excise), have not been entrusted with any cross-border pursuit power. The same is the case for the so-called special investigative services, like the AID and the ECD,[69] even though these seem to play an important role in investigating waste crime, EU-fraud and other typical cross-border offences.

6.2.3.3 Luxembourg

Both the Benelux Treaty and the Schengen Convention refer to the officers of the Luxembourg *gendarmerie* and police forces, the Benelux Treaty still mentioning the separation between the municipal police and the judicial police of the public prosecutor, of which nowadays's grand-ducal police is the merger. In bilateral agreements, this may be extended to customs officers, at least with respect to their powers regarding illicit traffic in narcotic drugs and psychotropic substances, traffic in arms and explosives and the illicit carriage of toxic and dangerous waste. An agreement of that kind has been concluded with France.[70]

6.2.3.4 France

As to France, the police officers competent for cross-border hot pursuits are the officers and criminal police officers (*officiers et agents de police judiciaire*) of the national police and the national *gendarmerie*, thus implying that police officers without such criminal investigative tasks, like the members of most of the rural municipal police forces, will not be allowed to carry out a cross-border hot pursuit. With respect to the illicit traffic in narcotic drugs and psychotropic substances, traffic in arms and explosives and the illicit carriage of toxic and dangerous waste, customs officers may be given this power by appropriate bilateral agreements. At the signing of the Schengen Convention, France concluded such agreements with Belgium, Luxembourg and Germany.[71]

---

68 Agreements of this kind do not exist to date.
69 With respect to these services, the investigation departments of the Ministries of Agriculture and of Economic Affairs, we refer to Buruma, 1995.
70 Schengen, June 19, 1990, J.O. 1995, 16444.
71 Schengen, June 19, 1990, J.O. 1995, 16443-16445.

6.2.3.5 Germany

All officers of the German provincial police forces as well as those of the federal criminal police (*Bundeskriminalamt*) and the federal border police (*Bundesgrenzschutz*) will be entitled to carry out cross-border hot pursuits. The same power has been created for members of the federal customs investigation service (*Zollfahndungsdienst*), but only with respect to the illegal traffic in narcotic drugs and psychotropic substances and arms traffic.

6.2.4 The Concept of "Apprehension in the Act"

The first paragraph of art. 41 SC restricts the possibility to carry out cross-border pursuits to the situation where the individual to be pursued has been "apprehended in the act," thus implying that the suspect must have been discovered "*in flagrante delicto*, found or apprehended in the act of committing the offence charged."[72] This seems to be a more severe restriction than the suspect having been caught "red-handed," which expression is often used in the same sense but should rather be interpreted as "with the marks of the crime on him."[73] However, the authentic versions of the Convention apply the much wider terminology of *heterdaad, en flagrant délit* and *auf frischer Tat*, all three of which include the suspect caught red-handed.

It should be noted that the text of the Convention does not demand that the officer who pursues the suspect also be the person by whom the suspect is apprehended. The offence might for instance be discovered in the act by a witness who warns the police immediately afterward. Because of the importance attached to the concept of being apprehended in the act, it is useful to study and compare this concept in the law of each of the five countries discussed in this context.

6.2.4.1 Belgium

According to art. 41 Sv, an offence has been discovered in the act (*op heterdaad* or *en flagrant délit*) if it was "discovered while being committed or immediately after it was committed." According to Belgian jurisprudence, this "immediately" implies that the "period between the commission of the offence and its acknowledgement by the authorities must be a short one." The state of *flagrante delicto* will continue existing "during the time that is reasonably necessary to enable the intervention of a competent officer."[74] In the words of the Belgian Court

---

72 In this sense Burke 1977.
73 Burke 1977.
74 Spriet, 1991, p. 22.

of cassation: "The time that passes between the commission and the beginning of the inquiry must not be longer that the time that is necessary to begin this inquiry."[75] Whether the time passed between the discovery of the crime and the start of the inquiry has been too long or not, is a question of fact rather than of law.[76] It is however not necessary that the offence be discovered by the investigative officers themselves; police officers who, having been warned by witnesses to a car accident, find a license plate on the spot, may act as if the offence was discovered in the act.[77]

In the second paragraph of art. 41 Sv, two situations have been put on the same level as the apprehension in the act: On the one hand the case that a suspect has been followed by the clamour of the crowd,[78] on the other hand that he is found shortly after the offence was committed with traces, instruments or fruits of the offence on him (a so-called red-handed suspect). The duration of "shortly" will depend on the specific circumstances of the case and its discovery.[79] In general, since the police and public prosecutor have more powers in case of apprehension of a suspect in the act than in other situations, the question whether or not one may speak of an *in flagrante delicto* must be interpreted restrictively.[80]

In case of a discovery in the act, the investigative officers may apply special procedures in which they have more powers than usual (for instance in art. 40 Sv), but this extension is restricted again to situations where the offence belongs to the category of *crimes*, which offences may be punished with imprisonment between 5 years and perpetuity.

6.2.4.2 The Netherlands

In Dutch law, a definition of a discovery in the act (*op heterdaad*) may be found in art. 128 par. 1 Sv, which mentions as such "an offence that is discovered while being committed or immediately after it was committed." The concept must be interpreted restrictively; according to the government it only concerns a "fresh situation."[81] The concept of a discovery in the act primarily applies to the situation where a criminal offence was eye-witnessed by someone, but may also apply to facts and circumstances. A police officer who sees that a

---

75   Cass., June 29, 1984, J.T. 1985, 407; R.D.P. 1985, 76.
76   Being a matter of fact, this cannot be answered by the Court of cassation. See Verstraeten, 1994, pp. 143-144; Cass. April 4, 1898, Pas. 1898, I, 145, and Cass. December 31, 1900, Pas. 1901, I, 89.
77   Cass. October 21, 1986, A.C. 1986/1987, 106.
78   *La clameur publique* or *het openbaar geroep.*
79   Verstraeten, 1994, p. 144.
80   Cass. September 22, 1981, R.W. 1981/1982, 1271.
81   In the same sense Melai, note 6 to art. 128.

person, walking through Amsterdam with a car radio in his one hand and a screwdriver in the other, starts running as soon as he notices the officer, may act as if the person was caught in the act, even if nobody has seen him actually steal the radio.[82] According to par. 2, one may also speak of an offence *in flagrante delicto* if the offence was discovered "shortly after it was committed." In that case, the "freshness" of the offence must be judged in the light of the traces that were left; central question will be, to what extend the freshness of the offence will be relevant for its investigation.[83] By whom the offence was discovered is of no importance, but there must be a relation between the discovery and the suspicion that has risen against a certain person.[84]

The Dutch Supreme Court once had to take a decision in a case where the offence of which the pursued was suspected turns out to be non-extraditable. It ruled that the officers must be considered incompetent and the information that was possibly gathered through the illegal apprehension is not accessible as evidence in court.[85] Remark that, in case of a hot pursuit by a foreign officer in the Netherlands, the legality of the pursuit will usually not be judged in the Netherlands and Dutch law will not be the main yardstick to be used.

6.2.4.3 Luxembourg

Art. 30 par. 1 of the Luxembourg Code of criminal procedure (CIC) defines an offence discovered in the act (*en flagrant délit*) as "an offence that is discovered while being or immediately after having been committed." Par. 2 adds to this the situation that the suspect of the offence is followed by the clamour of the crowd or found with traces, instruments or other objects on him that may sustain his involvement in the offence (red-handed). In art. 40 CIC, the application of the special procedures of *in flagrante delicto* is restricted to those cases where the offence discovered in the act is punishable with a prison sentence.

6.2.4.4 France

According to art. 53 CPP, an offence is discovered in the act (*en flagrant délit*) if it is discovered "during its commission or immediately after the commission." One may also speak of an offence *in flagrante delicto* if it has been committed recently and the suspect is followed by the clamour of the crowd or found in possession of objects or instruments related to the crime or other traces on him.

---

82 Example from Naeyé, 1990, p. 52.
83 Hof 's-Hertogenbosch, December 14, 1931, NJ 1932, 353; Naeyé, 1990, p. 55.
84 Naeyé, 1990, pp. 53-54.
85 In this sense HR April 26, 1988, NJ 1989, 186.

On the basis of case law of the French Cassation court, in each of these cases it is necessary that there be "clear indications" (*indices apparants*) in order to continue the *in flagrante delicto*-procedures. In general, these special procedures, granting more powers to the investigative officers than usually, may only be started if the offence involved may be punished with a deprivation of liberty (artt. 67 and 40 CP), which is the same condition as for pursuits exceeding the limits of the pursuing officer's *circonscription*.

6.2.4.5 Germany

Where the law of Germany speaks of offences and suspects discovered in the act (*auf frischer Tat* or *Flagranz*), it refers to offences that are discovered at the moment of their commission and suspects who are found immediately after the offence was committed at or around the spot of the crime.[86] In case certain clear indications, such as traces or objects, lead directly to a suspect, this person may also be considered discovered in the act. The terminology however only applies to criminal acts for which remand in custody of the suspect is allowed.

The person who starts the investigation or pursuit against the suspect must not necessarily be the same as the one who discovers the offence, nor must the discovery be followed by the pursuit immediately; the pursuer may for instance first get some help or technical support. Besides, it is not necessary either that the pursued stay in the sight of the pursuer, nor is there any restriction to the duration of the pursuit.[87]

6.2.5 Traffic Dispensations During Hot Pursuit

As we indicated above, it may occur that pursuing police officers are confronted with a fleeing suspect who ignores traffic provisions and obligations, such as speed limits and priority. The officers than have to face the dilemma of, on the one hand, loosing the pursued person and, on the other hand, breaking the law. To regulate such situations, the legislators of all five countries have created dispensations in their traffic legislation, thus offering an exception to the criminal and civil responsibility of their police officers.

According to art. 42 SC, "officers operating on the territory of another Contracting Party shall be regarded as officers of that Party with respect to

---

86   Those law texts mentioning the concept of apprehension in the act (artt. 104 and 127 StPO) do however not explain what is meant by this concept; such an explanation has been developed in case-law.

87   Kleinknecht/Meyer-Goßner, 1995, p. 431.

offences committed against or by them."[88] Thus, the dispensations the states have created will protect the cross-border pursuing officers of a neighbour state to the same extent as the police officers of the visited state. However, this does not exclude that the dispensations and therefore the protection and conditions of protection differ from state to state, so that it will be necessary to describe and compare the ways these dispensations have been given form.

6.2.5.1 Belgium

Central element of Belgian traffic law is the General Regulation on the Traffic Police (*Wegverkeersreglement* - WVR).[89] Art. 37 WVR states that, with regard to respecting traffic regulations, police vehicles may be considered as so-called priority vehicles (*véhicules prioritaires*). As a priority vehicle, they are obliged by art. 37 par. 2 WVR to use a blue flashing light while executing an urgent task, whereas they are allowed to use this light during any other task. Art. 37 par. 3 allows the use of a siren or "special sound set" during urgent tasks as well, but using the siren during a non-urgent task is not allowed. Technical requirements regarding the blue lights and sound sets do not exist.[90]

Priority vehicles using their blue lights may ignore the maximum speed (art. 59 par. 13 WVR) and use the bus lanes (art. 72.5 WVR). On the basis of the articles 59 par. 14 WVR, priority vehicles are also entitled to interrupt military parades and other columns, as well as sports events such as bicycle races. Art. 59 par. 13 WVR further allows that they ignore the special regulations for highway traffic, such as the minimum and maximum speed limits, they may use the central reserve and non-official exits, make U-turns and even drive backwards, all provided they use their blue lights and (possibly) their siren.[91]

When using siren and blue lights, the police may cross an intersection with a red traffic light, provided they have stopped first (art. 37 par. 4 WVR); slowing down instead of stopping completely is not sufficient.[92] The police car may not cause any danger to other traffic participants, including those who

---

88   Before it was overruled by the Schengen Convention, a similar provision could be found in art. 28 BET as well.

89   *Koninklijk Besluit houdende algemeen reglement op de politie van het wegverkeer*, Royal Decree of December 1, 1975, B.S. December 9, 1975, corrected in B.S. December 13, 18 and 20, 1975.

90   Poté, 1990, Chapter XVIII, pp. 3-4; Ruypers, 1989, pp. 53-59.

91   See Poté, 1990, Chapter XVIII, p. 9 and Ruypers, 1989, p. 55.

92   Cass. June 26, 1984, A.C. 1984-1985, 949.

ignore the police car's priority,[93] and those who have not been able to hear the siren in time.[94]

Drivers of priority vehicles do not enjoy other privileges than those provided explicitly in the Traffic Regulation. As a result, they have no general permission to ignore traffic signs or obligatory driving directions, nor may they drive on sidewalks, bike paths etc.[95] As a compensation of the dispensation for priority vehicles, art. 38 WVR provides an obligation for all other traffic participants: As soon as the sound of a siren announces the arrival of a priority vehicle, other users must give way and let this vehicle pass, and possibly they will have to stop.

Since Belgian traffic legislation does not make a difference between "urgent" and "normal" tasks, police officers must judge a situation themselves.[96] An urgent task must involve a higher goal than the protection of a normal traffic conduct but does not necessarily require the same urgency as the concept of urgency in criminal law.[97] However, in case one can speak of an urgency in the criminal law sense, the situation can certainly be considered as an urgent task in the sense of the Traffic Regulation.

6.2.5.2 The Netherlands

According to art. 146 of the 1994 Dutch Road Traffic Act (*Wegenverkeerswet - WVW*), the minister of traffic may create a general dispense from the rules provided by this statute for motor vehicles used by "public services." A ministerial decree of this kind is the Traffic rules and traffic signs regulation (*Reglement Verkeersregels en Verkeerstekens - RVV*). Art. 29 RVV states that drivers of police vehicles may use a blue flashing light and a two or three-tone horn in order to make clear that they fulfil an urgent task. Technical requirements regarding flashing light and siren can be found in art. 3 of the Decree on optical and sound signals (*Besluit optische en geluidssignalen*).[98] On the basis of art. 91 RVV, drivers of such a priority vehicle may deviate from the traffic rules as described in the entire Regulation.

A police officer using his signals may however only trust in his priority if he applies his special powers in a sufficiently careful way. In case the signals

---

93 Cass. March 13, 1985, A.C. 1983-1984, 1403.
94 This may be due to for instance street noise, local circumstances, wind, driving direction or the siren being turned on too late. Brussels, June 30, 1962, Bull. Ass. 1962; Corr. Brussels, April 22, 1988, VR 1988, 335; Brussels, May 25, 1971, J.T. 1972, 106; Cass. October 25, 1965, Pas. 1966, I, 273.
95 Poté, 1990, Chapter XVIII, pp. 13-14; Ruypers, 1989, p. 57.
96 Poté, 1990, Chapter XVIII, p. 5.
97 Poté, 1990, Chapter XVIII, p. 6.
98 October 1, 1991, Stcrt. 1991, 202.

have only been started 100 m before an intersection is crossed at 100 km/h, the driver may not expect that every other traffic participant is warned sufficiently.[99] In case the signals have only been started very shortly before, the driver must not trust that all other traffic participants have noticed him, even though he sees that he has been noticed by some participants.[100]

Finally, it should be noted that several police forces in the south of the Netherlands have created special service orders regarding cross-border pursuits into Belgium, which states that a police officer who crosses the border is not allowed to use any optical or sound signals. According to these orders, the Dutch officers could not benefit any priority or other special position in Belgian traffic, since the Benelux Treaty would only apply to police officers, not to the vehicles in which they cross the border.[101]

6.2.5.3 Luxembourg

Traffic law in Luxembourg contains several dispensations for vehicles of public services involved in urgent tasks, like police and *gendarmerie* officers pursuing persons to be arrested or apprehended. To indicate their involvement in such urgent tasks, their vehicles may be equipped with sirens and blue flashing lights (artt. 39 and 44 of the Grand-ducal Decree on road traffic (*Code de la Route*)).

According to art. 107 IV 10 of this Code, they may use bus lanes when using their siren, and art. 139 allows them to exceed speed limits when using blue lights, siren or both. With both siren and blue lights on, police service vehicles also have priority at street crossings and other intersections on the basis of art. 136 D, except when ordered differently by traffic police officers. On the same basis and provided they use siren and blue lights, they must be granted priority when changing lanes on multi-lane highways.

The fact that officers of public services may have priority or other specific rights in special circumstances does not imply that, in these cases, they can also claim their priority. They will always have to warrant the security of the other traffic participants.[102]

6.2.5.4 France

Art. 28 of the French Road Traffic Code (*Code de la route*) states that all traffic participants must give way to police vehicles announcing their approach by the use of the signals technically described in the artt. 92, 95, 175 and 181 of the

---

99   Rb Utrecht, April 13, 1994, NJ 1984, 783.
100   Hof Amsterdam, December 22, 1988, VR 1990, pp. 18-20.
101   On these instructions, see Naeyé, 1990, p. 446.
102   Information originating a member of the Luxembourg *police*.

same code. More detailed legal provisions regarding the right of the police to ignore traffic rules in cases of urgency could not be found.

According to a source in the *gendarmerie*, eventual problems with regard to a police vehicle ignoring a red traffic light or maximum speed limits would be solved through the general criminal law concept of urgency. This concept is not foreseen in legislation but has been formulated in jurisprudence as "a situation that does not allow any delay of intervention."[103] For the question as to whether or not such a situation exists, proportionality, opportunity and the presumption of legality of the intervention to be undertaken play a central role.[104]

6.2.5.5 Germany

Vehicles of public services such as the police are dispensed from all obligations and prohibitions mentioned in the German Road Traffic Regulation (*Straßenverkehrs-Ordnung* - StVO), as long as this is urgently necessary for the execution of their public task (art. 35 StVO). The necessity of a situation has to be judged by the officer who finds himself in the situation, within a certain margin of appreciation. Outside of this margin, the officer is criminally responsible for his deviant behaviour.[105] The immediate execution of the driver's public task must seem more important than obeying the involved traffic rules. The risks that are taken should not be disproportionately high: life or limb of other traffic participants must not be put in danger.[106]

Note that art. 35 StVO does not explicitly bind the dispensation from the traffic provisions to the use of flashing blue light or multi-tone horn. In itself, these devices may be used, but only in case of urgency, one of the examples for this mentioned in art. 38 StVO being the pursuit of a fugitive. According to art. 38 StVO, however, the use of these signals does at least oblige all other traffic participants to clear the road immediately. Requirements as to the technical state of flashing lights and horn have been described in detail in the artt. 52 and 55 Road Traffic Admission Regulation (*Straßenverkehrs-Zulassungs-Ordnung* - StVZO).

Notwithstanding the existing dispensation, according to constant case-law a driver of a vehicle as mentioned in art. 35 StVO may only expect priority at a red traffic light if those traffic participants facing a green light have been warned on time by a blue flashing light combined with the two-tone horn.[107]

---

103   Decocq, Montreuil & Buisson, 1991, p. 265.
104   Decocq, Montreuil & Buisson, 1991, p. 266.
105   OLG Celle, October 6, 1987, VRS 1988, Bd. 74, 220.
106   OLG Stuttgart, October 7, 1991, DAR 1992, 153.
107   KG (the Berlin OLG), February 3, 1986, VRS 1986 Bd. 70, 432.

When the driver of a priority vehicle with blue light and horn is not certain if he has been noticed by all traffic participants involved, he may only approach an intersection at a speed that allows him to possibly stop on time.[108]

6.3 Comparing National Norms

On the basis of the information provided above, a comparison between the five countries can be made. For this comparison, we will focus upon the aspects that we have distinguished to this police power already: Territorial restrictions, offence categories, competent officers, the concept of "apprehension in the act," and dispensations from traffic regulations.

6.3.1 Territorial Restrictions

Regarding the territorial powers of the police officers and the ways these powers have been restricted by the respective Schengen states, several different systems may be distinguished. The most generous systems may be found in Luxembourg and the Netherlands, both countries having created a national territorial competence for police officers in the execution of their general tasks. It should be added, however, that a Dutch police officer is supposed to refrain from operating outside his own region.

The most restrictive country with respect to the territorial restrictions of a police officer's activities is France. In this country, a suspect may only be pursued across the boundaries of the officer's circonscription if the person has been caught in the act of committing a *crime* or a *délit*, or in case the prevention of such an offence urges his intervention outside his own circonscription.

The systems of territorial competences for the Belgian and German police forces might be considered the most complicated ones of the five, since in both countries the regulations of territorial powers may differ from one police force to another. In Germany, the federal police forces have national power and may operate over the entire federal territory. The territorial restrictions to which the provincial police forces are subjected, depend on the legislation of the respective provinces. They may have power all through their province or only in their own district. Belgium's *gendarmerie* and judicial police (prosecutor's police) may be compared to Germany's federal police forces: All three are nationally competent. The territorial competence of officers of Belgium's municipal police forces is generally restricted to their own municipality or brigade.

However, when it comes to pursuing a person to be arrested, the police officers in all examined states are essentially competent to continue this pursuit

---

108 OLG Braunschweig, January 24, 1990, NZV 1990, 198.

over the entire territory of their state. This is especially the case for persons whose pursuit might be extended to the territory of a neighbouring Schengen state. In that case new restrictions must be faced, which are created by the country where the pursuit is continued and may again differ widely for almost every bilateral relation. The only country with a uniform regulation of cross-border pursuit on its territory is Germany, which has granted police officers from all of its western neighbour states the right to continue the pursuit over the entire Germany, for every extraditable offence and including the right to apprehend the pursued. By doing so, they have also shown to be the most generous Schengen member state for foreign pursuers. A uniform system also exists between the three Benelux member states, allowing cross-border pursuit in case of extraditable offences through the whole country, the right to apprehend being restricted to a 10 kilometre zone along the border. Toward their neighbours outside the Benelux, they seem to have been unable to maintain their uniformity: Belgium, the second least restrictive country with respect to cross-border pursuit, has imposed no time or distance limits to pursuits by German or French police officers, whereas The Netherlands submit German officers to a 10 kilometre zone and Luxembourg limits a pursuit by both German and French officers to a circle of 10 kilometres around the point of entry. France allows Belgian and German police officers to pursue over its entire territory, limiting the Luxembourg police to a 10 kilometre circle.

Finally, it should be noted that two specific cross-border pursuit relations have not been regulated at all: hot pursuit by Dutch officers in France and by French officers in the Netherlands. Even though such a pursuit is, doubtlessly, improbable to occur, it is not impossible or legally excluded. Both Dutch and French police officers may continue a pursuit over the entire territory of Belgium, in which case the pursued suspect might possibly lead them to the French respectively the Dutch border (by motorway, this would hardly take an hour), where they could be challenged to continue their pursuit across the border. Neither the French nor the Dutch government have made any declarations regarding this possibility. However, considering the French position as to the apprehension of a suspect by Belgian, German and Luxembourg officers, it is safe to conclude that a Dutch officer who would find himself in France after a hot pursuit through Belgium is not allowed to proceed to the apprehension of the suspect. On the other hand, a French police officer on Dutch territory would certainly not be allowed to apprehend the pursued person outside of the 10 kilometre zone along the border.

Within the 10 kilometre zone, the pursuing officer's position is less clear. Maybe it could be compared to the situation of a Luxembourg police officer pursuing into the Netherlands: These two countries do not have a common border either, but the pursuit and apprehension regulation of the Benelux Treaty apply to Dutch and Luxembourg police officers operating on their mutual territories as well.[109] However, in our opinion the legal position of a French police officer at the Dutch-Belgian border or on Dutch territory should be defined by a declaration of both governments before practice urges a judge to do so.

When evaluating the Schengen cross-border pursuit regulation, the first thing to be noticed is the enormous variety in conditions and limits that has been created, each bilateral relationship having its own regulation. This will certainly and unnecessarily lead to unclear situations, especially in those areas where three countries and three bilateral relationships meet. Secondly, as was noticed already in the discussion of the Schengen observation regulation, it is not entirely clear what should be understood by places not accessible to the public, especially as to those places which are accessible to the public, and thus to the pursuers.

Furthermore, it has been suggested that the limits of a 10 kilometre zone could be ignored or avoided by using the provisions for cross-border observation as a basis for cross-border pursuit.[110] However, this does not seem to be very likely or attractive, the practice of a pursuit (visibility, loudness and hurry) being almost the opposite of the essence of an observation (going unnoticed and calm). Furthermore, in the context of observation, the pursued's apprehension, the final aim of a pursuit, would be excluded. Finally, since in most bilateral relations the 10 kilometre limit has not been set to the pursuit itself but to the area where apprehension may take place, there is practically no reason for bypassing the pursuit restrictions.

The combination of the Schengen and Benelux regulation is another aspect that asks for attention. According to the Dutch ministry of Justice, the intention of the Schengen drafters was to ensure that the situation for the Benelux countries would certainly not become more restrictive under Schengen. The combination of the two that exists now is partly hard to understand and demands a great deal of interpretation, especially regarding the Schengen restriction to land borders, the Schengen obligation and Benelux allowance to be recognisable as a police officer, and the means of force and defence that a pursuing and apprehending officer may use. This would have been avoided easily if the Benelux pursuit regulation had been replaced entirely by the one in Schengen. The ministerial declarations referred to in art. 41 par. 9 SC could then still have been used for detailing and enlarging the scope of the Schengen regulation in the spirit of the Benelux Treaty.

---

109 As we stated above, the Benelux Treaty does not require that the countries involved be neighbour countries; see also Klip, 1996, p. 2 and footnote 7.

110 In this sense for instance Bönninghaus, 1992, p. 203. The Belgian ministries of justice and the interior seem to have thought about this as well, since in their Schengen circular (p. 7793) they have suggested that an observing police officer should bring in armband in order to be able to identify himself if the observation turns into a pursuit.

Besides these interpretation problems, it is obvious that there will remain some considerable differences between the pursuit regulation in the Schengen Convention and the one in the Benelux Extradition Treaty. On several aspects, the latter is more generous than the former, especially where it does not contain the Schengen provision that cross-border pursuit be reserved for situations of urgency. Furthermore, the Benelux regulation does allow the pursuit of suspects who have not been caught in the act, whereas it does not restrict the pursuit to land borders, a limitation with unclear extend that may be found in the Schengen Convention.

Table 6.1 National Territorial Police Competences and Restrictions

	Territorial competence	*Pursuit categories*	*"In the act"*
B	* *gendarmerie* + GPP: national * municipal police: brigade area (in general), national (pursuit)	* suspects * escapees	* while committed * immediately after commission * clamour of the crowd * red-handed suspect * not necessarily discovered by pursuer
NL	* national	* suspects * escapees	* i.d.
L	* national	* suspects * escapees	* i.d.
F	* circonscription (general), national (in case of pursuit of *crime/délit*)	* suspects of *crime/délit* (incl. escape) in the act	* i.d.
D	* BKA/BGS: national * provincial police: province or district (in general), national (pursuit)	* suspects * escapees	* i.d.

Concerning issues such as the group of persons who may be pursued, the Schengen Convention also contains an extension to the Benelux Treaty: The latter did not allow the pursuit of an escaped prisoner. Furthermore, Schengen has introduced a rather strict system of control and supervision which did not explicitly exist under the Benelux system either. From a practical point of view, it should be regretted that the Schengen Convention has been drafted in a so much more restrictive sense than the Benelux regulation. On the other hand, for the sake of the rule of law, the introduction of a control and supervision system by Schengen must be welcomed.

6.3.2   Offence Categories

As for the categories of offences allowing a cross-border pursuit, the first thing to be noted is that the Schengen drafters have created a choice between the large category of extraditable offences and the relatively small group of offences mentioned explicitly in a catalogue. The most restrictive choices with respect to this have been made by the French government, which has also created the most restrictive system of pursuit for their own police officers. These may only trespass the borders of their own circonscription for the pursuit of a person, caught in the act of a *crime* or *délit*; the commission of a misdemeanor may not lead to such a pursuit. At first sight, this seems to exclude the pursuit of escapees, but this gap has been provided in by a criminalization of escape as a *délit* in itself. Regarding cross-border pursuit by foreign officers, France is the only country among the five to have restricted this to those offences mentioned in the catalogue of art. 41 par. 4 sub a SC. The other four countries have all chosen to allow cross-border pursuit for all extraditable offences, except for a pursuit by French officers on Luxembourg or Belgian territory.[111]

The least restrictive offence categories for cross-border pursuit by foreign police officers apply within the Benelux territory. The three member states have chosen to allow such pursuit for all extraditable offences, which is essentially the same restriction as the one set by Germany, the only difference being that the category of extraditable offences according to the Benelux Treaty is significantly larger than the same category according to the European Extradition Treaty. Moreover, it is worthwhile noticing that the Benelux Treaty did not leave the member states a choice between one category or another.

The most problematic aspect of the offence categories might be their multitude: The fact that the police in the border regions must apply one out of four different categories of offences (national law, Benelux extraditable, Schengen extraditable and Schengen catalogue) forms a serious complication for the legal position of a pursuing officer in those areas where three countries meet. Not only will the officer be unsure where the pursuit will lead him, but it will also depend on the country to which it leads whether he may indeed continue pursuing. One does not need to be a pessimist to foresee problems like illegal pursuits and arrests, all the more since a pursuit could pass through a country where the pursuit may continue and end in a third country where the continuation is not allowed.

Other problems may occur during the cross-border pursuit of a person who has escaped from what the English translation of the Convention calls "provisional custody" and "custodial sentence." If the Dutch and German wordings

---

111   Somehow, this looks like a revenge or at least a reaction to the extremely strict attitude of the French government.

chosen for "provisional custody" are interpreted according to Dutch, Belgian and German law, the Convention seem to exclude the cross-border pursuit of escapees from police custody. In these systems, the words *voorlopige hechtenis* and *Untersuchungshaft* are used only for provisional deprivation of liberty ordered by a judge. In the French text of the Convention, the more general formula of *arrestation provisoire* (provisional arrest) has been used, which also seems to include all other forms of deprivation of liberty for judicial reasons, such as the custody at a police station.[112] Here, two of the three authentic languages exclude the pursuit of a escapee from police custody, although these are not necessarily less dangerous or severe criminals than those whose provisional custody has been ordered by a judge. Furthermore, it will be just as hard for a police officer to distinguish one group of provisional detainees from another as it is to distinguish one group of convicts from another. There is, however, no guarantee that a trial judge, forced to a decision by a defence lawyer, will consider that the cross-border pursuit of a person escaped from police custody is indeed covered by art. 41 SC.

Essentially, the formula "custodial sentence" is a very general term, meaning the same as the wordings in the German and French texts (*Strafhaft* and *peine privative de liberté*): In German, French and Luxembourg law, these formulas must be considered general descriptions of the concept of deprivation of liberty as a punitive sanction. The Dutch text, however, uses the word *gevangenisstraf*, a specific legal term which the Netherlands have reserved for a more severe and longer lasting form of deprivation of liberty, thus excluding the less severe form, *hechtenis*. The Dutch speaking part of Belgium on the other hand, the word *gevangenisstraf* in a legal sense stands for short custodial sanctions with a general maximum of 10 years.

One could argue that, in order to be practicable, differences like these should be left without consideration: For a pursuing police officer, it would be too complicated and often impossible to know whether a person has escaped from *gevangenisstraf* or from *hechtenis*, especially since both may be served in the same penitentiary centres. This interpretation, which follows from two of the three authentic languages, would of course be preferable in the light of the aim of the involved chapter of the Convention, the improvement of international police cooperation as a compensation of the abolition of border controls. Strictly spoken however, a lawyer defending an escapee from *hechtenis* in the Netherlands, arrested after a cross-border pursuit may perhaps plead successfully that his client was illegally pursued and arrested.

---

112 Note that in France, where artt. 434-27 and 434-28 CP criminalize the *délit* of escape (*évasion*), this concept does indeed include escape from the detention at a police station (*garde à vue*).

An aspect that should not be forgotten is, that the five countries do not necessarily give the same priority to the same offences. If the police of one country frequently carry out cross-border pursuits for offences that do not have a high priority in the neighbour country, this could irritate the authorities of the latter, who are obliged to spend their time cooperating and hearing the pursuing officers' account.

Finally, it should be noted that one specific cross-border pursuing situation has not been regulated: hot pursuit by Dutch officers in France and by French officers in the Netherlands. Even though such a pursuit is, doubtlessly, rather improbable to occur, it is not impossible or legally excluded. Both Dutch and French police officers may continue a pursuit over the entire territory of Belgium, so the pursued suspect might possibly lead them to the French respectively the Dutch border (by motorway, this would hardly take an hour), where they could be challenged to continue their pursuit across the border. Neither the French nor the Dutch government have made any declarations as to this possibility, but considering the French position as to the apprehension of a suspect by Belgian, German and Luxembourg officers, it is safe to conclude that a Dutch officer who finds himself in France after a hot pursuit through Belgium is not allowed to proceed to the apprehension of the suspect. On the other hand, a French police officer on Dutch territory would certainly not be allowed to apprehend the pursued person outside of the 10 kilometre zone along the border. In this context it is worthwhile to recall the fact that, although the Netherlands do not have a common border with Luxembourg, the Benelux Treaty does seem to cover a pursuit by Dutch police officers through Belgium into Luxembourg, where the Dutch police could apply the same powers as in Belgium.

6.3.3   Competent Officers

Concerning the police officers who have been given competence to execute cross-border pursuits, the Schengen Convention has been more generous than the Benelux Treaty. The latter contains the restriction that officers of the municipal police forces may only cross the border when pursuing if the municipality from which they originate is within 10 kilometres form the border. Furthermore, the Benelux Treaty did not mention any pursuing possibility for other investigation services than the regular police forces, whereas the regulation in the Schengen Convention concerns the customs services as well.

A cross-border pursuit power has however not been created for all customs services equally. Belgium, The Netherlands, Luxembourg and France only allow this on the basis of additional, bilateral agreements. This does not seem to be an innovative provision, since such bilateral agreements would have been possible without the Schengen Convention saying so. For the German customs investigation service, no additional regulation will be necessary, since they have been entrusted this power by the Convention directly. This leads to the situation that until today the German customs are the only ones who may exercise this cross-border power, for - as far as we know - such bilateral agreements as demanded for the other countries do not exist yet. However, different from their neighbour country counterparts, traffic in explosives and illicit carriage of toxic or dangerous waste have been excluded from their mandate.

6.3.4   The Concept of "Apprehension in the Act"

The basic sense of the concept of apprehension in the act is literally the same in all five countries: while the offence is being committed or immediately after its commission. Furthermore, all countries know certain extensions to this basic idea. But, although these extensions have been formulated and divided differently in the diverse legal systems, the result as a whole seems to be similar in all five countries. Together, the criteria of the red-handed suspect and the clamour of the crowd as mentioned in the laws of Belgium, France and Luxembourg seem to overlap the criterion of freshness (discovered shortly after the commission) under Dutch law. In German law, the criteria have not been explicitly prescribed by the legislator, but the criteria developed in German case-law seem to be identical to the ones applied in the other countries.

A remarkable difference is the fact that the extension of powers in case of a caught in the act situation is restricted to severe offences in all other countries than the Netherlands, the only country where this extension also applies to the commission of misdemeanours. However, since misdemeanours are excluded from cross-border hot pursuits anyway, this difference does not really play a role in this context.

Finally, it is worth recalling that a cross-border pursuit within the Benelux does not require that the suspect be caught in the act. Problems in this field may occur when such a suspect, pursued by a Luxembourg police officer across Belgian territory, decides to continue fleeing across the German border. In that case, a strict interpretation of the Schengen Convention would lead to the conclusion that the pursuit should stop there.

6.3.5   Traffic Dispensations

Among the five countries discussed, France is the only one that has not created an explicit statutory basis for its police officers trespassing general traffic obligations and prohibitions. Thus, with respect to this aspect of their administration and legislation, the French seem to infringe with the obligation to accept the rule of law as prescribed in the Statute of London. It is obvious that this does not lead to the conclusion that the French police must respect traffic rules to the same extent as other traffic participants. Since they only do so in urgent cases, they will plead the exception of urgency which, from a police officer, is easily accepted. As a result, different than those of other traffic participants, their case is not prosecuted and they evade control.

Table 6.2 Police Traffic Dispensations and Conditions

	B	NL	L	F	D
Ignoring speed limits					
Lights and siren obliged	-	+	-	-	-
Lights obliged, siren optional	+	-	-	-	-
Lights or siren obliged	-	-	+	-	-
Lights and siren optional	-	-	-	-	+
No specification	-	-	-	+	-
Ignoring priority					
Lights and siren obliged	+	+	+	-	-
Lights and siren are optional	-	-	-	-	+
Exception of urgency/no specification	-	-	-	+	-
Stopping obliged	+	+	-	-	-
Other traffic's security guaranteed	+	+	+	+	+
Other traffic must give way	+	+	+	+	+
Other dispensations					
Use of bus lane (lights)	+	-	-	-	-
Use of bus lane (siren)	-	-	+	-	-
Priority on highways (lights and siren)	+	-	+	-	-
Ignore all traffic rules (lights and siren)	-	+	-	-	-
Ignore all traffic rules (lights and siren optional)	-	-	-	-	+
Ignore all traffic rules (exception of urgency)	-	-	-	+	-

Belgium is the single country without any legislation on the technical requirements for the police vehicles' sirens and blue flashing lights. Therefore, it is hard to understand why some police service orders in the southern Netherlands prohibited exactly the use of these signals when pursuing into Belgium, the only country where it seems impossible for a technical apparatus not to meet the national standards.

As for the restrictions and conditions which the different countries have set for legally applying the dispensations, the following may be said. All countries allow that the applicable speed limits be ignored by police vehicles involved in urgent police tasks. According to the Dutch and Belgian regulations, police vehicles intending to ignore usual priority of other traffic participants, must stop before they do so. Luxembourg and German law do not go this far but demand that the safety of the other traffic participants be guaranteed. All countries, including France, know provisions obliging other traffic participants to give way to priority vehicles.

In the Netherlands, Germany and France, essentially all other traffic rules may be ignored as well, if this is necessary for the execution of police tasks. The only dispensations Luxembourg and Belgium know besides the ones mentioned above, are the use of bus lanes and the ignoring of the specific rules for highway traffic. As to the use of siren or blue lights, the Dutch regulation is the strictest one, imposing the use of both in order to benefit from the traffic dispensations. Luxembourg law imposes the use of both as well, except for exceeding the speed limits, the use of one of the two being sufficient in that case. In Belgium, both signals must be applied generally as well, but for exceeding the speed limits and using bus lanes the siren is optional. According to German law, the use of both warning devices is always optional, whereas the French legislations does not know any specific provisions with respect to this.

All in all, one must conclude that the French regulation is not only the least specific but, with the German one, also the least restrictive. Third in generosity are the Netherlands, where the same dispensations exist but, different from the former two, always under the condition that both siren and blue lights are used. The Belgian and Luxembourg safety regulations finally may be considered equally restrictive.

6.4 Conclusion

Resuming the results of the comparative analysis of cross-border pursuit between the Benelux countries, France and Germany, we may reach some conclusions.

Regarding the territorial restrictions to which pursuits are bound by national legislation, many differences between the various national systems were found but, thanks to the way the cross-border pursuit has been regulated, these differences are unlikely to have repercussions for cross-border pursuits. More problems may be caused by the fact that cross-border pursuits on the Schengen territory are regulated by two treaties instead of one. The combination and mutual interference of the Schengen and Benelux regulations has resulted in unnecessarily diverse and complicated legal situations. A similar, critical remark should be made with respect to the wide variety in conditions and limits for cross-border pursuits, that could emerge only thanks to the fact that the Schengen Convention leaves its Contracting Parties a great deal of liberty in choosing modalities. In our opinion, this will lead to a situation in which problems in practice will be inevitable.

In the field of offence categories that may lead to pursuits according to the national systems, only few differences between the five countries could be found as well. However, the choices the five countries have made with regard to the offences which may lead to cross-border pursuits vary widely and we estimate that their multitude may cause numerous practical problems. A problem of a more general nature that seems to play a role here, is the fact that the various terms applied in the three authentic versions of the Convention do not have corresponding meanings in the respective legal terminologies. The unclear situation that thus emerges is due to cause practical problems as well. A final aspect involving offence categories is the fact that cultural and political differences between the countries have led to different priorities for the investigation of many specific offences. This priority difference could be an important cause for friction between the authorities on both sides, especially since the authorities of the country on whose territory the pursuit ends are supposed to cooperate in the administrative part of handling the operation.

The regulation of the officers who are competent for executing cross-border pursuits must be considered clear. Especially since the assignment of the competent officers has been an entirely unilateral matter, this aspect seems to leave no room for discussion or doubt. It is, however, remarkable that the German customs investigation service have been given pursuing power directly by the Convention whereas for the customs services of Germany's partners this power still remains to be entrusted by bilateral agreements.

Our research of the concept of apprehension in the act has shown that, although it has been given form in several different ways this concept substantially seems to cover the same situations in all five countries. Therefore, it is unlikely that problems will arise caused by different interpretations of this concept. However, a problem for Belgian, Dutch and Luxembourg police officers might be that they may only continue a pursuit into Germany or France in case of an apprehension in the act, whereas the Benelux Treaty does not require this for pursuits within the Benelux.

Table 6.3 Police Powers During Cross-Border Pursuit[113]

to from	Belgium	The Nether-lands	Luxembourg	France	Germany
B		* no limit * extradit. off. * appr. in 10 km zone * transport to local author.	* no limit * extradit. off. * appr. in 10 km zone * transport to local author.	* no limit * offences ex art. 41 * no appre-hension	* no limit * extradit. offences * appre-hension
NL	* no limit * extradit. offences * appr. in 10 km zone * transp. to local auth.		* no limit * extraditable offences * appr. in 10 km zone * transport to local author.	* no com-mon border, no regula-tion	* no limit * extradit. offences * appre-hension
L	* no limit * extradit. offences * appr. in 10 km zone * transp. to local auth.	* no limit * extraditable offences * appr. in 10 km zone * transp. to local auth.		* 10 km ray * offences ex art. 41 * no appre-hension	* no limit * extradit. offences * appre-hension
F	* no limit * offences ex art. 41 * no appr.	* no common border, no regulation	* 10 km ray * offences ex art. 41 * no appr.		* no limit * extradit. offences * appr.
D	* no limit * extradit. offences * within 30 min.: appr.	* 10 km zone * extraditable offences * apprehen-sion	* 10 km ray * offences ex art. 41 * apprehension	* no limit * offences ex art. 41 * no appre-hension	

Regarding dispensations that have been created to allow that pursuing police officers disobey traffic regulations if necessary for the execution of their tasks, the first thing to be noticed is the fact that the situation in France, where dispensations do not have a legal basis, seems to collide with the rule of law that should be obeyed by all Council of Europe members. Secondly, we found that, between the five countries, there is a wide variety in generosity regarding dispensations and the conditions for them to apply. This variety may cause

---

113 Note that, although The Netherlands and Luxembourg do not have a common border, they do have a pursuit regulation.

unequal and therefore unclear situations, leading to a degree of uncertainty that must be considered undesirable, especially since this uncertainty also touches the individual civil and penal responsibility of each police officer involved in cross-border pursuit. It seems that this aspect of uncertainty will surely affect the confidence, well-being and well-functioning of the pursuing officers.

As a general conclusion of this subject, one may say that the main problem which police officers will be confronted with during cross-border pursuits will be the incredible diversity of rules, conditions and restrictions. It must be regretted that this multitude of provisions to be dealt with is not primarily caused by the combination of five national legislative systems, but rather by the combination of the two relevant treaties, and more specifically by the fact that the Schengen Convention has left too much choices to the individual Contracting Parties.

7 Apprehension, Arrest and Control of Identity

Both the 1990 Schengen Convention (SC) and the 1962 Benelux Extradition Treaty (BET) contain possibilities for foreign police officers to apprehend a person after a cross-border hot pursuit. During this cross-border operation, the pursuing officers must comply with the law of the country where they operate. Thus it will be important that they be aware of these provisions and of the differences between the law of their own and that of their neighbouring countries. In this chapter we will study and compare the law of the five countries with regard to this subject.

In both treaties, the measure of apprehension is closely related to the measures of control of identity and arrest. Since they seem to be closely related in the police practice and the law of all five countries as well, the three police powers will be analyzed together. In their declarations to art. 41 of the Convention, the Contracting Parties made some specific statements regarding the way cross-borders pursuits on their territory may be executed, including as to the question whether or not the pursuing officers are allowed to apprehend the suspect and if so, under which conditions. Since these statements differ importantly from one another, the special conditions the countries have set for apprehension by a foreign police officer on their territory will be discussed in this chapter as well.

7.1 International Norms

Before discussing and comparing the national norms regarding apprehension, control of identity and arrest after cross-border pursuits, it is useful sketch the international context. Therefore, we will make an analysis of the rules that the Schengen Convention and the Benelux Treaty have created on this subject.

7.1.1 International Norms on Police Cooperation

When the Schengen Convention was drafted, the negotiators did not just want to create a treaty basis for cross-border pursuits, but also a power for the pursuing police officer to stop the person he had been pursuing. However, some countries hesitated to go as far as allowing foreign police officers to physically exercise more than a mere pursuit; especially France did not want foreign police

289

officers to actually intervene against individuals. Therefore, art. 41 par. 1 SC states that

> At the request of the pursuing officers, the competent local authorities shall challenge the pursued person so as to establish his identity or to arrest him.

thus expressing the intention that the person who finally arrests the pursued should be a locally competent police officer.

However, for those treaty partners who were willing to give up a part of their sovereignty by allowing the physical intervention of a foreign officer, par. 2 provides a choice regarding the procedures to be followed during the pursuit. According to alternative (a), they could decide that

> The pursuing officers shall not have the right to apprehend.

whereas alternative (b) reads:

> If no request to cease the pursuit is made and if the competent authorities are unable to intervene quickly enough, the pursuing officers may apprehend the person pursued until the officers of the Contracting Party in the territory of which the pursuit is taking place, who must be informed without delay, are to establish his identity or to arrest him.

As we noticed already regarding other police powers mentioned in the Schengen Convention, the treaty itself does not contain a definition of apprehension or arrest. As a result, it does not become immediately clear what kind of operation a cross-border pursuing police officer is entitled to and which he is not allowed to do. According to par. 1, the suspect's arrest must be reserved for the locally competent police, but the suspect may be apprehended by his foreign pursuers. The question as to whether there is a difference between apprehension and arrest, and if so, what is this difference, becomes especially important when reading art. 41 par. 5 sub f:

> Once the pursued person has been **apprehended** as provided for in par. 2 sub b, for the purpose of bringing him before the competent local authorities he may be subjected only to a security search; handcuffs may be used during his transfer; objects carried by the pursued person may be seized.

The Schengen drafters seem to have assumed that the distinction between apprehension and arrest is such a clear one that it does not need further explanation. In combination with this assumption, apparently they have also considered the terminologies used for either measures in the three authentic languages to be equivalent.

Indeed, if this second assumption had been true, there would have been no doubt as to the distinction between apprehension and arrest, and the interpretation of what is allowed to police officers involved in cross-border pursuits would not cause any problems. However, the terminologies are not fully equivalent and, as a result, interpretation problems are not unlikely to occur. For this reason, we will analyze the wordings used in every one of the three languages, as well as the words of the non-authentic English translation provided by the Benelux/Schengen secretariat.

According to Jowitt's dictionary of legal terminology, the English word "apprehension" is "the capture of a person upon a criminal charge," whereas "arrest" stands for "the restraining of the liberty of a man's person in order to compel obedience to the order of a court of justice (or to prevent the commission of a crime) or to ensure that a person charged or suspected of a crime may be forthcoming to answer it." It is obvious that the latter is a rather formal, legal definition, in comparison to which the former must be considered a mere factual description of an activity; it should have not be forgotten that the English version of the treaty is not an authentic one. As far as the authentic versions of the convention are concerned, the terminological situation may be represented in the following table:

Table 7.1 Terminology Applied in Various Versions of art. 41 SC

	Dutch	**German**	**French**	**English**
par. 2 sub a	* *staande houden*	* *festhalten*	* *interpeller*	* apprehend
par. 2 sub b	* *staande houden* * *aanhouden*	* *festhalten* * *festnehmen*	* *interpeller* * *arrêter*	* apprehend * arrest
par. 5 sub f	* *aanhouden*	* *ergreifen*	* *appréhender*	* apprehend

As to the distinction of the two concepts according to the national legislation of the Contracting Parties, two remarks should be made. On the one hand, under Belgian, no police power with the name *appréhension* is known, whereas for the Dutch speaking part of Belgium, *staande houden* does not exist as a legal concept either. Therefore, hitherto Belgian law does not know a distinction between apprehension and arrest. In the Netherlands and Germany, on the other hand, legislation does know a difference between apprehension (*staande houden* respectively *anhalten*) and arrest (*aanhouding* respectively *Festnahme*). In both countries, the police power named apprehension is a restriction of liberty directly aiming at the control of identity, whereas arrest is a more general form of deprivation of liberty in the interest of an enquiry.[1]

---

1   See Bevers & Joubert, 1994, pp. 325-326.

The problem gets even more complicated when par. 5 sub f of art. 41 is included in the analysis. As we saw above, the English translation of this provision seems to entrust the measures of security search, use of handcuffs and seizure of objects to the officer who has carried out the apprehension. The Dutch version applies the word *aanhouding*, and thus seems to refer to the arrest by the local police officers. The German text allows this to be done by the person who has *ergriffen* the suspect, thereby introducing a third term. Finally, the French text also designates the competent officer by a new, third term, speaking about the person who has exercised the *appréhension*.

It seems that the apprehension mentioned in art. 41 SC cannot be the same as the measure meant in German and Dutch law, since in both countries this measure aims directly at the control of the suspect's identity, a measure that art. 41 par. 1 as well as par. 2 sub b SC explicitly reserve for the locally competent officers. Because of its context, the Schengen apprehension should rather be compared to the stopping and immobilizing of a person who has been caught in the act, a provisory form of arrest which is allowed to every individual, whether police officer or not.[2] The use of the word *ergreifen* (to seize, to catch) in the German version of the Convention also suggests that the activity meant is the factual stopping and catching of the pursued; furthermore, this would be the most literal interpretation of the Dutch *staande houden* as well.[3] With respect to this, it is interesting to see that for such situations, Luxembourg and French law do apply the term *appréhension*, as used in the French text of art. 41 par. 5 sub f SC, the provision referring to security search and other measures. Furthermore, the provision the Dutch legislator has created in order to elaborate the power of apprehension by foreign police officers on Dutch territory, the newly introduced fourth paragraph of art. 54 Sv, does not mention the Dutch equivalent of apprehension (*staande houden*) but the equivalent of arrest, *aanhouden*.[4] As a conclusion, the word apprehension in art. 41 SC should be interpreted as "provisory arrest," thus as a form of arrest.[5]

Finally, we must establish the relation between the generally existing national norm that, in case of *flagrante delicto*, every person may arrest the

---

2   We came to this conclusion already in Bevers & Joubert, 1994, pp. 325-326; in the same sense: Maring, who explains that the Schengen power of apprehension "includes nothing more than the right to hold the pursued person until the local police arrive" (Maring, 1995, p. 223).

3   Such a factual interpretation of *staande houden* has also been defended by Maring, 1995, p. 224.

4   Maring, 1995, p. 225.

5   This also implies that, in spite of the Dutch text using the word *aanhouding* in par. 5 sub f, the foreign pursuers would, after they have apprehended the pursued person, themselves be competent to subject him to a security search, to use handcuffs and to seize objects he carries with him. For a more detailed discussion of this matter, we refer to Chapter 8 of this study.

suspect, and art. 41 par. 2 SC, which prohibits such apprehension or at least restricts it to certain limits in space or time. In our opinion, the Schengen Convention, being a regulation of a higher rank and of a later date, changes the national provision in the following sense: Although essentially every person would be allowed to proceed to the arrest of a suspect who has been caught in the act, a foreign police officer would only be allowed to do so within the limits of the Schengen Conventions. Besides the time and distance limits that may be set according to art. 41 par. 3 sub b SC, this also includes the prohibition for observing police officers to proceed to the arrest of any person as mentioned in art. 40 par. 3 sub f SC. This general prohibition would be set aside in case the arrest is immediately necessary in order to prevent severe danger or harm. In such a case, the illegal intervention would be justified by the urgency of the situation.

The police power for cross-border pursuit that Belgium, the Netherlands and Luxembourg have created a in the 1962 Benelux Extradition Treaty also contains a possibility for the pursuing officers to stop the pursued person. This treaty does not, however, leave the Contracting Parties a choice as to whether they want to allow foreign police officers to actually intervene against individuals: The pursuing officers are simply allowed to do so. The terminology used for this intervention is the same as in the French and Dutch versions of the Schengen Convention, *staande houden* and *appréhender*. In this treaty as well, the starting-point is that the apprehension be done by the locally competent police, on request of the pursuers. These are, however, allowed to proceed to the apprehension of the pursued person themselves if the local authorities are unable to intervene in time. In that case, the foreign police officers must bring the apprehended person before the local authorities, who may establish his identity or proceed to his arrest.

In spite of the Dutch terminology the treaty drafters have chosen, this police power should be considered the same form of provisory arrest as the one in the Schengen Convention that was discussed above.[6] This follows from the combination of the French text and the function that the same drafters have entrusted to this power of apprehension in the context of the treaty. Furthermore, the fact that the drafters of the French version of the Benelux Treaty have explicitly referred to the French and Luxembourg legal terminology for provisory arrest implies that the Schengen regulation also addresses this measure. After all, the Schengen drafters primarily intended to create an extension of the Benelux regulation to Germany and France, not a restriction of the Benelux system.[7]

---

[6] In this sense also De Schutter, 1967/1968, p. 1942 and Maring, 1995, p. 232.
[7] In this sense also Maring, 1995, p. 232.

7.1.2   European Convention on Human Rights

The distinction between restriction and deprivation of a person's liberty of movement may be found in the European Convention on Human Rights and its Protocols as well.[8] The first paragraph of art. 5 of the Convention reads as follows:

> Everyone has the right to liberty and security of person. No one shall be deprived of his liberty save in the following cases and in accordance with a procedure prescribed by law: (....)

The term *deprivation of liberty* is not explained in the Convention nor has it ever been defined by the case-law, but the notion must at least contain elements of space and time as well as a certain degree of coercion, which elements must be given simultaneous consideration as they may influence each other. Typical examples of a deprivation of liberty in the sense of art. 5 are measures like arrest and detention, both elaborated in the same provision. Mere restrictions of liberty like stopping a person on the street are not covered by art. 5,[9] which, therefore does not concern the measure of apprehension as regulated under Dutch and German law.

Limits for a simple restriction of an individual's liberty of movement are given by the second article of the fourth Protocol, which provision can be considered a specification of art. 5:

> Everyone lawfully within the territory of a State shall, within that territory, have the right to liberty of movement.

In that case, of course, restrictions of the liberty of movement should still be in accordance with the law and necessary in a democratic society as well. Notwithstanding, according to the European Commission "the mere obligation to carry an identity card and to show this at every request of a police officer does not create an infringement with the right to liberty of movement".[10] In that case, it is difficult to imagine to which situations art. 2 of the fourth Protocol would apply, apart from the prohibition for a person to go to certain

---

8   Van Dijk & Van Hoof, 1990, p. 253; Trechsel, 1993, p. 285. A similar distinction between deprivation and restriction of liberty is made by German law as well, especially by art. 104 of the German Constitution. However, in German law apprehension is not considered a restriction of liberty in this sense; see for instance Drews/Wacke/Vogel/Martens, 1985, p. 187 and Heise/Tegtmeyer, 1990, pp. 104 and 130.

9   Trechsel, 1993, p. 285.

10   In this sense the Commission in Reijntjens v. Belgium (Request Nr. 16810/90), published in NJCM-bulletin 1993, pp. 337-341, annotated by A.W. Heringa.

places.[11] However, this necessarily leads to the conclusion that, according to the interpretation of the Commission, the European Convention does not contain any provision or guarantee with regard to the apprehension. As long as the measure is applied on the basis of a "lawful order of a court or in order to secure the fulfilment of any obligation prescribed by law" (art. 5 par. 1b) and "this obligation is sufficiently concrete and specific," a person who is unwilling to comply with the measure may even be arrested or detained.[12] Because the Convention apparently does not apply to apprehension, there is no common minimum standard with which the national rules on this subject could be compared. As a result, a comparison with regard to apprehension would be limited to a reciprocal research.

However, since the measure we are dealing with in the cross-border perspective should be considered a form of arrest rather than of apprehension, art. 5 ECHR is applicable. Therefore, we will discuss some aspects of the European Convention law, especially those aspects relevant in the context of international policing: the right to be informed (par. 2) and the right to be brought before a judge (par. 3).

The first condition to be fulfilled in order for an arrest to be lawful, is the right provided by par. 2 of art. 5 ECHR:

> Everyone who is arrested shall be informed promptly, in a language which he understands, of the reasons for his arrest and of any charge against him.

Regarding this right to be informed, it should be noted first that the word "promptly" in par 2 does not have the same meaning as the "promptly" used in par. 3, which refers to a time-period that may be extended to up to four days and six hours.[13] The difference is shown clearly by the fact that, in the French text, the two paragraphs apply different words: *dans le plus court délai* and *aussitôt*.[14] Yet this does not answer the question as to when and by whom the arrestee should be informed. According to us, it is preferable that the person carrying out the arrest also be the person to inform the arrestee on the reasons for his arrest.[15] Furthermore, in the same context of deprivation of liberty, art. 9 par. 2 ICCPR states that arrestees should be informed at the moment of the arrest,[16] thus implying that the information be given by the same person as the one who carries out the arrest.[17]

---

11   This was the case in Guzzardi, November 6, 1980, Series A 39.
12   According to the Commission in the case of Reijntjens v. Belgium, p. 338.
13   Brogan case, November 29, 1988, Series A 145; see Trechsel, 1993, pp. 335-336.
14   Trechsel, 1993, p. 317.
15   Van Dijk & Van Hoof, 1990, p. 272.
16   In this sense also Fijnaut, 1991a, p. 61.
17   Trechsel, 1993, p. 317.

This also seems to be in accordance with the rationale of the right to information in this context. Naturally, one reason to inform the arrestee of the reasons for his arrest is, to enable him to decide whether he should have the lawfulness of his deprivation of liberty controlled by a judge.[18] However, for humanitarian reasons, a person who is arrested "also has a fundamental need to know what is happening".[19] Even besides this elementary need to know, one may imagine that a person being arrested might be more cooperative for a police officer who explains the reasons for the arrest than for an officer who refuses to do so. Therefore, the person to inform an arrestee of the reasons for the arrest must in general be the officer carrying out the arrest, implying that after a cross-border hot pursuit ending in the pursued's apprehension according to art. 41 SC, the pursuing officer is the first person to inform the suspect. The only circumstance that could justify a delayed information is the need for an interpreter, in case the pursuer does not speak a language that the pursued understands, and he cannot be informed in a language which he understands. Finally, it should be acknowledged that the right to be informed promptly is closely related to another well-known right of a suspect, which the European Court has discovered in art. 6 par. 2 of the Convention, the right to remain silent.[20]

The second right an arrestee has on the basis of the European Convention is the right to be brought promptly before a judge or other officer authorized by law to exercise judicial powers (art. 5 par. 3). As was stated above, the word "promptly" in this paragraph (in French: *aussitôt*) refers to a time-period which, depending on national law, may last up to four days. Even in case the arrest is the result of a cross-border pursuit, the local authorities will certainly be able to take the arrestee from the foreign pursuer in time to make sure that they can bring the suspect before their local judge. It may be expected that these will be aware of the provisions of their own, national law that should be respected in addition to the demands of art. 5 ECHR. As for the time-period within which they have to bring their arrestee before a judge, it should be noted that this period starts at the moment of the apprehension by the foreign police officer, this being the start of the deprivation of liberty. However, since this provision of the European Convention does not directly affect the obligations of a cross-border pursuing police officer, it may be left out of consideration in the following. Therefore, for the comparison of arrest powers, art. 5 will serve as a common denominator as far as the right to be informed according to par. 2 is concerned. It must nevertheless be stressed that the obligation to inform an

---

18 Van Dijk & Van Hoof, 1990, p. 272; Trechsel, 1993, pp. 314-315.
19 In this sense also Trechsel, 1993, p. 315.
20 Funke v. France, decision of February 25, 1993, Series A 256; because of the central role this right plays in the context of the interrogation, it shall be dealt with in detail in Chapter 10 of this study.

arrestee is an obligation for concrete situations without being a demand for national legislations: It is quite well possible that the police respects this right of the suspect without a statutory basis existing in his national legislation.

Finally, we must examine the question as to whether the European Convention applies to the control of identity, this being one of the aims of the apprehension according to the Schengen Convention. Especially art. 8 ECHR, stating in its first paragraph that

> Everyone has the right to respect for his private and family life, his home and his correspondence.

could be considered relevant in this context.

Up to this date, the European Court was never asked to judge the compatibility of forms of control of identity with art. 8,[21] but the European Commission once had to decide about the question as to whether the Belgian obligation "to carry an identity card and to show this at every request of a police officer" was an infringement of the right to privacy as guaranteed by art. 8."[22] In its decision the Commission stated that, in itself, this was not the case "since the identity card concerned (did) not contain any information on the private life without the consent of the holder." It only mentioned the bearer's name, first names, gender, date and place of birth, address and name and first name of his spouse.[23] Thus the Commission implicitly decided that if an ID card were to contain more personal data, like a tax or social security number, an infringement of the right to privacy would be possible. The conclusion must be that art. 8 of the Convention essentially does apply to the control of identity.[24]

7.2 National Norms

In order to illustrate the context of the comparison of national norms on apprehension and arrest, as well as control of identity, in this paragraph we will discuss the legal situation with regard to these police powers per country. Aspects that will be focused upon especially are restrictions regarding the ways

---

21 The same was concluded by Wiarda, 1987, p. 7.
22 Commission, September 9, 1992, Reijntjens v. Belgium (Request Nr. 16810/90), NJCM-bulletin 1993-3, pp. 337-341, annotated by A.W. Heringa.
23 The Commission in the same decision, pp. 337-341.
24 This conclusion seems to concur with the opinion of for instance the Dutch government, since they asked former president of the European Court G.J. Wiarda to research whether an ID-obligation would be an infringement with art. 8. One can, however, wonder whether the right to privacy does not imply as well that a person can walk on a street without being asked for all this information. In this sense also Heringa, 1993, p. 340. Wiarda (1987, p. 11) refers to this as "the right to be let alone".

a person may be apprehended or arrested, the right to be informed and the conditions, methods and means to control a person's identity.

7.2.1   Apprehension and Arrest

In this section, we will analyze the conditions under which these two forms of restriction of liberty may be applied under the jurisdictions of the five countries studied. This analysis will include questions regarding the right to be informed promptly, such as when, how and by whom this should be realized.

7.2.1.1 Belgium

The authentic terms which the French, Dutch and German texts of the Schengen Convention apply for apprehension (*appréhender*, *staande houden* and *festhalten*) do not represent any police power regulated by Belgian statutory law.[25] Furthermore, Belgian jurisprudence and literature do not recognize, distinguish or describe any subsistent power under one of these terms either. Because of the link that was made above between the treaty term apprehension and the legal concept of arrest and provisory arrest in case of a caught-in-the-act-situation, we will examine the Belgian law regarding this police power. Furthermore, the word apprehension under Belgian law could perhaps be understood as being inherent in the police power to control a citizen's identity.

It was only in 1990 that Belgium introduced a new statutory legislation regarding arrest and other measures of deprivation of liberty, the Detention on Remand Act (*Wet betreffende de voorlopige hechtenis* - WVH). One of the themes regulated by this statute is the provisory arrest in a caught-in-the-act-situation. According to art. 1 WVH, the arrest of a suspect who has been caught in the act is only allowed in case the offence is a *misdaad* or a *wanbedrijf* (*crime* and *délit*), thus excluding the category of the least severe offences, *overtredingen* (misdemeanours).

Such an arrest may be carried out by both police officers (art. 1 sub 2 WVH) and civilians, who must in that case promptly denounce the arrest to the competent police authorities (art. 1 sub 3 WVH); in this context, the word promptly must be interpreted as "as soon as possible in the given circumstances."[26] Note that, on the basis of art. 2 sub 1 WVH, the decision to arrest a suspect of an offence that was not discovered in the act must be taken by a

---

25   It was expected that at least an explication or definition of the term would be given in the so-called Schengen-circular (*Interministeriële omzendbrief over de gevolgen van de Schengen-Overeenkomst in het domein van de grenscontrole en de politiële en gerechtelijke samenwerking*, March 16, 1995, B.S. March 28, 1995, p. 7785), but this turned out not to be the case.
26   Van Laethem, 1994, p. 118.

public prosecutor or an investigating judge. Unless the suspect was caught in the act, there is no legal basis in Belgian law for a deprivation of liberty by a Belgian police officer. This also involves those suspects arrested by a Luxembourg or Dutch police officer after a cross-border pursuit according to the Benelux Extradition Treaty, in case the pursued person was not caught in the act. If in those cases the foreign police officer guides the suspect before another authority than the public prosecutor or the examining judge, like for instance a police officer, the deprivation of liberty following may be illegal and might even constitute a criminal offence.[27]

In general, the factual arrest may be carried out by immobilizing the suspect in order to deprive him of his liberty to go where he wants to (in the words of art. 1 sub 1 WVH: to prevent his escape). In order to retain the suspect, he may be put under custodial measures, comparable to the *bewarende maatregelen* as mentioned in art. 2 sub 2 WVH. These measures may include threatening with a danger of some sort in order to prevent his escape, seizure of his ID card, restriction of his liberty of movement by holding him physically, maybe even with the help of a rope or handcuffs, or locking him up in a car or room, all as long as the measure stays within reasonable limits of legality, subsidiarity and proportionality.[28] After being arrested, art. 12 GW does restrict the maximum period during which the suspect may be detained to 24 hours. Art. 1 sub 2 and 3 WVH add that this period starts at the moment that, as a result of the intervention of a police officer, the arrestee can no longer decide for himself where to go. After the arrest, an auxiliary to the public prosecutor must be informed about the event immediately, unless the arresting police officer or the officer to whom the suspect has been handed over by a civilian is himself invested with this quality.

As to the right to be informed promptly, Belgian law does not contain much information. In case of an arrest following a court order, the arrestee is informed at the very moment of the arrest, since at that moment he must be given notice of the court order (art. 7 WVH), which must contain the reasons for the arrest (art. 3 WVH). In case of an arrest by a civilian, police officer or public prosecutor, the law does not provide any special rights for the arrestee.[29] Art. 2 WVH only prescribes that the arrestee be informed of the fact of his arrest, not of the reasons for the arrest.[30] Although the ECHR have never given an indication that this right must be codified in the national legislation, it is obvious that the right will be much more easily respected in case national legislations demands

27   Van den Wyngaert, 1994, p. 689.
28   Van Laethem, 1994, pp. 115-117.
29   Van den Wyngaert, 1994, p. 690.
30   Fijnaut 1991, p. 67-68.

so explicitly and in detail than if it is only a general provision of the European Convention.[31] Case-law regarding this matter does not seem to exist.

According to the Benelux Extradition Treaty, Dutch and Luxembourg police officers may, during a cross-border hot pursuit of a person under suspicion of a criminal offence for which he can be extradited, apprehend the pursued person on Belgian territory within a zone of 10 kilometres parallel to the common border. On the basis of the declarations made on the modality of the hot pursuit according to the Schengen Convention, German police officers are allowed to this apprehension as well, at least with regard to escaped prisoners and to red handed suspects of a criminal offence for which extradition according to the European Extradition Treaty is possible. The Belgian government has not adjudged this competence to French police officers who cross the Belgian border during a hot pursuit by virtue of the Schengen Convention: They must wait for the Belgian police to arrive.

7.2.1.2 The Netherlands

Under Dutch law, the position of the Schengen power of apprehension (*staande houden*) is a rather confusing one. This confusion is caused especially by the fact that the art. 52 of the Dutch Code of Criminal Procedure explicitly mentions a police power by the name of *staande houden*. The Dutch *staande houden* cannot be considered the same power as the Schengen apprehension, since the former aims exclusively at asking the apprehended person's personalia, whereas the latter explicitly leaves the identification of the suspect to the local police (art. 41 par. 2 sub b SC). A further distinction between the Dutch and the Schengen apprehension is that the latter implies that the suspect is guided to a place of interrogation (art. 41 par 6 SC), thus having exactly the same basic function as the arrest according to Dutch law.[32]

As a consequence, the Schengen power of apprehension seems to find its equivalent in the Dutch power of arrest rather than in the Dutch *staande houden*. This seems to be confirmed by the Dutch legislator as well, since the entire implementory legislation regarding this aspect of the Schengen Convention applies to those provisions regulating the arrest, the artt. 53 and 54 Sv.[33] The former is involved because it regulates the arrest of a suspect who has been caught in the act, the latter, regulating the arrest in other situations, has been enlarged with a new provision, especially regarding officers of a foreign state.

---

31 In the same sense Fijnaut, 1991, p. 61.
32 Naeyé, 1990, p. 59. For a brief outline of the Dutch proceedings and regulations of pre-trial detention after the arrest, we refer to Swart, 1993b, pp. 300-303.
33 This was one of the conclusions of the Schengen ratification and implementation debates; see TK 22 142 nrs. 1-2; TK 22 140 nr. 12, p. 51, and TK 22 142 nr. 3, pp. 3-4 and p. 14.

Of course, the question rises which one of these provisions should be applied in which kind of situations.

According to art. 53 Sv, every person may arrest a suspect who was caught in the act of committing a criminal offence, be it a crime or a misdemeanour. Regarding the applicability of art. 53 Sv in cases of cross-border pursuit ending on Dutch territory, the Dutch government has shown a strongly ambivalent position. On the one hand, during the ratification procedure they stated that the term *flagrante delicto* in art. 53 Sv only applies to offences committed within the jurisdiction of the Netherlands. On the other hand, in the parliamentary preparation of the Implementation Act they explained that the term would also include offences committed outside the Dutch jurisdiction, as long as they were criminalized under Dutch law.[34] It seems to us that the second interpretation is preferable. Firstly, it is the only one to be compatible with the Schengen regulation, which exactly intends the recognition of the interest of a foreign catch-in-the-act, considering it the only justification for a foreign police officer to operate on the territory of another country. Secondly, there seems to be no practical reason for a territorial restriction of caught-in-the-act-situations.[35] If the conditions art. 41 SC sets for the cross-border pursuit of a suspect are met, the same is the case for the conditions of art. 53 Sv.[36]

The newly introduced provision of art. 54 par. 4 Sv regulates the arrest on Dutch territory by officers of a foreign state after a border-crossing in accordance with international law, but only for situations where the suspect was **not** caught in the act. At first sight, this seems to be a rather strange provision, the Schengen pursuit being created especially for those situations which are excluded here. Besides, the other Schengen countries have not seen any necessity for a corresponding provision, whereas in the Benelux context such a provision was never judged necessary. This is the more remarkable where the Benelux Extradition Treaty is the only context that has also allowed cross-border pursuits of suspects who were not caught in the act, a context therefore where a provision such as art. 54 par. 4 Sv would have been useful for several decades already. However, in comparison to the Benelux regulation, Schengen did introduce at least one new aspect of cross-border pursuit, the pursuit of escaped prisoners. Since such pursuits were not allowed under the Benelux regime, art. 54 par. 4 Sv was not necessary in that context. Furthermore, the reason that The Netherlands, different from their Schengen partners, had to introduce a legal basis for the arrest of escaped persons is the fact that Dutch law is the only legal system in which escape from legal detention is not an offence and, as a result, the escapee cannot be caught in the act. His arrest would therefore not be

---

34 See also Maring, 1995, pp. 225-227.
35 Maring, 1995, p. 227.
36 In the same sense the Dutch government in TK 22 142 nr. 3, p. 14.

covered by art. 53 Sv,[37] whereas the provisions on arrest of convicted persons only regard arrest by Dutch officers on Dutch soil.[38]

Moreover, the argument that the concept of *flagrante delicto* in art. 53 Sv only applies to offences committed within the Dutch jurisdiction has also inspired the Dutch government to deny a foreign police officer to apprehend a suspect outside of the 10 kilometre zone, although basically every individual would be allowed to do so according to art. 53 Sv.[39] The argument used by the government in this case cannot be considered a very strong one. As we have shown in our discussion of the Schengen regulation, a better argument for such a prohibition could be found in the hierarchy of national and international or ancient and recent norms.

A provisory arrest in a caught-in-the-act-situation according to art. 53 Sv is allowed regarding suspects of all criminal acts, crimes as well as misdemeanours. In other than caught-in-the-act-situations, the suspect may be arrested only in case of an offence for which pre-trial custody is allowed (art. 54 par. 1 Sv). These offences, mentioned in art. 67 Sv, include severe crimes threatened by a liberty sanction of four years imprisonment or more, as well as some explicitly mentioned misdemeanours and less severe crimes. As we mentioned already, escape from legal detention is not an offence under Dutch law, and the legal basis for the arrest of escapees is provided by art. 564 Sv.

An arrest *in flagrante delicto* may be executed by every person, police officer or civilian, Dutchman or foreigner. Depending on the urgency of the intervention, par. 1, 2, and 3 of art. 54 Sv have reserved the arrest of other suspects than those who have been caught in the act for public prosecutors, their auxiliaries and (ordinary) police officers. In those cases, par. 3 of this provision also covers the deprivation of liberty of a person by an ordinary Dutch police officer to whom a person has been handed over after having been arrested by officers of another Benelux state. Persons who have escaped may be arrested on the basis of a police report, to be issued by the first police station informed about the escape. In addition to a telex message, such a report can also be distributed by means of telephone, telefax, radio or television.[40]

---

37 This can be deduced from the explanatory statement of the Dutch government to the Schengen Implementation Act, TK 22 142 nr. 3, p. 4. Note that, according to the Dutch government, the addition of par. 4 to art. 54 Sv only applies to the arrest of escaped prisoners after a cross-border pursuit. In that case, the only legal basis left for the arrest of a pursued suspect by a foreign police officer is indeed art. 53 Sv.

38 Provisions on this theme may be found in art. 564 Sv and two circulars that will be discussed hereafter.

39 Answering Statement to the Schengen Ratification Act, TK 22 140 nr. 12, p. 51.

40 The exact procedure to be followed in such cases has been regulated by two circulars of the ministry of justice, July 1, 1993, Stcrt. 1993, nrs. 127 and 128.

Dutch law does not contain any definition or description as to the way the arrest of a person should be executed. According to the explanatory statement, the term should be understood as "depriving the suspect of his liberty of movement in order to guide him before the police or judicial authorities." Such a deprivation includes that, in case the arrestee does not follow the arresting person's instructions voluntarily, physical force may be applied to stop the person and to bring him to "a place of interrogation" (the police station).[41] However, there is no obligation to cooperate with a police officer attempt to proceed to one's arrest; ignoring a request to stop or trying to escape from a police officer is not generally criminalized, unless this is done by violence or physical resistance against the officer, or the stopping order was given within the context of one of the police's control tasks, such as traffic policing.[42]

In case of an arrest *in flagrante delicto*, the arrestee must be guided before an auxiliary to the public prosecutor "as soon as possible" (art. 53 par. 2 Sv), in other cases this should be done "without delay" (art. 54 par. 2 and 3 Sv).[43] After having been guided before the auxiliary, the arrestee may be retained at the police station for a maximum period of 21 hours, consisting of a maximum of 6 hours for identification,[44] 6 hours for interrogation,[45] and a fixed period of 9 hours during the night time. Because the aims of the detention are identification and interrogation at the police station, this period does not include the time between the moment of the arrest and the arrival at the police station.[46]

Although Dutch law does not provide any explicit provision on the arrestee's right to be informed promptly, and this right seems to be ignored by the police frequently, its existence and validity are generally accepted.[47] Recently, this has been confirmed by the *Nationale ombudsman*, who stated that "as soon as an arrestee has been brought under the control of the police, he should be informed of the reasons for his arrest, at least in short and to-the-point wordings."[48]

In the Dutch declaration on the right to hot pursuit in art. 41 of the Schengen Convention, apprehension by a German police officer on the territory

---

41   Naeyé, 1990, p. 75.
42   An original method of arresting a suspect who tries to escape over the highway was revealed by member of parliament L. Sipkes: In order to prevent the suspect from leaving the highway, the police created a traffic jam from which he could not escape so that he could be arrested (TK 1995-1996, *Aanhangsel van de Handelingen* nr. 456).
43   Naeyé, 1990, p. 85.
44   This subject will be discussed later in this paragraph.
45   For this, we refer to Chapter 10 of this study.
46   In this sense HR May 24, 1988, NJ 1988, 918. See also Naeyé, 1990, p. 214, who refers to a number of circulars issued by the minister of justice.
47   Naeyé, 1990, p. 87.
48   Report 94/624, p. 21.

of the Netherlands is allowed when it concerns a suspect who is caught in the act during a criminal offence which can lead to extradition according to the 1957 European Treaty on Extradition. The apprehension may only take place within ten kilometres of the German border. On the basis of the Benelux Extradition Treaty, Belgian police officers are bound by the same distance limit for apprehending a suspect of an extraditable criminal offence who has been pursued from the Belgian side of the border. In that case, however, it is not necessary that the suspect be caught in the act.

7.2.1.3 Luxembourg

As we mentioned above, Luxembourg law does not know the term *interpeller* as applied by the French version of the Schengen Convention. However, a regulation involving a form of apprehension comparable to the deprivation of liberty meant by art. 41 SC may be found in art. 43 CIC under the name of *appréhender*. Note that this is the same term as the one applied by art. 41 par. 5 sub f SC and by art. 27 BET. Art. 43 CIC states that the apprehension is a provisory type of arrest which is possible in case a *crime* or a *délits* is discovered *in flagrante delicto*, as long as the offence in question may be punished with a liberty sanction.

Every person is entitled to proceed to an apprehension of this kind, under the condition that the apprehended person be brought before the closest police or judicial authorities. According to art. 39 CIC, an auxiliary to the public prosecutor may hold a person against whom exist serious suspicions (a criterion larger than being caught in the act) in arrest for a period not exceeding 24 hours. The 24 hour period starts at the moment the authorities lay their hands on the suspect (par. 2), and may be used for instance for his interrogation.[49] As to the way the apprehension or arrest should be realized or the apprehendee should be treated or informed, neither statutory law nor case-law provide any information and moreover, as far as we have been able to establish, subjects of this kind have never been more thoroughly described or discussed in jurisprudence.[50]

According to the Benelux Extradition Treaty, apprehension in Luxembourg is allowed to Belgian police officers pursuing a suspect of an extraditable offence, as long as the apprehension takes place within ten kilometres of the Belgian border. On the basis of the Luxembourg declaration to the Schengen Convention, German police officers may apprehend escaped prisoners or suspects of a criminal offence mentioned in art. 41 par. 4 sub a of the Convention after a hot pursuit to Germany. French police officers, pursuing an escaped

---

49   This subject is elaborated in more detail in paragraph 4.7 of this study.
50   For further information on detention on remand and other coercive measures under Luxembourg law, see Spielmann & Spielmann 1993, pp. 270-274.

prisoner or a suspect across the French-Luxembourg border, are not entitled to apprehend the pursued person, this being an exclusive jurisdiction of their Luxembourg colleagues.

7.2.1.4 France

In the French criminal legislation, no measure by the name of *interpellation* as used in art. 41 par. 2 SC exists. There is, however, one provision explicitly referring to the *appréhension* of a suspect as referred to by art. 41 par. 5 sub 5: art. 73 CPP, regulating the provisory arrest in a caught-in-the-act-situation. Such an apprehension is possible as a measure against persons who have been discovered while committing a *crime* or a *délit* liable to be punished by imprisonment, or immediately after the commission of such an offence (art. 53 CPP). The fact that afterward the offence is only punished with a fine does not affect the legality of the intervention.[51]

An offender who has been caught *in flagrante delicto* may be apprehended by every person, police officers as well as civilians. The law contains no further specification as to the actual realisation of the apprehension, except for the condition that the apprehended person must be brought before the closest police or judicial authorities. Instead of bringing him before the authorities, the person who has executed the apprehension may also retain the apprehendee until the arrival of a police officer, as long as the authorities have been warned as soon as allowed by the circumstances.[52] Depending on the severeness of the crime and the danger of the suspect, the apprehender may apply physical force in order to stop the pursued and proceed to his apprehension.[53] Once guided before the local auxiliary to the public prosecutor, a suspect against whom exists a serious suspicion may be held in custody (*garde à vue*) for a period not exceeding 24 hours (art. 63 CPP). Since this period only regards the custody, it does not include the time between the factual arrest and the beginning of the custody.

In the French system, the right of an apprehended person to be informed promptly of the reasons of his apprehension is not mentioned in any legal text, statute or case-law. Its insertion in the Code of criminal procedure was among the suggestions done by the Commission on Criminal Justice and Human Rights, but this has not led to any change of law.[54] Art. 63-1 CPP, which was also based on a proposal done by the Commission, mentions a number of rights of which a person must be informed when being put in police custody, but these

---

51 Crim. March 11, 1992, Bull. crim. 110.
52 Crim. October 1, 1979, Bull. crim. 263.
53 Civ. June 10, 1970, Rev. sc. crim. 1971, 420.
54 Commission, 1991, p. 209. For a more detailed discussion of the French *garde à vue*, we refer to Chapter 10.

rights, elaborated in artt. 63-2, 63-3 and 63-4 CPP, do not include the right to be informed promptly as addressed by art. 3 ECHR.[55] However, it is difficult to imagine that a person must be told his right to make a telephone call, to be examined by a medical doctor and (after 20 hours) to contact a lawyer, without telling him why he has been deprived of his liberty, especially since the same person must confirm in his own record that he has indeed been informed of all this.

In the French declaration on the way the right to hot pursuit as provided by the Schengen Convention must be carried out, apprehension is excluded from the scope of police powers that may be exercised by foreign police officers. The French government has intended to reserve this compulsory measure entirely for French officials.

7.2.1.5 Germany

The German version of art. 41 of the Schengen Convention uses the word *festhalten*, a term applied under German law for the temporary restriction of a person's liberty of movement in order to enable the application of (further) police measures.[56] With the same meaning, most provincial and federal legislation on the control of identity apply *anhalten*, a term which therefore can also be considered a German counterpart of apprehension.[57] The same is the case for the so-called provisory arrest (*vorläufige Festnahme*) as regulated in art. 127 StPO, especially since this kind of arrest does not require any particular form or procedure and therefore in fact concurs with the most common meaning of *festhalten*.

Although art. 127 StPO does not contain any restriction as to the offences for which a provisory arrest in caught-in-the-act-situations is possible, such a measure is allowed only in case the offence concerned may lead to the suspect's detention on remand or immediate internment in a mental hospital or institute according to artt. 112 and 126a StPO.[58] This implies, that there must be reasons to fear that the suspect would escape or commit collusion (art. 112 par. 2 StPO). An additional condition for the arrest to be legal is that the measure must be

---

55 The effects and results of the Commission's work on the French legislation have been discussed in detail by Joubert, 1994, pp. 248-271.

56 The term may be found in for instance artt. 163b StPO and 14 par. 1 MEPolG; see also Rachor, 1992, p. 282.

57 For instance in art. 12 NWPolG; see for other references Drews/Wacke/Vogel/Martens, 1985 p. 187; Rachor, 1992, p. 282.

58 In this sense Kleinknecht/Meyer-Goßner, 1995, p. 430. Löwe/Rosenberg (1989, art. 127, nr. 8) state that provisory arrest must be limited to the criminal offences, thus excluding administrative misdemeanours (*Ordnungswidrigkeiten*).

necessary to ensure the suspect's presence or establish his identity.[59] In case of more severe offences, the risk of escape or collusion is considered to exist implicitly.[60] For the same reason, art. 112 par. 3 StPO explicitly states that the additional conditions do not need to be fulfilled in case of typical forms of organized crime and terrorism.

The provisory arrest is a measure which art. 127 par. 1 StPO allows to be applied by every person, be he a police officer or a civilian. When proceeding to the arrest of a suspect *in flagrante delicto*, criminal law requires no formalities other than the suspect being told that he was provisorily arrested and for which reasons.[61] The law does, however, not mention any sanctions whatsoever for cases in which these rights were not respected.[62] The factual deprivation of the suspect's liberty of movement is sufficient; with this purpose, physical force may be applied within the limits of proportionality, in case of an apprehension by a police officer, the applied force may be based on the provincial and federal police acts.[63] After the apprehension, the police must be informed as soon as possible; if necessary, the apprehended person may be retained until the arrival of the police.[64] Art. 128 StPO prescribes that a person who has been provisorily arrested must be guided before a judge of the local court (*Amtsgericht*) before the end of the day following the arrest.

In the declarations made by the German government to the Schengen Convention concerning the modalities for cross-border hot pursuit, they generously adjudged the power of apprehension of a red-handed suspect of an extraditable criminal offence to every Dutch, Belgian, Luxembourg and French police officer. The hot pursuit and apprehension on German territory are not limited in time or distance.

---

59   Roxin, 1993, pp. 224-225.
60   Roxin, 1993, p. 225.
61   Thus was decided in several judgements referred to by Kleinknecht/Meyer-Goßner, 1995, p. 431. The provincial police acts explicitly mention the police officer's obligation to inform arrestees of the reasons for the arrest in case the measure is based on the provisions of this statute. This might be the case if a suspect must be established in order to proceed to his prosecution (in this sense artt. 15 and 20 NGefAG). Furthermore, reference may be made to artt. 37 NWPolG, 19 BayPAG, 28 par. 2 BWPG, 16 RhPfPVG and also, for the federal border police, to art. 41 BGSNeuRegG.
62   A defence of this kind was originally accepted by a Bavarian court, deciding that consequently the suspect's resistance against the arresting policing officers would not constitute a criminal offence; however this decision was crushed by the Bavarian Court of appeal; OLG München, March 3, 1960, NJW 1960-35, pp. 1583-1584.
63   Roxin, 1993, pp. 226-228; with regard to this force, we refer to Chapter 8 of this study.
64   Kleinknecht/Meyer-Goßner, 1995, pp. 431-432.

7.2.2   Control of Identity

Art. 41 par. 2 sub b SC leaves no doubt as to the authorities who may establish the apprehended person's identity: this is left explicitly to "the officers of the Contracting Party in the territory of which the pursuit is taking place." This clear restriction is not difficult to understand, since the control of identity is not a very urgent task. Usually, it may easily be postponed until it can be done better by those officers who are most familiar with the locally existing legal provisions. Nevertheless, it seems useful to study and compare the national norms regarding control of identity, this power being closely related to the apprehension because, under international as well as under national law, it is one of the reasons to proceed to the apprehension.

Aspects of control of identity that will be focused on in the following are the conditions justifying the control of a person's identity, the type of obligation for the individual citizen (sanctions), the information mentioned on the citizen's ID-card (identity card), compulsory methods the police may apply in order to establish the identity and the registration of the collected information.

7.2.2.1 Belgium

Most police powers regarding the control of identity may be found in special legislation on detailed subjects, such as Traffic Regulations and the Aliens' Act, but the recent Police Function Act (WPA)[65] also contains some general provisions in this field. These excepted, citizens of Belgium are subject to a legal obligation to carry an ID-card on them, containing information as the bearer's name, gender, date and place of birth, address and name of spouse (plus, on request, his population register number and the name of his late or ex-spouse).[66] The ID-card should be shown upon every request of a police officer and on every other occasion where a person is required to demonstrate his identity. Unwillingness or incapability to show the ID-card on request can be punished with a fine. Inherent in the police power to ask for a person's ID-card is the police power to apprehend a person with the purpose of summoning him to show his card. The person whose identity is being controlled may not be held longer than necessary for the verification of the ID-card, that must be handed over to the police officer (art. 34 par. 4 WPA).

Control of identity is only allowed under certain conditions: Besides the regulations contained in special legislation (such as concerning the control of foreigners, which will be left out of consideration), the measure is allowed firstly

---

65   August 5, 1992, B.S. December 22, 1992.
66   Royal Decree of July 29, 1985, published in B.S. September 7, 1985, correction B.S. October 3, 1985.

towards persons who are being deprived of their liberty or have committed a criminal offence; secondly towards persons who are, on the basis of their behaviour, tangible indications or circumstances of time and place, under suspicion of having committed or preparing the commission of a criminal offence, or who are threatening to disturb or actually disturbing public order (art. 34 par. 1 WPA). Thirdly, control of identity is permitted regarding persons willing to enter a place where public order is or can easily be endangered, such as football stadiums (art. 34 par. 2 WPA).

If a person whose identity has been asked is unable to show his ID-card, he may establish his identity in any other way. In case of unwillingness to cooperate he may be arrested and taken to the police station in order to have his identity established under supervision of an auxiliary to the public prosecutor. This is also possible when the controlling police officer is not convinced of the correctness of the alleged identity (art. 34 par. 4 WPA). At the police station his identity may be established with the help of a bodily search and search of luggage, photographs, fingerprints and a personal police description. The duration of this arrest may not exceed twelve hours. Information that is gathered on the controlled person may not be stored unless this is necessary for a purpose allowed by statutory law (art. 8 par. 1 sub 1 Protection of Privacy Act).[67]

7.2.2.2 The Netherlands

Under Dutch criminal law, apprehension (or more precisely, the counterpart of the terminology used in the Dutch version of the text of the Convention, *staande houden*) is closely and directly related to the establishing of a suspect's identity. The apprehension is considered the least infringing of the liberty restricting coercive means, finds its statutory basis in art. 52 Sv and may only be used by an investigating officer for the purpose of asking name, address and date and place of birth of a suspect or witness.[68] The person who is held up for this reason is not obliged to stand still.[69] However, if he is physically upheld by the police officer who wants to stop him, trying to escape by force might be punished as resistance.[70] An obligation to answer and reveal his identity does not exist either,[71] but if the apprehendee does answer, the provided information

---

67 *Wet tot bescherming van de persoonlijke levenssfeer ten opzichte van de verwerking van persoonsgegevens*, December 8, 1992, B.S. March 18, 1993.
68 HR November 11, 1947, NJ 1948, 126.
69 HR January 16, 1928, NJ 1928, 233; HR June 25, 1934, NJ 1934, 1038; HR November 26, 1957, NJ 1958, 356. Special regulations, especially in the field of traffic, might however contain an obligation to stand still, like art. 33 WVW 1935.
70 Art. 180 Sr; HR June 25, 1934, NJ 1934, 1034.
71 HR June 27, 1927, in NJ 1927, 926.

must be correct. Stating a false identity is sanctioned by art. 435 par. 4 Sr. The apprehension itself may not take more time then necessary for asking the question and answering or refusing to do so.[72] Since the only aim apprehension may be used for is asking a suspect's or witness' identity, apprehension of non-suspects and non-witnesses or of a person whose identity is known already, is not allowed.

Since World War II, Dutch law has never known a general obligation to possess, carry or show an official document establishing the bearer's identity, nor did an official ID-card exist. Until recently, the only generally accepted documents to demonstrate one's identity were passport and driver's license. In the last few years however, this situation has changed drasticly. After having already adopted a bill on measures to identify anonymous suspects,[73] parliament has also accepted bills introducing a (restricted) ID-obligation[74] and an ID-obligation for financial transactions.[75] In connection with these, a national ID-card is still planned to be introduced. This card will contain the bearer's name, surname, date and place of birth, address, citizenship and tax & social security number.[76] In particular the last items, aiming at the use of the ID-card as a single personal number, has raised many questions as to the necessity of the measure and the risks for private life.[77] However, even after the introduction of this card several other documents will be useful as ID-documents, such as a passport, tourist card, municipal ID-card, residence permits and driving licences, the use of the latter being restricted to those situations where the individual's nationality is of no relevance.[78]

In accordance with artt. 53 and 54 Sv, a suspect who refuses to mention or demonstrate his identity may be arrested and taken to the police station when

---

72   See Naeyé, 1990, p. 61.
73   March 24, 1993, Stb. 1993, 182.
74   ID-Act of December 9, 1993, Stb. 1993, 660, in force since June 1, 1994 according to a Royal decree of March 9, 1994, Stb. 1994, 190. The alleged restricted character of the regulation has been and still is subject to discussion.
75   *Wet identificatieplicht financiële transacties*, December 16, 1993, Stb. 1993, 704.
76   As a comparison, it is interesting to mention the data that can be found on the other two official documents already existing: Passports contain bearer's name and name of birth, date and place of birth, size, citizenship and colour of eyes, driver's licences mention bearer's name and name of birth, date and place of birth, address and type of license. According to the Dutch minister of justice during a parliamentary debate on June 17, 1993, it is likely that citizenship, status of residence and tax & social security number will be added to these data.
77   See the above mentioned judgment of the European Commission on Human Rights in the case Reijntjens v. Belgium (Request 16810/90), NJCM-bulletin 1993, pp. 337-341 and particularly the note by A.W. Heringa. See also *NJCM-commentaar op het wetsvoorstel identificatieplicht II*, in: NJCM-Bulletin 1993, p. 626 and Holvast & Mosshammer, 1993, pp. 63-73.
78   NJB 1994, p. 791.

310

he has been caught red-handed committing any offence or stands under suspicion of having committed an offence for which art. 67 Sv allows his remand in custody.[79] If neither of these is the case, the apprehended may not be arrested and may leave: No more coercive measures are allowed against witnesses and suspects of minor offences who have not been caught in the act. Once arrested, a public prosecutor or his auxiliary may decide that the suspect be submitted to several measures that intend to establish or verify his identity: Photographs and fingerprints may be taken and his body sizes measured (art. 61a par. 2 Sv). On the basis of the new art. 61c Sv, a bodily search is allowed as well. Unless his remand in custody is possible, the suspect may not be held at the police station for identification longer than twelve hours: six hours for interrogation and six for verification of identity (artt. 61 par. 2 in combination with 61b Sv). The information gathered through ID-control or verification may be registered as long as necessary for the goal for which it was gathered (art. 4 WPolR).

On the basis of the ID-Act, a (restricted) ID-obligation has been introduced for every person in certain situations: Every citizen is obliged to bring his ID-card to his working place and to show it at financial transactions and at every contact with tax and social security offices. A similar obligation exists for spectators to professional football games and for public transportation passengers who do not have a valid ticket. In the first three cases, not bearing your ID is not an offence in itself; in the other two, (extra) penal sanctions are provided.[80] Aliens, who were until recently submitted to an obligation to carry and show their ID and residence permit, may now establish their identity and residence status otherwise. Of this follows that, at least theoretically, they do no longer need to carry their documents on them but may leave them home. For alleged aliens, it is sufficient to make their Dutch citizenship conceivable.

7.2.2.3 Luxembourg

Setting aside the regulations for ID-control on the basis of special laws regarding subjects as traffic and foreigners, a Luxembourg citizen is obliged to carry an ID-card or passport at all times, which must be shown upon every request of a police officer.[81] The ID-cards mention the bearer's name, surname, citizen-

---

79 With some exceptions, this is only possible with regard to suspects of crimes that may be punished with detention of four years or more.

80 This questionable distinction was criticized upon by the Dutch Council of State in its report published in TK 22 694 B p. 7, as well as by Naeyé, 1993a, p. 56.

81 This obligation was introduced by a grand-ducal decree of August 30, 1939 (*Arrêté grand-ducal portant introduction de la carte d'identité obligatoire*), Mém. 1939, 846.

ship, gender and date and place of birth.[82] According to art. 45 of the Luxembourg CIC, a control of identity must be restricted to suspects and witnesses of a criminal act and persons whose assistance or information could be of importance for the investigation of such an act. Nevertheless, the Luxembourg *Cour de cassation* decided that art. 45 CIC did not replace the 1939 grand ducal order, so that on this basis a control of identity could still be allowed in other situations than those mentioned in art. 45, for example during a routine control or of a person who seems to be preparing the commission of an offence.[83]

An apprehended person who refuses or is unable to demonstrate his identity by all means and papers, may be punished with a fine for not carrying his ID-card (par. 5 of the 1939 order) and be arrested in order to have his identity established at a police station (art. 45 par. 2 CIC). Under supervision of a public prosecutor's auxiliary, he may be photographed, fingerprints may be taken and his body sizes measured. A suspect may also be submitted to a bodily search. In order to undergo these measures, the person may be held at the police station during no longer than four hours, unless he is the object of a severe suspicion: In that case, his being held in custody for identification may last up to twenty-four hours. The information concerning the identity of the controlled person may be registered and stored as long as necessary for the following proceedings. If no further proceedings follow, they must be destroyed within six months and under supervision of the public prosecutor (art. 45 par. 8 CIC).

7.2.2.4 France

Under French law, a person who is asked to reveal his identity may, according to art. 78-2 CPP, demonstrate his identity by all means, which includes passports, driver's licences, ID-cards and statements of witnesses. Although France does indeed know a national ID-card, there is no obligation to carry and show or even possess one.[84] However most French usually have and carry their ID-card, which mentions the bearer's name of birth, surnames, date and place of birth, gender, size, citizenship and address, as well as (on request), his family situation and eventual name that may be used according to the law (for instance the husband's name).[85]

---

82 Prescribed in art. 4 of the ministerial decree of June 12, 1989, Mém. 1989, 1309 (*Règlement ministériel du 12 juin 1989 déterminant le modèle de la carte d'identité obligatoire à délivrer par les administrations communales*).

83 Cass. April 22, 1993, *Jurisprudence Luxembourgeoise* 1993, 209. On this decision, see Spielmann, 1993a, pp. 950-951.

84 Art. 1 decree nr. 55-1397 *instituant la carte nationale d'identité*, October 22, 1955.

85 Art. 2 decree nr. 87-178 *portant création d'un système de fabrication et de gestion informatisée des cartes nationales d'identité*, March 19, 1987.

Art. 78-2 CPP allows that the identity be controlled of every person who is under suspicion of the commission or preparation of a criminal offence, likely to have information on the commission of a criminal offence or wanted by the judicial authorities. Under the same provision, every person can be subject to a control of identity when this is necessary in order to prevent a disturbance of the public order. Someone who does not cooperate or is unable to attest his identity in a credible manner may be arrested for verification of identity at a police station. This verification must be executed under supervision of an auxiliary public prosecutor and may include the making of photographs and fingerprints and the measuring of body sizes. The maximum duration of custody for identification is four hours. When it concerns a suspect, he may be held in custody for a longer period, in which case his person and luggage may also be searched. The gathered information can be stored 25 years if a criminal procedure follows. In case no further investigation arises, the data are to be destroyed under supervision of the public prosecutor within six months.[86]

7.2.2.5 Germany

Within the framework of the Code of criminal procedure, apprehension in order to control a person's identity is allowed regarding suspects and other persons whose cooperation is necessary for the investigation of a criminal offence, such as witnesses or victims (art. 163 StPO). Under provincial law, depending on the province, the control of identity and apprehension may also be exercised on suspects of the preparation of a criminal offence, (probable) disturbers of public order and even in certain places where the public order and safety is endangered in general.[87]

In case of control, a person may demonstrate his identity by all means. Usually, the apprehended person will use his personal ID-card which art. 1 PAuswG obliges every German citizen to possess (unless he has a passport).[88] However, there is no obligation that one of these documents be carried at all times. A person being summoned to show his identity may also be obliged to show his card to the authorities as soon as possible. If this obligation is neglected, he can be punished with a fine (art. 5 PAuswG). The German personal ID-card reads the bearer's name and name of birth, PhD degree, pen name or alias, date and place of birth, address, size, eye colour and citizenship (art. 1 par. 2 PAuswG), which information can be read electronically.

---

86 Art. 5 decree nr. 87-249 *relatif au fichier automatisé des empreintes digitales géré par le ministère de l'intérieur*, April 8, 1987.
87 See for instance art. 12 par. 1 NWPolG.
88 Act on the personal ID-card (*Gesetz über Personalausweise* - PAuswG), April 21, 1986, BGBl. I, 1986, 548.

If a police officer is unable to control the identity of the apprehended person on the spot, he may arrest him and bring him to the police station for the verification his identity. With this goal, all necessary methods may be applied to establish a suspect's identity: His person and luggage may be searched, photographs, fingerprints, foot prints, hand prints and body sizes may be taken, a description of external body features (such as tattoos or scars) or a voice recording may be made, a writing test may be given, a confrontation with witnesses is allowed and even a change of the person's beard or hairdo is possible.[89] If necessary he may be kept in custody for identification up to a maximum of twelve hours (art. 163c par. 3 StPO). For other than criminal investigation purposes, some provinces have a maximum of twenty-four hours. In that case, the person involved should be brought promptly before a judge, unless this would take more time than the verification of identity itself (art. 163 par. 1 StPO). With regard to non-suspects, identity verification measures other than photographs, fingerprints, body sizes, hand prints, description of external body features essentially are allowed only with the consent of the person concerned (art. 163b par. 2 StPO).[90]

In general, the information that is gathered during a control or verification of a person's identity may be stored as long as necessary for the goal it was collected for, unless other provisions justify that the data be registered.[91] Art. 163c par. 4 StPO prescribes that identity data with regard to non-suspects be destroyed immediately.

7.3 Comparing National Norms

On the basis of the information on the different regulations of the apprehension and control of identity, it is possible to compare the five countries. For this comparison, we will focus on nine aspects that can be distinguished to these police powers. Regarding apprehension and provisory arrest, we will compare the offences for which this measure may be applied, the maximum period a person may be deprived of his liberty after having been handed over to the authorities and the right to be informed. The aspects of control of identity that will be compared are: the conditions for ID-control, the types of ID-obligation, the kind of information given on the ID's, the compulsory measures for ID-verification and the registration of information.

---

89   See for instance artt. 81b StPO and 14 NWPolG; Löwe/Rosenberg, 1989, art. 81b, nr. 9; Kleinknecht/Meyer-Goßner, 1995, pp. 249-241; Roxin, 1993, pp. 230 and 237.

90   For more general information on identity verification methods, see Rachor, 1992, pp. 260-277.

91   Drews/Wacke/Vogel/Martens, 1985, p. 190; Götz, 1991, p. 201; art. 14 par. 2 NWPolG.

Table 7.2 Apprehension and Provisory Arrest in the Act

	B	NL	L	F	D
Arrestable offences					
All except misdemeanours	+	-	+	+	-
All offences, special provision for arrest of escapees	-	+	-	-	-
All offences liable to detention on remand (excludes minor offences)	-	-	-	-	+
Maximum detention after provisory arrest					
24 hours from arrest by police	+	-	-	-	-
15-21 hours from arrival at police station	-	+	-	-	-
24 hours from beginning custody at police station	-	-	+	+	-
No maximum specified; until end next day	-	-	-	-	+
Right to be informed					
Not regulated	+	+	+	+	-
Recognized by case-law	-	+	-	-	+
Regulated in police law	-	-	-	-	+

7.3.1 Arrestable Offences

Regarding the offences for which the apprehension of a suspect *in flagrante delicto* is allowed to every person, two details of the Dutch regulation will be remarked immediately. On the one hand, The Netherlands are the only country where the entire caught-in-the-act-procedure is not restricted to serious crimes and felonies but is possible also in case of less serious offences. On the other hand, they are the only country where escape from prison or other deprivative measures or sanctions is not a criminal offence. Therefore, the Dutch criminal procedure is the only one to provide a separate legal basis for the arrest of escapees.

Under the law of Luxembourg and France, the power to arrest a suspect who was caught in the act is recognized to every person only in case of the commission of those offences that may be punished with imprisonment. Belgian law has realized a similar result by generally excluding all misdemeanours from this special investigation form. The German situation is more complicated, allowing the provisory arrest of a suspect caught in the act only in case the suspect's detention on remand is possible. In practice however, this seems to be possible in all cases except for "small" offences.

Whatever these differences may be, it is unlikely that they will cause problems in the context of cross-border pursuits and police cooperation. Since the Schengen and Benelux categories of offences that may lead to cross-border pursuits are more restrictive than any of the national systems, police officers respecting the international regulations will automatically respect the national regulations. Furthermore, regarding this aspect, the legislation of all five countries seems to comply with the standards set by art. 5 ECHR with regard to the reasons for which the individual freedom of movement may be restricted.

7.3.2 Maximum Duration

As to the maximum duration a suspect may be held in custody on the basis of the original arresting decision of the first police officer involved, the five countries' regulations strongly differ. This difference becomes even stronger when the moment at which this period of deprivation of liberty starts, is included in the comparison.

Belgium, Luxembourg and France have all set maximum durations of 24 hours. However, in Belgium this period starts at the very beginning of the arrest by the police officer on the street, whereas according to Luxembourg and French law, the beginning is the moment of being put into custody at the police station. Thus in these two countries, the time between the factual deprivation of liberty (by the arrest) and the official beginning of the custody is not counted, although this period, that will usually include the transport from the place of the arrest to the police station, may have a considerable duration. The Netherlands do not count the hours before the arrival at the police station either, but under Dutch law the maximum duration of this provisory arrest, including the eventual 9 hours during the night, is limited to 15 hours, or 21 in case of a suspect who still needs to be identified.

The real outsider concerning this subject is Germany. German law does not mention any maximum duration for the arrest, but only demands that an arrestee be brought before a judge at last by the end of the day after the arrest took place. As a consequence, the maximum duration of the arrest is almost 48 hours, starting at the moment of the factual arrest. Although it is hard to say something about aspects such as transportation time, the frequency with which persons must be kept in custody for identification and the average duration of an arrest in Germany, it seems safe to consider Belgium and the Netherlands as the countries with the most restricted possibilities for the police keeping people arrested at police stations.

In general, international policing will not be hindered by the variety of national rules concerning the maximum duration of the police custody following the initial arrest, these periods being too long to cause problems. Furthermore, with the exception of Belgium and Germany, the period does not start before the arrestee's arrival at the police station. Therefore, in The Netherlands, Luxembourg and France, it lies entirely in the hands of the local police whether the maximum period is respected or not. This is not the case in Belgium and Germany, but it is unlikely that local police officers will be unable to intervene in time to avoid that the apprehension will last more than 24 hours respectively longer than until the end of the next day.

7.3.3 The Right to be Informed

From a criminal legislation point of view, the position of the right to be informed of the reasons of one's arrest is equal in all five studied countries: None of them has created a statutory obligation for their police officers to inform a person at the moment of his arrest about the reasons for this measure. In the cases of Belgium, Luxembourg and France, this seems to be all there is to say about the subject, whereas under Dutch and German law, this right seems to have at least a place in the legal framework in another way. In The Netherlands, it has been recognized by the national Ombudsman, which implies that not informing a suspect at the moment of his arrest must be considered improper or undue behaviour, without however having any procedural consequences. In Germany, the right to be informed has been codified for other situations than criminal investigation. The impact of this right on criminal procedure has also been acknowledged as such by several judgements of criminal courts, although it was never judged that neglecting this right should have as a consequence that the arrest would be illegal.

This difference could lead to practical problems in those cases where a suspect is arrested by a Belgian, Luxembourg or French police officer on Dutch or German territory. In those cases, the officers are bound to Dutch respectively German law and must therefore respect the arrestee's right to be informed of the reasons for the arrest, an obligation they are not familiar with under the law of their home countries. Although it is still unclear whether such neglection would have consequences, procedural sanctions such as the legality of the arrest or even the acceptability of evidence gathered by or thanks to the neglect do not seem to be impossible, whereas disciplinary measures against the neglectant officer might be applied as well.

Concerning the question as to whether or not the five countries comply with the conditions of art. 5 par. 2 ECHR on the suspect's right to be informed, the

German legislator is the only one to have created an explicit statutory obligation to do so. In The Netherlands, several judges and other institutions have recognized this right, but in our opinion it should nevertheless be codified or regulated as a reminder. Such a reminder would be useful in Belgian, Luxembourg and French law as well, particularly since in these countries the right neither seems to have been considered by legislators or judges nor by scholars. However, as we stated above, this does not necessarily imply that in concrete cases the right to be informed is disrespected by the police officers of these countries.

7.3.4   Conditions for ID-Control

It is possible to distinguish several categories of conditions under which the control of identity of a person is allowed in the studied countries as well as in the Schengen Convention and the Benelux Extradition Treaty. These conditions are most restricted in the law of The Netherlands, which only allows the control of identity of a suspect or witness of a criminal offence, limiting the possibilities of a routine control to the working place and to persons who are present or around professional football games. All other four countries also have legal bases for the control of identity of persons who are under suspicion of preparing a criminal offence,[92] who threaten to or actually do indeed disturb the public order and of persons on places where public order can be endangered in general (not just restriction to professional football matches).

Apprehension and the following control of identity according to art. 41 of the Schengen Convention are bound to much more restricted conditions than all five countries studied here: It only allows this measure after a cross-border pursuit of a person who was caught in the act of committing certain severe offences, that are either mentioned in the European Extradition Treaty or in the catalogue of art. 41 par. 4 of the Convention. The Benelux Extradition Treaty is less restrictive than the Schengen Convention and does not demand that the pursued suspect be caught in the act.

---

92   It should be noted however, that for severe offences, liable to imprisonment of 8 years or more, preparation of the offence may be a criminal offence itself.

Table 7.3 Control of Identity I

	B	NL	L	F	D
Conditions/situations					
Suspect	+	+	+	+	+
Witness	+	+	+	+	+
Preparation of crime	+	-	+	+	+
Football match	-	+	-	-	-
Public order	+	-	+	+	+
Working place	-	+	-	-	-
Type of obligation					
Carry	-	+	-	-	-
Carry + sanction	+	-	+	-	-
Show	-	+	-	-	-
Show + sanction	-	+	-	-	+
Demonstrate	-	+	-	+	-

7.3.5 Types of ID-Obligation

One can also distinguish several types of identification obligation: The most infringing is the obligation to carry an ID permanently, eventually accompanied by a fine for non-compliance with this obligation. Eventually, this can be combined with the obligation to show the ID at every request of a police or other official, which is the case in Belgian and Luxembourg law. In Germany, the ID-card or passport does not have to be carried all the time, but every citizen is obliged to possess at least one of them and show it to the authorities (e.g. at the police station) at every request. Refusal to do so is also liable to be punished with a fine. In France, a citizen who is asked by a police officer to demonstrate his identity may do so by all means: He can use his ID-card, passport or other document, but essentially he may use any other means as well. In the Netherlands, the situation is likely to become very complicated with the obligation to carry and show an ID at the working place (without any sanction), at football games (with a fine) and for clandestine public transportation passengers (where not carrying an ID constitutes an aggravating circumstance). In other than these situations, no obligation at all will be introduced.

7.3.6   Information on ID-Cards

Among the five countries studied, Germany is the only one that has prescribed by statute which information the ID-card should mention. In the other four countries, this prescription is done at a lower level of legislation, namely by (ministerial or royal) decree.

All ID-cards mention (or, as to the Netherlands, will mention) the bearer's name, date and place of birth and citizenship. The Luxembourg and German cards do not reveal the bearer's address whereas in the Netherlands and Germany the bearer's gender is not mentioned. The German and Belgian card give information on the bearer's marital status, the French card only does so on request. On request as well, the Belgian card may mention the name of the bearer's late or ex-spouse and his civil registration number. The Dutch card is likely to mention the bearer's tax and social security number without the bearer being able to object. The German card finally, is the only one to contain information on the eye colour, size and eventual pen name and PhD-degree of the bearer.

Although the German ID-card evidently contains more information than the other four, the Dutch card is the one that will contain the most confidential information, since it will be the only one that automatically mentions the bearer's tax and social security number, whereas the other cards cannot even mention this at request. Therefore, of these five ID-cards the Dutch card is the most close to infringing the right to privacy as guaranteed by art. 8 of the European Convention, especially since one can wonder if the extension of the use of this number to a single national personal number can be considered "necessary in a democratic society" as required by this provision.

7.3.7   Compulsory Measures

A person who is unwilling to cooperate with a legal control of identity or is unable to convince the controlling officer of his identity may be arrested for verification of his identity in Belgium, Luxembourg, France and Germany. In The Netherlands this is only allowed when it concerns a red handed suspect or someone under suspicion of a criminal offence severe enough to allow his being placed in custody.

With regard to the measures that may be applied to establish an arrested person's identity, the situation in the five countries is generally similar: All allow that the person be searched, photographed, his fingerprints be taken and his body be measured or described. Some differences exist in the periods of time the controlled person may be held in custody: This ranges from 4 hours in France and Luxembourg to 12 in Germany and Belgium or even 24 in some German provinces and in Luxembourg in case of a severe suspicion. In all countries, however, the duration of this custody may not exceed the necessary time for the verification of the identity.

Two details should be considered as especially remarkable: Firstly, in comparison with the other countries, the German police seem to dispose of a great number of methods for establishing a person's identity. They may use hand and foot prints, writing tests, voice recordings, cosmetic changes and actually all other methods as long as they are necessary, which also implies that they be in accordance with the principles of proportionality and subsidiarity. Secondly, Germany is the only country among the five where measures of identity verification may be executed without the direct responsibility of an auxiliary to the public prosecutor.

7.3.8   Registration of Information

When the person the identity of whom has been verified is under suspicion of a criminal offence, Belgium, the Netherlands, Luxembourg and Germany allow registration of the information on his subject as long as necessary for the following proceedings, whereas the French legislator has set a fix maximum period of 25 years. Information on a non-suspect must be destroyed immediately according to Belgian, Dutch and German law, unless another legal reason for storage of the data exists. France and Luxembourg essentially prescribe the destruction of the information within 6 months.[93]

---

93   For a more general discussion of the management of personal data by the police, we refer to Chapter 11 of our study.

Table 7.4 Control of Identity II

	B	NL	L	F	D
Information (besides name, date & place of birth, nationality)					
Address	+	+	-	+	-
Gender	+	-	+	+	-
Marital status	+	-	-	-	+
Marital status on request	-	-	-	+	-
Late or ex-spouse on request	+	-	-	-	-
Fiscal/social security number	-	+	-	-	-
Civil registration number	+	-	-	-	-
Eye colour	-	-	-	-	+
Size	-	-	-	-	+
PhD-degree	-	-	-	-	+
Pen name	-	-	-	-	+
Compulsory methods					
Arrest	+	-	+	+	+
Arrest (if custody allowed or in the act)	-	+	-	-	-
By (auxiliary) public prosecutor	+	+	+	+	-
Search, photo, fingerprint, description	+	+	+	+	-
All necessary methods	-	-	-	-	+
Maximum hours of custody	12	6	4	4	12

7.4 Conclusion

The first thing that should be noted is that a comparison of the national regulations for initial restrictions and deprivation of liberty in the context of a criminal investigation confirms our interpretation that the Schengen term "apprehension" should be read as "provisory arrest." Belgian legislation is the only one out of the five studied that does not know a counterpart of the terminology as applied by the Schengen Convention. The other four countries do know such counterparts in one or another form, although the Dutch, Luxembourg and French situations are rather complicated: In these countries, the regulation of the literal terminological counterparts (*staande houden* respectively *interpeller*) do not cover the Schengen power, whereas the regulation of *aanhouden* respectively *appréhender*, a power to which the Convention seems to refer in another context and that is also mentioned in the French version of art. 27 BET, apply perfectly. As a result, some practical confusion might occur, particularly in cross-border pursuit situations involving the Netherlands or Belgium. This is especially the case in combination with the power to use of handcuffs and to apply security searches and seizures on the suspect, this being reserved for the officers who have proceeded to the suspect's arrest.

Further, one may conclude that the conditions under which apprehension, (provisory) arrest and identity control are allowed are the most restricted in the Netherlands, the other four countries being strongly similar. However, it is important to add that even the Dutch conditions go far beyond the conditions for apprehension after cross-border pursuit as they are set by the Schengen and Benelux Treaties. Therefore, a pursuing police officer who complies with the provisions of these treaties generally will also comply with the law of the country on whose territory the operation is taking place.

It is remarkable that the right of the suspect that, thanks to American TV series and motion pictures, is probably his best-known right, the right to be informed of the reasons for his arrest, has not found recognition in any of the codes of criminal procedure studied, and only in some of the German provincial police acts. This right, which is clearly warranted by art. 5 par. 2 ECHR, should in principle be respected by every police officer proceeding to the arrest of a suspect, including police officer operating on foreign territory. Nevertheless, it was only explicit recognized in decisions of the Dutch Ombudsman and several German courts. It is true that the European Court or Commission has never judged a codification of the right to be informed of the reasons for arrest in national legislation necessary. Since it is obvious that this right will be much more easily respected if prescribed explicitly by national legislation, it must nevertheless be regretted that it still remains nothing but a general provision of the European Convention.

As for the control of identity, no problems for the international police cooperation are to be expected either, since both art. 27 BET and art. 41 Schengen Convention reserve the execution of this power exclusively for the locally competent police forces. Nevertheless, it may be interesting to compare the five countries' provisions in that field. This comparison shows that with regard to the existing type of ID-obligation, Belgium and Luxembourg are the most strict countries, whereas France is the least strict. Without any doubt the Netherlands will be the country with the most complicated regulation. The personal information given by the ID-cards in the different countries is the most restricted in France (no marital status mentioned unless on request) and in

Luxembourg (no address), whereas the card that will be introduced in the Netherlands will be the only one that automatically provides the bearer's tax and social security number.

In comparison with the other four countries, Germany seems to be the country where the most methods for verification of a person's identity may be used, even though it is possible, that all these methods be allowed in the other countries as well but have never been explicitly accepted by legislation or put to the test of the jurisprudence. In any case, Germany is also the only one of the five countries where verification of identity may take place without the interference of an auxiliary to the public prosecutor.

With regard to the registration of information it should be noted that all countries prescribe the destruction of data regarding non-suspects within a short delay. Information on a suspect may be stored as long as necessary for the proceedings; France is the only country that has set a maximum period: fifteen years.

Finally, the most remarkable and important conclusion to be drawn from the above might be that the drafters of the Dutch and French versions of the Schengen Convention would have better chosen to use the word *aanhouden* respectively *appréhender* instead of *staande houden* respectively *interpeller*. The means of coercion for which the Convention intends to create a cross-border power is in fact the provisory arrest of a person caught in the act (that all legislations allow to everyone). At present, the terminology applied by the Convention does not have a legal meaning in Belgium, Luxembourg and France, whereas in Germany and the Netherlands, the terminology is known but means something else than what the treaty intends to use it for.

8 Handcuffs, Service Weapons and Self Defence

In the course of their duty the police do not always come across the same degree of cooperation on the part of suspects or witnesses. In some cases the execution of certain powers, the prevention of an ongoing crime or dangerous situations will require that police officers make use of physical force. This may imply a simple tap on the shoulder or the use of handcuffs when arresting a suspect but sometimes also the use of a stick or even a firearm during, for instance, a robbery in progress. When a cross border operation brings foreign police officers in a situation where a certain degree of force must be used, it is of crucial importance to know whether force may be used and to which extent.

That conflicts may occur in cross border situations because of a lack of knowledge of international treaties on the one hand and of national legislation on the other hand is a fact well illustrated by the following anecdote: A hot pursuit of a car thief brought Belgian gendarmes onto Dutch territory. The Dutch police officers were informed of the pursuit and a patrol car proceeded to the site. Nevertheless, the Belgian officers found themselves in a tricky situation. One of the gendarmes located the suspect in an open field and proceeded after him on foot. It seems that while trying to apprehend the suspect, one of the gendarmes shot. The other gendarme who had remained in their vehicle joined him and they proceeded to the arrest of the suspect together. The suspect was seated in the vehicle and they all left the site for Belgium. Indeed, on their way back to Belgium, the gendarmes encountered the Dutch patrol car in which two police officers are seated. The Dutch police officers attempted to speak with the two gendarmes but there appeared to be a problem: The gendarmes only spoke French whereas the police officers only Dutch. The two gendarmes left with the suspect for Belgium.

Later, one of the gendarme was heard by the Dutch authorities on the shooting: He had shot twice in the air, firstly, because he wanted to indicate his position in the field to his colleague and secondly, because he wanted to keep the suspect from fleeing in one of the nearby vacation houses. He added that he was unaware of whether the suspect was armed or not. Indeed, the action of the Belgian gendarmes was judged completely illegal by the Dutch authorities and the suspect was eventually set free. Not only was the arrest illegal in the light of both the Benelux Treaty and the Schengen Convention, but shooting was completely out of line according to Dutch law.[1]

In this chapter we have made a distinction between means of constraint, coercion and means of physical force. Constraint is the most general term, designating both coercion and means of force as a whole. Coercion is used more specifically for labelling those means of constraint used to compel an arrestee to cooperate. Finally, force is used for the use of an array of service weapons in self defence or other strict situations of imminent danger. In our definition, handcuffs would be more a means of coercion while the use of the service weapon would be considered force. We have made this distinction to help classify means of constraint, being conscious of the fact that not all countries apply this distinction, let alone that this distinction would have any legal consequences. Because in other countries such a distinction is made and because such a distinction will help to define differences in conceptions between the studied countries, we have chosen to use this terminology.

8.1 International Norms

8.1.1 International Norms on Police Cooperation

The use of constraint and in particular the resort to physical force is by definition one of the police powers that is in principle exclusively reserved to the locally competent police officers. One may even state that the police hold a force monopoly within the national borders when it comes to executing their task and that this monopoly is detained exclusively by nationally competent authorities. This, however, needs to be tempered by the following: Although the Benelux Treaty as well as the Schengen Convention recognize this principle, they have also created some exceptions. Because art. 28 of the Benelux Extradition Treaty has been replaced by the relevant dispositions of the Schengen Convention, we will not leave the Benelux out of the discussion.[2] The Schengen Convention provides for rules concerning both coercion and force. Coercion is permitted by means of handcuffs or a security search when the competence to apprehend is present. In other words, coercion is permitted provided the officers have competence to apprehend. The conditions giving competence for apprehension are set out in art. 41 SC after a cross-border hot pursuit. As for the use of force, that is to say the use of the service weapon, it is permitted in the only circumstance of self defence, notwithstanding whether the foreign officers are acting during a cross-border observation or a cross-border hot pursuit (artt. 40 and 41 SC).

---

1   Timmer, Naeyé & Van der Steeg, 1996.
2   See sub-paragraph 6.1.1.2 where we explain this position.

Foreign police officers will therefore be able to use such means of coercion as handcuffs when necessary or force such as service weapons in self defence while nationally competent police officers will be given the possibility to exert constraint on the grounds of a suspicion risen on the territory of another country (art. 41 par. 5 sub f SC). The Schengen Convention explicitly gives foreign police officers the power to use handcuffs on the apprehended suspect after a cross-border hot pursuit. The Convention is, however, silent on the conditions applying to the actual resort to handcuffs by the foreign police officers. Consequently, it will be the relevant national law that will offer the remaining norms. Further, the Convention allows the resort to service weapons in self defence, but is silent as to the definition of the concept. National law will here again be determinant.

Besides authorizing the use of handcuffs on an apprehended suspect, the Schengen Convention (art. 40 par. 3 sub d on cross-border observation and 41 par. 5 sub e on cross-border hot pursuit) provides for rules regarding service weapons. These provisions stipulate that police officers may bring their service weapon as they cross the border, unless one of the Contracting Parties has indicated its disapproval. This is possible in the case of cross-border observation (art. 40 SC) only, but as far as known no country has officially used this possibility. During cross-border hot-pursuit, police officers are always authorized to bring their service weapons. Officers of another Schengen country are only authorized to use their service weapon in self defence.

Foreign police officers observing or pursuing a suspect onto another Schengen country will have to keep in mind that they are not only bound by the Convention itself, but also by the law of the country in which they operate. This will be important especially when it comes to the use of their service weapon since on the one hand, the potential consequences of the use of a weapon may be serious and on the other hand, the standard for self defence will be that of the country in which they are operating. Although the Schengen Convention provides the use of handcuffs with a legal basis in international law, this does not mean that they should be used systematically, nor does it mean that they must be used in the same way in every country. Indeed, the law of the country in which the officer is operating will have to be respected.

A Schengen working group has studied the question of cross-border use of service weapons in greater detail and has drawn up a memento on international cross-border cooperation.[3] In addition to a definition of what is considered a service weapon for each country, the working group has come up with a common definition of self defence. Concerning the concept of self defence police officers should use when operating in another Schengen country, the

---

3   Working group Schengen I "Police and Security", established in Brussels on June 2 1995, (SCH/I (94) 17, 8ème rév.)

working group proposes the following: In all cases, three conditions must be fulfilled. Firstly, the existence of an illegitimate and actual attack on the physical integrity, honour or goods of the officer in question or that of a third. The concept of illegitimate or illegal attack must be extended to include the case where a violation of the right of the victim or of a third is neither imposed nor authorized by any rule. Secondly, the intended reaction to the attack must be proportional and reasonably necessary to prevent or avert the aggression. Thirdly, the situation to be averted must not be the result of the will or the provocation of the aggressed party and the reaction of the latter must be impossible to avoid. We will study the different service weapons in each respective country as well as the concept of self defence when we take an inventoy of the different norms on the use of service weapons in the different countries.

8.1.2   European Convention on Human Rights

When searching minimum standards for the use of force by the police one must take the European Convention on Human Rights into account, especially since all the studied countries recognize its provisions as being law in their respective legal systems. Among all the different norms contained in the European Convention, artt. 2 (right to life), 8 (protection of physical integrity) and 3 (prohibition of torture, inhuman or degrading treatment) offer the most relevant provisions when it comes to the use of force by the police. Since we will discuss art. 3 extensively in Chapter 10 when dealing with police interrogation, we will concentrate here on art. 2 and mention some of the relevant aspects of art. 3. Moreover, given the restricted use of force authorized in the Schengen context, it is not likely that police officers will go so far as using force in a way that might be in violation of art. 3 ECHR. The protection against unduly violations of the physical integrity (art. 8) will be discussed further in Chapter 9 when we analyze bodily searches in the different countries.

8.1.2.1 Right to Life (art. 2)

The use of physical force by the police may in extreme cases result in injuries to or even death of the suspect or third party. Indeed it will rarely be the intention of the police official to induce harm but in the heat of the action accidents may happen. Art. 2 ECHR sets a minimum standard for the use of force by police authorities:

*1. Everyone's right to life shall be protected by law. No one shall be deprived of his life **intentionally** save in the execution of a sentence of a court following his conviction of a crime for which this penalty is provided by law.*

2. Deprivation of life shall not be regarded as inflicted in contravention of this article when it results from the use of force which is no more than absolutely necessary:
a. in defence of any person from unlawful violence;
b. in order to effect a lawful arrest or to prevent the escape of a person lawfully detained;
c. in action lawfully taken for the purpose of quelling a riot or insurrection.

Upon reading the whole of the article, one remarks firstly that par. 1 enacts the right and par. 2 the limitation. The fact that the limitations have been enacted exhaustively indicates that they must be interpreted restrictively. The second paragraph enumerates a number of situations in which force may be used. The first condition for the limitation is that the legitimate use of force should be no more than "absolutely necessary," which is to say that there must be proportionality between the "measure of force used and the purpose pursued."[4] This purpose must furthermore be one mentioned in art. 2: defence of a person (which in fact can be considered an expression of the principle of self defence), lawful arrest and quelling a riot. There must be proportionality between the force used and the particular interest at hand. In other words the death of a person will not be justified when there is no serious danger feared from the person.[5]

However, the Commission in the case X. v. Belgium interpreted "intentionally" in the wording of art. 2 par. 1 ECHR as excluding the case of unintentional death caused by a police officer.[6] The Commission had declared that the complaint was "manifestly ill-founded" because it was a case of self defence of a policeman who felt threatened. There were no reasons to believe that the policeman had intentionally wanted to kill the victim. Because of this reason the Commission felt that it was not necessary to look upon the question whether the force used was absolutely necessary. This interpretation of art. 2 however seems to limit its domain unduly since death occurring in those situations cited in art. 2 par. 2 will rarely be intentional. The wording "when it results from the use of force" supports this thesis.[7]

This was also the conclusion of the Commission in the case Stewart v. United Kingdom, deciding that the second paragraph of art. 2 does not enumerate a number of situations where it is allowed to kill someone, but rather a number of situations where the use of force is permitted and where death may

---

4   Van Dijk & Van Hoof, 1990, pp. 222 - 226.
5   See Van Dijk & Van Hoof, 1990, p. 223; Castberg, 1974, p. 82.
6   Appl. 2758/66, X. v. Belgium, Yearbook XII (1969), p. 174 (192).
7   See Van Dijk & Van Hoof, 1990, p. 223 where this thesis is more extensively discussed.

occur as an unintentional consequence. The use of force in this context must be absolutely necessary for one of the aims enumerated in sub-paragraphs a, b or c. "Absolutely necessary" designates a "pressing social need," the "necessity test" consisting of weighing the question of whether the use of force was appropriate to the legitimate purpose pursued. Finally, the combination of the word "necessary" with the word "absolutely" indicates that the test of necessity will be applied strictly and compellingly.[8] In assessing the question as to whether the means employed are proportional, the Commission acknowledged furthermore the relevancy of such factors as "the nature of the aim pursued, the dangers to life and limb inherent in the situation and the degree of risk that the force employed might result in the loss of life."[9]

The court has confirmed this vision of art. 2 in the recent Gibraltar case.[10] The court reaffirmed in its judgment that art. 2 not only guarantees the right to life but sets out circumstances where the use of lethal force may be justified. In that sense, the provisions of art. 2 should be "strictly construed."[11] The court continues by stating that art. 2 does not primarily enounce in which situations it is justified to intentionally kill a person, but rather that it is permitted to use force, even with as result that death might be the outcome. The test for the use of force contained in art. 2 is much stricter that contained in other provisions of the Convention. Indeed, the wording "absolutely necessary" must be understood as much stricter than "necessary in a democratic society." The court pursues that the force used "must be strictly proportionate to the achievement of the aims set out in sub-paragraphs 2a, 2b and 2c."[12] Finally, the court maintains:

> In keeping with the importance of this provision in a democratic society, the Court must, in making the assessment, subject deprivations of life to the most careful scrutiny, particularly where deliberate lethal force is used, taking into consideration not only the actions of the agents of the State who actually administer the force but also all the surrounding circumstances including such matters as the planning and control of the actions under examination.[13]

On the basis of what has been discussed above it is safe to assume that art. 2 par. 2 ECHR imposes a much stricter test of necessity to the use of force for

---

8   Van Dijk & Van Hoof, 1990, p. 224.
9   Appl. 10044/82, Stewart v. United Kingdom, D & R 39 (1986), p. 162 (169-171). See also Appl. 9013/80, Farrell v. United Kingdom, Yearbook XXV (1982), part. II, Ch. L.B., p. 124 (143).
10 Mc Cann and others v. the United Kingdom, September 24, 1995, Series A, 324.
11 Nr. 147 of the case.
12 Nr. 149 of the case.
13 Nr. 150 of the case.

the purpose of defending anyone from unlawful violence, arresting an individual or to prevent escape or for the purpose of suppressing a riot, independent of the question of intention. It follows that the proportionality of the force used will be weighed against the aim pursued. This will be particularly important when lethal force will be used in situations of self defence. The question of specially trained and specially equipped sharp shooters and their control and supervision will be crucial.

8.1.2.2 Prohibition of Torture and Inhuman or Degrading Treatment (art. 3)

Since the content and the case-law regarding this article will be discussed extensively in Chapter 10 on police interrogation, we will limit ourselves here to a number of important points. Art. 3 ECHR reads as follows:

No one shall be subject to torture or to inhuman or degrading treatment or punishment.

Any use of force contrary to one of these three interdictions would be an element of violation of art. 3. In this case it is not the degree of force that is measured to see whether it is in accordance with the European Convention on Human Rights, but rather the fact that a certain practice can be considered as torture, inhuman treatment or degrading. This article has no second paragraph allowing derogation provided there be a sufficient basis in domestic law. Indeed, since it can never be an aim in a democratic society to have laws permitting torture or inhuman treatment, this prohibition will apply to practices to that effect, notwithstanding their eventual basis in domestic law. Even a limited amount of force can be considered contrary to art. 3, but it is a question of evaluating in each case whether a practice can be considered torture or inhuman or degrading treatment.

The Commission refers to degrading treatment or punishment as measures "which constitute an insult to the applicants' human dignity."[14] In a case where the applicant claimed to have been brutalized during his arrest while he was already handcuffed and to have been attacked by a police dog, the Commission determined that the request was ill-founded. The Commission concluded that the applicant was brutalized after he had become violent and assaulted the police officer holding the dog.[15] This does not mean that the Commission found that it was correct to brutalize a handcuffed suspect, rather that it was not severe

---

14 Appl. 8930/80, *X, Y and C v. Belgium* (not published), referred to in Van Dijk & Van Hoof, 1990, p. 228.
15 Appl. 4220/69, Rec. 37, p. 51.

enough a treatment to constitute an inhuman treatment. The Court requires a minimum degree of severity to fall within the scope of art. 3.[16]

However, in our opinion, such practices as the arrest of an unarmed suspect for instance, by a team of specially trained police officers, in his home while taking a shower, subsequently being handcuffed and brought outside while sirens of a number of police cars are blowing, in so doing awaking the neighbours who all gather around the scene might, in our opinion, be considered an inhuman or degrading treatment, notwithstanding the fact that such a practice would have sufficient basis in national law.

In short, one could see a gradation between artt. 2, 3 and 8 ECHR as to the use of force by the police. Use of force resulting in a violation of art. 3 would not be allowed under any circumstances, whereas force resulting in death (as an unwanted consequence) would only be justified in the cases enumerated in art. 2 of the Convention. Finally, use of force resulting in the violation of the right to privacy and discussed in the following Chapter 9, would only be authorized under the conditions set out in art. 8 ECHR.

8.2 National Norms

When describing the national norms applicable to the use of constraint, coercion and force, one comes across a vast array of regulated subjects: general theories, use of technical means of restraint such as handcuffs, tear gas, chains, use of firearms and sticks. In analyzing these types of norms, one can distinguish between norms that create a competence and norms that regulate the scope and domain of the competence. In this system of analysis, means of constraint represent the competence (for example arrest, control of identity, search and seizure or interrogation) while coercion and force represent the instruments to accomplish these competencies effectively. In an effort to present these norms in an orderly fashion we have divided this paragraph in five sections, following the Schengen system of analysis. We will look upon constraint in general (section 8.2.1), upon the use of handcuffs (section 8.2.2), upon the use of service weapons (section 8.2.3) and finally upon the concepts of self defence with that of the actual use of service weapons (section 8.2.4). This will allow us not only to compare norms with each other but also to analyze cross-border consequences of the disparities between the different countries.

16   See further Van Dijk & Van Hoof, 1990, pp. 230-241.

8.2.1 Constraint in General

Most countries have general principles police officials must know and respect when deciding whether constraint should be used in a particular situation. The purpose of this section is to sketch the different general principles applicable to the use of constraint in the studied countries.

When a police officer is not competent to carry out certain acts, the suspect is in most countries allowed not to cooperate. We have decided, however, to leave the comparative inventorization and analysis of the legal concept of "resistance" out of the scope of this study for the following reason. This study focuses on the powers of competent police officers during cross-border operations. It is not the purpose of this study to analyze to which degree citizens may or may not resist.[17]

8.2.1.1 Belgium

In the Police Function Act, Belgian law distinguishes between constraint and force. Although no definition is given of the two concepts, the explanatory statement states that force must be interpreted extensively and designates all means that may be used to physically compel a person. It designates a vast array of measures, from the simple arm grip to the deadly shot. The concept of constraint designates not only physical constraint, but also all violations of individual liberties such as arrest, identity control, police custody and searches.[18] The Belgian police officers may use physical force when performing their duty.[19] The intensity of the force may vary between the use of handcuffs on a suspect resisting arrest and the use of firearms in extreme cases. One may also think of stopping an ongoing vehicle with the help of barricades, ropes or other technical means.

Belgian law foresees a number of very different provisions considering the use of force by police officials. Art. 37 WPA is a general provision stipulating that physical force may only be used when it serves to accomplish a legitimate aim, that the use of force must be proportional to the importance of the aim and that a warning must be given prior to the use of such force. The concept of

---

17 The legitimacy of resistance being the complement of incompetent police action, a study of one already implies the study of the other. Moreover, a study of the consequences of incompetent police action would call for a study of all these consequences and would exceed the scope of the present study. Indeed, a study of the consequences of incompetent police action, illegal gathering of evidence and nullities would form a natural complement of the present study and would logically flow from its conclusions.

18 See Bourdoux & De Valkeneer, 1993, p. 174.

19 See: Six, 1984, pp. 2065-2090; Bruggeman & De Lentdecker, 1987, pp. 399-423 (contains information on statistics); Geerits, 1989, pp. 51-64; De Valkeneer, 1991, pp. 87-93.

legitimate aim or legitimate reasons has yet to be developed by the case law. However there is no doubt that factors like the individual interest of physical integrity and that of the safety and peace in the society in general must be carefully weighed.[20] Further the use of force by police officers may be legitimized by the existence of a state of emergency or *force majeure*,[21] self defence[22] and legal provisions.[23] Moreover, principles such as the principle of opportuneness, proportionality and subsidiarity will be important in relation to the use of force by the police.[24]

8.2.1.2 The Netherlands

Dutch law makes a distinction between means of coercion, regulated in both the Code of criminal procedure and the Police Act, and physical force (*geweld*: violence) the legal competence of which is regulated in the Police Act (PolW) and the application of which is worked out in lower forms of regulations (*Ambtsinstructie*, further called Police Instruction).[25] Means of coercion found in the Code of criminal procedure rest on general legal provisions granting police officers competence to compel suspects for the purpose of the criminal enquiry: arrest, search and seizure, interrogation. Force may be needed to physically compel suspects to cooperate, in which case Dutch law speaks of "violence." We will refer to this type of physical force simply with the use of the word "force," for the sake of convenience. The central concepts a Dutch police official will have to bare in mind are the concepts of proportionality and subsidiarity during the legitimate exercise of this duty. Art. 8 PolW explicitly authorizes police officials to make use of force in the legitimate execution of their duties. According to the explanatory statement, each application of force of more than a superficial manner on persons, objects or animals is considered

---

20 Bruggeman & De Lentdecker, 1987, p. 407; Geerits, 1989, p. 52.
21 In the Belgian criminal code the existence of a state of emergency is not seen as legitimization for the violation of a legal norm in situations where a higher norm renders this necessary. Nevertheless the courts recognize this principle; see Van den Wyngaert, 1994, pp. 188-196.
22 This legal exception provided for by artt. 416-417 Sw and 38 par. 1 sub 1 WPA will be discussed more closely in this chapter.
23 See art. 70 Sw; see also Van den Wyngaert, 1994, pp. 196-203.
24 See Luypaers, 1993, pp. 260-263.
25 These are the Police Act of 1993 (*Wet van 9 december 1993 tot vaststelling van een nieuwe politiewet - Politiewet 1993*, Stb. 1993, 724) and the Instructions for the police of april 8, 1994 (*Ambtsinstructie voor de politie, de Koninklijke marechaussee en de buitengewoon opsporingsambtenaren - Besluit van 8 april houdende regels met betrekking tot een nieuwe Ambtsinstructie voor de politie, de Koninklijke marechaussee en de buitengewoon opsporings- ambtenaren en de maatregelen waaraan rechten van hun vrijheid beroofde personen kunnen worden onderworpen*, Stb. 1994, 275); For an overview on the use of force by the police, see Elzinga, Van Rest & De Valk, 1995, pp. 81-139.

force in the context of police duty.[26] The use of force is subjected to three conditions: The officer must be legitimately executing his duty and his actions must be compa-tible with the principles of proportionality, subsidiarity, reasonability and measure. Is any one of these conditions absent, the police officer will not be able to invoke art. 8 PolW and his actions will be assessed on the hand of the regular criminal law. Indeed his actions may eventually be justified by criminal exceptions such as that of *force majeure* and of self defence (artt. 40 and 41 Sr).

Furthermore, the concept of proportionality demands a reasonable weighing of interests: The contemplated aim must justify the means employed in relation to the possible danger that can result of the use of force. In weighing the danger of the acts one must not only look at the consequences that are certainly expected but also at the consequences that can reasonably be expected. For the use of firearms for instance, this means that one must not only look at the possible consequences for a suspect caught red handed but also at the reasonable consequence that third parties might get hurt by stray bullets. Finally, the principle of subsidiarity implies that force may only be used when there are reasons to believe that the aim could not be achieved with other less drastic means. Art. 8 par. 2 PolW also states that the use of force must be preceded by a warning. In the light of the subsidiarity principle, one may wonder whether kicking a car, stopped because it had been speeding, aiming to divert the driver's attention from a police colleague approaching the car from the other side, will be among the generally acceptable forms of physical force.[27]

8.2.1.3 Luxembourg

Luxembourg law distinguishes between coercion, a competence worked out mainly in the Code of criminal procedure, and force, worked out in a separate statute. This statute, the 1973 Act Regulating the Use of Force (*Loi réglant l'usage des armes et des moyens de contrainte*), further designated Force Act, regulates the use of service weapons and specific technical means of force by the members of the public force.[28] Other non regulated forms of physical coercion (such as the use of handcuffs) are seen as basic police measures that do not require a specific legal basis. The most important principle for the use of force by Luxembourg police officers is absolute necessity.

---

26 Explanatory statement on art. 33a of the Police Act 1957, renumbered art. 8 PolW 1993 (TK 1985-1986, 19 535, nr. 3).
27 A case of such police operations was provided to us by our colleague J. Timmer.
28 Mem. 1973, 1094, July 28, 1973.

8.2.1.4 France

French law regulates means of constraint mainly in the code of criminal procedure. Physical force as such is not regulated as such in any statute. However, a general theory on the use of constraint (constraint here being used as an expression englobing coercion and force) set out by case law and literature partly regulates the use of both coercion and force.[29] According to this theory the use of coercion is regarded as an essential power of the police. The police is expected to act in reaction to different factors, for instance to disturbances of the peace or to crime. In order to be able to exercise physical coercion in a legitimate manner, the police officer will first acknowledge that such a disturbance is taking place. Then he will ask himself whether he is competent to take action. The legitimate use of coercion is subject to two conditions: the existence of a fact leading to the use of constraint and the presence of an officer legitimately in function.[30] Finally, there must be the existence of a state of necessity or emergency. These two expressions have no legal meaning but are used by the courts as a legitimacy test for the use of constraint. The two expressions indicate that there must be a need to act quickly.

The use of coercion is further subjected to principles such as proportionality, presumption of legality and opportuneness. The latter two are considered by the doctrine as complementary principles since they are not *per se* inherent to the rule of law. The principle of proportionality however is more fundamental since it sets the basis of police action as a whole: There must be balance between the aim of the action and the means used to reach that aim. The police may only use the appropriate means that are necessary to reach the legitimate aim.[31]

According to the principle of proportionality, the actual conduct of a suspect caught in the act or the circumstances surrounding the action will, for instance, influence the police officer: In the presence of many witnesses, the simple words: "Please, come with us" may be sufficient to force the suspect to follow the officers. In other circumstances it might be necessary for the officer to put his hand on the suspect's shoulder or even use more force to constrain the suspect to follow him. The use of all means of coercion, from the use of handcuffs to that of firearms, is subject to these principles.[32]

As for the two complementary principles, the presumption of legality and the opportuneness, they find their importance in the weighing of the interest of effective police action and that of avoiding systematic use of force by the

---

29   See Buisson, 1988, pp. 531-723 on the *théorie générale de la contrainte*.
30   Called *titre de contrainte*; see: Decocq, Montreuil & Buisson, 1991, p. 255.
31   Decocq, Montreuil & Buisson, 1991, p. 267.
32   Decocq, Montreuil & Buisson, 1991, p. 268.

police. From the presumption of legality follows that police actions are *prima facie* considered legitimate. The case law has held since the 1830's the opinion that in principle citizens must passively endure police actions.[33] The *Cour de cassation* has followed this line since then and in theory the citizen is only allowed a certain degree of resistance when the police action is blatantly illegal. This means that the passive cooperation expected of the citizen is only one of a short duration, necessary for the maintaining of the public order.

8.2.1.5 Germany

German law categorizes very strictly between coercion and force, but both are worked out systematically in statutes, federal or provincial, depending on the aim of the action (before or after criminal suspicion). Because the use of force by the public authorities usually implies a certain violation of the personal freedom and liberties of an individual, art. 2 GG demands a legal basis.[34] This demand has been mainly fulfilled by the legislations of the different provinces, each of which have adopted rules for the legitimate use of constraint by police officers. Indeed these statutes basically only apply to police officers of the respective province. A special place is created for the *Spezialeinsatz-Kommandos* (SEK's), consisting in heavily armed officers of each province, which are especially called upon in cases of kidnapping, terrorism and violent crime. For officers of the federal police forces (the *Bundesgrenzschutz* and the *Bundeskriminalamt*), this subject is regulated by a federal statute on the use of direct force (*Gesetz über den unmittelbaren Zwang bei Ausübung öffentlicher Gewalt durch Vollzugsbeamte des Bundes* - UZwG).

The federal and provincial legislation concern the conditions justifying the use of force, the kind of force and the extent to which one is habilitated to apply it. In general this legislation distinguishes between three forms of physical force: physical force, physical force with the use of material aids (*Hilfsmittel der körperlichen Gewalt*) and the use of arms.[35] An example of the first situation is the bringing an arrested suspect by the arm, the second makes reference to the use of handcuffs or other material means to immobilize a suspect, as well as the use of water canons, tear gas, dogs, horses and vehicles. To the third category, the use of arms, belong the use of arms to hit and poke and the use

---

33   Crim. January 5 1831; see also Decocq, Montreuil & Buisson, 1991, p. 268; Vitu & Montreuil, artt. 209-221.
34   Vogel & Martens, 1985, p. 541.
35   Roxin, 1993, pp. 227-228.

of firearms, including explosives.[36] When applying direct physical force, the principles of subsidiarity and proportionality play an important, even a double role: Not only one must use the least severe means, but the means used must be proportional to the cause.[37]

8.2.2 Handcuffs

Of all means of physical coercion available to the police, handcuffs are the most known. They belong, with the firearm and the stick, to the basic equipment of a police officer. Used most often for reasons of safety, opinions differ on the question whether they should be used systematically or exceptionally, and whether their use should be regulated legally.

When thinking about handcuffs, the first thing that comes to mind are the conventional metallic handcuffs, but throughout the years other types of cuffs have appeared such as tapes, the so-called tie-raps, and special foot and hand cuffs for dangerous suspects. Because neither the legislation of the different studied countries nor the text of he Schengen Convention distinguish between these different means of physical restraint, we will limit our study to the use of handcuffs in general.

8.2.2.1 Belgium

Belgian law does not provide for specific rules for the use of handcuffs by the police.[38] With a few exceptions the literature has paid little attention to this means of restraint.[39] Various legal provisions of a more general nature authorize police officials to make use of force while performing their duty. The first legal exception that comes to mind is the existence of emergency or *force majeure* combined with a legitimate aim: On many occasions the police will use handcuffs for reasons of safety, in order to fulfil an obligation such as the obligation of inquest ex artt. 8 Sv and 15 WPA or to execute an order originating a superior officer (such as the arrest of a particular individual). Further it is possible to read in artt. 257 Sw and 37 WPA an indication that police officers will not be acting illegally when using force for legitimate reasons or in order

---

36 Vogel & Martens, 1985, p. 543; for statistical information on the deadly use of firearms by the police in Germany see for instance the chronicles in B & P, 1991-1, pp. 71-74, 1992-1, pp. 61-63; 1993-1, pp. 79-85, 1994-1, pp. 59-64 and 1995-1, pp. 69-71.

37 The so-called *doppelte Verhältnismäßigkeit*; see Roxin, 1993, pp. 227-228.

38 Glorie, 1991, p. 141 seems to suggest that the *gendarmerie*, the judicial police and a number of corps of the municipal police have their own internal regulations on that matter.

39 See Glorie, 1991, pp. 140-141; De Valkeneer, 1991, p. 81; the only work paying some attention is *Politiepraktijk*, a book essentially concentrating on police practice. A substantial part of this paragraph is based on information originating this book.

to attain a legitimate aim. It is conceivable that such a reason or aim may be found in legal provisions containing the description of their tasks.

An important condition for to the use of handcuffs can be found in the principle of subsidiarity: When there are other less forceful means to achieve the same goals police officers may not use this instrument of restraint. In this view for instance it does not seem necessary to systematically handcuff a person in cases of administrative arrest.[40] It seems, however, that the control of the use of handcuffs in the light of the principle of subsidiarity is difficult in practice because of the fact that the conditions in which handcuffs are being used can hardly be controlled *a postiori*. In fact it is possible to distinguish two due causes for the use of handcuffs: to prevent any danger of escape and to guarantee the safety of enacting police officers or that of third parties.[41] In practice, police officers will make use of handcuffs in the following situations: During the arrest, whether it be after catching the suspect in the act or following a warrant for arrest, on persons that have been arrested administratively, in cases where it can be reasonably assumed that it is the only means of preventing a suspect from committing a criminal offence, during the transfer of a prisoner and for suspects cooperating during a reconstruction, a search or other inquests at the *locus delicti*.

For the transfer of minors[42] no handcuffs may be used in principle unless the public prosecutor has given his written authorization.[43] Note that on the grounds of art. 310 Sv suspects must be brought before the provincial court (*Hof van Assisen*) uncuffed.[44] Were the court to decide that a reconstruction of some sort must take place then the suspect may be handcuffed for reasons of safety and to make sure he will not make use of the opportunity to get away.[45]

One situation which the use of handcuffs is explicitly provided for is cross-border hot pursuit. In the event that a hot-pursuit takes place from the Netherlands, Luxembourg or Germany into Belgium, the pursuing officers may make use of handcuffs on the apprehended suspect in the conditions stated by Belgian law. The foreign police officers are habilitated to use handcuffs on the basis of the Schengen Convention, but will have to respect Belgian legislation on this matter. This means that they will have to act according to the dispositions of the WPA: Prior to resorting to the application of handcuffs on the suspect, the

---

40   Glorie, 1991, p. 140; on administrative arrest see paragraph 7.2.1.
41   De Valkeneer, 1991, p. 81.
42   In Belgium, one is major at the age of 18.
43   Ministerial circular, September 1, 1966.
44   The *Hof van Assisen*, one being present in each province, are colleges of judges formed *ad hoc* out of three professional judges and twelve laymen (known as the jury). They siege in first and last instances for the trial of severe criminal offences as well as of political and journalistic offences; see Van den Wyngaert, 1994, p. 449.
45   Cass., August 17, 1872, Pas. 1972, I, 1033.

officers will ask themselves whether the aim may be obtained in another, less forceful, way (the above-mentioned principle of subsidiarity). Where the suspect is fleeing out of France, the use of handcuffs is excluded since the French police officers do not have the power to apprehend a suspect on Belgian grounds.[46]

8.2.2.2 The Netherlands

Before the adoption of the 1994 Police Instructions there was no legal basis for the use of handcuffs in the Netherlands. Because of this, the use of such methods varied from precinct to precinct and from region to region. Some police corps used them systematically while others let it depend on the circumstances.[47] The conditions could differ depending whether the use of handcuffs was perceived as a safety measure (for instance during a ride to the police station) or as a means of constraint. In a circular dated December 20, 1991 the ministers of justice and of the interior had set a number of criteria for the legitimate use of handcuffs,[48] in which the systematic use of handcuffs for safety reasons was not considered reasonable. Further it obliged each corps to adopt instructions regulating the use of handcuffs, which instructions had to be made public.

According to art. 22 of the 1994 Police Instructions, police officers may use handcuffs when transferring a legally arrested person. This measure may only be taken when the facts and circumstances of the case give reasonable cause to do so, considering factors such as the risk of escape and danger for security or life of the arrested person, the officer or others. This measure is only allowed against a person who is legally deprived of his liberty and in relation to the circumstances of the deprivation of liberty and that of the transfer. Whether in a particular case handcuffs should be used is said to depend on the personal situation of the suspect (for instance his behaviour during arrest or any past experience with this particular suspect), whether the police automobile is specially equipped, the conditions in which the transport must take place and the possibility of reaching the same result with less drastic means. In any case the situation must be evaluated by the particular police officer.

Foreign police officers pursuing a suspect onto Dutch territory are bound to the Schengen Convention as well as to the law of the Netherlands. Of this

---

46 See the declaration of the ministers and secretaries of State in conformity to art. 41 par. 9 SC.

47 See Naeyé, 1990, pp. 314-315; note that the national ombudsman of the Netherlands had already judged several times that handcuffs should not be used systematically; see over this subject for instance reports nr. 286, 451 and 465, as well as Naeyé, 1992.

48 Circular nr. 175794/91/POL, *Onderzoek aan kleding en aanleggen van handboeien in relatie tot het recht op de onaantastbaarheid van het lichaam*, Stcrt. 1991, nr. 250.

follows not only that German and Belgian police officers will have the power to apprehend and use handcuffs on the suspect, but also that the conditions applying to the use of handcuffs in the Netherlands will have to be present. This means that the police officer must be acting in the legitimate exercise of his police task and that the use of handcuffs be proportional and subsidiary.

8.2.2.3 Luxembourg

The use of handcuffs by the Luxembourg police is not regulated by any legal provision since it is not considered as a use of physical force by the legislator of 1973.[49] We find this expressed in the explanatory statement of the statute on the use of physical force by the members of the public force. The use of handcuffs is said to be a matter to be regulated by internal instructions.[50]

A 1975 circular of the public prosecutor's department stresses, however, that the use of handcuffs should remain an exceptional measure. According to the circular the use of handcuffs should be restricted to suspects caught in the act, taking into account different factors such as the circumstances of the case, the suspect's personality and the nature of the crime. Furthermore, the judge may state in a warrant for the bringing of a suspect or for presentation at trial whether the use of particular measure, such as handcuffs, is justified. When the judge has given no indication to that effect, the police officer may use his own judgement in assessing whether to use handcuffs.

A Belgian or German police officer pursuing a suspect across the Luxembourg border have been given the power to use handcuffs on fleeing suspects, provided all the conditions contained in the Schengen Convention and Luxembourg law are fulfilled. This means that in relation to Luxembourg law, the circumstances of the particular case, the suspect's personality and the nature of the crime will have to be assessed when evaluating the opportuneness of the measure.

8.2.2.4 France

The first principle concerning means of constraint in France is that of the *non-coercion*: When operating in a regular enquiry the police must refrain from using any means of constraint. However, in cases where a suspect has been caught red-handed, the use of means of constraint, handcuffs included, will be authorized. Nevertheless there is no legal provision regulating the use of instruments such as handcuffs as a whole and, consequently, it is generally accepted that

---

49   *Loi réglant l'usage des armes et des autres moyens de contrainte par les membres de la force publique dans la lutte contre la criminalité*, July 28, 1973.
50   Explanatory statement (*Exposé des motifs*) nr. 1640, November 1972, p. 979.

the decision to use handcuffs will be left to the discretion of each police officer. In answer to a question of the *Assemblée Nationale*, the minister of justice stated in 1978 that in cases where the suspect had been caught in the act, handcuffs could and should be used, especially when the circumstances of a particular case justify special care. Circumstances as the time and place of the arrest, the personality of the suspect, danger for the arresting officer, third parties or the arrested suspect or the risk of escape are considered as such. [51]

The only written rule on the use of handcuffs by the police is that contained in art. D.294 CPP, a decree on the application of the Code of criminal procedure concerning the transfer of prisoners and, *mutatis mutandi*, to arrestees. The use of handcuffs in that case is authorized when police officers are executing an arrest warrant. In that case the police officers should have the warrant or a copy thereof in their possession in order to show it to the person to be arrested. In practice, however, the police officers will seldom have the warrant or even a copy in their possession since many of these warrants are issued by telephone. The legitimacy of the actions of police officers is presumed until the contrary has been established. Therefore, the arrested suspect may not resist the use of handcuffs, even though the arresting officers do not have the warrant on them. [52]

After a cross-border hot-pursuit the police officers may have to use handcuffs on an apprehended suspect. According to the interpretation we have retained of art. 41 par. 5 sub f SC, this would be possible for those foreign police officers who also dispose of the power to apprehend the pursued suspect. However, the French government in its declaration concerning the exercise of hot-pursuit has denied all foreign police officers the power to apprehend pursued suspects in France and in so doing has excluded all means of constraint.

8.2.2.5 Germany

Of common use when arresting suspects, two kinds of handcuffs are used in the Federal Republic. The classic metal cuffs garnished with a lock (*Handschellen*) but also disposable tie-raps (very often designated by the general appellation *Fesseln*) are both used in Germany. [53] Rules concerning conditions under which and cases where handcuffs may be used are contained in the *Landespolizeigesetzen* as well as for the federal police forces in the federal *Unmittelbare Zwangsgesetz* (UZwG).

---

51   J.O. déb. Ass. Nat., October 12, 1978, p. 6034; see also Cass. crim, August 8, 1900, Recueil Dalloz-Sirey 1902, I, 267; Trib. corr. Paris, July 1, 1969.

52   Vitu & Montreuil; Decocq, Montreuil & Buisson, 1991, p. 463.

53   The word *Fesseln*, generally meaning "something to tie up," is used in most of the legislation texts.

As an example, the provincial Police Act of Nordrhein-Westfalen (NWPolG) in art. 62 authorizes police officers to use handcuffs when arresting a person, bringing him before a judicial authority or transporting him. This is allowed when it is feared that the arrested person will injure the police officer or third parties, that he will resist arrest, that he will attempt to escape or that he will attempt to commit suicide.[54] It is not permitted to use handcuff-like objects in order to prevent an event that cannot possibly be foreseen objectively: The assumption that one of the dangers mentioned above is imminent must be assessed on the basis of concrete facts and actual circumstances.[55]

As for the use of physical force in general, the principle of proportionality applies to the use of handcuffs. In practice, this means primarily that handcuffs may not be used when this is not in proportion to the severity of the case and the necessity in the actual situation.[56] One must take the necessary precautions in order to prevent any permanent physical damage such as internal bleeding or wounds caused by handcuffs fastened too tightly.[57] Handcuffing a number of persons together must be avoided when this could have adversary effects on the further conduct of the enquiry, when this could pose health hazards for one or more of the prisoners or when this would constitute a degrading treatment. Men and women should as much as possible be handcuffed separately from one another.[58]

The German code of criminal procedure contains a virtually identical provision as that contained in the provincial statutes and in art. 8 UZwG. Like its counterparts, art. 119 par. 5 StPO applies to persons being held in custody (whether it be police custody, remand or even detention) and is particularly relevant when this detainee is provisionally placed under police responsibility, for instance during an interrogation. Although this provision is taken from the provincial police law, it does not exclusively apply to the prevention of danger (*Gefahrenabwehr*), but also to the domain of the prosecution of criminal offences.[59]

When Dutch, Belgian, Luxembourg or French police officers pursue a suspect into Germany they will be allowed to not only apprehend the suspect, but also to use handcuffs. This power is neither restricted in time nor in distance. Note, however, that the pursuing officers will have to respect the conditions of application of handcuffs as set out by German law. This means that there must

---

54 Similar provisions are found, for instance, in artt. 8 UZwG, 65 BayPAG, 59 HSOG, 62 RhPfPVG and 55 SPolG.
55 Heise/Tegtmeyer, 1990, p. 388; Kleinknecht/Meyer-Goßner, 1995, p. 405.
56 Especially the duration of the handcuffing ought to be monitored closely; Heise/Tegtmeyer, 1990, p. 388.
57 VVPolGNW 62.02.
58 VVPolGNW 62.03.
59 Heise/Tegtmeyer, 1990, p. 388.

be an imminent danger present for the safety or for escape, resting on actual facts and circumstances. The use of handcuffs must moreover be proportional to the circumstances.

8.2.3   Service Weapons

When one thinks of service weapons one thinks in the first place of firearms. Although in the framework of the Schengen Convention the expression service weapon is used, the same assumption may be tempting. Indeed, police officers may choose to use other objects to force a person to obey an order or to avert an assault. In that respect, sticks, teargas, dogs, water canons and even barbed wire and barricades to stop a fleeing vehicle could be mentioned. Other than for the use of handcuffs, the Schengen Convention does not restrict the use of the service weapon to cross-border hot pursuit, but authorizes it also for cross-border observation. The key condition is that it be in self defence. However, in the case of cross-border observation, the Convention does authorize the Contracting Parties to express reserves as to the use of service weapons. To this date, no Party has made such a reserve officially, although it appears that France and The Netherlands have done so in a memento drawn by the Schengen working group. In this section we will sketch the applicable legislation to the use of service weapons by the police in the studied countries and mention which arms are considered by these countries as service weapons for the purpose of the Schengen Convention.

8.2.3.1 Belgium

According to art. 38 par. 1 sub 3 WPA, Belgian police officers are authorized to use service weapons in order to protect the safety of objects and persons under their responsibility if this cannot be achieved otherwise. In principle police officers must first make use of other - less severe - means such as sticks, sabres, tear gas, water canons, dogs or horses. Resorting to firearms is only authorized at the latest moment possible and after a distinct warning has been given.[60]

Resorting to the above-mentioned techniques to stop fleeing vehicles may, however, only be justified in cases of banditism (robbery, organized crime), fleeing suspect vehicles and police alarm. It would not be justified to resort to such extreme techniques in cases of traffic infractions because of the principle of proportionality.[61] In principle, for public safety reasons, the G-strings will not be used on highways where traffic flows at high speed, nor at intersections

---

60   De Valkeneer, 1991, p. 92; see also Bourdoux & Brammertz, 1995, pp. 385-399.
61   According to pp. 17-18 of the *gendarmerie* course material.

that are difficult to see or that are very busy.[62] The final decision is left to the locally competent chief. Note that officers of the *gendarmerie* assisting customs officials may use their arms on the grounds of art. 192 the General Customs Act (*Algemene Douanewet*). According to this provision they are authorized to use their firearms for instance against persons who have just robbed a bank, attempt to escape, re-possess seized goods or free arrested suspects.[63]

Until recently there was no provision in Belgian law concerning the use of firearms during the hot pursuit of a vehicle. Before, the case law had decided (without any particular reasoning) that police officers have a large amount of discretion when deciding upon the use of force in general. The courts stated that there is illegal use of force when a police officer shoots on the tires of a fleeing vehicle if the driver seems not to be willing to obey the summon and escape the control.[64] Since January 1, 1993 a provision granting a legal basis for the use of force can be found in art. 38 par. 2 WPA. According to this provision the use of firearms is authorized against armed persons and their vehicles. Further there must be question of a serious criminal offence where it can be presumed that the suspect will make use of his firearms against persons.

In addition to the use of firearms as mentioned above, police officers may also be forced to resort to this kind of force when executing their task of judicial police, for instance when forcing a fleeing automobile to a halt in order to arrest the passengers. When stopping an ongoing vehicle, police officials may proceed to set up a barricade with the help of fences, gates or light cones. According to artt. 4.1, 4.2 and 4.3 of the Royal decree on the road police, even the use of devices to render cars physically unable to ride such as nails, G-strings and other sharp objects on the ground may be allowed. As this seems necessary, a police service car may be placed across the road, as well as other available material.

One finds little discussion in the literature on the so-called "shoot to kill." The law, however, authorizes the resort to firearms in case of brutal hold-ups, particularly violent aggressions, hostage taking or acts of terrorism.[65] It seems that in this manner, the legislator has created situations which are to be assimilated to cases of self defence. There is a special unit of the Belgian *gendarmerie*, the *Speciaal Interventie Eskader* (SIE) which are trained for the use of precision

---

62 G-strings are a kind of spike-mats that can be unrolled across a road; they are very damaging to tires. KB December 1, 1975, B.S. December 12, 1975. This information originates course material of the *gendarmerie* as well as from Geerits, 1989, p. 64, note 7.

63 Bruggeman & De Lentdecker, 1989, pp. 408-409.

64 HvB Brussels, June 6, 1973, J.T. 1973, 537; HvB Brussels, January 21, 1974, J.T. 1974, 352; HvB Bergen, May 28, 1976, J.T. 1977, 591.

65 *Gedrukte stukken* 1991-1992, nr. 364/2; Bourdoux & De Valkeneer, 1993, p. 179; see explanatory statement, p. 63 and Luypaers, 1993, p. 266.

weapons and the carrying out of such delicate operations.[66] The final decision is taken by the *beleidsstaf*, composed of members of both the police and the magistrature, as well as by the responsible magistrate leading the operation. In more politically sensitive cases, the decision must be authorized by the minister of justice.[67]

A foreign officer wanting to use his firearm in Belgium will have to take the following rules into account. Whether the observing or pursuing officer is Luxembourg, Belgian, Dutch, French or German, they will be subject to the Schengen Convention as well as to Belgian law concerning the concept of service weapon. Concerning the service weapon, the working group Schengen I (Police and Security), Belgium considers hand guns, sticks and tear gas spray as such.

8.2.3.2 The Netherlands

The Police Instructions, the *Ambtsinstructie* based on art. 8 PolW, came forth in 1994,[68] and contain a number of provisions regulating the use of certain service weapons specifically. They begin by expressing a number of general provisions on the use of force in general, before they pursue in regulating the use of firearms (the service pistol, the use of automatic weapons and finally the use of precision firearms) and the use of other means such as tear-gas, water-canons and electrical stick.

Art. 4 Police Instructions expresses the general principle and stipulates that the use of force is permitted only for the use of legally authorized means and for those police officers who are specially trained for the use of that means of force.[69] If the police officer is acting under the responsibility of a superior officer, he may only use force at the latter's explicit request, unless otherwise has been determined ahead of time or in situations of self defence (art. 41 Sr).

---

66   It seems that some larger municipalities such as Antwerp have tried to set up such specialized operational units.

67   Instructions of the minister of justice on the application of artt. 1, 37 and 38 WPA and circulars of December 13, 1993 and February 25, 1994 on the use of weapons and ammunition by the police (nrs. DOAD/Ops/12/C and DOAD/Ops/17/C) for the *gendarmerie*; the use of such precision firearms was confirmed and explained to us by the head of the division of international police cooperation of the APSD, P. Zanders.

68   KB 8, 1994, Stb. 1994, 275 (*Besluit houdende regels met betrekking tot een nieuwe Ambtsins-tructie voor de politie, de Koninklijke Marechaussee en de buitengewone opsporingsambtenaar en de maatregelen waaran rechtens van hun vrijheid beroofde personen kunnen worden onderworpen*); adopted by the ministers of justice and of the interior and commented in a letter addressed to the president of the second legislative chamber (*Tweede Kamer*) and dated December 14, 1992; for a general overview of the use of arms in The Netherlands, see Bourdoux & Brammertz, 1995, pp. 370-385.

69   See also Van Kooten, 1994, pp. 20-23.

The Police Instructions of 1994 stipulate as well that the superior officer, indeed when present, must indicate which means of constraint should be used (art. 5). Further service weapons should not be used against persons or vehicles in which persons might find themselves unless may be reasonably expected that these persons are immediately capable of using firearms against others.

The Police Instructions continue by regulating a number of means of force: firearms (artt. 7-12), tear gas (art. 13), water canons (art. 14), police dogs (art. 15) and electrical police sticks (art. 16). The Police Instructions distinguish between a firearm with which cannot be fired automatically (art.7), a firearm with which can be fired automatically (art. 8) and long-distance precision firearms (art.9).

Firearms with which cannot be fired aut ₁atically may be used in the following cases (art. 7): to compel an uncooperative suspect of a serious crime to cooperate with his arrest or other legitimate restriction of liberty when it can be reasonably expected that he is armed and will use his weapon against persons (par. a), to arrest a person who has or who is illuding arrest and who is suspected to have committed a crime constituting a gross violation of the legal order (par. b) or for quelling a riot (par. c). However, in all these cases there will be no use of force authorized, when the identity of the suspect is known and delaying the arrest would not cause unreasonable danger (art. 7 par. 3). Use of automatic weapons, on the other hand, is only authorized in situations where there is a serious danger of immediate and illegal assault against persons, when arresting dangerous suspects and to guard persons and objects. The transport of such automatic weapons is only allowed according explicit authorization of the public prosecutor and with written procuration of the minister of justice. Finally, the use of precision firearms is authorized exclusively in case of severe crimes and to prevent direct danger for the life of others.[70] Transporting such weapons is only permitted by the competent authority and with a written procuration of the minister of justice.

A police officer is allowed to draw his firearm as a preventive measure for his own safety or that of others in cases where he reasonably expects the use of a firearm to be allowed (art. 10). This is, however, not considered use of force by the instructions (art. 1). To aim his firearm, there must be a situation where the use of firearms is authorized (art. 11). The officer must give a distinct warning, eventually a warning shot, before he proceeds to use his firearm.

When a police officer has been compelled to use physical force (including of his service weapon), he must report it in writing and without delay to his superior officer along with the reasons that led to the use of force. When the

---

70 Whether shoot to kill is given a legal basis by this provision may be disputed. However, it does create a legal basis for the precise aiming at someone in certain circumstances to neutralize this person. This will be discussed further below.

use of force has resulted in significant harm or injury or when a firearm has been used, it must not only be reported to the superior officer, but also to the public prosecutor of the district where the incident has taken place. A complete report must be drawn up within 48 hours when, in the opinion of the superior officer, the consequences of the use of force justifies it or the use of force has resulted in death (artt. 17 - 19).

In cases where it may reasonably be expected that persons will resist arrest in a violent way and may even resort to using weapons, the Dutch police may resort to sending an arrest-team. Arrest-teams consist of specially equipped and trained police officers who, not taking any chances with their lives and the lives of others, arrest suspects using an increased level of physical force. This implies for instance the use of rams to open doors, noise-grenades (the so-called stun grenade), handcuffs, automatic weapons and bags to cover the head of the suspect.[71]

The police are further authorized to use different techniques and means to stop a fleeing vehicle. In practice, the police officer limits himself to the use of a stop sign. If the vehicle omits to stop, the police officer may take note of his licence plate number and the driver will be fined subsequently. However it is possible that the police officer decides to pursue the vehicle or use roadblocks.[72] In this case the police officer must keep in mind that he must act according to the principles of subsidiarity and of proportionality.[73]

The regulation of the "shoot to kill" procedure seems to be found in art. 9 of the 1994 Police Instructions, where the use of long-distance precision firearms is regulated. As we have stated above, the use of such weapons is only authorized in the case of very severe crimes to avert immediate danger for the life of persons and when used by officers specially trained to handle these weapons. The use of such firearms is only authorized under the orders of the commanding officer. The decision to transport or carry such firearms is only authorized either for the purpose of training or the actual repression of very severe crimes for which there is a direct life threatening situations. Carrying such arms is only permitted after authorization of the local mayor and written approbation of the minister of justice. Although the text of the decree does not explicitly mention whether this approbation also covers the actual use of

---

71   Circular of the ministry of the interior concerning arrestation teams (*Circulaire van de Minister van Binnenlandse zaken van 25 september 1979, nr. EA 79/U 1384, OOV, Directie Politie, Afdeling O en U, aan de Commissarissen der Koningin, betreffende arrestatieteams*); cases of the national ombudsman nr. 106 and 167, in Naeyé, 1992.

72   Naeyé, 1990, p. 443.

73   HR December 12, 1978, NJ 1979, 142; see further Naeyé, 1990, pp. 465 *et seq.*

precision firearms, it seems logical that this final decision is delegated to the commanding officer.[74]

German, Luxembourg and Belgian police officers on Dutch territory will be subject to the Schengen Convention. According to the above mentioned memento on cross-border cooperation, Dutch police officers dispose of two service weapons: a stick and a semi-automatic handgun. Foreign police officers acting on Dutch territory during an observation are only authorized to carry these two weapons. Carrying other weapons is only authorized, as long as these other weapons are part of the standard equipment of police officers of that member state, in the case of cross-border hot pursuit in urgent case not necessiting prior authorization.

8.2.3.3 Luxembourg

The use of weapons by the members of the Luxembourg public force is regulated by the Force Act of 1973 (*Loi règlant l'usage des armes et des moyens de contrainte*).[75] This statute restricts the use of weapons to a number of circumstances. The use of firearms and of other weapons bearing blades (for instance a bayonet) or sticks (*armes blanches*)[76] is authorized in four situations: When violence is being done towards a police officer, when life, physical integrity or goods are being threatened, when it proves impossible to defend a place against an armed assault in any other way and to stop someone who has been summoned to do so. Furthermore the statute states that police officers are authorized to use their weapons to stop the completion of a criminal offence.

The fact that one of these situations occurs does not automatically mean that the use of a weapon is legitimate. Case law states that even when the police notices one of these situations, the decision to use weapons is subjected to another criterion: self defence.[77] Art. 416 CP states that self defence is the situation where physical force is immediately necessary to defend oneself or another or when it is used against a night burglar or armed robber (art. 417 CP).

Police officers may use weapons in self defence when they are on duty. Considered as one of these situations is the hot pursuit of a suspect who has been summoned to stop. When the suspect refuses to stop after having been warned twice with the words: "*Halte! Police!*" or "*Halte! Gendarmerie!*" he may be stopped with the help of a weapon. Indeed a person stopped in that way must be seriously suspected of a severe criminal offence for which he is wanted by the judicial authorities, a warrant for his arrest having been issued or he must

---

74   See on the "shoot to kill" question: Boek, 1995, pp. 217-225.
75   Mém. 1973, 1094, July 28, 1973.
76   The explanatory statement considers knives and sticks as *armes blanches*.
77   Tr. Arr. Luxembourg, July 10, 1981, ref.: 480/81.

be an escaped convict (art. 1 par. 4 Force Act). Further weapons may be used against a fleeing robber who has ignored repeated calls to stop or to stop a vehicle that causes danger to the life or the physical integrity of a person (art. 2 par. 1 Force Act).

During a control operation or an enquiry it may prove necessary to stop a vehicle. Art. 8 Force Act states that officers of the police or of the *gendarmerie* may use special equipment at the order of a superior officer or, the judicial authority or at their own initiative. They may use cables, fences, barbed wire, nets and other similar means. According to the explanatory statement the expression "other similar means" (*autres moyens analogues*) designates other material that may be found on the spot. In extreme cases it may be authorized to shoot at a fleeing vehicle when it seems that this is the only way to bring it to a stop. This may especially be the case of suspect vehicles that are trying to avoid the road block. (art. 2 par. 3 Force Act).

It is unknown whether the so-called "shoot to kill" with high precision firearms is authorized or specifically regulated in Luxembourg. However, further analysis of the Force Act seems at the very least not to explicitly exclude the resort to such means. In that case, the use of service weapons in that way would have to be in accordance of the provisions contained in the Force Act. The use of service weapons in that way must be compatible with the conditions stated above (art. 1 Force Act). Art. 2 par. 4 Force Act authorizes to use service weapons in order to stop the imminent commission of a severe criminal offence or its continuation when according to the circumstances, it constitutes either a *crime* or a *délit* committed with the help of arms or explosives. Sources in the police have confirmed the existence in Luxembourg of specially trained units that, in the occurrence of facts and circumstances justifying such an intervention, stand ready to act. Because of the absence of a specific text on the procedure to be followed in such sensitive situations, the question of who will take the responsibility for the final - deadly - decision remains unanswered. It is likely that this decision will be taken by one of the political figures responsible.

In the event that German, Belgian or French police officers observing or pursuing a suspect onto Luxembourg territory, these will only be authorized to carry blank or fire arms as carried by members of their own police corps. In any case this seems to be the consequence of the memento drawn by the Schengen working group. The only restriction made by the Luxembourg authorities is that the service weapons be put at the disposal of the police by a hierarchic superior. There is no further specification as to the type of weapon in the above mentioned memento on cross border cooperation. This implies the absence of restrictions as to the weapon that may be carried by foreign police officers during cross border operations.

8.2.3.4 France

In principle French police officers may only use their weapons in self defence.[78] One situation where the modalities of the use of service weapons by officers habilitated to make summons is regulated is that of the dispersion of a crowd. After two summons the public force may disperse a crowd (art. 431-3 NCP). The article states that the resort to the use of force will only be justified when there is danger of violence against the officers or when there is no other way to defend the place they are occupying, thus expressing the principle of subsidiarity. According to a circular of 1961 the use of constraint is not limited to the use of service weapons but includes all forms of constraint and physical force in general against persons, such as force used during charges.[79]

An important disposition for the use of weapons is art. 3 of the *ordonnance* of December 23, 1958 concerning the use of weapons and the instalment of barricades by the *Police Nationale*.[80] With this disposition the police officers are authorized to force a person to stop when this person has ignored a summon. For officers of the *gendarmerie* another disposition applies, namely that of art. 174 of the organic decree of May 20, 1903.[81] This disposition authorizes the use of weapons in certain circumstances, such as the situation where a suspect does not stop after having been summoned with the words: "*Halte gendarmerie!*" and it does not seem possible to stop him any other way. One could speak here of a kind of principle of subsidiarity. Another provision of the above mentioned *ordonnance* authorizes officers of the *Police Nationale* to set up road blocks, to use cables and other technical means such as barbed wire and nets when trying to force a fleeing vehicle to stop. The use of weapons to this end is, however, prohibited for the *policiers* but not for the *gendarmes*. Indeed the latter are authorized to do so after having summoned the suspect to stop.[82]

Whether shooting with the aim to kill is authorized formally in France is doubtful, even though this seems to happen in practice.[83] One may imagine

---

78 Decocq, Montreuil & Buisson, 1991, p. 265; see also Machielse, 1986, pp. 289-481.
79 Circular nr. 198, April 22, 1961; see further Decocq, Montreuil & Buisson, 1991, p. 401 *et seq.*
80 *Ordonnance du 23 décembre 1958 relative à l'usage des armes et à l'établissement de barrages de circulations par le personnel de la police*, nr. 58-1309.
81 Modified by the *décret* of July 22, 1943.
82 Art. 174 of the before-mentioned *décret* van May 20, 1903.
83 An example of this was given by the outcome of the kidnapping in the Parisian suburb Neuilly in May 1993: police officers of the *Unité de recherche, d'assistance, d'intervention et de dissuasion* (RAID) shot a kidnapper in his sleep. See on this operation the Dutch weekly *Panorama*, November 25, 1993; another example is given by the outcome of the man-chase organized to catch Khaleb Kelkal, the chief suspect in the series of bombings in the Paris metro. Kelkal was shot dead by units of the *gendarmerie*. The official version alleges that the officers shot Kelkal in self defence, although an amateur film tape shows Kelkal on the

that such situations are considered a state of emergency but shoot to kill actions find no basis in domestic law. However, both the Police National and the gendarmerie have their specially trained and specially equipped sharp shooters for those special situations. Information on these special units are classified tactical information and can only be found in non official documentary sources.

Police officers originating Germany, Belgium or Luxembourg who must operate on French territory will be authorized to carry his service weapon. According to the memento on cross border cooperation, this designates in France a hand gun, a tear gas grenade, a stick and hand cuffs. In the course of a cross border observation as regulated by art. 40 SC, foreign police officers will not be authorized to carry other weapons than those carried by French police officers. However, this implies that in the case of cross border hot pursuit (with or without prior authorization) other weapons may be carried.

8.2.3.5 Germany

The federal *Strafvollzugsgesetz* (StVollzG) contains general provisions as well as specific regulations on the use of firearms.[84] According to art. 99 par. 1 of this statute, police officers may only use their firearms when other - less drastic - means have proved ineffective, while application against persons is only authorized when application against objects has no effect. The second paragraph adds a supplementary condition to the effect that the use of firearms is only permitted to avert a possible assault or to prevent the suspect's escape. Firearms may not be used when this may result in great risks for the safety of third parties, unless this is the only way the life of a third party can be saved.[85] Par. 3 states finally that prior to any directed shot the officers must give a warning (eventually in the form of a warning shot). Shooting without warning is only authorized in cases of self defence of life and limb of oneself or others. Art. 100 StVollzG allows the possibility to use firearms against violent, rebelling or fleeing prisoners as well as against anyone trying to help prisoners escape.[86]

German police officers are further authorized to use technical instruments of force (*Hilfsmittel der körperlichen Gewalt*). These are worked out in provincial statutes, most of which have been taken over from the Model Statute for

---

ground while an unidentified voice orders to finish him off. See de Volkskrant, Octobre 4, 1995.

84 *Gesetz über den Vollzug der Freiheitsstrafe und der freiheitsentziehenden Maßregeln der Besserung und Sicherung.*

85 Götz, 1991, p. 164; because of the fact that such a use of firearms is considered preventive police work the *Staatsanwalt* is not competent to give indications or orders to use firearms in such a manner.

86 For a general overview of the use of arms in Germany, see Bourdoux & Brammertz, 1995, pp. 348-369.

a Uniform Police Act (*Musterentwurf* - MEPolG). These include such technical means as water canons, road block attributes and drugs to temporarily knock persons out of conscience. This list is not exhaustive and such tools as crowbars for opening doors, agents to limit the sight (fogging agents). The use of these technical means are subjected to the same prerequisites as the use of force. Force may be used when it is necessary to avert an actual danger, especially when other means are not possible or are not expected to be successful and when the police officer is competent.[87]

The use of firearms in order to execute an arrest is in most of the provinces only permitted in cases of *Verbrechen*, with the additional condition that other less drastic means do not suffice to realize the arrest and that the actual use of the firearm is preceded by a warning.[88] A directed shot with the purpose to kill a kidnapper (*gezielter Todesschuß*) may in certain circumstances be authorized when this seems to be the only way to render the person harmless and to eliminate danger for others.[89]

Although the above mentioned memento on cross border cooperation only mentions what is considered a service weapon in Germany without specifying which weapon will be considered as such when carried by foreign police officers acting in the framework of a cross border operation, one may suppose that these will be the same. As far as the use of the service weapon is concerned, the foreign police officer acting in the framework of the Schengen Convention will be admitted to carry any weapon used by a police force and placed at the disposition of the police officers by their hierarchic superiors. In all of the German provinces, these include the stick, the hand gun, the revolver and the automatic hand gun. There is no restriction mentioned as to whether these may be carried only during an observation or during a cross border hot pursuit.

8.2.4 Concepts of Self Defence and Use of Service Weapons

The Schengen Convention authorizes the use of the service weapon in self defence, bringing about two important questions. Firstly, what is self defence and secondly, what is actual use. Because the Schengen Convention does not offer any definition of these two concepts and short of a common negociated definition, the answer will be found in the different national law systems.

---

87 Rachor, 1992, pp. 348-349; see for instance artt. 50 and 57 *et seq.* NWPolG.
88 Roxin, 1993, p. 228; see for instance art. 64 NWPolG; Heise/Tegtmeyer, 1990, pp. 389-402. For statistical information on the deadly use of firearms by the police in Germany, we refer to B & P 1991-1, pp. 71-74, 1992-1, pp. 61-63; 1993-1, pp. 79-85, 1994-1, pp. 59-64 and 1995-1, pp. 69-71.
89 Götz, 1991, p. 163.

During the Schengen debates in The Netherlands, the christian-democratic fraction of the Dutch parliament asked the government what was meant with the expression "self defence" in artt. 40 par. 3 sub d and 41 par. 5 sub e of the Convention. The government replied that the notion of self defence was limited to situations where there is an acute threat to the life of oneself or another. The government continued: "Though the different countries know detail differences in their national law relating to the concept of self defence, this interpretation of the expression proved to be practicable."[90]

This interpretation of the concept of self defence, however, is supported neither by the Convention nor by any subsequent - official - declaration of the Contracting Parties. That the differences of interpretation of this notion in the different countries only be detail differences is an affirmation that must be verified. Although some differences may appear to be detail differences, they can prove to have more practical consequences.

The concept of self defence as an exception or defence for the use of force against a person, which use of force might otherwise be considered a criminal offence, is developed in different ways in the studied countries. Although one may consider the right to self defence as an expression of the natural right one should have to defend oneself against illegitimate assaults, different law systems may view this right more or less restrictively, including or excluding different aspects such as provoked assaults or defence against someone acting in a state of mind where intention is absent. It is relevant to look more closely at the different views on self defence in studying the use of physical force. Indeed this can have significant consequences when it comes to cross-border operations by the police since the officers will be subject to the law of the country they are entering. They will often have to face a different definition of self defence than the one they are used to.

When studying and summarizing the different theories relevant to self defence, one often comes across the concept of excessive self defence (*noodweer-exces*). Self defence may be considered a justifying fact, legitimizing the use of force while excessive self defence may be considered an excuse for the disproportional use of self defence. The former is thus an objective factor while the latter is a subjective one. Furthermore, self defence exists when a number of external objective factors are present (an assault), while excessive self defence

---

90 " *Ondanks detailverschillen in interpretatie van het begrip noodweer in het nationale recht van Partijen bleek deze invulling van het begrip praktisch hanteerbaar..*" TK 1991-1992, 22 140, nr. 12, p. 34. This interpretation also proved later to be inaccurate since members of a Schengen working group quoted above have worked out the definition of self defence in a Schengen memento: It seems that instead of taking the most restrictive view on self defence as the standard, the parties seem to favour the more extensive definition, allowing the self defence of goods as well as of life and limb. We will return to this point later.

may be invoked as an excuse when a number of subjective factors are present (fear, desperation). However, since the text of the Schengen Convention does not mention this excuse, which is actually very logical since it does not constitute a justifying factor for the use of force, we will restrict our study to the concept of self defence as such.

Further, we will address the question of the actual use of the service weapon in the various countries. This, for an important reason: The Schengen Convention authorizes use of service weapons in case of self defence. Is use of service weapons exclusively shooting with a firearm or throwing a tear gas grenade, or is the mere threat to do so considered use of service weapons as well. What is to say of taking a weapon in one's hand as a preventive measure? If it is not considered use of service weapons, it will be authorized even outside self defence situations. This is of great importance in those tense moments where self defence is not (yet) an issue.

8.2.4.1 Belgium

Self Defence

One speaks of self defence (*wettige verdediging* or *légitime défense*) in a situation where a person, in order to defend himself or another person, averts an illegitimate assault with the help of beating, wounding or manslaughter (art. 416 Sw).[91] Art. 416 Sw treats such a situation as a criminal exception when the beating, wounding or manslaughter is the result of the immediate necessity of self defence or of defence of another. In the doctrine it is stressed that self defence should be considered not as a general but as a specific justification, the application of which is limited to beating, wounding and manslaughter. Note as well that this justification may only be invoked in situation of illegitimate assault on persons. It represents no justification in situations of illegitimate assault on material goods.[92]

The assault must be illegitimate in order to justify the exception of self defence. This means to say that one is not entitled to avert an assault that would be considered legitimate, for instance when a police officer tries to arrest someone legally. In this situation the arrest by the police officer could not be interpreted as an illegitimate assault and the arrested person would not be able to invoke the exception of self defence if he were to harm the officer. Furthermore the illegitimate assault must be inevitable in the sense that the assaulted

---

91   "*Er is noch misdaad, noch wanbedrijf, wanneer de doodslag, de verwondingen en de slagen geboden zijn door de ogenblikkelijke noodzaak van de wettige verdediging van zich zelf of van een ander.*" See also Van den Wyngaert, 1994, p. 184.

92   Van den Wyngaert, 1994, p. 184; see also on the concept of self defence and the use of firearms in Belgium Bourdoux & Brammertz, 1995, pp. 396-399.

person has no possibility to respond otherwise than with the use of violence. This has to do with the wording of art. 416 Sw that uses the words "immediately necessary" (*actuellement nécessaire* or *ogenblikkelijk noodzakelijk*). It must be an assault on persons whether it be himself or another. The assault must (potentially) jeopardize the personal integrity of those against whom the assault is directed: This is the case not only when the physical integrity of a person is at stake, but also his freedom or virtue (*honneur* or *eerbaarheid*).[93]

The act of defence must be immediately necessary. This means that it would not have been possible to avert the assault in another way. In this we can see an expression of the principle of subsidiarity. Whether this means that there would be an obligation, where possible, to flee for the assaulted person is unclear. According to some this would be the case, but it would depend on the factual circumstances.[94] The defence must furthermore be in proportion to the assault. These two principles must be seen as complementary to each other since if an assault could have been averted in another way, it will be considered as non-proportional. The reverse is also true: When an act of defence can be considered disproportional, then the assault could have been averted in another way.[95]

The act of defence must have taken place prior to or during the assault, not after. Indeed an act of defence after the assault is over cannot be seen as a defence that is "immediately necessary." One would then speak of revenge rather than of defence. This means that a person shooting a fleeing assaulter will not be able to invoke the criminal exception of self defence.[96] A woman killing her husband during his sleep after he has been beating her in drunken rage is not considered by the Belgian case law as acting in self defence either.[97]

Whether the definition of self defence discussed above is also valid for police officers acting in cross-border hot pursuit may be the subject of some discussions on the hand of what has been said by the Dutch government during the Schengen debate. However, it is likely that the above-mentioned conditions for self defence will play a role in determining whether foreign police officials have indeed acted in self defence. Conditions such as an illegitimate assault, subsidiarity, proportionality and necessity, as well as the condition that the defence must occur during the illegitimate assault are of such a general nature

---

93 Antwerp, May 27, 1981, R.W. 1983-84, 1989, with note by P. Arnou.
94 Van den Wyngaert, 1994, p. 185.
95 See Cass. December 23, 1986, A.Cc, 1986/87, 577; Corr. Tongeren, June 21, 1990, R.W., 1990/91, with note by B. Spriet.
96 Corr. Luik, March 21, 1980, Jur. Liège, 1981, 37, note F. Piedboeuf.
97 Gent, December 11, 1963, R.W., 1963/64, 1656.

that they may be considered to apply to the actions of foreign police officers as well.

Actual Use of Service Weapons

As for the use of service weapons as such, neither in the artt. 37 *et seq.* nor the literature offers any details as to what is considered use of service weapons. However, especially in the light of art. 38 WPA *in fine* where it is stated that before service weapons may be used the police officers must give a warning, either orally and distinctly or with a warning shot. Considering the fact that such a warning shot is not - yet - considered "use" of service weapons as such since it belongs to the preliminary phase of the resort to force, then *a contrario* it must be concluded that actual use cannot be less than the directed use of the service weapon.

8.2.4.2 The Netherlands

Self Defence

Self defence (*noodweer*) is an exception to criminal responsibility because it justifies the offence that has been committed.[98] Art. 41 Sr states that one who commits a criminal offence commanded by the necessary defence of the physical integrity, virtue (*eerbaarheid*) or goods of oneself or of others against an immediate illegitimate assault will not be criminally responsible.[99] As the text states, the Dutch legislator has set limits to the exercise of this exception of self defence. Indeed there must be an assault that is on the verge of immediately being committed and this assault must be illegitimate. Furthermore, only physical integrity, virtue and material things may be defended and not rights such as the domestic peace.[100] With the expressions physical integrity (*lijf*), virtue and goods, the article aims to protect life, physical integrity, sexual virtue and physical goods in the sense of civil law.[101]

Firstly, the act of self defence must be weighed against the principle of subsidiarity: Was there not another action possible that would have been less damaging? Secondly, the defence action must be proportional to the assault: The means used to defend one's interest must be proportional to the means of assault. The wording of the article "commanded by the necessary defence"

---

98 For a detailed study on self defence, see Machielse, 1986.
99 *"Niet strafbaar is hij, die een feit begaat, geboden door de noodzakelijke verdediging van eigen of een anders lijf, eerbaarheid of goed tegen ogenblikkelijke, wederrechtelijke aanranding."*
100 HR May 7, 1974, NJ 1974, 300; see also Jörg & Kelk, 1992, pp. 128 *et seq..*
101 Wemes, 1994, p. 202; see also on the concept of self defence and the use of firearms in The Netherlands Bourdoux & Brammertz, 1995, pp. 380-384.

(*geboden door de noodzakelijke verdediging*) indicates the weight given to the condition of proportionality and subsidiarity.[102]

When reading the explanatory statement, one notes that the legislator established three conditions for the exercise of self defence as an excuse for the use of physical force. Firstly, there is no self defence without an illegitimate assault, secondly, there must be an immediate danger for one's physical integrity, virtue or good or that of another and thirdly, it must be necessary to use force in order to avert the actual and inevitable danger.[103]

The concept of assault (*aanranding*) is not limited to the only factual physical aggression on the integrity, virtue or goods of a person but may also include the behaviour that poses an immediate menace of danger.[104] Although the assault does not have to constitute a criminal offence in itself, there can be no assault when the victim is consenting. Furthermore the only fear of an assault is not enough to justify any acts of self defence.[105] The assault must be immediate (*ogenblikkelijk*). This means that the act of self defence will be justified at the moment the assault is beginning or is imminent. Indeed there can be no self defence once the assault has come to an end, and any act of self defence after the assault has ended will not be considered self defence.[106] The assault must also be illegitimate, which means without right or competence, illegal or unlawful. For instance one may not invoke the exception of self defence when averting an assault constituting an act of self defence in itself. In that case the assault would be legitimate.[107]

When it comes to the use of force in any situation, whether the person using the force be a citizen or a police officer, the principles of proportionality and subsidiarity play a crucial role in the legitimacy of the force used. In the context of self defence these two principles are embodied as we have stated above in the wording "commanded by the necessary defence." The use of the word "necessary" indicates that the defence must be appropriate. Although it is difficult to draw a clear line between the concepts of proportionality and subsidiarity in this article, one may note that the idea of proportionality lies with the word "necessary" while the subsidiarity rather insists on the idea of "commanded."[108] At any rate one should be aware that there must be a balance between the aim (averting the assault), the severity of the assault and the means.

102 See HR June 13 1989, NJ 1990, 193; see also Jörg & Kelk, 1992, p. 129.
103 See Machielse, 1986, pp. 481 *et seq.* for an in depth analysis of the concept of self defence in the Netherlands; Jörg & Kelk, 1992, p. 129; Wemes, 1994, pp. 200 *et seq.*
104 HR February 2, 1965, NJ 1965, 262; HR March 30, 1976, NJ 1976, 322.
105 See HR February 8 1932, NJ 1932, 617; HR January 8, 1974, NJ 1974, 131; HR June 24, 1975, NJ 1976, 60; HR September 18, 1989, NJ 1990, 291.
106 HR November 22, 1949, NJ 1950, 179; see also Wemes, 1994, p. 201.
107 HR May 27, 1986, NJ 1987, 6; Wemes, 1994, p. 201.
108 See Machielse, 1986, pp. 647 *et seq.*; Wemes, 1994, p. 202.

When assessing the subsidiarity one must ask oneself whether the aim could have been attained with another, less forceful means. In the idea of subsidiarity the choice of the means plays a crucial role.

Actual Use of Service Weapons

In the Netherlands, a police officer is considered using his service weapon at the moment he is drawing it with the intention of using it, which, in turn, is only authorized in situations where actual use is allowed. The Instructions for the police distinguish, rather ambivalently, between taking a weapon in the hand as a prevention measure and drawing a weapon in situations where the use of weapons is allowed (artt. 10 and 11 Police Instructions).[109] According to art. 1 par. 3 sub c Police Instructions, taking a weapon in your hand as a prevention measure is not considered use of force. Consequently, the only logical interpretation of the Instructions lies in for which reason the officer takes his weapon. Drawing his weapon, without aiming is only allowed as a preventive measure in cases where he suspects that a situation in which he will be authorized to use his weapon will occur. Actually using the weapon goes one step further. The use of a firearms is considered aiming and holding at aim of a firearm (art. 1 par. 3 sub j Police Instructions), while art. 11 Police Instructions states that drawing the firearm is only allowed in circumstances where using the firearm is authorized. Therefore, using a firearm begins with the movement of drawing the firearm with the intention of using it.

8.2.4.3 Luxembourg

Self Defence

Self defence as a justification for resorting to physical force is accepted in Luxembourg only when it comes to legitimately defending oneself or another when homicide, wounds or blows were commanded by the actual necessity (art. 417 CP).[110] One cannot speak of self defence when defending a material good, although the case law does indeed recognize a certain right to defend one's property when the means used are proportional to the attack.[111] The physical force used by a police officer while on duty is legitimate when it is necessary for the enforcement of law and judicial decisions as long as they do not transgress what is strictly necessary.[112] Self defence may only be invoked

---

109 Although the text makes a slight textual distinction between "taking in the hand for prevention" (*uit voorzorg ter hand nemen*) and "drawing" (*trekken*) the factual consequences, the actual movement of the officer, will probably be difficult to distinguish from one another.

110 "*Il n'y a ni crime ni délit lorsque l'homicide, les blessures et les coups étaient commandés par la nécessité actuelle de la légitime défense de soi-même ou d'autrui.*"

111 Cour December 6, 1974, Pas. 23. 235; see also art. 417 CP.

112 Cour May 1, 1897, Pas. 4. 438.

when the assault is unjustified. From this follows that resisting arrest with violence cannot be qualified as self defence when the use of force by the officers was rendered necessary in order to enforce the law. This is also valid for the enforcement of warrants and judgements.[113]

Actual Use of Service Weapons

As for the use of service weapons as such, there are no provisions explicitly stating at which moment an officer is considered to have used his weapon. However, the wording of artt. 1 *et seq*. Force act as well as the fact that no article specifies what is to be understood with "use," suggest that actually shooting should be considered as actual using.

8.2.4.4 France

Self Defence

According to art. 122-5 CP one speaks of self defence when a person is forced to use force to defend himself, another person or a good against an unjustified assault, when this force is commanded by the necessity of self defence and as long as the force used is not disproportionate to the severity of the assault.[114] Further a person who attempts to stop the commission of a criminal offence against a good with an act of defence other than a voluntary homicide, is not criminally responsible when this act of defence is necessary for the pursued aim and the means employed are proportional to the severity of the criminal offence.[115] Another provision (art. 122-7 CP) states that someone is not criminally responsible when facing an immediate danger menacing himself, others or a good and accomplishes an act necessary for the safeguard of the person or the good, except when the force used is disproportionate to the severity of the menace.[116]

---

113 Cass. June 26, 1980, P. 25. 11.

114 Art. 122-5 CP reads "*N'est pas pénalement responsible la personne qui, devant une atteinte injustifiée envers elle-même ou autrui, accomplit, dans le même temps, un acte commandé par la nécessité de la légitime défense d'elle-même ou d'autrui, sauf s'il y a disproportion entre les moyens de défense employés et la gravité de l'atteinte.*"

115 Art. 122-5 par. 2 CP: "*N'est pas pénalement responsable la personne qui, pour interrompre l'execution d'un crime ou d'un délit contre un bien, accomplit un acte de défense, autre qu'un homicide volontaire, lorsque cet acte est strictement nécessaire au but poursuivi dès lors que les moyens employés sont proportionnés à la gravité de l'infraction.*"

116 Art. 122-7 CP: "*N'est pas pénalement responsable la personne qui, face à un danger actuel ou imminent qui menace elle-même, autrui ou un bien, accomplit un acte nécessaire à la sauvegarde de la personne ou du bien, sauf s'il y a disproportion entre les moyens employés et la gravité de la menace.*"

The predecessor of the present code was especially vague in its distinction between self defence of persons and self defence of goods. The new code, in force since March 1, 1994, was partly successful in clarifying the situation. For unjustified assault on persons it kept the former conditions of immediacy, necessity and proportionality whereas for averting a *crime* or *délit* against a good the conditions of strict necessity and proportionality are demanded. This means for instance that voluntary manslaughter is explicitly excluded to avert assaults on goods.[117]

It is likely that the case law relating to the former definition of self defence of a person will keep its validity as an interpretation tool under the new disposition.[118] Self defence may apply not only to *crimes* and *délits* but also to *contraventions* with light violence.[119] It is only authorized to avert an actual danger because only at that moment defence becomes necessary.[120] It is not necessary that the victim be threatened by death in order to invoke self defence but the assault must have a certain degree of severity.[121] The assault must be unjustified: A person may not invoke self defence when he has resisted arrest and in so doing wounded police officers.[122] Furthermore, the actions of the police as such, even supposing they were illegal, may not be considered as actual necessity justifying self defence and resort to violence.[123]

Actual Use of Service Weapons
The police officer is using his service weapon when he is actually shooting it. Some authors see in the wording of art. D. 7 CP combined with a circular dated March 4, 1987[124] that actually firing an service weapon (or throwing a teargas grenade) is considered using it as such.[125]

---

117 See Poncella, 1993, p. 460.
118 See further on self-defence according to the former legislation: Rassat, 1987, pp. 398-407; Machielse, 1986.
119 Crim. November 20 1956, Bull. crim. nr. 761.
120 Crim. June 27, 1927, S. 1929 1. 356.
121 Crim. October 11, 1956, Bull. Crim. nr. 630; Crim. May 22, 1959, Bull. crim. nr. 268.
122 Crim. February 9, 1972, Bull. Crim. nr. 54.
123 Crim. September 15, 1864, S. 1865 1. 152.
124 NOR:*MIDSD8700057C*; the circular states that use of force must be preceeded by warnings and sommations.
125 See Decocq, Montreuil & Buisson, 1991, p. 403 (nr. 867 note 2).

8.2.4.5 Germany

Self Defence

A police officer legitimately performing an arrest may in some cases invoke the exception of self defence (*Notwehr*).[126] On the basis of art. 32 StGB, self defence is the use of physical force necessary to avert an actual assault against one self or another.[127]

An assault is an actual threat of harm or harm that has not yet been achieved to a subjective right or interest (*Rechtsgut*), even when the resulting harm is not the intention of the assailant. Self defence can exist even in cases where the assault is not the result of any fault or where the assailant is not aware of his actions. The assailant must be a human being.[128] The assault must further be directed against any interest, whether it be life, limb, liberty or virtue (*Ehre*), reputation (*Recht am eigenen Bild*), intimacy (*Intimsphäre*), property or possession (*Eigentum oder Besitz*).[129] The assault must furthermore be actual, which means that it does not suffice that the assault be probable: it must be imminent.[130] The case law gives as examples when the assailant reaches for his weapon or when he aims at the victim. The intention to harm the interest of someone must be apparent in fact. The assault must be illegitimate as well, which means that the assailant must lack the competence for his actions. In other words, if the assailant is legitimately using force, for instance as a police officer, the victim cannot invoke self defence.[131]

The action to avert the assault must consist in a defensive action and must be necessary. The person trying to avert the assault must act with the intention of defending his interest and direct his action against the assailant.[132] The action must also be necessary to avert the assault. It must be necessary in the objective situation and not only in the imagination of the alleged victim.[133] It must be proportional at the moment of the assault from the point of view of the victim and furthermore proportional considering the whole of the circumstances. The victim may use the means he has at hand. Proportionality must only exist between the assault and the defence and not between the importance of

---

126 Kleinknecht/Meyer-Goßner, 1995, pp. 432 and 589; see on the concept of self defence and the use of firearms in Germany also Bourdoux & Brammertz, 1995, pp. 362-365.

127 "*Wer eine Tat begeht, die durch Notwehr geboten ist, handelt nicht rechtswidrig. Notwehr ist die Verteidigung, die erforderlich ist, um einen gegenwärtigen rechtswidrigen Angriff von sich oder einem anderen abzuwenden.*"

128 Dreher/Tröndle, 1993, p. 234.

129 See for more examples Dreher/Tröndle, 1993, pp. 234-235.

130 RG 64, 101.

131 See further Dreher/Tröndle, 1993, pp. 236-237.

132 Dreher/Tröndle, 1993, p. 238.

133 BGH 3, 196.

the assaulted interest and the danger it ran on the one hand and the importance of the interest menaced by the defence action and the danger it ran on the other hand. Finally, the action of defence must be one that imposes itself.[134]

Actual Use of Service Weapons
One finds in art. 99 par. 2 StVollzG an indication of what is meant by use of service weapons in German law. This provision states that before the use of service weapons, there must be a warning. This warning may also consist in a warning shot, implying that this warning shot does not (yet) consist in actual use of a firearm. The actual use of the service weapon is therefore the actual shooting. In the same way, the use of direct force must be announced (art. 98 StVollzG), indicating that use of force as such consists in the actual use of force.

8.3 Comparing National Norms

Comparing the norms is very helpful when trying to understand the complicated material of the use of physical force inside the Schengen territory. Police officers crossing the border during an observation operation or in hot pursuit will indeed have to keep a lot in mind when assessing whether and for which type of force application they are competent.

8.3.1 Constraint in General

All of the studied countries have regulated means of constraint at least in general statutes such as their respective codes of criminal procedure.

Table 8.1 Regulation of Constraint and Force in General

	B	NL	L	F	D
Constraint					
Statute	+	+	+	+	+
Force					
Statute	+	+	+	-	+
Decree	-	+	-	-	-
Case-law and literature	-	-	-	+	-

---

134   Dreher/Tröndle, 1993, pp. 238-241.

All but one country, France, have regulated use of coercion and other means of physical constraint in statutes (*Table 8.1*). France does not seem to distinguish between constraint and force, or at least seems to consider force as tactical means to be regulated internally or left to the personal appreciation of the police officer himself or of his superior (see *Table 8.2*). This means that use of physical force will be limited by general provisions of criminal law. The case law and the literature have developed a number of principles applicable to the use of physical force by the police. In the other countries the use of physical force will be allowed when it is exercised according to a number of conditions set in the law.

Table 8.2 Force in General

	B	NL	L	F	D
Principles					
Legitimate aim	+	+	-	+	-
Proportionality	+	+	-	+	+
Subsidiarity	-	+	+	-	+
Warning	+	+	-	-	-
Absolute necessity	-	-	+	-	-
Presumption of legality	-	-	-	+	-
Opportuneness	-	-	-	+	-
Conditions/situations					
Force majeure	+	+	-	-	-
Legal provision	+	-	-	-	-
Self-defence	+	+	+	+	+
After summoning or after robbery	-	-	+	-	-
Aversion of recovery of confiscated goods, or evasion of prisoner	-	-	+	-	-
Stop fleeing vehicle	-	-	+	-	-
Stop commission of offence	-	-	+	-	-
Necessity or emergency	-	-	-	+	+

Most of the countries seem to hold proportionality as a golden rule for the use of physical force in general. Subsidiarity is a second key principle in the Netherlands and Germany. Luxembourg sees absolute necessity as a prerequisite for the use of service weapons, which may be seen as similar to the subsidiarity principle. France demands opportuneness in the use of physical force in general. The exact distinction between the two terms seems to lie in that the former refers to an absolute necessity and the latter seems to suggest a greater degree of discretion on the part of the police officer in question.

The concept of legitimate aim is explicitly present in Belgium, the Netherlands and France.[135] The concept of emergency or *force majeure* play an important role in determining in which circumstances physical force may be used in Belgium, The Netherlands and France.

8.3.2   *Handcuffs*

Most countries do not have any legal provision formally regulating the use of handcuffs by the police, suggesting that it is not considered force in these countries. Only Germany provides for formal legislation in statutes for the use of handcuffs, on a federal as well as a provincial level, whereas The Netherlands regulates the use of handcuffs in a decree (see *Table 8.3*).

The practice of using handcuffs seems to be generalized in all studied countries. Handcuffs are generally seen as safety measures and mostly seen as exceptional, depending on the personality of the suspect, on circumstances, of conditions of transport etc. Only France seems a bit vague on prerequisites concerning the use of handcuffs, leaving its use to the sole appreciation of the police officer.

---

135   Expressed in France by the expression *titre de contrainte*.

Table 8.3 Handcuffs

	B	NL	L	F	D
Type of norm					
Statutes	-	-	-	+	+
Decree	+	+	-	-	+
Circular	-	+	-	+	+
Internal instructions					
No specification	-	+	-	-	+
Cases when use authorized					
During police task	+	+	+	+	+
Force majeure	+	-	-	-	-
Legitimate aim	+	-	-	-	-
Subsidiarity	+	+	-	-	-
Prevention of danger or escape	+	-	-	-	-
During arrest	+	-	-	-	-
Depending on circumstances of person and situation	+	+	+	+	+
Arrest in the act	-	-	-	+	-
Proportionality	-	-	-	-	+

8.3.3   Service Weapons

Most of the studied countries provide for formal legislation regarding the use of service weapons by the police. France stands alone in that the use of service weapons is regulated by a general theory developed by the case law and the literature (see *Table 8.3*). All five countries recognize self defence as a valid justification for the use of service weapons (explicitly or implicitly). Most countries consider arrests, safety (prevention in general), stopping a fleeing vehicle. All countries have the possibility to resort to other means of force such as sticks, water canons and tear gas grenades, France being the only country where these are not formally regulated at all. Shoot to kill seems to be formally regulated in Germany and in The Netherlands, although it seems that all the remaining countries have specially trained and equipped units of sharp shooters.

When comparing the definition of service weapon as contained in the Schengen memento on cross-border cooperation, one comes across important differences. Both Belgium and France see tear gas as part of the standard equipment of police officers, whereas in Luxembourg, Germany and The Netherlands, these are not mentioned. Only France and The Netherlands have expressed reserves as to the service weapons that may be carried by foreign police officers during cross-border observation. In both cases, the use of a weapon other than those carried by national police officers is forbidden. However, in the case of The Netherlands, the use of other weapons than those carried by Dutch police officers is restricted to urgent cases where cross border hot pursuit may occur without prior authorization of the locally competent authorities.

Table 8.4 Arms

	B	NL	L	F	D
Type of norm					
Statute	+	+	+	-	+
Theory in literature	-	-	-	+	-
Cases when allowed					
Against (allegedly) armed persons and their vehicles	+	+	-	-	-
Arrest	+	+	-	-	+
Compelling non-cooperative suspects	-	+	+	+	-
Proportionality	-	+	-	-	-
Subsidiarity	+	-	-	-	+
Warning	+	+	-	-	+
Shoot to kill (basis in statute)	-	+	-	-	+
Shoot to kill (no basis)	+	-	+	+	-
Self-defence/safety persons and objects	+	+	+	+	+
Depending on circumstances	+	+	+	+	+
Stop summoned person	-	+	+	+	-
Prevent (severe) criminal offence	-	-	+	-	+
Service weapons					
Pistol	+	-	-	+	+
Semi-automatic pistol	-	+	-	-	-
Automatic pistol	-	-	-	-	-
Revolver	-	-	-	-	+
Pistol or revolver	-	-	-	+	-
Tear gas spray	+	-	-	+	-
Stick	+	+	-	+	+
Individual or collective arms (firearms or blades)	-	-	+	-	-

368

8.3.4 Concepts of Self Defence and Use of Service Weapons

Although the acts excused by the exception of self defence resemble one another in the different studied countries. The most significant difference between the countries is the fact that in one group self defence includes the aversion of assaults on goods (The Netherlands, Germany and France) while in the other group (Belgium, Luxembourg) self defence is restricted to assaults on human beings (see *Table 8.5*). Indeed it is possible that the various Contracting Parties to the Schengen Convention agree on one definition of self defence in order to avoid conflict of interpretation between the different countries. However we have found no evidence supporting this thesis. One may not forget that police officers operating on foreign territories are subject to the law of the country in which they are operating. This means for instance that a French police officer may find himself arrested for manslaughter after trying to defend goods against an assault in Belgium, even though this would have been authorized in France. To this date no international agreement has been published, which means that police officers must be aware of the different definitions of self defence before they decide to use their weapon in another country.

Indeed it is possible that the different Contracting Parties to the Schengen Convention agree on one definition of self defence in order to avoid conflicts of interpretation between the different countries. Incidentally, the above mentioned Schengen working group has been set up precisely to discuss the practice of such questions as the common concepts on cross-border operations. The working group has retained the following common definition of self defence: There must be an illegal and actual assault against physical integrity, honour or goods of the police officer or of a third party, the means to avert the assault must be proportional and necessary and finally, the situation must not have been provoked and it must not be possible to avoid the defence reaction.

Table 8.5 Self Defence

	B	NL	L	F	D
Justified acts					
Beating	-	-	-	+	+
Wounding	+	+	-	-	+
Manslaughter	-	+	-	+	+
Any criminal offence					
Use of physical force	-	+	-	-	+
Definition					
Defence of oneself	+	+	+	+	+
Defence of others	+	+	+	+	+
Defence of goods	-	+	-	+	-
Defence of virtue	-	+	-	-	-
Illegitimate assault	+	+	+	+	+
Proportionality/necessity	+	+	+	+	+

Comparing the different notions of use of service weapons, it seems that only The Netherlands differ from the other studied countries. Indeed, this country sees as "use" of service weapons the aiming of the weapon, even without actually shooting. In all of the other countries, this distinction is not made. Use of service weapons is therefore seen as the actual using of the weapon: such as shooting with firearm or with tear gas grenade or hitting with stick. Of this follows that taking a weapon in the hand as a preventive measure, for instance for the purpose of apprehending the suspect, is not seen as use of service weapons in any of the countries. Even in other situations as self defence, it will be possible to carry a weapon for prevention purposes. However, a foreign police officer will have to think twice before drawing his weapon and aiming it in The Netherlands. This will only be allowed in self defence.

8.4 Conclusion

On the hand of what has been discussed above we would like to attempt to answer two questions: Firstly whether the observed differences in legislation with regards to the use of physical force will have consequences for the international police cooperation and secondly whether the different legislations are compatible with the norms expressed by the European Convention on Human Rights. In doing so, we will address these two questions following the pattern we have used in this chapter: We will focus on the use of physical force in general before we move on to the use of handcuffs and of firearms in particular. Further we will consider the differences in conceptions of self defence and use of service weapons.

As we have stated above, the Schengen Convention foresees certain rules for the application of means of constraint in general. Coercion, that is in the case of the Convention the use of handcuffs and the eventual security search (studied in Chapter 9), is only authorized after a cross-border hot pursuit when police officers are competent to apprehend the suspect. National norms will complement these rules. Force, on the other hand, will only be authorized in self defence, whether it be during a cross-border observation or hot pursuit.

The most important problem border crossing police officers will have to face is the lack of knowledge of the legal norms, statutes and customs of the neighbouring countries. Although cross-border observation or hot pursuit will probably never be everyday practice, they are police situations which are likely to be one of the most stressful for the enacting officers. They will have to ask themselves whether and for which acts they are competent, all in a very limited time. For this reason is it important to clearly evaluate the situation. Table 8.6 gives an overview of the legal and tactical situation on the hand of the different national norms, the Schengen Convention and results of the Schengen working group I (Police and Security) of June 2, 1995. This overview gives us an idea of how complicated the matter is.

Table 8.6 Restrictions for Cross-Border Use of Service Weapons[136]

to / from	Belgium	The Netherlands	Luxembourg	France	Germany
B		* semi-automatic pistol or revolver, stick; other only if urgent and part of equipment * no aiming	* collective or individual firearms or blade weapons	* observation only same weapons as France: revolver, pistol, tear gas, stick, handcuffs	* all weapons legally put at officer's disposal
NL	* pistol, stick and tear gas		* collective or individual firearms or blade weapons	* no common border, no regulation	* all weapons legally put at officer's disposal
L	* collective or individual firearms or blade weapons	* semi-automatic pistol or revolver, stick; other only if urgent and part of equipment * no aiming		* observation only same weapons as France: revolver, pistol, tear gas, stick, handcuffs	* all weapons legally put at officer's disposal
F	* revolver or pistol, tear gas, stick, handcuffs	* no common border	* revolver or pistol, tear gas, stick, handcuffs		* all weapons legally put at officer's disposal
D	* pistol, automatic pistol, revolver, stick	* semi-automatic pistol or revolver, other weapon only if urgent and part of equipment * no aiming	* pistol, automatic pistol, revolver, stick	* observation only same weapons as France: revolver, pistol, tear gas, stick, handcuffs	

136   Although Luxembourg and The Netherlands have no common borders, they do have a pursuit and observation regulation and, consequently, will in theory be in a position to use their service weapons in self defence.

The only country with explicit and formal statutes on the subject of handcuffs is Germany. Although the practice of using handcuffs is generalized in all of the remaining countries, these do not have any statute on the subject. The Dutch Police Instructions is a decree and does not have, therefore, the status of formal statute. Most countries have provided for a series of criteria, be it on the hand of case law or set out in lower forms of legislation, on the basis of which one can evaluate whether the use of handcuffs is opportune. Indeed, in our opinion, the only fact that an international treaty permits the use of handcuffs is not a legitimation for systematic use of handcuffs and cannot compensate for the lack of statutory norms. Some countries (Belgium, France and Germany) name arrest as a situation where the use of handcuffs is opportune. Nevertheless, countries such as the Netherlands and Luxembourg insist that arrest alone is not enough of a reason to resort to handcuffs. The personal situation of the suspect and the circumstances of the case are other important factors to be regarded. Whether these differences are liable to cause great problems for the international police cooperation is doubtful.

It is opportune, however, to ask the question as to whether the use of handcuffs should be regulated in statutes, be worked out in lower forms of legislation or whether principles set out by case law are sufficient. In our opinion, considering the impact the use of handcuffs may have on the personal situation of a suspect and the situation in which handcuffs can be used, the rule of law demands that their use be regulated. In our opinion, because the use of handcuffs constitute at the very least a violation of the physical integrity, art. 8 ECHR disposes that their use should be regulated in accessible and foreseeable regulations. Criteria set out in case law have the disadvantage of being more difficult of access and subject to interpretation, which could not be practical in situations of cross-border operations. The Dutch solution - a general provision for the use of force worked out in lower regulations - seems to us a minimum for both these criteria. Moreover, such accessible and foreseeable norms are ideal to help the international cross-border cooperation.

The definitions of service weapon contained in the Schengen memento on cross border cooperation has helped clear up some potential problems. However, the fact that The Netherlands and France have voiced reserves as to the type of service weapon that may be carried on their territory is both a blessing and a source of conflict. It is in one way a blessing because it may initiate discussion as to which service weapons are necessary in a democratic society. The fact that the officers of one country dispose of riot guns, for instance, is not necessarily a reason for each European police officer to carry one. Moreover, the fact that officers of all countries carry riot guns is no reason to let these weapons be carried by foreign officers on your own territory. Indeed, this might be a source of problems in cross border hot pursuit situations: Even if it is not an urgent case and there is time to solicit authorization from the locally competent author-ities, will there be time to stop somewhere to deposit one's tear gas spray?

Considering the concept of "use" of service weapons, The Netherlands is the only country assimilating aiming and holding the weapon at aim with using it. All remaining studied countries consider more or less explicitly that there can only be "use" of service weapons when there is also actual - directed - use. This will most certainly have consequences for the cross border police cooper-ation. Indeed, German or Belgian police officers on Dutch territory will have to think twice before drawing their weapon since they have not been trained to think and react as to assimilating drawing their weapon with using them. Giving a warning shot in the air, something not only authorized in their legislations but even encouraged, will be considered "using" their service weapons. We suspect that these differences are liable to cause problems for the cross-border police cooperation.

As stated above, actual use of the service weapon in a foreign country during a cross-border operation is only authorized in a situation of self defence. In all countries, taking a weapon in the hand as a preventive measure is not considered actual use. Foreign police officers will have to make note of the fact that they are not allowed to aim as a preventive measure, unless all conditions of self defence are present. In theory, Dutch police officers will be confronted with a new situation in other countries, as they will be allowed to aim their pistol at someone in a preventive manner, without having neither the intention to shoot, nor the legitimacy of self defence.

Knowledge of the concepts of the use of service weapons and of self defence will therefore be very important. As we have seen above, there are some differences in the different countries as to what is considered self defence, the most important of which being the fact that in some countries averting an assault on goods may be considered as such while in other countries it is not. A satisfactory solution would be to allow the use physical force exclusively in the situations set forth by the European Convention on Human Rights.[137] Another solution might be to adopt a protocol to the Schengen Convention containing a common definition of self defence.

A common definition was indeed proposed by the Schengen working group on cross border cooperation.[138] As we have seen above, it was decided to include the aversion of an attack against goods and the honour, the most permissive common denominator, instead of excluding this situation, which would have constituted the restrictive common denominator. Moreover, the standard to be respected is that of the reasonable necessity, as opposed to the

---

137 This solution would join the interpretation of the Dutch government discussed above, in section 8.2.4.
138 See section 8.1.1 of this study.

absolute necessity. In our opinion, this decision is contrary to the principles expressed in the European Convention on Human Rights.

As we have seen above in section 8.1.2 and in contrary to the proposal of the Schengen working group on the definition of self defence, the European Convention sets as minimum standard for the use of physical force by public officers that it be absolutely necessary (subsidiarity) for defending **someone**, when performing a lawful arrest or quelling a riot. We have seen that most of the studied countries authorize the use of force when protecting goods against an assault and that the Schengen working group takes this common denominator for cross-border operations. Consequently, in our opinion, all countries should have rather proceeded to adapt their legislation in order to be in line with the European Convention on Human Rights and only allow the use of physical force, or at the very least the use of service weapons, in the conditions set out by art. 2 ECHR. This is of particular importance when one notes the existence in each country of specially trained and specially equipped units for the use of lethal force. As their acts are often legally given the justification of self defence, the lack of sufficient legal framework, nationally and internationally, is evident. Indeed, we acknowledge the fact that it is probably more convenient for the practice of cross-border police cooperation to enlarge the definition of self defence to its largest common denominator, acting as an umbrella to catch all possible automatic reactions of police officers especially considering the high risks involved with these operations for the acting police officer, but the potential consequences for such a definition of self defence in this context can prove difficult to endorse. Despite these eventual practical advantages, we remain of opinion that the European Convention on Human Rights, signed and ratified by all the Schengen Contracting Parties, should and does serve as a more suitable guide for common denominators for the police practice, particularly in this time when the rights of the suspect are increasingly absent from international documents.

9 Security Search and Investigative Bodily Search

The bodily search of a suspect may serve two principal purposes. On the one hand it is a safety measure destined to make sure the suspect is not carrying any objects or substances that may be used to harm himself or others and on the other hand, it may be a useful investigation technique in the search for evidence. In both cases it may consist of a simple search of the pockets of the suspect or of the bag he or she is carrying, but in the case of an investigative search it may also extend to a strip-search, involving investigations in the natural openings of the body or even the special bodily investigations.

In the following paragraph we will first consider the international norms concerning bodily search, addressing both the issue of the norms provided by the Schengen Convention and the Benelux Extradition Treaty (section 9.1.1) as the guarantees offered by the European Convention on Human Rights (section 9.1.2). Second, we will look into the different national norms provided by the studied countries with regard to security search and investigation search (sections 9.2.1 and 9.2.2). Third we will compare the different norms with one another (paragraph 9.3) and we will conclude by examining whether the observed differences may constitute a barrier to international police cooperation and whether the different national norms stand the test set up by the European Convention on Human Rights (paragraph 9.4).

9.1 International Norms

9.1.1 International Norms on Police Cooperation

As we have stated in Chapter 6, art. 41 SC will replace the Benelux Extradition Treaty concerning all topics not foreseen by the latter, unless this leads to a restriction of the actual practice in the Benelux related to the competence to apprehend, the territorial habilitation and the criminal offences leading to the application of the treaty. As far as there are differences between the Benelux countries on the one hand and the Schengen countries on the other, note that within the Benelux countries there is no necessity for an offence to have been caught in the act, nor is there an urgent character needed to pursue a suspect into another Benelux country. Further, the Schengen Convention will add the possibility to pursue formally detained or imprisoned escapees, whereas with the Benelux Extradion Treaty the pursuit may also take place across other than land borders. One restriction to the situation that existed before the coming into force of the Schengen Convention that will exist, is that foreign police officers must now be recognizable as police officers. The use of force and in particular the use of the service weapon is now restricted to self-defence.[1] The Schengen Convention permits foreign police officers competent to apprehend to carry out a security search on the apprehended suspect. In that case the Convention specifies that foreign officers may seize the objects found on the suspect (art. 41 par. 5 sub f *in fine*), illustrating how closely related these two measures are.

We have shown in Chapter 6 that the different versions of art. 41 SC may be seen as contradictory, the Dutch text reserving actions as the use of handcuffs and security search to the officers habilitated to arrest the suspect. Without restating the argumentation set out in that sub-section, note that both treaties authorize foreign police officers to make a security search on the suspect they have been pursuing. The question is of a totally other nature with regard to more thorough searches on the body of the suspect. Neither treaty provides for regulations concerning more extensive forms of searches, although the Schengen Convention does mention the possibility of seizing objects on the person of the suspect. In that case, however, it is probable that one speaks solely of objects incidently found on the person of the suspect during the security search, such as weapons or seringes. In our opinion, bodily searches involving more than a superficial palpation of the suspect's body would require the intervention of nationally competent authorities, especially in cases where the investigation requires the use of some sort of technical means or is reserved by law to specific authorities. Moreover, our interpretation of the relationship between the Benelux Extradition Treaty and the Schengen Convention leads to conclude that the Schengen partners have ruled to exclude this possibility by not continuing art. 28 BET.[2]

9.1.2   European Convention on Human Rights

There is a gradation of severity between the different forms of bodily search done by the police. While an extensive bodily search, for instance a strip-search, may in certain circumstances, for instance in public, be qualified as an unhuman treatment and constitute a violation of art. 3 ECHR, other more superficial forms of bodily search may constitute a "mere" violation of the physical integrity and a violation of art. 8 ECHR: The former should, as an unhuman treatment, be avoided altogether while the latter should have sufficient basis in domestic law

---

1   See paragraph 4.3 for details.
2   Art. 28 BET could be understood, with the expression "use of force" it contains, as including the performance of a more extensive bodily search.

and be subject to a number of legal formalities. Indeed, where a bodily search constitutes a violation of the physical integrity, it should only be authorized on the basis of a formal law, therefore in accordance with the criteria exposed in the cases Kruslin and Huvig.

This view is supported by Resolution 428 (1970) of the Consultative (Parliamentary) Assembly of the Council of Europe, stating that the "right to privacy consists essentially to live one's life with a minimum of interference. It concerns private, family and home life, **physical and moral integrity**, honour and reputation (...)."[3] In addition, the European Court on Human Rights does not exclude the possibility that "there might be circumstances in which art. 8 could be regarded as affording in relation to 'measures involving physical integrity' a protection which goes beyond that given in art. 3."[4] In other words, a violation of physical integrity may in extreme cases be protected by the prohibition of unhuman treatment expressed in art. 3 but in other cases, the dispositions guaranteeing the respect of the private life may serve as a minimum protection for invasions of the physical integrity of a suspect by a police officer.

As we have stated in Chapters 4 and 5, according to the Court an interference of a public authority in an individual's private life does not violate art. 8 ECHR when it is done

in accordance with the law, pursues one or more legitimate aims referred to in par. 2 and furthermore is necessary in a democratic society in order to achieve them.[5]

Further, in par. 2, it

requires firstly that the impugned measure should have more basis in domestic law; it also refers to the quality of the law in question, requiring that it should be accessible to the person concerned, who must be moreover be able to foresee its consequences for him, and compatible with the rule of law.

Indeed, this is true for measures interfering with the respect of one's physical integrity as it is true with the respect of one's private conversations.

Some special investigation techniques involving the introduction of foreign instruments in the natural openings of the body or the collecting of bodily samples bring us one step further. Firstly because they involve the actual physical collecting of samples on or in the body; secondly, in the use of genetic samples, because the scope of the information contained is not yet fully delimited. Indeed, these techniques may offer advantages to the criminal justice

---

3   Council of Europe, Cons. Ass., Twenty-First Ordinary session (Third Part), Texts adopted (1970); Council of Europe, Collected Texts, Strasbourg 1979.
4   Costello-Roberts v. U.K., March 25, 1993, Series A 247C, nr. 36, p. 12.
5   *Kruslin & Huvig v. France*, April 24, 1990, Series A 176.

system, especially when it comes to the determination of innocence or guilt, but may bare great consequences for the victim or the suspect for instance when it comes to an AIDS test. However, because of the possible repercussions of the results of these tests and because external factors such as laboratory conditions may have an impact of these results, these techniques should

> be carried out in a reliable manner, (...) take full account of and not contravene such fundamental principles as the inherent dignity of the individual and the respect for the human body, the rights of the defence and the principle of proportionality in the carrying out of criminal justice.[6]

However interesting and useful a study of the different national norms on the subject of special bodily investigations would be for the international cooperation in criminal matters as a whole, it would exceed the scope of this work which, as we have mentioned earlier, concentrates on the direct international police cooperation. Because police officers themselves will not directly be confronted with the collecting of such bodily samples, we will not consider special bodily investigations in this study.

9.2 National Norms

This paragraph will focus on the description of the legal framework in the different countries concerning bodily seach. We have chosen a distinction between the different forms of bodily search according firstly to the aim of the search and, secondly, according to the degree, although this distinction may seem artificial to practionners. This distinction is, moreover, not one to be necessarily found in the law and in many cases, police officers will go from one type of search to another without making note of it. For this reason, we will not only discuss the security search, which has its explicit basisin art. 41 SC, but also the investigative search, although the Schengen Convention does not mention this power at all. We will discuss the so-called security search in section 9.2.1, and pursue with the investigative bodily search in section 9.2.2.

9.2.1   Security Search

The expression "security search" will be used here to designate the bodily search carried out for safety reasons: either for the controlled person's own safety or for that of the acting police officer or third persons. It is the only form of bodily

---

6   See Recommendation R (92) 1, adopted by the Council of Europe Committee of Ministers on February 10, 1992, regarding the use of analysis of deoxyribonucleic acid (DNA) within the framework of the criminal justice system.

search that may be carried out by foreign police officers acting in another Schengen country than their own.

The text of both the Benelux Extradition Treaty and the Schengen Convention provide for a legal basis for the carrying out of a security search in a partner country by foreign police officers. As long as the concerned police officer has the power to apprehend the suspect, he will have the power to carry out a security search. Indeed, the objects he will come across may be seized according to art. 41 par. 5 sub f SC.

9.2.1.1 Belgium

Until the beginning of 1993, Belgian legislation did not foresee any provision regarding security search, also known as administrative search. This certainly did not mean that such a search was not practised before that time: This particular form of bodily search was regulated in a number of special statutes regarding such specific areas as customs law, penitentiary law, aviation law and the legislation concerning doping in sports.[7] There was no legal basis for a security search done outside the scope of these statutes, which led to the adoption of art. 28 of the Police Function Act (*Wet op het politieambt/Loi sur la fonction de police* - WPA).[8]

This new statute aims to restrict the use of security searches to a limited number of cases set up in the act: firstly, to the situation where, during an identity control, the behaviour of the controlled person, material clues or circumstances give reasons to fear that he is carrying a weapon or other dangerous object (art. 28 par. 1 sub 1 WPA); secondly, on persons being arrested within an administrative or judicial context (sub 2). Finally, the safety search is authorized on persons participating in public meetings posing a threat to the public order (sub 3). The explanatory statement specifies that the mere threat to the public order is sufficient to motivate a security search and that it is not necessary that an actual menace be awaited. Also, such a bodily search may be done at the entrance of places where the public order is threatened (sub 4), for instance at the entrance of a court of justice where a politically sensitive trial is taking place or places considered as potential targets for terrorist actions.[9] Finally, art. 28 par. 3 WPA provides for the possibility to carry out a security search on persons being locked up in a cell (*insluitingsfouillering*).

Art. 28 WPA also foresees rules regarding the way the security search should be carried out: Theoretically, it will be carried out by feeling the body

---

7 Arnou, 1982, pp. 134-137.
8 According to the explanatory statement (pp. 48-49), this general form of security search is comparable to searches done at airports.
9 Explanatory statement, p. 48.

and clothes of the person. Indeed, while it is possible that the person be searched after he has been undressed, it will not be done very often in this way. The explanatory statement indicates that the investigative search will be carried out in a more thoroughful manner than the security search and that even for an investigation search, the need to undress the person must be established on the basis of facts and circumstances. If this is the case for the investigative search, it will certainly be true, if not more so, for the security search.[10] During a security search, the luggage one is carrying may be searched as well. The controlled person may not be upheld longer than the necessary time and in any case, no longer than an hour.

Security searches carried out in predictable cases, for instance that to be carried out at the entrance of a court of justice or before locking a person up in a cell, ought to be carried out only following an order and under the supervision of a superior officer (art. 28 par. 3, sub 2 and 3 WPA). They must be carried out by a person of the same sex as that of the controlled person, even in cases where the eventuality of a search was not predictable.[11]

The explanatory statement adds further that the security search may be carried out with the help of technical means, such as metal detectors.[12] Although it mentions this possibility concerning the security search being carried out on persons participating in public meetings potentially forming a threat to the public order or in places where the public order may potentially be disturbed, it is conceivable that it be permitted before locking a suspect up in a cell as well since all these situations are ones that remain predictable. It remains somewhat peculiar that the explanatory statement does not mention this possibility. When, during a security search, objects are found on the controlled person that may constitute a threat to a good or or the life or the physical integrity of a person, they may be seized in virtue of art. 30 WPA.

French and German police officers who have pursued a suspect accross the border will have to respect the conditions established by the Schengen Convention and by the Belgian government in its declaration made in accordance with art. 41 par. 9 SC. This means that although both French and German police officers will be competent to pursue the fleeing suspect, only German police officers will be competent to apprehend the suspect, hence giving them the competence to carry out a security search. Moreover, the conditions giving way to cross-border hot pursuit will have to be present. Consequently, German police officers may apprehend and carry out a security search on a fleeing escaped

---

10 Explanatory statement, p. 50.
11 Indeed this might prove difficult at times, but the fact remains that all must be done in order to follow this imperative; see D'Haese, 1993, p. 151.
12 Explanatory statement, p. 50.

prisonner or a suspect that has been caught in the act of an extraditable offence as long as this occurs within 30 minutes of crossing the border.[13]

On Belgian territory, police officers pursuing a suspect out of another Benelux country will be competent to apprehend and carry out a security search on the suspect. Indeed they will be subject to the different conditions applying to the Benelux area: apprehension inside a 10 kilometre zone from the border and no restriction as to offences caught in the act. In comparison to the situation existing before the coming into force of the Schengen Convention, they will furthermore be subject to a number of additional conditions, for instance the obligation to be recognizable as a police officer.

9.2.1.2 The Netherlands

For a long time, a bodily search for reasons of safety did not have any legal basis in The Netherlands. At that time this practice was authorized on the basis of a decision of the *Hoge Raad*.[14] It was not before the constitutional amendment of 1983 introducing the right to privacy as a fundamental right that the necessity of a legal basis for carrying out a security search was recognized. Art. 33a PolW 1957, later renumbered art. 8 PolW 1993, created a legal basis for the carrying out of a security search on the clothing of a suspect by all police officers and on his body by superior officers, auxiliaries of the public prosecutor (*hulpofficier van justitie*).

Art. 8 par. 3 PolW stipulates that the police officer, "employed to carry out the police task, is competent to search the clothes of a person, when legally exercising one of his competences prescribed by law or the general police task when, on the basis of facts or circumstances, there appears to be an immediate threat for his own life or safety, that of the officer personally or that of third parties and when the search is necessary to avert this threat."[15] Par. 4 of the same article adds that the auxiliary of the public prosecutor before whom a suspect is being presented is competent to have the suspect's body searched. Art. 8 par. 5 PolW adds furthermore that the search must be in proportion to the aim, reasonable and measured. Of all this follows that this measure is not meant to be carried out as a standard procedure, but that its necessity in each situation must be assessed on the hand of the different interests. Note that the

---

13   See Chapter 6 for more information on the conditions of cross-border hot pursuit.
14   HR 16 December, 1975, NJ 1976, 491.
15   The Dutch text states: "*De ambtenaar van politie die is aangesteld voor de uitvoering van de politietaak is bevoegd tot het onderzoek aan de kleding van personen bij de uitoefening van een van hem wettelijk toegekende bevoegdheid of bij een handeling ter uitvoering van de politietaak, indien uit feiten en omstandigheden blijkt dat een onmiddelijk gevaar dreigt voor hun leven of veiligheid, die van de ambtenaar zelf of van derden en dit onderzoek noodzakelijk is ter afwending van dit gevaar.*"

provisions of art. 8 PolW not only apply to regular police officers but also to the corps of the *Koninklijke marechaussee*.[16] Art. 21 *Ambtsinstructie* adds that a police report must be drawn up for every security search carried out.

As the security search is considered a bodily search carried out with the intention to discover dangerous objects on the body of a suspect, the search consists essentially in the palpation of the clothes with the hands. However, there is a gradation in the different forms this type of search may take. It can be informally carried out upon entering the police car by superficially feel places where weapons could be hidden, but it can also consist in forcing the suspect to take a special position (leaning on a vehicle or a wall with hand up and legs spread). In the latter case, the suspect is searched by palpating the body through the clothes from head to toes in such a way that potentially dangerous objects can be localized. Further, it is even possible to search the suspect according to the afore described method, handcuff the suspect and once at the police station, to carry out a more detailled security search. Finally, dangerous suspects may be searched while being held at aim by police officers.[17] The law is silent as to whether luggage or bags may be searched for security reasons.

In the police practice it is also customary to carry out a security search before a person is locked up in a cell. With this measure one aims to collect objects that may pose a threat to the life and physical integrity of the arrested person himself, that of the police officer or of thirds. This type of search finds its original justification in art. 15 par. 4 of the Dutch Constitution (GW): a person being lawfully deprived of his liberty may be restricted in the exercise of his fundamental rights. A person being remanded in custody may be searched for security reasons on the basis of artt. 62 par. 1 Sv and 225 ISv.

The police instructions of 1994 work out the detail of the security search as foreseen in art. 8 PolW.[18] A security search carried out by ordinary police officers consists in a superficial palpation of the clothes. As much as possible, it must be carried out by an officer of the same sex as that of the searched person. In the case of the security search ordered by the public prosecutor or one of his auxiliaries, it must be carried out by an officer of the same sex as that of the searched person (art. 20 *Ambtsinstructie*).

German police officers operating on Dutch territory after a cross-border hot pursuit will have to respect the conditions established by the Schengen Convention and by the Dutch government in their declaration made in accordance with art. 41 par. 9 SC. Of this follows that German police officers will

16 Explanatory statement, TK 1991-1992, 22 562 nr. 3, p. 22.
17 See Naeyé, 1990, pp. 147-149 and Elzinga, Van Rest & De Valk, 1995, pp. 118-131; see also artt. 11 and 20 *Ambtsinstructie*.
18 *Amsbtsinstructie voor de politie, de Koninklijke mareechaussee en de buitengewoon opsporingsambtenaar*, Decree of April 8, 1994, Stb. 1994, 275.

be competent to apprehend the fleeing suspect in a 10 kilometre zone of the common border, giving them the competence to carry out a security search as well. That is, as long as the other conditions giving way to cross-border hot pursuit have been fulfilled: The fleeing suspect of an extraditable offence must have been caught in the act.[19]

Police officers of another Benelux country pursuing a suspect on Dutch territory will be competent to apprehend and carry out a security search on the suspect. Indeed they will be subject to the different conditions applying to the Benelux area: apprehension inside a 10 kilometre zone from the border, no restriction as to offences caught in the act, no urgent character required etc. They will furthermore be subject to a number of additional conditions foreseen by the Schengen Convention, for instance the obligation to be recognizable as a member of the public force and the use of their service weapon in self-defence only.

9.2.1.3 Luxembourg

The only legal basis for a bodily search in Luxembourg is the investigative search carried out at the beginning of the remand in police custody (art. 39 CIC). In practice, police officers do carry out searches for security reasons in other occasions, the so-called *Durchsuchung zur Eigensicherung*,[20] destined to protect their own safety.

Art. 39 par. 5 CIC stipulates that a suspect caught in the act may be searched prior to his remand in custody, when it is expected that he has on his person objects that may interest the investigation or that may harm himself or others. With this provision, the Luxembourg legislator has given both the security search prior to the suspect's confinement in a cell and the investigative search (the so-called *perquisition*) a legal basis. The security search of art. 39 CIC must be carried out by a person of the same sex as that of the suspect. The law does not provide for a solution to the situation where such a person cannot be found. Because of the fact that such a search is also an investigative search, it is likely that it must be carried out under the supervision of an auxiliary to the public prosecutor (*officier de police judiciaire*). Art. 39 CIC does not, however, state this explicitly.

---

19 See Chapter 6 for more details, in particular on the extradition relationship between The Netherlands and Germany.

20 This is a good example of the difference between "police language" and "legal language" in Luxembourg: As we have mentioned in Chapter 3, the daily language in Luxembourg may well be *Letzebuergisch*, but the language used in police reports and instructions is German. Moreover, French is the language used for all legal texts and for court proceedings.

It is conceivable that security searches of persons outside the situation covered by art. 39 CIC may be carried out by ordinary *policiers* or *gendarmes* as this measure is destined to protect the safety of the police officers themselves or that of the public in general. In practice, a security search is carried out when someone is arrested or prior to confining a suspect in a cell. In most cases, the controlled person will be asked to empty his bag(s) and pocket(s) before the police officers carry out a search of his clothes and body. A so-called security palpation of clothes and body may even be carried out in public. In practice, the carrying out of such a measure seems to be encouraged since it increases the safety of the officers as well as that of the public. These security searches must probably be performed by persons of the same sex as the controlled person. Male officers may ask a female suspect to remove her jacket or empty her handbag or pockets, but in principle shey may not touch her. When necessary, she may eventually be submitted to a superficial palpation. Because of a lack of women in both police corps in the past, civil personnel was often required to perform on these occasions. However, this practice is discouraged since this civil personnel has neither relevant training in the police field nor is there a relevant hierarchical supervision or responsibility possible.[21]

German and French police officers pursuing a suspect accross the border onto Luxembourg territory will have to respect the conditions established by the Schengen Convention and by the Luxembourg government in its declaration made in accordance with art. 41 par. 9 SC. Of this follows that cross-border hot pursuit will be limited to the cases where the suspect is either an escaped prisoner or has been caught in the act committing one of the offences mentionned in art. 41 par. 4 sub a SC. While the pursuit by both French and German police officers may take place in a 10 kilometre zone of the common border, only German police officers will be competent to apprehend the fleeing suspect and consequently to carry out a security search.[22] As French police officers do not have jurisdiction to apprehend the suspect, they will not be able to carry out security search.[23]

Belgian police officers pursuing a suspect on Luxembourg territory will be competent to apprehend and carry out a security search on the suspect. Indeed as police officers of a member State of the Benelux, they will be subject to the different conditions applying to the Benelux area: Apprehension of the suspect will have to take place inside a 10 kilometre zone from the border an Schengen restrictions as to offences being caught in the act or as to the required urgent character will not apply. However, they will be subject to a number of condi-

---

21 This was confirmed by sources in the *police* as well as in the *gendarmerie grand-ducale*.
22 See Chapter 6 for more details on cross-border hot pursuit.
23 This probably because the French government has not given this competence to Luxembourg police officers pursuing a suspect into France.

tions foreseen by the Schengen Convention which were not present in the past years of the Benelux Union: They will be obliged to be recognizable as police officers. Once the suspect has been apprehended, he may be submitted to a security search and the objects found on him seized.

9.2.1.4 France

The French courts consider that investigations on clothes and body must be regarded as *perquisitions*, which is to say that they are subjected to the same formalities as searches in a house.[24] This, however, can only be said of the investigative bodily search, the security search (*palpation de sécurité*) being considered a simple police act and having no basis in formal French law.[25] Officers and auxiliaries of the public prosecutor of all ranks, as well as simple citizens may carry out a simple security search for instance after they have caught a suspect in the act. In this case, all potentially dangerous objects may be seized in order to be handed over to the higher ranked auxiliary of the public prosecutor (*officier de police judicaire*), who will take all necessary subsequent steps.

A security search may be performed at different moments: For instance, agents or officers of judiciary police who are requested by a judge to arrest an individual, may submit him to a security search prior to his appearance before the judge.[26] The measure may also be carried out during an identity control. After he has been remanded in custody (*garde à vue*), the suspect must be subjected to a security search on his clothes and his body. In this case, art. C.117 IG states that someone being remanded in custody may be subjected to a search if he is suspected to carry dangerous objects or objects that may be useful to the investigation. This provision confuses bodily searches done for security reasons with those done for the investigation. The search must be carried out by a person of the same sex as that of the suspect, in the absence of which civilian personnel may be used.[27] An important distinction between a *perquisition* and a security search is the fact that with the latter, the respect of the legal hours is not mandatory.[28] The searched person may be undressed, for instance for the purpose of examining his clothes, and the objects found

---

24 Aix-en-Provence, June 28, 1978, Gaz. Pal. 1979, 1, 79.
25 Paris, January 12, 1954, Receuil Dalloz-Sirey 1954, 71; Cass. crim. September 22, 1988, Gaz. Pal., April 14, 1989, somm. p. 17: The case reports on a knife that was lawfully found and seized on the body of a suspect during a security search carried out by a lower ranked police officer (*agents de police judicaire*).
26 Decocq, Montreuil & Buisson, 1991, pp. 462 and 467.
27 Decocq, Montreuil & Buisson, 1991, p. 301.
28 See Decocq, Montreuil & Buisson, 1990, pp. 289 and 301. Legal hours, in France between 06:00 and 21:00, must in principle be respected when carrying out investigative searches.

during the search may be seized.[29] Both the law and the litterature are silent on the question as to whether luggage may be searched as well.

After having pursued a suspect across the French border, foreign police officers habilitated to apprehend the suspect will have the power to carry on a security search (art. 41 par. 5 sub. f SC). Nonetheless, because of the fact that the French government in its declaration made according to art. 41 par. 9 SC concerning the conditions applicable to hot-pursuit on French territory has denied all foreign police officers the faculty to apprehend a pursued suspect, this provision will have no effect on French territory.

9.2.1.5 Germany

When it comes to bodily search, German law provides for rules on a federal level as well as on a provincial level. The provincial statutes are mostly modeled on the example furnished by art. 17 MEPolG and foresee explicit provisions for the security search (*Durchsuchung zur Eigensicherung*).[30] Art. 43 par. 3 and 4 of the 1994 Federal Border Police Act (*Gesetz zur Neuregelung der Vorschriften über den Bundesgrenzschutz* - BGSNeuRegG) enacts rules for the carrying out of a security security search by both the federal police, the BGS and the BKA.[31] Because the security search is not aimed at investigating criminal offences, there is no explicit provision contained in the German criminal code (*Strafprozeßordnung*) concerning this measure. However, when the identity of a suspect is being controlled on the hand of art. 163b StPO, this provision may also serve as a basis for carrying out a security search.[32]

The security search is a police measure that may be carried out on a person whose identity must be established or who must be brought to another location to be presented to an official. This person may then be searched to control whether he is carrying dangerous objects such as weapons and explosives; this is possible when it is necessary for the safety of the controlling officer or that of others. The safety of the controlled person himself may be reason enough to perform a security search as well.[33]

---

29 Decocq, Montreuil & Buisson, 1991, p. 301.

30 This is true in any case for the "old" western provinces of Germany; Drews/Wacke/Vogel/Martens, 1985, p. 201; since most of the "new" eastern provinces have modelled their police law on existing legislation in other western provinces, one may expect this to be the case for them as well. See also Heise/Tegtmeyer, 1990, p. 293.

31 BGBl. I, 1994, 2978.

32 Kleinknecht/Meyer-Goßner, 1995, p. 599.

33 Heise/Tegtmeyer, 1990, p. 290; provisions concerning the bodily search for security reasons are, among others: artt. 39 par. 2 NWPolG, 18 par. 2 RhPfPVG, 36 par. 3 HSOG, 21 par. 2 BayPAG and 17 par. 2 SPolG.

Systematically carrying out of security searches with every identity control is not authorized: Facts and circumstances must give reason to believe the existence of danger, the situation at hand being determinant.[34] It is not necessary that the danger be imminent: The threat of a dangerous situation developing is sufficient. In that case, the principle of proportionality (*Verhältnismäßigkeitsprinzip*) must be kept in mind.[35]

Every police officer with investigative powers is authorized to perform a security search as well as an identity control, since both measures are closely linked. It is not necessary that they be habilitated auxiliaries of the public prosecutor (*Hilfsbeamte der Staatsanwaltschaft*). The condition that the search must be performed by a person of the same sex as that of the controlled person applies also to the security search, although less strictly than for the investigative bodily search.[36] It will mostly depend on the presence or availability of (fe)-male police officers.

Since the security search will often be carried out prior to the arrest of a suspect, it may be carried out in public.[37] As this measure aims to find weapons and other dangerous objects relatively difficult to conceal in comparison to for instance drugs or jewelry, it will be carried out in a more superficial manner than the investigative bodily search.[38] During a security search, personal belongings such as luggage or a vehicle may be searched as well.[39] All seizable objects encountered by coincidence during the search may be seized, thus not only the ones that have given cause to the search.[40]

In the event that a foreign police officer would cross the German border in order to pursue a suspect, they would be subject to art. 41 SC. Combining art. 41 par. 5 sub f SC with the declaration made by the German government concerning the modalities that must be followed by foreign police officers whiLe acting in cross-border hot pursuit on German territory, it is to be concluded that French, Belgian, Luxembourg and Dutch police officers will be habilitated to carry out a security search on a suspect they have apprehended in Germany.

9.2.2 Investigative Bodily Search

Investigative bodily searches are an important source of evidence during criminal investigations. Although foreign police officers, according to present interna-

---

34 Heise/Tegtmeyer, 1990, p. 293.
35 Heise/Tegtmeyer, 1990, p. 290.
36 Kleinknecht/Meyer-Goßner, 1995, p. 599; see also artt. 39 par. 3 NWPolG, 18 par. 3 RhPfPVG, 36 par. 4 HSOG, 21 par. 3 BayPAG and 17 par. 3 SPolG.
37 Heise/Tegtmeyer, 1990, p. 292.
38 Heise/Tegtmeyer, 1990, p. 293.
39 Kleinknecht/Meyer-Goßner, 1995, p. 599.
40 Roxin, 1993, pp. 255-256; Heise/Tegtmeyer, 1990, p. 320.

tional law, are not authorized to carry out investigative bodily searches on a suspect they have followed across the border, the study of this measure seems important to us for two reasons. Firstly because national competent authorities will in these cases carry out an investigative bodily search on the basis of a suspicion that has risen in a foreign country, a suspicion of which they have no personal actual knowledge, and secondly, because investigative bodily searches carried out in one country may be of importance for investigations taking place in another. Results of these may be exchanged on the hand of police cooperation and, in a broader context, may even be used as evidence (after the necessary request for mutual legal assistance).

9.2.2.1 Belgium

The judicial investigative search (of the body as well as of places not accessible to the public) finds its legal basis in art. 28 par. 2 WPA. This provision authorizes the carrying out of investigative bodily searches on persons suspected of having evidence or other clues related to a criminal offence (*misdaad* or *wanbedrijf*) on them.[41] In the case of contraventions, a search is thus not permitted. Further it is possible to carry out a search on someone who has been placed under administrative arrest.[42]

The time spent on the investigative bodily search should be limited to what is necessary, while the period of time during which the concerned person may be held must not exceed 6 hours. The search must be carried out following guidelines and under the responsibility of an auxiliary of the public prosecutor; whether this officer must be present during the search is unclear. The search must also be carried out as much as possible by someone of the same sex as that of the person being searched. Because of practical reasons, this condition is not seen as a rule to be strictly followed. Further, the Belgian legislator aims at preventing abuses during bodily searches: The necessity to have the person undress for the purpose of a search must appear out of "general instructions and special circumstances of fact",[43] while the use of force during the search is only authorized in the extent of art. 36 WPA.[44]

The fact that Belgian law did not provide for rules regarding bodily search before the adoption of the Police Fuction Act has led to the development of an abundant case law on the subject and which, for a substantial part, remains

---

41   It is not necessary that there be more than elements indicating the possible detention of such evidence or clues. See D'Haese, 1993, p. 154.

42   For more details on investigative bodily searches under Belgian law, we refer to Bourdoux & De Valkeneer, 1993, pp. 217-233.

43   *"uit algemene onderrichtingen en bijzondere feitelijke omstandigheden."*

44   Explanatory statement, pp. 49-50.

relevant. The *Hof van Cassatie* ruled for instance, that during a bodily search police officers were authorized to search in or under the clothes for the purpose of determining whether objects are being hidden. This was interpreted rather extensively by the court as to allow police officers to compel suspects to undress completely and take special bodily positions such as bending over legs spread apart.[45] Although the court did not rule on other conditions concerning the way a search must be carried out, the police practice holds that this method of bodily search should be reserved for situations where it is reasonably opportune, which means to say when there are reasons to believe that the suspect is indeed hiding trafficable goods such as drugs or jewelry.[46] It is considered highly preferable that the suspect take the prescribed position of his own will (that is to say without the resort to force).

The possibility of a bodily search is not restricted to the suspect. A third party may be subjected to a bodily search when there exists a reasonable certainty that this person carries evidence or clues on him.[47] Both agents and officers of judicial police, auxiliaries of the public prosecutor, have the power to carry out an investigative bodily search. In cases where the particular situation calls for the search to be carried out by other persons than police officers, for instance because the suspect is female and there are no female police officers present, the court requires that it take place under the supervision and responsibility of an auxiliary of the public prosecutor.[48]

9.2.2.2 The Netherlands

Concerning investigative bodily search, Dutch law distinguishes between investigation on the clothes (*onderzoek aan de kleding*) and investigation on the body (*onderzoek aan het lichaam*). As we have said earlier, bodily searches infringe two fundamental rights: the right to privacy (artt. 10 GW and 8 ECHR) and the protection of the physical integrity (artt. 11 GW and 3 ECHR). Both provisions authorize a restriction of these rights as long as there exists a sufficient basis in formal law. When it comes to bodily search in criminal investigations, this mostly concerns the Code of Criminal Procedure (Sv), the Opium Act (OW) and the Weapons and Ammunition Act (WWM).

An investigation on the clothes of a suspect involves a search of the clothes, in the course of which police officers are looking for objects concealed in or between the clothes. Investigating objects worn on the body, such as bags (when they are worn on the body), jewelry or a watch, also belongs to an investigation

---

45   Cass. October 27, 1987, R.W. 1988-1989, p. 1025.
46   According to the police instruction book *Politiepraktijk*.
47   Arnou, 1982, p. 129.
48   Cass. October 27, 1987, R.W. 1988-1989, p. 1025.

of the clothes. The investigation may even lead to a search of the lining of a piece of clothing, soles and heels, that may be opened. The search of hand luggage is, however, not permitted in this context since it must first be seized before it can be investigated.[49]

An investigation on the body is primarily aimed at the search of objects concealed on the body of the suspect.[50] It not clear whether the search for clues of the commission of criminal offences is permitted. In 1988, the *Hoge Raad* stated that the natural openings of the body (such as mouth, ear, nose, anus and vagina) may also be investigated during an investigation on the body of a suspect.[51] However, an investigation of the body does not include the possibility to collect bodily samples such as hair or skin cells for the purpose of submitting them to special methods of identification such as DNA analysis. A medical investigation where (a part of) the body itself is investigated for forensic purposes is in principle authorized, although it may only be carried out with the explicit consent of the suspect as long as no legal basis for the investigation exists.[52]

A bodily search may be ordered after the arrest of a suspect: moreover, a bodily search carried out in virtue of art. 56 par. 1 Sv is only authorized on an arrested suspect. This means that a bodily search carried out on a suspect that was not caught in the act will only be authorized for criminal offences where remand in custody is possible. In cases concerning drugs or weapon offences, artt. 9 par. 5 OW and 52 par. 2 WWM authorize bodily searches even prior to the arrestation of the suspect.[53]

For the carrying out of a bodily search, it is, however, mandatory that there be a aggravated suspicion (*ernstige bezwaren*) against the suspect. This means on the one hand that there must be a suspicion reaching further than a reasonable assumption of culpability (*redelijk vermoeden van schuld*) and, on the other hand, this aggravated suspicion ought to be relevant to the aim of the bodily search. For instance, it is not likely that evidence for the theft of a motorcycle will be found during a bodily search. In this case there would be no aggravated suspicion justifying the bodily search of the suspect.[54]

An investigative bodily search may not only be carried out on a suspect. The examining judge may on the basis of art. 195 Sv, of his own initiative or

---

49 Naeyé, 1990, pp. 282-284.
50 Tak, 1990, p. 2.
51 The so-called *Rectaal fouilleren-arrest* ("rectal search-case") HR November 8, 1988, NJ 1989, 667 with a note by T.M. Schalken; see also Naeyé, 1989, p. 880; Swart, 1989, p. 780; Rozemond, 1992, pp. 131-132.
52 Rb Maastricht, October 4, 1989, NJ 1989, 914 (DNA analysis); Rb Haarlem December 5, 1986, NJ 1987, 549 (X-ray investigations).
53 Hendriks *et al.*, 1992, p. 124.
54 See: Naeyé, 1990, pp. 129-130.

upon the request of the public prosecutor, order to have all persons searched who are suspected of carrying on their body or clothes any evidence of the criminal offence. Prior to this search, the persons must be presented to the examining judge in order to be heard. If they refuse to be searched, the search may only be carried out after a court order has been issued.

Indeed, an investigative bodily search may always be carried out when the concerned person agrees to this.[55] This does not mean, however, that with the authorization of the concerned person everything is permitted. Especially when lower ranked police officers obtain the authorization to carry out powers that the legislator has reserved for the public prosecutor or his auxiliaries.[56]

Art. 56 par. 1 Sv reserves the power to order an investigative bodily search to the (auxiliary) public prosecutor, while according to par. 2 of the same article, ordinary police officers are empowered to carry out investigative searches on the clothing. This difference is not followed by artt. 9 par. 5 OW and 52 par. 2 WWM: These provisions authorize police officers of all ranks to carry out investigative searches of the clothes and body of a suspect, as long as there is a aggravated suspicion that he has committed an offence relevant to these provisions. According to the above-mentioned "rectal search-case", this enables police officers to search all the natural body openings as well. There is no provision in Dutch law on the obligation to have a bodily search on a female suspect carried out by a female officer (or citizen).

Searches in such natural openings of the body as mouth, nose and ears are not considered to be medical acts and may therefore be carried out without the assistance of a medical doctor. On the other hand, searches in the anus or the vagina are considered to belong to the (para)medical field since the risk of causing damage to tissues is higher and, in that respect, must be carried out by a doctor.[57] It seems that the fact that the search had been carried out by a doctor was determinant in the fore-mentioned "rectal search-case." The (auxiliary) public prosecutor will in that case deliver a request to that purpose. The use of special equipment (such as a speculum) is in all cases only permitted with the express authorization of the concerned person.[58]

The investigative bodily search will most often be carried out in the police station. In the case of a search carried out in virtue of the Opium Act or the Weapon and Amunition Act, it may be carried out in other places, even in public. The suspect is not obliged to cooperate with the investigative bodily search being carried out. He must, however, endure that this search is being carried out though he may not be obliged to take any prescribed position or to

---

55   HR June 26, 1962, NJ 1962, 470 (Blood test-II).
56   Naeyé, 1990. p. 124.
57   Naeyé, 1990, pp. 133-138.
58   Naeyé, 1990, p. 133.

undress.[59] In cases where it is necessary to examine the inside of a heel or to take pieces of clothing apart, this will take place, for obvious practical reasons, at the police station. Although this type of search constitutes a search of the clothing that may be carried out by regular police officers, it will in most cases be ordered by an (auxiliary) public prosecutor.[60]

9.2.2.3 Luxembourg

In general, Luxembourg law does not distinguish between searches done on premises and those done on persons, both being designated under the name *perquisitions*. It is the purpose of the search that is determinant: the search for evidence. Both forms of search must be carried out by or under the supervision of an auxiliary to the public prosecutor.

The Luxembourg code of criminal procedure mentions only once the possibility to carry out a bodily search, when a suspect is to be remanded in police custody. In that case he will be searched if there is reason to believe that he is carrying objects or substances that may be of interest for the investigation or that may be considered dangerous for himself or for others, in this making no difference between an investigative search and a security search. The text of art. 39 CIC is so general that it appears that both an investigative search on and in the body may be based on that provision.[61] This measure must be carried out by a person of the same sex as that of the suspect. The situation is unclear as to the procedure to follow when such a person cannot be found. It seems to be possible to resort to civilians to carry out such investigations, indeed under the supervision of members of the public force. This problem seems to become increasingly less significant as more women are employed by the public force as police officers.[62]

Investigative searches in general (of persons as well as of houses) are regulated by art. 33 CIC and consequently, an investigative search carried out in violation of this provision is illegal. Of this follows that objects found during an illegal search must be excluded from the evidence.[63] In principle, investigative searches may only be carried out during the day, between 6:00 and 20:00 hours. However, in analogy to the provisions of French law and the position of the literature on the subject, it is likely that investigative bodily searches are

---

59 Naeyé, 1990, p. 130.
60 Naeyé, 1990, p. 131.
61 Art. 39 CIC: "*Si la personne retenue est suspectée de dissimuler des objets utiles à la manifestation de la vérité ou des objets dangereux pour elle-même ou pour autrui, il peut être procédé à sa fouille corporelle.*"
62 This was related to us by members of the public force in Luxembourg.
63 Tr. Arr. Luxembourg, March 11, 1907.

not bound by this provision. When the suspect is caught in the act, the investigative search may be carried out at all times of the day or night. A police report must be drawn and signed by the concerned person as well as by the acting police officers. In case the suspect refuses to sign the police report, this is mentioned in the report.

When the suspect has not been caught in the act or he is being suspected of a criminal offence related to illicit drugs, a *perquisition* may only be carried out with the express authorization of the suspect. According to art. 47 par. 1 CIC, this authorization must be hand-written by the suspect. In the event that he is unable to write, this is recorded in the police report. For the manner in which the search ought to be carried out, the article refers to the provisions of art. 33 CIC.

Whether the suspect has been caught in the act or not the main officers habilitated to carry out investigative searches are auxiliaries of the public prosecutor, of their own initiative or on request of the public prosecutor (artt. 33 and 47 par. 3 CIC). The examining judge may carry out investigative searches personally, even when the suspect has not been caught in the act. In that case he must inform the public prosecutor before hand (art. 65 par. 2 CIC). The investigative search carried out by the examining judge must follow the same rules as other investigative searches.

9.2.2.4 France

An investigative search of clothes or body (*fouille corporelle*) is seen in France as a *perquisition*, which means that it is assimilated to an investigative search carried out on private premises. Of this follows that the artt. 56 *et seq.* CPP will apply to bodily searches as they apply to all forms of *perquisitions*. Each search will be required to be carried out with the express authorization of the concerned person, except in cases where a suspect has been caught in the act.[64] In the course of the criminal procedure, we find three moments where an investigative search may be carried out: in *flagrante delicto*, which is to say when a suspect has been caught in the act,[65] when a suspect is being remanded in custody (the so-called *garde à vue*) and on request of the examining judge having issued an order (*commission rogatoire générale* or *spéciale*).

Hence, the French code of criminal procedure does not foresee any specific provision for investigative searches of the clothes and body and the provisions concerning investigative searches of premises apply, *mutatis mutandis*, to those

---

64 Cass. crim. January 22, 1953, J.C.P. 53, II, 7456; Aix-en-Provence, June 13, 1975, Gaz. Pal. 1975, 2, 711; Decocq, Montreuil & Buisson, 1991, p. 301.

65 During the so-called *enquête de flagrance*, a person may be searched on the spot if there is reason to believe that he carries objects that may be important to the investigation.

carried out on persons. Indeed, the acting officers are not bound to the respect of the so-called legal hours: Other than in the case of investigative searches of private premises, investigative bodily searches may be carried out between 21:00 and 6:00.[66] As we have stated above, the express authorization of the suspect is necessary for searches being carried out (art. 76 CPP), unless the investigation takes place in *flagrante delicto* or the examining judge has issued an order to that effect.[67] The order must be hand-written by the concerned person or, if he or she does not know how to write, mention of this must be recorded in the police report. The procedure described in artt. 56 and 59 CPP must be followed, meaning that only the auxiliary of the public prosecutor is habilitated to peruse the found objects, along with the eventual technical experts he called upon in virtue of art. 60 CPP. With the authorization of the public prosecutor, he only seizes the objects that may be relevant to the discovery of the truth (art. 56 *in fine* CPP).

The investigative bodily search may be carried out on the suspect as well as on persons who are suspected to carry objects that may be relevant for the investigation (art. 56 CPP). The search will be performed by an officer auxiliary of the public prosecutor or, under his orders and supervision, by lower ranked auxiliaries of the same sex as that of the concerned person (art. C.117 IG). In the event that a female police officer is not present at that time, it seems possible to have the search be carried out by a female civil employee.[68]

After a person has been remanded in custody, an investigative bodily search may be carried out if he or she is suspected to carry objects that may be relevant for the investigation or that may be dangerous for himself or for others (art. C.117 IG). In that way, the law makes no apparent difference between a search carried out for investigative reasons and that carried out for security reasons.[69] Force may eventually be used and, if necessary, the person may be undressed in order to examine his clothing thoroughly. The concerned person is then confronted with the objects found before they are seized and sealed. A detailed police report must be drawn from the whole procedure.

In the course of a criminal investigation led by an examining judge, it is possible for him to order that certain investigations be carried out. With a so-called letter rogatory *générale* or *spéciale* he may give orders to auxiliaries of the public prosecutor, who may then carry out investigative searches at all places

---

66   Decocq, Montreuil & Buisson, 1991, p. 325. The position of the *Cour de cassation* is commented by the Court of appeal in Aix-en-Provence, January 13, 1975, Gaz. Pal. 1975, 2, 711.
67   Tak & Lensing, 1990, p. 44.
68   See Decocq, Montreuil & Buisson, 1991, p. 301.
69   See artt. 203 and 215 *Arrêté du ministre de l'intérieur* nr. 334, May 7, 1974, *portant réglement intérieur des gradés et gardiens de la paix des polices urbaines.*

and at all times where it is suspected that relevant objects for the investigation may be found.

9.2.2.5 Germany

In German criminal procedure, both investigative searches of the clothes and of the body are considered specific forms of investigative search (*Durchsuchung*), as are searches of private premises. This means that, in principle, the same conditions apply to all forms of investigative searches. Investigative bodily searches being carried out on a special place, the human body, they will be subject to special protection on the basis of art. 2 par. 2 GG. Of the fundamental right guaranteed by this provision, the protection of the physical integrity (*körperliche Unversehrheit*), it follows that an infringement of this right must find sufficient basis in formal law.

The aim of the search regulated by artt. 102 and 103 StPO is to search for objects or clues that one expects to encounter: It is an investigative search (*Ermittlungsdurchsuchung*).[70] The measures described in these two articles may be carried out on suspects. Like other measures implying physical force, the principle of proportionality (*Verhältnismäßigkeitsgrundsatz*) must be taken into account. This does not mean, however, that an investigative search will never be carried out in the case of a petty offence or always in the case of a more serious crime.[71]

In the course of an investigative bodily search, the police officer is habilitated to search for objects that may help the investigation in or under the clothes or on the body of the concerned person.[72] The officers are even permitted to inspect the natural body openings, as long as they are accessible without medical assistance.[73] In that way the officer may look in the mouth, nose and ears, but also in the anus and vagina.[74] The person being searched may be obliged to undress or to let himself be undressed.

When a person is being searched, the objects he is carrying with him may be examined for clues as well.[75] In principle, this is also the case for the vehicle he is using, unless it is being used as domicile in which case the particular rules applying to the search of domicile mustbe observed. The search

---

70   Besides foreseeing provisions on the *Ermittlungsdurchsuchung*, these two articles also regulate the *Ergreifungsdurchsuchung* that aims to find the suspect in order to arrest him. See about the *Ermittlungsdurchsuchung* for instance Tak, 1990, pp. 29-31 and Mols, 1990a, pp. 110-111.
71   Löwe/Rosenberg, 1989, art. 102, nrs. 36-38.
72   See also the different provincial police statutes (*Landespolizeigesetze*), for instance art. 39 NWPolG, VVPolGNW 39.02 and Heise/Tegtmeyer, 1990, p. 289.
73   Kleinknecht/Meyer-Goßner, 1995, p. 308.
74   Löwe/Rosenberg, 1989, art. 81a, nr. 16.
75   Löwe/Rosenberg, 1989, art. 102, nr. 35.

must be tolerated by the person being searched. In encountering resistance, the officers carrying out the investigation may use force and, if necessary, the searched person may be brought to the police station.[76] In the occurrence that the searched person does not cooperate in opening his luggage or the trunk of his car, these may be opened forcefully. Indeed, these situations will bring about the particular question of proportionality.[77]

In order for the search to be legal, two conditions must be fulfilled: The person to be searched must be suspected of being involved in the commission of a criminal offence and it must be expected that the search will help finding evidence related to that offence.[78] The presumption of culpability does not have to rest on specific facts, but may be the result of a certain "criminological experience."[79] It must be at least likely on the basis of legally obtained police information.[80] This extensive interpretation of the concept of suspicion may lead to the situation where a person originally being heard as a witness and not (yet) as a suspect (and who has not yet been informed of his right to silence), will have risen the sufficient degree of suspicion on his behalf to justify an investigative bodily search.[81] Neither the law nor case-law provide a definite rule determining the place where an investigative bodily search should take place. It is, however, possible to deduct from the aim of the measure as well as from the principle of proportionality, that an investigative bodily search on the street will rarely be considered legal.

It is generally concurred that the investigative bodily search of a non-suspect may be based on art. 103 StPO, as long as there are factual elements present to suggest that the person potentially carries evidence or clues on him. Because of the fact that art. 103 StPO, where the search of non-suspects is regulated, mentions only the search of places instead of also mentioning the search of persons as in art. 102 StPO, there is somewhat discussion on the possibility of carrying out investigative bodily searches on non-suspects.[82] However, considering the fact that special bodily investigations (*körperliche Untersuchung*) may be carried out on non-suspects, although these constitute a greater violation of the physical integrity, it is generally agreed on that investigative bodily searches on non-suspects are authorized as well.[83] Since searches carried out in virtue of art. 102 StPO are only permitted on charged

---

76 Löwe/Rosenberg, 1989, art. 105, nr. 29a.
77 Löwe/Rosenberg, 1989, art. 111, nr. 29.
78 Löwe/Rosenberg, 1989, art. 102, nr. 25.
79 Roxin, 1993, p. 254.
80 Löwe/Rosenberg, 1989, art. 102, nr. 14.
81 Kleinknecht/Meyer-Goßner, 1995, p. 308.
82 Roxin, 1993, pp. 256-257.
83 Löwe/Rosenberg, 1989, art. 103, nr. 13; Roxin, 1993, p. 257; Kleinknecht/Meyer-Goßner, 1995, p. 310.

persons (*Beschuldigte*), they may not be carried out on minors and other persons that cannot be held criminally responsible.[84]

A specific competence for carrying out an investigative bodily search flows from art. 111 StPO: When the commission of terrorist crimes is suspected, the police may set up control posts where the identity of every person passing may be controlled. This control must be tolerated and may be extended to investigative bodily searches and the search of the objects one is carrying.[85] However, according to artt. 163b and 163c StPO referred to by art. 111 par. 3 StPO, non-suspects may not be searched against their will.[86]

Other than in the code of criminal procedure, where both the bodily search and the search of premises are regulated in the same provisions, most of the provincial police statutes foresee specific provisions for investigative bodily searches.[87] Consistent with general police law, these provincial provisions may only aim the non-judicial police sphere: This means for instance that they may only be aimed at the prevention of danger, identity controls related to this aim, the seizure of dangerous objects and substances and controls in places prone to danger.[88]

In conformity to art. 105 StPO, the judge is first competent to order an investigative bodily search, a competence that is extended to the public prosecutor and his auxiliaries in urgent cases. This competence includes also the faculty to establish control posts on the basis of art. 111 StPO. An investigative bodily search must be carried out by a person of the same sex as the searched person, unless being carried out by a doctor.[89] This rule has also been adopted by the various provincial statutes. The woman carrying out a bodily search on the basis of this rule does not have to be a police officer.[90]

84   Pfeiffer *et al*, 1982, p. 246.
85   Vehicles may also be searched based on this provision; Löwe/Rosenberg, 1989, art. 111, nr. 29.
86   Roxin, 1993, p. 258; Löwe/Rosenberg, 1989, art. 111 nrs. 26-28.
87   For instance artt. 39 NWPolG, 17 SPolG and 18 RhPfPVG.
88   Heise/Tegtmeyer, 1990, pp. 288-294; Drews/Wacke/Vogel/Martens, 1985, pp. 201 *et seq.*; Götz, 1991, p. 196.
89   Kleinknecht/Meyer-Goßner, 1995, p. 599.
90   Löwe/Rosenberg, 1989, art. 81a, nr. 5; although this comment relates to the special bodily investigations (*körperliche Untersuchung*), it also applies to the investigative bodily search (*Durchsuchung*).

9.3 Comparing National Norms

9.3.1   Security Search

One notes here a distinction in two groups as to the way security searches are regulated: group one (Belgium, The Netherlands and Germany) providing for a formal basis in domestic law and group two (France and Luxembourg) having no distinct norm (*Table 9.1*). Nevertheless, the conditions in which this search may be done are comparable in all countries. In none of the countries, systematic use of security searches is considered acceptable. One of the most important differences in the execution of the search is the possibility to undress the person concerned. This may constitute a greater violation of one's physical integrity as well as constitute a inhuman treatment when performed in public (*Table 9.1*).

Table 9.1 Security Search

	B	NL	L	F	D
Type of norm					
Statute	+	-	+	-	+
Lower legislation	-	+	-	+	-
Published	+	+	+	+	+
Content					
Palpation of body & clothes	+	+	+	+	+
Palpation of clothes only	-	+	-	-	-
Undress	+	-	-	-	-
Luggage	+	-	-	-	+
Systematically	-	-	-	-	-
Officer same sex as suspect	+	+	+	+	-
Applicability					
Identity control	+	-	-	+	+
Arrest	+	-	+	-	-
Confinement/remand in custody	+	+	+	+	-
Transport	-	-	-	-	+
Public assemblies	+	-	-	-	-
Exercise of legal competence	-	+	-	-	-
Suspect consisting danger to officer or others	-	+	-	-	+
Caught in the act	-	-	-	+	-
Proportionality/subsidiarity	-	+	-	-	-

9.3.2   *Investigative Bodily Search*

Belgium, The Netherlands and Germany know specific legislation regarding investigative bodily searches. These statutes are all published and in that way relatively accessible to the general public. Luxembourg and France on the contrary do not provide specific legislation on bodily searches, these being regulated by the provisions concerning search in general (*perquisition*). This means that questions such as what may be done during a bodily search and in which way it may be carried out cannot be answered clearly and easily, this having consequences for the accessibility of the norms (*Table 9.1*).

Looking more closely at the situations where investigative searches may be carried out in the different countries, we notice that most countries demand that the crime in question be serious enough to justify the measure or in any case that the suspicion resting on the suspect be of a serious nature (*Table 9.2*). We see for instance that Belgium does not admit investigative bodily searches for simple offences (misdemeanours). The Netherlands demand that the crime leading to the measure be one justifying remand in custody. Even France and Luxembourg see remand in custody as a moment where an investigative bodily search ought to be carried out. Moreover, these two countries are very strict as to the fact that authorization of the suspect is needed when he has not been caught in the act. Other cases are left to the appreciation of the judge. Germany seems to be less strict on these conditions since it only demands a suspicion based on criminological experience.

As for the way the investigative bodily search may be carried out, the various countries provide for an array of different norms. If most countries see the investigative bodily search as a search being carried out in or under the clothes, different countries have a distinct idea of how far a search may be carried out in the intimate sphere of the body. The Netherlands and Germany, for instance, are clear in allowing the search to be carried out also in the natural openings of the body, unless medical know-how or special instruments are needed, in which case the investigations are to be carried out by a doctor. In Belgium and in The Netherlands, the suspect may be asked to undress and take certain positions to enable the officers to observe all possible hiding places on the body. Note that Belgium and The Netherlands are the only countries providing for a time limit for the length of the search. Non-suspects may be searched in Belgium, The Netherlands (upon request of the examining judge), France and Germany. The search must be carried out by a person of the same sex as the searched person in Luxembourg, Belgium and France. Germany foresees the same obligation, unless the search is being carried out by a doctor (*Table 9.2*).

Table 9.2 Investigative Bodily Search

	B	NL	L	F	D
Type of norm					
Statute	+	+	+	+	+
Lower legislation	-	-	-	-	-
Content					
In or under clothes	+	+	+	+	+
On the body	-	+	-	-	-
In natural openings of body	+	-	-	-	-
Take special bodily positions	+	-	-	-	+
Use force permitted	-	-	-	-	-
Officer same sex as suspect	+	+	+	+	-
Applicability					
On suspects	+	+	+	+	+
Arrest	+	-	-	-	-
Identity control	-	-	-	-	+
Confinement/remand in custody	-	+	+	+	-
Authorization of the suspect necessary	-	-	+	+	-
Court order necessary	-	-	+	+	+
Caught in the act	-	-	+	+	-

9.4 Conclusion

When looking at present international law on police cooperation, the security search as mentioned in art. 41 SC is the most relevant form of bodily search as it may, in certain circumstances, be performed by foreign police officers. This is not to say that the other studied forms of bodily search are not: They will be relevant when assessing the evidence obtained in another country. Moreover, in the context of cross-border hot pursuit, they might be performed on the grounds of a suspicion risen in another country.

Looking at which officers may carry out security searches on which territory,[91] note that the officers of the Benelux countries will have to adapt to the new situation created by the Schengen Convention, since they will have to restrict the use of force to what is provided by art. 41 SC, which use of force is subject to the acquisition of the power to apprehend in another country. Moreover, since according to the Schengen Convention the officers of the different parties are subject not only to the law of the Convention itself, but also to the law of the party on which they are operating, the officers will have to have sufficient knowledge of the rules applying to the execution of a security search. Indeed, the fact that a foreign police officer has the power to apprehend a suspect on the territory of another Schengen country does not necessarily mean that this country authorizes the systematic application of security searches. In many cases, they will have to weigh the opportuneness of such an operation.

Dutch and Luxembourg police officers will be restricted to a 10 kilometre zone when it comes to the power of apprehending and carrying out a security search on a suspect pursued on Belgian territory. On the other hand, German officers will have thirty minutes to apprehend a suspect in the same circumstances. The officers of these three countries will, however, be subjected to Belgian law when it comes to the carrying out of the security search on Belgian territory. Of this follows that the suspect may not be held up more than the time necessary to carry out the search, never exceeding the time of 1 hour. The officers carrying out the search will have to be of the same sex as the suspect being searched (*Table 9.1*).

Belgian and German police officers will have the power to apprehend a suspect on Dutch territory within a 10 km zone of the Dutch-Belgian border. When doing so they may carry out a security search, provided they first take into account the conditions set out by Dutch law. This means that systematically carrying out a security searches on suspects is excluded on Dutch territory. The facts and circumstances will have to be carefully weighed with regard to the reasonability and the proportionality of the measure (*Table 9.1*).

Belgian and German police officers pursuing a suspect onto Luxembourg territory will have the power to apprehend this person within a 10 kilometre zone from their respective common borders. Luxembourg does not have any distinct legislation on the way security searches may be carried out. It seems that it would be possible there to carry out security searches systematically since an arrest is considered sufficient ground for this measure. Luxembourg officers are, moreover, very specific about the necessity of having a security search carried out by a person of the same sex as the suspect as a very crucial one (*Table 9.1*).

---

91   See Chapters 6 and 7 for a detailed look at hot pursuit and apprehension.

Because of the fact that the French government has not given the power to apprehend a suspect on French ground to any foreign officer, it is not necessary here to study the French legislation on that subject, if only in an academic effort to subsequently test this legislation on the hand of international norms (paragraph 9.1). French law does not foresee in any provision regulating the use of security searches by police officers. Considered as a "simple police act," it is likely that it may be carried out in a systematic manner (*Table 9.1*).

Dutch, Belgian, Luxembourg and French police officers have been granted by the German government the power to pursue suspects from their respective territories into Germany, with no restriction of time or distance. When apprehending a suspect on German ground, the foreign police officer will have to keep the following in mind when carrying out a security search: It may not be carried out in a systematic way and its opportuneness must rest on facts and circumstances (*Table 9.1*).

In the context of cross-border hot pursuit, apprehension and security search, the extent the different countries allow security searches to take place may potentially cause clashes. Whether a pursuing Belgian police officer will actually go so far as to have an apprehended suspect undress on Dutch or German territory is doubtful. It is, however, important to stress these differences in the light of international cooperation. Another point is whether the luggage or the automobile of a person being searched for security reasons may be searched as well. It seems plausible that in all the countries a superficial search of these may be done, as long as this can be justified in the light of safety. Taking the case of a vehicle apart will be difficult to defend as having done for security reasons. Indeed, the lack of specific provisions on the way or the extent to which a security search may be carried out is liable to cause problems.

Whether the acknowledged differences will have an impact on international police cooperation. As we have seen in section 9.1.1, the only search foreign police officers are habilitated to perform is the security search. Although the law of all the countries limit the security search to a palpation of the clothes and a superficial search of bags and other objects carried, one important difference remains which may trouble the smooth execution of such a search in another country. Foreign officers of Belgian and Luxembourg territory will have to respect the fact that security searches may only be done by an officer of the same sex of that of the pursued suspect. Whether this will cause important problems in the future is a question yet to be answered. Once the suspect has been apprehended and the competent authorities warned, it might not always be possible to wait for the local police authorities: Is it wise to expect that pursued suspect will have the same amount patience as the arresting officers?

Whether the different national law are conform to the prescriptions of the European Convention on Human Rights is the next question we will attempt to answer here. As the introducing statement of the Convention acknowledges, the parties to the Convention all share a common heritage in the rule of law. Consequently, public authorities such as the police are subject to the law in the same way as are the states and their citizens. Is there a legal basis needed for bodily searches?

The answer to the question lies in the form or the moment these searches are done. There is a clear gradation in the different bodily searches as we have shown above. A security search done on a red-handed suspect upon apprehension and limited to the palpation of the body and the clothes of the suspect may not need a legal basis as in a country where this may be done by a citizen in the same circumstances. However, this is a special situation, an exception to the general principle that no one may be compelled to undergo a bodily search. In this sense, the rule of law prescribes the necessity of a set of rules, democratically controlled by parliament, especially when these competences concern extra-territorial jurisdiction. As was stated by the European Court on Human Rights, a violation of a fundamental right, in this case the physical integrity, must be accordance with the law, pursue a legitimate aim and be necessary in a democratic society. The law must, moreover, be accessible and its consequences must be foreseeable for the citizens. This is true especially with certain forms of security searches, for instance a so-called strip search, where the physical integrity of a person is clearly violated. Furthermore, security searches should only be possible when they are regulated by law, whether they be carried out by police officers or by regular citizens.

As for investigative bodily searches, it is clear that the greater the violation of the physical integrity, the greater the need for special and detailed regulations in domestic law. As we have stated in section 9.1.2, there is a gradation of severity between the different forms of bodily search. While simple violations of physical integrity should be subject to a number of formalities prescribed by law, certain unreasonable bodily searches should to be avoided altogether as unhuman treatment. When a bodily search constitutes a violation of the physical integrity, it should indeed be based on sufficient national law as was defined by the European Court on Human Rights in the cases Kruslin and Huvig. This means that this basis should to consist in more than case law. Further, it should to be accessible and sufficiently detailed as the concerned person must be able to foresee its consequences for him. Finally, it must be compatible with the rule of law.

Do the national laws of the different studied countries comply with the requisites of the European Convention on Human Rights? As acknowledged above, the countries may be divided in two categories: one with countries that have adopted laws (Belgium, The Netherlands and Germany) and one with countries which have not (Luxembourg and France). Despite the fact that a security search may be executed by civilians acting in hot-pursuit in most of the countries, it must be treated as an exception to the common rule that no one

406

may be forced to endure such close physical contact. A legal basis is needed for the actions of the civilian as for the acts of police authorities. For those reasons, the national laws of France and Luxembourg are not sufficient in our opinion.

The national laws on the investigative bodily searches are closer to the prerequisites of the European Convention on Human Rights. They are all contained in statutes. However, the extent to which the concept of investigative bodily search flows into that of investigative searches of a house suggests a lack of accessibility: Is it possible for the citizen to clearly foresee the consequences for him upon the lecture of the legal provisions? In any case, the laws of France and Luxembourg would gain in clarity if special statutes for investigative bodily searches were adopted.

In short, the limit and the conditions in which bodily searches should be done by the police should be set out in clear provisions of formal law. Indeed, the degree of infringement in one's physical integrity, the fact that it might be carried out in public, that one might be obliged to undress, that one may be searched by an official of the opposite sex or that the suspect may be compelled to endure special investigations or that samples be collected are all factors to influence the degree of formality to be observed. What is important to keep in mind is that clear statutes will not only improve the accessibility of the rules, but the international cooperation as well. As stated in other paragraphs, statutes are public and easy to consult when attempting to elaborate conflict rules or to evaluate the value of evidence gathered in another country.

10 Police Interrogation

A very important source of information for the police, interrogation may be considered a moment where suspects are particularly vulnerable to pressure, stress and other factors that may affect the quality of the resulting declaration. For this reason many states have set rules and elaborated guidelines for the treatment of suspects and witnesses during interrogation while international law has set standards guiding the different national authorities towards ideals of the rule of law.

Interrogation of a suspect, but also that of a witness, occurs often in the early stages of the police enquiry since it is necessary to gather as much information as possible as soon as possible. While interrogation of a witness as a source of information will rarely be subjected to a great degree of formalism, the interrogation of a suspect will be more delicate: On the first hand because the suspect might make incriminative declarations that may be used later in court and on the second hand, and partly because of this, the suspect is placed in a particularly weak situation. Indeed in early stages of the enquiry, the suspect will be confronted with the police, with witnesses, maybe even with the victim. The police seem to be more free to influence the suspect, while interrogation at a later stage of an officially charged suspect, for instance by the judiciary, may prove more difficult since in principle it will be subject to a greater degree of formalism and control. For these reasons it is important to set rules in order to guarantee due process and make sure abuses of power do not occur.

We will first consider international standards concerning police interrogation and then we will study the law of the different countries in the light of these international standards.

10.1 International Norms

10.1.1 International Norms on Police Cooperation

Although questioning suspects after a cross border pursuit is in principle the exclusive privilege of those authorities locally competent, some treaties have addressed the issue, be it in very general terms. The Benelux Extradition Treaty and the Schengen Convention mention the possibility of interrogation but offer few details. Art. 27 par. 2 *in fine* combined with par. 1 BET, as well as art. 41 par. 4 sub f SC provide for the bringing of suspects to the local public authorities after a cross border pursuit. The actual apprehension for questioning of the suspects will then be reserved to the locally competent authorities and will be executed in accordance to the law of the state where the pursuit has taken place (art. 41 par. 6 SC).

It is worth mentionning that the question of the police interrogation of the pursued suspect has been the suspect of misconceptions in the past. In 1993, according to a newspaper clipping, French officers had heard a suspect after a cross border pursuit in Belgium. It was at the time thought that this was allowed because of the Schengen Convention. At the time, the Schengen Convention was not yet in force, but even if it would have been, There is no doubt as to the fact that police interrogation excluded from the scope of the Schengen Convention. Furthermore, the Belgian government abusively stated in the Schengen Explanatory statement for the Senate, that the pursuing police officers disposed of the power to interrogate the suspect.[1]

The situation is not as clear as it appears. It seems that the power reserved to the locally competent authorities ia not as much the interrogation in itself, but rather the retention for the purpose of interrogation.[2] There is, indeed, nothing standing in the way of police officers legally in a foreign country to question the apprehended suspect. That is, provided they are in the lawful execution of their tasks, are legally on the foreign territory and they dispose of the right to apprehend. The Schengen Convention offers police officers a legal basis to find themselves in a foreign country. In our opinion, police officers that have legally apprehended a suspect according to art. 41 par. 5 sub f SC, will, indeed, have the faculty to ask questions and in that way "hear" the suspect. Spontaneous declarations done by the pursued or observed suspect may be collected.[3] Moreover, nothing stands in the way of them accompanying the locally competent police officers to the police station where they may participate to the interrogation. In that case, however, they will be subject to the cooperation of their foreign colleagues. This should not pose much problems in practice.

When questionning suspects after a cross border hot pursuit, police officers will have to respect national law. As we have often repeated in the course of this book, the Schengen Convention imposes on the foreign police officers the

---

1   *Gedrukte stukken* 1991-1992, nr. 464/1, p. 17; the text litterally says: "*In een verklaring (...) heeft elke Staat (...) toepassingsmodaliteiten bepaald met betrekking tot het recht om de betrokkene te ondervragen (...)*"; this inaccurate statement was not taken over by the Belgian circular.

2   In the text, litterally:" *être retenue aux fins d'audition*," "*voor verhoor worden opgehouden*" and "*zum Zwecke der Vernehmung festgehalten werden.*"

3   This interpretation is confirmed by the French circular on the application of the Schengen Convention (NOR:*JUSA9500149C*, June 23, 1995).

obligation to respect the law of the country where they operate. In this chapter, we will give an overview of what this law is.

10.1.2 European Convention on Human Rights

The existing international norms as standard minimum for national states do not offer detailed regulations regarding the way the interrogation of a suspect ought to take place. They do offer however some fundamental principles that are to be respected. The problem lays mainly in the fact that the different principles do not concern each moment of the criminal procedure. The prohibition of torture and degrading or inhuman treatment or punishment for instance is guaranteed to everyone at all times, independent from the fact whether one has been charged or found guilty of an offence (art. 3 ECHR). The guarantees of artt. 5 (liberty and security of the person) and 6 ECHR (fair and public trial) on the other hand only concern certain moments in the criminal procedure: starting at the moment of the deprivation of liberty or at the moment one charged with a criminal offence. This goes for other norms offering a minimum standard for the treatment of suspects: the right to be informed promptly of the reasons of one's arrest as guaranteed by art. 5 par. 2 ECHR and the right to be brought promptly before a judge as guaranteed by par. 3 of art. 5 ECHR.

One of the most important problems posed by these guarantees is the moment they begin to take effect. The problem of characterizing police interrogation in the different countries in order to place it under one of the categories provided for by the European Convention on Human Rights may render the enforcement of these provisions difficult.

10.1.2.1 Prohibition of Torture and Inhuman or Degrading Treatment (art. 3)

Applied to the particular issue of the interrogation of suspects, the prohibition of torture and inhuman or degrading treatment or punishment as guaranteed by art. 3 ECHR prohibits the use of certain police techniques to obtain a confession or incriminating information on oneself or others. Art. 3 ECHR reads:

No one shall be subject to torture or to inhuman or degrading treatment or punishment.

When reading this article, one notes that there is a gradation between the different actions prohibited by art. 3. In the Greek case the Commission developed the concept of inhuman treatment and stated that it "covers at least such treatment as deliberately causes severe suffering, mental or physical, which inhuman treatment with a purpose such as to obtain information or a confession whereas punishment would be an aggravated form of inhuman treatment. Degrading would be said of treatment or punishment that grossly humiliate the person subject to it before others or drive "him to act against his conscience."[5]

This definition was used by the Court in the Ireland v. Great-Britain case on deciding whether the english techniques of interrogation suspects, known as the five techniques, were compatible with art. 3 ECHR. The Court started by emphasizing that "ill-treatment must attain a minimum level of severity if it is to fall within the scope of art. 3."[6] The techniques - consisting in obliging interrogated persons to stand for a long period on their toes against the wall, covering their heads with black hoods, subjecting them to constant intense "hissing" noise, depriving them of sleep and sufficient food and drink - were indeed considered by the Court as being inhuman treatment.[7] It did not constitute torture because it was not a "deliberate inhuman treatment causing very serious and cruel suffering" and it "did not occasion suffering of the particular intensity and cruelty implied by the word torture as so understood."[8] Furthermore, the circumstances must be examined not at the moment of the signing of the Convention but at the present moment since "the Convention is a living instrument which (...) must be interpreted in the light of the present-day views."[9]

More recently the Court was asked in the Tomasi case to pronounce itself on claims of ill-treatment by the police during police custody (*garde à vue*) in France. The Court distinguished two questions, one of which concerning the question of the causality existing between the alleged ill-treatment and the observed injuries and the other one concerning the severity of the ill-treatment in relation to art. 3.[10]

The first question was answered in the affirmative since medical reports indicated that the injuries occurred during the period when the defendant was in police custody. It seemed determinant for the Court that the defendant was examined by four independent physicians.[11]

---

5   The Greek case, p. 186; see on art. 3 further Van Dijk & Van Hoof, pp. 226 *et seq.* and Swart, 1993a, p. 184.
6   Ireland v. Great Britain, January 18, 1978, Series A 25, pp. 60 *et seq.*
7   Ireland v. Great Britain, p. 65.
8   Ireland v. Great Britain, pp. 66-67.
9   Tyrer case, April 25, 1978, Series A 26, p. 15.
10 Tomasi v. France, August 27, 1992, Series A 241A.
11 This poses a particular question related to the right to a medical examination as guaranteed for example by the French *Code de procédure pénale*: In the last reform the right to a medical examination by a physician of one's choice was restricted to include only those physicians appearing on a list set up by the public prosecutor; see on this subject further Joubert, 1994.

Although the Court did not feel it ought to examine neither the system of the *garde à vue* in France nor the frequency and the length of the interrogation, it did pronounce itself on the severity of the ill-treatment as established by the medical reports. These reports indeed establish the intensity and the multiplicity of the blows suffered by Mr Tomasi. These are two elements that provide serious clues when establishing whether ill-treatment may be considered inhuman or degrading. The Court adds that neither the necessities of the enquiry nor the evident difficulties encountered by the police in its fight against crime may justify the resort to methods endangering the physical integrity of the person.[12]

10.1.2.2   Right to Liberty and Security of Person (art. 5)

Without entering the debate concerning the difference between detention and restriction of liberty as addressed by art. 5 of the Convention, one may note that some forms of police custody, like the *garde à vue* in France or the *ophouden voor verhoor* and *inverzekeringstelling* in The Netherlands, pose a specific problem as they constitute a hybrid form of detention: As long as the time of deprivation does not exceed the limit stated in the Brogan case[13] one may argue that the right to be informed promptly of the reasons of one's arrest (art. 5 par. 2) or to be brought promptly before a judge (art. 5 par. 3) have not been violated. However, upon reading art. 5 par. 2 ECHR:

> *Everyone who is arrested shall be informed promptly, in a language which he understands, of the reasons for his arrest and of any charge against him.*

One notes the use of the word "arrested" instead of the words "deprived of its liberty" which suggests that art. 5 par. 2 may also apply to restrictions of liberty, including being brought in the police station for interrogation before having been formally charged.[14] In any case it seems relevant to state that a person detained for interrogation should be at one point informed of the reasons of his or her arrest and, should this person be detained longer than necessary for interrogation, be brought promptly before a judge. This seems to find a basis in par. 1 sub c, which states as a lawful deprivation of liberty the "arrest or detention of a person effected for the purpose of bringing him before the competent legal authority on reasonable suspicion of having committed an offence." The crucial point being in this case the moment when a questioned person becomes a suspect. At least from this moment on he should have the right to be informed

---

12 Tomasi v. France, p. 45.
13 Brogan case, November 29, 1988, Series A 145/B.
14 The ECHR estimates this moment as being the moment where the suspect is being told by a competent authority that he has committed an offence; see Eckle case, July 15, 1982, Series A 51 and the Fox, Campbell and Hartley case, December 10, 1982, Series A 182.

suspect. At least from this moment on he should have the right to be informed promptly of the reasons of his arrest, if this has not been already done, since the omission of such information would result in a violation of his right to remain silent as guaranteed by art. 6 par. 2.[15]

Considering the right to be brought promptly before a judge or other officer authorized by law to exercise judicial power as guaranteed by art. 5 par. 3 ECHR:

> *Everyone arrested or detained in accordance with the provisions of par. 1c of this article shall be brought promptly before a judge or other officer authorized by law to exercise judicial power (...),*

it is relevant to examine the function of the different officials charged with the appreciation of the legality of the police custody. Since this question has been examined in greater detail in paragraph 4.7 of this book, it is not relevant at this point to make extensive note of some of the criteria stated in the Brogan case. Let us however point out one aspect of this case that is especially relevant to the control function a judge may have when seeing the suspect after a number of hours of police interrogation. The Court states in Brogan that "Judicial control of interferences by the executive with the individual's right to liberty is an essential feature of the guarantee of art. 5 par. 3, which is intended to minimise the risk of arbitrariness."[16] In this way, it is relevant to examine whether the official competent to decide on the maintaining of the custody and responsible for the factual revision of the legality of the custody is a representative of the public prosecutor or an impartial judge within the meaning of the European Convention on Human Rights.

10.1.2.3   Presumption of Innocence and Right to Silence

As for the presumption of innocence as guaranteed by art. 6 par. 2 with regards to police interrogation:

> *Everyone charged with a criminal offence shall be presumed innocent until proven guilty according to law.*

The Court includes the right to remain silent in the presumption of innocence. In its judgement in the Funke case, the Court stated that the obligation for the

---

15 The Commission has stated that art. 5 par. 2 extends to all forms of arrest effected in accordance with any of the provisions sub a to f; see Report of July 14, 1988, par. 105-107 and teh Court in the Bouamar case, February 29, 1988, Series A 129, both cited in Van Dijk & Van Hoof, 1990, pp. 273-274.

16 Brogan case, nr. 58.

have obtained another way, was equivalent to furnishing evidence of alleged infractions himself. This, the Court said, was incompatible with the presumption of innocence and the inherent right to remain silent.[17] The question as to the moment this guarantee starts to exist finds its answer in the wording of par. 2: when the person is "charged with a criminal offence." Strictly speaking, this guarantee would not apply to the particular issue of police interrogation since one cannot at this point speak of a person "charged with a criminal offence". However, the Commission stated in the Neumeister case that the relevant stage of the procedure "is that at which the situation of the person concerned has been substantially affected as a result of a suspicion against him."[18] Indeed one may wonder on the interpretation to be given to the word "substantially" in this context, but one may indeed argue that from the moment a suspect is deprived of his freedom to come and to go as he wishes, that his situation has been "substantially affected as a result of a suspicion against him." Moreover, one could go one step further and consider any questionning situation by the police. This could include, for instance, the situation where an infiltrating police officer is questionning an unaware suspect. In our opinion, this suspect is in great need of protection as the infiltrating officer, acting undercover, is in a position to manipulate his intention. This protection can be considered as not absolute, but in that case a legal basis is needed to restrict it.[19]

Art. 6 par. 2 ECHR does not impose on the authorities the obligation to inform the suspect of his right to remain silent. On the other hand it would be difficult to argue that an obligation to testify existing in the former text of art. 62 par 2 of the French *Code de procédure pénale*[20] for example would be compatible with art. 6 par. 2 ECHR. However, it is doubtful whether the presumption of innocence would have any sense by denying it to those who are suspects but not yet formally charged.

Art. 6 par. 3 ECHR recognizes other rights as well, the right to legal counsel being one that has been discussed greatly by many scholars in Europe.[21]:

> *Everyone charged with a criminal offence has the following minimum rights: (....) to defend himself in person or through legal assistance of his own choosing or, if he has not sufficient means to pay for legal assistance, to be given it free when the interests of justice so require.*

---

17 Funke v. France, February 25, 1993, Series A 256, p. 18.
18 Report of May 27, 1966, Neumeister, B.6 (1966-1969, p. 81.); see also Van Dijk & Van Hoof, 1990, p. 329.
19 See further Chapter 5.
20 "*Les personnes convoquées sont tenues de comparaître et de déposer.*" The words "*et de déposer*" have been however excluded in the last reform of 1993.
21 See for instance Lensing, 1988; Fijnaut, 1988; Delmas-Marty, 1991.

Although the right to legal counsel may be regarded as a safeguard for the rights of the suspect discussed above, the European Convention on Human Rights only recognizes this right to the suspect at the moment he has been officially charged. Where the right to remain silent becomes illusionary by its late revelation to the suspect, the right to legal counsel may palliate this irregularity by enabling the suspect to be aware of his rights via his legal counsel.[22] However the fact that this right is guaranteed only once the suspect has been officially charged dampers the impact of this right considerably. The Commission considers the right to legal counsel as a right that may be restricted in that this right does not imply that the legal counsel be given free access to all confidential papers nor that the suspect be given the opportunity to consult his lawyer at all times he wishes to do so.[23] Be that as it may, the Commission has also questioned the value of a incriminative declaration made before the suspect had the opportunity to consult his legal counsel.[24] In the evaluation of the whole of the criminal procedure the presence of the lawyer will further be a determinant factor.[25]

It may be argued that the different rights offered by the legislation of a state ought to be regarded as a whole when assessing the compliance of one system with the requisites of art. 6 of the Convention. This means to say that the right to a legal counsel in this context might be more important as other rights, such as the right to silence, the right to be informed or the right to be brought before a judge, are given less significance. The relative weight of the right to legal counsel as guaranteed by art. 6 ECHR was reiterated in the case Imbrioscia v. Switzerland[26] where the court stated that: "the right set out in paragraph 3 (c) of article 6 is one element, amongst others, of the concept of a fair trial in criminal preceedings (...) [It] does not specify the manner of exercising this right. It thus leaves to the Contracting States the choice of the means of ensuring that it is secured in their judicial systems, the Court's task being only to ascertain whether the method they have chosen is consistent with the requirements of a fair trial."[27]

---

22 Furthermore, the right to legal counsel may work as a deterrent for authorities conducting interrogations that may otherwise get carried away by the heat of the moment.

23 Bonzi v. Switzerland, July 12, 1978; Shertenleib v. Switzerland, July 12, 1979; Kurup v. Denmark, July 10, 1985.

24 Barbera, Messegué and Jabardo-case, December 6, 1988, Series A 146; Moudefo v. France, Report of July 8, 1987; see also Lensing, 1988, pp. 107 *et seq.*

25 Requests nr. 8022, 8025 and 8027/77, March 18, 1981.

26 November 24, 1993, Series A 275.

27 Imbrioscia v. Switzerland, nr. 37 and 38.

10.2   National Norms

Regarding the particular issue of police interrogation, one must note that the norms regarding police custody must also be observed. The question of police custody has been discussed in Chapter 7. In this chapter we will discuss the different norms regarding police interrogation in general in the light of the minimum standards offered by the European Convention on Human Rights and the principles discussed above and of the question as to whether these differences are liable to cause problems for police officers operating in a foreign country. After this we will compare the norms as we have done in the preceding chapters and comment their compatibility with the European Convention on Human Rights which will permit us to draw some conclusions.

10.2.1   Guarantees Against Torture and Inhuman or Degrading Treatment

Since it is hardly imaginable that the legislation of a civilized country provides their police with powers that would explicitly authorize torture or inhuman or degrading treatment as an aid to police interrogation, one must consider the safeguards provided by national laws that may render the resort to such techniques difficult. One may think here for instance of the obligation for police officers to make a detailed report of each interrogation, mentioning for instance all periods of interrogation and rest, the placing of the interrogation under control of a judicial authority or even audio or video taping of the interrogation. One may think as well of the right to have one's legal counsel present during police interrogation or eventually the possibility to have oneself examined by a physician during police custody.

10.2.1.1   General

Belgium
As we have seen in the preceding chapter, a person that has been arrested, whether it be administratively or judicially, may be held in police custody for a period not exceeding 24 hours. Belgian law only provides for rules regarding interrogation by the investigating judge.

The most important provision concerning interrogation before the preliminary instruction (enquiry by the investigating judge) is art. 16 VHW which concerns the interrogation prior to the issuing of a warrant for arrest. According to par. 2 sub 1 of this provision the investigating judge must, prior to issuing the court order, interrogate the suspect on the alleged charges and receive any comment he might have concerning the charges. The suspect is in no way obliged to answer any question directed to him (art. 14 par. 3 sub g ITCPR) but the authority conducting the interrogation is not obliged to point this out to the suspect. The suspect has no obligation to speak the truth and will therefore not testify under oath.[28]

Art. 16 par. 2 obliges the investigating judge to inform the suspect that a warrant for his arrest may be issued. The judge must hear his reaction to this information. The judge must also inform the suspect of his right to consult a legal counsel of his choice with whom he will be able to communicate freely after the first period of interrogation (art. 20 VHW).[29] The first period of interrogation by the investigating judge is in principle conducted without a lawyer being present.[30]

The provisions of art. 16 VHW concern in theory the only interrogation by the investigating judge prior to the issuing of a warrant for arrest. The interrogation during police enquiry is generally considered a deontological obligation.[31] The Belgian legislator has not given any guidelines concerning the interrogation of suspects by the police or officers of the public prosecutor's department. This is due to the fact that the whole of the police enquiry, contrarily to the judicial enquiry by the investigating judge, is not regulated.[32]

In important cases the interrogation will mostly be done by the investigating judge personally but in other cases the interrogation may also be left to the senior police officers (*officiers de police judiciaire*).[33] In general it will be the officer leading the enquiry who will also conduct the interrogation, eventually delegating this task to hierarchical subordinates and even to the BOB.

Despite this absence of rules one may consider that the interrogation by police officials ought to be conducted in the same way as the interrogation by the investigating judge. Firstly because of the fact that most of these obligations originate from international obligations: This is the case for instance of the right to silence.[34] Every deprivation of liberty and interrogation must furthermore be accounted for in a detailed and regularly updated report (artt. 1 and 2 VHW). The suspect must also be presented to the investigating judge before the 24 hour limit. Indeed according to the exclusionary rule, evidence obtained with the help of any form of undue pressure or intimidation will be excluded.

To complete the information gathered by the interrogation one may also think of confrontations, where methods as Oslo confrontations are meant as well as

---

28 Fijnaut, 1988, p. 38; Van den Wyngaert, 1994, pp. 6638-640.
29 De Nauw, 1991, pp. 113-115.
30 See Fijnaut, 1988, pp. 37-40.
31 Van den Wyngaert, 1994, p. 638.
32 See Chapter 3; see also Fijnaut, 1988, p. 37.
33 Van den Wyngaert, 1994, pp. 607, 638; however the questioning must be done by the examining magistrate when the question regards whether a court order of arrest ought to be issued (art. 2 VHW); see Van den Wyngaert, 1994, pp. 696-697 and De Nauw, 1991, pp. 111-112.
34 Note that neither the examining judge nor the police official is obliged to point out to the suspect, see also Fijnaut, 1988, pp. 37-40.

methods where a number of persons are heard in the presence of one another. Like other forms of interrogation the person conducting the enquiry ought to draw up a detailed and updated report of all events.

The Netherlands

After his arrest, the suspect must be taken to the police station where he may be retained before he is to be brought before the public prosecutor or one of his auxiliaries. This higher ranking police officer will then determine whether the suspect ought to be kept in custody for interrogation.[35] The retention may not last more than six hours, by the computing of which the time between 00:00 and 9:00 do not count (art. 61 Sv). After a maximum duration of fifteen hours (at the latest) the auxiliary public prosecutor must decide whether the suspect must be placed in (police) custody (*inverzekeringstelling*) in conformity to art. 57 Sv or whether he must be brought before an investigating judge (*rechter-commissaris*) as to have him remanded in pre-trial custody (*bewaring*). If the police custody is not followed by the placing of the suspect in security custody or his appearance before the investigating judge, he must be freed (art. 61 par. 2 Sv).

A suspect may be interrogated during the preliminary phase as well as during the enquiry before the court.[36] During the preliminary phase the interrogation will mostly be used during the apprehension and retention for interrogation (*ophouden voor verhoor*) and the police custody which does not mean that its use will be excluded in later phases of the criminal process.

The aim of the interrogation is to gather information related to the committed crime and to the role of the interrogated person in its commission. The final aim is to shine light on the truth and to gather evidence or clues.[37] Every question by an enquiring police officer or judicial official to the suspect in relation to his role by the commission of a criminal offence must be considered an interrogation according to the law.[38] From that moment on the suspect must be informed that he is not obliged to answer any question.[39] Only facts that the interrogated person has experienced first hand, facts of his own knowledge or known to him personally may be the object of a declaration (art. 341 Sv).

---

35 Naeyé, 1990, p. 55; Bossink *et al.*, 1986, pp. 155-161.
36 For an extensive study of interrogation see Naeyé, 1990, pp. 225-262 and especially Lensing, 1988.
37 The aim is not to obtain a confession! see Naeyé, 1990, pp. 236-238.
38 For instance HR October 2, 1979, NJ 1980, 243, with note by G.E. Mulder; Hendriks *et al.*, 1992, p. 115.
39 See Naeyé, 1990, pp. 231 and 249; we will discuss this further in sub-section 10.2.3.2.

Luxembourg

The Luxembourg law does not provide for norms regarding the manner in which a suspect may be interrogated. It does however offer some guidelines destined to ensure the fulfilment of certain formalities.

Although the interrogation of a suspect may take place anywhere, the only form of interrogation that is addressed in the code of criminal procedure is the one following the placing in police custody ex art. 39 CIC.[40] Paragraph 1 states that a person against whom serious and corroborating suspicion has risen, the nature of which may justify criminal charges against him, may be placed in police custody for a period not exceeding 24 hours. This period is calculated starting from the moment the suspect's physical freedom has been taken.

Luxembourg law does not foresee the possibility to prolong the period of 24 hours. After the termination of the police custody the judge is competent to decide on the placing of the suspect in preliminary detention.

France

A French police officer has the power to hold a person in custody for a period not exceeding 24 hours. This period of police custody, called *garde à vue*, is submitted to strict procedural rules that have been reviewed and completed by the laws of January and August 1993 in an effort to make them more compatible with the European Convention on Human Rights.[41]

The expression "*garde à vue*," literally meaning "guard in sight" designates the period during which the suspect or a witness spends his time during police interrogation. If the *garde à vue* is exercised in a police station, the guarded person will be placed in a cell where the guards will observe him during rest periods through a large window located in every cell door. From this cell he will be brought before the officers responsible for his interrogation. The *garde à vue* may in principle also be exercised anywhere, even in hospitals that are sometimes equipped with specially prepared *garde à vue* locals. This form of police custody is possible in three phases of the enquiry: during the police enquiry *in flagrante delicto* (artt. 63-65 CPP), during the regular police enquiry (artt. 77 and 78 CPP) and after the opening of an enquiry by the investigating judge (art. 154 CPP).

---

40 Although many of Luxembourg's legal dispositions seem to have been borrowed from the French legislator, the Luxembourg legislator explicitly did not intend to borrow the French concept of *garde à vue*, but indeed intended to regulate a practice that in fact existed for a long time, the placing in custody of suspects by the police for periods of time not exceeding 24 hours. See the explanatory statement on art. 39 CIC, bill of law nr. 2859 (5), September 9, 1989.

41 Law nr. 93-2, January 4, 1993, *portant réforme de la procédure pénale* and law nr. 93-1013, August 24, 1993, *modifiant la loi 93-2 portant réforme de la procédure pénale*; see on the recent developments regarding the *garde à vue* in France also Boyer, 1993, p. 6; Pradel, 1993a, p. 39; Pradel, 1993b, pp. 229 *et seq.*; Jansen, 1994, pp. 122-138; Joubert, 1994, pp. 248-271.

The decision to place someone in custody is taken by the officer of judicial police, in turn supervised by the public prosecutor's department. As was stated above he has in flagrancy cases the power to place anyone in police custody whom he suspects to detain relevant information for the ongoing enquiry (artt. 62 CPP).[42] In the absence of flagrance he may only do so if elements exist against the person in question that may lead to the presumption that he has committed or attempted to commit a criminal act (art. 77 CPP). However, if there are reasons to believe that someone may have relevant information for the enquiry, he may summon this person to appear before him (art. 78 CPP). The person summoned in that way is then obliged to present himself before the auxiliary of the public prosecutor. If he omits or refuses to do so, the auxiliary of the public prosecutor will inform the public prosecutor (*procureur de la République*) who may order to have the person brought by force.

Once a person is placed in custody, the public prosecutor must be informed in the best possible time (artt. 63 and 77 CPP), the proof that this has indeed been done being established by the mention of it in the police report.[43] The suspect must be brought before the *procureur de la République* at the end of the first twenty-four hours.

The *garde à vue* of persons against whom there are no elements justifying the presumption that they have committed or attempted to commit a criminal offence may not exceed the time necessary for their declaration (art. 64 par. 2 CPP). The *garde à vue* of those against whom such elements exist may be prolonged for another period of twenty-four hours after written authorization has been given by the public prosecutor. If the reproached facts were not caught in the act the prolongation of maximum twenty-four hours is subject to the prior presentation of the suspect before the *procureur de la République* (art. 77 CPP). However this presentation may in exceptional cases be accorded in writing without the prior presentation of the suspect. In flagrant cases the public prosecutor may decide whether this authorization ought to be subjected to the bringing of the person before him (art. 63 par. 3 CPP). In cases where the reproached facts are related to drug trafficking or terrorism offences, the suspect may be kept for another period of forty-eight hours, bringing the maximum period to seventy-two hours (artt. 627-1 CSP, 706-23 CPP).

---

42 Note that according to the Schengen circular of June 23, 1995 (NOR:JUSA9500149C), the public prosecutor will have to control whether the offence caught in the act in a foreign country corresponds to the caught in the act situation in France.

43 The text states: "*dans les meilleurs délais.*" For a summary on the relation between the law of January 1993 and the law of August 1993, see Pradel, 1993a, pp. 299 *et seq.*; Jansen, 1994, p. 125; and Joubert, 1994, p. 264. See also *Circulaire relative à la présentation de l'ensemble des dispositions de la loi du 4 janvier 1993 et commentaire analytique de celles d'entre elles qui modifient le Code de procédure pénale (...)*, January 27, 1993, J.O., January 31, 1993, p. 1687.

The beginning of the *garde à vue* is calculated starting from the moment a person presents himself to the auxiliary of the public prosecutor when he has been summoned to do so. Otherwise the beginning of the *garde à vue* is calculated from the moment the person is physically forced by the *force publique* to appear (art. C.115 IG). When a person is summoned in cases of flagrance to stay on the scene of the crime, the start of the *garde à vue* is calculated from the moment this person is not free to come and to go, whether he be at this point informed of the measure taken against him or not.[44]

The suspect that has been placed in *garde a vue* has been recognized a number of rights with the passing of the law of January 4 modified by the law of August 24 1993.[45] According to art. 63-1 CPP he must be immediately informed by the auxiliary of the public prosecutor or, under his supervision by an agent of judicial police, of the rights guaranteed by artt. 63-2 (the right to inform someone with whom one usually lives), 63-3 (the right to be examined by a physician), 63-4 (the right to confer with a legal counsel) and of the dispositions regarding the length of the *garde à vue*. This information must be given to him in a language which he understands (art. 63-1 CPP *in fine*).

Although a previous version of art. 63-2 CPP guaranteed the right to inform by telephone a member of the suspect's family, whether he live with the suspect or not, the version of art. 63-2 CPP actually in force since the law of August 1993 foresees the calling of only those with whom the suspect usually lives. The new law also considers direct family members, brothers or sisters or employer of the suspect as potential persons to be informed. The law of January 1993 was thought not specific enough because it only stated family members as potential persons to be informed, increasing according to some the risk of collusion.[46] However this risk does not seem to have been neutralized by the new text since it is just as difficult to control the identity of an alleged family member as it is of a person allegedly living with the suspect, a direct family member, brothers, sisters or alleged employer. It is nevertheless true that by adding the employer to the list, the legislator of August 1993 has increased the number of persons to be potentially informed of the measure.

Germany

A suspect may be interrogated (*Vernehmung*) after he has been placed in police custody following a preliminary arrest (*vorläufige Festnahme*) or the issuing of a warrant for his arrest (*Haftbefehl*). It is also possible that he be summoned

---

44 Decocq, Buisson & Montreuil, 1991, p. 316.
45 For an overview of these modifications, see Jansen, 1994, pp. 122-138; Joubert, 1994, pp. 248-271.
46 Pradel, 1993a, feared for instance that this would increase the risk of collusion since the identity of the person contacted cannot be controlled.

by the public prosecutor (*Staatsanwalt*) to appear before him in order to be questioned (art. 163a par. 3 StPO). Finally no provisions stand in the way of simply asking the suspect to cooperate on a voluntary basis and present himself at the police station to be interrogated. It is also possible to subject a simple witness to an interrogation. This interrogation is possible at any stage of the enquiry and the same norms are valid for the interrogation of witnesses as of suspects. For the specifics, one may refer to artt. 48-93 StPO.[47]

The first paragraph of art. 163a StPO stipulates that the suspect ought to be questioned in any case before the closing of the police enquiry. This however does not impeach the police officials to question the suspect at an earlier time, in some cases this even being mandatory (for instance artt. 115 and 128 StPO by the investigating judge (*Ermittlungsrichter*) before the placing of the suspect in (preventive) custody). The police and the public prosecutor are also competent to subject the suspect to an interrogation (art. 163a par. 3, 4, and 5 StPO).

In all cases the interrogation will in principle take the same form (art. 136 StPO): First of all the suspect will be informed of the facts reproached to him, following which he will be asked to state his personals. What exactly is meant by personals and whether the suspect is obliged to respond is a controversial topic of discussion.[48] The suspect will be thereafter informed of the fact that he is not obliged to respond to the alleged commission of criminal offences by him (*Belehrung*), that he may submit a written statement and that he may confer with a legal counsel before he is submitted to the interrogation.[49] The suspect may then be interrogated on the reproached facts, during which interrogation he will first be asked to make a coherent statement concerning the facts; this may be followed by more directed questions. The suspect may further submit information *à décharge* and, depending on the nature of the alleged criminal offence, give his written opinion on the reproached facts.[50] Whether the suspect

---

47 See on the position of the suspect with respect to the witness, Roxin, 1993, pp. 175-176 and on the difference between witness, expert-witness and expert, Roxin, 1993, pp. 193-194.
48 Art. 11 OWiG includes not only the name, but also the date of birth, the marital status, the profession, the address and the nationality to the giving of personals (*Namenangabe*). According to Roxin (1993, p. 169) the profession does not automatically belong to the personals. However Kleinknecht/Meyer-Goßner (1995, p. 449) state that the profession, even along with information on matters such as religion, origin, race and political preference may sometimes be seen as part as the personals.
49 See on this topic Fijnaut, 1987b, pp. 101-135.
50 Löwe/Rosenberg, 1989, art. 136; Fijnaut, 1991, p. 71; Roxin, 1993, pp. 167-171; Kleinknecht/-Meyer-Goßner, 1995, pp. 448-453.

is obliged to make a statement relating the truth calls for a difference of opinion among authors.[51]

In execution of the prohibition enclosed in art. 1 par. 1 GG protecting the dignity of the human being, the German legislator has explicitly prohibited certain interrogation techniques (art. 136a StPO): It is forbidden to violate the free will of the suspect with mistreatment, fatigue, bodily harm, the giving of substances, aggravation, misleading or hypnosis. Force may only be used in those cases permitted by law. Threatening the suspect with measures not provided for by law and promising the suspect advantages not provided for by law are also prohibited (par. 1). Measures that disadvantage the capacity of the suspect are not permitted (par. 2). Violations of paragraphs 1 and 2 are not permitted even when the suspect agrees with the violation. Depositions made in violation of these provisions may not be used even with the authorization of the suspect (par. 3).

10.2.1.2 Police Report

Belgium
A detailed report of each interrogation period must be drawn up and art. 16 par. 7 VHW stipulates the obligation to state the beginning, the end and each interruption of the interrogation periods. Each declaration ought to be, as much as possible, literally written over and not summarized in order to prevent undue or improper interpretation. After the interrogation the declaration will be read and signed by the suspect. If he refuses to do so, the reason of this refusal must be written down in the report. If the suspect declares wanting to go back on his declaration the first report will not be amended but completed with the new declaration. From these obligations may be supposed that unduly long periods of interrogations or interrogations during the night should be restricted to only these cases where such is strictly necessary.[52]

The Netherlands
The third paragraph of art. 29 Sv states that the words of the suspect's declaration made during or after an interrogation must be typed out in the police report as accurately as possible. After the interrogation the declaration will be read and signed (or not) by the suspect. The suspect may go back on his declaration

---

51 One may presume that such an obligation does not exist although this situation in no way creates a right to lie. In this way it is possible and permitted that the interrogator confront the suspect with the internal incoherences in his deposition and that he tell the suspect that an eventual confession may have a substantial effect on his sentence. See Roxin, 1993, p. 169 and Kleinknecht/Meyer-Goßner, 1995, p. 452.

52 Instructions originating study material for the *gendarmerie*-school.

after it has been made and may even withdraw it. The judge will determine which consequences will be drawn from this withdrawal.[53]

Luxembourg
Art. 39 par 8 CIC states specifically that all interrogations must be extensively accounted for in a detailed police report. All periods of interrogation and rest must be noted as well as the date and hour of the privation of liberty and time and date that the suspect was freed or led before a judge.

France
The judicial police is obliged to make a certain number of annotations in the police report. Art. 64 CPP obliges the auxiliaries of the public prosecutor to mention the length of the interrogation, periods of rest, date and time of the beginning of the *garde à vue* as well as the fact that the suspect has been brought before the public prosecutor. These annotations must also be made in the special register kept at the place where the police custody is being spent. All requests made according to artt. 63-2, 63-3 and 63-4 and whether they have been honoured must appear in the police report as well, which annotations will be signed by the suspect (art. 64 CPP). If he refuses to sign, the police report will mention that fact. In all cases the reason for the *garde à vue* will appear on the police report. The annotations prescribed by the first paragraph of art. 64 concerning the dates and time of the *garde à vue*, the length of the interrogation and the rest periods between interrogation, must also appear in the special *garde à vue* register kept in all police or *gendarmerie* locals susceptible to be used as *garde à vue* locals (art. 65 CPP).

Germany
Police officers conducting the interrogation must draw up a detailed report from each interrogation which may in the first place consist of a preliminary report to be worked out at a later time (art. 168a StPO). The final police report will be presented to the suspect who will be requested to read and sign it, should he agree with its contents. Should he refuse to sign his deposition it will be mentioned in the report.

10.2.1.3   The Right to Legal Counsel

Belgium
In principle, the suspect may ask to be assisted by a legal counsel after he has been informed of this right by the investigating judge. It is however possible according to art. 22 VHW to have a legal counsel present during the "summar-

---

53 Naeyé, 1990, pp. 228-229.

izing interrogation" (*samenvattende ondervraging*). In this case the suspect and his legal counsel will be authorized to consult the record two days prior to the interrogation.[54] Contact with others than the legal counsel is possible but may be suspended for a single period of three days on the grounds of a motivated decision by the investigating judge in the interest of the enquiry.[55]

The Netherlands
The suspect may at all times be assisted by a legal counsel and art. 57 par. 2 Sv states this explicitly for the interrogation. Nevertheless, if the suspect does not already have a legal counsel and one has to be appointed to him, it can only be done once the suspect has been placed in custody (art. 40 Sv). This means that the presence of a legal counsel during interrogation prior to police custody is not possible for suspects that do not have their own (paid) lawyer.[56]

Luxembourg
Luxembourg is one of the few European countries to provide for the right to a legal counsel prior to the interrogation by police officials. A person that has been placed in custody in accordance with art. 39 CIC must be informed of his right to be assisted by a lawyer prior to his interrogation (art. 39 par. 7 CIC). According to art. 39 par. 3 CIC the suspect that has been placed in police custody may chose to have a person of his choice informed of the measure taken against him unless there is reason to believe that this would endanger the course of the investigation.

France
Upon the expiration of the first twenty hours of custody the person in *garde à vue* may request to confer with a legal counsel for a period not exceeding thirty minutes. If he is not able to designate a legal counsel or if the one he has chosen cannot be contacted in due time, he may request that the dean of the Bar Association designate one for him. The dean is informed of this request by all means possible and without delay. If the person is being subjected to a *garde à vue* liable to be prolonged according to the special provisions stated above, he may only request to contact his legal counsel after the expiration of the first forty-eight hours (art. 63-4 CPP).

The designated counsel may communicate with the suspect in circumstances guaranteeing the confidentiality. He is informed by the auxiliary of the public prosecutor or, under his supervision, by the agent of judicial police of the nature

54 See on the Belgian law concerning the presence and absence of lawyers during questioning by the police, Fijnaut, 1988, pp. 37-40.
55 De Nauw, 1991, pp. 124-128.
56 See Fijnaut, 1987b; Fijnaut, 1988; Naeyé, 1990, pp. 573-577.

of the ongoing enquiry. After the expiration of the thirty minutes the legal counsel may have his written observations be adjoined to the file. The law prohibits further that the legal counsel disclose the content of his conversation with the suspect to anybody. This disposition appears to suggest that not only the suspect but also the state is the beneficiary of the right to the confidentiality of the conversation. In that way, it seems impossible for the suspect to relieve his legal counsel from his obligation to silence.

The period of twenty hours mentioned in the first paragraph is extended to thirty-six hours when the suspicion concerns participation to a criminal association (artt. 265, 266 CP), aggravated procuring or extortion (artt. 334-I to 335 and 400 CP) or criminal actions committed in organized groups (artt. 257-3, 384 and 435 CP).

Germany
After the suspect has been notified of the reasons of his arrest he is informed of his right, by virtue of art. 136 StPO, to designate and consult a lawyer. He may decide to make a declaration but he is free to wait for a consultation with his legal counsel before he does so. If the suspect expresses the will to speak with his legal counsel, he must be given the opportunity to contact him by means of telephone.[57]

10.2.1.4   Medical Examination

Belgium
There are no provisions concerning an eventual right for the suspect to have himself examined by a doctor although he may address such a request to the investigating judge. The only provision mentioning a medical examination is art. 90bis Sv. This art. states that notwithstanding flagrancy situations the only medical examination that may be ordered are the ones requested by the Court in chambers (*raadkamer*), the chamber responsible for charging the suspect and the Court that acquired knowledge of the facts. In that case the suspect may require to have the examination witnessed by a medical expert of his own choice. The victim has the same privilege. The fact that there are no other provisions mentioning the possibility of the suspect being examined if he so wishes does not appear to stand in the way of granting this wish. It does not however create an obligation for the investigating judge to honour the request. It will probably depend on circumstances such as the availability of a doctor, the time of the request and the seriousness of the suspect's condition.

---

57 Kleinknecht/Meyer-Goßner, 1995, pp. 450-451.

The Netherlands

Although most enquiring techniques involving a certain violation of the physical integrity of the suspect (to a greater extent than a superficial body search) will be executed by a physician, the law does not formally foresee any right for the suspect to ask to be examined by a physician to establish his physical capacity to undergo the police interrogation. However, art. 32 of the new police instructions provide for the possibility to have a suspect examined by a physician when they feel the suspect seems to have some difficulties. If the detained suspect requests to consult a doctor or asks for specific medicine, the officer consults the doctor. In case the suspect requests to be examined by his own doctor, the officer informs the doctor.

Luxembourg

The right to a medical examination is considered as one belonging to the suspect and a prerogative of the public prosecutor. According to art. 39 par. 6 CIC, the prosecutor may at all times decide, automatically or at the request of a family member, to designate a physician to examine the suspect.

France

The person that has been placed in *garde à vue* disposes in addition of the right to have himself examined by a physician designated by the public prosecutor or his auxiliary. In case of prolongation of the *garde à vue*, he may request to be examined a second time (art. 63-3 CPP). The prosecutor may at any time decide to have the person in *garde à vue* examined by a physician. In the absence of a request from the part of the person in *garde à vue*, from the prosecutor or an auxiliary, a member of the family may request that a physical examination be carried out. The physician is designated by the prosecutor or his auxiliary (art. 63-3 CPP). The January legislator had left the choice of the investigating physician to the person placed in *garde à vue*. The decision to leave the choice of the physician to instances as the (auxiliary) of the public prosecutor may have an impact on the independent character of the examination although one may be tempted to pose the independence of physicians as a premise. One should remember that this independent character played an important role in the Tomasi v. France-case cited above.

Germany

The first provision concerning the medical examination of the suspect is found in the Code of criminal procedure. Artt. 81a and 81c par. 6 second sentence StPO may be interpreted together as giving the judge (as well as the prosecutor and his auxiliaries in case waiting for the judge would endanger the enquiry) the right to request that the suspect be examined by a doctor, either at the police station or in a hospital.[58] Although a right for the suspect to have himself examined by a doctor is not explicitly provided for in the law, nothing seems to stand in the way of an examination requested by the suspect. Art. A 14 RiStBV does even mention the possibility of having the suspect hospitalized when this seems necessary. A right for the suspect, corresponding to an obligation on the part of the judicial or police authorities, does however not exist.

10.2.2 Guarantees Regarding the Right to be Informed Promptly

The right to be informed promptly and in a language that one understands of the reasons of one's arrest is guaranteed by art. 5 par. 2 ECHR. As we have seen above this right may be considered to be guaranteed to persons being held in custody by the police, at least from the moment they are considered suspects. This guarantee is very important in consideration of the suspects right to silence guaranteed by the presumption of innocence. Indeed from this moment on the suspect is able more or less to appreciate the consequences of the words he does decide to pronounce.

10.2.2.1   Belgium

There are no provisions in Belgian law explicitly prescribing that the suspect be informed of the reasons of his arrest. Thus the investigating judge is not obliged to inform the suspect of the exact content of the charges against him.[59] Although in general the doctrine seems to agree on the fact that art. 6 par. 3 ECHR does not apply at this phase of the procedure,[60] the situation is not as clear with regards to art. 5 par. 2 ECHR. Since the only regulated form of interrogation is the interrogation of the suspect by the investigating judge, it seems arguable that at least the guarantee of art. 5 par. 2 ECHR will apply. Indeed at this point of the procedure, the judge may issue a warrant for arrest making the deprivation of liberty more formal than interrogation by the police. It is doubtful whether these provisions apply to the interrogation by the police officials before the starting of a judicial enquiry by the investigating judge.

10.2.2.2   The Netherlands

In the Netherlands the right guaranteed by art. 5 par. 2 and by art. 6 par. 3 sub a ECHR is recognized to the suspect at this early hour of the criminal procedure.

---

58 Roxin, 1993, p. 236.
59 Mons, March 21, 1989, Rev. Liège, 1989, 987.
60 See Van den Wyngaert, 1994, p. 639.

Prior to the interrogation, the suspect must be informed of the reasons of his arrest or the nature and reasons of the charge against him.[61]

10.2.2.3   Luxembourg

On the grounds of art. 6 par. 3 ECHR the Luxembourg district court decided that the suspect had the right to be informed of the charges against him. The declarations of the suspect were declared invalid in this case because they had been done during police interrogation and again before the investigating judge while the suspect had not yet been informed of the charges against him. According to the court this endangered the rights of the defence.[62]

10.2.2.4   France

Although the *Commission justice pénale et droits de l'homme* had proposed to give the suspect placed in *garde à vue* the right to be informed of the reasons of his detention the French legislator did not follow its recommendations.[63] Neither the law passed in January 1993 nor that of August 1993 mention the right of the suspect to be informed of the reasons of his arrest.

10.2.2.5   Germany

After a German police officer has arrested a suspect and before he informs him of his rights, the suspect will be told the reasons of his arrest. This information must be given to him in a way he will be able to comprehend and will help him in his defence. However the information given ought not to go so far as to jeopardize the efficiency of the investigation (art. 136 StPO).[64]

10.2.3 Presumption of Innocence and Right to Silence

One may consider the right to silence as a right implicitly understood in the principle of the presumption of innocence. Indeed the presumption of innocence sees its actual expression in a number of guarantees among which the *nemo tenetur*-principle and the right to silence may be counted. As we have seen

---

61 See Naeyé, 1990, pp. 225 *et seq.*
62 Tr. Arr. Luxembourg, March 4, 1987; see also M.P. v. K. & W., arrest nr. 337/87, VI, November 5, 1987; Spielmann & Weitzel, 1991, pp. 418-421.
63 This commission was set up to make recommendations in order to revise the *Code de procédure pénale*. On the rights of the person placed in *garde à vue* see the commission's recommendations in Delmas-Marty, 1991, pp. 209-210.
64 Kleinknecht/Meyer-Goßner, 1995, p. 450.

earlier this view is shared by the European Court on Human Rights.[65] However, the question is still open as to whether this right also includes the obligation on the part of the authorities to inform the suspect of this right. As we will see the studied countries differ in views on that subject.

10.2.3.1   Belgium

Although Belgian law does not mention this right explicitly, practitioners consider in general that because of the obligations contained in the European Convention on Human Rights and in art. 14 par. 3 ITCPR the suspect may not be forced to testify. In the present Belgian courts do not consider it mandatory that the instances interrogating the suspect inform him of this right. However the rights of the defence may not be rendered illusionary by actions of the authority interrogating the suspect.[66] In this way the Belgian *Cour de cassation* decided that promises to the suspect that no charges would be held against him should he make some specific declarations, had violated the right of the suspect to silence and frustrated the rights of the defence.[67]

10.2.3.2   The Netherlands

During the interrogation there may be no unduly pressure or other methods exercised against the suspect that may endanger the free and voluntary character of the declaration. Violence, menaces, unduly long periods of interrogation, trick questions, deception, use of lie detectors, presents, promises, misuse of authority among others. are not permitted during interrogations (art. 29 par. 1 Sv). The suspect may not be obliged to incriminate himself (*nemo tenetur*-principle). In the execution of the *nemo tenetur*-principle, the officer will inform the suspect prior to his interrogation that he is not obliged to answer any question (art. 29 par. 2 Sv). This is called the caution (*cautie*). However this obligation to inform the suspect exists only when the person to be interrogated can be considered a suspect according to the law.[68] The obligation of the caution is subject to the existence of a reasonable suspicion of guilt regarding the person to be interrogated. Although the suspect has no obligation to cooperate to his interrogation, he has the obligation to passively tolerate it.[69] There is however no doubt that one cannot speak here of real freedom. The officers responsible for the interro-

---

65 See the case of Funke, cited above.
66 Van den Wyngaert, 1994, pp. 557-558.
67 Cass. May 13, 1986, R.D.P. 1986, 905.
68 HR September 29, 1981, NJ 1982, 258.
69 In relation to the material gathering of evidence he may be subjected to various methods of investigation. See Naeyé, 1990, p. 227.

gation will certainly exert the allowed pressure on the suspect in order to help him make a confession.[70]

Omission to inform the suspect of his right to silence may lead to the exclusion of his declaration as evidence if the omission has damaged the suspect's interests.[71] To evaluate whether the suspect's interests have been damaged by the omission, the court looks upon relevant factors such as the fact that the suspect was aware or may be presumed to have been aware of his right not to cooperate with his interrogation or the fact that he has, in a later declaration where this information was indeed given to him, made another declaration to the same effect as the first one, or when he was assisted by a lawyer during the interrogation. Neglect to inform the suspect during the enquiry before the court may lead to annulment of the process and of the judgement if the suspect's interests can reasonably be expected to have been damaged.[72] If the suspect has been subjected to unduly pressure during his interrogation his declaration or confession may be annulled and excluded from the evidence because it has been obtained unlawfully.

10.2.3.3   Luxembourg

There are no provisions in Luxembourg law regarding the right of the suspect to silence. If the suspect refuses to sign a declaration he has made to the police, he will be brought before the investigating judge. Although the silence of the suspect may not work in his disadvantage in theory,[73] in practice this may be used against him as aggravating circumstances. Refusing to sign a declaration or making a false declaration may have the same consequences.[74]

10.2.3.4   France

The *Commission Justice pénale et droits de l'homme* recommended to give the suspect the right to refuse the interrogation before having had the possibility to consult his legal counsel.[75] The legislator did not follow this recommendation which means that the law still does not mention the eventual right of the suspect to remain silent, even less does it provide for an obligation for the police officers to inform the suspect of this right.

---

70 See also Naeyé, 1990, pp. 226 and 231-233; however, the line between duly and unduly pressure is not always clear; see Naeyé, 1990, p. 235.
71 See among others HR June 26, 1979, NJ 1979, 567 with note Th.W. Van Veen.
72 Naeyé, 1990, pp. 248-253; Hendriks *et al.*, 1992, pp. 113-115.
73 See Spielmann, 1993, p. 994.
74 This information was reported by officials of the *police grand-ducale*.
75 Delmas-Marty, 1991, p. 209.

10.2.3.5   Germany

The German criminal procedure law recognizes explicitly the principle that the suspect cannot be compelled to testify against himself during police custody. On the one hand art. 136a StPO states this clearly[76] and on the other hand the Federal Court recognizes that this principle belongs to the basic principles of German law.[77] However one should not speak here of a right to silence, since silence may imply a renouncement to the right to orally defend one self, but rather of a liberty to testify.[78] The suspect may choose to restrict the scope of the questions he is willing to answer, he may withdraw answers or even refuse to answer one or more particular questions.[79]

10.2.4   *Guarantees Regarding the Right to be Brought Promptly Before a Judge*

As we have seen in the introduction, guaranteeing the right to be brought promptly before a judge brings about a number of considerations. If the law of most countries does provide for the bringing of the suspect before a superior police officer upon deciding on the placing of the suspect in police custody, one may note that the time one may be held in custody without being brought before an impartial judge varies considerably.

10.2.4.1   Belgium

Since the only regulated form of interrogation is that being conducted by the investigating judge, one does not find in the Belgian code of criminal procedure any provision explicitly obliging the police to bring a suspect before him. However, a person may not be held in police custody more than 24 hours (art. 1 VHW). After this period, the suspect will be set free unless there are reasons to keep him for further enquiry. If this is the case, he will be presented to the court in chambers, who will decide on his detention (artt. 21 *et seq.* VHW).

10.2.4.2   The Netherlands

The police is in virtue of art. 61 Sv authorized to retain a suspect for a period of six hours (not including the period between 24:00 and 9:00) after which time

---

76 "He (the suspect) must be informed that he is free in virtue of the law to express himself on the facts held against him or not to be heard on that matter." (*Er ist darauf hinzuweisen, daß es ihm nach dem Gesetz freistehe, sich zur Beschuldiging zu aüßern oder nicht zur Sache auszusagen (...)*)
77 BGH 14, 358, 364.
78 KG VRS 45, 287.
79 Kleinknecht/Meyer-Goßner, 1993, p. 541.

he must be presented to an (auxiliary to the) public prosecutor or set free. After the suspect is presented to the officer in question, he may be placed in police custody if this appears in the interest of the enquiry. This is the case for instance when the six hours prove not to have been enough to conclude the interrogation, when the suspect is needed for a confrontation or when there is fear for collusion. This type of police custody is only authorized for suspects of crimes which, according to law, may justify preventive detention. Prior to the order for police custody the suspect must be questioned by the (auxiliary of the) public prosecutor.[80] At this point it is possible that the suspect be assisted by a legal counsel (art. 24 Sv).[81]

The suspect must be set free as soon as the interest of the enquiry is not jeopardized. An order for police custody holds according to art. 58 Sv for a period of three days, after which it may be prolonged by the public prosecutor for another two days (art. 58 Sv).[82] After the police custody or directly after the apprehension, the suspect may be brought before the investigating judge. After interrogating him he may decide to remand him for custody, keeping him at the disposition of the judicial authorities.[83]

10.2.4.3   Luxembourg

Art. 39 CIC provides for a legal basis for the police custody. The police officers may keep a suspect for twenty-four hours before he is either set free or presented to the investigating judge who will then decide on his preventive detention. This form of police custody is only possible concerning a person against whom severe and corroborating elements would justify charges (art. 39 par. 1 CIC). The period of retention is calculated starting from the moment of the actual restriction of freedom.

---

80 Melai, note 3 on art. 57 Sv.
81 See Melai, note 4-6 on art. 57 Sv; Sjöcrona, 1995b, pp. 65-67.
82 Since the arrest of the European Court on Human Rights in the case of Brogan and others, ruling that a detention period of four days and six hours without any appearance before a judge was in violation of art. 5 par. 3 ECHR this situation has changed. In consequence of this judgement, the assembly of prosecutors general decided on a general line of conduct for the public prosecutor's department according to which the suspect ought to be presented before the investigating judge before the end of the third day (this means three times twenty-four hours after the beginning of the police custody). If the suspect is not presented before the judge after the third day he must be set free. The law has been modified since then.
83 Melai, note 2 on artt. 63-92 Sv.

10.2.4.4   France

As we have seen the suspect placed in *garde à vue* must be brought before the public prosecutor at the end of the first period of twenty-four hours. Upon the placing of the individual in police custody, the public prosecutor must be informed in the best possible time. This must appear in the police report. However, according to the principles discussed above concerning the Brogan case, the *procureur de la République* cannot be considered a judge in the sense of the European Convention on Human Rights. A suspect will finally be brought before an investigating judge after the end of the *garde à vue* (artt. 144 et seq. CPP) who will decide on the placing of the suspect in preventive detention (*détention provisoire*). This means in fact that in some cases the suspect will not be presented before a judge before the expiration of the maximum duration of the *garde à vue* (twenty-four hours in regular cases, forty-eight in cases of prolongation but up to seventy-two hours - four days - in case of terrorism or drug trafficking). All of these terms ought to be considered in accordance with the Brogan case.

10.2.4.5   Germany

Art. 104 GG reserves the power to suspend the freedom of a person exclusively to a judge. Only in some exceptional cases is it possible to resort to the (temporary) arrest of a suspect, for instance when a person is caught in the act. However even in this case the suspect must be brought as soon as possible before a judge who will decide at this point (at the request of the public prosecutor or at his own initiative) whether the suspect may be kept in custody (art. 128 StPO). When a suspect is held by the police he must be brought before a judge at the latest at the end of the day after his arrest (art. 104 par. 2 GG). When a number of conditions are fulfilled the judge may decide to place the suspect in preventive custody (*Untersuchungshaft*): If this is necessary to prevent the danger of escape, recidivism and collusion (artt. 112, 112a and 113 StPO). The severity of the offence also plays a role.

10.3   Comparing National Norms

Most of the studied countries provide for a certain number of norms regarding police interrogation. However in one country, Belgium, there are no provisions at all setting formal rules for this phase of the enquiry. That does not mean that the police do not have the implicit power to question the suspect, it only means that interrogation is not formally subjected to any guidelines, although the doctrine seems to agree that interrogation should be bound to the same rules whether they be done by police officials or by investigating judges.

Whether police officials are required to produce a written report may be one of those formalities that may perhaps be seen as guaranteeing a certain degree of abidance by the law. The more mandatory details in the report and the more control its content is subjected to, the more it may be difficult to go beyond the scope of the law. For example it may be safe to assume that the fact that French police officials must produce a written report of all periods of interrogation and that this report must correspond to a special record placed under the responsibility of yet another official ensures a certain degree of controllability of police actions. These reports are required to state details regarding the length of interrogations, periods of rest, the fact that the suspect has been informed of his rights, these being countersigned by the suspect. Although the other countries provide for the obligation to produce a report for most of the acts posed by the police during the enquiry, they do not for the most part specify the mandatory content of the report (see *Table 10.2*).

Only two countries, Germany and Luxembourg, allow the suspect to consult a legal counsel of his choice prior to the police interrogation. In France this is possible after 20 hours of interrogation and in Belgium after the interrogations by both the police and the investigating judge. The situation in The Netherlands is somewhat different. If a person already has a lawyer and this lawyer is being paid by the suspect, the lawyer may be consulted before or be present during the interrogation. However, if this is not the case a lawyer will only be appointed after the first six hours, when the suspect has been placed in police custody (see *Table 10.1*).

The possibility to have oneself examined by a physician may serve many purposes. On the one hand it may be used by police or judicial officials to have certain tests done,[84] but also to have the suspect examined in order to determine whether his physical state allows extensive interrogation or demands certain precautions or to refute allegations of ill-treatment. A physical examination may also be used by the suspect himself if he is feeling ill or to establish ill-treatment. Most of the countries consider the medical examination as a prerogative for the judicial officials although medical examinations at the request of suspects may be performed. However in Belgium the suspect may have his own medical expert present during the examination. Only in France and Luxembourg is this right considered one belonging (at least in part) to the suspect.

Another guarantee that may play an important role in the legal security of the suspect is the right to be informed, in a language he understands of the reasons of his arrest and eventually of a number of other rights implicitly or explicitly recognized to him. Three of the five studied of the countries (the

---

84 Such as the analysis of blood, a DNA-analysis, or an analysis of the content of the stomach.

436

Netherlands, Luxembourg and Germany) recognize this right explicitly prior to the interrogation by the police. Others, like France and Belgium, do not recognize this right explicitly. Since there are no formal rules regarding police enquiry in Belgium, there is no explicit obligation to inform the suspect of the reasons of his arrest. Although no provision stands in the way of the investigating judge to inform the suspect of this right before interrogation, there is no obligation either. French law does not mention this right either, although it is safe to assume that lawyers will inform their clients when they are finally able to consult with them after the twentieth hour of police custody. Indeed the lawyer will only be able to inform his client of what he knows.

Table 10.1 Police Interrogation

	B	NL	L	F	D
Type of norm					
Statute	-	+	+	+	+
Procedural rights and guarantees					
Legal counsel prior to interrogation	-	-	+	-	+
Legal counsel during interrogation	-	-	-	-	-
Legal counsel after interrogation	+	+	-	+	-
Informed of right to remain silent	-	+	-	-	+
Informed of reasons of suspicion	-	+	+	-	+
Brought before a judge within 24 hours	+	-	+	-	+
Brought before judge later	-	+	-	+	-
Mandatory content of police report	-	-	-	+	-
Right to medical examination	+	-	+	+	-

Provisions explicitly obliging police officials to inform the suspect of his right to silence are scarce in the studied countries. Yet, it is a right that plays an important role in the early stages of the enquiry and is likely to have great implications for the further course of events. The Netherlands and Germany are the only countries to explicitly require the suspect be informed of this right before he be questioned. Although Belgian law does not mention this right explicitly, practitioners insist that international obligations require it be done at least before the interrogation by the investigating judge. France and Luxembourg make no mention of this obligation during the police enquiry either. However the Netherlands and Germany consider this information crucial for the validity of the police interrogation.

How long a suspect may be held in custody without being brought before a judge varies considerably depending on the studied countries. Although Belgium and Luxembourg consider the suspect ought to be brought before an impartial judge in a relatively short period of time (twenty-four hours), most other countries vary their time according to circumstances and the severity of the offence. This is the case for instance for the Netherlands and France, where police custody may be prolonged if certain conditions are fulfilled. In Germany the suspect must be brought before a judge as soon as possible, but not later that the end of the day following the arrest.

Table 10.2 Interrogation Formalities to be Observed

	Formalities in police report	*Other formalities*
B	* detailed report, including hours of interrogation * literal transcription of declaration * declaration signed by suspect	* investigating judge must inform suspect that arrest warrant may be issued and that he may consult legal counsel
NL	* declaration as accurately as possible * declaration signed by suspect	* suspect must be informed of right to silence
L	* detailed report, including hours of interrogation * beginning and end custody	* authorization by *procureur d'État* * suspect may inform person of choice and consult legal counsel
F	* reason of *garde à vue* * date and hours of *garde à vue* * whether suspect has been brought before public prosecutor * requests made by suspect and whether they have been granted * report signed by suspect * all forementioned in special register	* *procureur de la République* must be informed
D	* report of each interrogation * report signed by suspect	* suspect must be interrogated before end of enquiry * suspect must be informed of facts, of right to silence, right to consult legal counsel and right to produce written statement

10.4   Conclusion

We have discussed a number of possible procedural safeguards against treatments in the criminal system that may be seen as degrading or unhuman. The

438

more an enquiry will be open and subject to formal procedures, the more difficult it may prove to go around the law. More formality has also the advantage of setting guidelines for police officials informing them of the exact content and scope of their powers. moreover, the presence of a legally trained defender on the side of the suspect as a counterpart to police interrogation techniques may also be seen as a guarantee. As some police officers state that an innocent party has no need for legal counsel before or during police interrogation, the suspect may state that profesionnal police officers need not feel threatened or empeached by the presence of legal counsel of the suspect. Regrettably, only two countries, Luxembourg and Germany, recognize the right to consult with a legal counsel before the police interrogation. In the context of cross-border apprehension, this aspect can cause discrepencies between, for instance, suspects apprehended in France and those apprehended in Germany. This might even lead to a particular type of forum shopping where authorities will, in the elaboration of international strategies on crime repression, chose the country where the suspect has less rights in order to have him interrogated there.

Not all studied countries provide for basic safeguards or controls for a good and fair execution of the police interrogation. Some countries such as France provide for specific formal rules regarding the phase of police interrogation while other countries seem to privilege a more flexible approach based on the confidence in the ethics of the police. Given the stressful situations police officers are subjected to, one may question whether controls and safeguards are not necessary to help officials in their quest for the truth without letting them glide to legally difficult situations. Whether formalities may be considered effective safeguards against abuses of authority in practice is a question that only an extensive field research can answer. However, it is safe to assume that formalities provide for a number of thresholds making it more difficult to blatantly ignore principles of law and justice. Further it is important to note that formalities such as informing the suspect of possible charges against him or of his right to silence also play an important role in guiding officials in the exercise of their discretionary power, making interrogations a useable (and more reliable) source in the gathering of evidence. In that sense, the presence of the legal counsel prior to or during police interrogation may serve as an efficient guardian of due process.

Furthermore, these differences in formalities between the different countries may cause problems in international cooperation since the lack of formality in one country may cause some declarations to be unfit as evidence in other countries. The court of one country may decide either to exclude possible evidence originating a foreign country or to refuse to test its validity because of the lack of information on foreign legal systems. A good example of this would be the declaration of a suspect in France or Belgium that have not been told of his right to silence. In theory this declaration would be seen as void for

Dutch or German courts. However examples of this in practice have shown that judges often chose not to control the legality of evidence gathered outside the country. In Belgium for instance judges refuse to test the legality of enquiry methods used in a foreign country because they consider that they are not able of doing so. This seems to lead to a double standards system: "If foreign police officials have done it we don't have to test its validity."[85]

This topic is one that has initiated a great deal of discussion in many countries regarding which rights ought to be recognized to suspects held in custody. In weighing the interest of an effective crime-fighting against that of due process one notes that the rights of the arrested suspect seem all too often to be neglected while the new generation of international treaties on cooperation in criminal matters do not seem to consider these rights as essential components to these treaties. The fact that these rights are neglected does not necessarily have to do with the fact that a number of legal principles (such as the presumption of innocence) would have become less important over the years but perhaps because of the fact that a discrepancy appears between these principles and the actual position of the suspect in this phase of the criminal process.[86] One may suggest that at least one of the causes of this discrepancy be the pressure the society puts on the judicial apparatus to cope with the changing forms of criminality.

Whether the placing of a suspect in police custody ought to be considered the moment when principles such as the presumption of innocence ought to be materialized in actual procedural consequences is a question of great importance. One notes in that context that procedural guarantees such as informing the suspect of his right to silence is crucial, precisely at this moment of the criminal procedure. Indeed reserving this formality to a latter phase of the procedure would have the effect of rendering this right illusionary. What is left of the importance of the right to silence when a suspects declaration during police custody can be used in court?[87] If the presumption of innocence should have some meaning, is it not only logical that it be guaranteed with actual procedural consequences even at the beginning of the placing in police custody?

In our opinion, the question as to whether a suspect must be informed of his right to remain silent is a crucial one in the context of cross border hot pursuit. It seems that it should be seen as a minimal guarantee in the light of the European Convention on Human Rights. Indeed, foreign police officers operating on Dutch and German territory will be subject to national Dutch and German law and formally to this obligation. The question, however, as to whether the deposition of a suspect will in fact be used even when done in

---

85 For an overview of these problems in Belgium, see Hutsebaut, 1991, pp. 49-94.
86 This is suggested by Fijnaut, 1987b; see also Fijnaut, 1988, pp. 19 et seq.
87 See Fijnaut, 1988, pp. 19-20; Naeyé, 1988, pp. 114 et seq.; Schalken, 1988, pp. 136 et seq.

violation of this right is one that only future case studies will answer. One can only hope, since the question as to procedural rights of suspects is one that has been neglected in recent years in international treaties, that the right to be informed of the right to remain silent will be seen as a minimal procedural guarantee.

11 Mutual Legal Aid by Police Officers

The origin and the aim of practically every criminal procedure, information is the alpha and omega of police work. The opening of most investigations is inspired by some sort of information coming to the attention of the police, and the final purpose of every investigation will usually be to gather as much information as possible in order to enable a well-founded decision on the possibilities and opportuneness of a successful prosecution. In the context of an international enquiry, the importance of information is the same, but the accessibility will usually be a lot more complicated. Essentially, the police will not be entitled and therefore be unable to gather information on the territory of another State. For this reason, the exchange of information between police services, which does already take a central place in the national police field, is even more important in international policing.

In general, it is important for the police that the person on whom they collect information does not know what information the police has already collected. This is particularly, but not exclusively the case for investigations against persons who are not (yet) aware of their suspect status. Because of this confidential, secret character, the exchange of information and other forms of data processing by the police may be considered a covert policing technique, like observation and infiltration are covert methods as well.

For several reasons, such as national sovereignty, the security and secrecy of the information and the police work in general and (the last decades) also the protection of the citizen's privacy, the international exchange of police information was never really regulated. The only official ways to obtain foreign information for police investigations have been for a very long period on the one hand through the international police organisation Interpol and on the other hand with an international letter rogatory by the judicial authorities. Especially between the Western European countries, who were getting used to more and more cross-border traffic, communication and criminal activities, the former was more and more considered as being inefficient and slow.[1] The latter way usually takes even more time, since it must not only pass through the judicial authorities but also through the embassies of both countries concerned; it is however still

---

1   A more detailed presentation of Interpol may be found in Chapter 2 of this study and the
     works referred to in that context.

the only way to obtain foreign information or objects that may serve as evidence in a criminal procedure.

In order to enable closing the investigation within the shortest delay possible, the police have been trying to find quicker ways for the exchange of information with their foreign counterparts. Especially in the border areas, where it is no exception for a police officer to know several police colleagues across the border personally, informal ways for the international exchange of police information emerged. Two central concepts for the functioning of this informal exchange of information are reliability and reciprocity: As long as X will provide some information to Y, he may be rather certain that in the future Y will provide him information in return.[2] When asking his colleague for the information, he may also suggest or promise that he immediately has some information in return. If necessary, the real source of the information is hidden under such general phrases as "In the context of a good cooperation between several police forces we have received the following information from a serious and reliable source."[3] An aspect of informational policing that, even though it cannot be worked out in detail here, must not remain unmentioned is the so-called Old-boys-network. This network of police officers, former colleagues and other acquaintances mainly employed in branches where information takes a central place (such as banks, insurance companies and the private security sector) often appears to be an efficient forum for the informal exchange of police information.[4]

The twilight zone in which this kind of informational police cooperation takes place may easily result in problematic and undesirable situations. Some examples from the past are worth mentioning briefly. It once occurred that, while information on a certain suspect had been provided to a foreign police service, the Dutch authorities prosecuted the same person for the same reasons. In another case, police reports that had played a role in acquittals or even convictions of a person were sent abroad in the same case against the same person.[5] The informal character of some exchanges of information does not only involve a risk for suspects, but might also turn back on the police officers. Before Belgium had its privacy legislation, some Belgian police officers mentioned in their records who were the reliable (German or Dutch) sources who had provided them with the information they could use so well. When the sources were punished with disciplinary sanctions, their cooperative attitude disappeared entirely.[6]

2   Hofstede *et al.*, 1993, p. 23; Brammertz *et al.*, 1993, p. 23.
3   Hofstede *et al.*, 1993, p. 54.
4   For a thorough study of this "police complex" in construction, we refer to Hoogenboom, 1994.
5   Both examples were taken from Orie, 1986, p. 173.
6   Brammertz *et al.*, 1993, p. 23.

Another problem is that, to an even greater extent than within one country, the possibilities of international exchange of police information may easily lead to "data laundering." The Dutch police may for instance distribute an information of some kind to several foreign police services and not much later issue a request for this kind of information through another channel. If the request is replied, this can be considered an unsuspicious confirmation of the information, which increases its status and reliability.[7] Furthermore, priorities which are set by national police forces (and are a direct expression of the dominant culture in that country or force), may frustrate the efficiency of cross-border cooperation in a way that cannot be encountered by an extension of the international regulatory system. This was stressed by witnesses before the parliamentary enquiry committee in The Netherlands, who explained that "the national CID regularly receives foreign information about criminal organizations in The Netherlands, for instance from liaison officers abroad. Often, the regional police forces put the information that was forwarded to them aside because it does not fit into their own priorities."[8] A concrete example of different priorities is the case of two French police officers who spontaneously provided the Rotterdam police with names, addresses and phone numbers of two Rotterdam heroin dealers. After several months without a reaction they were told that the information had not resulted in an intervention, because for the Rotterdam police, arresting two small dealers does not have much priority.[9]

Information, especially the information collected and used by the police, may originate countless sources, which may have such a strong influence on the reliability and controllability of the information,[10] as well as on the acceptibility of the methods used to collect the information. This was recently illustrated during a trial before a Dutch court, where the defence counsel demonstrated that, after a Dutch request for information, the Turkish police had applied torture and undue physical pressure against witnesses in police custody.[11] But it should not be neglected that information provided by more "western" police forces can be incorrect as well. The Dutch Registration Chamber concluded for instance that police registers were seriously polluted with information on former suspects that had not been removed after their acquittals.[12]

---

7   This risk was also constated in the report of the parliamentary working group Van Traa, 1994, pp. 37-40 and 43.
8   In this sense B.N. Barendregt and H.J.C.M. Theeuwes of the national coordination of criminal intelligence department during their interrogation on September 14, 1995; see Van Traa, 1996, App. II, pp. 359-378.
9   Example taken from *Dralen op de drugsroute*, in: NRC-Handelsblad March 9, 1996.
10 In this sense also Van Traa, 1996, pp. 275-302.
11 *'Turkse politie heeft in drugsonderzoek gemarteld'*, de Volkskrant, February 7, 1996.
12 *Politieregisters 'vervuild' door nalatigheid OM*, in: Stcrt. February 15, 1996.

In order to prevent legal problems in connection with the international exchange of information by the police, many new regulations and powers have been introduced during the last decade. These new instruments give the police, particularly within the framework of Schengen, not only a more regulated and therefore restricted position, but also more autonomy and independence in the international mutual assistance in criminal matters.[13]

Furthermore, police information may be distinguished according to the purposes for which it was collected: operational information, that may soon lead to an intervention, and information with a strategic character (intelligence), that is not intended to be operationalized within a short period of time. Within the concept of intelligence, one can distinguish hard intelligence (facts) and soft intelligence (other forms of information, such as opinions, personal assessments, suspicions and allegations).

Information exchanges do not only take place between individual police officers, but also (and maybe more often) between police services. In order to obtain interesting and useful information, it may be fructuous to use liaison officers. These police officers of one police force or service stationed in another may function as a bridge between two services, establishing and maintaining structural contacts for their home force with the foreign force in which they work and the environment in which they live. Since their functioning is not based on specific national or international legal provisions and exchanges of information with liaison officers are usually subjected to the same provisions and restrictions as informational cooperation in another setting, we consider them an institutional aspect that does not need special attention in a chapter on police powers.

In the context of this chapter, we intend to mainly restrict ourselves to the bilateral exchange of police information in more or less concrete cases, thus excluding institutions used for placing information at the police's disposal in general, such as Interpol, the Schengen Information System and Europol, which are being dealt with briefly in the second chapter of this study. It should be noted however that until this day all police officers working within the context of Europol still have a liaison officers status and operate according to their respective national laws. Their position with respect to the international exchange of information is therefore comparable to those of liaison officers stationed in for instance embassies.

---

13   In this sense, and advocating an even more autonomous position of the police in this context, Heimans, 1994, pp. 139-142.

11.1   International Norms

In general, the information management within the police forces is subject to restrictions imposed by national law for reasons of, on the one hand, national security and sovereignty, and on the other hand, privacy.[14] The former aim the protection of the confidential character of police information, whereas the latter, partly inspired by international agreements, envisages the protection of the individual citizen's right to control the flow of personal data about him. In an international context, exceptions to most of these restrictions have been created, offering a basis for international exchange of information. In this paragraph, we will focus upon the role the Schengen Convention and Benelux Extradition Treaty have had in introducing police powers in this field, as well as upon the restrictions and exceptions existing within the framework of the Council of Europe, in particular the European Convention on Human Rights.

11.1.1   International Norms on Police Cooperation

To encounter the police organisations' desire for possibilities to exchange information more directly and therefore faster, the Schengen partners have drafted and introduced two provisions on mutual legal aid by police officers. Art. 39 SC deals with exchanging information on request of a foreign police service, whereas art. 46 focuses on sending information to a foreign police service spontaneously. In order to enable a joint discussion of these provisions to show the relevant common points and differences, we will first repeat both articles.[15]

Art. 39 SC reads:

1. The Contracting Parties undertake to ensure that their police authorities shall, in compliance with national legislation and within the limits of their responsibilities, assist each other for the purposes of preventing and detecting criminal offences, in sofar as national law does not stipulate that the request is to be made to the legal authorities and provided the request or the implementation thereof does not involve the application of coercive measures by the requested Contracting Party. Where the requested police authorities do not have jurisdiction to implement a request, they shall forward it to the competent authorities.

2. The written information provided by the requested Contracting Party under paragraph 1 may not be used by the requesting Contracting Party as evidence of the criminal offence other than with the agreement of the relevant legal authorities of the requested Contracting Party.

14   Raab, 1994, pp. 123-126.
15   The English translation has been taken from Meijers *et al.*, 1991 and was written by the Schengen/Benelux secretariat in Brussels.

3. Requests for assistance referred to in paragraph 1 and the replies to such requests may be exchanged between the central bodies responsible in each Contracting Party for international police cooperation. Where the request cannot be made in good time by the above procedure, it may be addressed by the police authorities of the requesting Contracting Party directly to the competent authorities of the requested Party, which may reply directly. In such cases, the requesting police authority shall as soon as possible inform the central body responsible in the requested Contracting Party for international police cooperation of its direct application.

4. In border regions, cooperation may be covered by arrangements between the responsible Ministers of the Contracting Parties.

5. The provisions of this Article shall not preclude more detailed present or future bilateral agreements between Contracting Parties with a common border. The Contracting Parties shall inform each other of such agreements.

Art. 46 SC reads as follows:

1. In particular cases, each Contracting Party may, in compliance with its national legislation and without being asked, send the Contracting Party concerned any information which may be of interest to it in helping prevent future crime and to prevent offences against or threats to public order and security.

2. Information shall be exchanged, without prejudice to the arrangements for cooperation in border areas referred to in Article 39(4), through a central body to be designated. In particularly urgent cases, the exchange of information within the meaning of this Article may take place directly between the police authorities concerned, save where national provisions provide otherwise. The central body shall be informed of this as soon as possible.

Both provisions show clearly that, whatever the intentions of international cooperation in this field may be, even between the Schengen countries national law will continue prevailing: the Schengen provisions do not add powers to those which police officers already have according to their national legislation.[16] In spite of this, it is necessary to make some remarks on the international provisions as well, since after all they do function as a framework for cross-border assistance, in particular exchanges of information by police services.[17]

Firstly it should be noted that, other than artt. 40 and 41 SC, the provisions discussed here do not specify the police forces or officers who are entitled to apply the cooperation instrument dealt with. It must, therefore, be assumed that

---

16 Swart, 1991b, p. 98.
17 Swart (1991b, p. 98) notes that the term "assistance" has not been defined and many other forms of assistance than the mere providing of information are conceivable. In this context, we will however restrict our discussion to the exchange of information. On the one hand, this is the most basic and important form of cross-border police assistance in criminal matters, whereas on the other hand, more operational forms of assistance are being dealt with in more detail in artt. 40 and 41 of the Convention and Chapters 4-10 of this study.

it is an exclusive matter of domestic law to decide which police services may provide police information to foreign police services. Furthermore, neither art. 39 nor art. 46 SC contains elements as to the nature of the information for which this exchange context was created: "typical" police information only or general information as well? It occurs to us that general information from publicly accessible sources may be exchanged outside of any procedure, whereas the goal of artt. 39 and 46 SC is rather to facilitate the exchange of typical police information, such as intelligence, results of investigative measures and suspect's antecedents.[18] Requesting this kind of information through a formal letter rogatory procedure would often take too much time and work, whereas the character of the data to be exchanged would not be compatible with an entirely informal transmission.

As to the form of a request for cross-border assistance, the text of the first sentence of art. 39 is not very clear: Should this be written or is a question on the telephone sufficient? Since it should be avoided that police authorities base their work on weak grounds (and provide information to others than they intend to do), it could be justified to demand a written request.[19] Further, one could even defend that, in case of an oral request, the requested authorities are incompetent to provide assistance.[20] Likewise, the second sentence of both the Dutch text and the English translation suggest such an interpretation by the words "*zenden*" and "forward," which can hardly apply to anything else but written documents (including modern versions such as telex and telefax messages and printed e-mail).[21] However, the equivalents of this word in German and French are less specific: *weiterleiten* and *transmettre* may apply to all kinds of transmissible messages. Furthermore, the fact that art. 39 par. 2, other than par. 1 specifically mentions "written" information, implies that the information asked for may be provided in other forms as well.[22] In that case, why would a request for this information need to be written in order to be

---

18 Since (strictly interpreted) they do not contain police information, judicial records and their exchange will be left out of consideration.
19 In this sense Sjöcrona, 1990, p. 74.
20 Sjöcrona, 1995a, p. 1039.
21 Sometimes the police do have the possibility to modernize; in the Euregion Scheldemond (the region of the Dutch-Belgian Schelde Delta), the police are preparing an on-line connection between the data banks of the Zeeland police region and the *gendarmerie* of East Flanders in Gendt. A similar project is being developed along the border of The Netherlands with the German province of Niedersachsen, whereas the Dutch, Belgian and German police in the Maastricht-Liège-Aachen area will be able to communicate via a computerized video system within two years; see De Limburger, October 26, 1995.
22 Even if a written form would be preferable for reasons of exactitude and controllability, it may be in the interest of "quick and efficient policing" that oral messages are done; in this sense a report of the Dutch *Nationale ombudsman* (April 2, 1991, 91/R119), and Hofstee & Schalken, 1991, pp. 61-63.

acceptable, provided the requested authority has no doubt about the source and reliability of the request? Finally, one should not forget that Schengen also guides the police into a new era of operational cooperation, and it is obvious that during a joint pursuit or a common observation by two police officers from different countries, the exchange of information between them will be inevitable, often necessary and never written.

What is important to establish is the context in which these forms of exchange of information may take place, a context which is outlined by the purposes mentioned in the text. Another reason to pay some attention to these purposes is the fact that the legal or illegal character of the exchange of information depends on the aim of this exchange (the principle of finality).[23] According to the English translation, information may be provided on request for "preventing and detecting criminal offences", whereas the police may spontaneously send information to another Contracting Party's police force in order to "prevent future crime" and "to prevent offences against or threats to public order and security." Since these terms should be interpreted and understood on the basis of the authentic versions of the convention, a common presentation may be useful.

Table 11.1 Terminology in Various Versions of artt. 39 and 46 SC

	German	French	Dutch	English
art. 39	* *vorbeugende Bekämpfung* * *Aufklärung* * *strafbaren Handlungen*	* *prévention* * *recherche* * *faits punissables*	* *voorkoming* * *opsporing* * *strafbare feiten*	* preventing * detecting criminal offences
art. 46	* *Bekämpfung zukünftiger Straftaten* * *Verhütung von Straftaten* * *Abwehr von Gefahren*	* *répression d'infractions futures* * *prévention d'infractions* * *prévention de menaces*	* *bestrijding toekomstige strafbare feiten* * *voorkoming strafbare feiten* * *afwending gevaar openbare orde*	* prevent future crime * prevent offences against or threats to public order and security

Considering that both provisions intend to facilitate the exchange of information between two police services on different sides of the border, the question rises as to what is the meaning of the differences in terminology applied for both

---

23 This rule, that seems to be an application of the *détournement de pouvoir* (abuse of power) provision of art. 18 ECHR, was stressed for instance in Recommendation R (87) 15 of 17 September 1987 of the Committee of Ministers of the Council of Europe.

information exchange instruments. It occurs to us that the purposes mentioned in art. 39 ("preventing and detecting criminal offences" and their authentic counterparts) are so general that they cover the entire criminal police task, whereas the enumeration in art. 46 is a much more specific one. It explicitly mentions proactive policing (instead of the pleonastic "prevention of future crime" it would have been more appropriate to translate the authentic texts by "repression of future crime") the prevention of "offences against or threats to public order and security," thus excluding the investigation (detection) of criminal offences while adding a public order task. One can only guess why the investigation of criminal offences was excluded as a purpose of spontaneous exchange of information. Maybe the idea was that, without a request for information, a police service would not be aware of the investigations the police across the border were involved in. It is however not difficult to imagine that information about current or recent events crosses the border in other manners than through official requests (newspapers, radio, television), thus inspiring the police to think of their spontaneous information as possibly being helpful.

It is surprising to see that art. 39 makes no further specification as to the categories of "criminal offences" for which information may be exchanged. Apparently, this instrument of cooperation may be applied in cases of shop lifting, bike theft and traffic offences as well in cases of murder, EC fraud and bank robbery. At first sight, the words used in art. 46 seem to be more detailed, but in fact the concepts of "future crime" and "offences" are no more specific than art. 39 is, whereas "threats to public order and security"[24] must be considered an extension rather than a restriction.[25] The fact that both provisions seem to mention an enumerative number of purposes for data exchange might however suggest a more restrictive regulation than is really the case. On the one hand, the purposes mentioned cover almost the entire range of police activities, whereas on the other hand the information to be provided does not need to be necessary for these purposes. The information may already be provided if it can be useful for one of these purposes.[26] Yet more remarkable is that neither art. 39 nor art. 46 mention anything about the relation between the purposes for which the information to be provided was demanded and the purposes of its

---

24 The English translation confusingly reads "offences **against or** threats to public order and security," thus relating "offences" to "public order and security"; besides being pleonastic (as long as offences may still be prevented, they are threats), the translation does not mention the purpose of "preventing offences" (*Verhütung von Straftaten*, *prévention d'infractions* respectively *voorkoming van strafbare feiten*).

25 Indeed, according to the Dutch government, the aim of art. 46 is to encourage the enforcement of criminal law and public order in general; explanatory statement, TK 1990-1991, 22 140 nr. 3, p. 30.

26 In the same sense Verhey, 1991, p. 126.

originally being gathered.[27] It seems that the treaty drafters have intended to leave this subject entirely to the national legislator's discretion.

Furthermore, one might wonder whether it is necessary that the purpose for which the information is requested or provided, or even the case for which the information is needed, be mentioned at the moment of request or reply. In our opinion, in case the requested party (or, in case of a spontaneous sending as referred to in art. 46, the sending party) explicitly mentions a specific purpose or case the provided information may be used for, this should be considered a restriction to which the requesting party is bound. Although the speciality rule might not yet be generally accepted with respect to mutual legal assistance,[28] it has been recognized by several provisions of the Schengen Convention and, in the form of the principle of finality, it does apply in case of police data exchange.[29] A form of this speciality rule may also be found in art. 39 par. 2 SC, that demands prior permission of the judicial authorities of the requested State before the information provided may be used as evidence in a criminal procedure. This restriction was added in order to avoid the international police cooperation replacing the usual mutual legal assistance in criminal matters,[30] provided by the judicial authorities according to treaties such as the European Convention on mutual assistance in criminal matters.[31] It must be considered a matter of national law to decide which authorities are competent to give this permission.[32] The use of the information for other than police tasks in practice might be warranted by measures such as marking each page with a stamped warning "For police use only!" This has however shown to be ineffective several times, the stamp being hidden by a sticker, correction fluid or otherwise before the text was photocopied.[33]

The agreement of the judicial authorities could be considered as a fictitious form of judicial mutual assistance: After the police authorities have provided the information for police purposes, the judicial authorities fictitiously provide

---

27   Scheller, 1992, p. 167.
28   Orie et al., 1991, p. 109-110; Haentjens, 1992, pp. 71, 74. In matters of extradition, Stanbrook & Stanbrook (1980, p. 47) have defined the speciality rule as "the rule of international practice which prohibits a requesting state from trying a returned person for any offence committed before his return other than one for which he was returned."
29   In this sense for instance artt. 50 par. 3 and 126 par. 3 sub a SC.
30   Explanatory statement of the Dutch government, TK 1990-1991, 22 140, p. 25-26.
31   Strasbourg, April 20, 1959, Trb. 1965, 10.
32   At least, this seems to be the reasoning the Dutch government has followed when stating that within The Netherlands this would be a task for the public prosecutor of the requested district; Answering statement to the Schengen Implementation Act, TK 22 142, 6, p. 26. Later, this idea was confirmed by the French government in the Schengen circular, that will be dealt with later.
33   This example was mentioned in the Nijmegen LL.M. thesis of an officer of the National Central Bureau Interpol in The Netherlands; see Mangelaars, 1992, p. 13.

the same information once again for judicial purposes. Note that the restriction only mentions "written information," thus suggesting that it does not apply to other forms of communication. However, fax messages and (print-outs of) electronic mail and on-line information could be considered "written information" as well. Oral (telephone) messages on the contrary, will usually need a written confirmation before being used as evidence. The agreement of the relevant authorities as referred to in par. 2 may also enable that information originally provided for the purpose of prevention be used as evidence against the person who finally committed the offence that could not be prevented. A provision of this kind cannot be found in art. 46, but since this provision does not cover the exchange of information for investigative purposes, that is no surprise. On the other hand, it is not unthinkable that information provided for a preventive or proactive purpose may eventually be helpful for investigation and evidence. In that case, a supplementary permission (analogous to art. 39 par. 2) seems to be necessary because of the speciality rule and the finality principle mentioned above. Of course, proceeding to an additional request for mutual assistance by the judicial authorities will still be possible as well.

The Schengen provisions do not mention any sanctions for the situation that art. 39 par. 2 has been ignored and written information has indeed been used as evidence or otherwise in judicial procedures.[34] Obviously, this is another aspect of international policing that is left to national legislation and discretion. Finally, police information may well be excluded from procedures without additional permission, but it should not be forgotten that it may help obtaining information that could serve as evidence: One may think of an interrogating police officer confronting a denying suspect with information showing that the police know that he has committed similar offences elsewhere.[35]

A restriction requested police authorities must comply with on the basis of art. 39 par. 1 SC, is the situation that the assistance asked involves the use of coercive measures. Since the concept of coercive measures has not been explained or defined in detail in the Convention, national law will decide as to whether a specific activity is a coercive measure. In the case that national law does not allow the police to reply, the request must be forwarded to the competent authorities, designated by national law, who will deal with it as a normal request for mutual legal assistance. Since it is unlikely that the police of one country will use coercive measures in order to enable itself to spontaneously send information to the police in another country, it is logical that art. 46 SC does not contain a similar provision.

---

34 Answering statement to the Schengen Ratification Act, TK 22 140, 12, pp. 50-51.
35 Brammertz *et al.*, 1994, p. 25.

Another question to be discussed is, whether a requested country is entitled to impose additional conditions before replying the request. One may imagine that a replying country would appreciate being kept informed about the affair or, in case the information provided would lead to the arrest of a citizen of the requested country in the requesting country, the former would like the latter to transfer the proceedings or the execution of the criminal judgment. Although it is likely and comprehensible that such wishes exist, they hardly seem compatible with the fact that the police forces of the Schengen partners are obliged to assist each other and therefore may not refuse to do so in case additional conditions are not fulfilled.[36] They would however be able to refuse the assistance for such reasons if their national legislation would only allow the assistance to be provided under such conditions. It would furthermore be difficult to establish whether a requested party refuses to provide information because they do not have it or because they do not want to provide it. Note that as long as the conditions imposed by the requested party are in the field of mutual police assistance as well, the conditions could be considered as a counter-request for assistance, which should be replied to by the counter-requested party as well.

As to the delay within which a request in this context must be honoured, art. 39 contains no details. On the one hand this is self-evident because of the variety of requests that is to be expected. On the other hand it would not have been impossible to mention a maximum reaction period in such a way that the requesting police force would at least have an idea as to how much time the final answering will take.[37]

Essentially, according to art. 39 par. 3 SC the international police assistance must be exercised by "the central bodies responsible in each Contracting Party for international police cooperation." However, for urgent cases the same provision also creates the possibility that the entire exchange (from request to reply) be done by local police authorities. The second paragraph of art. 46 states that the spontaneous exchange of information must be realised through "a central body to be designated" (not necessarily the same as the body referred to in art. 39), unless in case of "particularly urgent cases" or "arrangements for cooper-

---

36 Note that the strictness of the obligation to assist is shown more clearly by the wordings used in German, French and Dutch (*verpflichten sich, daß ihre Polizeidienste (...) Hilfe leisten, s'engagent à ce que leurs services de police s'accordent (...) l'assistance* and *verbinden zich ertoe dat hun politiediensten elkaar (...) wederzijds bijstand verlenen*) than by the English translation "undertake to ensure that their police authorities shall (...) assist each other."

37 In a memorandum on the Schengen information exchange regulation, G. Van Gestel proposed that, in case a reply would not follow within a week, the requesting service would be informed about the delay to be expected and the reasons for this (*Eindrapport Werkgroep grensverleggend politieoverleg; Bijlage 5: Nederlandse uitwerking artt. 39 en 46 Accoord van Schengen*; April 14, 1993).

ation in border areas referred to in Article 39(4)." The fact that the information must be exchanged through a central body does however not imply that the decision to spontaneously send information must be taken by this body as well. On the contrary, this may very well be decided by the local police in the border areas,[38] who are far better aware of the possible needs and interests of the cross-border colleagues. Note that the concept of "urgent cases" is a very flexible one, that may be extended in various directions. Apparently the Contracting Parties have realized this as well, since in June 1995 a Schengen working group paid some attention to the interpretation of the urgency of requests. In their memento they state that a request must be considered urgent if the delay caused by sending the information through the central body would endanger the success of the prevention or investigation it was meant for.[39]

The Schengen Convention contains several specific provisions to enable the exchange of police information to be supervised by other authorities. Firstly, if a request for information is addressed to the competent authorities directly because the urgency of a situation does not permit sending it to the central authority, the requesting authorities must inform the central authority of the requested state as soon as possible (artt. 39 par. 3 and 46 par. 2 SC). Furthermore, art. 126 par. 3 sub e SC requires that every transmission and receipt of personal data in the context of the Convention "must be recorded both in the data file from which they originated and in the file in which they are incorporated."

The fourth and fifth paragraph of art. 39 deal with the possibility that neighbour Schengen countries bilaterally apply less restrictive regulations of exchange of information by their police forces. Par. 4 allows that the scope of the cooperation in border areas be enlarged by arrangements between the responsible Ministers of the Contracting Parties. This provision was added because in border areas, generally a more intensive cooperation may be expected. However, since the exact need for structure and powers might differ from region to region, it should be possible to adapt and elaborate the applicable regulations according to the local circumstances.[40] Their restricted geographical scope does nevertheless not necessarily impede that police officers outside these areas benefit from the same arrangements: The Hamburg police (no border area) could for instance ask the police in Aachen (in the German-Dutch-Belgian border triangle) for some information the Maastricht or Eupen police could have. The Aachen police would then contact their colleagues across the border and forward the obtained information to Hamburg.[41] However, police officers with

---

38 Answering statement to the Schengen Ratification Act, TK 22 140, nr. 12, pp. 84-85.
39 *Groupe de travail I, "Police et sécurité"*, Bruxelles, June 2, 1995, SCH/I (94) 17, 8th revision.
40 Explanatory statement of the Dutch government, TK 1990-1991, 22 140, p. 26.
41 An example of this kind was referred to by Brammertz *et al.*, 1993, p. 62.

similar experiences have warned that the success of such detour border cooperation might also become an impediment for the cooperation itself, because of the risk that the border area police services finally become the unique and full-time contact services for the other police forces in their country.[42]

Meanwhile, additional arrangements in the sense of art. 39 have been concluded or negotiated for police forces in the border regions of the five original Schengen partners.[43] Note that the Convention itself does not contain any specification as to what should be considered a border region or area or what size this should have. In our opinion, this might depend from one country to another, or even from one region to another, and consequently the determination of the territorial scope of these arrangements must be left to the respective responsible Ministers.

As indicated by art. 46 par. 2 SC, these border area arrangements may also apply to spontaneous cross-border data communications. Art. 39 par. 5 states that the provisions of art. 39 shall not preclude more detailed present or future bilateral agreements between Contracting Parties with a common border, and obliges the Contracting Parties to inform each other of such agreements. In spite of the addition "with a common border," according to us the Convention would not preclude an agreement of this kind between for instance France and The Netherlands, nor would it preclude a multilateral agreement between for instance the Benelux partners. If the basic possibility of data exchange is not restricted to neighbour countries, it does not seem logical to subject an extension of this possibility to such a restriction.

Strictly spoken, the Benelux Extradition Treaty does not offer a formal basis for data exchanges by police officers. Art. 26 BET (as do artt. 3 and 4 of the European Convention on Mutual Assistance in Criminal Matters) allows however that, in the context of a letters rogatory of their own judicial authorities, according to the law of the country of their origin, police officers of the requesting country assist at the carrying out of the letters rogatory by the authorities of the requested country. It seems to be a logical consequence of such events that police officers of both countries exchange views, experiences and other kinds of information on the case concerned. Furthermore, the spontaneous and requested exchange of information in criminal matters between "the competent authorities" is mentioned by art. 18 of the 1969 Benelux Convention on Administrative and Criminal Cooperation,[44] without any indication that these authorities would include the police.

---

42 This was refered to us by L. Van Heek, regional coordinator of international affairs of the Groningen regional police.

43 We will discuss and compare these regulations and their implications for each country in paragraphs 11.2 and 11.3.

44 The Hague, April 29, 1969, Trb. 1969, 124.

The difference in nature between this kind of exchange of information and the instruments offered by the Schengen Convention is clearly illustrated by the fact that, unlike the situation with respect to cross-border pursuit, the Schengen Convention does not refer to provisions of the Benelux Treaty that will or will not be changed or influenced by the Schengen regulation. Because of the different character and lack of legal safeguards of this form of data exchange, it seems to go without saying that such data may not be used in procedures without additional permission of the judicial authorities.

Within the Benelux territory, although not within the official framework of the Benelux Economic Union, numerous agreements on police cooperation have existed for a long time. According to a 1949 Belgian-Dutch border agreement for instance, the commanders of the *Rijkswacht* and the *Rijkspolitie* were allowed to inform each other directly about suspects in the border areas and to warn each other in case of severe offences of which the perpetrators are still hiding in the border area.[45] The question whether this border agreement has been inherited by the regional police forces after the reorganization of the Dutch police,[46] seems to have lost its importance anymore, since the possibilities introduced by the agreement have been subsumed by the relevant provisions of the Schengen Convention.

11.1.2 European Convention on Human Rights

Within the framework of the Council of Europe, several instruments have been created that may be applied to data and privacy protection with respect to the collection and registration of information by the police. Here, we will discuss the European Convention on Human Rights, in particular art. 8, the Council of Europe Convention of 28 January, 1981 for the Protection of Individuals with regard to Automatic Processing of Personal Data (Data Protection Convention), and Recommendation R (87) 15 of the Committee of Ministers to Member States regulating the use of Personal Data in the Police Sector (Recommendation). The subject of international data and privacy protection is a fairly complex and to some extent rather technical one, that has however been discussed profoundly in numerous previous publications.[47] In this context we will therefore confine ourselves to a rather limited discussion of the matter, mainly restricted to the criteria the international exchange of police information should comply with.

The first thing to be established is the relation between the three international legal instruments mentioned above, as well as their mutual statuses. Art.

---

45 The full text of the agreement may be found in for instance Fijnaut, 1992a, p. 213.
46 Which is stated by for instance Hofstede *et al.*, 1993, p. 25, footnote 51.
47 Reference may be made to studies like Nugter, 1990; Korff, 1990; Verhey, 1991; Raab, 1994.

8 ECHR offers a general protection of the individual citizen's right to respect for his privacy, the second paragraph describing the conditions under which an infringement with this right may take place legally. The aim of the 1981 Data Protection Convention was to improve the privacy protection as offered by art. 8 and to ease the restrictions on international communication of personal data that existed at that moment.[48] Note that, other than art. 8 ECHR, "the 1981 Convention does not have direct effect within the national legal systems and therefore no directly enforceable rights can be derived from it."[49] As to the Recommendation, this was drafted by the Committee of Ministers with the intention to plug the hole in the Convention caused by the possibilities of derogation to national legislators, a purpose leading to "a special set of data protection principles for the classic and crucial tasks of the police." Therefore, not just the 1981 Convention, but also the 1987 Recommendation could be considered an elaboration of the European Convention,[50] and both may be applied to reach a more detailed interpretation of art. 8 ECHR.[51]

As to the applicability of art. 8 ECHR to the use of personal data in the police sector, reference may be made to a strong development in the Strasbourg case-law. In 1972, the European Commission on Human Rights stated that registration by police and judiciary did not conflict with art. 8, not even when the registration concerns persons without a criminal record.[52] In a more recent case however, the Commission implicitly judged art. 8 applicable to the transmission of personal data by the police to the criminal court,[53] whereas in the Leander and Gaskin cases, the European Court explicitly decided that art. 8 applies directly to registration and management of personal data by the police.[54] With respect to the applicability of the Data Protection Convention and the Recommendation to exchanges of information within the Schengen framework, it should be mentioned that both instruments are being referred to explicitly by artt. 115 and 117 SC. On the basis of these provisions, both data protection instruments are directly applicable to data exchanges over the Schengen Information System. Direct applicability to other automated information exchanges in a Schengen context is prescribed by art. 126 SC, while art. 127 explicitly extends the applicability of art. 126 to non-automated data files transmitted through the provisions of the Convention. Furthermore, since art. 117 obliges the Contracting Parties to adapt their legislation on computerized

---

48   Raab, 1994, p. 123.
49   Verhey, 1991, p. 112.
50   Verhey, 1991, p. 111; Raab, 1994, p. 126.
51   As Korff, 1990, p. 68 deduced from the Court's judgments in the Leander and Gaskin cases.
52   Appl. 5877/72, X. v. United Kingdom, Yearbook XVI (1973), p. 328.
53   Appl. 8170/78, X. v. Austria, Yearbook XXII (1979), p. 308.
54   Respectively March 16, 1987, Series A 116 and July 7, 1989, Series A 160; see also Van Dijk & Van Hoof, 1990, pp. 369-371.

data management to this Convention and Recommendation, both instruments will also touch automated data exchanges in other than SIS contexts, and are likely to indirectly influence the exchange of other kinds of data as well.[55]

Under art. 8 ECHR, the police commit an interference with fundamental rights by collecting, using and exchanging information that refers or may be retraced to individual citizens.[56] In order to be justified, art. 8 par. 2 demands that the interference be "authorized by law" and "necessary in a democratic society" in the interest of a legitimate aim, such as "public safety or the prevention of crime." This also implies that there must be "proportionality" between the aim pursued and the seriousness of the interference. This proportionality can be interpreted in more detail with the help of the Data Protection Convention and the Recommendation on Police Data. These instruments provide rules regarding subjects such as the kind of data which may or may not be collected, the quality of the data which is collected and the passing on of data.[57]

As to the collection and quality of the data, art. 5 of the Convention states that personal data shall be obtained and stored for legitimate purposes and not used in a way incompatible to those purposes. They must be adequate, relevant and not excessive to those purposes, accurate and kept up to date and identification of the data subjects should not be possible for longer than required for the purposes for which it was collected. Principle 2.1 of the Recommendation limits the collection of personal data for police use further to "such as is necessary for the prevention of a real danger or the suppression of a specific criminal offence," except for further specifications in national law. The collection of data by the police should be based on reasonable suspicions and open-ended, indiscriminate collection of data should be avoided. Art. 6 of the Convention and principle 2.4 of the Recommendation contain special safeguards for the collection of certain particularly sensitive data, such as religion, sexual behaviour or political opinions, data which may only be collected "if absolutely necessary for the purposes of a particular enquiry," based on "strong grounds for believing that serious criminal offences have been or may be committed." Concerning the storage of data, principle 3.1 stipulates that this "should be limited to accurate data and to such as are necessary to allow police bodies to perform their lawful tasks" according to national and international law. The latter expressly intends to include international cooperation through Interpol and could be extended to

---

55   In this sense also Korff, 1990, p. 68.
56   The following is mainly based upon Korff, 1990, pp. 71-74.
57   The question of rights of data subjects, which has been paid detailed attention to in the same regulations, will be left out of consideration here because it does not concern in the first place a matter of police cooperation. The subject has been dealt with in detail by Korff, 1990, pp. 74-83.

the Schengen cooperation without any problem. When storing the data, they should as much as possible be distinguished and classified according to "their degree of accuracy or reliability and, in particular, data based on facts should be distinguished from data based on opinions or personal assessments" (principle 3.2). The data should therefore not include vague aspersions and unsubstantiated suspicions.[58]

For the subject at hand, the cross-border exchange of police information, the most important provisions are to be found in principle 5 of the Recommendation. Within the national police sector, principle 5.1 intends to limit such communications to situations in which exists "a legitimate interest (...) within the framework of the legal powers of these bodies." International exchanges, mentioned in principle 5.4, should not be possible to other authorities than police bodies and, unless necessary for the prevention of a serious and imminent danger or the suppression of a serious criminal offence, they should be based upon a clear provision under national or international law. Furthermore, international exchange of information should not infringe with national regulations for the protection of the person. Some final remarks must be made with respect to the modalities of international communication of police data, an aspect dealt with in principles 5.5.i. through 5.5.iii. Requests for such communications should indicate the requesting body or person as well as the reason and objective for the request, the quality and accuracy of the data should be checked before communication, and in case inaccurate data have been communicated, the recipients must be informed as far as possible. Finally, the information provided should not be used for other purposes than those indicated, unless prior agreement of the communicating body.

11.2   National Norms

In the following paragraph, we will briefly outline the national regulations with respect to the provision of information by police forces to their foreign counterparts. Before discussing this, the legal system of information management and data processing by the police will be sketched, including such subjects as categories of police data, data collection and data storage. As far as possible, the discussion will also include elaborations of international data exchange by the police in border areas. Although originally we did have the intention to

---

58   It speaks for itself that these criteria are in the interest of an adequate functioning of the police as well.

illustrate the legal information with some practical experiences, we did not manage to collect a sufficient amount of information to realize this intention.[59]

11.2.1 Legal Framework

11.2.1.1 Belgium

The legal framework the Belgian legislator has created for the international informational police cooperation may in general be characterized as a moderately detailed one. The regulations that do exist are almost without exception very recent, most of them being inspired or even imposed by the Schengen Convention and developments within the European Union, particularly TREVI and Europol. The only provision of Belgian law regarding international legal cooperation that pre-existed these international instruments was art. 11 of the Judicial Code (*Gerechtelijk Wetboek* - GWb), stating that Belgian judicial authorities are entitled to request information, legal assistance and investigations from foreign judicial authorities. Belgian criminal law and procedure do not pay any attention to the subject, but some general provisions may be found in the Police Function Act and the Royal decree installing the General Police Support Service (*Algemene Politiesteundienst* - APSD).[60] More detailed provisions on the processing and exchange of information in general may be found in the Procession of Personal Data Act (*Wet verwerking persoonsgegevens* - WVP),[61] and in a number of decrees based upon it. This Personal Data Act does not only apply to the processing and storage of computerized personal data, but also to manual registers and documentations. Furthermore, it applies to Interpol and Schengen databanks, since these are accessible from Belgian territory as well.[62] Finally, regulations regarding the exchange of information may also be found

---

59   This is partly due to the short period of time Schengen has been in force; before, most police services were more reticent in registering international contacts in their records. Furthermore, common police information system in The Netherlands do not yet register cross-border incidents as such, and as a result it is impossible to select them systematically. It is nevertheless interesting to note that in one of the Dutch border regions, during the first seven months of Schengen being operational, more than 700 foreign requests were received, 70 % of which concerned license plates in combination with criminal antecedents. Most of the requests were done and answered by individual police officers over the telephone; in general, the requested service did not ask nor receive any feedback on the use and results of the information.

60   July 11, 1994, published in B.S. July 30, 1994, 19658. The decree will be referred to as KB APSD.

61   *Wet ter bescherming van de persoonlijke levenssfeer ten opzichte van de verwerking van gegevens*, December 8, 1992, B.S. March 18, 1993, 5801.

62   De Schutter & De Hert, 1994, p. 7-8.

in the Circular on special policing techniques and the Belgian Schengen circular.[63]

General conditions regarding the treatment of personal information may be found in art. 5 WVP: The processing of personal information is allowed only for clearly described and legal purposes and, with respect to these purposes, the processing must be done in a sufficient, accurate and proportionate manner. The Belgian government specified that "the purposes must be well-indicated and known at the beginning of the processing."[64]

Combined with art. 1 par. 3 and 4, art. 2 WVP stipulates that private life must be respected when processing or collecting data, although it is worth remarking that there is no further specification of methods that enable personal data to be collected without infringing with private life. The privacy protection legislator has also paid some attention to the cross-border provision of information, art. 22 WVP stipulating that international exchanges must take place according to specifications elaborated in Royal decrees. This has meanwhile resulted in four decrees concerning data protection and processing in general, one of them (to be refered to in the following as KB nr. 8) focussing especially on the international exchange of police data.[65]

Registers in which personal data are stored must be reported to the Committee for the protection of private life (art. 17 WVP). When reporting the existence of the register, the eventuality of international exchanges of information contained in the register must be mentioned to the Committee as well (par. 6). This obligation exists regardless of the form the exchange will have, computerized or not.[66] The same Committee plays a role in realizing the rights of data subjects in case of police registers. In general, artt. 9-15 WVP guarantee the data subject's right to notification, access, control and rectification of the information that was stored with regard to him. Art. 11 sub 2 WVP however excludes police registers from these general rights of the data subject, the Committee being entrusted to look after his interests through a system of indirect access, control and rectification.

According to art. 8 WVP, the processing of police and judicial information involving personal data is only allowed for purposes mentioned in or based upon the law, such as those referred to in art. 39 WPA.[67] In order to specify this, the government stated that the collecting and processing of information as

---

63 Respectively April 24, 1990, 7/SDP/690/MN NIX/RB6/6 and March 16, 1995, B.S. March 28, 1995.

64 Explanatory statement, *Gedrukte stukken* 1990-1991, nr. 1610/1; note that the explanation was given to art. 6, which was later renumbered art. 5.

65 Together with KB's nr. 7, 9 and 12, this decree of February 7, 1995 was finally published in B.S. February 28, 1995, pp. 4453-4455.

66 De Schutter & De Hert, pp. 12-13.

67 Bourdoux & De Valkeneer, 1993, p. 275.

referred to in art. 39 WPA must be restricted to the prevention of concrete dangers and the repression of concrete crimes.[68] The third paragraph of art. 39 WPA deals with the information provision to third parties and specifies that information may be provided to other police forces only if these have, within their powers, a legal interest in obtaining the information.[69]

With respect to the types of information, it is worth noticing that Belgian law does not make a distinction between soft and hard information or intelligence. A familiar, legal distinction is the one between judicial and administrative police tasks, but the existence of this distinction has not yet led to a separate processing and storage of judicial and administrative police data.[70] A basic condition regarding the collection and storage of information that the legislator apparently found so self-evident that it would not need mentioning in art. 39 WPA, is that only legally obtained information may be processed.[71] In spite of the lack of recognition in formal regulations, Belgian police practice does seem to make a distinction between soft and hard information, the collection of intelligence being considered a specific task for the district investigation offices of the *gendarmerie* (DBO).[72] For this task, they stand in contact with a specialized public prosecutor, who also coordinates proactive operations.[73]

In general, police registers may contain all kinds of information with respect to events, groups of people and individuals.[74] There are however some restrictions as for the subjects information may be processed on, restrictions that can mainly be found in the artt. 6, 7 and 8 WVP (regulating the so-called "conditional data"). These provisions in principle prohibit the processing of sensitive data regarding the individual (such as religion, ethnicity, sexual behaviour, political or philosophical conviction and activities and membership of labour unions and health insurances),[75] regarding his medical status and regarding his criminal convictions, suspicions and other judicial information. Exceptions to this rule may be made by law and must be restricted to purposes established by law and may be found especially in the above mentioned Royal decrees KB nr. 7 and 8. On the basis of one of these exceptions, the police may collect such data as long as this is necessary for the police task as described in the Police

---

68   Explanatory statement, *Gedrukte stukken* 1990-1991, nr. 1637/1 p. 65.
69   Explanatory statement, *Gedrukte stukken* 1990-1991, nr. 1637/1 p. 66.
70   De Schutter & De Hert, 1994, p. 8.
71   Bourdoux & De Valkeneer, 1993, p. 273.
72   This was confirmed by for instance the commissary-general of the judicial police forces; see *Commissaris-Generaal Christian De Vroom: "België heeft één gerechtelijke, één federale en één basispolitie nodig"* in: Politeia, 1995-6, p. 12.
73   Thus was reported by Van Traa, 1996, App. VI, p. 458.
74   Bourdoux & De Valkeneer, 1993, p. 271.
75   The last two categories are added especially because in Belgium these institutions often have a religious or political character; Robben, 1995, p. 91.

Function Act, particularly in art. 39. The government added that no collecting of sensitive data is allowed for the mere reason for which they are sensitive.[76] In general, in order to be legal, the collecting of sensitive data must be necessary for a concrete interest. It is "allowed from the very moment that the information relates to criminal offences or disturbances of the public order that are actual or likely to happen according to precise and internally consistent indications" and the "exploratory investigation of information without any concrete purpose or police reason is therefore excluded."[77] Furthermore, in case a type of processing sensitive data is not allowed in Belgium within the limits of artt. 6-8 WVP and the additional Royal decrees, then consequently art. 4 par. 2 WVP also prohibits that these data be collected in Belgium for the same type of processing abroad.[78]

11.2.1.2   The Netherlands

With respect to data processing and communication by the police, The Netherlands have a rather extended system of statutory and other legislation.[79] If a foreign request for assistance or mutual legal aid is received by the Dutch police instead of the judicial authorities, the general regulation to be applied may be found in art. 552i Sv, a provision that was adapted by the Schengen Implementation Act. Does the requested assistance concern personal data from police records, then further provisions and conditions may be found in the privacy and data legislation.[80]

The legal framework for data storage, processing and exchange in The Netherlands strongly resembles a funnel. The most general regulations may be found in the Data Protection Act (*Wet persoonsregistraties* - WPR),[81] that however explicitly excludes the entire police sector from its application (art. 2 par. 3 WPR), with the exception of the supervising and advisory task of the Registration Chamber. For this sector, a special Police Records Act (*Wet politieregisters* - WPolR) was drafted,[82] which has been elaborated in more

---

76   Explanatory statement, *Gedrukte stukken* 1990-1991 nr. 1637/1, p. 65.
77   Bourdoux & De Valkeneer, 1993, p. 272.
78   De Schutter & De Hert, 1994, p. 13.
79   Although this seems exagerated, the Van Traa committee registered the complaint that "the rules are so complete that one does not even know whether one respects them" (Van Traa, 1996, App. VI, pp. 97-98).
80   The latter must be considered a *lex specialis* in relation to the former; in this sense the Dutch government in their answering statement, TK 22 140 nr. 12, pp. 84-85; Sjöcrona, 1995a, pp. 1043-1044.
81   December 28, 1988, Stb. 1988, 665. See Nugter, 1990, pp. 145-179.
82   June 21, 1990, Stb. 1990, 414.

detail in the Police records decree (*Besluit politieregisters* - BPolR).[83] Police Records Act and Decree contain detailed provisions on the storage, processing and exchange of personal data for police purposes. They also contain provisions regarding the verification and erasure of inaccurate data, but nevertheless police records seem be seriously polluted, for instance by data on suspects who have been acquitted.[84] Art. 5 WPolR explicitly prohibits the storage of sensitive data (religious, political or other conviction, ethnicity, sexuality, intimate behaviour or medical and psychological characteristics), unless this is necessary in addition to other data. Specific provisions on cross-border exchange of police data can be found in art. 18 WPolR, stating that the international exchange of police information must be regulated by decree, the result of which may be found in art. 13 BPolR.[85]

Furthermore, the storage and processing of personal data that must be considered criminal intelligence by the Criminal intelligence departments (*Criminele inlichtingendiensten* - CID) has been regulated in the 1994 CID Regulation (*CID-Regeling*).[86] This ministerial decree addresses the gathering, collection and verification of CID-information in CID and grey field-registers as well as a differentiated access regulation. CID-information may concern "CID-subjects" (natural or legal persons who are or might reasonably become involved as a suspect in severe, frequent or organized crime) and "grey field-subjects" (similar persons who are not yet registered as CID-subjects). This hard respectively soft intelligence is stored in separate registers, the soft intelligence being verified at least every six months, at which occasion the information must be deleted or transferred to the CID-register.[87]

---

83 February 14, 1991, Stb. 1991, 56.
84 This was concluded after a research by the Registration Chamber in several police regions; see *Politieregisters 'vervuild' door nalatigheid OM*, Stcrt. February 15, 1996.
85 Note that artt. 18 WPolR and 13 BPolR only apply to information from registers the police uses for the exercise of their task as formulated in art. 2 PolW ("to maintain legal order and provide assistance to any who may require"). Since this does not include administrative and control functions and registers, the exchange of information from registers concerning such divers subjects as personnel and firearms licences must take place according to artt. 11 and 18 WPR (Mangelaars, 1992, p. 22). This implies that the provision of these data to third persons is allowed only if based on the aim of the register or on a legal provision; in case of mutual legal aid by police services, such provisions may be found in artt. 39 SC and 552i Sv.
86 March 31, 1995, Stcrt. 1995, 74. The place and functioning of the Dutch criminal intelligence departments have been discussed in detail by Van der Heijden, 1993; see also Klerks, 1995, pp. 107-115.
87 More information on the Dutch CID's may be found in Van Traa, 1996, pp. 303-318, who also judge that the sensitive character of the CID tasks would require that they work on a more specific legal basis.

11.2.1.3   Luxembourg

The legal framework applicable to the processing and transmitting of personal data by the police consists of two elements, a general and a specific one. Since 1979, Luxembourg knows a statute regulating the use of personal data in automated processing (hereafter Automated Data Act),[88] which was amended in 1992, when it was also significantly extended with specific new rules concerning respectively police data and medical data.[89] Supervision and advise with respect to the application of the statute have been entrusted to a committee set up by art. 30. On the basis of art. 12-1 Automated Data Act, a specific decree concerning police databases was created (hereafter Police data decree).[90] Altogether, however, these two regulations are still not very extensive or detailed, and since case-law, guidelines and doctrine are practically non-existent, some central information on this subject is primarily based on interviews and correspondence with key persons in the Luxembourg criminal law enforcement practice.

As to the collection, storage and exchange of personal data by the police, it should be noted that both the Automated Data Act and the Police Data Decree only apply to computerized information, not offering any protection whatsoever in the field of manually processed data.[91] Furthermore, neither the Act nor the Decree contains a specification of different forms of processing. Both only refer to data processing in a general sense, stating that the police and the *gendarmerie* are entitled to create and exploit, in joint ownership, personal databases for the purposes of prevention, investigation, establishment and prosecution of criminal offences.

According to art. 2 par. 1 Police data decree, the police database will consist of three parts: a register of wanted persons and objects, accessible for all Luxembourg police officers, a documentation register, accessible for police chiefs and judiciary police officers who are auxiliaries to the public prosecutor, and an archives register, accessible only with permission of or on behalf of the prosecutor general. The documentation register contains information on cases that have not yet been solved and on persons who are object of a police record or an investigation involving a criminal offence (art. 5 par. 1 Police Data Decree).[92] Various contact persons in Luxembourg have explained us that this documentation register will also be used for storing soft intelligence.

---

88   *Loi du 31 mars 1979 réglementant l'utilisation des données nominatives dans les traitements informatiques.*

89   Korff, 1993, L.1.

90   *Règlement grand-ducal du 2 octobre 1992 rélatif à la création et à l'exploitation d'une banque de données nominatives de police générale.*

91   Vermeulen *et al.*, 1994, p. 40.

92   According to a letter of October 3, 1995 of the *gendarmerie* captain R. Genson, in September 1995 the police database was still being developed and not yet completely operational.

11.2.1.4   France

The framework French domestic law offers for the international exchange of information by the police only has a limited size.[93] It mainly consists of the Data Processing, Databases and Liberties Act (*Loi relative à l'informatique, aux fichiers et aux libertés* (hereafter Data Protection Act or LIFL).[94] In general, the French Data Protection Act may be considered a rather vague and broad statute,[95] entrusting practically all central advisory, supervisory, consultative and even regulatory task to an independent committee of state,[96] the National Data Processing and Liberties Committee (*Commission Nationale de l'Informatique et des Libertés*, hereafter Committee). The impression of vagueness of the Data Protection Act increases when focusing on its provisions concerning the treatment of personal data by the police: It does not mention the function or task of the police once, and only refers to public purposes, State security and public safety in a very general sense, leaving all further regulation of the matter to the Committee.

According to art. 4 LIFL, the statute does not only apply to automated databases but also to manual ones.[97] Furthermore, it applies to public as well as private data collections, both being supervised by the Committee (art. 14 LIFL). Automated databases for public purposes, (thus including those used by the police), must be authorized by decree or, in some cases, by statutory law (art. 15 LIFL). The latter is the case when the database concerns individual liberties that may only be infringed by the legislator; the Computerization of Judicial Records Act forms an example of this.[98] Before an authorization is given, the opinion of the Committee must be asked (art. 15 par. 1 LIFL) and the Committee's decision as well as the application it was based upon shall be kept available to the public (art. 22 LIFL).

As to the collection of data, art. 25 LIFL rather superfluently emphasizes that it is prohibited to do so by use of any fraudulent, dishonest or illegal means. Furthermore, according to art. 19 par. 1 LIFL the collection, storage, exchange

---

93   It must be hoped that our own experiences with the collection of material for this paragraph were no indication of the way foreign requests for information will be dealt with by the French police and judicial authorities: Even the French public prosecutor seconded in The Hague as a liaison magistrate, Ms E. Pelsez, who fully and cordially cooperated, was forced to wait more than three months for some general information she requested from her colleagues in Paris. The information we finally received surprisingly consisted of hardly anything else but a French copy of the relevant Schengen provisions.
94   January 6, 1978, J.O. January 25, 1978; most recent amendment March 11, 1988.
95   Korff, 1993, F.5.
96   Nugter, 1990, p. 78; Vermeulen *et al.*, 1994, p. 41.
97   Nugter, 1990, p. 78-79.
98   See Picard, 1993, p. 294.

and other forms of data processing must be mentioned in the application for the Committee's opinion. However, par. 2 allows that these conditions be omitted for reasons of State security (*Sureté*), defence and public safety (*Sécurité*). For automated databases in the field of State security, defence and public safety, the Council of State (*Conseil d'État*) may allow that these authorizations and the conditions they are subjected to do not have to be published (art. 20 par. 2 LIFL).[99] As a result, the French police forces may use secret databases of which the contents, purposes and regime are unknown to the public.

In the field of criminal policing, no formal distinction between soft intelligence and other kinds of information is made. When it comes to security policing, the *Renseignements Généraux* (general intelligence service) within the *Police Nationale* may be mentioned as a police service with the sole task of collecting (mainly political) intelligence for State security and public safety. At request, these data may be communicated to other police services as well.[100]

Regarding so-called sensitive data, art. 31 LIFL states that data referring to a person's racial origin, political, religious or philosophical opinion, union membership and moral behaviour may only be collected with the explicit permission of the concerned person. However, according to par. 3, for reasons of public interest, a decree may allow that exceptions to this prohibition are made, which has been done in several decrees. These exceptions particularly refer to the activities of the *Renseignements Généraux* intelligence service in the field of combating violent crime and terrorism. In cases of violent crime and after a written request, these informations may also be communicated to other services of the police.[101]

11.2.1.5 Germany

In 1983, the Constitutional Court caused a tremendous change in German privacy protection law. In its so-called census decision (*Volkszählungsurteil*), the Court judged that the combination of the constitutional rights of individual dignity (art. 1 par. 1 GG) and individual freedom (art. 2 par. 1 GG) implies an underlying constitutional right to individual self-determination.[102] As a result, every act by which the state or its organs deal with personal data without the

---

99 This does not imply that they are never published; Picard (1993, p. 294) refers to some decrees that have indeed been published, adding that it is (of course) hard to know the contents of unpublished decrees. Another decree has been published in J.O. March 9, 1995. It also happens that the fact of a new decree being introduced is announced, whereas its contents remain unpublished.
100 Picard, 1993, p. 295.
101 Picard, 1993, pp. 294-295.
102 BVerfG December 15, 1983, BVerfGE 65, 1, also published in NJW 1984, pp. 419-428.

explicit consent of the individual concerned, must be based upon statutory law. Since police work is mainly a matter of collecting, storing, combining and processing information on individual citizens, the police sector was maybe more thoroughly affected than any other part of the German society. Every form of policing involving personal data would in the future (after a period of so-called transition bonus) require its own specific legal basis.[103]

Being a matter of administrative nature, the subject of data protection in Germany is in the first place part of the task of the provincial legislator. As a result, for the entire German police exist altogether sixteen provincial data protection statutes (*Landesdatenschutzgesetze*) and a Federal Data Protection Act (*Bundesdatenschutzgesetz* - BDSG), whereas more specific regulations with respect to the police use of data may also be found in the legislation on provincial as well as federal police forces. These Police Acts contain detailed provisions on collecting, storing, transmitting, blocking, changing, combining and erasing personal data and the conditions required for these forms of police data management. As long as no such specific provisions apply, the police must respect the general data protection legislation, which also implies the competence of the Provincial data protection controller (*Landesdatenschutzbeauftragter*) or, for the federal police forces, the Federal data protection controller (*Bundesdatenschutzbeauftragter*) to control the storage and use of personal data by the police.[104]

The management and regulation of police information under German law is dominated by the dichotomy that characterizes the German police tasks in general, the separation between criminal law enforcement on the one hand and pure police tasks (prevention of danger and proactive policing) on the other.[105] As a result, as far as the international exchange of police information is concerned, several levels and sorts of legislation must be taken into account. Regarding the exchange of information in criminal matters, regulations can be found in the Act on the Federal Criminal Police Office (*Gesetz über die Einrichtung eines Bundeskriminalamtes* - BKAG), the International Legal Assistance in Criminal Matters Act (*Gesetz über die internationale Rechtshilfe in Strafsachen* - IRG), and the joint federal and provincial Guidelines on foreign

---

103 Bäumler, 1992, pp. 509-511.
104 Due to a lack of capacity, the Data protection controllers yet seem to have been unable to exercise any form of control of most police data; in this sense Bäumler, 1992, pp. 528-529.
105 Bäumler, 1992, p. 521. The difficulty to separate one category from another is illustrated clearly by Dautert (1989, pp. 61-64), who shows that data concerning the criminal past of a person may serve the prevention of more crime by this person as well as his future prosecution in case the prevention fails. However, as we explained in Chapter 4, the question whether proactive policing should be regulated in (federal) criminal procedure or in (provincial) police law is still a subject of fierce debates; see for instance Weßlau, 1989; Wolter, 1991, pp. 30-33; Hund, 1991; Kniesel, 1992; Denninger, 1992, pp. 169-173; Busch, 1995, 169-179.

contacts in criminal matters (*Richtlinien für den Verkehr mit dem Ausland in strafrechtlichen Angelegenheiten* - RiVASt).[106] The subject of international exchange of information for pure (preventive and proactive) police tasks has been addressed by most provincial and federal police statutes.

Partly because of the federal organisation, partly because of specialisation, and certainly also as a result of the strict legal separation between pure police task and criminal investigation, Germany knows numerous kinds of police data bases. Some of these are managed and used by the federal and the provincial police forces together, others by the federal or the provincial police, some are used for typically preventive tasks, others serve mainly proactive or investigative purposes, some only contain information on pre-trial and other detention, others have been created especially for border control etc.[107] A strict separation between "hard" and "soft" data cannot be made, but some data bases (especially the so-called PIOS and SPUDOK data bases,[108] containing investigative and proactive information on suspects, possible suspects and their contacts) do indeed contain more vague, unconfirmed and therefore soft data than others (such as those containing information on detained persons or unwanted aliens).[109] One might therefore conclude that in fact there is indeed a difference between information in general and intelligence in particular.[110]

The storage of information is generally allowed for those purposes for which the data were or could have been collected (the finality principle),[111] with however a central role for the principles of proportionality and subsidiarity.[112] A general basis for the collection and storage of information for criminal investigative purposes (thus after the discovery of a criminal offence) may be found in art. 163 StPO,[113] whereas all methods of preventive and proactive data gathering have been addressed by police law. Regarding the transmission of data and the use of these data by the foreign service to which

---

106 Published in for instance Grützner/Pötz.

107 Bäumler, 1992, p. 536-544.

108 PIOS stands for *Personen, Institutionen, Objekte, Sachen* (persons, institutions, targets, objects) and SPUDOK for *Spurendokumentationssystem* (trace documentation system).

109 Bäumler, 1992, p. 535.

110 This topic is also addressed by Strunk, 1994, pp. 16-22.

111 In general, this follows from artt. 13 and 14 BDSG; Bäumler, 1992, p. 610.

112 Bäumler, 1992, pp. 608-609.

113 This general provisions only covers investigations for which no specific legal basis exists or is required.

they have been provided, the finality principle must be respected as well,[114] although exceptions seem to be possible.[115]

11.2.2 International Data Exchange by the Police

11.2.2.1   Belgium

When it comes to the provision of police information to foreign police services, Belgian law seems to make no distinction between the provision of information on request and the spontaneous provision of information. Specifications of this kind not only seem to be unknown to legislation, regulations or case-law, but in spite of the fact that the Schengen Convention, which does make this distinction, has been discussed profoundly, it is even ignored by doctrine.

Art. 39 WPA does not contain a specification of the police services with whom information may or may not be exchanged; therefore, providing information to foreign police services does not seem to be excluded at forehand.[116] In general, this is confirmed by art. 22 WVP, a provision that has however been explained and elaborated restrictively in the above mentioned Royal decree nr. 8. The Belgian regulation of international exchange of police data does not know a general restriction of its territorial scope, although specific countries may or must be treated in a different way than others. As every other type of processing, the international exchange of the conditional data referred to in artt. 6, 7 and 8 WVP is bound to special restrictions.[117] The conditional data mentioned in art. 6 WVP, data concerning religion, ethnicity etcetera, may be processed and exchanged only on the basis of a legal obligation in Belgium or the receiving country, signatory to the 1981 Data Protection Convention and with data protection standards equal to those in Belgium. It may be done only by officers who have been mentioned by name on a list that is accessible for the Committee (art. 8 KB nr. 7). According to KB nr. 8, the cross-border provision of judicial and police data is only allowed on the basis of an intergovernmental agreement (such as Schengen and Europol) or within an international organisation for police cooperation (Interpol). The exchange of information with or provision of information to countries without a sufficient privacy protection system is not excluded,[118] but art. 1 par. 2 KB nr. 8 subjects such exchanges to more severe

---

114 Bäumler, 1992, p. 611.
115 Art. 26 par. 1 PolGNW for instance states that the finality principle must be respected, unless the transmission "(1) has an explicit legal basis or (2) is necessary for the prevention of danger and it is impossible or disproportionally difficult for the requesting authority to collect the information elsewhere."
116 In this sense also Bourdoux & De Valkeneer, 1993, p. 277.
117 De Schutter & De Hert, 1995, p. 13.
118 De Schutter et al., 1992/1993, p. 1153; Vermeulen et al., 1994, p. 44.

conditions and restrictions. More specifically, there must be a severe or imminent danger, it must be in the interest of the repression of a criminal act more severe than a misdemeanour, or it must be necessary for the police task in one of the countries involved. Furthermore, the categories of information that may be provided to such countries have been reduced as well.[119] A list of countries that do offer an equal or otherwise sufficient protection will be established by Royal decree.[120]

The purposes for which a Belgian police force may provide information to a foreign police force are described in the most general sense by art. 39 par. 1 WPA, stating "when exercising the tasks entrusted to them." This remarkably large description might be considered some kind of a finality principle,[121] but makes no distinction whatsoever between the administrative and the judicial or criminal police task. It does not address the distinction between preventive, repressive and proactive purposes either; none of them seems to be excluded at forehand.[122] Note however that, in accordance with art. 14 WPA, only the *gendarmerie* and the municipal police may collect and process general intelligence in order to prevent crime, since the public prosecutor's judicial police does not have any preventive tasks or powers. In order to make sure that the purpose information has been asked for is in conformity with the aims for which the requested information was collected (the finality principle), the requested service must judge the legality of the request before providing the requested information.[123] To enable this, the requesting party will have to specify the reasons why they need that specific information, which may include some of the context of the investigation involved.

On occasion, the police may be incompetent to reply a foreign request for police information themselves, and obliged to forward the request to the judicial authorities. The Schengen circular of the Belgian ministers of justice and the interior repeats art. 39 SC by stating that this is especially the case if the request involves the use of coercive measures or such measures are necessary in order to obtain the requested information. Although no further specification of the concept of coercive measures could be found in Belgian law, circulars, case-law or doctrine,[124] it seems safe to assume that investigative activities which

---

119 According to art. 1 par. 2, information regarding subjects as administrative and civil cases, out-of-court-settlements, youth protection measures, pre-trial custody and mental health measures may not be provided.

120 Robben, 1995, p. 96 and footnote 66.

121 Vermeulen *et al.*, 1994, p. 45.

122 Vermeulen *et al.*, 1994, p. 44.

123 Bourdoux & De Valkeneer, 1993, p. 276.

124 It should be acknowledged that there is one exception to this: Bourdoux *et al.*, (1995, pp. 11-12) argue that as coercive measures should be considered all physical force plus all other infringements with individual liberties and freedoms.

respect the individual citizen's freedom and liberties may be used in order to reply the request. One can think about such measures as interrogating a voluntarily cooperating suspect or witness or establishing the factual situation at a place that is accessible for the public.

11.2.2.2   The Netherlands

As mentioned above, the first provision of Dutch law that applies to legal assistance by the police on foreign request is art. 552i Sv. This provision states that foreign requests for mutual legal assistance, received by police, must be sent to the public prosecutor (par. 1), unless the request only asks for information that may be obtained and provided without using coercive measures (par. 2). Because of the importance and complexity of the matter, the prosecutors-general have drafted a circular containing guidelines on how the police should handle requests for legal assistance.[125] A central provision in these guidelines states that, in case the request concerns the provision of information, additional conditions may be found in art. 13 BPolR. Notwithstanding the fact that this decree was originally introduced for automated data, art. 13 has been declared explicitly applicable to other than computerized information as well. For this reason and because this chapter focuses on informational rather than operational cooperation, it occurs to us that a joint discussion of the artt. 552i Sv and 13 BPolR is preferable to a separate one.[126]

The first remark to be made regarding the Dutch regulation of the exchange and international provision of information by police officers concerns its territorial scope. Since Dutch law does not demand a treaty basis for this form of mutual legal aid, it may also be applied in the relation with other than Schengen countries and is therefore less strict than the provisions of artt. 39 and 46 SC, on which the Dutch provisions were inspired.

Furthermore, in general art. 13 par. 1 BPolR restricts the provision of police information to foreign services to situations in which this is necessary for the Dutch police task, and the prevention of a serious and imminent danger or investigation of a crime that has shocked the legal order, or (as long as the assistance is based on a request regarding a specific person or case) the police task in the requesting country. In order to enable establishing the necessity, the foreign authority must indicate in their request why the solicited information is needed. The Dutch authorities will then be able to weigh the interest of the investigation against the interest of privacy protection. Before providing their colleagues with information, the Dutch police authorities must take the privacy

---

125   *Richtlijn wederzijdse rechtshulp in strafzaken*, November 23, 1994, Stcrt. 1994, 242.
126   A general discussion of mutual legal assistance by Dutch police and judicial authorities may be found in Van Traa, 1996, App. V, pp. 422-432.

standards in the requesting country into account (art. 13 par. 4 BPolR). In general, this restriction does not seem to apply to the Schengen partners since they are considered sufficiently reliable regarding the protection of the privacy and other aspects of data protection.[127] However, since most of them do not know so strict a separation between hard and soft intelligence as The Netherlands do, the precautions to be taken must always depend on the character of the information to be provided and the aim of the provision.

Although in general the existence of a foreign request is a constitutive condition without which no legal assistance in criminal matters may take place,[128] artt. 46 SC and 13 par. 2 BPolR also allow the spontaneous provision of information by the Dutch police to their cross-border colleagues. It is not surprising to see that this spontaneous sending of information has not been subjected to explicit restrictions regarding means of coercion, since the spontaneous use of means of coercion or investigation in order to enable a spontaneous provision of information for the police in a neighbour country does not have to be expected. In case such a situation does however occur, the guidelines stipulate that the spontaneous provision of information is bound to the same conditions as the transmission on request.

The spontaneous exchange of information according to art. 46 SC and 13 par. 2 BPolR may be given some structural character, even between two non-neighbouring countries, such as France and The Netherlands. In the field of drug crime, the Dutch authorities will consistently report all license plates of French cars that have been seen in some specific neighbourhoods of Dordrecht and Rotterdam to the French authorities.[129] Another example from the practice shows that the spontaneous sending of information may to some extent also be provoked: As an example of this, we may mention that the Dutch police district "Achterhoek" receives a daily report of all events that have occupied their German colleagues just across the border, which might inspire them to spontaneously send information that might help the German police.

In the Answering statement to the Schengen Ratification Act, the Dutch government stated that, since spontaneous sendings of information in principle need to be send through the CRI, a general check of the exchange by a third would be guaranteed.[130] This raises the question to which extent the CRI may carry out such a check and whether they will be able to intervene and prevent the exchange. In our opinion, since the main aim of the Schengen Convention was to improve the speed and efficiency of the international exchange of police

---

127 In art. 126 SC, they have committed themselves to realizing a system of privacy protection that is at least equal to that of the 1981 Data Protection Convention.

128 Sjöcrona, 1995a, p. 1038.

129 Jaarverslag Contactofficier van Justitie Parijs, referred to in *Opportuun* 1995-5, p. 6.

130 TK 22 40, nr. 12, p. 85.

information, this check may only be a marginal one. In the light of the coordinatory and advisory task of the CRI, the main criterion should then be whether the provision of this information in the concrete case would frustrate other investigations, especially if these are of a larger scale. The practical experience of the CRI however seems to indicate that decentral police services only send their information through the CRI if they believe that the central body will be able to add something essential to the information. As a result, the coordinatory function of the CRI is seriously frustrated, which regularly leads to collisions when two or more regional police forces suddenly notice that they are investigating the same case.[131]

11.2.2.3 Luxembourg

As far as the transmission of police data from the Luxembourg police to foreign police authorities is concerned, art. 10 sub d Police Data Decree explains that this is allowed within the framework of an international convention, an intergovernmental agreement or through Interpol. Practically, this implies that a direct exchange of police information is possible with police services of all Schengen partners under the same conditions, whereas with other countries all police information must be exchanged through Interpol. It is likely that in the future an exchange with all European Union members will be enabled through Europol as well, at least from the moment the (intergovernmental) Europol Convention comes into force. Note that the Luxembourg legislation itself does not make a distinction between the exchange of information on request and the spontaneous provision of such information to foreign authorities. Since it does not contain a specification of the purposes for which information may be communicated, such communications may take place for repressive as well as for preventive and proactive purposes in general, as mentioned in artt. 39 and 46 SC.[132] The subject of spontaneous sendings remains unmentioned in Luxembourg law. In general, it will be left up to the individual police officers to judge, within the limits of the law, the necessity and opportunity of a spontaneous transmission of information to a foreign police service.[133]

---

131 This complaint was related to us by CRI data protection specialist P. Tazelaar. For us, it also implied that, in spite of our original hope, the CRI would not be a complete and reliable source of information on national experiences with international legal assistance by the police.
132 This was confirmed in the letter by captain Genson.
133 In this sense captain Genson in his letter of October 3, 1995.

11.2.2.4   France

French law does not contain many specific provisions on international data exchange. Besides the Schengen provisions, only two official documents deal with the subject of informational police cooperation. The first one is a Schengen circular, explaining some provisions of this Convention in more detail.[134] The circular only addresses the authorization procedure for the police providing written information that might serve as evidence, as referred to in art. 39 par. 2 SC. The Data Protection Act does not contain any restrictions with respect to the territorial scope of exchange of police information. Such restrictions may however be mentioned in the conditions belonging to the authorization, since the intention of cross-border forwarding of information must be specified in the application for the Committee's opinion according to art. 19 par. 1 LIFL.

The second document of French law which explicitly addresses the international exchange of police information is a Decree entrusting the Interpol tasks for France to the *Direction centrale de la police judiciaire* of the *Police nationale*.[135] This decree does not contain any specification of situations in which or purposes for which such exchange may take place, but only refers to the Interpol Constitution. As a result, the international exchange of police information will be allowed within the limits set by international law, in particular the Schengen Convention (artt. 39 and 46 SC: "prevention and detection of criminal offences, future crime and threats to public order and security"), possibly completed and elaborated by the conditions set for the authorization of individual databases.

11.2.2.5   Germany

Because of the legality principle, that takes a central position in German law, the general obligation to prosecute every criminal offence reported, the police must forward all information concerning a concretely committed offence to the judicial authorities (art. 163 par. 2 StPO). This however does not stand in the way of the police keeping copies of all information for police use.[136] This is also illustrated by the fact that the mere sending of a file to the judicial authorities does not imply that the police work on the case concerned is finished or must be stopped.[137] The discussion is still in progress, whether data for

---

134 *Circulaire du 23 juin 1995 commentant les dispositions des articles 39, 40 et 41 de la convention signée à Schengen le 19 juin 1990*, June 23, 1995, NOR:*JUSA9500149C*.

135 *Décret fixant les attributions du bureau central national de l'Organisation internationale de police criminelle (Interpol)*, May 26, 1975, J.O. June 4, 1975, hereafter NCB-Decree.

136 Bäumler, 1992, p. 561.

137 Kleinknecht/Meyer-Goßner, 1995, p. 588.

proactive purposes, particularly those data that might possibly serve as evidence in future prosecutions, should be forwarded to the public prosecutor or could stay in the possession of the police for preventive purposes.[138] As for the provision of information to the German police, the legality principle is said to cause a certain reticence among foreign police services to provide information that they do not want to be used for prosecution.[139] As a practical solution for this problem, foreign police officers transmitting intelligence to their German counterparts seem to ascertain that the information provided is not enough to base an official suspicion upon.

A distinction between the provision of information on request of a foreign police service versus the spontaneous cross-border provision of information may be found in several provincial police statutes. The distinction is related to the purposes for which information may be provided. Spontaneous provision is allowed only if this is necessary for the fulfilment of the providing police service's tasks. This distinction seems to be a logical one since, without a request, the only necessity that a providing service can judge is indeed the necessity for itself.

As to the field of application of the International Legal Assistance Act, it should be stressed that this statute intends to cover all forms of international legal assistance in criminal matters, most of its provisions regulating issues such as extradition and execution of foreign sentences. A small number of provisions has however been devoted to "other forms of assistance" in criminal matters, such as the exchange of evidence or information. Although, according to the text of art. 59 IRG, this only applies to legal assistance on request, the law however does not stand in the way of spontaneously providing information to other states, which could inspire them to file a request afterward.[140] Art. 59 IRG does also apply to police cooperation, as long as it concerns strictly criminal matters, thus excluding preventive and proactive policing.[141] Once a foreign request for legal assistance has been received, it should be interpreted largely and in a flexible manner. If a witness who is interrogated on request does not give any the essential information but mentions another person who might be a more useful witness, the interrogation of the latter may be considered to be necessary within the context of the same request.[142]

The exchange of criminal information according to art. 59 IRG has been subjected to no specific territorial restrictions whatsoever. As for the exchange

---

138 Bäumler, 1992, pp. 575-576.
139 Thus was reported to us by numerous Dutch and Belgian police officers in the areas along the German border; confirmation may be found in for instance Hofstede *et al.*, 1993, p. 52.
140 Vogler/Wilkitzki, § 59, p. 4.
141 Vogler/Wilkitzki, § 59, p. 12.
142 Vogler/Wilkitzki, § 59, p. 4.

of pure police information, this will mainly depend on the provincial law concerned. Furthermore, in general the data protection standards of the receiving country must be verified; in case the information will be provided to another Schengen partner, it may be assumed that these standards will be sufficient.[143]

The cross-border provision of information by a German police service is allowed for several reasons, some of which may be found on the German side, some on the foreign side. Firstly, police information may be provided to a foreign police service if this is necessary for the provider's (the German police's) task.[144] Secondly, police data may also be exchanged if necessary in the interest of the foreign police service's task; this kind of exchange is usually limited to requested assistance, as expressed explicitly in for example artt. 40 par. 5 BayPAG and 28 par. 4 NWPolG.[145] Situations justifying the provision of police information on request are the necessity for the prevention of serious danger[146] or of severe criminal offences in the receiving country,[147] and situations where the provision is prescribed or regulated by international agreements.[148] Furthermore, the speciality principle prohibits that the information provided be applied for other purposes than it was provided for.[149] In order to enable the establishment of the purposes for which information must be provided, a request should contain sufficient information with respect to the case and intentions of the requesting police service.[150]

In the so-called *Zuständigkeitsvereinbarung* 1993, an agreement based on art. 74 par. 2 IRG, the German federal and provincial governments have separated their powers as far as mutual legal assistance in criminal matters is concerned.[151] On the basis of this agreement, most of the mutual legal assistance has been delegated to the governments of the provinces, who may subdelegate it to their respective provincial authorities. As an elaboration of the former *Zuständigkeitsvereinbarung* (1983), most provinces have introduced detailed regulations regarding this subdelegation, which also foresee a specifica-

---

143 Bäumler, 1992, p. 614. In this sense also art. 43 par. 4 NGefAG, the most recent provincial regulation with respect to this matter.
144 See for instance artt. 32 par. 3 sub 1 BGSNeuRegG, 34 par. 2 sub 1 SPolG, 28 par. 1 NWPolG, 43 par. 2 sub 2 NGefAG, 40 par. 2 BayPAG.
145 In this sense also Heise/Tegtmeyer, 1990, p. 230.
146 Artt. 32 par. 3 sub 2 BGSNeuRegG, 34 par. 2 sub 2 SPolG, 28 par. 4 NWPolG, 43 par. 2 sub 2 NGefAG, 40 par. 5 sub 2 BayPAG.
147 Art. 32 par. 3 sub 2 BGSNeuRegG.
148 Artt. 43 par. 2 sub 1 NGefAG, 40 par. 5 sub 1 BayPAG.
149 In this sense for instance artt. 33 par. 6 BGSNeuRegG, art. 52 par. 5 SPolG, 26 NWPolG, 39 NGefAG, and 39 par. 2 BayPAG.
150 In this sense for instance art. 32 par. 4 SPolG.
151 More completely named *Vereinbarung zwischen der Bundesregierung und den Landesregierungen (...) über die Zuständigkeit im Rechtshilfeverkehr mit dem Ausland in strafrechtlichen Angelegenheiten*, July 1, 1993, published in for instance Grützner/Pötz.

tion of cases in which the police, especially the respective province's criminal police office (*Landeskriminalamt*, hereafter LKA), may independently reply to requests for police information.[152]

11.2.3 Exceptions to Data Exchange by the Police

11.2.3.1 Belgium

Oddly enough, the Belgian Schengen circular does not pay any substantial attention to requests which must be dealt with by the judicial authorities instead of by the police. It only states (once more inspired by art. 39 SC), that the police are incompetent to reply requests concerning or involving an exclusive power of the judicial authorities.[153] Regrettably, it does not specify the situations in which such is the case, and Belgium's national legislation does not contain any provisions with respect to this either. Altogether, not a single substantial exception to the informational police cooperation has been made explicitly. It seems however that a detailed circular concerning the international exchange of information by the police is in preparation and will deal with this question as well.[154] In the meantime, some exceptions might be deduced from the general system of Belgian international criminal law.

Traditionally, mutual legal assistance in criminal matters, which has never known a systematic legal basis in Belgian law, was always closely related to the extradition.[155] Conditions that must be fulfilled in order to enable a person's extradition by Belgium are: double incrimination and a certain minimum severeness of the offence concerned, and no extradition of Belgian citizens. Further, extradition is prohibited for political or fiscal offences, in case a discriminatory prosecution may be feared, if it is unlikely that the extradited's human right will be respected and if there is a risk that the death penalty will

---

152 These provincial elaborations, that have not been renewed, still fit in the new frame and seem to have stayed in force. They may be found in Grützner/Pötz as well.

153 It seems that, according to the assembly of prosecutors general, all information the police may use in their investigations is judicial information; as a consequence, informational police cooperation in criminal matters would be impossible.

154 In this sense the head of the APSD-division international police cooperation, P. Zanders. Meanwhile, restrictions and possibilities to extradition and international mutual legal assistance between Belgium and its Schengen partners have been updated and specified in a circular issued by the minister of justice (*Ministeriële omzendbrief met betrekking tot de uitlevering en de wederzijdse rechtshulp in strafzaken tussen de lidstaten van de Uitvoeringsovereenkomst van het Akkoord van Schengen van 19 juni 1990*, April 24, 1995, B.S. June 2, 1995, pp. 15762-15779, but this circular does not address the topic of informational assistance by the police.

155 Van den Wyngaert, 1994, pp. 839-843.

be imposed and executed.[156] The political susceptibility of what should be understood by political offences was clearly illustrated when the Belgian Council of State prohibited the extradition to Spain of two alleged ETA members who had asked for political asylum in Belgium. As a reaction, Spain withdrew its ambassador and suspended all police and judicial cooperation with Belgium.[157] As a consequence of art. 9 of the 1957 European Convention on Extradition, which is in force between Belgium and its direct neighbour countries according to art. 60 SC, extradition is also excluded if the person involved has been tried for the same facts already (international application of the *non bis in idem*-principle).[158]

Some of these grounds for refusal however, do not apply to mutual legal assistance. This is especially the case for the condition of double incrimination and the minimum severeness of the offence concerned, whereas the speciality principle does not apply to the same extent as in cases of extradition. On the one hand, it is true that this principle is difficult to apply in the informational phase of mutual legal assistance, since this form of cooperation often plays a role in the beginning of an investigation, when still little is known about facts and suspects.[159] On the other hand, where the Schengen circular states that the information may not be used for other purposes than those for which it was provided, the heart of the speciality principle seems to have indeed been recognized.

Remaining grounds for refusal are the political or fiscal character of the offence (art. 2 of the 1959 European Convention on Mutual Assistance in Criminal Matters),[160] the situation that replying the request would be against Belgium's own public order,[161] and the risk of the death penalty being imposed or executed on the basis of the information provided. Regarding the principle *non bis in idem*, Belgium has recognized in art. 22 par. 2 sub b BET the incompatibility of a request for mutual legal assistance with the *non bis in*

---

156 Van den Wyngaert, 1994, pp. 829-835. Note that the last ground for refusal is somewhat surprising in the light of the fact that, until this day, Belgium has not officially abolished the death penalty in their own criminal law yet. It is the more remarkable in the light of the fact that (according to De Ruyver & Hutsebaut, 1995, p. 367) there are countries which refuse extradition to Belgium because of the same risk.

157 *Spanje roept ambassadeur uit België terug*, de Volkskrant, February 7, 1996. Note that in a letter of February 29, 1996, the Dutch government states that the Belgian-Spanish cooperation in criminal matters has not been suspended; see TK 19 326, nr. 136.

158 Vermeulen, 1994, pp. 228-229. Regarding this principle *in extenso*, we refer to Wyngaert, 1994, pp. 511-515.

159 In this sense Van den Wyngaert, 1994, p. 842.

160 Although Belgium has signed the 1978 Protocol on non-refusal of assistance for the mere fiscal character of the offence, it has not proceeded to its ratification yet.

161 Van den Wyngaert, 1994, p. 842.

idem-principle as a facultative ground for refusal.[162] Furthermore, Belgium has made a similar reservation with respect to the applicability of the Mutual Assistance Convention.[163] Other Belgian reservations concern a reasonable fear for discriminatory prosecution and violation of human rights, and the prosecution of a person who is being prosecuted for the same facts in Belgium. Since soft intelligence does not have a special status in the Belgian data protection and provision system, it is no surprise that the circular does not mention a special exception or regulation for the international exchange of such information. The single indication that could be found regarding the exchange of soft intelligence is, that nrs. 3.5.1-3.5.5 of the Circular on special policing techniques would not allow that information provided by police informers be exchanged without the National Magistrate's consent.[164]

In short, it seems safe to state that, in the event that of the police receiving a foreign request for information to which one of the grounds for refusal applies, the APSD-division international police cooperation will have to decide in accordance with the Schengen circular whether and how the request should be forwarded to the judicial authorities. In that case, the circular recalls that the judicial authority charged with the international police cooperation and legal assistance in criminal matters is the National magistrate, notwithstanding the competence of the prosecutors general in case of cross-border crime between neighbour countries.[165]

11.2.3.2   The Netherlands

Under Dutch law, there are several situations in which a request for mutual legal assistance received by the police must be sent to the judicial authorities, more precisely the public prosecutor. In the first place this must be done in case the request implies the use of coercive means (art. 552i Sv). This term, that may be found in art. 39 par. 1 SC as well, has not been defined or specified by law, but the Schengen implementation legislator did indeed pay some attention to its further interpretation. Before the implementation of Schengen, art. 552i Sv contained a prohibition to apply all investigative acts (*opsporingshandelingen*), a much more general concept that includes both coercive means and non-coercive investigative acts. The police were only entitled to independently answering a foreign request for assistance in case the request involved informa-

---

162 Vermeulen, 1994a, p. 232.
163 Reservation regarding art. 2 sub b: "in so far as it concerns a prosecution or proceedings incompatible with the principle non bis in idem;" published in Trb. 1977, 21.
164 This was confirmed by the head of the APSD-division international police cooperation, P. Zanders.
165 This competence has however not been specified yet; it will probably be dealt with in special agreements on international police cooperation in border areas.

tion they disposed of already or generally accessible information.[166] The Schengen Implementation Act has however changed this and under the new art. 552i Sv, investigative means that do not involve coercion may be applied on request without interference of the judicial authorities.[167] Elaborating this amendment, the prosecutors-general have now specified in their guidelines that not only requests for the use of "classical" coercive means (such as search and seizure or arrest) must be forwarded, but also requests involving modern, covert means of investigation, such as wire tapping, controlled delivery, observation, infiltration and the use of informers.[168]

Since requests involving non-coercive means of investigation may be answered by the police without being sent to the judicial authorities, the police are entitled to provide their foreign colleagues with information resulting from the use of coercive means in the past, but they can also collect new information in order to answer the request. They may for instance interrogate persons (suspects as well as witnesses) in order to reply a foreign request, as long as this interrogation does not require a declaration under oath or a deprivation or restriction of liberty against the consent of the person to be interrogated.[169] The same seems to be the case for collecting information in private domiciles and at places not accessible to the public, provided that they enter with the explicit permission of the inhabitants.[170] It should however be stressed that, on the basis of a request for mutual assistance the police are never entitled to more than what they would be entitled to according to national law already. In this sense, the request does not have a constitutive character, but only an inspiring one.[171]

As we have shown above, according to art. 39 SC the Dutch police are obliged to assist their foreign colleagues. This may raise the question whether the Dutch police have the obligation to use (non-coercive) investigative means if that is the only way to provide their requesting colleagues with the solicited information. In our opinion this is indeed the case, since the only exceptions to the assisting duty are, as mentions art. 39 SC, the use of coercive means and national law. Since Dutch law does not seem to oppose the use of non-coercive

166 Rb. Utrecht, June 16, 1987, NJ 1987, 922; Sjöcrona, 1990, pp. 128-133.
167 Answering statement, TK 22 142, 6, p. 28; Sjöcrona, 1995a, p. 1046.
168 Note that, unless clearly and overtly reported, it will always be hard to establish whether one of these covert means has been applied across the border, be it with or without a prior request for assistance.
169 Answering statement, TK 22 142, 6, pp. 26-27.
170 Although situations such as this one might in practice be exceptional, it must be regretted that these kinds of non-coercive investigative means have not been dealt with in the circular by the prosecutors-general.
171 Sjöcrona, 1995a, p. 1043; Dutch government's reaction to final report, TK 22 142 nr. 8, p. 11.

investigative means and as far as no other legal reasons for refusal may be invoked, such obligation does exist. Practically spoken however, as we stated before, it will be tedious for the requesting party to establish the distinction between not being able to comply with this obligation and not wanting to.[172]

Art. 13 par. 8 BPolR contains exceptions from the possibility of information provision by the police, mentioning the situations and cases in which a foreign request must be forwarded to the judicial authorities. In the first place, this must be done if there are reasons to fear that the information will be used for an enquiry, prosecution or punishment because of a person's religious or political conviction, citizenship, race or ethnic origin, or an otherwise discriminatory prosecution might be expected.[173] Note that, The Netherlands being a party to the Sixth Protocol to the European Convention (abolition of the death penalty), a request for assistance must be rejected in case of an imminent risk that the person concerned will be condemned to the death penalty.[174]

In principle, according to guideline 1.3, the information may be provided regardless of the risk of prosecution or trial for inhabitants of The Netherlands, thus implying a certain risk for disguised extradition of Dutch citizens. In general, such a disguised extradition, an infringement with art. 2 lid 3 GW, would take place if for instance the Dutch police and justice authorities would cooperate in a plan to have a Dutchman arrested and tried in Germany.[175] However, according to the Dutch *Hoge Raad*, there was no disguised extradition to the USA when a Dutch citizen was attracted to a third country with the help of information provided by Dutch police or justice,[176] nor when the attracted person was already intending to leave for the country were he was put to trial.[177] Therefore, in international investigations some forum shopping seems to be possible, depending on the prosecution interests in the participating countries. In a recent case, two Dutch travelled abroad in order to import cannabis into The Netherlands, and although the foreign authorities could have be informed to enable the suspects' arrest abroad, it was decided not to do so because the scale of the Dutch investigation was bigger than the foreign

---

172 According to a data protection specialist of the Dutch NCB Interpol, it is inevitable that priorities will be set.
173 These exceptions go back to the 1969 reservations the Dutch government made to the applicability of the European Convention on Mutual Legal Assistance in criminal matters. Note that, during the parliamentary enquiry on police investigation methods, it has turned out that the Dutch police themselves do have registers of suspects and CID-subjects based on mere ethnicity.
174 Orie *et al.*, 1991, p. 113; HR March 30, 1990, RvdW 1990, 76.
175 Pres. Rb. The Hague, June 29, 1984, NJ 1985, 815.
176 HR June 6, 1988, NJ 1988, 1041.
177 HR September 9, 1994, NJ 1995, 44.

one.[178] An alternative possibility to prevent disguised extradition in this example would have been to add a condition that both suspects should be transferred to The Netherlands in order to have their sanction executed in their home country.[179]

Another reason for the police to send a foreign request for assistance to the judicial authorities is the fear that the involved person is or has been subject of a Dutch investigation, pursuit or trial concerning the same case, in short a fear for *bis in idem*. To us, it occurs that the reasons for such a fear will be hard to judge for a police officer, unless he is familiar with the details of the case or the suspect has a lawyer who is well-informed. It is true that the Schengen Convention foresees a procedure for establishing wether or not this risk is real (artt. 56-57), but this procedure only applies to the prosecution stage of the enquiry, not to the police investigation. Another type of request for legal assistance or information that must not be handled by the police independently are those concerning political or fiscal crime; requests of this kind may be fulfilled only with permission of the minister of justice.

Two categories of information are subjected to special restrictions regarding their provision to foreign police services: sensitive data and CID-information. The former, data with respect to a person's religious or political conviction, citizenship, race or ethnic origin, sexual preference and psychologic or medical situation, may be provided only in case this is inevitable for answering the request correctly, and only in combination with other information. Furthermore, the reply must in this case contain an indication of the reliability of the sensitive data (art. 13 par. 6 BPolR). According to art. 13 *CID-regeling*, data forthcoming from CID-registers may be provided internationally only after consulting the public prosecutor for the CID (*CID-officier*).

Regarding the use of the information provided by the Dutch police to police services abroad, art. 13 par. 5 BPolR repeats the general condition of finality: The information may be used only for the goal it has been provided for, save with additional permission. In order for the police assistance to be allowed, it is not necessary that there be double incrimination.[180] This may be of particular importance in case of requests and investigations concerning acts that are not criminalized under Dutch law. Dutch police officers might in this context be obliged to assist in the prosecution of for instance abortion and euthanasia

---

178 This case is mentioned by Van Dijk & Demmink, 1995, p. 15.
179 On forum shopping by the Dutch police, see Van Traa, 1996, App. V, pp. 404-442, who also sees a connection with provocation of Dutch citizens by foreign police services abroad.
180 Sjöcrona, 1995a, p. 1040.

as well as several forms of drug use (such as cannabis and qat),[181] moral behaviour (such as homosexual contacts between two consenting adults) and the possession of pornographic material,[182] all of these being acts that are more or less entirely accepted in the Dutch society.

11.2.3.3 Luxembourg

In general, the Luxembourg police must be considered incompetent to reply to a foreign request independently in case the request involves the use of coercive measures or *contrainte*, investigative measures against the involved person's will.[183] The interrogation of a person who is willing to provide information is therefore allowed, as is the provision of information from police databases collected with the use of coercive measures in the past. Requests involving the use of coercive measures specifically for the occasion of the request must however be forwarded to the judicial authorities. The same is the case for requests which, in the eyes of the police, seem to involve any of the forms of legal assistance dealt with by or in the context of the European Convention on Mutual Legal Assistance, which all have been reserved explicitly for the judicial authorities.[184] For this reason, the general grounds for refusal of judicial assistance according to art. 2 of this Convention (political or fiscal offences) will apply to police legal assistance as well. Additionally, in 1977 Luxembourg has made several reservations to this Convention, stressing that legal assistance will not be provided if there is a reasonable fear for discriminatory prosecution or prosecution incompatible with the principle *non bis in idem*, or in case of a current prosecution for the same acts in Luxembourg. The same will be the case for the risk of the death penalty, Luxembourg being a signatory to the 6th Protocol to the ECHR. Finally, it is worth adding that a double incrimination of the offence for which the assistance is requested, is not necessary.

An important question is, whether and under which conditions the Luxembourg police may exchange so-called sensitive data with their foreign counterparts. Art. 15 Automated Data Act generally prohibits the collection and storage in databases of data concerning a person's political, trade-union, philosophical or religious activities, data concerning the intimacy of private life or data revealing the racial origin of the individual, without making an exception for police or judicial databases. The suggestion that, as a result, the police would

---

181 In its decision of November 29, 1994 (NJ 1995, 292; with note by A.C. 't Hart), the Supreme Court judged that the scope of the Opium Act did not cover the psychotropic substance "qat," which is especially popular among people from Somalia, Kenya and Yemen. Hereafter, the government decided that they did not intend to extend the scope of the legislation at this point.
182 This example was mentioned in Orie, 1986, p. 171.
183 As referred to in the letter by captain Genson.
184 In this sense captain Genson.

not be allowed to process such data either, is confirmed by the Police data decree. According to artt. 3 and 5 of the Decree, the wanted persons register and the documentation register may not contain any more information than the wanted or documented person's personal particulars and the reasons for his being wanted respectively documented. As a logical consequence, the Luxembourg police will be unable to exchange personal data with a more sensitive character than these.

Regarding the foreign use of information provided by the Luxembourg police, no specific limitations of speciality or finality seem to apply. Besides the restriction in art. 1 Police data decree, that all police data exploitation must serve one of the four purposes of crime prevention, investigation, establishment and prosecution, no mention is made of a speciality or finality principle. However, it should be reminded that according to art. 39 par. 2 SC, information provided for police use may not be applied for prosecution purposes.

11.2.3.4   France

In a number of situations, the French police will be incompetent to independently reply to a foreign request for information, and obliged to forward the request to the judicial authorities. As mentioned in art. 39 par. 1 SC, this is the case if the request involves the use of coercive measures or *contrainte*, which implies that something is done to a person without his consent or without him knowing. According to information from French police and judicial authorities, this implies that the only international assistance the police may provide would be verbal or written transmissions of information that is in their possession already. Furthermore, before providing information that has been gathered during an enquiry led or directed by a *procureur de la République* or a *juge d'instruction*, the judicial authority involved must be contacted. Another exception to the independent replying power of the police may be found in art. 2 of the European Mutual Assistance Convention, excluding political and fiscal offences from mutual legal assistance. By joining the 1978 Additional Protocol, France has however expressed that it would not refuse assistance for the mere reason of an offence's fiscal character. Further, besides the fact that France has ratified the Sixth Protocol to the European Convention and thus abolished the death penalty, with respect to the fields of application of mutual legal assistance have not been made.

The principle *non bis in idem* may especially form an impediment in case the information also plays a role in an investigation that is carried out in France already. The Schengen circular explicitly states that, in case the information is requested for evidence purposes, it may only be provided under the condition that the French investigation will not be harmed.[185] If the information requested is intended for prosecution and use as evidence in a judicial procedure, the forementioned Schengen circular prescribes a procedure regarding the authorities who must permit that the information be provided: This authorization must be given by the investigating judge in the event that he was the authority who issued the documents concerned, and by the public prosecutor in all other cases. This restriction might also be considered an international application of the finality principle as expressed by art. 22 LIFL.

11.2.3.5   Germany

In general, German law does not consider the political, military or fiscal character of a case, the risk of the death penalty being imposed or applied, foreign prosecution of a German national,[186] or a current or past prosecution of the same person for the same facts (*bis in idem*) an obstacle for the provision of the requested legal assistance.[187] Factors of this kind may however have consequences for the level of administration that has to deal with the request: Among the cases in which the decisive power to reply to a foreign request is excepted from delegation to the provincial authorities, requests concerning political or military offences take a central position (art. 4 sub b *Zuständigkeits-vereinbarung*). Furthermore, does a particular request involve a special importance for political, factual or legal reasons, then at least the federal government or authorities must be consulted (art. 7 *Zuständigkeitsvereinbarung*). This is particularly the case if there are reasons to believe that the death penalty will be imposed or executed or basic principles of German *ordre public* will be neglected (nr. 13.1 RiVASt). The provision of data is not allowed in case this would indeed cause a risk for purposes of German law;[188] according to art. 73 IRG, a request for assistance must be rejected if the assistance would be against the German legal order or *ordre public*. This would only be the case if there is a risk of infringement with principles recognized by all democratic States that abide by the rule of law, such as the prohibition of torture or inhuman treatment, unfair trial, or in general, common ECHR standards.[189]

---

185   For the place and impact of the non bis in idem-principle in French law, we refer to Stefani *et al.*, 1993, pp. 791-810.
186   Although art. 16 par. 2 GG prohibits the extradition of German citizens, this would therefore not necessarily be considered a disguised illegal extradition.
187   Vogler/Wilkitzki, *Vor* § 59, p. 5. Germany is a partner to the European Mutual Assistance Convention and the 1978 Protocol concerning the non-refusal of mutual assistance for fiscal offences; apparently the German policy also includes a unilateral non-refusal for political and connex (related) offences.
188   Bäumler, 1992, pp. 555, 613.
189   Vogler/Wilkitzki, § 73, pp. 7-24.

Although these exceptions were originally drafted for requests for extradition in particular, to some extent they seem to apply to other legal assistance as well.[190]

As far as mutual legal assistance is concerned, double incrimination of the investigated offences is not required, unless the request involves the use of coercion.[191] In general, requests involving that originals of police records be sent abroad must be dealt with by the highest judicial or administrative authorities. However, this is not obligatory in case of a request from Belgium, The Netherlands, Luxembourg, France and Germany's other western European neighbours (nr. 83 RiVASt). Finally, reasons of disproportionality may also lead to a rejection in case the offence concerned is too harmless according to German standards.[192]

Different from its predecessor, the BDSG 1977,[193] today's Federal Data Protection Act does not prescribe any specific treatment for particularly sensitive data regarding political, religious, sexual or other intimate aspects of private life.[194] Instead, art. 31 BDSG intends to protect all information with respect to an individual and information that might be individualized. The appropriate degree of protection may subsequently be warranted by the principles of proportionality and subsidiarity.

In general, the concept of coercion in German data protection law is a particularly wide one, relating to every form of data management that is done without the concerned individual's content.[195] Therefore, it is safe to state that, besides those exchanges of information without the individual's consent but based on an explicit legal basis, the police may also exchange information that has been collected with the individual's cooperation, for instance by a voluntary interrogation. In general, the information requested by and provided to a foreign authority may include results of investigations and interrogations, examinations of proper or foreign reports, registers and information etcetera.[196] In their elaborations of the *Zuständigkeitsvereinbarung*, provincial legislators have

---

190 Vogler/Wilkitzki, *Vor* § 59, p. 6.
191 Vogler/Wilkitzki, *Vor* § 59, pp. 3-4.
192 Vogler/Wilkitzki, *Vor* § 59, p. 6.
193 Discussed in Nugter, 1990, p. 59.
194 This is confirmed by Ordemann/Schomerus (1992, p. 83), who do not distinguish general personal data such as name, address and family situation form sensitive data such as health and religious or political conviction either.
195 Bäumler, 1992, p. 507.
196 Vogler/Wilkitzki, § 59, p. 12. This seems to be confirmed by nr. 77 RiVASt, that states that interrogations must be done by court if this follows from the request; a contrario, one may assume that in other than such cases interrogation may take place by the police, especially if the request was addressed to the police and the person to be interrogated is willing to cooperate voluntarily.

indeed also restricted the answering of foreign requests for police information by their police forces to requests that do not involve the use of coercion in the sense of the Code of criminal procedure.

11.2.4 Competent Police Authorities

11.2.4.1   Belgium

Basically, the international exchange of police information must be carried out through a central body, and for Belgium this has been entrusted to the APSD-division for international police cooperation as introduced by art. 2 KB APSD. According to art. 4 par. 2 sub 4 of this Decree, this department was installed to become the central body in the sense of artt. 39, 40 and 46 SC. It will be competent for all international exchanges of police information, and according to par. 1 sub 1 KB APSD it will be the central contact office for foreign correspondents and contacts. Nevertheless, there are some exceptions to this domination by the central body. Firstly, the Schengen-circular allows that in urgent cases a foreign request be replied directly by the police service that received request. Note that, when referring to art. 39 WPA as a legal basis for the international exchange of police information, the number of police services entitled to such exchanges is restricted to six: According to art. 2 WPA, the Police Function Act only applies to the regular police services *gendarmerie*, municipal police and judiciary police, as well as the railway police, maritime police and air police (special police forces). Secondly, an agreement signed between the Belgian ministers of justice and the interior on July 4, 1994 entrusts the exchange of police information in border areas to the gendarmerie districts in those areas, which will in general function as contact offices for the foreign police.[197] In the future, these operational contact points (OIPG's) along the Belgian-French border (in Kortrijk) and the Belgian-German border (in Eupen) should also serve as common international offices (*gemeenschappelijke commissariaten*) where, partly on the basis of art. 47 SC, liaison officers will be stationed permanently.[198]

---

197 In this sense and with this task, these *operationele invalspunten in de grensregio's* (OIPG) or *points de contact opérationel* (PCO) are also referred to in the Schengen-circular.
198 This was announced by the Belgian minister of the interior, J. Vande Lanotte, during a conference on Schengen in Kortrijk on March 4, 1996.

11.2.4.2   The Netherlands

As does art. 39 SC, the Dutch art. 13 par. 7 BPolR prescribes that foreign requests for information by the police must be replied by a central body, more specifically the National police services agency (KLPD), where the CRI (NCB-Interpol) houses. However, on the basis of other arrangements with foreign police authorities, approved by the minister of justice or the interior, the communication of information may also be decentralized. With respect to the authority entitled to provide the information, note that Dutch law and guidelines do not mention the urgency of a situation as a justification to exchange the information without intervention of the central body. Since art. 39 SC does make such a distinction, Dutch law must be considered to contain a restriction to the Schengen regulation at this point. In practice, however, this is not likely to pose a problem because in every border region the exchange of information may be carried out directly anyway on the basis of regional arrangements. In addition, some special arrangements have been created by national legislation as well: Information on unusual financial transactions (especially concerning money laundering) may be communicated by the Unusual transactions office (*Meldpunt ongebruikelijke transacties* - MOT) to their foreign counterparts directly (art. 13 par. 3 BPolR), and the international provision of CID-intelligence may be done through the National criminal intelligence department (another part of KLPD) or, on the basis of specific arrangements as mentioned by art. 13 BPolR, locally. Finally, special arrangements may be made also for foreign liaison officers stationed with Dutch police forces (art. 13 par. 10 BPolR). Data exchange with Dutch liaison officers stationed with foreign police forces is covered by the general provisions (par. 11).

As to the question which of the Dutch police services may provide international legal assistance, no explicit mention has been made. For this reason, it seems reasonable that, without a further restriction existing, all (regular and special) police services will essentially be entitled to such exchanges. It should nevertheless be noted that the role of the Royal marechaussee in this form of international police cooperation seems will be limited by the general position of this force, that has regular police tasks in the civil society only if specially ordered or requested, and only in assistance of the regular police. In the same sense, the role which the special enforcement agencies may play in the international police data exchange will be restricted to their own respective domains. Finally, it is worth recalling that the Police records Act and Decree only apply to the regional police forces, which is also the case for the special arrangements for police cooperation in the border areas.

11.2.4.3   Luxembourg

The Luxembourg body assigned for the task of a central body through which cross-border exchanges of police information must take place, is the *Service de Transmission et de Traitements des Informations* (STTI). This joint police and *gendarmerie* body is entrusted with the transmission and processing of police information and also houses the National Central Bureau of Interpol.[199] Exceptions to this centralized transmission have not been created, besides the possibility of direct exchanges in urgent cases as provided in artt. 39 par. 3 and 46 par. 2 SC.

11.2.4.4   France

Within the *Police Nationale*, central, regional and local services have been entrusted with research and appliance of scientific methods of investigation, including databases;[200] to some extent all of these services process judicial information and keep a wanted persons register.[201] As far as the *gendarmerie* is concerned, within the *Direction Générale* exists a technical centre with such services as a judicial information centre and a database of wanted persons.[202] Because the separation of the two databases within the *Police* and the *gendarmerie* may evidently result in considerable disadvantages,[203] an automatic exchange of information takes place every day.[204]

As stated by artt. 39 and 46 SC, foreign requests for police information must in principle be replied through a central body. For this purpose, France has assigned the forementioned National Central Bureau of Interpol France.[205] In domestic law, an exception to this rule is foreseen in art. 4 NCB-Decree, allowing that, in urgent cases, French police services directly contact their counterparts in France's neighbour countries. As the exception formulated by the Schengen Convention, this provision also includes that, through the regional judicial police services (*Service régional de police judiciaire*), the central authority must be informed of every international exchange of data by other police bodies.

---

199 This service was assigned in for instance the *Note du groupe de travail I "police et sécurité"*, Bruxelles, June 2, 1995, SCH/I (94), 8th revision.

200 A general statutory basis for this may be found in the *Loi portant création d'un service de police technique* of November 27, 1943.

201 For more information we refer to Decocq, Montreuil & Buisson, 1991, pp. 123-127.

202 Decocq, Montreuil & Buisson, 1991, pp. 138.

203 As recalled in Decocq, Montreuil & Buisson, 1991, p. 138, footnote 277-1.

204 Thus was related to us by several sources in both police forces.

205 *Note du groupe de travail I "police et sécurité"*, Bruxelles, June 2, 1995, SCH/I (94) 17, 8th revision.

11.2.4.5   Germany

The federative constitutional system of Germany continually causes fierce discussions about which authorities must be competent for the international police cooperation, including the exchange of information. Federal government and BKA stress that a centralisation of such tasks is more practical and would guarantee a better overview of activities, and moreover, international affairs are a federal task. Several provinces, promoting their LKA, state that a decentralized cooperation would go faster and would be in accordance with the constitution, according to which the police (in its widest sense) is in the first place a provincial task.[206] Art. 10 BKAG entrusts the international communication in the field of criminal law enforcement primarily to the federal criminal police office (*Bundeskriminalamt*, hereafter BKA).[207] Nevertheless, according to the second part of art. 10 BKAG, exceptions for the international communication in border areas may be made by the federal minister of the interior and the highest administrative authorities in the provinces.[208] In this context, the above-mentioned *Zuständigkeitsvereinbarung* and its respective provincial elaborations state that in general the provincial LKA's are competent for international matters, unless the BKA is exclusively competent. This is the case for the cooperation in the sense of art. 39 par. 1-3 SC is, for which the German government has exclusively assigned the BKA in Wiesbaden, which is also Germany's National Central Bureau of Interpol.[209] It is no more than logical that, within this context, the government has not mentioned the exchange of information on the basis of art. 46 SC. Since this provision exclusively concerns the spontaneous exchange of information for preventive and proactive purposes and excludes criminal investigations, this task has not been entrusted to the federal but only to the provincial police services.

As mentioned above, information in other than criminal matters may in general be exchanged internationally by the provincial polices and the *Bundesgrenzschutz* according to the respective legislations and for the proactive and preventive purposes. Some provincial legislators have elaborated these rules in more detailed regulations. On the basis of art. 27 NWPolG for example, a ministerial decree has been created for the police in the province of Nordrhein-

---

206   This forms an interesting paradox: As a result of its federative nature, Germany seems to be much more centralist in its foreign relations than many unitary states.

207   Vogler/Wilkitzki, § 59, p. 6.

208   The draft version of a new BKAG seems to extend this exception by entrusting the provincial police authorities with the communication with their direct neighbour countries; a critical comment to this extension may be found in Steinke, 1995, p. 216.

209   In this sense *Note du groupe de travail I "police et sécurité"*, Bruxelles, June 2, 1995, SCH/I (94), 8th revision.

Westfalen,[210] which regulates the data exchange between the four *Polizeipräsi-dium* areas along Germany's border on the one side, and the neighbouring Dutch police regions and Belgian *gendarmerie* district on the other. In urgent cases, information may also be exchanged between the highest police authorities in the border *Kreisen*, the *Oberkreisdirektoren*, and their nearest counterparts in The Netherlands or Belgium. Art. 3 PolDÜVNW entrusts the LKA in Düsseldorf with the exchange of data that may not be exchanged by lower police authorities directly.

11.2.5   Supervision and Control

11.2.5.1   Belgium

In order to enable the international exchange of information by the Belgian police to be supervised, the APSD-division for international police cooperation must be informed of all direct replies by other police authorities. Furthermore, the APSD must store the name of the requesting authority and the reason for the request during at least 6 months (art. 4 sub 4 KB nr. 8).[211] Note that the mere existence of this obligation suggests that the request must contain the reasons why it was done, which would enable some sort of controllability of the purposes for the requested service and thus realise part of the speciality principle. No mention is made of any form of report to the judicial authorities, but since the APSD fulfils its judicial task under the supervision of the ministry of justice, the judicial authorities may exercise a certain control anyway.[212]

11.2.5.2   The Netherlands

A possibility for the judicial authorities to supervise and control the exchange of information by the Dutch police has been foreseen in the third paragraph of art. 552i Sv. Every time the police deals with a foreign request for information themselves instead of sending it to the public prosecutor, the event must be reported and registered on a special form, mentioning such details as the nature of the case, the requesting authority, the replying officer, the contents of the reply or the reasons for rejecting the request.[213] Besides this obligation, every provision of information from a police register must be marked in the register

---

210   *Verordnung über die Zulassung der Datenübermittlung von der Polizei and ausländische Polizeibehörden* - PolDÜVNW; October 22, 1994, GVNW November 11, 1994.
211   See also Robben, 1995, pp. 96-97.
212   Note that this subject will be dealt with in detail in the future Circular on police information exchange.
213   A model form has been published in Stcrt. 1993, 252.

itself on the basis of art. 16 par. 2 BPolR. However, despite its rather clear and detailed regulation, the registration obligation does not really seem to be respected.[214]

More restrictions and conditions for mutual legal aid by the police may be set by the local judicial authorities on the basis of art. 552i par. 4 Sv. Within this context, the local public prosecutor's departments are enabled to develop their own policies, also concerning the question who will be competent to agree that information provided according to art. 39 SC may be used in judicial procedures.

11.2.5.3   Luxembourg

In order to enable the international exchanges of information by the Luxembourg police forces to be supervised and controlled, the exchange must be reported to the judicial authorities and the NCB must be informed of direct exchanges in urgent cases. Furthermore, as soon as the database will be completely operational, every use of personal data must be registered in the database according to art. 2 par. 2 Police data decree.

11.2.5.4   France

Specific provisions of French law addressing supervision or control of the judicial authorities in case of international information exchanges are unknown, but this seems to be covered by the general obligation of art. 19 CPP that the police must report all their investigating activities to the judicial authorities. Besides, as we have discussed above, in a great deal of cases the information asked for will have been gathered during a judiciary enquiry, and in that case the judicial authorities must even be informed before the transmission.

Indeed, it cannot be excluded that one or more of the unpublished decrees contain more specific information regarding this matter. The same is the case for the question, whether the fact that information has been provided must be marked in a register. If it concerns information provided by the *Renseignements Généraux* to another French police service, this must be marked indeed and the *fiche de consultation* must be kept for two years.[215]

11.2.5.5   Germany

Supervision and control of mutual legal assistance provided by the police are subject to the central dichotomy in German policing. In case of informational

---

214   Van Traa, 1996, App. V, p. 424.
215   Picard, 1993, p. 295.

police cooperation in criminal matters, a report of the reply must be sent to the judicial or administrative authorities according to nrs. 11 and 12 RiVASt. Furthermore, most of the provincial elaborations of the *Zuständigkeitsvereinbarung* prescribe that the exchange be marked in a register. Occasion, contents, receiving party and date of transmission must be registered in case of exchanges of information for preventive and proactive purposes as well (see for instance art. 33 par. 2 BGSNeuRegG).

11.2.6 Special Border Arrangements

11.2.6.1 Belgium

As for special border arrangements concerning Belgium in the sense of art. 39 par. 4 SC, which will regulate in more detail the exchange of police information and other forms of international cooperation, a distinction per neighbour country will have to be made. With The Netherlands, reverse agreements have been developed within the Belgian-Dutch Police and Border Concertation (*Politieel Grensoverleg*) and include agreements on radio contact in border areas. They will be introduced soon, after The Netherlands have already specified their possibilities and powers in the border area cooperation.

In the border areas, that have been defined as "those zones within the border provinces which are confronted with border-bound phenomena," cooperation will take place on the basis of the ministerial agreements of July 4, 1994 as mentioned above. This implies that the informational cooperation in the border provinces has been entrusted to the *gendarmerie* district offices, unless the scope of the request exceeds their geographical or functional responsibilities, in which case it must be sent to the APSD. Between Belgium and Germany, an agreement has been in force since 1960, introducing a joint communication service for the border area, as well as an exchange between police authorities of information on criminals residing or staying in the border area.[216] A more modern border area agreement with France has been concluded recently,[217] whereas agreements with Germany and Luxembourg are still being negotiated.[218]

---

216 January 13/26, 1960, published in for instance Vogler/Wilkitzki.
217 According to P. Zanders, the agreement was signed on March 16, 1995.
218 The first has been referred to us in a letter from the Luxembourg *gendarmerie* captain Genson (October 3, 1995), the second in a letter from the ministry of the interior of Rheinland-Pfalz of September 7, 1995.

11.2.6.2   The Netherlands

As mentioned before, both art. 39 SC and the Dutch art. 13 par. 7 BPolR create the possibility to elaborate the informational police cooperation in the border areas by introducing special arrangements. For The Netherlands, a committee has drafted two model arrangements (convenants) on request of the Ministers of Justice and Interior, one model specifically for the border regions, the other for the other Schengen territory. Both models are equal as to their contents, except that the purposes allowing the international data provision are formulated in a more general and larger sense in the border region model than in the model for the larger Schengen area. Note that the model concerning the larger Schengen area has not been implemented yet.

As for the area that is considered to be a border area or border region in the sense of artt. 39 and 46 SC, the Dutch convenants have restricted this to the police regions at the internal border with Belgium and Germany; counterpart on the Belgian side is the province, whereas Germany has decided to entrust this to their provinces as well. The Dutch choice to restrict the interpretation of a border area to the police regions along the border has been subject to criticism. Some of the other police regions are situated so close to the border (Brabant-Noord, situated less than 10 kilometre from the German border) or have such an important international function (especially Rotterdam-Rijnmond and Zuid-Holland-Zuid), that there would be good reasons to allow them to directly exchange information with foreign services as well. One could even wonder why, as far as communication is concerned, the whole of The Netherlands could not be considered one border area. After all, the entire country has about the same size as one single German province.

Evidently, the main aim of the convenants is to enable the direct, spontaneous or requested, international provision of information from one police service to another, instead of having to go through a central body such as the CRI. However, there seems to be one further difference between the convenants and the general regulation. The convenants further state that CID-intelligence from grey-field registers may be provided with the consent of or on behalf of the regional police manager. The convenants furthermore prescribe that, on request of the providing authorities, the receiving authorities must inform the former about the use that has been made of the data provided. As to the organisational aspects of the international provision of information, most regions have established some sort of a centralized regional communication and information centre (RCIC) in order a enable a 24 hour service and quick processing of relevant information and requests.

Note that the convenants that have been introduced at the southern border only concern information provided by The Netherlands to a foreign police service. Arrangements regulating the provision of information to the Dutch police do not exist yet, but are being prepared.[219] The convenants at the eastern border were originally intended to be joint Dutch-German arrangements that would cover both directions immediately, but this turned out to be impossible due to German domestic law.[220] Now, the convenants at the eastern border have the same contents as the ones with Belgium and only bind the Dutch institutions. The one-way effect of the convenants corresponds to the fact that art. 552i Sv does not apply to Dutch requests for foreign legal assistance. This is a matter of law of the foreign country to which the request is addressed.[221] The Dutch police will probably need some trial and error before becoming familiar with the possibilities and problems for foreign police forces to deal with mutual legal assistance.

11.2.6.3   Luxembourg

Until this day, Luxembourg has not yet signed any special border arrangements as referred to in artt. 39 and 46 SC.[222] Agreements with Germany and Belgium are due to be signed before the end of 1995, whereas for the border with France, possibilities for an agreement are being studied. Although the Schengen Convention introduced the possibility of special arrangements especially for border areas, Luxembourg has not chosen for a structured decentralization of border area cooperation. Because of the small size of the country, the entire country could be considered a border area; in the draft agreement between Luxembourg and Germany, this is indeed the choice that has been made. Within the context of this arrangement, that regulates the common border between Luxembourg and two German provinces (Rheinland-Pfalz and Saarland), several topics have been dealt with. Firstly, a direct cooperation has been foreseen for the purpose of prevention of danger for public order and safety. Secondly, regarding the exchange of information, the Luxembourg STTI and the German *Polizeipräsidium* in Trier, *Polizeidirektion West* in Saarlouis and *Grenzschutz- und Bahnpolizeiamt* in Saarbrücken provide each other with all information that is important for the criminal law enforcement in the border area, unless it concerns a case for which the provincial LKA has explicitly been assigned. Besides the exchange of police information, the agreement mainly contains organisational and structural topics: The services where a request for operational assistance must be addressed to, elaboration and explication of several aspects

---

219 This task has been entrusted to the *Belgisch-Nederlands Politieel Grensoverleg* mentioned above.
220 Thus was related to us by several of the regional police officers entrusted with the international police cooperation in border areas.
221 Van Dijk & Demmink, 1995, p. 13.
222 Thus was related to us by Colonel F. Diederich, Commander of the Luxembourg *gendarmerie*, in a letter of September 18, 1995. See also Diederich, 1994, pp. 69-88.

of cross-border pursuit and observation, exchange of communication equipment, common schooling etcetera. The agreement with Belgium, especially regulating the border cooperation between the Luxembourg STTI and the Belgian gendarmerie district office (PCO) in Arlon will cover the same topics; it is hoped that a future agreement with France will have a similar content.[223]

11.2.6.4   France

Bilateral border agreements between France and Belgium or Luxembourg do not exist yet, but particularly in the French-German relationship, some special border arrangements address the subject of international exchange of police information. One dates from 1977 and deals with the exchange of information between the police forces in the German provinces Baden-Württemberg, Rheinland-Pfalz and Saarland and the French departments Bas-Rhin, Haut-Rhin and Moselle.[224] Communication must take place through the National Central Bureaux of Interpol or, in urgent cases, directly between the local police services. In this case however, the NCB Interpol must be informed. This agreement was elaborated in 1992 by a second one, addressing such themes as the exchange of general information and statistics, joint schooling and language courses, exchange of police officers, joint police stations at border, participation of individual officers in foreign investigations of illegal immigration, assignment of contact persons with knowledge of the other country's language, exchange of information on individual actions and events with cross-border effects, joint exercises, exchange of equipment and installation of direct international communication lines, assignment of coordination offices and participation in foreign observation operations.[225] Note that neither of the two is based upon art. 39 SC and as a result neither of them introduces new international legal obligations.[226]

11.2.6.5   Germany

Until this day, special border arrangements in the sense of artt. 39 and 46 SC regulating the informational cooperation between Germany and The Netherlands have not been concluded yet, mostly because some time was lost trying to make one arrangement for both German provinces (Niedersachsen and Nordrhein-Westfalen) and all nine Dutch police regions involved. Since this attempt has failed, new arrangements will have to be worked out on the German side, this

---

223 Thus was related to us by captain Genson in his letter of October 3, 1995.
224 Paris, February 3, 1977, BGBl. II, 1978, 1402, also published in Vogler/Wilkitzki.
225 Metz, October 12, 1992; publication unknown.
226 In this sense a letter from the ministry of the interior of Rheinland-Pfalz of September 7, 1995.

time by each of the provinces separately. In this context, we might once again refer to the forementioned ministerial decree on the basis of art. 27 par. 2 NWPolG, which facilitates the exchange of information in border regions, more specifically to the *Polizeipräsidium* areas along the border, in urgent cases even to the border *Kreisen* and their authorities (artt. 1 and 2 PolDÜVNW). With France, Germany has concluded an agreement in 1977 which was elaborated in 1992 and discussed in the paragraph on France above. With Belgium and Luxembourg, similar arrangements are being negotiated.[227]

11.3   Comparing National Norms

11.3.1   Legal framework

A first comparative remark that could be made with respect to the general character of the legal framework created for the protection of personal data, concerns its detail. This seems to be highest in Germany and The Netherlands, followed by Belgium (with a moderately detailed regulation), Luxembourg (rather basic) and France, which takes a particular position due to the fact that parts of the regulation have been embodied in secret (or at least non-published) decrees. Furthermore, In all countries, formal statutory law mainly contains the general principles of data protection, whereas the detailed elaboration of these may be found in more flexible legislation, such as royal or ministerial decrees. Luxembourg is the only country where the data protection law exclusively applies to automated data. In the other countries, the collection, storage, processing and exchange of non-automated data is part of the scope of the law as well. Finally, each country has created a supervisory and advisory task for an external, independent authority.

The regulation regarding the collection, storage and processing of and access to personal data by the police is most extended in Germany. This is partly due to the federal character with its statutory separation of police tasks, the role and place of provincial legislation therein and also to the active role of the courts, particularly the Federal Constitutional Court. With their special statute and decrees on different types of police registers, The Netherlands also have a quite extended body of legislation. The system in Belgium, with several special decrees on police data, is still rather detailed. In Luxembourg, in spite of the decree dividing the police database in three separate parts, it is rather basic but still clear. In France however, important roles in the regulation process have been created for the supervising authority and the Council of State, resulting in the situation that many relevant legal texts, especially decrees

---

227   In this sense a letter from the ministry of the interior of Rheinland-Pfalz of September 7, 1995.

concerning police, security and public safety have not been published and are therefore unknown.

The subject of processing sensitive data has lead to the widest possible differences between the five studied countries. In Luxembourg, the collection and every type of processing of such information is prohibited, without any exception, whereas German law does not regard sensitive data as a separate category at all. If necessary, extra protection will be warranted by the principles of proportionality and subsidiarity only. The other three countries seem to be somewhere between these extreme positions. In Belgium, the police are entitled to work with sensitive data as long as this is necessary in order to fulfil their task. Dutch law has combined this condition with the requirement that sensitive data be processed only in combination with other, non-sensitive data. The French position is that sensitive data may only be dealt with if based on a decree and in the public interest.

In Belgium, Luxembourg, France, and Germany, there is no legal distinction between (hard and soft) intelligence and other, more operational police information. In The Netherlands, such a distinction does exist and even a rather strict separation is made. For police intelligence, a proper and rather detailed regulation with its own access regime has been created, whereas for the informational cooperation in border areas, this distinction is still refined by also separating hard and soft intelligence. These distinctions and classifications of data according to their degree of accuracy or reliability seem to correspond well to the requirements of Principle 3.2 of the Council of Europe Recommendation R (87) 15.

11.3.2 International Data Exchange by the Police

Germany disposes of the most extended regulation on the exchange of police data in general, particularly since the German separation of police tasks also implies a differentiation of purposes. Furthermore, Germany distinguishes spontaneous and requested transmissions and is the only country where the matter has a rather detailed basis at the level of statutory legislation, in the four other countries this may almost entirely be found in decrees. In addition to these decrees, the Belgian and Dutch authorities as well as some German provinces have issued circulars with practice guidelines on international exchanges. In Luxembourg, this is only referred to by the Police Data Decree, that does not contain any more information than the context of the exchange, which must be within the framework of an international or intergovernmental organisation or agreement. The same criterion may be found in Belgian law, which adds that the requesting party must have a legal interest in obtaining the information. Possible French conditions for police data exchange are inaccessible due to the secret character of relevant decrees, whereas the Schengen circular of the French government only addresses the exchange of judicial, not police information. However, in spite of the extended character of the German regulations, when focusing on the international situation the Dutch regulation seems to be the most detailed one. The Netherlands being the only country that has actually amended its statutory legislation in order to implement the Schengen Convention, its legislation distinguishes requested and spontaneous assistance. Moreover, it is unique in containing a specification of what is coercion and requires an interference of the judicial authorities.

Possibilities for international exchanges of police information may contain restrictions with regard to their territorial scope, implying that police officers can cooperate more easily with colleagues from one country than from another. These restrictions may be more or less formal or substantive. The Dutch regulation seems to have the largest territorial scope, setting no explicit restrictions, allowing substantive differentiation from case to case but also obliging the police to weigh the data protection interests against the investigative interests. In Germany every police level essentially knows its own territorial scope, the main general rule being that sufficient data protection in the receiving country is required. Belgian law is more differentiated, requiring that for the exchange of sensitive (or conditional) data in general, a legal basis must exist in either the requesting or the requested country. Furthermore, it does not allow that police data be transmitted other than at a treaty basis or through Interpol, and in case the receiving country does not offer a sufficient legal data protection, additional conditions must be set before replying. Luxembourg and French law are the most strict countries with respect to the territorial scope: They only allow the exchange of police data through international treaties and organizations such as Schengen and Interpol. There seems to be a considerable difference between a substantive approach, offering more flexibility, and a formal approach, warranting a better foreseeability. However, in our opinion no important differences in their practical impact need to be expected since, as far as the Schengen partners are concerned, all will be covered by both approaches.

Table 11.2 International Exchange of Police Information I

	B	NL	L	F	D
Regulation quality					
Detailed statute(s)	-	+	-	-	+
Basic statute(s)	+	-	+	+	-
Detailed decree(s)	+	+	-	-	+
Basic decree(s)	-	-	+	+	-
Detailed circular(s)/directive(s)	-	+	-	-	-
Basic circular(s)/directive(s)	+	-	-	+	-
Secret decrees	-	-	-	+	-
Transmission purposes & use of data					
General police task in requested country	+	+	-	-	+
General police task in requesting country	-	+	-	-	-
Prevention of danger, detection of severe crime in requesting country	-	+	-	-	+
Detection, prevention and proactive policing (ex artt. 39 & 46 SC)	+	-	+	+	-
Finality principle	+	+	-	-	+
Police incompetent					
Coercion necessary	+	+	+	+	+
Political offence	+	+	+	+	+
Fiscal offence	+	+	+	-	-
Bis in idem/current enquiry or prosecution	+	+	+	+	-
Fear for discriminatory prosecution	+	+	+	-	+
Risk of death penalty	+	+	+	+	+

As for the purposes of informational police cooperation, Belgian law generally states that information may be exchanged or transmitted if this is necessary within the police task, without any further specification. Dutch and German law are slightly more specific where they state that it must be necessary for the Dutch respectively the German or for the foreign police task. More specified, in both countries reference is made to the prevention, detection and repression of a serious and imminent danger or a crime that has shocked the legal order. Luxembourg and French domestic law do not mention any specification of the purposes for which the police may exchange information. Since however both countries only allow international exchanges in a Schengen or Interpol context, the purposes as mentioned in the Schengen Convention may be considered those of Luxembourg and French law. Indeed, for France it is always possible that these purposes have been completed or restricted in a non-published decree.

11.3.3 Exceptions to Data Exchange by the Police

Furthermore, Belgian, Dutch and German law explicitly require that, regarding the use of the provided information, the requesting country must respect the principle of finality. In order to enable the requested authorities to establish the purposes for the request, these three countries also state that requests must specify the reasons and the context of the cases involved. In French and Luxembourg law, provisions asking such specifications are unknown.

In several types of situations, the police will not be entitled to reply a foreign request without interference of the judicial authorities. The reasons for this may be divided in three categories, one of which is linked to the aim of the request, one is related to the type of assistance requested, and one found in the nature of the case. The police's incompetence to independently reply a foreign request for information because of the aim of the request follows from art. 39 par. 2 SC and may therefore be found in each of the five legal systems: The case that the information is necessary for judicial proceedings. In France, Belgium and The Netherlands, the procedure to be followed in that case has been addressed in a circular, The Netherlands still leaving a margin of discretion for the local prosecution departments in the border regions.

The second reason for the police to be obliged to forward the request to the judicial authorities also follows from art. 39 SC. It is related to the type of assistance requested and concerns the case that replying the request implies the use of coercive measures. Belgian, Luxembourg and German law do not contain a specification of which police actions must be considered coercion and therefore an impediment for the police to independently reply a foreign request for information. In France, the police may not engage in any investigation whatsoever in order to answer a foreign request for information, whereas in The Netherlands, the subject has been specified at several levels. Firstly, the statutory law has been amended by replacing a wide restriction (investigative measures) with a limited restriction (coercive measures); secondly, the Dutch government has explained that a foreign request involving non-coercive investigations may be replied by the police without interference of the judicial authorities; thirdly the Dutch circular specifies that requests must be forwarded if they involve classical coercive means or modern, covert means of investigation, which even in domestic investigations may be applied with permission of the judicial authorities.

Cases in which the nature of the case involved may be an impediment for the police to provide the requested assistance are mainly rooted in general provisions on mutual legal assistance in criminal matters, which may reserve some requests for the judicial authorities or even prohibited them to be fulfilled at all. They are most numerous in Belgian, Dutch and Luxembourg law, which mention fear for a discriminatory prosecution, the political or fiscal character of the offence, fear for *bis in idem* and fear for the death penalty being imposed or executed. In essential, France has recognized the same exceptions as the Benelux countries, but does not consider the fiscal character of an offence as an impediment. An entirely different approach is followed by Germany. The main element there is that the federal government or administrative authorities must be consulted before replying a request that may have a special importance for political, factual or legal reasons, which is the case for political offences, fear for the death penalty and for the respect of basic human rights standards (which seems to include fear for discriminatory prosecution). Furthermore, German law prescribes that legal assistance be denied if it would be disproportional to indeed provide the assistance.

For some specific categories of police data, the international transmission may be subjected to special regimes. The Netherlands being the only country with a special regime for police intelligence, it is the only country with special restrictions for the transmission of such data: this is allowed only after consulting the CID-prosecutor. In border areas, hard intelligence may be provided without such consult.

Table 11.3 International Exchange of Police Information II

	B	NL	L	F	D
Transmission of intelligence					
Consultation of public prosecutor	-	+	-	-	-
Sufficient data protection required	-	+	-	-	-
On written request only	-	-	-	+	-
No special legal position	+	-	+	-	+
Transmission of sensitive data					
Legal or treaty obligation	+	-	-	-	-
If inevitable for reply, combined with other data only	-	+	-	-	-
No processing allowed	-	-	+	-	-
No processing allowed, safe scarce exceptions	-	-	-	+	-
No special legal position	-	-	-	-	+
Central body and exceptions					
NCB-Interpol	+	+	+	+	+
Provincial central bodies	-	-	-	-	+
Regional bodies in border areas	+	+	-	-	-
Local police in border areas	-	-	-	+	+
All police in urgent cases	+	+	+	+	+
Supervision and control					
NCB informed of decentral transmission	+	+	-	+	-
Central authorities informed	-	-	-	-	+
Transmission marked in register	+	+	+	-	+
Transmission reported to judicial authorities	-	+	+	+	-
Transmission reported to judicial or adm. authorities	-	-	-	-	+

For sensitive data, the most extreme countries are Luxembourg, which cannot provide such data to foreign services since their collection, storage and processing are generally prohibited, and Germany, where the only special treatment for sensitive data is their being subjected to higher standards of proportionality. Belgium seems to have the most restricted regime for the international provision of sensitive data: This may be done only by a restricted group of specially assigned police officers and must have a legal basis in either the requesting or the requested country. Dutch law allows the international provision of sensitive data, like every other treatment of such information, only if it is inevitable in the individual case and only in combination with other data. As for France, nothing specific regarding this subject is known; if there is a regulation and what contents it has depends entirely on non-published and thus unknown decrees.

11.3.4 Competent Police Authorities

In all five countries, the task of international transmission of police information has been entrusted primarily to the National Central Bureau of Interpol, in Germany combined with the Bureau's provincial counterparts, the LKA's. There are however some exceptions to this rule. In all five countries, urgent requests for information may be replied directly by the receiving decentral police service. In addition, in special border arrangements Belgium, The Netherlands, France and Germany have assigned decentral police services for the exchange of information in the border areas or will do so. Luxembourg being such a small country that it could be considered a border area as it is has not institutionalized such a decentralization.

11.3.5 Supervision and Control

In order to ensure the hierarchical and legal control to be fulfilled, various mechanisms of supervision by other or higher authorities have been foreseen. In all countries, direct exchanges must be reported to the National Central Bureau, this being the central body for international police contacts. In The Netherlands, a special provision has been created on control by the judicial authorities, for which also a special form has been prescribed. Under German law, the international exchange of police information in criminal matters must be reported to the judicial authorities. In other than criminal matters, the German police have a more independent position and are not obliged to report to others. Luxembourg and French law do not specify a duty to report to the judiciary, but in these countries such a duty may be deduced from the general obligation to keep the judicial authorities informed. The same may be said about Belgium, but there a circular containing more detailed information is being prepared. Control afterward of what has occurred is possible thanks to the fact that, in all countries, a report about the transmission must be stored in a register. In Belgium, this is done by the central body, whereas in the other four countries (in France, at least for the RG), this must be done in the register where the information originates from.

11.3.6 Special Border Arrangements

The subject of developing and introducing special border arrangements as addressed by art. 39 SC is most advanced in The Netherlands. Both for the Dutch-German and the Dutch-Belgian data communication, Schengen border arrangements are actually being applied. In the other four countries, arrangements are under preparation and negotiation, while between Germany and Belgium respectively Germany and France, some pre-Schengen agreements are still in force.

11.4   Conclusion

On the European continent, the Schengen Convention is the first multilateral legal instrument explicitly addressing the subject of international legal assistance by police services. Although it was in many ways a predecessor of the Schengen cooperation, not even the cooperation framework of the Benelux contained regulations of this kind. As a consequence of the formula "in compliance with the national legislation," which may be found in both art. 39 and 46 SC, the real legal meaning of both provisions is nevertheless meagre. If the national legislation is more restricted, then Schengen does not add anything because it must be in compliance with the national legislation. Does the scope of national legislation go beyond that of Schengen, then the latter will respect this and artt. 39 and 46 SC do not change anything about it either (art. 39 par. 4 and 5 SC). One might nevertheless say that, rather than having a legal impact, Schengen did have a political impact by encouraging national legislators to enlarge the possibilities of national legislation.

Schengen leaves the responsibility to restrict or specify which police officers are entitled to carry out international exchanges of information to the national legislator. Although none of the studied countries has specified this, the situation in Luxembourg, France and Germany appears to be perfectly clear: there are only one or two different police services and all of them may handle foreign requests for information. The Netherlands and Belgium on the contrary each know a number of public services with police tasks but have not made a strict specification either. Thus in these two countries all public authorities with police tasks can be considered entitled to exchange police information with their foreign counterparts, as long as this happens within the limits of their domestic task and powers. Other police forces than the regular ones will however only play a role in the direct transmission of information in urgent cases, since the basic procedure leads through the NCB's of Interpol, which is housed by (one of) the regular police forces. In the framework both countries have created for a structural police cooperation in the border areas, a similar restriction has been created by entrusting this to a central body in each of the border regions or districts.

Neither the Schengen Convention nor any of the studied countries binds a request for foreign police assistance to conditions regarding its form. The source and reliability of the request must nevertheless be beyond any doubt. The Convention does not pay any attention to the contents of a request for foreign information. According to Dutch, Belgian and German law, the requested party must at least be informed about the purpose of the request and the context of the case involved. Furthermore, an international request may concern generally available information as well as typical police data. The Convention allows the exchange of data for purposes of a preventive, proactive or repressive kind, purposes which can also be found in Dutch, Belgian and German law. Other than Belgian law and the Convention, which do not contain any restriction of offence categories cross-border data exchanges may be used for, Dutch and German law initially restricts such exchanges to serious and imminent dangers and crimes that have shocked the legal order. In border area arrangements however, this extra restriction has been dropped again.

Art. 39 SC prescribes that foreign requests soliciting the use of coercive measures must be forwarded to the judicial authorities, but does not specify what is meant by coercive measures. As a result, it may be unclear whether the police are entitled to independently and directly reply a foreign request. As we have shown above, among the five original Schengen partners The Netherlands are yet the only one where this gap is filled by domestic regulations. The cross-border exchange of information by the police is also prohibited if national law has reserved the request concerned to the judicial authorities or does not allow to reply the request at all. In all five countries this is the case for requests involving a political offence, fear for a discriminatory prosecution, or the risk of the death penalty being applied. Different from France and Germany, the Benelux countries also consider the fiscal character of an offence a reason to refuse legal assistance by the police, and with the exception of Germany, all countries consider fear for *bis in idem* as such a reason.

Regarding the international exchange of police data within the Schengen context, the finality principle must be respected. This implies that, if certain data have been provided for police use, they must not be used as evidence or otherwise in judicial proceedings. It is however not easy to ascertain if indeed this principle is respected. Simple methods such as marking the police purpose of the information have proven insufficient. The problem is enlarged by the fact that the Schengen Convention does not suggest any sanctions in case police information is indeed used in proceedings without judicial permission. The Schengen drafters have left this matter entirely to the domestic legislator, who has ignored it completely and left it to the judges in individual cases. These seem to be tempted to accept foreign evidence rather easily, perhaps because they would have problems controlling whether the foreign legislation has indeed been respected. Maybe it would be a solution if, instead of accepting every piece of evidence that does not mention to be intended for police use only, judges would only accept documents that are explicitly intended to be used as evidence.

According to both the Schengen Convention and national law in all five countries, the basic procedure for a foreign request for police information is to send it to the National Central Bureau of Interpol in the requested country; in Germany, it might also be sent to a Provincial criminal police office (LKA). Since urgent requests may be sent directly to and answered directly by another police service than the central body, it is useful to establish that urgent cases are those of which the success would be endangered by the delay caused by sending the request through the central authority. Besides the case of an urgent request, The Netherlands, Belgium, France and Germany have also expressed the intention to create possibilities for a decentralized data exchange in their respective border areas. The implementation of arrangements with this content seems to be most advanced in The Netherlands.

In general, we regret that all five countries tolerate the possibility of forum shopping or disguised extradition by police officers, which for The Netherlands has even been acknowledged officially in the data exchange guidelines. This seems to have been compensated somewhat by the fact that the investigative interests in all involved countries must be weighed before information is provided. For a police officer or service who is only partly aware of the investigative interests of his own country, it will nevertheless be difficult to weigh these against the even less known interests of another country, and the same problem seems to exist for the judge on trial. In this context it could be interesting to have a reply accompanied by the condition that a suspected resident be extradited for prosecution or execution of the sanction. In general however, the requested police service may not impose any additional conditions before replying, unless these conditions follow from national legislation. Since the respective national legislations do not mention such conditions, it seems legally impossible for the police to subject their reply to any conditions.

The informational cooperation as provided by the Schengen Convention does not require the existence of a double incrimination, nor is this required by the legislations of the participating countries. Since the condition of double incrimination is not even imposed on informational cooperation by the judicial authorities, this is not surprising. Nevertheless, it might lead to the undesirable situation that a country is obliged to contribute to the investigation and perhaps even prosecution and condemnation of a person whose conduct is not considered wrong according to its own legislation. Since this will especially occur in cases of moral or immoral intimate behaviour and petty offences regarding psychotropic substances, it might cause some international commotion. Therefore, it would be preferable that requests concerning cases in which the existence of a double incrimination is not clear, be forwarded to the judicial authorities instead of being replied by the police. This is even more recommandable in cases where the exchange might result in a disguised extradition.

In general, one may distinguish several types of risks occurring in the context of international informational exchanges by the police. The existence of cultural differences and differing priorities may for instance lead to the frustration of an efficient cooperation as well as of the police officers involved. We may also recall the risk of "data laundering," the complex of possibilities to hide the real origin of certain informations and to have the value of information upgraded by multiplying the number of confirmations.

Furthermore, there are various participants in the investigative process who run risks. The requesting police might become disappointed or even frustrated by the results of their request, which may be avoided by the best possible adaptation of their requests to the legal provisions of the requested country. They may also have or obtain problems due to a lack of controllability of the foreign information's legality and accuracy. The requested police might provide more assistance than they are entitled to and therefore run the risk of disciplinary measures, which may be avoided by a better knowledge of their own legal system. Finally, the person whose personal data are being transferred may, when eventually being put to trial, have problems tracing the origins and controlling the legality of information used against him. This might be avoided by improving the internal openness of the international aspects of the proceedings, a better way of ensuring that the finality principle will be respected and a more critical approach of his judges, also with regard to the foreign part of the investigation.

Finally, we have put the five countries to the test of the human rights standards as elaborated within the Council of Europe. In general, since the use of personal data by the police constitutes an infringement with the individual's right to privacy as protected by art. 8 ECHR, the conditions of art. 8 par. 2 must be met. This implies that the infringement must be authorized by law and necessary in a democratic society in the interest of public safety or the prevention of crime. The legality aspect has been elaborated by the Court in the Kruslin and Huvig decisions, explaining that the authorizing law must have certain qualities, especially of accessibility and foreseeability.

Furthermore, the legal systems must be in compliance with the Data Protection Convention and the Recommendation on Personal Data in the Police Sector, both being referred to directly in the Schengen Convention. This foremostly implies that the storage of personal data is only allowed if necessary to perform the lawful police tasks, a condition all countries seem to fulfil. The condition that special safeguards must be created for sensitive data is respected in the most extreme sense in Luxembourg, where the collection and processing of such data is entirely prohibited. In The Netherlands, Belgium and France, legislation has created various types of safeguards, whereas in Germany, a special protection must be warranted by the influence of the principles of proportionality and subsidiarity in individual cases. A data protection condition met by Dutch law only is the distinction of soft and hard police data, especially intelligence.

The exchange of police data is only allowed if there is a legitimate interest, and the international exchange must be limited to situations where this is necessary for the prevention or investigation of a serious danger or crime or based upon a clear provision of national or international law. This condition is, at least in some form, respected by each of the national systems as well as by the Schengen Convention itself. According to international standards, requests should indicate the reasons why and context in which they are done, and the use of data transmitted from abroad must be bound to the finality principle: Data must not be used for other cases than the ones it was provided for. Both these standards may be found in Belgian, Dutch and German, but not in Luxembourg or French law.

A final and partly additional standard of a more general nature, finding its origin in basic principles of the rule of law, is the possibility of hierarchical supervision and control afterwards. At least to some extent, this standard is met by all countries. As a result, German, Dutch and Belgian law are likely to pass the test of most of the data protection criteria without too much problems. Luxembourg law might also be sufficient, but the French system seems to be too basic. With all its elaborations in non-published decrees, it can not be considered to meet the necessary standards of accessibility and foreseeability.

Part III

Conclusions and Recommendations

12   Conclusions and Recommendations

Confusing the aim with the means, many law enforcement practionners see in uniformization a means to achieve an effective cooperation. A few days before the Schengen Convention would come into force, the Twente regional police chief and former president of the Dutch assembly of police chiefs P. IJzerman stated that Schengen would not stop crime. Even with Schengen, the impediments for an optimal cross-border law enforcement cooperation would remain numerous. He mentioned differences in legislation, insufficient knowledge of nature and size of organized crime on a European level and problematic exchange of information, complex procedures, differences in informational technologies, different languages and cultural differences.[1]

In addition to the fact that, even with all these impediments eliminated, crime would still succeed to exist, some of his remarks are worth discussing in this context. Firstly, as we have shown and will recall hereafter, the legislation of the studied countries with respect to the more basic police powers does not vary dramatically. Furthermore, most of the remaining impediments are of another than legal nature: lack of knowledge, differences in informational technologies, different languages and cultural differences all have in common that law is unable to change them. The last two even occur to be such autonomous phenomena that neither politics nor law will be capable of abolishing or even influencing them. They might however be the most important aspects of international cooperation, differences in national culture still leading to a different application of the law enforcement system in every single country, even with the criminal legislations entirely uniformized.[2]

It is illusionary to believe that uniform legislation is the key to smooth and effective cross-border police cooperation. On the one hand, there are many examples of structured cooperation in the world where no uniformization has been implemented. The United States of America are perhaps the best-known example, but close cooperation exists as well between the Swiss cantons which all have autonomy in criminal law, within the United Kingdom, where Scotland is the only member with a codified criminal system, between the Scandinavian

---

1   *Schengen kan criminaliteit niet stoppen*; De Gelderlander, March 19, 1995.
2   See Hofstede, 1980; Blankenburg & Bruinsma, 1994; Van Twuyver & Soeters, 1995, pp. 247-249 and Verbruggen, 1995, pp. 199-200.

countries. We can further mention the vast experience and system of international private law.

Moreover and on the other hand, a uniform legal system is not a guarantee for a uniform application of the law. It is common knowledge that law enforcement in urban areas of The Netherlands, for instance, is not the same as law enforcement in the countryside. In Germany, law enforcement in Nordrhein-Westfalen is not the same as in Bayern. Judges of the Ontario Court of Appeal in Canada do not necessarily decide a case the same way as judges of the Québec Court of Appeal. Finally, imposed harmonization of criminal law systems can be a greater source of tensions between the States than the situation it is trying to improve. International treaties may offer conflict rules, as the Schengen Convention does by stating that police officers acting in a foreign country are bound by the law of that country, and have a harmonizing effect by stating that rules have to be implemented in each State to permit controlled delivery. In doing so, harmonization itself, at best, can only be a distant aim achieved by accident, as an effect of very many years of effective cooperation.

Uniformization is not a means to achieve well-grinded police cooperation, knowledge is. Lack of mutual knowledge seems to be the most important impediment to a well-grinded cross-border police cooperation. Better mutual knowledge of language, law, culture and customs can provide a better cooperation in all domains. A good framework is also essential but its potential in regulating police cooperation will remain limited without a good and structural knowledge of language, culture and law.

We have structured this concluding chapter as follows. First we will recapitulate the aim and problem definition (par. 12.1), and give a review of the standards used throughout our study. We sketch and summarize our interpretation of the Schengen Convention in relation to the Benelux Extradition Treaty (section 12.2.1) and the rule of law as incorporated in the European Convention on Human Rights (section 12.2.2). After a review of the conclusions we have drawn for each of the police powers studied (sections 12.3.1-12.3.9), we will conclude with some general conclusions in the field of cross-border police cooperation (par. 12.4).

12.1   Review of Aim and Problem Definition

One may wonder - and we have been asked regularly - to what extent the international regulations of cross-border policing are acceptable for police officers in practice. To this matter, at least two aspects may be distinguished: Does the legal framework that has been created correspond to the needs of the police practice, and do police officers have problems accepting the infringement with national sovereignty caused by foreign police officers operating on their territory. Regarding the former, we may note that most of the regulations introduced now have been based on the practice as is has developed during the preceding decades. Thus, they might be considered to meet the daily needs of the police practice. The latter aspect does not seem to cause any problems because of what we would like to call here "the international colleague concept," the fact that police officers throughout the world always seem to refer to police officers elsewhere, known or unknown, as being their "colleagues," thus expressing a strong sentiment of internal unity, alliance, and solidarity. As a result, they most often seem to be willing to cooperate or, at least in border areas, do not object against a certain degree of foreign police activities on their territory.

As we have stated in the introduction, fighting cross-border crime is best achieved with an efficient and well-grinded cross-border police cooperation and mutual knowledge of rules and regulations in policing powers is indeed essential to achieve this goal. The central matters examined in this study can be reduced to the following questions: Firstly, which is the law in Belgium, The Netherlands, Luxembourg, France and Germany concerning those police powers that play a substantial role in operational international police cooperation? Secondly, in which way and to which extent must differences between the national systems be considered a potential impeachment for efficient police cooperation? Thirdly, how does Schengen provide for solutions? And fourthly, can the European Convention on Human Rights play a role as a central standard in international police cooperation?

We have answered the first question in Chapters 3 through 11, where we have sketched the positive law in force in the studied countries concerning a number of police powers. The police powers we have chosen for our analysis are those which, in our opinion, will play a direct role in cross-border police cooperation. Although we have given some answers in these chapters already, we will give an overview of our findings and answer the questions more directly in this chapter.

12.2 Review of Standards

In order to test the different policing techniques it is useful to find a common standard of interpretation. This has the advantage of forming a common denominator for the study of subjects that otherwise may be qualified apples and pears. Furthermore, a common interpretation seems to be an essential condition for a smooth cooperation between the treaty partners. A first standard we have chosen is a common interpretation of two international treaties on cross-border police cooperation, the 1990 Schengen Convention and the 1962 Benelux Extradition Treaty. All Contracting Parties will in the first place read and understand these treaties in their own language(s) and within the context of their own legal systems. In order to find a common interpretation of the various authentic versions of both treaties, we have therefore analyzed and compared the corresponding police powers in each of the legal systems. As a tool for the standard interpretation and as a source of solutions to unanswered questions of cross-border policing, we have chosen the rule of law as incorporated in the European Convention on Human Rights.

12.2.1 Schengen Convention and Benelux Extradition Treaty, a Combined Interpretation

The Schengen Convention is not exempt from confusing elements as to its interpretation. When interpreting the Convention in its relation with the Benelux Extradition Treaty and the law of each of the studied countries, we have chosen an approach which is conform to art. 33 par. 4 of the Vienna Convention on the Interpretation of Treaties, as well as to the principle *lex posterior derogat legi anteriori*.[3] Neither treaty foresees in solving language-related interpretation problems and the parties have not agreed on consulting a version in another (unofficial) language. Because of this, and after in some occasions having consulted secondary sources such as explanatory statements, we have presumed that the different versions of the Convention have all the same meaning and have interpretated both treaties in the way that would reconcile them best, taking factors such as aim and purpose of the Convention into account. Moreover, the Contracting Parties having set in the Single European Act such goals as the realization of the free circulation of persons and merchandise and acknowledging that the realization of such a borderless area needs compensatory measures,[4] we have concluded to opt for an interpretation of the treaty which will serve police cooperation best.

12.2.2 The European Convention on Human Rights as a Standard for the Rule of Law

As we have stated in the preceding paragraph, we have chosen to interpret the Schengen Convention in the way that serves international policing most. Because all the Contracting Parties have also ratified the European Convention on Human Rights, we have used the latter as a minimum standard for cross-border police actions. One of the most important standard expressed by the European Convention on Human Rights is the rule of law.

In Chapter 1, we have distinguished two main components of the rule of law. The first is a formal one, inspired by the many provisions of the European

---

3   "The later law amends the earlier one;" this adage has also been expressed in art. 30 par. 3 Vienna Treaty Convention.
4   In this sense the preamble to the Schengen Convention.

Convention on Human Rights permitting a restriction of a right or freedom when this is done in accordance with the law. What is meant by "law" has been analyzed by the European Court on Human Rights in for instance the cases of Kruslin and Huvig: A restriction of one of the rights or freedoms guaranteed by the Convention must have a basis in domestic law, the law itself should be accessible to the person concerned, and this person must be able to foresee the restriction's consequences for him.

The second component is a more material one. A basis in domestic law does not necessarily justify a violation or restriction of a fundamental right or freedom guaranteed by the Convention. In general, the restriction must pursue a legitimate aim and be necessary in a democratic society in order to achieve this aim. Moreover, it must be compatible with the rule of law as well, and the aims of the restriction in themselves must be compatible with the essence of the European Convention on Human Rights. Note that the restriction of some rights, such as the right to life and the right to liberty will be subject to yet stricter tests or even entirely exclude (the prohibition of torture).

The rule of law is a combination of these two aspects. Not only is the State obliged to create a legal basis for each violation of a fundamental right or freedom and for any activities which, if they were done by ordinary citizens, would be prosecuted, but it must, moreover, respect the essence of the European Convention on Human Rights. We have chosen to test the different police powers according to the criteria the Court has identified in the cases of Kruslin and Huvig. The regulations containing the restriction must be accessible and their consequences foreseeable for the general public. To these criterium developped by the court, we have added another dimension. The text of the Convention states that the restrictions must be necessary in a democratic society. In our opinion, this implies the necessity of democratic control: The demonstration of the necessity of the restriction of the right guaranteed by the Convention should be done in a public debate in parliament, as representative body of this democratic society. The restriction should be assessed by the elected representatives and voted on. Only formal statutes offer a guarantee that this democratic control has taken place.

12.3   Review of the Findings

One of the most important differences between the studied countries concerns indeed the availability and accessibility of information on police, security and public order. This is perhaps the consequence of what we have called in our first study an "open" or "closed" police culture.[5] In an open police culture, the police practice, organization and powers are set out in numerous rules which

---

5   Bevers & Joubert, 1994, p. 318.

are both clear and published, either in statutes or in circulars. The more open the police culture, the more it answers to the criteria we have set out in this study: accessibility, foreseeability and democratic control. A closed police culture regards the police practice as a tactical field of State security and is therefore better served with secrecy. The two extremes are represented by Germany and France, whereas The Netherlands follow Germany closely. Belgium and Luxembourg evolve somewhere in the middle, at times closer to France, other times closer to Germany.

Besides this difference of a rather general nature and all other, more specific differences we have found during our reserch, it also seems interesting to recall a remarkable general similarity between the studied countries. In all five, police and criminal law in the largest possible sense have been subject to impressive reconstructions and recalibrations. This development, that is still continuing, seems to be due to two causes: on the one hand the increasing internationalization of both the legal and the illegal economy, and on the other hand the growing influence of the European Convention on Human Rights. It is obvious that this similarity between the studied countries may not only be presented as a conclusion of our study but also as a problem during the research, since in some countries laws were changed so easily and often that it was almost impossible to stay up-to-date. Furthermore, we have no indications that these legislative developments have stopped or will stop in the near future; on the contrary, criminal law in this part of Europe seems to be moving more and more.

12.3.1 General Structure of Law Enforcement

In Chapter 3 we proceeded to describe the general structure of law enforcement in the five countries. We began with an overview of the legal framework applying to the actors of the first phase of the criminal procedure: the police, the public prosecutor, the examining judge and the suspect. We pursued by sketching the preliminary enquiry, its general principles and the general course of the enquiry. In this overview of our findings we will only summarize these findings which may have an impact on cross-border operational police cooperation.

12.3.1.1   Actors of Law Enforcement

One of the first characteristics of the police forces in the different countries is the plurality of forces working at law enforcement in each country. In countries such as France and Belgium, the plurality of forces is paired with an overlapping of police powers and jurisdiction, sometimes leading to a certain degree of competition. One notes, however, that with the influence of international police cooperation most countries are tending to diminish this plurality and, most important, the disparity between the forces and their overlapping jurisdictions. The most apparent[6] cohesion may be found in The Netherlands and in Luxembourg, whereas the situation in Germany is of a different order: It shows a plurality of independent police forces, with a strict division, in theory, between the federal and the provincial polices.

As a consequence of this disparity for the international police cooperation, it is tedious to determine with whom one is actually cooperating on the border. It will be easier to determine the competent local authority in a country with more internal cohesion in its police force then in a country with more separated police forces. However, the provisions contained in artt. 40 and 41 SC seem to form a good framework to counter the negative effects of the disparity of police forces. Remaining problems must be solved through more mutual knowledge of each other's police organization.

The public prosecutor's department in all of the countries is organized as a hierarchical agency. The executive members of the department are all magistrates who have, in principle, the direction of the pre-trial enquiry of the police. Although they have investigative powers in all countries, in practice, they seldom carry out investigationd themselves. The most significant difference lies in their discretionary power to prosecute: All but one country apply the principle of opportuneness of criminal proceedings. Germany is the only country where the discretionary power of the public prosecutor is limited by the principle of legality. Whereas in the other countries, the prosecutor will prosecute only if it is opportune, in Germany he will prosecute unless matters of law or fact renders this impossible.

A first consequence of this discrepancy for the international police cooperation will lie in the priority given to the investigation of particular offences. While in most countries the public prosecutor, and as a consequence the police, will have discretion as to whether a particular offence will be investigated, in Germany the police is likely, in theory, to investigate all criminal offences regardless of their seriousness. This situation is liable to cause frictions between cooperating police forces and at a higher, institutional or political level. In spite of the complexity caused by the "menu" choice they offer for the criminal offences which give competence to pursue across the border (catalogue or extraditable offences), the provisions set out in artt. 40 and 41 SC have the potential of diminishing these frictions. They indicate that at least all countries have agreed on types of offences which may open the door to cross-border policing and cooperation.

---

6   The expression apparent is used because it seems that competition between services is very difficult to eliminate.

12.3.1.2   Structures of Criminal Law Enforcement

Another difference worth mentioning is the categorization between criminal offences the studied countries make. The fact that every country knows its own offence categories (such as *crimes, délits, contraventions, misdrijven, misdaden, wanbedrijven, overtredingen, Verbrechen, Vergehen*), shows that an offence category is not a practical criterion for international police cooperation, as it will create a definition problem. The choice made by the Schengen Convention, either the extraditable offence criterion or a catalogue, seems, although complicated and arbitrary, a practical one.

As we have mentioned in earlier chapters, the essential difference in the pre-trial phase between pro-active and re-active police action lies in the question whether a criminal offence has or has not been committed. The fact that rules are set to determine police powers implies that they have a restricting as well as a permitting side. Because of this, one might imagine that there is a difference in independence or liberty to act between police officers in countries where pre-trial enquiry is hardly regulated and police officers in countries with more rules. With respect to this, an evolution seems to have taken place in the last decades.

Originally, the existence of less legal provisions suggested less restrictions for the police, who had more powers and thus more independence from the judicial authorities. The influence of the European Convention on Human Rights and the case-law of the Court and the Commission, have increasingly emphasized the importance of legality and explicit legislation. As a result, the use of several police powers (especially those infringing with the individual's rights and freedoms) was prohibited unless it had a legal basis. In the exercise of such powers, the police was bound to a warrant issued by the judicial authorities according to a procedure provided by law. In the new situation, the existence of more, and more detailed, provisions implies more powers for the police and thus more independence.

Countries with few rules on the pre-trial police enquiry, such as Belgium, France and Luxembourg, still prohibit the use of most forms of coercive measure in that first phase of the enquiry. Evidence and information gathered in violation of this principle may, in theory, only be used before the examining judge for justifying the use of more coercive measures. In countries with more rules on the police enquiry (The Netherlands and Germany), the law demands a certain degree of suspicion that a criminal offence has been committed as a prerequisite for the use of coercive means. Nevertheless, in all of the studied countries, the police have great liberty in their investigations, as long as no means of coercion are used.

Whatever these differences may be and whether they do indeed have an impact on the cross-border police cooperation is difficult to assess since it would require more empirical information instead of exclusively theoretical material.

However, it seems likely that these differences will have an impact on the mentality of the police officers, their approach of a situation and on the degree of initiative they might show. Therefore, in order to improve the development of an efficient policy of international police cooperation, it would be useful to have a thorough study of police and criminal law cultures in the involved countries carried out.

12.3.2 Observation

The studied countries all permit the use of observation as an investigating method in the police enquiry, at least to a certain extent. We note, however, that there is a huge difference in the formal legal framework enacted in each country, caused by different approaches of the question whether such policing techniques should be regulated, be it in statutes or otherwise. Furthermore, they do not all seem to attribute the same importance to the distinction of pro-active and re-active policing, which has already led to different interpretations of the Schengen provisions on observation. Both for the police officers involved and for the citizen's fundamental right, it were desirable if such differences in interpretation would be replaced by a common interpretation.

Germany seems to be the only country to consider observation techniques as such a violation of the right to privacy that it imposes the creation of a legal basis. This position has led to a vast and detailed legislation on the subject which could serve as an example for democracies abiding by the rule of law. Moreover, Germany is the only country fulfilling all the conditions set out by art. 8 ECHR and the European Court. Its legislation is accessible and its consequences are foreseeable for the enforcing police officers as well as for the general public. Further the regulations are embodied in statutes, giving them quality as they have been the object of public debates. The absence of regulations in the remaining countries or the secrecy of such regulations cause them to score poorly on these three criteria. Being not accessible (inexistent or secret), their consequences are not foreseeable, and not being embodied in statutes, they do not have the quality one expects in a democratic society.

In addition to the argument of the rule of law for the necessity of statutes one notes that explicit and clear statutes would also be practical for solving problems in terminology caused by the Schengen Convention. Moreover, clear and published statutes have the advantage of rendering important information accessible to all parties involved, which could certainly improve cross-border cooperation. In some countries for example, the use of specific technical devices during an observation is bound to more and other conditions than those mentioned in art. 40 SC. These differences, that may eventually lead to the illegal gathering of information that might be excluded from the evidence in court, are so detailed that it will be indispensable for the observing officers to be aware of the national regulations. In order to enable this, the national legislators must ensure that police officers of their neighbour countries are or may be aware of restrictions and conditions for cross-border observation, for instance by publication. Further, this would improve not only the position of the cross-border observing officers but also the controllability of the operations by the competent national and international authorities. This aspect is especially important in the highly sensible field between the common interest of criminal investigation and the individual interest of privacy protection.

12.3.3 Controlled Delivery, Infiltration and Informers

Here again, there is no consensus among the studied countries on the necessity of having detailed legislation on that matter, nor do they agree on the form an eventual regulation should have. Regulation of such techniques often occurs by accident, in any case not directly because of a deep concern for the rule of law. The only two countries with formal statutes on these techniques are Germany and France. In these countries, the resort to techniques such as controlled delivery or infiltration is seen as an exception not only to the protection of privacy and the presumption of innocence guaranteed by art. 8 and 6 par. 2 ECHR, but also to the national law in general.

In countries such as The Netherlands, Luxembourg and Belgium, these techniques are, when regulated at all, confined in circulars and directives.[7] These circulars and directives can be secret, in which case their controllability by an impartial agency is non-existent, but they can also be published, in which case their controllability can be assured. Directives may be easily modified, which is a practical advantage, but also have the disadvantage of eluding direct political control, even though there is a need for political discussion on whether these methods should be used at all. When methods are not regulated, be it by statute or otherwise, it is left to the courts to decide whether police officials have transgressed their limits. Due to the covert character of the methods involved, the courts are dependent on the good will of the police and the public prosecutor for information on these methods. In assessing the legality of such methods, the courts often tend to resort to flexible criteria which vary according to the seriousness of the offence.

All methods discussed in Chapter 5, controlled deliveries or transports, infiltration and the use of informers, are interlinked and intertwined. The practice increasingly tends to use informers who commit acts which the police do not want to commit. The concept of informer is, furthermore, a concept subject to

---

7   Note that The Netherlands will probably move towards formal legislation with the results of the parliamentary enquiry committee Van Traa, which gave a good idea of how wrong things can go; see Van Traa, 1996.

strong variations. Whether one speaks of an incidental informer or of "running" an informer may be the entire difference between a simple observation and long-term infiltration. This poses difficult ethical questions as the State, either via a police officer or an informer, may be committing serious crimes. Moreover, both police officers and informers are confronted with enormous amounts of money, against which the State cannot compete. One must therefore seriously ask oneself whether resorting to these methods is proportional, considering the high ethical and operational risks and the limited results. The importance of these matters for the legal nature of the State are such, that a democratic parliament cannot allow itself to leave these methods and their impact on society undiscussed.

Once a country has answered the question whether these methods are compatible with the needs of a democratic society and necessary to solve the problems of organized crime, it will need formal statutes to regulate the techniques and limit the ethical risks. Because of the secret character of the techniques, it is difficult to get a clear view on this part of the international police cooperation. It is however probable that the hermetical character of some regulations is an impediment for a good cooperation. Clear formal statutes are important to increase both the accessibility of the norms and the mutual knowledge. Finally, because resorting to these methods on a purely national level is not realistic in Europe, a solid international framework is needed to prevent international conflicts in this field.

12.3.4 Hot Pursuit

The most important problem of cross-border hot pursuit will not be formed by the plurality of rules in the different countries, but rather by the combination of all rules that are applicable. Besides the rules found in the Schengen Convention and the Benelux Extradition Treaty, the Schengen Convention has left a large margin of discretion to the States as to the choices of the different rules that may apply. The Convention permits to choose "à la carte" which set of rules may apply to cross-border hot pursuit, not only specifying the respective scopes of the pursuit (10 kilometre zone, 10 kilometre distance, 30 minutes, entire territory) but also differentiating the police officers form different countries. This renders an overview of the complete legal framework tedious and thus the situation difficult to manage.

Another important problem is that the legal meaning of single terms used in the three authentic versions of the Schengen Convention does not seem to correspond with the legal terminology in each country. This is especially the case with the various authentic versions of the English translation "escaped from custodial sentence," some of which include escapes from police offices, while others exclude this. It is likely that this discrepancy will cause practical problems, as will the fact that the countries each have their own priority lists as to which criminal offences must be investigated first. This could have a serious impact on the degree of cooperation of the locally competent authorities in a cross-border hot pursuit situation.

The rules designating for each country which police officers will be competent to carry out cross-border hot pursuits seem to be clear and not likely to cause much problems. The different concepts of apprehension in the act all cover basically the same situations, despite the differences in terminology. These rules are an improbable cause for problems. What might become a source of difficulties is the fact that the Benelux Extradition Treaty does not require a caught in the act-situation, whereas the Schengen Convention does. Police officers used to working with the Benelux Treaty may have a problem with this restriction, although it is unlikely to be substantial.

With regard to traffic regulations dispensations for pursuing officers, France is the only country that has not regulated these on a legal basis. This may be considered against the rule of law, traffic violations being generally punishable unless an exception has been created. Further, in our study we have shown a wide variety of dispensations and conditions for traffic violations in each country. We suspect that this will cause inequalities and unclear situations, leading to uncertainty and problems for cross-border hot pursuit. It would perhaps be wise to either adopt a series of harmonized international rules on the subject, or to increase the accessibility and availability of the existing national rules. This could be done within the police education.

12.3.5 Apprehension, Arrest and Control of Identity

Having compared the national norms on initial restrictions and deprivations of liberty during a criminal investigation, one notes in first instance that the Schengen term "apprehension" must be interpreted as meaning "provisory arrest." This confirms the result of a reasonable interpretation of "apprehension" in its context in the Convention. The conditions under which apprehension, provisory arrest by police officers and identity control are authorized are most restrictive in The Netherlands, although the other four countries are rather similar. Note, however, that the Dutch regulations stay far under the prerequisites for apprehension of the Schengen Convention and the Benelux Treaty for cross-border hot pursuit. Thus a pursuing officer complying with the provisions of these treaties, will normally stay in accordance with the law of the country where he is operating.

An important right art. 5 ECHR guarantees an arrested person, is the right to be informed promptly of the reasons for his arrest. Unless impossible, this information should be provided at the moment of the arrest and therefore mostly by the arresting police officer. In case of a cross-border pursuit, this could also be a foreign officer. This right, which (thanks to the American film and TV industry) is probably the best-known of the suspect's rights, has not been codified, except in German police law, which does not apply to judicial arrests. It has further been recognized by the Dutch Ombudsman and several German criminal courts, but as far as known, no consequences for the procedure or whatsoever were ever attached to neglecting this right. This might however change after an eventual complaint at the European Court and in that sense it is a certain risk for cross-border policing, especially when Belgian, Luxembourg or French police officers must proceed to an arrest on German or Dutch territory. It therefore seems wise if administrative or judicial authorities in all participating countries would regulate this right one way or another, be it only in a circular or guideline to inform the police of their obligation in this respect, especially also in cross-border pursuit cases.

The most important conclusion that can be drawn regarding apprehension and arrest, may be that the drafters of both the Dutch and the French version of the Schengen Convention would have better used the expressions *aanhouden* and *appréhender* rather than *staande houden* and *interpeller*. After all, the means of coercion they intended to regulate was indeed the provisory arrest of a person who has been caught in the act. Now that this terminological uncertainty does exist, it would be recommended to the national governments to explain exactly what they will understand by the expressions that have been applied.

Concerning regulations on the control of identity, there are numerous differences between the five countries. Belgium and Luxembourg are the most strict countries, both obliging their citizens to always carry their ID. France is the least strict, since its law explicitly allows the citizens to demonstrate their identity by any means. Without any doubt the Netherlands will be the country with the most complicated regulation, a mixture of obligations that may vary from no obligation at all to an obligation to carry, all depending on the situation. As to their contents, the French and Luxembourg ID-cards bear the least information, whereas the card which The Netherlands want to introduce will be the only one that provides the bearer's tax and social security number. Further, Germany has the most detailed regulation of methods for the verification of a person's identity, and is also the only one of the five countries where such a verification may take place without the interference of an assistant public prosecutor. None of these differences will however cause a problems for the international police cooperation, since both art. 27 BET and art. 41 SC have reserved the control of identity exclusively for the locally competent police forces.

12.3.6   Handcuffs, Service Weapons and Self Defence

Regarding the use of force, France is the only country without any statutory regulation on the subject. All four remaining countries have either a general law worked out in lower legislation (The Netherlands and Germany) or statutes regulating certain means of force in particular (Belgium and Luxembourg). However different the norms, all countries seem to hold proportionality and subsidiarity (absolute necessity) as a ground rule, as well as the necessity of the legitimate aim.

Considered a safety measure, the use of handcuffs has only become the explicit subject of statutes in Germany and The Netherlands. In most countries, it is seen as an exceptional measure, the use of which must depend on such factors as the personality of the suspect or the circumstances of a situation. The Schengen Convention does not mention any conditions for the use of handcuffs, it only mentions that a pursuing officer who is entitled to apprehend (= provisorily arrest) the suspect on foreign territory, may use them. Note that, when using handcuffs, a pursuing officer must respect the law of the country on which territory they operate. This implies that, for the sake of the foreign pursuing officer, clear regulations are required. Moreover, the rule of law demands that such regulation be accessible, foreseeable and have a certain quality.

Use of the service weapon according to the Schengen Convention is only possible in self defence. In most cases this service weapon will be a firearm, but it may also be tear-gas or a stick. The fact that its use is only authorized in self defence will represent for most foreign police officers a restriction of their normal use of service weapons. In most countries, the use of service weapons is not only authorized in self defence, but also while carrying out lawful arrests or as a preventive method. Again, France is the only country that does not provide for formal legislation regarding the use of arms by the police.

With respect to the use of service weapons during cross-border cooperation, there are three questions that should be answered: What is meant with "service weapon," what is meant with "self defence" and what is meant with "use." The Schengen memento of the working group I on cross-border cooperation gives an overview of which weapons are considered service weapons in each country. Belgium and France consider tear-gas as belonging to their standard police equipment whereas Luxembourg, The Netherlands and Germany do not. The Netherlands and France are the only two countries which have expressed reservations as to the type of weaponry that may be carried by foreign police officers during a cross-border operation. They have stated that, save in urgent hot pursuit cases, carrying another weapon than the types used by their local police officers is excluded. This means that in other than urgent hot pursuit cases, for instance during an observation, Belgian police officers with tear-gas in their service vehicles will be obliged to stop somewhere in order to deposit the unauthorized weapon before crossing the border. It is obvious that this may cause practical problems at moments when time is tight, problems which can only be avoided by clear and adequate information for police officers in border areas.

One of the most significant differences is the definition given in each country to the concept of self defence. In one group of countries (The Netherlands, Germany and France), this includes the aversion of assaults on goods, while in Belgium and Luxembourg, self defence is restricted to assaults on human beings. The difference between these two definitions could lead to problematic situations, that might be avoided by also implying the definition of self-defence offered by the European Convention on Human Rights. According to art. 2 ECHR, "the deprivation of life shall not be regarded as inflicted in contravention of this article when it results from the use of force which is no more than absolutely necessary in defence of any person from unlawful violence." Considering the fact that most use of a service weapon may result in the loss of life, these should be suiting criteria for resorting to physical force. However, the Contracting Parties seem to have chosen another path in the Schengen memento as to include the defence of goods in all countries, instead of excluding it. In our opinion, this contravenes both the letter and the spirit of the European Convention.

Finally, there seems to be one major difference between the regulation of the use of service weapons in The Netherlands on the one side, and the other countries on the other. The Dutch regulation is the one to pay attention to the concept of "use" of firearms, a concept which does not only cover shooting, but includes drawing the firearm with the intention to use it (aiming or threatening). In the other countries this distinction is not made and using a firearm or any other service weapon seems to only refer to the actual using of the weapon (actually shooting, throwing, hitting or otherwise using). As a consequence, foreign police officers operating on Dutch territory and bound by Dutch law, will have to be alert and only draw their firearm (with the intention to use) in self-defence. However, taking a firearm or other service weapon in the hand as a preventive measure (without aiming or threatening) is not considered "use" and thus seems to be implicitly authorized by the Schengen Convention and the law of the studied countries. Altogether, the particular legal situation in The Netherlands is liable to cause problems, especially when foreign police officers aim their weapon with preventive intentions outside the situation of self-defence. The Dutch authorities could help minimizing problems of this kind by ensuring that foreign police officers are aware of this particularity of Dutch law.

12.3.7 Security Search and Investigative Bodily Search

Carrying out security searches is subjected to more or less the same conditions in the studied countries, although only Belgium, The Netherlands and Germany foresee specific norms in formal law, be it in statutes or in lower legal provisions. France and Luxembourg have no distinct norms for this measure, but in Luxembourg the Code of criminal procedure mentions a bodily search for both security and investigative purposes. Systematic use of security search is not allowed in any country. The most important difference concerns the way a security search should be carried out: In some countries for instance, a person subjected to a security search may be undressed (Belgium). In the context of cross-border hot pursuit, apprehension and security search, this is the only difference which may potentially cause clashes.

As for the investigative bodily search, Belgium, The Netherlands and Germany have specific provisions in statutory law. France, on the contrary, has no specific provision for investigative bodily searches, it being assimilated with the search of private premises. Luxembourg has only one provision, serving both security and investigative purposes. Most countries demand, however, either that the suspicion be sufficiently serious or that the criminal offence giving cause for the search be severe enough to justify the measure (proportionality). In most countries, the investigative bodily search includes at least the search in or under the clothes. The Netherlands and Germany are the countries of which the legislation permits the most intimate bodily search: It may be carried out in the natural openings of the body, unless medical expertise is needed. In Belgium and The Netherlands, the suspect may be asked to undress and take special positions to enable the officers to observe all possible hiding places on and of the body. In the practice of cross-border hot pursuit and apprehension, it is not likely that the differences in regulation of the bodily investigative search will give problems: The Schengen Convention reserves this type of search to the locally competent police officers.

Whether a pursuing Belgian police officer will actually go so far as to have an apprehended suspect undress on Dutch or German territory is doubtful. It is, however, important to stress these differences in the light of international cooperation. Another point is whether the luggage or the vehicle of a person being searched for security reasons may be searched as well. It is plausible that in all the countries a superficial search of these may be done, as long as this can be justified in the light of safety.

All types of bodily searches, as an intrusion of one's physical integrity, are likely to violate the right to privacy as guaranteed by art. 8 ECHR. All the studied countries agree that even a security search should be carried out systematically. In that way, they all agree that even a security search is liable to violate a person's physical integrity. Concerning the security search, there are two groups, one of which has set provisions in specific statutes and the other which has not. Belgium, The Netherlands and Germany all have adopted statutes on security searches. The regulations in these countries fulfil all the prerequisites of the European Convention on Human Rights as they are accessible, foreseeable and their necessity has been demonstrated in a democratic society through their adoption by the different parliament. France and Luxembourg should adopt formal statutes on this subject as well in order to fulfil these conditions as well as facilitate cross-border operation.

Comparing the norms for the investigative bodily search, all the countries have a type of provision regulating investigative searches, although not all respect the conditions of accessibility, foreseeability and quality. In short, in our opinion, the conditions and limits in which bodily searches may be done by the police, should be set out in clear provisions in statutes. A bodily search, for security as well as for investigative purposes, reaches such a degree of infringement in one's physical integrity that it renders a legal basis necessary for the sake of the rule of law. Such a provision should answer such questions as whether it might be carried out in public, whether persons may be obliged to undress, whether the search may be carried out by an official of the opposite sex, whether a person may be compelled to endure special investigations and whether samples from his body may be collected. Moreover, clear published provisions will not only improve the accessibility and foreseeability of the rules, but the international cooperation as well.

12.3.8 Police Interrogation

Some formalism, such as the obligation to draw a written report of an interrogation can contribute to a certain degree of controllability of the police by the judge. Most of the studied countries provide for a certain number of norms regarding police interrogation, each of the countries enacting a varying level of formality. Belgium is the only country to have no provisions at all for this phase of the enquiry.

Most countries recognize a certain number of rights to the suspect being held in custody, although at different stages of the procedure. Only two countries recognize the right to see a lawyer prior to the police interrogation: Luxembourg and Germany. In principle, none of the countries explicitly recognize the right to have an attorney present during the interrogation. The right of the suspect to be informed in a language he understands of the reasons of his arrest and eventually of a number of other implicit or explicit rights is not unanimously recognized. The Netherlands, Luxembourg and Germany explicitly guarantee this right prior to the police interrogation, whereas France and Belgium do not do so.

The right to silence is undoubtedly the right which will have the most impact on cross-border police operations. When apprehending a suspect after a cross-border hot pursuit, it will be easy to ask a few questions, which would otherwise only be possible after a request for mutual legal assistance. Provisions concerning this right are scarce in the countries. Only The Netherlands and Germany explicitly require the police to inform the suspect of this right before he be questioned. The moment when principles such as the presumption of innocence should be materialized in actual procedural consequences such as the right to silence is a question of great importance. Informing the suspect of his right to silence later than strictly necessary would have the effect of rendering this right illusionary. Not much is left of the importance of the right to silence when a suspect's declaration to the police without this right can be used in court.

The European Court on Human Rights in the case Funke has declared the importance of the presumption of innocence and the right to silence. Moreover, it is in our opinion inherent to the presumption of innocence that it be present the moment one is a suspect. In the situation of cross-border hot pursuit and considering the conditions contained in the Schengen Convention for crossing the border, one can be certain that the pursued person will very much be a suspect. It is essential to the presumption of innocence that the right to silence be recognized at this stage of the procedure since recognizing it only at a later date would have the effect of robbing this guarantee of its content.

Procedural differences between the studied countries in cross-border apprehension situations may have considerable consequences for the suspect and for court proceedings: The lack of formality in one country may cause some declarations to be unfit as evidence in other countries. The court of one country may decide either to exclude possible evidence originating a foreign country or to refuse to test its validity because of the lack of knowledge of foreign legal systems.

12.3.9 Mutual Legal Aid by Police Officers

Strictly spoken, the Schengen regulation for cross-border exchange of information by the police does not have any direct impact on the legal situation. Since restrictions as well as extensions of national law must be respected, it does not change the possibilities offered by national legislation. If the Convention has influenced the legal situation, it was rather in encouraging the national legislators to enlarge the possibilities offered by national law. The purposes for which information may be exchanged according to both the Schengen Convention and Belgian, Dutch and German national law include preventive, pro-active and repressive policing. In other than border areas, The Netherlands and Germany exclude the exchange of information for less severe offences.

The international exchange of police information has basically been entrusted to the National Central Bureaus of Interpol, in Germany also to the NCB's provincial counterparts. In urgent cases, local police services may communicate across the border directly, and the police in the Dutch, Belgian, French and German border areas are in general entitled to such direct exchanges according to special border arrangements.

The Netherlands are the only country that has specified when requested investigative measures become coercive measures and as such an impediment for an independent reply by the police. France on the other hand is the only country that seems to exclude that their police officers engage in any investigative activity in order to reply to a foreign request. The French police may only transmit information they have already, and this only if the information does not originate from any judicial enquiry. In all countries, replying a foreign by the police is also excluded if the request involves a political offence, or there is a fear for discriminatory prosecution or the death penalty. The Benelux countries further consider the fiscal character of an offence as an exception, and together with France, the fear for *bis in idem*. In general however, it would be desirable if all countries would explicitly state which types of request may or may not be replied directly and independently by their police authorities.

The Schengen Convention and all five countries require that the finality principle be respected, without however indicating what will be the consequences if for instance police information is used as evidence without consent of the judicial authorities. The authority who will eventually be obliged to solve this problem is the court judge, who will hardly be able to control if foreign legislation has been respected or ignored. This impediment to the controllability is also a problem in the light of the possibility of forum shopping or disguised extradition by the police, who can influence the country where a person will be put to trial. Weighing the interests of prosecution in both countries concerned will be a difficult task for an individual police officer and *a fortiori* for the judge on trial. Since they are obliged to provide assistance, the replying police service is not allowed to attach conditions regarding extradition for execution or transmission of prosecution to their answer, unless these have their basis in national law. However, none of the countries studied know such conditions.

Another risk resulting from the diminished controllability is the risk of data laundering by the police, upgrading the value of information by sending it to and requesting it from foreign police services. It is obvious that this also enlarges the risk that a suspect will be unable to trace the sources and check the real credibility of the information he is confronted with on trial.

Some international commotion might be caused by the fact that neither the Convention nor national law requires double incrimination of the offence for which information is requested. This could force a country to assist in the investigation or prosecution of a suspect who, according to their own laws, has not committed any offence at all. Furthermore, the existence of different priorities and police cultures in the countries is likely to become (or remain) an important source of frustration in the field of international cooperation. More frustrations for the police might be caused by insufficient knowledge of the information exchange possibilities of their cross-border colleagues or even of their own law.

As to art. 8 ECHR and other international legal instruments regarding the protection of data in the police sector, we can conclude that Germany and The Netherlands, which have the most elaborated systems, as well as Belgium seem to meet their standards easily. Particularly concerning the police sector, Luxembourg law is a great deal less detailed but, nevertheless, it may be considered sufficient. The French system, however, is dominated by general expressions and secret elaborations in non-published decrees and, as a result, it fails to meet even the most elementary standards of accessibility and foreseeability.

12.4   General Conclusions

The amount of data collected in this study is eclectic and vast: Finding a consistent path through the heterogenous information is a trying enterprise. In order to assist in structuring the information, it can be helpful to recapitulate the central questions of this study.

The first question addresses the law in the studied countries concerning police powers playing a substantial role in operational international police cooperation. We feel that we have answered to this question in sufficient detail in Chapters 4 through 11. We have, moreover, recapitulated the different conclusions and their potential impact on police cooperation in paragraph 12.3. In doing so, the second question has been answered as well: In which way and to which extent must differences between the national systems be considered a potential impeachment for efficient police cooperation? We have analyzed the solutions offered by Schengen as well as its potentially problematic interpretation throughout the same chapters, but we will pursue this discussion in the following section (12.4.1). The last question, relating to the role the European Convention on Human Rights can play as a central standard in international police cooperation, has been woven into all the preceding chapters. The Convention is to be considered a minimum norm in the interpretation of the treaties addressing cross-border police cooperation.

Analyzing police powers, one can make many distinctions with the purpose of classifying them. One distinction that can be made is between conventional and non-conventional policing methods. Conventional methods consist mostly in basic investigation methods such as arrest, questioning, search and seizure and just looking around for clues (observation in its simplest form). Non-conventional policing consists in more hidden police powers such as looking around with technical means, infiltrating, using informers and collecting sensitive data on potential suspects. This distinction, which is related to a distinction between several types of criminal offences that we discussed in Chapter 1, shows the difficulty of classifying policing methods: As time passes, police methods that once were non-conventional, may be considered conventional methods. Other usable categories relate to the covert or overt character of a policing method. This seems to us the most relevant distinction in the context of cross-border operational cooperation between police officers, as it exposes the sensitive issue of control. The policing powers then easily fall in one or another category according to their covert or overt character: Observation, infiltration and data exchange on the one hand and arrest, physical force and search on the other, to name only those police posers which have been the subject of our study. In evaluating the Schengen Convention, we will follow this distinction.

12.4.1 Evaluating Schengen and the State of Legislation

Before we continue the evaluation of the Schengen framework, we will take a short look at what we call the state of the legislation in the studied countries on the hand of the European Convention on Human Rights. In *Table 12.1*, we have evaluated the different legal systems with the help of a number of criteria, each represented by + or -. The first criterion is the accessibility of the norm, expressing whether the content of the norm is accessible for the police and the general public. The question as to whether a norm is published (+) or not (-) plays a central role in this context. The second criterion is the foreseeability. In this context, the clarity and the detail of the existing norm play the central role (+ for more, - for less clear and detailed). The third criterion concerns what we have called the democratic control of the norm. The central question will be whether the norm has its basis in lower or in higher legislation. As restrictions of human rights must be necessary in a democratic society, this criterion addresses the central question of whether the necessity of the power has been the object of public debate. Formal statutes offer the best guarantee that this control has taken place. Police powers determined by statutes have obtained a + in the table whereas countries where the particular power is not determined in a statute have obtained a -. However, the absence of formal statutes can be an indication that the technique is not being used and, therefore not needing to be regulated.

Table 12.1 The State of Legislation and the Rule of Law

	D	NL	B	L	F	Total +/-
Overt methods						
Apprehension, arrest + control of identity	+ + +	+ + +	+ + +	+ + +	+ + +	15/0
Investigative search	+ + +	+ + +	+ + +	+ + +	+ + +	15/0
Physical force + use of arms	+ + +	+ + +	+ + +	+ + +	- - -	12/3
Interrogation	+ + +	+ + +	- - -	+ + +	+ + +	12/3
Security search	+ + +	+ + +	+ + +	- - -	- - -	9/6
Sub-total overt +/-	15/0	15/0	12/3	12/3	9/6	63/12
Covert methods						
Wire taps	+ + +	+ + +	+ + +	+ + +	+ + +	15/0
Mutual legal aid by police	+ + +	+ + +	+ + +	+ - +	- - -	11/4
Informers	+ + +	- + -	- + -	+ - +	+ - +	9/6
Infiltration	+ + +	+ + -	- + -	- - -	+ - +	8/7
Controlled delivery	+ + -	+ + -	- + -	- - -	+ - +	7/8
Observation	+ + +	+ + -	- + -	- - -	- - -	6/9
Sub-total covert +/-	17/1	13/5	10/8	7/11	9/9	56/34
Total +/-	**32/1**	**28/5**	**22/11**	**19/14**	**18/15**	

This manner of processing data gives a rather digital overview of the difference in the studied countries on the one hand, and the differences between covert and overt policing methods on the other hand. Indeed, it is not our pretention to present a quantified system of analysis of the quality - in the moral sense of good or bad - of the legal systems we have studied. Rather, we consider this an instrument to help us sort out eclectic data. The table gives us an indication of the actual state of legislation and its relation to the criteria we have developed above. Although the criteria can be considered objective as they flow from decisions of the European Court on Human Rights, their application in this manner is one-sided, as the evaluation only rests on + or -, ignoring all nuances.

A rapid look at the table exposes two extremes between, on the one hand Germany with a very good score of almost only + and, on the other hand France, which scores quite poorly. What is particularly interesting is to look at differences in the relationship +/- between covert and overt policing methods. The difference between + and - in the covert methods sector is smaller than this difference in the overt methods sector. Moreover, the number of - diminishes sharply concerning overt methods. The accessibility and foreseeability of the content of the norms is less present than in overt methods. When regulated at all, covert policing methods are, in general, regulated in lower forms of regulations. This can be an indication of the difficulty to control the actual application of the existing norms.

12.4.1.1 Overt Policing Methods

The overt policing methods of which we have sketched the legal framework are apprehension, arrest, control of identity, the use of physical force and arms, security search, investigative search and police interrogation, with cross-border hot pursuit as an international framework of the methods. Carried out in public, their controllabity will cause less problems. Most of these methods are regulated in statutes in the studied countries and, although the norms may differ, they seem to be carried out in similar manner.

What is liable to cause more problems is the aspect of the terminology used in the Schengen Convention. A number of expressions and terms used in the Convention would gain in clarity by being explained in all official languages, taking in consideration the fact that some of these languages are used in more than one legal system and, consequently, may have a different legal meaning in these countries. This explanation should preferably be given in general terms, free of national legal implications, without using terms which have a legal meaning in any of the countries.

Nonwithstanding the terminological inconsequences and the necessary critical comments on the judiciary and democratic control, the chapter on the police contained in the Schengen Convention is admirably detailed. Since the police powers used in cross-border operations discussed in this study do not differ very much in regulation, it seems that further uniformization is not necessary. What is, however, essential is mutual knowledge of each other's cultural and legal frameworks on the one hand and, on the other hand, a standard interpretation of the Convention's terminology consistent with the different legal frameworks.

12.4.1.2   Covert Policing Methods

The covert policing methods we have analyzed in this study are observation, controlled delivery, infiltration, the use of informers and data collecting, processing and exchange. A crucial question when it comes to policing methods carried out in secret concerns their controllability. In the case of infiltration, for instance, police officers who must mingle so closely with criminals, adopting their ways in order to entrap them, sufficient steps must be taken to ensure an adequate control. Moreover, having representatives of the State engage in such close contact with the criminals they are trying to investigate have great ethical consequences, is highly risky and difficult to control.

In the studied countries, the role of the public prosecutor in the control of these secretive methods is predominant. In the absence of clear regulations, this control is even essential. However, because of this secret character, it is very difficult - even for the public prosecutor - to get a clear view of the methods employed. In this context and because of the discretion this magistrate has in instigating criminal procedures, one can question the degree of control he may exercise. Is it wise to expect such a degree of impartialness of a magistrate charged with the control of both the enquiry and the prosecution? How can a person have the amount of impartiality required to judge its own operation? Moreover, the public prosecutor must rely on police reports in order to be able to take a decision. Police officers may chose to be silent on methods they know are questionable and public prosecutors may be tempted not to ask too many questions. Control is therefore very difficult.

Because the criminality investigated and prosecuted with these methods is not limited to the national borders, these control problems are multiplied when seen in their international context. The absence of an international legal framework renders control illusionary. Indeed, some will argue that the control will be exercised by locally competent authorities, but the above mentioned problems of the controllability of these secretive methods remain evident. In this context, Schengen provides very few answers. Ironically and although reliable statistics on this subject are difficult to obtain, one can imagine that cross-border infiltration operations are more often carried out than cross-border hot pursuits, although the latter has a much more clear basis in international law.

12.4.2 *Final Conclusions*

It must be acknowledged that in general the Schengen regulation of international police cooperation is a unique, original and well-structured international legal instrument. Will the disappearance of border control facilitate illegal trafficking? Criminal organizations have never had great problems with border controls, on the contrary, they have even been advantaged by the existence of borders.

Indeed, borders are there to delimitate the scope of national law and jurisdiction but "have never been a very intelligent means of investigation."[8] The disappearance of border controls has brought about a degree of cooperation between police and judicial authorities never reached before.

In order to optimalize the Schengen framework some basic recommendations have been made, the most important of which have to do with the improvement of mutual knowledge and the setting of national rules in formal statutes. In the covert policing fields, setting norms in formal statutes will have a positive effect on the improving of accessibility and therefore, of the mutual knowlwdge and on the democratic control of the norm. More precisely, one could imagine a harmonized interpretation of the Schengen Convention in areas such as hot pursuit and the meanings to be given to expressions as apprehension, service weapon and self-defence. These harmonized definitions should then be given publicity. In that sense, joint police training programs, joint border region policing teams and a European police academy are all measures that could help Schengen become more succesfull.

It will not be a surprise that some critical remarks must be made. It is likely that the Schengen Information System (like Europol) will almost exclusively be used for the repression of drug trafficking and EC fraud. These are problems which, according to many, could be solved much better by other strategies. A well-considered, gradual decriminalization of drugs seems to be a necessary condition to encounter drug problems and related organized crime, whereas an important part of EC fraud is due to the subsidy system itself and could only be neutralized by rendering subsidy rules less permeable to fraud, or even (partly) abolishing them. Because most of the cross-border exchanges of police data and criminal intelligence will be related to these two types of criminal offences, it is not likely that this order of priority will change in the near future. If such a change of priority were to occur, it would be reasonable to expect an over-capacity of the political - and indeed financial - capacity in the domain of cross-border cooperation in criminal matters.

Concerning the contents of the Schengen Convention, an important subject as the position of the defence and his possibilities to examine and control the international cooperation has been left unmentioned. This forms a strong contrast with the size and the remarkably well-elaborated details of the part of the Convention addressing control, investigation, and prosecution by the police and judicial authorities (almost 90 out of 142 articles). Since in practice it has always been difficult for the defence to develop more than an impression of what has happened in the context of international cooperation, this would have been a good opportunity to improve its position, instead of leaving this entirely to the

---

8   In this sense the former German minister of the interior, W. Schäuble: "*Der Schlagbaum ist kein besonderes intelligentes Fahndungsinstrument.*"

national legislator. If the position of a police officer in international cooperation can be harmonized and improved, why not the position of the defence as well? Regrettably, the absence of a number of rights of the defence in one country, for instance the right to legal counsel, is liable to cause a particular type of forum shopping, where responsible authorities will arrange to have a oerson apprehended in one country rather than in another because of the relative absence of formalities in favour of the defence. Because of the relative difficulty of control of the procedure by the trial judge, this may lead to a loss of quality of the evidence.

Since the Schengen Convention stipulates that a police officer operating in a foreign country must comply with the law of that country, we suppose that practical problems are likely to arise if this law were to differ importantly from the legal system in which he was trained. However, in general the differences found between the five legal systems are rather limited, in number and in size as well as in possible impact on a successful police cooperation.

The most striking and possibly problematic differences may be found among the operational covert policing methods of observation and infiltration. The former may be illustrated by stressing the fact that in Germany and Belgium, technical devices may be used to overhear a conversation in a public place, whereas in France, this is criminalized. As to the latter, we must add that the Schengen Convention does not explicitly address infiltration, but only implicitly refers to it by mentioning controlled delivery. Nevertheless, the differences in regulating this technique may also lead to problematic situations, since France does not allow transports of illicit goods to be accompanied (controlled) by a foreign infiltrator. As a result, a Belgian infiltrator on a transport from Munich via Paris to Brussels will be forced to leave the transport at the German-French border and allowed to join it again at the French-Belgian border. Furthermore, particularly regarding covert methods of policing, the availability of information varied widely from one country to another, which may have resulted in a partly incomplete and outbalanced overview of regulations. Moreover, covert policing methods cause specific problems of controlling and judging what has actually happened.

With respect to overt police powers, differences are far less striking and it is unlikely that they will lead to practical problems. If problems occur during or after the cross-border exercise of overt policing, they will rather be due to other factors. The most important of these factors might be the fact that the combination of authentic texts of the Schengen Convention may lead to significantly different interpretations of police powers. A clear example of this is, that one interpretation will allow a police officer who has apprehended a suspect after a cross-border hot pursuit to carry out a security search, whereas according to another interpretation such a security search could be done only by the locally competent officers.

The second factor which might become a source of practical problems is the variety in police and legal cultures between the countries concerned. This fact, that is likely to also have an catalytic effect on the differences of interpretation, is easily illustrated by the differences in police autonomy and the relation between the police and the judicial and administrative authorities. Other examples worth referring to are the importance attached to statutory legislation and its detailedness, as well as the differences in substantive criminal law, particularly where it concerns moral behaviour.

Furthermore, due to unclear terminology, there is among police officers and police unions a considerable uncertainty of the exact extent of police powers during cross-border cooperation. This leads to a negative influence on the motivation of police officers, particularly in border areas, since they are not confident whether and how they may exercise some of their most basic powers and do not want to put their legal and disciplinary position at stake. This uncertainty and demotivation could be encountered (at least temporarily) if the supervising authorities would inform the police about the interpretations they will use when judging the police activities. In the beginning, the authorities could do so regardless of any interpretation by a judge at all, and after such judgements the interpretation can be adapted if necessary.

Perhaps the most important question regarding the practical value of the Schengen framework for international police cooperation is, whether and how the judicial authorities will judge the results of this cooperation. A central aspect of this question is, how the courts in the countries involved, once they are able to control the events, will judge irregularities during the cooperation, and to which extent this might influence the legality and admissibility of the evidence that was gathered. This question cannot be answered without a thorough study of the respective systems of evaluation of evidence, particularly of evidence collected abroad or by foreign police officers. However, besides the fact that there is no case-law concerning the Schengen provisions yet, such a study would have been too extended to be possible within the context of this project. As was stressed already by various participants to the expert meeting in 1993 (see Chapter 1), this judicial control in court is, both from a practical and from a legal science point of view, so essential that we must recommend strongly that such a research be carried out in the future.

As we have shown in our study, possible differences in interpretation may be eliminated and problems avoided or solved by clearly studying and interpreting the combination of all authentic versions of the treaty and all national legislation and case-law with respect to a police power in an individual case. Nevertheless, the interpretative choices we have made do not have any legal force and may only serve as suggestions. As long as the only judges who will interpret the Schengen Convention will be national judges, there is no guarantee that the provisions of the Convention will be interpreted and applied equally in all participating countries. A harmonized interpretation seems nevertheless in the interest of both the police officers who must work with the Convention and the citizens who may be confronted with its cross-border application. Indeed, the role of the European Court of Human Rights as a common, international judge in criminal matters must not be neglected, but the main task of this body is not to guarantee a harmonized interpretation of police powers but to safeguard a minimum level of protection of human rights.

As we have discussed, the Benelux partners continue stressing that the European Court must be given a role in the Europol Convention, for the sake of a good and harmonized interpretation as well as the protection of individual citizens. Some aspects of the Schengen Convention, particularly the operational police powers on foreign territory and the Schengen Information System, reach far beyond the scope of the Europol Convention. Furthermore, different from the Europol Convention, Schengen is in force already, whereas Europol still functions on the provisory basis of ministerial agreement. Therefore, at this moment a good and harmonized interpretation of the Schengen Convention by an international judicial body is even more urging.

For practical reasons, one could think of a procedure of prejudicial decision by one of the international courts existing within Europe. As soon as the European Court of Justice has been entrusted with Europol affairs, it is preferable that the same court will also be entrusted with the Schengen jurisdiction. Meanwhile, this judicial control could perhaps be exercised by the Benelux Court. Evidently, an international court entrusted with the task of a harmonizing interpretation of an international treaty or convention will have a harmonizing effect. However, this cannot be compared to a complete uniformization of substantial and procedural criminal law. This will only be a gradual and partial harmonization, limited to the interpretation of an international agreement that (as far as operational policing is concerned) contains mainly conflict rules and gives priority to national law by leaving the national legislators a serious margin of discretion.

Index of Comparative Tables

Bibliography

Anderson, M., *Policing the world. Interpol and the Politics of International Police Co-operation*; Clarendon Press, Oxford, 1989.
- & Den Boer, M., (eds.), *European police co-operation*, University of Edinburgh, Department of Politics, Edinburgh, 1992.
- & Den Boer, M., (eds.), *Policing across National Boundaries*, Pinter, London/New York, 1994.
Arnou, L., *Strafrechtspleging voor de 21e eeuw*; in: R.W. 1990/1991, pp. 969-977.
Arnou, P., *Het fouilleren van een persoon en het doorzoeken van zijn bagage en/of zijn voertuig*; in: Pan. 1982, pp. 123-140.

Baldwin-Edwards, M. & Habenton, B., *Will SIS be Europe's 'Big Brother'?*; in: Anderson & Den Boer, 1994, pp. 137-157.
Bandisch, G., *Zum Entwurf eines Kriminalitätsbekämpfungsgesetzes der Fraktionen der CDU/CSU und FDP vom 4.1.1994*, in: StV 1994, pp. 153-159.
Bäumler, H., *Polizeiliche Informationsverarbeitung*; in: Lisken/Denninger, 1992, pp. 501-618.
Benyon, J., Turnbull, L., Willis, A., Woodward, R. & Beck, A., *Police Co-operation in Europe: An Investigation*; Centre for the Study of Public Order, Leicester, 1993.
Berkmoes, H., *Georganiseerde criminaliteit in België*; in: Revue van de Rijkswacht 1994-128, pp. 4-11.
Bevers, H., *Police Observation and the 1990 Schengen Convention*; in: EJCPR 1993-4, pp. 83-107.
- *Regionalization. The Dutch Police and their Reorganization*; in: The Police Journal 1994, pp. 326-334 (1994a).
- *The Role of the Police in the Dutch Legal System*; in: Groenhuijsen & Veldt, 1995, pp. 45-59.
- & Joubert, C., *Politiële samenwerking in Europa*, Gouda Quint/Kluwer Rechtswetenschappen, Arnhem/Antwerpen, 1994.
Blaauw, J.A., *Infiltratie als nieuw specialisme: aanvaardbaar of hellend vlak?*, in: APB 1985, pp. 243-253.
Blankenburg, E. & Bruinsma, F., *Dutch Legal Culture*; Kluwer, Deventer, 2nd ed. 1994.
Blom, T. & Mevis, P., *Ziende blind? Een beschouwing over inkijkoperaties*; in: DD 25 (1995), pp. 5-27.

Blonk, G.N.M., Fijnaut, C.J.C.F. & De Kerf, E.L.A.M. (eds.), *Grensverleggende recherche*; Van den Brink, Lochem, 1990.

Blontrock, P. & De Hert, P., *Telefoontap: Tournet, Peureau, Derrien, Huvig, Kruslin et les autres* in: R.W. 1991/1992, pp. 865-871.

Boek, J.L.M., *Organisatie, functie en bevoegdheden van politie in Nederland. Juridische beschouwingen over het politiebestel en het politiebedrijf in historisch perspectief*, Kluwer/Gouda Quint, Antwerpen/Arnhem, 1995.

Boeles, P., *Schengen and the rule of law*; in: Meijers *et al.*, 1991, pp. 135-146.
   - *Data Exchange, Privacy and Legal Protection; Especially Regarding Aliens*; in: Schermers *et al.*, 1993, pp. 52-57.

Bolten, J.J., *From Schengen to Dublin: The new frontiers of refugee law*; in: Meijers *et al.*, 1991, pp. 8-36.

Bönninghaus, H., *Die polizeiliche Zusammenarbeit im Dreiländereck*; in: Fijnaut, 1992a, pp. 201-204.

Boon, K., Kaminski, D., Brion, F. & Cappelle, J., *Opsporingsdiensten bij de gemeentepolitie; een studie naar de gerechtelijke opdrachten van de gemeentepolitie*, Vanden Broele, Brugge, 1991, (also published in French).

Borsboom, A. & Spronken, T., *Geruchtmakende zaken. Politie hört mit*, in: Van Almelo, L. *et al.* (eds.), *Crimineel Jaarboek 1993*, pp. 157-169.

Bosly, H.-D. & Vandermeersch, D., *La loi belge du 30 juin 1994 relative à la potection de la vie privée contre les écoutes, la prise de connaissance et l'enregistrement de communications et de télécommunications privées*; in: RDP 1995, pp. 301-343.

Bossink, I., Draijer, H., Graumans, G., Hoeven, G. van & Zorko, P., *NPA-studenten onderzochten functioneren hulpofficier*; in: APB 1986, pp. 155-161.

Böttger, A., & Pfeiffer, Chr., *Der Lauschangriff in den USA und in Deutschland*, in: ZRP 1994, pp. 7-17.

Bourdoux, G.L. & De Valkeneer, C., *La loi sur la fonction de police*; Larcier, Bruxelles, 1993.
   -, De Raedt, E., Duchatel, A. & Seurynck, J., *De wet op het politieambt*; in: Revue van de Rijkswacht, 1995-130, pp. 11-14.
   - & Brammertz, S., *L'Usage de la force et des armes à feu par le fonctionnaires de police dans l'Eurégio Meuse-Rhin*, in: RDP 1995, pp. 344-408.

Boyer, J., *Présentation de la loi n. 93-2 du 4 janvier 1993 portant réforme de la procédure pénale*; in: La Semaine Juridique, February 10, 1993, p. 6.

Brammertz, S., De Vreese, S. & Thys, J., *Internationale Politiesamenwerking*; Politeia, Brussel, 1993 (also published in French).

Brants, C & Field, S., *Participation Rights and Proactive Policing. Convergence and drift in European criminal process*; Kluwer, Deventer, 1995.

Bresler, F., *Interpol*, M & P Uitgeverij, Weert, 1992.

Bruggeman, W., *Naar een vernieuwde statistiek voor de reguliere politiediensten in België*; Politeia, Brussel, 1992.
   - *Rubriek Opsporing en politie*, in: Pan. 1995, pp. 239-240 (1995a).

- *Rubriek Opsporing en politie*, in: Pan. 1995, pp. 451-452 (1995b).
- & De Lentdecker, J., *Gebruik van geweld & wapens door de politie-diensten*; in: Pan. 1987, pp. 399-424.

Brun, H. & Tremblay, G., *Droit constitutionnel*, Les Éditions Yvon Blais, Inc., Cowansville, 1985.

Buisson, J., *L'acte de police*; Thèse, Lyon, 1988.

Burke, J., *Jowitt's Dictionary of English Law*, Sweet & Maxwell, London 1977.

Buruma, Y., *EC Law and the National Enformcement Agencies*, in: Groenhuijsen & Veldt, 1995 p. 73-84.

Busch, H., *Von Interpol zu TREVI*; in: Bürgerrechte und Polizei 1988-2, pp. 38-55.
- *Grenzenlose Polizei? Neue Grenzen und polizeiliche Zusammenarbeit in Europa*; Westfälisches Dampfboot, Münster, 1995.

Buytaert, M., *Bevoegdheid opstellen processen-verbaal*; in: De Politieofficier 1988-8, pp. 41-49 (followed by the French version).

Caesar, P., *Das Gesetz gegen die organisierte Kriminalität - eine unendliche Geschichte?* in: ZRP 1991, pp. 241-246.

Cameron-Waller, S., *Interpol's Point of View*; in: Pauly, 1993, pp. 101-110.

Castberg, F., *The European Convention on Human Rights*, Leyden, 1974.

Claus, F., *Grenzen verleggen. Juridische beletselen voor politiële beleidssamenwerking tussen Nederland en België*; Universitaire Pers, Maastricht, 1995.

Cleiren, C.P.M. *De openheid van de wet, de geslotenheid van het recht*, Gouda Quint, Arnhem, 1992.

Cohen-Jonathan, G., *Respect for Private and Family Life*, in: Macdonald *et al.*, 1993, pp. 405-444.

Corstens, G.J.M., (red.), *Rapporten herijking strafvordering 1989-1992*, Gouda Quint, Arnhem, 1993.
- *Inbreken in de rechtsstaat*; in: NJB 1994, pp. 497-498 (1994a).
- *Rapport over in Frankrijk gebezigde opsporingsmethoden met betrekking tot georganiseerde criminaliteit*; in: Appendix 4 to Van Traa, 1994 (1994b).
- *Het Nederlandse Strafprocesrecht*, Gouda Quint, Arnhem, 2nd ed. 1995.
- & Roording, J.F.L., *L'instruction préparatoire aux Pays-Bas*, in: Rev. sc. crim. 1995, pp. 247-255.

Coveliers, H., *Twee jaar Bendecommissie. Een schimmengevecht*; Hadewijch, Antwerpen/Baarn, 1992.

Creifelds, C. & Meyer-Goßner, L. (eds.), *Rechtswörterbuch*, C.H. Beck, München, 1988.

Curtin, D. & Meijers, H., *The Principle of Open Government in Schengen and the Euroepan Union: Democratic Retrogression?*; in: CMLR 1995, pp. 391-442.

D'Haenens, J., *Belgisch strafprocesrecht*; E. Story-Scientia, Gent, 1985.
- & De Ruyver, B. (eds.), *Schengen en de praktijk*; Mys & Breesch, Gent, 1992.

D'Haese, Chr., *De regeling van de fouillering en de identiteitscontrole*; in: Fijnaut & Hutsebaut, 1993, pp. 147-170.

Daniels, B.P., *Veiligheidssituatie in België*; in: TvP 1989, pp. 445-451.

Danwitz, K.-S. von, *Anmerkungen zu einem Irrweg in der Bekämpfung der Drogenkriminalität*, in: StV 1995, pp. 431-437.

Dautert, U., *Zulässigkeit verdeckter Ermittlungen (Rechtsgrundlagen, Gesetzesinitiativen)*; in: *Schlußbericht über das Seminar Verdeckte Ermittlungen - Rechtliche und taktische Probleme*; Polizei-Führungsakademie, Münster, 1989, pp. 53-74.

De Doelder, H. & Mul, V. (eds.), *samenwerking baat. Amerikaans-Nederlandse strafrechtelijke samenwerking*; Vermande, Lelystad, 1994.

De Doelder, H., Foqué, R.M.G.E., Gerding, R.A.F. & Van Russen Groen, P.M., *Taak en functioneren van het OM*; Sanders Instituut/Gouda Quint, Rotterdam/Arnhem, 1994.

De Feo, M.A., *The US Experience in Federal Policing, a Model for Europe?* in: DD 24 (1994), pp. 475-484.

De Hert, P., *Het verzamelen en gebruiken van visuele informatie: foto's, videosurveille en verkeersradars*; in: Politeia, 1994-8, pp. 8-18.
- & Vanderborght, J., *Magistraten met aanleg voor politiewerk: de nationale magistraten*; in: Vigiles - Tijdschrift voor Politierecht, 1996-1, pp. 1-19.

De Nauw, A., *De toelaatbaarheid van de politiële infiltratie in België*; in: Enschedé, Ch.J. et al., *Naar eer en geweten. Remmelink-bundel*; Gouda Quint, Arnhem, 1987, pp. 443-454.
- *De beoordelingsruimte van de politie in het strafprocesrecht*; in: R.W. 1990/1991, pp. 65-74.
- *De opsporing en de vaststellingsbevoegdheid van de gerechtelijke politie en de recente rechtspraak van het Hof van Cassatie*; in: *Liber Amicorum Marc Châtel*; Kluwer, Antwerpen, 1991, pp. 109-116.

De Ruyver, B., *Politie, veiligheid en justitie in het federaal regeringsprogram*; in: Politeia 1995-7, pp. 14-16.
- & Hutsebaut, F., *De onverminderde actualiteitswaarde van de discussie over de doodstraf*; in: Pan. 1995, pp. 365-368.

De Schutter, B., *Bij het in werking treden van het Beneluxverdrag aangaande uitlevering en rechtshulp in strafzaken*; in: R.W. 1967/1968, pp. 1937-1946.
-, De Keyser, K., Brison, F. & Gutwirth, S., *De Belgische privacy-wetgeving, een eerste analyse*; in: R.W. 1992/1993, pp. 1145-1154.
- & De Hert, P., *Het politioneel gebruik van informatie en de Pricaywet*; in: Politeia 1994-6, pp. 7-14.

De Valkeneer, C., *Le droit de la police. La loi, l'institution et la société*; De Boeck Université, Brussel, 1991.
- & Winants, A., *L'arrestation*; in: Dejemeppe, 1992, pp. 43-88.

De Wilde, L., *Anonimiteit in het strafproces*; in: De Nauw, A., D'Haenens, J. & Storme, M., *Actuele problemen van strafrecht (XIVe Postuniversitaire cyclus*

W. Delva 1987-1988); Kluwer/Gouda Quint, Antwerpen/Arnhem, 1988, pp. 58-86.

De Wit, L., *Interimadvies Infiltratie; rapport van de werkgroep De Wit*, 1994.

Declerq, R., *Beginselen van Strafrechtspleging*; Kluwer Rechtswetenschappen België, Deurne, 1994.

- & Verstraeten, R. (eds.), *Voorlopige hechtenis. De Wet van 20 juli 1990*; Acco, Leuven, 1991.

Decocq, A., Montreuil, J. & Buisson, J., *Le droit de la police*; Litec, Paris, 1991.

Dejemeppe, B. (ed.), *La détention préventive*; Maison Larcier, Brussel, 1992.

Delmas-Marty, M. (pres.), *La mise en état des affaires pénales, rapports de la Commission justice pénale et droits de l'homme (Commission Delmas-Marty)*; La Documentation Française, Paris 1991.

Demanet, G., *Quelques problèmes pratiques générés par la loi du 5 août 1992 sur la fonction de police*, in: RDP 1994, pp. 140-158.

Den Boer, M., *Schengen: Intergovernmental Scenario for European Police Co-operation*, in: Working Paper Series "A System of European Police Co-operation after 1992" Department of Politics, University of Edinburgh, Edinburgh, 1991.

Den Boer, M., *Police cooperation in the TEU: Tiger in a Trojan Horse?* in: CMLR 1995, pp. 555-578.

Denis, G., *L'enquête préliminaire. Étude théorique et pratique*; Police-Revue, 1974.

Denis, F., *Voor een modern en efficiënt veiligheidsbeleid en veiligheidssysteem*; in: Denis, F. et al., *De politiediensten in België. Vier commentaren op het rapport van Team Consult*; Kluwer/Gouda Quint, Antwerpen/Arnhem, 1989, pp. 1-22.

Denninger, E., *Polizeiaufgaben*, in: Lisken/Denninger, 1992, pp. 169-170.

Deruyck, F., *De wet van 11 februari 1991 tot invoeging van een artikel 88bis in het Wetboek van Strafvordering betreffende het opsporen van telefonische mededelingen*, in: R.W. 1991/1992, pp. 10-15.

Diedcrich, F., *La coopération policière*; in: Pauly, 1994, pp. 69-88.

Dierkens, R., Bruggeman, R., De Ruyver B. en Zanders, P., *Grensoverschrijdende criminaliteit*, Rijksuniversiteit Gent, Gent, 1991.

Doorenbos, D.R. & Verweij, R.J., *Hercodificatie Wetboek van Strafvordering: Tijd voor een integrale herziening?*; Ars Aequi Libri, Nijmegen, 1991.

Drews/Wacke/Vogel/Martens: Vogel, K. & Martens, W., *Gefahrenabwehr*; Carl Heymanns Verlag KG, Köln, 1985.

Dreher, E. & Tröndle, H., *Strafgesetzbuch und Nebengesetze*; C.H. Beck'sche Verlagsbuchhandlung, München, 46th ed. 1993.

Dworkin, R., *Law's Empire*, Fontana Press, London, 1986.

EC Commission (ed.), *The system of administrative and penal sanctions in the member states of the European Communities*, Brussels/Luxembourg, 1994 (bilingual edition).

Elzinga, D.J., Van Rest, P.H.S. & De Valk, J, *Het Nederlandse politierecht*; W.E.J. Tjeenk Willink, Zwolle, 1995.

Enschedé, Ch.J. *Een uniform Europees strafrecht? Over grenzen en nationale identiteit*; Gouda Quint, Arnhem, 1990 (reprint of *Model Penal Code for Europe*, Amsterdam, 1971).

Favoreu, L. & Philip, L., *Les grandes décisions du conseil constitutionnel*, Sirey, Paris, 1991.

Fennell, P., Harding, C., Jörg, N. & Swart, B. (eds.), *Criminal Justice in Europe - Comparative Study*; Clarendon Press, Oxford, 1995.

Fijnaut, C.J.C.F., *De zaak François, Beschouwingen naar aanleiding van het vonnis* Kluwer, Antwerpen, 1983.
   - *De internationalisering van de opsporing in westelijk Europa*; in: Pan. 1987, pp. 300-320 (1987a).
   - *De toelating van raadslieden tot het politieverhoor*; Kluwer/Gouda Quint, Antwerpen/Arnhem, 1987 (1987b).
   - *De raadsman (al dan niet) bij het politieverhoor; een overzicht van de situatie op het Westeuropese vasteland*, in: Fijnaut & Blonk, 1988, pp. 31-58.
   - *De politionele vrijheidsbeneming in het kader van het vooronderzoek in strafzaken. Een rechtsvergelijkende beschouwing in het licht van het EVRM* in: Declerq & Verstraeten, 1991, pp. 49-87 (1991a).
   - *De regeling van de politiële samenwerking: implicaties voor de politie in Nederland*; in: DD 21 (1991), pp. 771-781 (1991b).
   - *Observatie en infiltratie, toe aan een wettelijke regeling* in: Doorenbos, D.R. & Verweij, R.J. (eds.), *Hercodificatie Wetboek van Strafvordering: Tijd voor een integrale herziening?* Ars Aequi Libri, 1991, pp. 69-85 (1991c).
   - (ed.), *De reguliere politiediensten in België en Nederland; hun reorganisatie en onderlinge samenwerking*; Kluwer/Gouda Quint, Deurne/Arnhem, 1992 (1992a).
   - *Naar een 'Gemeenschap-pelijke' regeling van de politiële samenwerking en de justitiële rechtshulp*; in: Fijnaut et al., 1992, pp. 89-117 (1992b).
   - *De normering van het informatieve vooronderzoek in constitutioneel perspectief*; Kluwer, Deventer, 1994 (1994a).
   - *International Policing in Europe: Present and Future*; in: ELR 1994, pp. 599-619 (1994b).
   - *Vergelijkende politiestudies als voorwaarde voor behoorlijke internationale samenwerking*; in: *Internationalisering door Grenzeloze Samenwerking* Transpol/Koninklijke Vermande, Lelystad 1994, pp. 95-100 (1994c).
   - *Een kleine geschiedenis van de huidige organisatie van het Belgische politiewezen*; Kluwer/Gouda Quint, Antwerpen/Arnhem, 1995.
   - & Kolthoff, E. (eds.), *Afschaffing van het gerechtelijk vooronderzoek*; Gouda Quint, Arnhem, 1991.

-, Stuyck, J. & Wytinck, P. (eds.), *Schengen: Proeftuin voor de Europese Gemeenschap?*; Kluwer/Gouda Quint, Deurne/Arnhem, 1992.

- & Blonk, G.N.M. (eds.), *De advocaat bij het politieverhoor*; Van den Brink/Gouda Quint, Lochem/Arnhem, 1988.

- & Hermans (eds.), *Police Co-operation in Europe: Lectures t the International Symposium on Surveillance*; Van den Brink, Lochem, 1987.

- & Hutsebaut, F. (eds.), *De nieuwe politiewetgeving in België*; Kluwer/Gouda Quint, Antwerpen/Arnhem, 1993.

- & J. Jacobs (eds.), *Organized Crime and its Containment*, Kluwer, Deventer/Boston, 1991.

- & Marx, G.T., *Undercover. Police Surveillance in Comparative Perspective*; Kluwer Law International, The Hague/London/Boston, 1995 (1995a).

- & Marx, G.T., *Introduction: The Normalization of Undercover Policing in the West: Historical and Comtemporary Perspectives*; in: Fijnaut & Marx, 1995a, pp. 1-27 (1995b).

Fischer, T., *Tatprovozierendes Verhalten als polizeiliche Ermittlungsmaßnahme*; in: NStZ 1992, pp. 7-13.

Fiselier, J., Gunther Moor, L. & Tak, P. (eds.), *De staat van justitite. Criminaliteit en strafrechtelijk bedrijf: een stand van zaken*, SUN, Nijmegen, 1992.

Florijn, N.A., *Leidraad voor zinvolle rechtsvergelijking* CDWO-SAW, Den Haag, 1994.

Fode, H., *Co-operation on Law Enforcement, Criminal Justice and Legislation in Europe; Nordic Experience*; in: Schermers *et al.*, 1993, pp. 61-69.

Franchimont, M. (pres.), *Commissie strafprocesrecht; verslag van de commissie-Franchimont*; Faculté de Droit de Liège/Maklu, Liège/Antwerpen, 1994.

Fransen, H., *Enkele beschouwingen over de gerechtelijke politietaak van de rijkswacht*; in: Pan. 1986, pp. 8-36.

Fransen, J.H., *Grensoverschrijdende recherche: een visie vanuit de Euregio*; in: Blonk *et al.*, 1990, pp. 158-162.

Frielink, P.M. *Infiltratie in het strafrecht*, Kluwer/Gouda Quint, Antwerpen/Arnhem, 1990.

- *Het openbaar ministerie*; in: Fiselier *et al.*, 1992, pp. 93-104.

Gallas, A., *Interpol*; in: Bernhardt, R. (ed.), *Encyclopedia of Public International Law, Instalment 1*, North Holland, Amsterdam, 1981, pp. 187-188.

Garé, D., *Het onmiddelijkheidsbeginsel in het Nederlandse strafproces*, Gouda Quint, Arnhem, 1994.

Geerits, M., *Schieten op vluchtende personen en voertuigen*; in: De Politieofficier 1987-7, pp. 51-64 (followed by the French version).

Glorie, J., *De nieuwe Gemeentewet in de Praktijk. De Gemeentepolitie; Deel 1: Organisatie en opdrachten; Deel 2: Personeel - diverse bepalingen*; Vanden Broele, Brugge, 1991 (loose-leaf).

Gössner, R., *Die neue Polizei?* in: Neue Kriminalpolitik, 1992-4, p. 19.

Götz, V., *Allgemeines Polizei- und Ordnungsrecht*; Vandenhoeck & Ruprecht, Göttingen, 10e druk 1991.

Groenendijk, C.A., *Three questions about Free Movement of Persons and Democracy in Europe*; in: Schermers *et al.*, 1993, pp. 391-402.

Groenhuijsen, M.S. & Veldt, M.I. (eds.), *The Dutch Approach in Tackling EC Fraud*, Kluwer, The Hague/London/Boston, 1995.

Gropp, W. (ed.), *Besondere Ermittlungsmaßnahmen zur Bekämpfung der Organisierten Kriminalität*; Max Planck Institut, Freiburg im Breisgau, 1993 (1993a).

- *Methods of Investigation for Combatting Organized Crime* in: (1993) 1, Eur.J. Crime Cr.L. Cr.J., pp. 20-39 (1993b).

Grützner, H. & Pötz, P.-G. (eds.), *Internationaler Rechtshilfeverkehr in Strafsachen. Die für die Rechtsbeziehungen der Bundesrepublik Deutschland mit dem Ausland in Strafsachen maßgeblichen Bestimmungen*; R. v. Decker, Heidelberg (loose-leaf).

Gutwirth, P. *Nineteen Ninety-Five! Hoog tijd om cameratoezicht te beperken;* in: R & K 1995, pp. 3-11.

Haentjens, R.C.P., *Schets van het Nederlandse kleine rechtshulprecht in strafzaken*, Gouda Quint, Arnhem, 1992.

Hart, H.L.A., *The concept of law*, Oxford 1961.

Harteveld, A.E., Keulen, B.F. & Krabbe, H.G.M., *Het EVRM en het Nederlandse Strafprocesrecht*, Wolters-Noordhoff, Groningen, 1992.

Heimans, D., *Internationale uitwisseling van politieinformatie: het grensvlak tussen rechtshulp en privacybescherming*; in: DD (24) 1994, pp. 125-142.

Heise, C., Tegtmeyer, H. & Braun, K.-H., *Polizeigesetz Nordrhein-Westfalen mit Erläuterungen*; Richard Boorberg Verlag, Stuttgart/München/Hannover, 7th ed. 1990.

Helsdingen, R., *The Development of Surveillance within the Dutch Police*; in Fijnaut & Hermans, 1987, pp. 22-25.

Hendriks, L.E.M., Klifman, J.H., Mols, G.P.M.F., De Roos, Th.A. & Wöretshofer, J., *Hoofdstukken strafprocesrecht*; Samson H.D. Tjeenk Willink, Alphen aan den Rijn, 1992.

Heringa, A.W., *Belgische identificatieplicht en artikel 8 EVRM*; in: NJCM-Bulletin 1993, pp. 337-341.

Hermann, I., *Darum geht es! Europol*; in: Der Kriminalist 1988, pp. 226-228.

Hilger, H., *Neues Strafverfahrensrecht durch das OrgKG*, in: NStZ 1992, pp. 457-463 and 523-526.

Hirsch-Ballin, E.M.H., *Vorming Europese politie is nog ver weg*; in: Stcrt. 1990-69, p. 1.

Hofe, G., *Abschied vom weitem Wohnungsbegriff des Art. GG?* in: ZRP 1995, pp. 169-171.

Hofman, J.A., *Vertrouwelijke communicatie*, diss. VU, Amsterdam, 1995 (commercial edition: Kluwer, Deventer, 1995).

Hofstede, G., *Culture's consequences: international differences in work-related values*; Sage Publications, Beverly Hills/London, 1980.

-, Van Twuyver, M., Kapp, B., De Vries, H., Faure, M., Claus, F. & Van der Wel, J., *Grensoverschrijdende politiesamenwerking tussen België, Duitsland en Nederland met speciale aandacht voor de Euregio Maas-Rijn*; Universitaire Pers, Maastricht, 1993.

Hofstee, E.J. & Schalken, T.M., *Strafrecht binnen het koninkrijk*, Gouda Quint, Arnhem, 1991.

Holsters, D., *Bewijsmiddelen in strafzaken*; in: *Strafrecht en strafvordering, commentaar met overzicht van rechtspraak en rechtsleer*; Kluwer, Antwerpen (loose-leaf).

Holvast, J. & Mosshammer, A., *Identificatieplicht en de technocratische samenleving*; in: Holvast, J. & Mosshammer, A., *Identificatieplicht. Het baat niet, maar het schaadt wel*; Jan van Arkel, Utrecht, 1993, pp. 63-73.

Hoogenboom, T., *Free movement of non-EC nationals, Schengen and beyond*; in: Meijers *et al.*, 1991, pp. 74-95.

Hoogenboom, A.B., *Het Politiecomplex. Over de samenwerking tussen politie, bijzondere opsporingsdiensten en particuliere recherche*; Gouda Quint/Kluwer, Arnhem/Antwerpen, 1994.

Hubin, J., *Considerations prospectives sur la loi du 5 août 1992 sur la fonction de police*, in: RDP 1994, pp. 130-139.

Huizing, B., *Werkplek*; in: Politie Magazine, 1994-10, p. 17.

Hund, H., *Polizeiliches Effektivitätsdenken contra Rechtsstaat*, in: ZRP 1991, pp. 463-467.

- *Der Einsatz technischer Mittel in Wohnungen*; in: ZRP 1995, pp. 334-338.

Hutsebaut, F., *Het onrechtmatig verkregen bewijs en zijn gevolgen*; in: Dupont, L. & Spriet, B., *Strafrecht voor rechtspractici IV*; Acco, Leuven/Amersfoort, 1991, pp. 47-94.

- *De Wet op het politieambt: naar een autonoom politierecht?* in: Fijnaut & Hutsebaut, 1993, pp. 91-124.

Huybrechts, L., *De "hot pursuit" van de gemeentepolitie*, in: R.W. 1988/1989, pp. 331-333.

- *Het gerechtelijk afluisteren in het Belgisch recht na de nieuwe Afluisterwet*; in: Pan. 1995, pp. 41-57.

Jammes, J.R.P., *European Insights; Effective Policing: The French Gendarmerie*; M.C.B. Publications, 1982.

Jansen, P., *Overzicht van de recente hervormingen in het Franse strafproces*, in: Pan. 1994, pp. 122-138.

Jessurun d'Oliveira, H.U., *Fortress Europe and (Extra-Communitarian) Refugees: Cooperation in Sealing Off the External Borders*; in: Schermers *et al.*, 1993, pp. 166-182.

- *Expanding External and Shrinking Internal Borders: Europe's Defence Mechanisms in the Areas of Free Movement, Immigration and Asylum*; in: O'Keeffe & Twomey, 1994, pp. 261-278.

Jörg, N. & Kelk, C., *Strafrecht met mate*, Samson H.D. Tjeenk Willink, Alphen aan de Rijn, 1992.

Joubert, C.M., *Nieuwe rechten van de verdachte tijdens de garde à vue in de Code de procédure pénale: een overzicht van de herziening van de Franse strafvordering*, in: DD 24 (1994), pp. 248-271.

Kaiser, G. & H.-J. Albrecht (eds.), *Crime and Criminal Policy in Europe*, Freiburg, 1990.

Keraudren, P., *Réticences et obstacles français face à Schengen: la logique de la politique de sécurité*; in: Pauly, 1994, pp. 123-144.

Keyser-Ringnalda, L.F., *European Integration with regard to the Confiscation of the Proceeds of Crime*; in: ELR 1992, pp. 499-515.

- *Boef en buit. De ontneming van wederrechtelijk verkregen vermogen*; Gouda Quint, Arnhem, 1994.

King, M., *Policing refugees and asylum seekers in 'greater Europe': towards a reconceptualisation of control*; in: Anderson & Den Boer, 1994, pp. 69-84.

Kleinknecht/Meyer-Goßner: Meyer-Goßner, L., *Strafprozeßordnung*, C.H. Beck'sche Verlagsbuchhandlung, München, 42nd ed. 1995.

Klerks, P, *Covert Policing in The Netherlands*; in: Fijnaut & Marx, 1995a, pp. 103-140.

Klesczewski, D., *Das Auskunftsersuchen an die Post: die wohlfeile Dauerkontrolle von Fernmeldeanschlüssen?*, in: StV 1993, pp. 382-389.

Klip, A., *Extraterritoriale strafvordering*; in: DD 25 (1995), pp. 1056-1078.

Kniesel, M., *Vorbeugende Bekämpfung von Straftaten im juristischen Meinungsstreit - eine unendliche Geschichte*, in: ZRP 1992, pp. 164-167.

Knoester, J.A.W., *De candid camera van Crime Time. De verborgen camara van Crime Time in een juridisch zoeklicht*; in: AAe 1994, pp. 564-569.

Koopmans, T. *Understanding political systems: A comment on methods of comparative research;* in: Georgia Journal of International and Comparative Law 1986, pp. 261-269.

Korff, D., *The Schengen Information System: also a question of data protection*; in: Mols, 1990b, pp. 67-96.

- (ed.), *Data protection law in practice in the European Union*; Federation of European Direct Marketing, 1993.

Körner, H.H., *Betäubungsmittelgesetz*, C.H. Beck'sche Verlagsbuchhandlung, München, 1985.

Körner, H. H., *Staatsanwaltschaft und Kriminalpolizei*; in: Kriminalistik 1992, pp. 130-135.

Kramer, B., *Videoaufnahmen und andere Eingriffe in das Allgemeine Persönlichkeitsrecht auf der Grundlage des § 163 StPO?* in: NJW 1992, pp. 2732-2738.

Kruijtbosch, E.D.J., *Benelux Experiences in the Abolition of Border Controls*; in: Schermers *et al.*, 1993, pp. 31-38.

Kruse, G., *Bundesrepublik Deutschland*; in: Gropp, 1993a, pp. 105-209.

Kühne, H.-H., *Verdacht*; in: Ulsamer, G. (ed.), *Lexikon des Rechts: Strafrecht/Strafverfahrensrecht*; Hermann Luchterhand Verlag, Neuwied, 1989, pp. 971-972.

    - *Germany*; in: Van den Wyngaert, 1993a, pp. 137-162.

Kuijvenhoven, A., *Europese politiekorpsen vergeleken*; in: TvP 1990, pp. 335-341.

Lasalle, J.-Y., *Enquête préliminaire, juris-classeur procédure pénale, art. 75-78 CPP, commentaires*; Paris, 1990.

Le Jeune, P., *La coopération policière européenne contre le terrorisme*; Bruylant, Bruxelles, 1992.

Leclerc, H., *Les limites de la liberté de la preuve. Aspects actuels en France*; Rev. sc. crim. 1992, pp. 15-29.

Lemmens, P., *De verwerking van persoonsgegevens door politiediensten en de eerbiediging van de persoonlijke levenssfeer*; in: *Liber Amicorum Jules D'Haenens*, Mys & Breesch, Gent 1993, pp. 205-218.

Lensing, J.A.W., *Het verhoor in strafzaken*; Gouda Quint, Arnhem, 1988.

    - *The Federalization of Europe: Towards a Federal System of Criminal Justice*; in: (1993) 1 Eur.J. Crime Cr.L. Cr.J., pp. 212-229.

Lesch, H.H., *Soll die Begehung milieutypischer Straftaten durch verdeckte Ermittler erlaubt werden?* in: StV 1993, pp. 94-97.

Lévy, R., *Du suspect au coupable: Le travail de police judiciaire*, Éditions Médecine et Hygiène, Méridiens Klincksieck, 1987.

Lisken/Caesar: Lisken, H., *Plädoyer gegen den großen Lauschangriff (ZRP-Rechtsgespräch mit Peter Caesar)*, in: ZRP 1993, pp. 67-69.

    - & Denninger, E. (eds.), *Handbuch des Polizeirechts*; C.H. Beck'sche Verlagsbuchhandlung, München, 1992.

Lorenz, F.L. *Frankreich*, in: Gropp, 1993a, pp. 301-363.

Löwe/Rosenberg: Rieß, P. (ed.), *Die Strafprozeßordnung und das Gerichtsverfassungsgezetz - Großkommentar*; Walter de Gruyter, Berlin/New York, 1989.

Luypaers, P., *De nieuwe regeling van het gebruik van geweld en (vuur)wapens*; in: Fijnaut & Hutsebaut, 1993, pp. 251-268.

Macdonald, R.St.J., *The Margin of Appreciation*, in: MacDonald *et al.*, 1993, pp. 83-124.

    - Matscher, F. & Petzold, H. (eds.), *The European System for the Protection of Human Rights*; Martinus Nijhoff Publishers, Dordrecht/Boston/London 1993.

Machielse, A.J.M., *Noodweer in het strafrecht*; Stichting Onderzoek Recht en Beleid, Amsterdam, 1986.

Mangelaars, G.A.H., *Internationale politiesamenwerking door middel van gegevensuitwisseling*; Katholieke Universiteit, Nijmegen, 1992.

Mann, T. & Müller, R.-G., *Präventiver Lauschangriff via Telefon?*; in: ZRP 1995, pp. 180-185.

Manual of the Council of Europe, Stevens & Sons Limited, London, 1970.

Maring, R.B., *Achtervolgen en aanhouden over de grens*; in: DD 25 (1995), pp. 222-232.

Marx, G.T., *Undercover: Police Surveillance in America*, University of California Press, Beverley Hills/Los Angeles/London, 1988.

Meertens, C., *Das Gesetz gegen die organisierte Kriminalität, eine unerträgliche Geschichte!* in: ZRP 1992, p. 205-208.

Meijers, H. *Schengen: Introduction*; in: Meijers *et al.*, 1991, pp. 1-7.
- *et al.*, *Schengen. Internationalisation of central chapters of the law on aliens, refugees, privacy, security and the police*; W.E.J. Tjeenk Willink/-Kluwer Law and Taxation, Zwolle/Deventer, 1991.

Melai: Groenhuijsen, M.S. (ed.), *Het Wetboek van Strafvordering*; Gouda Quint, Arnhem (loose-leaf).

Metzner, M, *Polizei und Legalitätsprinzip - Neue Gedanken zum alten Thema*; in: Die Polizei 1992-3, pp. 64-66.

Meyzonnier, Patrice, *Les forces de police dans l'Union Européenne*, L'Harmattan, Paris, 1994.

Middelburg, B. & Van Es, K., *Operatie Delta; hoe de drugsmafia het IRT opblies*, Veen, Amsterdam, 1994.

Minkenhof/Reijntjes: Reijntjes, J.M. (ed.), *De Nederlandse Strafvordering*; Gouda Quint, Arnhem, 1990.

Mols, G.P.M.F., *Onderzoek van kleding en lichaam*; in: Mols, G.P.M.F. (ed.), *Justitieel onderzoek aan en in het lichaam*; Kluwer, Deventer, 1990 (1990a)
- (ed.), *Dissonanten bij het akkoord van Schengen*; Kluwer, Deventer, 1990 (1990b).
- *Toezicht op interstatelijke politiesamenwerking; een aanzet voor internationale controle*; in: JV 1995-1, pp. 84-93.
- & Spronken, T.N.B.M., *Europa 1992, een moeras voor verdachte en verdediging?* in: Mols, 1990b, pp. 36-59.

Montreuil, J., *Crimes et délits flagrants, enquête de police*; in: Juris-classeur Procédure pénale, Fascicule 1, 3 (1982), updated 1989.

Moréas, G., *Un flic de l'intérieur*; Éditions Stock/Édition numéro 1, Paris, 1985.

Morié, R., Murck, M. & Schulte, R. (eds.), *Auf dem Weg zu einer europäischen Polizei. Rahmenbedingungen, Aufgaben und berufliches Selbstverständnis*; Richard Boorberg Verlag, Stuttgart/München/Hannover/Berlin/Weimar, 1992.

Mulder, C.F. & Rüter, C.F., *Het Scandinavische model; samenwerken met behoud van identiteit*; in: JV 1995-1, pp. 20-36.

Nadelmann, E.A., *Cops Across Borders. The Internationalization of U.S. Criminal Law Enforcement*, Pennsylvania State University Press, University Park PA, 1993.

Naeyé, J., *Een advocatenbalie op het politiebureau? Juridische consultatie voor verdachten en slachtoffers*; in: Fijnaut & Blonk, 1988, pp. 114-125.
- *Rectaal fouilleren?*, in: NJB 1989, pp. 880-886.
- *Heterdaad. Politiebevoegdheden bij ontdekking op heterdaad in theorie en praktijk*; Gouda Quint/Van den Brink, Arnhem/Lochem, 2nd ed. 1990.
- (ed.), *Nationale ombudsman en politie, jaarboek 1991*; Gouda Quint, Arnhem, 1992.
- *De nieuwe aanpak van anonieme verdachten, zwartrijders en vermoedelijke vreemdelingen*; in: De Doelder, H. & Zwetsloot, F.J.M., *Identificatieplicht. Aspecten van de invoering van een identificatieplicht*; Gouda Quint, Arnhem, 1993, pp. 21-57.
- *Het politieel vooronderzoek in strafzaken*, Gouda Quint, 1995 (1995a).
- *De reikwijdte van fundamentele rechten in strafzaken - enkele thema's*; in: Alkema, E.A., Groen, H.A., Wattel, P.J. & Naeyé, J., *De reikwijdte van fundamentele rechten (Handelingen Nederlandse Juristen-Vereniging)*; W.E.J. Tjeenk Willink, Zwolle, 1995, pp. 223-302 (1995b).

Nijboer, J.F., *Een verkenning in het vergelijkend straf- en strafprocesrecht*, Gouda Quint, Arnhem, 1994.

Noyon/Langemeijer/Remmelink: Remmelink, J., *Het Wetboek van Strafrecht*, Gouda Quint, Arnhem (loose-leaf).

Nugter, A.C.M., *Transborder Flow of Personal Data within the EC. A comparative analysis of the privacy statutes of the Federal Republic of Germany, France, the United Kingdom and The Netherlands and their impact on the private sector*; Kluwer, Deventer, 1990.

O'Keeffe, D., *Recasting the Third Pillar*; in: CMLR 1995, pp. 893-920.
- & Twomey, P.M., *Legal Issues of the Maastricht Treaty*; Chancery, London, 1994.

Ordemann/Schomerus: Schomerus, R. & Gola, P., *BDSG - Bundesdatenschutzgesetz mit Erläuterungen*; C.H. Beck, München, 1992.

Orie, A.A.M., *Internationale opsporing*; in: *Internationalisering van het strafrecht*, Ars Aequi Libri, Nijmegen, 1986, pp. 165-179.
- *Justitiële samenwerking*; in: DD 21 (1991), pp. 754-761.
-, Van der Meijs, J.G. & Smit, A.M.G., *Internationaal strafrecht*, Tjeenk Willink, Zwolle, 1991.

Osner, N., Quinn, A. & Crown, G., *The Royal Commission on Criminal Justice. Criminal Justice in Other Jurisdiction Systems*; HMSO, London, 1993.

Pauly, A. (ed.), *Schengen en panne*; Institut Européen d'Administration Publique, Maastricht, 1994.

Pels, P., *De vette jaren van een infiltrant*, in: Politie Magazine, July-September 1993, pp. 4-7.

Perrick, F., *The Netherlands*; in: Kurian, G.T. (ed.), *World Encyclopedia of Police Forces and Penal Sytems*, Facts on File, New York/Oxford, 1989, pp. 272-281.

Pfeiffer, G. (ed.), *Karlsruher Kommentar Strafprozeßordnung und Gerichtsverfassungsgesetz*; C.H. Beck'sche Verlagsbuchhandlung, München, 1982.

Picard, E., *La police et le secret des données d'ordre personnel en droit français*; in: Rev. sc. crim. 1993, pp. 275-310.

Pieroth, B. & Schlink, B., *Grundrechte - Staatsrecht II*; C.F. Müller, Heidelberg, 1989.

Pieters, J.J.Th.M. & Revis, C.J.P.M., *Het wettelijk kader voor 'kijkoperaties'*; in: NJB, 1994-11, pp. 401-407.

Pijl, D., *Geen deals met criminelen*; in: APB 1988, pp. 411-416.

Poncela, P., *Livre 1, Dispositions générales*, in: Rev. sc. crim. 1993, pp. 455-469.

Ponsaers, P., *Nationale Magistraten: "365 dagen, 24 uur op 24, all-round-men zijn"*; in: Politeia, February 1992, pp. 8-11.

- & Dupont, G., *De Bende; een documentaire*; Epo, Antwerpen, 1986.

Poté, R., *Handboek Verkeerswetgeving*, Acco, Leuven/Amersfoort, 1990.

Poulantzas, N.M. *The Right of Hot Pursuit in International Law*; A.W. Sijthoff, Leiden 1969.

Pradel, J., *Trafic de drogues, provocation délictueuse des agents de l'autorité et permission de la loi (commentaire de la loi no. 91-1264 du 19 dec. 1991 relative au renforcement de la lutte contre le trafic de stupéfiants)*; in: RDS 1992, pp. 229-234.

- *Observations brèves sur une loi à refaire (à propos de la loi du 4 janvier 1993 sur la procédure pénale)*; in: RDS 1993, pp. 39-40 (1993a).

- *Les droits de la personne suspecte ou poursuivie depuis la loi no. 93-1013 du 24 août 1993 modifiant celle du 4 janvier précédent. Un législateur se muant en Pénélope ou se faisant perfectionniste?* Recueil Dalloz-Sirey, 1993, pp. 299-306 (1993b).

- *France*; in: Van den Wyngaert, 1993a, pp. 105-136 (1993c).

- *Droit pénal comparé*, Éditions Dalloz, Paris, 1995.

Prakke, L. & Kortmann, C.A.J.M., (ed.) *Het staatsrecht van de landen der Europese Gemeenschappen*; Kluwer, Deventer, 1993.

Raab, C.D., *Police cooperation: The prospects for privacy*, in: Anderson & Den Boer, 1994, pp. 121-136.

Rachor, F., *Polizeihandeln*; in: Lisken/Denninger, 1992, pp. 193-375.

Rambach, P.H.M., *Luxemburg*, in: Gropp, 1993a, pp. 462-463.

Rassat, M.-L., *Procédure pénale*; Presses Universitaires de France, Paris, 1990.

Remmelink, J., *Iets over strafrechtsvergelijking*, in: DD (23) 1993, pp. 424-438.

Ring, W.M., *Die Befugnis der Polizei zur verdeckten Ermittlung*, in: StV 1990, pp. 372-379.

Robben, F., *De verwerking van gevoelige en gerechtelijke gegevens in het licht van de Belgische Wet Verwerking Persoonsgegevens*; in: CR 1995-3, pp. 90-99.

Roest, F., *Het belonen van informanten (I & II)*; in: TvP 1991, pp. 275-279 & 325-327.

Roxin, C., *Strafverfahrensrecht*; C.H. Beck'sche Verlagsbuchhandlung, München, 1993.

Rozemond, K., *Het DNA-onderzoek in strafzaken en het nemo tenetur-beginsel*; in: NJB 1992, pp. 125-132.

Rüter, C.F., *Opsporingsmethoden: regulering en controle in Duitsland*; in: DD 25 (1995), pp. 594-604.
- *De grote verdwijntruc*; in: NJB 1996, pp. 81-86.

Ruypers, H., *Politietaken en het verkeersreglement*; in: De politieofficier 1989-8, pp. 53-59 (followed by the French version).

Schalken, T.M., *Het taboe van art. 5 RO*; in: Trema¨ 1991, pp. 179-194.
- *Zelfkant van de rechtshandhaving, over onrechtmatig verkregen bewijs in strafzaken*; Gouda Quint, Arnhem, 1981.
- *Het politie-sepot en de mandaatsverhouding tussen openbaar ministerie en politie*; in: TvP 1984, pp. 5-11.
- *Euthanasie en handhaving van recht. Normatieve, procedurele en strafrechtspolitieke aspecten van het vervolgingsbeleid*; in: *Euthanasie: recht, ethiek en medische praktijk*; Kluwer, Deventer, 1985, pp. 154-173.
- *Een voorlopige analyse en enkele concrete voorstellen*; in: Fijnaut & Blonk, 1988, pp. 136-138.

Schattenberg, B., *The Schengen Information System: Privacy and Legal Protection*; in: Schermers *et al.*, 1993, pp. 43-52.

Scheller, S., *Legal problems of the Schengen Information System*, in: Anderson & Den Boer, 1992, pp. 157-168.

Schelter, K., *Verbrechensbekämpfung mit elektronischen Mitteln - ein Tabu?* in: ZRP 1994, pp. 52-57.

Schermers, H.G., Flinterman, C., Kellerman, A.E., Haersolte, J.C. van & Meent, G.W. van de (eds.), *Free Movement of Persons in Europe. Legal Problems and Experiences*; Martinus Nijhoff Publishers, Dordrecht/Boston/London, 1993.

Schürmann, D., *Verdeckte Ermittler und V-Personen (I & II)*, in: Die Neue Polizei 1995, pp. 348-351 & 383-387.

Seifert, J., *Vom Lauschangriff zum "Großen Lauschangriff"* in: KJ 1992, pp. 355-363.

Semerak, A. & Kratz, G., *Die Polizeien in Westeuropa*; Richard Boorberg Verlag, Stuttgart/München/Hannover, 1989.

Sieber, U., *European Unification and European Criminal Law*; in: (1994) 2 Eur.J. Crime Cr.L. Cr.J., pp. 85-104.

Sjöcrona, J.M., *De kleine rechtshulp. Nederlands procesrecht ten behoeve van buitenlandse justitie en politie. Een onderzoek naar de betekenis van de artikelen 552h-552q van het Wetboek van Strafvordering*; Gouda Quint, Arnhem, 1990.
  - *Internationale rechtshulp*; in: Cleiren, C.P.M. & Nijboer, J.F., *Tekst & Commentaar Strafvordering*; Kluwer, Deventer, 1995 pp. 1031-1077 (1995a).
  - *Dutch Criminal Procedure from the Point of View of the Defence*; in: Groenhuijsen & Veldt, 1995, pp. 61-70 (1995b).
Soeteman, A., *Boekbespreking: C.P.M. Cleiren, De openheid van de wet, de geslotenheid van het recht*, in: DD 24 (1994), pp. 69-73.
Spielmann, D., *Les mouvements de réforme de la procédure pénale et la protection des droits de l'homme (Rapport Luxembourgeois)*; in: RDP 1993, pp. 984-997.
  - *Des récentes réformes du Code d'instruction criminelle luxembourgeois. Un bilan de six ans*; in: RDP 1993, pp. 943-983 (1993a).
Spielmann, A. & Spielmann, D., *Luxembourg*; in: Van den Wyngaert, 1993, pp. 261-278.
  - & Weitzel, A., *La Convention européenne des droits de l'homme et le droit luxembourgeois*, Nemesis, Brussels, 1991.
Spriet, B., *De aanhouding en het bevel tot medebrenging*; in: Declerq & Verstraeten, 1991, pp. 17-47.
Stanbrook, I. & Stanbrook, C., *The Law and Practice of Extradition*; Barry Rose, Chicester/London, 1980.
Steenbergen, J.D.M., *Schengen and the movement of persons*; in: Meijers *et al.*, 1991, pp. 57-73.
Stefani, G., Levasseur, G. & Bouloc, B., *Procédure pénale*; Dalloz, Paris, 1993.
Steinke, W.D., *Der Einwurf für ein neues BKA-Gesetz*, in: ZRP 1995, pp. 212-216.
Strate, G., *Stellungnahme des Strafrechtsausschusses des Deutschen Anwaltvereins zum EOrgKG*, in: StV 1992, pp. 29-37.
Strunk, S., *Polizeiliche Intelligence - Informationsverarbeitung und -auswertung als neue Strategie*; in: B & P 1994-3, pp. 16-22.
Swart, A.H.J., *Onderzoek aan het lichaam*; in: AAe 1989, pp. 780-788.
  - *Afluisteren van telefoons*, in: AAe 1991, pp. 160-168 (1991a).
  - *Police and Security in the Schengen Agreement and Schengen Convention*; in: H. Meijers *et al.*, 1991, pp. 96-109 (1991b).
  - *The Case-Law of the European Convention on Human Rights in 1992*, in: (1993) 1 Eur.J. Crime Cr.L. Cr.J., pp. 167-184 (1993a).
  - *The Netherlands*; in: Van den Wyngaert, 1993, pp. 279-316 (1993b).
  - *De toekomst van Europol*; in: JV 1995-1, pp. 61-83.
Tabarelli, W., *Baltica 86, An International Exercise on Controlled Deliveries*, in: Fijnaut & Hermans, 1987, pp. 79-84.
Tak, P.J.P., *DNA en strafproces*; Gouda Quint, Arnhem, 1990.

- *Het strafproces, een overzicht*; in: Fiselier, Gunther Moor & Tak, 1992a, pp. 43-64.
- *OM en rechter in het Duitse vooronderzoek*; in: DD 22 (1992), pp. 673-684 (1992b).
- *De Kroongetuige en de georganiseerde misdaad*; Gouda Quint, Arnhem, 1994.
- & Lensing, J.A.W., *Het vooronderzoek rechtsvergelijkend onderzocht*; Gouda Quint, Arnhem, 1990.
-, Van Eikema Hommes, G.A., Manunza, E.R. & Mulder, C.F., *Bijzondere opsporingsmethoden. De normering van bijzondere opsporingsmethoden in buitenlandse rechtsstelsels*; Ministerie van Justitie, 's-Gravenhage, 1996.

Thiry, R., *Précis d'Instruction Criminelle en Droit Luxembourgeois (I & II)*, Lucien de Bourcy, Luxembourg, 1971 & 1984.

Thomas, F., *De Europese rechtshulpverdragen in strafzaken*, Story Scientia, Gent, 1980.

Timmer, J., Naeyé, J. & Van der Steeg, M., *Politieel vuurwapengebruik*, 1996 (forthcoming).

Tobback, L., *De coördinatie van de politie in België: Hoe meer politiediensten, hoe meer veiligheid?* in: De Politieofficier 1989-2, pp. 5-19 (followed by the French version).

Trechsel, S., *Liberty and Security of the Person*; in: Macdonald *et al.*, 1993, pp. 277-344.

Van de Reyt, I.W.D.M., *Die Niederlande*, in: Gropp, 1993a, pp. 485-565.

Van de Vijver, C.D., Broer, W., Hoogenboom, A.B. & Naeyé, J., *De politie*; in: Fiselier, Gunther Moor & Tak, 1992, pp. 73-92.

Van den Wyngaert, C., (ed.), *Criminal Procedure Systems in the European Community*; Butterworths, London/Brussels/Dublin/Edinburgh, 1993 (1993a).
- *Belgium*; in: Van den Wyngaert, 1993a, pp. 1-50 (1993b).
- *Strafrecht en strafprocesrecht in hoofdlijnen*; Maklu, Antwerpen, 2nd ed. 1994.

Van der Grinten, M.F.L.M., *The Role of the udge and the Public Prosecutor in the Dutch Criminal System*; in: Groenhuijsen & Veldt, 1995, pp. 21-36.

Van der Heijden, A.W.M. (ed.), *Criminele inlichtingen: De rol van de Criminele Inlichtingendiensten bij de aanpak van de georganiseerde misdaad*; VUGA, 's-Gravenhage, 1993.

Van der Vegt, M.G., *Recherche in het milieu*; in: Wilzing *et al.*, 1989, pp. 43-60.

Van der Wel, J.E., & Bruggeman, W., *Europese politiële samenwerking. Internationale gremia*; Politeia, Brussel, 1993.

Van Dijk, W. & Demmink, G., *Richtlijn wederzijdse rechtshulp in strafzaken. De toepassing van art. 552i Strafvordering*; in: APB 1995-7, pp. 13-15.

Van Dijk, P. & Van Hoof, G.J.H., *Theory and Practice of the European Convention on Human Rights*, Kluwer Law and Taxation, Deventer/Boston, 2nd ed. 1990

Van Duyne, P.C., Kouwenberg, R.F. & Romeijn, G., *Misdaadondernemingen*, Gouda Quint, Arnhem, 1990.

Van Es, A., *Schengen, of De nieuwe deling van Europa*; Van Gennep, Amsterdam, 1991.

Van Kastel, J.A.P., *Pseudokoop*; in: Wilzing *et al.*, 1989, pp. 205-218.

Van Kooten, J.N., *Ambtsinstructie. Nieuwe ambtsinstructie van kracht*; in: APB 1994-11, pp. 20-23.

Van Laethem, W., *Het vattingsrecht van particulieren*; in: Pan. 1994, pp. 112-121.

Van Muylem, E., *Geldigheid en bewijswaarde van het proces verbaal*, in: R.W. 1994/1995, pp. 1431-1434.

Van Outrive, L., *La démilitarisation de la gendarmerie belge*; in: Cahiers de la sécurité intérieure, 11 (November 1992-January 1993), pp. 125-128.

-, Cartuyvels, Y. & Ponsaers, P., *Sire, ik ben ongerust. Geschiedenis van de Belgische politie 1794-1991*; Kritak, Leuven, 1992 (also published in French).

- & Enhus, E., *Internationale politiesamenwerking - Europol*; Centrum voor Politiestudies, Brussel, 1994.

Van Parys, T. & Laurent, J. (rapp.), *Bendecommissie. Parlementair onderzoek naar de wijze waarop de bestrijding van het banditisme en het terrorisme georganiseerd wordt*, in: *Gedrukte Stukken* 1989-1990, 59/8-10 (also published in French).

Van Traa, M. (pres.), *Opsporing gezocht. Rapport van de werkgroep vooronderzoek opsporingsmethoden*; TK 1994-1995, 23 945 (1994).

-, *Inzake opsporing. Enquetecommissie opsporingsmethoden*; Sdu, Den Haag, 1996; with Appendices I-XI, TK 24 072 nrs. 12-20.

Vandeplas, A., *Vergelijkend onderzoek naar enige dwangmiddelen tijdens de opsporing*; Ministerie van Justitie, 's-Gravenhage, 1979.

Veerman, G.J., Paulides, G. & Hofstee, E.J., *Ik zal eens even vragen naar zijn naam*; Gouda Quint, Arnhem, 1989.

Verbraak, C., *Tipgeld in strafzaken*; in: Elsevier, May 4, 1991, pp. 24-25.

Verbruggen, F., *Eurocops? Just Say Maybe. European Lessons from the 1993 Reshuffle of US Drug Enforcement*; in: (1995) 3 Eur.J. Crime Cr.L. Cr.J., pp. 150-201.

Verhey, L.F.M., *Privacy Aspects of the Convention Applying the Schengen Agreement*; in: Meijers *et al.*, 1991, pp. 110-134.

Vermeulen, G., *Het beginsel ne bis in idem in het internationaal strafrecht*; in: Pan. 1994, pp. 217-235.

-, Vander Beken, T., Zanders, P. & De Ruyver, B., *Internationale samenwerking in strafzaken en rechtsbescherming. Pleidooi voor een geïntegreerde nationale en internationale benadering*; Universiteit Gent, 1994 (commercial edition: Politeia, Brussel, 1994).

Verstraeten, R.A.F., *Handboek Strafvordering*, Maklu, Antwerpen/Apeldoorn 1994.

- *Opsporingsmethoden: regulering en controle in België en Frankrijk*; in: DD 25 (1995), pp. 610-621.

Vitu, M., Montreuil, J., *Rébellion*; in: Juris-Classeur Pénal, artt. 209 à 221 (looseleaf).

Vogler, T. & Wilkitzki, P., *Gesetz über die internationale Rechtshilfe in Strafsachen (IRG) - Kommentar*; in: Grützner/Pötz.

Wächtler, H., *Der autoritäre Strafprozeß - das beschleunigte Verfahren neuer Art im Entwurf eines sogenannten Kriminalitätsbekämpfungsgesetzes von CDU/CSU und FDP*, in: StV 1994, pp. 159-161.

Welp, J., *Kriminalpolitik in der Krise - Der SPD-Entwurf eines Zweiten Gesetzes zur Bekämpfung der organisierten Kriminalität*, in: StV 1994, pp. 161-168.

Wemes, L.T., *Noodweer*; in: Cleiren, C.P.M. & Nijboer, J.F., *Tekst & Commentaar Strafrecht*; Kluwer, Deventer, 1994, pp. 200-206.

Weßlau, E., *Vorfeldermittlungen. Probleme der Legalisierung vorbeugender Verbrechensbekämpfung aus strafprozeßlicher Sicht*, Duncker & Humblot, Berlin, 1989.

- *Zum "Entwurf eines Gesetzes zur Bekämpfung der organisierten Kriminalität"* in: B & P, 1991-2, pp. 42-48.

Wesselius, E.T., *Vaktechnische vragen. Gebruik van camera's in winkels*, in: APB 1994-10, p. 18.

Wiarda, G.J., *Advies betreffende de verenigbaarheid van een eventueel in te voeren identificatieplicht met internationale en nationale bepalingen inzake grondrechten*; June 2, 1987, Appendix to TK 1986-1987, 19 991.

Wilzing, J. et al., *Inkijk in: Criminele Inlichtingendiensten, Misdaadanalyse en Pseudokoop*; Rechercheschool, Zutphen, 1989.

Wolter, J., *Heimliche und automatisierte Informationseingriffe wider Datengrundrechtsschutz (I & II)*, in: GA 1988, pp. 49-90 & 129-142.

- *Aspekte einer Strafprozeßreform bis 2007*; C.H. Beck Verlag, München, 1991.

Index